DATE DUE

OC 22 '04			

DEMCO 38-296

THE COLLECTED WORKS OF JUSTICE HOLMES

OLIVER WENDELL HOLMES

Reproduced by permission of Harvard Law Art Collection.

THE COLLECTED WORKS OF

Justice Holmes

Complete Public Writings
and Selected Judicial Opinions of
Oliver Wendell Holmes

EDITED BY

Sheldon M. Novick

WITH A FOREWORD BY

Erwin N. Griswold

The Holmes Devise Memorial Edition

VOLUME 1

THE UNIVERSITY OF CHICAGO PRESS

CHICAGO AND LONDON

cholar in residence at Vermont Law School. He is
norable Justice: The Life of Oliver Wendell Holmes

The University of Chicago Press, Chicago 60637
The University of Chicago Press, Ltd., London
© 1995 by Sheldon M. Novick
Foreword © 1995 by The University of Chicago
All rights reserved. Vols. 1–3 published 1995
Printed in the United States of America

02 01 00 99 98 97 96 95 1 2 3 4 5

ISBN (cloth): 0-226-34963-2 (vol. 1)
0-226-34966-7 (the set)

Library of Congress Cataloging-in-Publication Data

Holmes, Oliver Wendell, 1841–1935.
   [Works. 1995]
   The collected works of Justice Holmes: complete published writings
and selected judicial opinions of Oliver Wendell Holmes / edited by Sheldon M. Novick; with a foreword by Erwin N. Griswold.
     p. cm.
   Includes bibliographical references and index.
    1. Law—United States.   I. Novick, Sheldon M.   II. Title.
KF213.H6N68   1995
349.73—dc20
[347.3]   94-33345
                                        CIP

To Carolyn

How simple a type is the soldier and gentleman—how adorable. Unquestionably entitled to admission to the enclosure—yet—inadequate for final sympathy. A wretched worm, not entitled to live in the same world with him but having the compound twist, is closer to us. What is the compound twist do you ask dear Hibernian? I don't think you do ask. What is it that is *troubloux*—What is it that is the union of irreconcilables, of enthusiasm and irony?

Justice Holmes to Lady Castletown,
August 24, 1896.

Contents

Volume 1

Summary Contents of Volumes 2–5

Volume 2

NONJUDICIAL WORKS (continued)

Volume 3

NONJUDICIAL WORKS (continued)

Volumes 4 and 5

SELECTED JUDICIAL OPINIONS

Foreword

Oliver Wendell Holmes was surely one of our greatest judicial thinkers and a virtually unique legal writer. He retired as a judge early in 1932 and died a few years later, at the age of ninety-three. It is not surprising that he should be controversial. Most justices of the Supreme Court are, in one way or another. But thinking and writing about Holmes is widespread and probably will persist for a long period in the future.

During his life, Holmes left many "fragments of my fleece," as he said in the preface to his "Collected Legal Papers"—books, speeches, opinions, letters, not to mention records made in diaries, or by persons who knew him or otherwise came in contact with him. Until now, though, these materials have been widely scattered, and many of them are hard to locate, even if one has available the resources of a comprehensive library. It is for that reason that scholars of the law and students of the Supreme Court, and many others, should be grateful to Sheldon M. Novick for his labors in gathering these materials and bringing them together in a set of books that will make them conveniently available in many libraries. Mr. Novick has himself written an admirable biography of Holmes—*Honorable Justice,* published in 1989. In addition, Mr. Novick has prepared for this edition a "Brief Biography of Justice Holmes." He has also written an informative chapter on "Holmes's Philosophy and Jurisprudence," and has added a thoughtful "Critical Appraisal" in which he gives his own analysis of Holmes's work.

I write with some feeling, because I am one of those who knew Holmes—not intimately, but through a number of contacts which still stand out vividly in my mind. I had heard much about Holmes during my student days at the Harvard Law School and was fascinated by his portrait, which hangs in Langdell Hall there. I first saw him, sitting on the Supreme Court, on December 2, 1929. Thereafter, I participated in a number of cases, as a junior in the Solicitor General's office, when he was a sitting member of the Court. I never presented an oral argument before him, as the rules limiting appearances to members of the bar of the Supreme Court were strictly enforced in those days. One could not be a member of the Supreme Court bar until one had been admitted to practice in a state for three years. I was admitted in Ohio on April 17, 1929, and lost no time in gaining admission to the Supreme Court when the three years had expired. April 17, 1932, was a Sunday: my certificate shows that I was admitted to practice before the bar of the Supreme Court on April 18, 1932. Although Holmes had retired by that time, he still had law clerks, including H. Chapman Rose (clerk in 1931–32), who later became my partner, and in a later year, Mark DeWolfe Howe (clerk in 1933–34).

Through the law clerks, occasional meetings with Justice Holmes were arranged that were attended by a few young lawyers in the Department of Justice. Holmes was always very kind and gracious with us, although he displayed a bit of "show-off" at times. I remember one occasion when he picked up a thick brief and said: "One hundred and sixteen pages. I do not read them when they are that long, and I don't care who knows it"—as he threw the brief into a wastebasket. (One may speculate as to whether it was later retrieved.)

On some of these visits, we were received in the Justice's upstairs study. One of the pieces of furniture there was a stand-up desk, which Justice Holmes had inherited from his mother. It had been first acquired by Justice Jackson of the Supreme Judicial Court of Massachusetts in the early nineteenth century. Justice Jackson was the father of Justice Holmes's mother, and thus Holmes's grandfather. Holmes told us that he wrote most of his opinions at that desk, adding, "There is nothing so conducive to brevity as a feeling of weakness in the knees." I would have been very much surprised if I had then known that that desk would eventually come to the office of the dean of the Harvard Law School and that I would use it there. It is surely a treasure of legal history.

Holmes generally wrote short opinions, in longhand. For example, his opinion in the important case of *Lucas v. Earl*, 281 U.S. 111 (1930), occupied less than two printed pages. The equally important decision in *Corliss v. Bowers*, 281 U.S. 376 (1930), was no longer. His opinion in *United States v. Kirby Lumber Co.*, 284 U.S. 1 (1931), was even shorter. These came at the end of his judicial career, but Holmes had, throughout his life, a pervading capacity for concise statement that is worthy of current consideration.

Holmes not only wrote short opinions; he was a great phrase-maker. Often his phrases cast a bright light on the problem he was considering. "The Fourteenth Amendment does not enact Mr. Herbert Spencer's Social Statics." "General propositions do not decide concrete cases." Both of these quotations come from his dissenting opinion in *Lochner v. New York*, 198 U.S. 45, 75, 76 (1905), but there are many other illustrations—"The common law is not a brooding omnipresence in the sky," *Southern Pacific Co. v. Jenson*, 244 U.S. 205, 222 (1917), is an example.

Anecdotes about Holmes are abundant. The one I like best was told by Thomas G. Corcoran, who gained fame as a speechwriter and adviser to President Franklin D. Roosevelt. Corcoran was a law clerk to Justice Holmes in 1926–27. (I first met him in the Lakes of the Clouds Hut on Mount Washington in 1919 when, during the summer in his student days at Brown University, he was a hut boy for the Appalachian Mountain Club.) Corcoran recounted that occasionally the Justice took drives in his motor car through the back roads of northern Virginia, which was then a completely rural area. Sometimes the Justice asked Corcoran to go along. At that time, there were many signs put up along the roads by the Virginia Highway Department. Understandably, these were laudatory of Confederate troops, such as: "Near this spot, on June 14, 1862, Captain Smith, with three companies, defeated General Brown of the northern army, with three regiments under his command." (This, of course, is not an exact quotation.) At each of these signs, Holmes would get out of the car, walk to the sign, and read it aloud. Then he would come back to the automobile, without comment. When the trip was finished and Holmes was returned to his residence at 1720 I Street, N.W., he put a hand on Corcoran's shoulder and said: "Sonny, if you read those signs you would think that the rebels won a lot of battles. But we won the ——— —— war!"

The building on I Street is now gone. A stone-fronted bank occupies the space. The house was rather narrow and several floors in height. According to Mrs. Bancroft, the mother-in-law of Attorney General William D. Mitchell, who grew up in Boston, it was "the only place in Washington that smelled like Beacon Hill."

One time when my mother visited me in Washington, probably early in 1930, I told her of my admiration for Holmes. When she returned to Cleveland, she wrote a letter to the Justice, thanking him for the inspiration he provided for a young lawyer, her son. Holmes responded in a longhand letter, thanking her for her letter to him and saying that he greatly valued what she had written, for, in his words, "If you become a minority of one, they lock you up." I still have that letter, carefully protected in the pages of my copy of *The Common Law.*

I was married in late December 1931 and brought my bride to Washington. She arrived just after Holmes's retirement, so that she did not see him sitting on the bench. Some weeks later, though, I was able to arrange for her to come with me for a call on Holmes. Holmes was then over ninety, but he insisted on rising when she came into the room. He asked her where she came from, and she said she had grown up in California. Holmes's response to this was, "The last stand of the frontier was when I saw a top hat at the Cliff House in San Francisco."

Since his death, Holmes has often been subjected to vigorous, sometimes intemperate, criticism. There are surely some decisions which, as of today, seem hard to justify, such as the "Three generations of imbeciles are enough" opinion in *Buck v. Bell,* 274 U.S. 200, 207 (1927). It seems not unlikely that this was a reflection of the Darwinism that was widely accepted among the families and teachers he knew while he was growing up. And it may be noted, too, that we still breed racehorses and petunias. The "Stop, Look, and Listen" opinion in *Baltimore & Ohio Railway v. Goodman,* 275 U.S. 66, 69 (1927), may be another throwback. As to both of these, it can be observed that great men, like the rest of us, have their failings from time to time. More important, it should be recalled, too, that Holmes's early experience, for nearly twenty years, was on the Supreme Judicial Court of Massachusetts, where he was constantly dealing with questions of state power and state law. Understandably, it was his view that this law was generally to be made by the state legislature and that within wide limits his own conclusion about the legislature's wisdom in enacting the law was irrelevant.

Holmes left most of his legal papers to the Harvard Law School Library. Beginning in the 1940s, these papers were assembled and organized, with intense effort, by his one-time clerk, Professor Mark DeWolfe Howe. He first prepared, edited, and published the massive collection of correspondence known as the Holmes-Pollock letters, containing many significant personal observations by Holmes. This was followed by the Holmes-Laski letters, making available the extensive correspondence between Holmes and Harold Laski, one of the younger men who had attached themselves to Holmes in the second decade of this century. Mark and I often talked about various items he had found in the papers and problems he had encountered. Among other things, Mark Howe found some statements in the letters written by Laski which, to put it politely, were not so, and these items are among the matters Mark discussed with me. Mark had them printed as they were, with appropriate comments in a footnote.

After completing the compilation of these two sets of correspondence, Mark, being then deeply steeped in Holmes, began work on his biography. In the process of preparing the biography, Mark found that the Holmes papers were widely scattered. He had continually come across new lots of letters and other items, and this consumed much time. The work that Mark Howe did in organizing the materials has been a great help to subsequent biographers and has been generously acknowledged.

In my own experience, I knew many of the Holmes quotations, but it was hard to find their precise source. When that happened, I would walk down the hall to Mark and he would immediately tell me where that quotation could be found. Unfortunately, Mark died far too young, before he could get into the judicial part of the Holmes biography. I was greatly saddened when he was taken, and I have since missed his encyclopedic knowledge of Holmes's often-penetrating phrases. When there is a comprehensive edition of Holmes's works, including his letters and unpublished papers, with an electronic concordance for the whole, with the help of computers we will be able to approach Mark Howe's unaided memory.

Following Catherine Drinker Bowen's perhaps somewhat freely written *Yankee from Olympus,* there have been, in recent years, a number of biographies of Holmes: in addition to Mr. Novick's book, there has been Liva Baker's *The Justice from Beacon Hill,* Gary J. Aichele's *Oliver Wendell Holmes, Jr.: Soldier, Scholar, Judge,* and G. Edward White's *Justice Oliver Wendell Holmes: Law and the Inner Self.* The present work by Mr. Novick, gathering together all of the Holmes materials, will make it possible for other writers to familiarize themselves in detail with Holmes's writings, and to continue the process of depicting his career and analyzing his thought. To paraphrase Thoreau, persons who did not know Holmes will be enabled, through Mr. Novick's efforts, to march to the drumbeat of his thought.

This collection of the public writings of Justice Holmes includes his notices in the *American Law Review,* many of which had been published anonymously and had not been identified as his until now; his comprehensive notes to Kent's *Commentaries;* the full text of *The Common Law,* with Holmes's annotations for a new edition and the text of the final summary lecture, which had been lost; his speeches, including some never before published; and a selection of his opinions in the Supreme Judicial Court of Massachusetts and in the United States Supreme Court. Thus, through the careful work of Mr. Novick, both the admirers of Holmes and his critics will have all of the relevant materials available to use in developing further studies of Holmes's unique role in the development of American law. For this new facility, we are all much indebted to Mr. Novick, to the Holmes Devise Committee, and to the University of Chicago Press, which has supported the project and has so effectively carried it out.

Erwin N. Griswold

Preface

About ten years ago, I began work on a book about Holmes. It was to be about his friendships and disagreements, especially with William and Henry James; I thought these would give dramatic life to ideas that otherwise would have had to be teased out of treatises and presented in abstract form. But Holmes proved to be remarkably elusive; the only well-known book about him, Catherine Drinker Bowen's *Yankee from Olympus,* published in 1944, proved to be a fictionalized account; the authorized biography by Mark DeWolfe Howe had been interrupted when barely a third complete by Howe's death, and his successor, Grant Gilmore, had died without adding to it. There was no adequate history of the Supreme Court during Holmes's years. (Some of the reasons for this state of affairs are given in chapter 1.)

I decided to defer my book on Holmes and the Jameses, and to begin by writing a biography of Holmes alone. I was given access to Holmes's papers at the Harvard Law School Library and, with the aid of these materials, found and read all of Holmes's published work, which, far from being collected, had never been adequately identified. I prepared for my own use an outline of Holmes's thought at various stages of his development and, with that in hand, proceeded to write the story of his life. The result was *Honorable Justice: The Life of Oliver Wendell Holmes* (Little, Brown and Company, 1989). If Holmes's work is to be fully accessible, it has to be assembled and translated, as it were, into modern language, so that it can be understood without years of effort devoted to re-creating the context in which it was written. This edition fulfills that duty, and I hope that the reader will bear its origins in mind and forgive the occasional references to my own previous work and to work in progress on Henry James. The subject is Holmes alone, but it is better to be frank about the fact that an editor, like a judge, has the "sovereign prerogative of choice." Writing, like painting, long ago adopted the device of single-point perspective, and no landscape is really comprehensible now without it.

The criteria I used for deciding what to include in this edition are described in the following section, "Editorial Principles," which also contains information about the texts used and changes made. Instead of adding a great many isolated footnotes to Holmes's text to explain the context, I have collected this material in connected essays in chapters 2–4, which give the outline of Holmes's life and thought. Holmes's work is all of a piece, and it is difficult to follow any one article or speech until it has been set in the context of his overall effort. The introductory chapters therefore treat Holmes's lifelong work as a whole, which I believe is how he saw it.

An edition of this size is the work of many people. The first and principal acknowledgment must go to Claire Reinhardt, managing editor of this edition, who also assisted me in the preparation of *Honorable Justice.* Reinhardt brought a rare combination of intelligence, creativity, and meticulous care to this edition, as she has to all her work. She participated in every decision and supervised every step that she did not carry out herself in the long process of converting thousands of sheets of paper and note cards into these orderly volumes. Her fine judgment and editorial skills are reflected throughout the introductory chapters as well. Karen McLaughlin gave me her invaluable assistance, as lawyer and editor, in the final stages of the work.

My thanks to Dr. James H. Hutson, chief of the Manuscripts Division of the Library of Congress, and to the editor of the Holmes Devise history of the Supreme Court, Professor Stanley N. Katz, for their encouragement and support. My thanks also to the members of the Permanent Committee on the Oliver Wendell Holmes Devise when this project began: James H. Billington, librarian of Congress; Gerhard Casper, then provost of the University of Chicago; and Judge Robert H. Bork, for financial support from the Holmes Devise that helped make this edition possible.

I am once again indebted to Harry S. Martin III, librarian, and Judith W. Mellins, manuscripts associate, of the Harvard Law School Library, for giving me continued, unrestricted access to the Holmes papers while preparing this edition; to Mrs. Mellins and the other able staff of the library for their manifold kindnesses and assistance over the years: David R. Warrington, librarian for Special Collections; David de Lorenzo, curator of manuscripts and archives; David A. Ferris, curator of Rare Books; Mary L. Person, Special Collections Reading Room supervisor, and David Jenkins, Special Collections Stack supervisor; and to Bernice Loss, keeper of the Treasure Room, and Steven R. Smith, curatorial associate for the Art Collection, for helping to find and granting permission for the use of the photograph of Justice Holmes in this edition.

At the Library of Congress, where hundreds of Holmes's books remain in storage, I am grateful for the assistance once more of Drs. Billington and Hutson; of Peter van Wingen, director of the Rare Book Division; and of Chris Wright, director of the Loan Division. My thanks also go to Ray Richardson, foreman of the Landover warehouse; and Mary Yarnell, of the Loan Division.

My thanks for comments on draft portions of the introductory chapters to Judge Richard A. Posner, of the United States Court of Appeals for the Seventh Circuit, and Professor Albert W. Alschuler. As the reader will easily recognize, the introductory chapters owe a great deal more to Judge Posner's *Cardozo: A Study in Judicial Reputation* than specific citations can convey. I am glad once more to be able to acknowledge my debt to the late Professor Mark DeWolfe Howe, whose meticulous labors in assembling Holmes's papers and publications, and whose sadly incomplete biography of the justice, were the premise for this work; and to Mrs. Faneuil Adams, who so many years ago granted me access to Professor Howe's papers and Holmes materials.

I am grateful to David Pickman, secretary of the Tavern Club, Jim Ryder, alumni director of the Porcellian Club, and Carter Hood, also of the Porcellian Club, for providing access to and assistance with their respective collections.

For translations of Holmes's Greek, my thanks to David D. Coffin and Alexander Sens, and for scanning a large part of the text of this edition, to Diana Shannon of Sharon, Vermont. For keyboarding with miraculous precision the notes to Kent's *Commentaries,* I am grateful to the anonymous staff of Quadrant Technologies, of

Nashua, New Hampshire. For careful proofreading, my thanks go to Darren Defoe, Sally Defoe, Kate Ffolliot, David Graves, Caitlin Hawkins, Kevin Hogan, Judith Ianelli, Peter Keller, Bridget Linehan, Siobhan Linehan, Kristine McDonald, Cynthia Miller, Michael O'Reilly, Ron Resetarits, Jennifer Spry, Martha Stewart, Tricia Thompson, Judith Walker, and Sundee Webster. My thanks also to Jennifer Donovan, who located Holmes's copies of the *American Law Review* at the Library of Congress.

Portions of the introductory chapters have appeared, in substantially different form, in the *William and Mary Law Review, The Supreme Court Review, Washington University Law Quarterly,* the *Oxford Companion to the Supreme Court,* my *Honorable Justice: The Life of Oliver Wendell Holmes* (1989), and my preface to the Dover edition of *The Common Law.*

Once again I am glad to acknowledge my debt to the deans, the faculty, and the staff of Vermont Law School, and to my students in seminars on Justice Holmes and the history of the Supreme Court, who have helped me in numberless ways over the years. And I am most deeply indebted of all to Carolyn M. Clinton, to whom these volumes are dedicated.

Editorial Principles

The works collected in this edition cover a span of seventy-six years, from Holmes's first publication as a college sophomore, "Books" (5.1), in 1858, to a letter written shortly before his death in 1935 (10.31).

The compilation of a complete bibliography, with publication history and the identification of a copy text, was the first step in the preparation of this edition. It comprises, ultimately, everything that Holmes wrote which was intended either for print publication or for delivery to an audience, as well as a generous selection of his judicial opinions. Working from the Holmes Papers at the Harvard Law School Library and from Holmes's personal library, which he bequeathed to the Library of Congress, I have compiled a complete bibliography of those nonjudicial writings. Thus I have included speeches that existed only in manuscript form and a few letters that were plainly intended to be read at public meetings or to be published by their recipients. I have included all the work actually published, including newspaper reports of his talks where his copy shows that he approved the text.

Although all of Holmes's works were in a certain sense preparation for his opinions, I decided to include only a selection of Holmes's judicial writings from this edition for several reasons. Of course, there are questions of practicality. Holmes's more than 2,200 published, signed opinions are available in every major law library, and most of his decisions after 1890 are easily accessible through WestLaw and LEXIS. Although it would be convenient to have them all bound together with his other published writings, with a common index, the expense and difficulty does not seem justified at this point, nor does it seem to have been contemplated at any stage of the memorial edition's long history (see Chap. 1). Instead, in Volumes 4 and 5 of this edition, I have included a selection of Holmes's published opinions that shows the full development of his thought, and an index of all his published opinions.

Holmes also wrote a number of opinions, memoranda, orders, and jury instructions in the Massachusetts Supreme Judicial Court and the United States Supreme Court that were never published and that have survived in various collections. I hope to assemble these and publish them, but this edition did not seem the appropriate place, and as the effort and expense will be considerable it seemed better to publish these as a separate work when time and funds are available, rather than to risk further delays and mishaps in an already long-delayed enterprise.

The copy text for this edition in every case is the last version approved by Holmes. Details as to the copy texts are given below; publication histories of individual texts appear in the citation which accompanies the text. A few general remarks may help to describe the edition as a whole.

I have either included or appended all the variations among editions of his work published in Holmes's lifetime, and all corrections he marked on his own copies of his works—with one large class of exceptions. Holmes used his published works as a basic reference library which he kept up to date by adding annotations of cases as he came upon them. The margins of his copies of his own books and articles therefore contain a mass of nearly indecipherable marginal notations in a tiny precise hand; Holmes kept a fine-pointed pen for such annotations, much more legible than the rusty, sputtering pens he often used for his letters (or the quill pens he used for a while, in the 1880s, to write his opinions).

Holmes carried on this practice of collecting citations in the margins of his own work from the time of his earliest publications; even his undergraduate essay on Plato is annotated with citations. He bound his articles and judicial opinions into books and kept these annotated copies near his desk, along with his similarly annotated copies of Kent's *Commentaries* and *The Common Law*. This practice helps to explain the extraordinary persistence of ideas and even of specific language in Holmes's work over a period of fifty years. Holmes's published works provided the structure for his memory of law, and he added each new bit of learning to the overall structure.

It would be interesting and useful to have an edition of Holmes's works that included these marginal citations, but even setting aside considerations of practicality, this does not seem consistent with the original plan. The citations of research do not represent material Holmes ever thought of publishing; he did not cite "strings" of citations like those common in modern law reviews. His marginal citations in most cases were certainly meant for his own use, and do not belong in his published works. If Holmes's papers as a whole are published, however, these will be a valuable adjunct to or concordance of his writings.

Of course, there have been a great many judgments to make on individual citations, especially those that begin with "but" or some similar qualifier. Generally I have included marginal notations that had any textual component but have omitted pure citations of cases and texts. Many of Holmes's changes correct errors or make clarifications that he plainly would have included in any later edition of his work. He seems in fact to have planned a revised edition of *The Common Law* at one time, a plan that was not carried out during his lifetime. (See Chap. 9, Intro.) I have noted all of the places Holmes marked as needing revision, and all the changes in the text where Holmes marked them as definite. These annotations are a uniquely valuable guide to Holmes's intention, and most of them have not appeared before in print.

For Holmes's published work there is generally only one version. He systematically destroyed his first drafts, and in any case rarely made more than one for the printer. As his letters and judicial opinions show, he trained himself to write as he spoke, without revision. His printed articles, like his published speeches, were meant to show his thoughts still alive and wriggling. With few exceptions, his articles were published once and not reprinted during his lifetime. (For the exceptions, see Chap. 10, Intro.) Although his ideas did change somewhat over a seventy-year career, he rarely marked any changes of substance in his previously published work. Where he did mark changes, they were almost without exception corrections of errors in citations or quotes—more rarely he corrected errors of grammar or syntax or expanded or clarified terse passages.

Holmes extensively revised some of his long essay notes in Kent's *Commentaries,* apparently for his own convenience; in two cases he had the notes reset in type and tipped the new pages into his copy. These revisions I have included as notes to this edition, although it is not likely that Holmes intended to publish them.

Holmes's edition of Kent's *Commentaries* posed other difficulties. His essay notes were his first effort to restate the common law as a whole and were important in his thinking; they also represented a unique document, an encounter between natural law thinking and Holmes's empirical jurisprudence. The picture of this encounter is worth a dozen books of intellectual history. The few surviving copies of the original edition are now in a state of serious decay, and it therefore seemed important to include both Holmes's notes and enough of the text of *Kent* to provide a context for Holmes's reaction.

Those addresses that I have included from Holmes's book *Speeches* are reprinted from the last edition approved by him (the 1913 edition); I have retained not only the text but also the format. The only exceptions are that the subtitles—the occasion and date—which were originally in small capitals have been reset in italics; and I have ignored the small capitals in which the first word or two of each speech was printed. I have also left *Speeches* intact, leaving out the publication history which accompanies other texts and arranging in a subsequent chapter (Chap. 12, immediately following *Speeches,* Chap. 11) those addresses which were not included in it rather than inserting them in chronological order. *Speeches* is not really an anthology, but a single cohesive work, and should be treated as such.

For those addresses not included in *Speeches,* where more than one version has survived, I have used for copy text the last manuscript version. Holmes would write out his speeches beforehand and then deliver them from memory. After an address was given, he usually copied it into a scrapbook, sometimes making alterations. Holmes seems to have intended the scrapbook version to represent the text as delivered, rather than as written out beforehand; in a few cases, however, he simply inserted the prepared text into the scrapbook and noted that he had delivered it more or less as written. (Rarely does *Speeches* differ from the scrapbook version.) In a few cases, there is no version in Holmes's hand, but he retained a newspaper clipping, usually annotated or at least initialed. The nature of the copy text is given in the citation.

Because the copy texts for Chapter 12 are taken from manuscripts and newspaper clippings, their format was variable. I have therefore used the format of *Speeches* as a model, and have standardized the layout of the hitherto unpublished speeches accordingly.

Some of the addresses in Chapter 12 were collected by Mark DeWolfe Howe in *The Occasional Speeches of Justice Oliver Wendell Holmes.* I have not indicated where this edition varies from his, for the simple reason that the *Occasional Speeches* was never seen or approved by Holmes. It has, however, been until now the only publicly available version of these addresses; those readers familiar with it will notice differences between it and the present edition. These deserve a brief explanation here, since they are not treated elsewhere. The difference which will be most apparent is that I have abandoned Howe's titles, which were entirely his own invention. Where Holmes left a piece untitled, I have simply used the title "Address," or, in the case of tributes or obituaries, the name of the subject, followed by the occasion and date of delivery. The other differences between this edition and Howe's arise from two circumstances. In cases where there is more than one surviving manuscript, Howe seems sometimes to have selected as his copy text a draft other than the last; whether this is because later drafts had not come to light, or because he considered earlier drafts "better" in some way is unknown. Other differences arise from the fact that Howe, like others who have edited Holmes's work, felt free to alter punctuation, spelling, and syntax.

Most of Holmes's articles were printed only once in his lifetime. Virtually the only exceptions are those works which were reprinted in *Collected Legal Papers,* edited by Harold Laski and published in 1920. It appeared during his lifetime and with his approval, but Holmes says in the Preface (see vol. 3, p. 449, below) that he was "unable to do more than run my eye over" the manuscript. His letters to Harold Laski suggest that he actually read the proofs carefully, and submitted corrections to Laski; but Laski had the final say, and, as he was not scrupulous in such matters, it is impossible to know whether the final text is Holmes's. There are a great many uncorrected errors, and many of the changes made in the *Collected Legal Papers* alter Holmes's usual style, so it seems unlikely that he would have made them. Accordingly, I rejected the *Collected Legal Papers* as a copy text, and worked instead from earlier printed versions. However, because the *Collected Legal Papers* was published with Holmes's endorsement, and has been widely used as a definitive and approved work, I have treated it as a variant text in this edition.

Laski (or the publisher) was a consistent, if overenthusiastic, editor, and the bulk of his alterations can be summarized in a few words. They tend to be what Laski must have thought of as stylistic adjustments: commas added or deleted, resulting in changes in syntax and sometimes in meaning; spelling and forms of citation "modernized" and standardized; references to other works italicized or set in quotes. I have not made individual notations of this type of alteration. It is worth noting that the *Collected Legal Papers* was rather carelessly set; variations born of obvious typographical errors in the reprint are not noted. Any variations in word order and the not-infrequent changes in actual content are gathered at the end of each chapter. This is true of addresses included in *Speeches* as well as articles. If an article was reprinted in *Collected Legal Papers,* it is so indicated in the publication history which precedes the text. This was not practicable for the speeches, which lack individual citations; publication history for *Speeches* is given in the Introduction to Chapter 11.

In the few instances of a work republished in Holmes's lifetime other than in the *Collected Legal Papers,* any substantive deviation from the copy text is listed, along with the variations of the *Collected Legal Papers,* at the ends of chapters.

To the extent that it has been possible, I have preserved the original, exactly as represented in the copy text. Thus, the reader will notice stylistic inconsistencies and variations in spelling, not to mention a wild heterogeneity in citation form, from text to text. No effort has been made to standardize most inconsistencies.

However, some changes have been made, some out of necessity, others because usage has changed so radically in the one-hundred-and-thirty-odd years since Holmes began publishing that the original now seems jarring. These are enumerated below.

First, though, a word as to layout. I have standardized the manner in which the text is presented on the page. Even here, I have tried to follow Holmes's lead. Thus, the speeches in Chapter 12 mirror as closely as possible those in Chapter 11. Similarly, all book reviews appear in the form used by *The American Law Review,* in which most of them appeared. Letters are set in a form which closely resembles that used for speeches. The salutation, if there is one, is in small capitals, followed by a dash. Like the speeches in Chapter 12, letters have been titled as discreetly as possible, simply identifying the recipient, with the occasion and date providing a subtitle. Articles retain their titles; in cases where they were untitled, as when they formed part of a section of a journal, they have been given purely descriptive headings. The design of the opening of each text, which varied widely in the originals, has been standardized.

I return to the changes within texts. Case names, of which there are thousands, and which originally appeared in virtually every possible combination of roman and italic fonts, have been made uniform; in this edition they are all italicized, both in Holmes's text and in his footnotes, except the notes to Kent's *Commentaries,* where they are in roman type. The footnoting system has also been standardized. Holmes's footnotes are indicated with asterisks and are placed at the bottom of the page. My own notes are numbered, gathered at the end of each text, and preceded by the phrase, "Editor's Notes."

There were two matters in which the originals seemed joltingly archaic. Ligatures in Latin and Greek words and Latin- and Greek-derived words have been split, and, when necessary (as in the case of Æncyclopedia), the spelling has been modernized. Ligatures in Northern European names, however, have been retained. The other modernization which seemed necessary was the deletion of periods after titles of articles and after roman numerals in the text ("It was said that under Henry V., that a lease. . ."). These periods have been retained in the citations, where they seemed less obtrusive (Y.B. 13 Ed. IV. 9, 10. pl. 5;. . .).

Holmes's footnotes provided a myriad of problems. The font of the original has been preserved, despite both inter- and intratextual inconsistencies. So have Holmes's abbreviations, which are likewise inconsistent, and occasionally terse to the point of being fairly cryptic, a problem compounded by the fact that many of the texts to which he refers are no longer widely read or even available. Perhaps the most frustrating difficulty presented by the footnotes was unraveling the spacing—the small point size and narrow, justified columns of the original footnotes sometimes made it impossible to tell where there were spaces. Holmes's citation form being already inconsistent and difficult, it proved necessary to impose some external standards. I have followed the standards of *The Chicago Manual of Style,* clarified and expanded by editors at the University of Chicago Press.

Most of the decisions I made are summarized above. There were others—Should I replace two asterisks, indicating a passage deleted within a quote, with an ellipsis? I did, and where the omissions had any substantive effect, I made some indication of them in a note or at the end of the chapter. The double brackets used occasionally in the text or notes indicate either editorial insertions or page numbers that have been changed to refer to the present edition.

In some ways the present edition resembles the "New York Edition" of his own work that Henry James published. Like James, Holmes thought of his work as a single evolving corpus, and if he had been more like James, he might himself have published this annotated set as a single vast restatement of his thought. But Holmes always sought a distillation—the Japanese master's brush stroke that suggests a whole distant landscape. James's big, brightly colored Chinese scroll was not for him. And so at the end I cannot say that this edition exactly represents Holmes's intention. Every detail is his work, and this edition shows more of the inner machinery of Holmes's thought than has yet been seen, but in the end it is the brief, stunning opinions that worked the magic, and this whole invisible machinery was the preparation for that.

INTRODUCTION

1

The History of This Edition

This edition of Justice Holmes's works has a long history. In 1932, shortly after Holmes retired from the United States Supreme Court, Sherman F. Mittell proposed to publish an edition of the justice's complete works.[1] Mittell was organizing the National Home Library Foundation; Felix Frankfurter, then a professor at Harvard Law School, helped Mittell to raise money and secure distinguished sponsors for the foundation, which published inexpensive editions of the classics of political thought. I suppose it is fair to say that the foundation had a New Deal inclination; among its early editions, along with the Federalist Papers, were Henry Demarest Lloyd's *Wealth against Commonwealth* and Justice Louis D. Brandeis's *Other People's Money.*

Frankfurter, although at first not formally associated with the foundation, actively advised Mittell and apparently encouraged him to propose an edition of Holmes's works. (Frankfurter himself had already published a partial list of Holmes's early writings, along with reproductions of a few brief articles.)[2] For many years, Frankfurter had also selected a Harvard Law School graduate to serve as Holmes's secretary. On July 15, 1932, Holmes's secretary for that year, Horace Chapman Rose, wrote to Mittell saying that Justice Holmes was "much pleased to hear of your desire to make a more extensive publication of his writings. Although he cannot very well attend to such matters himself, he has left the making of further arrangements in my hands for the present." Rose said that he would consult with Holmes's friends, and from his letters it was plain that his principal adviser was Felix Frankfurter. With Frankfurter's help, Rose compiled a list of all Holmes's published works, including some of the anonymous notes and articles Holmes had written for the *American Law Review.* On August 13, Rose wrote to say that the justice was "thrilled" at the prospect Mittell would undertake to publish his complete works. Mittell suggested a four-volume format, and the details of the table of contents and the division into volumes were hammered out. It is not clear how much Holmes, who was ninety-one and in ill health when the discussions began, participated in the decisions. A list of Holmes's publications was drawn up which did not include all of Holmes's works; but whether this was because not all of the work had been found or because Holmes, Frankfurter, or Rose had decided to omit some of the pieces is not known.

The edition was not yet ready when Holmes died in 1935. His will appointed a literary executor, John G. Palfrey, who had been Holmes's personal attorney, but the Mittell project was set aside for some time. The executor's attention, and Frankfurter's, was directed to the task of preparing two biographies of Holmes. The justice had expected that Frankfurter would write a book on his work as a judge and that Palfrey would commission another author to write a traditional life-and-letters.

In preparation for the latter volume, Palfrey assiduously collected Holmes's private papers, even retrieving three hundred letters Holmes had left in books bequeathed to the Library of Congress and directing that no copies be made before the letters were returned to him.

In 1939, Palfrey commissioned Mark DeWolfe Howe, an able young Harvard law professor who had been Holmes's clerk and a Frankfurter protégé, to edit a two-volume edition of Holmes's correspondence with Frederick Pollock. It seems to have been understood that Howe would eventually write the biography. Howe continued the process of assembling Holmes's personal papers, while Frankfurter assembled materials in preparation for his own volume on Holmes's work as a judge. In 1941, Frankfurter proposed to Mark Howe that they work together on a single unified biography of Holmes. Frankfurter then seems to have gradually found himself too busy to do anything further, and when Howe returned from military service after the war he was the sole authorized biographer.

Holmes's will made some modest, specific bequests and named the United States of America as residuary legatee, to receive the bulk of his estate. The bequest amounted to approximately $250,000, and there was some uncertainty as to how it should be used. A number of proposals were made to Congress, including one to endow a chair of jurisprudence at the Library of Congress. The four-volume Mittell project, which seemed dependent on Frankfurter, remained suspended.

The wheels of government ground slowly. Congress asked the Supreme Court to make recommendations on disposition of the bequest. Justice Brandeis ordinarily would have played a part in the Court's response, but he too was failing and he resigned from the Court in 1939. Nothing had yet been done about Holmes's bequest when Felix Frankfurter was appointed to Brandeis's seat. He then joined Chief Justice Harlan F. Stone and Justice Roberts on a temporary committee concerning the bequest, and the committee was immediately invigorated. Frankfurter submitted a report recommending that the Holmes bequest be used to publish a volume of Holmes's writings, to consist of his general, nontechnical writings—speeches, a few of his articles, and a few of his better-known dissenting opinions. The volume would be published by the Government Printing Office at a low price to make it broadly available to the general public.

Mittell was given a copy of this report and submitted a rebuttal memorandum to the committee. He was evidently exasperated that Frankfurter had abandoned the collected works project, and Mittell's long, emotional memorandum is preserved among his papers. But on May 25, 1939, the committee of justices met briefly in the Court's large conference room and accepted Frankfurter's report. The committee recommended publishing the single volume for a wide audience; but as this plainly would leave the larger part of Holmes's bequest untouched, the committee also recommended using the balance of the fund to improve a park or square in Washington. Holmes had been very fond of walks and drives in Washington parks, and this would have been a suitable memorial.

Mittell abandoned his more ambitious project, apparently unable to proceed without Frankfurter's support. A memorial volume of Holmes's writings and the creation of a park were authorized by Congress in 1940,[3] but no action was taken on the park proposal for many years, and even the book project was set aside when war broke out a few months later.

No further action was taken on the Holmes bequest for nearly fifteen years, a delay that seems to have been due partly to continued disagreement over the proper use of the funds. In 1955, Congress established a new committee to advise it on disposition of the bequest. The committee was chaired by Chief Justice Earl Warren, and the other members included Associate Justices Hugo Black and Felix Frankfurter.[4] This committee reported promptly, and Congress adopted its report, essentially unchanged, the same year, establishing a Permanent Committee of the Oliver Wendell Holmes Devise to supervise the use of the bequest.[5] The Permanent Committee had five members, and the intensity of the struggle over Holmes's memory was reflected in the elaborate procedure for appointing them. The Librarian of Congress served *ex officio* as chairman of the committee; the other members were to be appointed by the president of the United States from panels submitted to him by the Association of American Law Schools, the American Philosophical Society, the American Historical Society, and the Association of American Universities. The appointees served single staggered terms of eight years. This elaborate structure was presumably designed to ensure scholarly objectivity in the administration of Holmes's legacy.

The memorial park was ignored, and Congress directed that the Holmes bequest be used to subsidize three scholarly projects: a history of the Supreme Court, a series of lectures to be known as the Oliver Wendell Holmes Lectures, and a memorial volume of Holmes's writings. (In 1980, Congress authorized acquisition of land for a park adjoining the Supreme Court building to be maintained as a memorial park, which has since been done with appropriated funds.)[6]

Holmes's executor, John G. Palfrey, had died, and his beneficial interest in Holmes's copyrights passed under his will to the Harvard Law School, which for many years thereafter undertook the duties of literary executor. Although scholars were routinely given access to the papers for research, the law school blocked access to Holmes's papers for any biography except one approved by them. Mark DeWolfe Howe, as already noted, was authorized to write the biography of Holmes. Catherine Drinker Bowen, who attempted to write a biography in the 1940s, was denied access to the papers and was refused permission to quote from copyrighted materials. She was obliged to rely on reminiscences of Holmes's clerks and surviving relations, and ultimately wrote a fictionalized account of Holmes and his family.[7]

The Holmes Devise Committee meanwhile had decided that the history of the Supreme Court Congress had authorized should be a multivolume work with numerous authors. Another Frankfurter protégé, Professor Paul A. Freund of Harvard, was named general editor, and the committee chose authors for the individual volumes of the history. The Holmes lectures, given annually at various universities, began in 1960.

Frankfurter himself eventually published a brief biography of Holmes, together with a summary of Holmes's constitutional opinions for the Supreme Court, in which Frankfurter emphasized and perhaps exaggerated the importance of Holmes's dissents on behalf of organized labor and the power of government to regulate business.[8] In his account, Frankfurter ignored Holmes's lifelong loyalty to the Republican party, his free-market economics, and his conservative political views and portrayed him as a tolerant godfather to the New Deal (see chap. 4.3.2, below).

Delays and bad luck have afflicted the other Holmes projects gathered under Frankfurter's aegis. The multivolume history of the Supreme Court has not been completed: the late Paul Freund, for many years general editor and designated author of a key volume, resigned with little of the work completed; other authors resigned or died without completing their assigned tasks. (However, under the present general editor, Professor Stanley N. Katz, the project has been reinvigorated and the long-delayed volumes have resumed their steady progress.)

Mark Howe published two volumes of his biography, covering Holmes's life to his fortieth year. At some point, Howe also began work on an edition of Holmes's complete works, but this was never carried past the early stages. In 1962, Howe published *The Occasional Speeches of Justice Oliver Wendell Holmes*, which consisted of Holmes's *Speeches* (see chap. 11) and some, but not all, of his unpublished addresses. In 1963, Howe published a new edition of *The Common Law* (see chap. 9). He made a partial list of Holmes's articles and had them retyped as if for publication, but the funds available from the Holmes Devise Committee were fully taken up by the history and lecture series, and Howe was more than fully occupied with editions of Holmes's letters, his biography of Holmes, and his teaching duties. Overtaxed as he was and discouraged by what seemed to him the bleakness of Holmes's character, Professor Howe left the biography of Holmes unfinished, and the collected works barely begun.

Harvard Law School then named Yale law professor Grant Gilmore to be Howe's successor. Soon thereafter the curator of the Holmes papers, Erika S. Chadbourn, began preparing an exhibition for the fortieth anniversary of Holmes's death. Gilmore wrote a brief essay on *The Common Law* for the catalog of the exhibit, but his essay was strongly critical of Holmes. Gilmore's piece was harsh—he called *The Common Law* "an elaborate joke."[9] Efforts to compromise differences over what was appropriate on the occasion were not successful, and Gilmore's piece was not published. An essay by Professor Freund appeared in the catalog of the exhibition instead, which like the exhibition itself was a landmark in Holmes scholarship. Gilmore abandoned work on the Holmes biography shortly before his untimely death in 1982, apparently at least in part because he anticipated further disagreement with the Harvard Law School.[10] The collected works of Justice Holmes seemed to have been forgotten.

Nothing further was done until I began work on the present edition. After Gilmore's death, Harvard Law School opened Holmes's papers to qualified scholars, and in 1984 I was given unrestricted access to Holmes's papers for the purpose of writing a biography. When the biography was complete,[11] I proposed to the Permanent Committee on the Oliver Wendell Holmes Devise that I undertake the long-delayed memorial edition of Holmes's work as well, returning to the original plan of collecting essentially all of Holmes's published work. This was approved, and support from the Holmes Devise helped make the present edition possible. The Harvard Law School again granted access to the Holmes papers, and the committee and the Law School have given me complete editorial freedom in preparation of this edition.

More than fifty years after Holmes's death, therefore, there has been a complete biography, and with the current volumes Holmes's published works are available to both scholars and the general public. Justice Frankfurter's efforts ultimately made these books possible, although it was also partly his efforts that so long delayed them. Whether they are the life and works that either Frankfurter or Holmes wanted us to remember, no one can say, and perhaps it does not matter now. I think we do Holmes the honor appropriate to a memorial by presenting an objective account of his work, written with only that degree of sympathy required for understanding.

Editor's Notes

1. See the Sherman F. Mittell Papers, Harvard Law School Library, for the correspondence discussed in the text.

2. Felix Frankfurter, *The Early Writings of O. W. Holmes, Jr.*, 44 HARV. L. REV. 717 (1931). (The same selections were reproduced yet again in FREDERIC ROGERS KELLOGG, THE FORMATIVE ESSAYS OF JUSTICE HOLMES: THE MAKING OF AN AMERICAN LEGAL PHILOSOPHY [Greenwood Press, 1984].) Frankfurter's list omitted half Holmes's articles and book notices for the AMERICAN LAW REVIEW, about sixty items, silently lopping off the entire first three years of Holmes's work on that journal, 1867–70, when his ideas were first forming. Frankfurter referred to the later work as "these earliest of [Holmes's] legal writings," ibid at 718, conveying a distinct impression that the list was complete. He then added a page of description to emphasize the influence on Holmes of the early pragmatism being developed in the 1870s. This surprising set of errors (Holmes himself, or at least his library, were available for an accurate list) had the unfortunate effect of persuading two generations of commentators that Holmes developed his central ideas "during the early 1870's at the same time that he was attending the meetings of the Metaphysical Club at which the pragmatic movement was founded." Thomas Grey, *Holmes and Legal Pragmatism*, 41 STANF. L. REV. 787, 826 (1989). But the Metaphysical Club was largely imaginary, and Holmes had set his course years before. (See chap. 4.3.2, below.)

3. 54 Stat. 7206 (1940).

4. See the QUARTERLY LEGAL HISTORIAN, March, 1963, p. 3.

5. Act of August 5, 1955, 69 Stat. 533 (1955).

6. Act of December 18, 1980, 94 Stat. 3130; Act of December 29, 1982, 96 Stat. 1958.

7. YANKEE FROM OLYMPUS: JUSTICE HOLMES AND HIS FAMILY (Little, Brown and Co., 1944).

8. MR. JUSTICE HOLMES AND THE SUPREME COURT (Harvard University Press, 2d ed. 1961).

9. The essay is apparently preserved in Gilmore's papers at the Harvard Law School, B1 F3. Paul Freund's version of the incident is given in Freund, *Dark Equanimity*, 59 AMER. SCHOLAR 303 (1990).

10. Freund's account is that Gilmore became disenchanted with his subject. Ibid. One of the curiosities of the tale is the decision to appoint Gilmore, whose negative view of Holmes was well known, and one of Gilmore's friends thinks he may have become disenchanted with Harvard.

11. HONORABLE JUSTICE: THE LIFE OF OLIVER WENDELL HOLMES (Little, Brown and Co., 1989).

2

A Brief Biography of Justice Holmes

2.1
NEW ENGLAND BOYHOOD

Oliver Wendell Holmes was born on March 8, 1841, in Boston, Massachusetts, to a family of moderate means.[1] His father, for whom he was named, was a physician and *littérateur* who supplemented his income from a meager Boston medical practice by lecturing on anatomy at the Harvard Medical School and lecturing on literary subjects to general audiences. Doctor Holmes was a gifted conversationalist and a compulsive writer of light verse; when his son was just entering college in 1856, the doctor began writing a series of essays and poems, collectively titled "The Autocrat of the Breakfast Table," for the *Atlantic Monthly* that became immensely popular in Great Britain and the United States and made Dr. Holmes a public figure. Like the doctor, Wendell Holmes was intensely talkative, with a light, combative manner and a knack for verse rhythms and imagery.

Mrs. Holmes, born Amelia Lee Jackson, the daughter of prominent Boston lawyer and judge Charles Jackson, devoted herself to her husband and three children, of whom the future Supreme Court justice was the first, and to charitable work in Boston. She was one of the leaders in organizing volunteer work in Boston to support the Union Army during the Civil War.

Wendell Holmes—tall, thin, lantern-jawed—resembled his mother more than his short, round-faced father and was deeply affected by her. He was her favorite and acquired a secure self-confidence as a result. He received also from his mother a powerful sense of duty and a talent for strong, warmly affectionate friendships. With his sense of duty came an unyielding adherence to the factual, a sharp skepticism for all but the self-evident, and a near-mystical acceptance of whatever in life seemed irrevocably given.

Holmes attended private schools and Harvard College, but the principal influences on his intellectual development were outside the classroom. He acquired early, as an article of faith, belief in a pre-Darwinian doctrine of evolution compounded of Malthus and German Romanticism. In later life, Holmes said that the great figures of his youth were Ruskin, Carlyle, and Emerson. He probably absorbed their ideas as much from conversation in his father's house, where Emerson and other literary figures were occasional callers, as from his reading. Emerson passed the "ferment" of philosophical inquiry on to Holmes, partly by encouraging his combative independence of mind. Holmes's first published essay, "Books" (see this volume, chap. 5.1), was an emulation of Emerson's essay of the same title. In 1860, while still an undergraduate, Holmes published essays on Plato's philosophy (5.5) and Dürer's engravings (5.6). The Dürer essay was a graceful homage to Emerson, but the essay on Plato was an attack. The attack was based on Holmes's belief that science had proven the truth of materialism and evolution, so that Plato's—and Emerson's—idealism had been proven wrong.

Holmes later recalled that while he had not yet read Darwin, evolutionism was in the air. The atmosphere was as much affected by Hegel as by Darwin, and Holmes's image of society as a conflict of collective wills owes as much to German philosophy as to English empirical science. Holmes's version of evolutionism also was partly inspired by R. A. Vaughan's *Hours with the Mystics,* which he read while working on the Plato essay. Vaughan gave a historical, evolutionary account of religion.

In his undergraduate essay on Dürer (5.6), Holmes announced the need for a "rational" explanation of duty, a sort of scientific substitute for religion which he sought in a scientific account of both history and philosophy.

The other great influence on his youth was a revival of chivalry then sweeping over the United States and Great Britain, partly inspired by Tennyson and Sir Walter Scott. Like many of his contemporaries, Holmes acquired a lifelong commitment to courtly ideals and conduct. Chivalry was the code of duty for which he sought—and ultimately believed he had found—scientific justification.

In July, 1861, at the age of twenty, Holmes enlisted in the federal army and obtained a commission as a lieutenant. He served for two years in the Twentieth Massachusetts Volunteer Infantry at Ball's Bluff, the Peninsula Campaign, and Antietam. In those two years he was wounded three times, twice near fatally, and suffered from dysentery. Exhausted, and reluctant to assume a command for which he had little aptitude, in the winter of 1863–64 Holmes accepted a post as aide to General Wright (and then to General Sedgwick) of the Sixth Corps. In the relative leisure of winter quarters, he turned to philosophical writing (in notebooks he later destroyed), developing his combat experience into a materialist, evolutionist philosophy steeped in conflicts between rival nations and races, and governed by the rules of chivalry.

He served through the Wilderness Campaign and the siege of Vicksburg, and then, exhausted and telling himself that his duty lay in pursuing his philosophy, he left the army when his three-year term of enlistment was up. His parents urged him to reenlist for the duration of the war, but he returned home to Boston.

2.2
THE COMMON LAW

Holmes attended Harvard Law School for a little more than one year, in 1864–65. In the summer of 1866, to complete his education, he traveled to Great Britain and the Continent. He began his long assault on London polite society, was invited to a great many homes, and made lasting friendships. One of his most important friendships was with Leslie Stephen, who greatly reinforced Holmes's interest in rationalist philosophy, evolution, and chivalry. Stephen had also undertaken to find a scientific basis for morality and believed for a time that Darwinism was the key. Holmes's diary of his 1866 journey shows that he and Stephen spent weeks climbing in Switzerland, talking philosophy.

Holmes returned to London for the summer social season whenever he could, and kept up a very energetic and extensive correspondence with English and Irish friends between visits, especially with young married women, who were more open to the traditions of courtly love than their Boston counterparts.

On his return to Boston, Holmes entered a clerkship and was admitted to the bar in 1867. He briefly practiced with a Boston law firm, but he devoted his spare time to writing for the *American Law Review.* In 1870, he resigned from the firm and attempted a career as an independent scholar, writing dozens of brief articles and reviews (see chap. 6), editing the twelfth edition of Chancellor James Kent's *Commentaries on American Law* (chap. 7), and writing occasional poems (chap. 5). Elements of his later thought were formed in these years, but he did not put them into coherent form. Among the fundamental ideas he arrived at in this time was his theory of the judicial function. Judges decided cases first and found reasons afterward. Holmes believed that judges' decisions were choices, often unconsciously made, between contending principles and that the decisions were more revealing than the opinions written to explain them. The decisions marked out the legal territory dominated by competing principles and eventually fixed the boundary between them, but the judges' opinions only offered rationalizations for the largely unconscious process of choice.

During the five years of his independent scholarship, he lived with his parents and supported himself with fees from lectures at Harvard College, from the occasional practice of law, and from editing Kent's *Commentaries.* In 1872, he married a childhood friend, Fanny Dixwell, and as his income from writing was insufficient to maintain a separate household, he gave up his scholarly work and joined a Boston law firm, with a busy commercial and admiralty practice, that became Shattuck, Holmes, and Munroe.

Fanny Holmes became seriously ill with rheumatic fever shortly after their marriage, and Holmes devoted himself to her and to his law practice for several years. They were never to have children.

He gradually returned to scholarly work in his spare hours, and in 1876, with "Primitive Notions in Modern Law" (8.1), he began a series of essays that presented a systematic analysis of the common law. He completed the series, somewhat hastily, and gave them as the Lowell Lectures (see 8.10) in November–December, 1880, and published them as a book, *The Common Law* (chap. 9), in 1881, a few days before his fortieth birthday.

The Common Law has been called the greatest work of American legal scholarship. It became one of the founding documents of the sociological and then the realist schools of jurisprudence, and more recently of legal pragmatism and the study of the economic basis of the law. It had a considerable impact on tort and contract law in both the United States and Great Britain, and formed the basis of Holmes's later work on the Supreme Court.

In Holmes's view, acquired in fifteen years of law practice and study, the actual grounds of judges' decisions were inarticulate views of social policy, the "felt necessities" of their time, as much as precedent or the logical rationalizations offered in opinions. Consciously or unconsciously, judges expressed the wishes of their class: "[L]aw . . . expresses the beliefs and wishes of the dominant force of the community," as he put it later. The relentless operation of natural selection would erase any lawmaking group that did not serve the survival interests of the dominant power.

Law accordingly was both an instrument and the result of natural selection. If law was simply an instrument to accomplish certain material ends, it followed that the law should concern itself solely with external behavior, and Holmes argued that he could discern in the developing common law a trend toward complete reliance on "external standards" of behavior rather than on subjective states of mind or personal culpability. A society which successfully expressed its true self-interest in laws would flourish in the struggle for survival.

This evolutionist argument is now of only historical interest, but to it Holmes added a truly original insight. Law writers, including Holmes himself through 1880, the year of his Lowell Lectures, had tried but failed to make sense of the multitudinous rules of conduct that courts seemed to recognize and enforce. A landowner had a duty to guests but not to trespassers; railroad companies had complex duties toward their passengers, the owners of their freight, and pedestrians crossing their tracks. Holmes had labored unsuccessfully, like his predecessors, to make sense of this tangled mass of duties and correlative rights. In 1880, however, he seems to have seen a new organizing principle. The question in every case, Holmes realized, was whether liability would be imposed. His great insight was to examine, not the rules themselves, but the circumstances under which a breach of the rule would be punished. By looking at the circumstances in which liability was imposed and ignoring rationalizations about duty and rules of conduct, Holmes was able to make general statements about law and its relation to society. The general organizing principle of *The Common Law* then became clear. It was the famous "external standard," the single basis for all liability in the common law: s breach of duty would be inferred, and liability would be imposed, when injuries resulted from behavior that an ordinary person would have foreseen would be damaging.

The law accordingly was founded on a policy of avoiding foreseeable, and therefore unjustified, harms. In *The Common Law,* Holmes argued that law had evolved from more primitive origins toward this still partly unconscious "external standard" of liability and that law would continue to evolve toward a fully self-aware instrument of social purpose. Holmes's book itself, presumably, was an important step in this evolution toward self-awareness.

2.3
AN OBSCURE JUDGE

After *The Common Law* appeared, in March, 1881, Holmes taught for a single semester at Harvard Law School and then accepted appointment as an associate justice of the Supreme Judicial Court of Massachusetts. He became chief justice in 1899.

Holmes wrote approximately thirteen hundred opinions for the Massachusetts court, most of them deciding common law questions or construing statutes in light of the common law. In his early opinions he relentlessly worked through the thesis of *The Common Law.* Until he became chief justice, Holmes generally avoided writing opinions in constitutional cases, but when obliged to state a view, he usually expressed deference to the legislature. His opinions and letters of the time make clear that he based this deference on the English constitutional principle that the legislature was omnipotent, a principle that in his view was modified in the United States only to the extent that written constitutions contained clear limitations on legislative authority. This was the reasoning of Cooley's famous treatise *Constitutional Limitations,* a book Holmes had favorably reviewed (6.53) and used when teaching, but it would have been a natural enough conclusion from his own approach to jurisprudence.

Beginning in 1884, with his well-known "Memorial Day Address" (11.1), Holmes also began giving carefully prepared public lectures in which he expressed his personal philosophy. Ralph Waldo Emerson was evidently the model for this form of essay-lecture. Holmes had some of these addresses bound into a slim book, *Speeches* (chap. 11), presenting both a self-portrait and a philosophy. Holmes dwelt heavily on the lesson he had drawn from the Civil War, the duty of self-sacrifice in the interest of ideals, which he attempted to mesh with his evolutionism by supposing an instinct of self-sacrifice in the service of the higher purposes of evolution: humanity was like "the grub that prepares a chamber for the winged thing it has never seen but is to be" (11.20). Holmes identified his own sense of duty and his code of honor with this instinctive sense of service to a higher purpose. To reconcile his ambition with his sense of duty, he put forward the belief that personal ambition is only an illusion through which nature extracts effort in aid of its unknowable purposes. He called his personal philosophy "mystical materialism."

In the 1890s, Fanny Holmes had suffered a recurrence of her rheumatic fever and, isolated in their Boston home, became markedly eccentric. Holmes's younger brother and sister, his mother and father, died, leaving him and a nephew the only survivors of his father's family. Principled but unpopular dissents he had written seemed to cut off any prospect of promotion to the United States Supreme Court. His own health was uncertain, and he seemed destined to end as an obscure, quickly forgotten judge. During this difficult period, Holmes made one last major addition to his legal writings.

In "Privilege, Malice, and Intent" (10.5), published in 1894, Holmes discussed libel and slander cases in which liability was based, at least in part, on the defendant's state of mind—actual malice—rather than on an external standard of foreseeable harm. In these cases, Holmes argued, a common-law privilege to do harm—like the privilege accorded to truthful speech—was based on a social policy favoring freedom of speech, but the privilege would be withdrawn when used for a malicious purpose. The defendant's subjective state of mind, and not just the objective standard of foreseeable harm, could be considered by the courts. This was a significant departure from the thesis of *The Common Law* and had ramifications through all of his thinking. Holmes now was obliged to say that the external standard of liability was just one element of a more complex standard. The more general question was whether, taking into account both what he had done and what he intended, the defendant's behavior in a particular case created an unacceptable risk of harm.

Holmes would later incorporate this more general standard into his opinions on the First Amendment. In 1896, he applied the new refinement of his theory in dissenting opinions in which he argued that a privilege should be extended to trade unions to organize and picket peacefully so long as these activities were carried on not for the purpose of doing harm but for a justifiable self-advantage.

Holmes suggested that, in English and American cases in which the right of unions to conduct strikes or boycotts had been denied, the judges had been biased by class prejudice. He argued forcefully that it was the duty of a judge to decide cases fairly, even if the result appeared dangerous to that judge's class interests.

This argument seemed inconsistent with Holmes's theory that judges were instruments of the dominant force in society, but in his legal writings he never acknowledged or explained the seeming contradiction of his view that natural selection over the long run would keep judges from expressing any interest but that of the dominant class, a view he continued to affirm. He attempted to reconcile the two only in his philosophical addresses, as in "The Soldier's Faith" (11.12) and "Law and the Court" (11.20), where he urged faith in the higher and more distant goals of human evolution. In his opinions, Holmes struck a new note—his own duty, as a judge, to set aside his loyalties and to decide cases fairly even if that meant the extinction of his race.

Holmes devoted himself to work and to Fanny's care, but he spent his summer vacations in Great Britain, dining out in London and visiting country houses, returning to Boston in the autumn. He said often that his compressed, forceful style of writing owed much to London dinner conversation. When abroad, he conducted courtly flirtations that he continued through correspondence after his return to the states. Holmes's letters to Lady Castletown, whom he visited in the summers of 1896 and 1898, have been preserved and contain a record of a moving and frank affection. He expressed his personal philosophy in letters to women more clearly than in any other medium, and often worked his ideas through for the first time in these letters and the conversations they reflected.

In 1899, when he became chief justice of Massachusetts, Holmes began to write many more opinions in constitutional cases, apparently to help clear the docket of numerous challenges to state regulatory statutes. In the three years before his appointment to the United States Supreme Court, he worked through in some detail his view that both state and federal constitutions should be construed in light of the common law.

2.4
MASTER OF HIS ART

The assassination of President McKinley and the incapacity of Supreme Court justice Horace Gray opened an unexpected prospect of promotion. On August 11, 1902, President Theodore Roosevelt nominated Holmes to the United States Supreme Court. He took his seat on December 8, 1902, and thereafter both Holmes and Fanny seemed to come into their own. Fanny had recovered her health, and in Washington she had a social position and could share in Holmes's career. His post imposed a great many social obligations on them both, which she met on their joint behalf with great energy and success. She also had responsibility for raising an orphaned niece, Dorothy Upham, who came to live with the Holmeses shortly after their arrival in Washington.

Holmes too was happy. After thirty-five years of trying to extract philosophical principles from the most meager materials, petty disputes, and sordid crimes, now for the first time he was addressing great questions of public life and national policy. With a new self-confidence, he developed opinion writing into an art peculiar to himself; and while his opinions were often difficult to follow and have always been criticized for undue brevity and obscurity, they often achieved a unique beauty and power.

Holmes served on the Supreme Court for thirty years, under four chief justices. Through longevity and an immense appetite for work, Holmes succeeded in writing 873 opinions for the Court, far more than any other justice has ever written. Key to his early success on the Court was his close friendship with Chief Justice Melville Fuller, who treated Holmes as a deputy and assigned to him many of the important constitutional cases that were decided between 1902 and Fuller's death in 1910. Fuller and Holmes agreed in most decisions, and from environmental law to constitutional questions their collaboration dominated the Court during Fuller's tenure.

Holmes wrote proportionately fewer dissents than many justices, but as these were particularly forceful and well written they are the best known of his opinions. A handful of his dissents, especially in substantive due process and free speech cases, are now cited as precedent.

Holmes expressed in his opinions the usually inarticulate premises on which decisions were based, striving to make the law more self-aware and scientific. This struggle to touch the inner reasons of decision gave his opinions much of their power.

In cases where precedent was not decisive, the choice was fundamentally one between competing social policies, and the judge's task was to choose wisely. He accordingly stated his own philosophy and his views on economics when these seemed pertinent, and freely exposed his brother justices' willingness to write their inarticulate assumptions into the Constitution.

The basis of his economic views was a conventional belief in the free market. His often-expressed conviction was that the "stream of products," by which he meant something like the gross national product, was fixed at any one time and that any increase would be quickly absorbed by the growth of population. He believed further that the share of products withdrawn by the wealthy capitalist class for its own consumption was minuscule in comparison to the total. If essentially all the wealth in society was consumed by the large mass of its citizens, it seemed to follow that workers competed with each other, not with capitalists, for a larger share of the national product and that prices reflected, not costs or competition, but the share of the product that consumers were willing to give to any one commodity. Proposals for economic reform, redistribution of wealth, and enhanced competition therefore seemed to him equally wrong. He believed that the Sherman Antitrust Act was an "imbecile statute"—"which aims at making everyone fight and forbidding anyone to be victorious." He insisted that the only hope for improved living conditions lay in eugenics and population control—"taking life in hand"—a view brutally expressed in his letters and in his opinion in *Buck v. Bell,* upholding Virginia's compulsory sterilization law.

2.5
THE DUTY TO CHOOSE FAIRLY

Holmes's most important opinions concerned constitutional law. In his view, the general terms of the Constitution—freedom of speech, due process of law—were to be understood as embodying "relatively fundamental principles of right" found in the common law. As that law was changing, so too were the meanings of constitutional terms—"a word is not a crystal, transparent and unchanging, but the skin of a living thought." Fundamental principles were to be viewed from the perspective of centuries, a perspective from which universal suffrage was a recent innovation, and property rights were by no means fixed or eternal.

To Holmes, the fundamental guarantees revolved around fairness in judicial proceedings. It was his opinion that the unrestrained investigations of the Interstate Commerce Commission, to which he objected, seemed to compel self-incriminating testimony. He refused to accept a procedure of empty forms when African-American and Jewish defendants were tried in lynch-mob settings. He insisted on the right of the federal courts to intervene in state proceedings by writ of habeas corpus. He wrote opinions limiting court power to punish contempt summarily, without trial, and in 1906 he managed the only criminal contempt trial that had ever been held in the Supreme Court, *United States v. Shipp,* against a state official who had conspired in a lynching.

Holmes was much more deferential to the states and to the other branches of government with regard to substantive guarantees of the Constitution. Holmes did not take an expansive view of constitutional rights. He had grown up in a world in which the right to vote was still limited to men of property, and his views of the power of government were formed in the Civil War. Although he had nearly given his life in the Abolitionist cause and was as nearly free of racial prejudice as anyone in public life in his time, he repeatedly avoided making any defense of the right of African-Americans to vote. He did not believe that wiretaps were unreasonable searches and seizures forbidden by the Fourth Amendment, and he rejected a right of privacy based on the Fourth and Fifth Amendments.

If he took a narrow view of civil rights, he took a similarly restrained approach to rights of property. He believed that property rights were created by the legislatures and could be undone pretty much at will, the only question usually being whether compensation was owed when the government destroyed a form of property.

Of all Holmes's opinions, the most important and the most controversial were in cases concerning the First Amendment's guarantee of freedom of speech.

During the First World War the federal government had prosecuted thousands of men and women who opposed or resisted mobilization. The first of these cases to be decided by the Court concerned speeches and leaflets that the government claimed were intended to obstruct the draft, in violation of the Espionage Act. In *Schenck v. United States* and two similar cases, Holmes writing for a unanimous Court said that Congress had the power to forbid speeches and publications that threatened to interfere with the draft. Freedom of speech was not absolute: a man might be punished for falsely crying fire in a theater and causing a panic. As Congress could make it a crime to obstruct the draft, so it might also punish speech that was intended to and did pose a "clear and present danger" of having this forbidden result. This was simply the common-law standard of liability, based on risk of harm, that he had added to his theory in the 1890s.

In a second group of cases, beginning in 1918, the Court had voted to affirm convictions for obstructing the war effort but Holmes had dissented. It appeared to him that in this second group of cases, the federal government had broadened its campaign of prosecutions to include political dissidents as well as draft resisters, and that these defendants were being convicted and sentenced to terms of up to twenty years' imprisonment for their socialist and anarchist ideas rather than for acts intended or likely to harm the war effort. The first of these cases was withdrawn by the government, apparently because the Justice Department had learned of Holmes's strongly worded dissent. The Court's unanimous opinion in *Schenck,* accordingly, was the first to be announced. But in 1919, in *Abrams v. United States,* the first of the political speech cases to be published, Holmes delivered a dissenting opinion in which he restated the "clear and present danger" test in more detail. The defendants' privilege to speak freely on political questions, and to cause foreseeable harms, might be defeated by an actual intent to do harm. But neither by the external standard of foreseeability, nor by the test of actual intent, did the defendants' acts pose a clear and present danger to the war effort.

Holmes went on to give his statement of the policy that he believed underlay the privilege afforded by the Constitution to honest expressions of opinion. Free speech was tolerated by the governing power in order to ensure that the ideas that offered the best hope of victory in the struggle for life were given their chance.

> [W]hen men have realized that time has upset many fighting faiths, they may come to believe even more than they believe the very foundations of their own conduct that the ultimate good desired is better reached by free trade in ideas—that the best test of truth is the power of the thought to get itself accepted in the competition of the market, and that truth is the only ground upon which our wishes safely can be carried out. That, at any rate, is the theory of our Constitution. It is an experiment, as all life is an experiment.

Although Holmes appeared willing to see some restrictions on free speech, he repeated again and again his view that political dissent was to be freely allowed; it was precisely those ideas that challenged and tested the principles of American society in the free competition of discourse that were to be most jealously protected: "[I]f there is any principle of the Constitution that more imperatively calls for attachment than any other it is the principle of free thought—not free thought for those who agree with us but freedom for the thought that we hate."

Holmes's constitutional opinions fit into a coherent view of the American system evolved from his own experiences and his studies of the common law. Holmes believed that the law of the English-speaking peoples was an experiment in peaceful evolution in which a fair hearing in court substituted for the violent combat of more primitive societies. In the American federal system, a refinement of this experiment, the states provided "insulated chambers" for experiments in law and political economy; these experiments were to be tolerated as long as they were conducted in accordance with the rules for making fair decisions about the outcome. Experiments even in socialism were not foreclosed by any principle fundamental to the law. Nor did Holmes believe that any religious or ethical precepts were fundamental. The Constitution, like the common law from which it had grown, was simply an evolving system of discourse in which the survival of rival groups and classes was determined by peaceful competition.

To Holmes, life was a continual clash of groups—nations, races, classes—representing great conflicting principles, struggling for survival in a world of limited resources. The task of the judge was to choose fairly between contending forces. Political truth was to be worked out in the competition of the marketplace and not imposed by armies or police.

The inconsistency in Holmes's idea of the judge's role became more marked as he grew older. The quasi-scientific system of *The Common Law* required judges to serve the survival of their own class or nation. Yet in the constitutional law Holmes described as he grew older, the judge was obliged to set aside his personal loyalties and views, and decide cases fairly even when that would mean death to the existing order.

Holmes's self-denying sense of duty, his loyalty to the future of humanity rather than to its present order, that to him reconciled the contradiction, apparently was founded on something outside the evolutionary system of law. It could not be reconciled with Holmes's system except by a mystical faith in the unknowable purposes of evolution. As Holmes grew older, his sense of duty came to predominate, so that his opinions seemed to be the impersonal voice of duty itself.

Fanny died in 1929, and Holmes's health failed in the summer of 1931. On January 11, 1932, at the suggestion of Chief Justice Charles Evans Hughes, he submitted his resignation to the president. He died of pneumonia at his home in Washington, D.C., in the early hours of March 6, 1935.

3

Holmes's Philosophy and Jurisprudence: Origin and Development of Principal Themes

---

3.1
INTRODUCTION

Holmes wanted to be remembered as a thinker. As he told Nina Gray, he would not have done much more than walk across the street to be promoted from justice to chief justice, but he wanted to be the greatest legal thinker who had ever lived.[1] It was a complex ambition, for he wished also to be an artist and a gentleman, as if to combine Sir Philip Sidney and Baruch Spinoza, whose qualities he believed ordinarily were incompatible.

To reconcile them, Holmes chose to embed his philosophical discoveries in forms acceptable to polite society. Poetry, he found, was not his medium, but he was a brilliant conversationalist; and so, odd as it seems, he spun out his theories in sparkling talk and courtly letters to young women, and then set them in more precisely faceted, formal addresses, delivered to surely somewhat startled audiences in rural New Hampshire and Massachusetts. He presented nicely bound copies of his *Speeches* (chap. 11) to English women of good family, and eventually the most carefully tested of his ideas could be detected beneath the surface of his judicial opinions.

This method precluded anything so dull and underbred as explanation. Not that there was any secret about his ideas. "Spinoza is the boy," he wrote to Felix Frankfurter, "he sees the world as I see it—and he alone of all the old ones that I know."[2] But Spinoza's quasi-mathematical deductions, like all formal systems, were both boring and vulnerable to attack. To the philosopher Morris R. Cohen, whom he greatly admired, Holmes wrote in his best swordsman's manner: "Systems are forgotten—only a man's aperçus are remembered. I used to say—extravagantly of course—that Kant could have told his main points to a young lady in ten minutes after dinner."[3]

So Holmes never made any systematic presentation of his thought. He labored patiently at technical philosophy—while on circuit in Massachusetts, in a hotel room with no books available, he wrote out for Anna Lyman Gray a careful outline of Kant's *Critique of Pure Reason*—but he did not emulate the academic philosophers. Impact, not dead pull, did the job, he liked to say. He found and carefully polished a few images that conveyed his meaning, but were highly resistant to analysis or refutation. He compared these images to a complicated mechanism that had gradually been refined into a single, smooth, oddly shaped brass part.

In my biography of Justice Holmes[4] it seemed proper to let him have his effects. But explanation also has its place, if only below decks; so while Holmes lightly touches the helm, we may now trudge down to the engine room and have a look at the machinery.

3.2
HOLMES'S GENERAL DEVELOPMENT

3.2.1 New England Boyhood. Holmes's father, the doctor, for whom he was named, was an eighteenth-century man, an optimist and an admirer of Leibniz; we must imagine him debating with his young son whether there were absolute truths. *The Autocrat of the Breakfast Table,* published in 1858, began with a combative exchange over Leibniz between the Autocrat and the "divinity student"—a transparent disguise for serious, seventeen-year-old Wendell Holmes.[5]

The doctor believed in reason and was something of a skeptic in religion; but he liked to reserve a little green room for free will, and kept an open mind on spiritualism and whether Bacon wrote Shakespeare. As the son said later,

> [T]here was with him as with the rest of his generation a certain softness of attitude toward the interstitial miracle . . . that I did not feel. The difference was in the air, although perhaps only the few of my time felt it. The Origin of Species I think came out when I was in college—H. Spencer announced his intention of putting the universe into our pockets—I hadn't read either of them to be sure, but as I say it was in the air. I did read Buckle—now almost forgotten—but making a noise in his day. . . . Emerson and Ruskin were the men that set me on fire. Probably a skeptical temperament that I got from my mother had something to do with my way of thinking. Then I was in with the Abolitionists, some or many of whom were skeptics as well as dogmatists. But I think science was at the bottom.[6]

The scientific atmosphere was a wind sweeping in from Germany. Holmes's friends Henry and William James, Henry and Brooks Adams, made their pilgrimage to the German universities. Ralph Waldo Emerson and Henry James, Sr., joined the St. Louis Philosophical Society, in seeking to combine Hegel and American transcendentalism.[7] "Science" in this world meant two things. First, as it still does today in socialist countries, "science" meant the study of hidden, fundamental forces or principles of history. Emerson said,

> Beside all the small reasons we assign, there is a great reason for the existence of every extant fact; a reason which lies grand and immovable, often unsuspected, behind it in silence. The Times are the masquerade of the Eternities; trivial to the dull, tokens of noble and majestic agents to the wise; the receptacle in which the Past leaves its history; the quarry out of which the genius of today is building up the Future.[8]

(Seventy years later, Holmes, reflecting on his own career, said, "My chief interest in the law has been in the effort to show the universal in the particular—That has kept me alive.")[9] In this view Plato and Kant were figures in the history of science. Second, science meant evolution. Scientific inquiry into the spirit of the time showed that the world was developing, progressing, through the struggle of contending ideas. Emerson again:

> What is the scholar, what is the man *for*, but for hospitality to every new thought of his time? . . . You shall be the asylum of and patron of every new thought, every unproven opinion, every untried project which proceeds out of good will and honest seeking. All the newspapers, all the tongues of today will of course at first defame what is noble . . . the highest compliment man ever receives from heaven is the sending to him its disguised and discredited angels.[10]

Both Emerson and Carlyle inspired Holmes with their vivid pictures of history as evolution, as the embodiment of advancing ideas, and with their implicit call to heroic accomplishment. Both Carlyle's *The French Revolution* and his *Sartor Resartus* were read and admired by Holmes, and when his father asked him the parlor-game question, what book he would take with him to a desert island, Holmes answered, *"The French Revolution."*[11]

But Emerson was the great inspiration of Holmes's development. One cannot trace particular ideas in Holmes's later works to Emerson, but the older man certainly inspired Holmes to write, and confirmed in him the attitudes and assumption that were the context of his work. In the 1850s, Holmes recalled, when he himself was in his teens, he saw Emerson on the other side of the street. Holmes ran over and said, "If I ever do anything, I shall owe a great deal of it to you."[12] In middle life, when he had written the first article setting out his mature philosophy of law, he sent a copy to Emerson:

> It seems to me that I have learned, after a laborious and somewhat painful period of probation, that the law opens a way to philosophy as well as anything else, if pursued far enough, and I hope to prove it before I die. Accept this little piece as written in that faith, and as [a] slight mark of the gratitude and respect I feel for you who more than anyone else first started the philosophical ferment in my mind.[13]

Toward the end of his life, Holmes said, "The only firebrand of my youth that burns to me as brightly as ever is Emerson."[14]

Emerson encouraged Holmes to exercise his individual judgment and to test all tradition by his own measure; Emerson embodied the solitary search for principle that to Holmes was the scientific method. He also introduced Holmes to Plato, another lasting influence in manifold ways. Holmes—who always exemplified Harold Bloom's anxiety of influence—reacted by opposing Plato's and Emerson's idealism, but he bore the marks of their method all his life. Especially did he become committed to the Socratic techniques of investigation—the *reductio ad absurdum* above all. This became his characteristic test of arguments, in law as in philosophy. Rights, for instance, were not ultimate, because taken to their extremes they were absurd; only the power of the state could be extended without limit and without contradiction.

Holmes summarized his understanding of this world view in two essays, written in the summer following his junior year at college. In an essay on Plato, he described philosophy as a search for empirical principles in the material world, and Plato as an early, long-outmoded scientist (5.5). In an essay on Dürer, written about the same time, he used his understanding of scientific principles to describe the development of art, as shown in the evolution of engraving technique and subject matter (5.6). In this remarkable work, Holmes treats works of art—as he would later treat judicial opinions—as unconscious expressions of the mentality of their time. The scientific historian studying these data, rather than the artist himself, understood the principles being revealed.

From his mother, Holmes acquired what he called a skeptical temperament, by which he seemed to mean a sense of acceptance of what was immediately given, and a doubt of anything that did not seem obvious. He also acquired from her a rigid sense of duty, a sense of obligation to accomplish something definite in each twenty-four hours. She smiled on his Abolitionism, and at his twentieth birthday, on the eve of the Civil War, she gave him a life of Sir Philip Sidney, the chivalric model of a gentleman. Holmes believed in scientific evolution as the latest stage in the development of philosophy, as he believed that science would find a new justification for morality, which was to say, for duty (see chap. 5). He was two generations removed from orthodox Christianity, and his table of duties was taken not from the Bible but from the code of chivalry. Like many in his time and circumstances, the manners of a gentleman or lady were his true morality; but he had more candor and self-awareness in this matter than most.

His mother was pleased when he enlisted in the Union Army; his father, who was not an Abolitionist, was not pleased at first. But when the war had begun in earnest the doctor became one of its principal propogandists. After three years of infantry combat, thrice wounded and often ill, Holmes wished to leave the army, but both his parents urged him to reenlist until the war's end, although that seemed to him to mean almost certain death. He began the war with a sense that duty meant ultimate self-sacrifice: Tennyson's "do and die." At first he was willing enough, but he could not continue in this way. He grew weary, and he grew older. After his second year of combat he left his regiment—one of its few surviving officers—for a safer staff position. In the winter of 1863–64, at relative leisure in staff headquarters, he talked compulsively with fellow officers and composed a series of essays in which he tried to make philosophic sense of his experiences in battle, above all trying to understand the duty of self-sacrifice.

He destroyed nearly all of the notebooks of this period, but enough can be gathered from remaining fragments and his contemporaneous letters to say that he came out of the army a thorough materialist and a mechanist who thought that human beings acted largely on unconscious impulse. The war taught him that government was founded on violence. And like the veterans of a later war, he ended with a deep-seated existentialist conviction that there was no external or absolute moral order, that he was free to be what he chose.

As the war ground on, he came at last to feel that his true duty was in the development of these philosophical ideas rather than in the anonymous death which in all probability awaited him if he remained in the army. And with this rationale to comfort him, he left the war after his first term of enlistment had ended and his regiment had ceased to exist.

3.2.2 Early Writings. Despite Holmes's determination to pursue philosophy (and art) his father made it plain that his son would have to earn a living, and Holmes trained for the bar. But law school was a perfunctory affair then, and Holmes's diaries and letters of the time show he was principally immersed in philosophy.

We have no record of Holmes's conversations and only a few of his letters from this period. His diaries contain a list of his reading,[15] but it isn't likely Holmes was ever deeply influenced by a book. The reading list is a record, not of influences, but of a preconceived program of study which suggests both his interest and, I would guess, the conclusion he hoped to arrive at. He read the utilitarian writers, especially Austin and Mill; but nearly all the reading is historical or on the theory of evolution. He read a number of histories of philosophy: the Hegelian historian of law, von Savigny, and the French anthropologist of ancient law, Fustel de Coulanges; Henry Maine's evolutionist account, *Ancient Law;* Stirling's *Secret of Hegel.* He read Herbert Spencer's *First Principles* of evolutionary philosophy and Chauncey Wright's positive review in the *North American Review* of Spencer's works. Holmes warmly recalled Wright's influence. It was Wright who confirmed in him the belief that logical arguments were not absolute; that, as he had told his father, one could not say "necessary" to the cosmos. Holmes probably also read and heard Chauncey Wright arguing that consciousness resulted from material, mechanistic evolution.[16]

In addition to history and evolution, Holmes read a good deal of Kant, and of post-Kantian investigations into the structure of language and thought. He reread Hamilton's version of Kant and Mill's commentary on Hamilton's Kant. A small army of European scholars were turning Kant's philosophy into psychology and logic; Holmes read Alexander Bain on the psychological basis of logic and several books on the new historical studies of language in which structural linguistics was getting its start, like Pictet's study in French of *Indo-European Origins,* subtitled *An Essay in Linguistic Paleontology.* He seemed to be heading toward an evolutionary account of the basic ideas or structures of thought, something like what was attempted in Herbert Spencer's *Principles of Sociology,* published serially in the 1870s, which described among many other things the evolution of "primitive ideas" of animistic societies.

In 1866, to complete his education, he visited England, where all his complex ambition was excited and confirmed. In the first of the many London seasons in which he would take part, he found himself at home among the gentry, and in a parlor game described himself as a sort of Sir Walter Raleigh. During two weeks of climbing in the Alps, he formed a long and intimate friendship with Leslie Stephen and certainly had his philosophical readings confirmed. Stephen, nine years his senior and a gifted teacher, had himself embarked on a long struggle to replace his lost religion with a belief in Darwinist evolution.[17]

An intermission in Holmes's philosophic studies occurred from 1867 to 1872 while he served as an editor of the new *American Law Review* (chap. 6) and edited the twelfth edition of Chancellor James Kent's *Commentaries on American Law* (chap. 7). He brought a historical, philosophic perspective to his writings on the law; by 1873, in "The Gas Stoker's Strike" (6.81), Holmes gave an explicitly Darwinist description of law, as an expression of the justified self-interest of the dominant forces in the community. This, he forcefully noted, was not consistent with the Liberal, utilitarian assumption of the "solidarity of society."

There was nothing distinctively his own about this evolutionism, as his very frequent citations to Maine, Savigny, and Jhering attested. And it was very awkwardly married to an arrangement of the law according to duties (6.20, 6.75). Holmes was struggling, as yet unsuccessfully, toward a study of law on scientific principles that would be like his brief study of Dürer's engravings. But he had learned an immense amount about the common law, and he had achieved critical insights into the nature of law and how judges did their work. The law was what judges did in particular circumstances. No one, not even the judges, could consciously state the principle on which they were acting at the time. Only after studying numerous decisions could one expose the unconscious forces at work (6.20). The scholar was a scientist delving into the fossil remains of the law, trying to trace the lines of its evolution.

3.2.3 The Common Law. There was a further intermission in his studies after he married, while he devoted himself to the practice of law. But in 1876 Holmes returned to scholarly studies. With characteristic method, he began a new quarto-sized notebook in which he recorded his systematic reading, a record that eventually was reduced to a simple list of books read every summer, but which at first included detailed pages of notes and citations arranged by topic. In the next five years he continued his reading in philosophy, anthropology, and language. He read Herbert Spencer's new books and the newer German historical studies of law by von Jhering. For the first time he read extensively on ethics, studying Kant's ethics and Wake's two-volume *Evolution of Morality*. He read with great care, and took detailed notes on, *Essays in Anglo-Saxon Law,* edited by Henry Adams and written by his students, reviewing it for the *American Law Review* (see 8.2). These essays enriched Holmes's historical knowledge of the law and encouraged him by tracing a line of development from the institutions of "primitive" Germanic tribes to the law of his own day. Prominent among the headings in this new notebook once again were von Jhering, von Savigny, and Fustel de Coulanges. The British utilitarians had all but vanished.

Holmes began a new series of articles in 1876, beginning with "Primitive Notions in Modern Law" (8.1). These articles were the basis for the Lowell Lectures he gave in the winter of 1880–81 (8.10), which were adapted in turn for his one great sustained theoretical work, *The Common Law* (chap. 9). As might be expected from his systematic studies, Holmes in these essays and lectures described law as the fossil deposit of an organic, evolving society. Law was the record of the evolving morality of society, its development traceable in the changing contours of unconscious elements or structures of thought and language. (For a more detailed discussion, see section 6, below.)

With completion of *The Common Law* in 1881, and his appointment to the bench the following year, Holmes's systematic studies were ended for a time. In the 1890s, he undertook a new course of reading in political economy which would confirm his belief that nations and classes were engaged in a Malthusian struggle for survival.

In those difficult years, when members of his immediate family were dying, his wife was chronically ill, and it seemed his career was ending in obscurity, he added an important new component to his thought. His ten years' experience on the bench, and perhaps also his greater maturity, helped him to dredge up from the depths of his difficulties an important addition to his thinking. Overlain upon the common law, the result of the judges' decisions, was the duty of the judge himself. Setting aside everything that was merely personal and temporary, setting aside also the special interests of his own class, the judge decided fairly who should be the victor in the peaceful, honorable struggle for life under the rule of law. (See "Privilege, Malice, and Intent," 10.5.) This final complex addition to Holmes's jurisprudence was to be the core of some of his most famous and important opinions, and is discussed at greater length in section 7, below.

3.3
PHILOSOPHY

3.3.1 Metaphysics. Holmes was a realist. Like modern realist philosophers he assumed the existence of an external world because its existence was the premise of all thought and speech. "At the outset of our philosophy we take the step of supreme faith—we admit that we are not God. When I admit you, I announce that I am not dreaming the universe but am existing in it as less than it."[18] If one thinks at all, one must think about a real world that is to some extent amenable to understanding. But this belief in a reality independent of thought cannot be justified by reason, and so it is an act of faith. "I have always said that every wise man was at bottom a mystic, but one must get one's mysticism like one's miracles in the right place—right at the beginning or end."[19]

There was a strong flavor in this of the spirit of acceptance of the unavoidable, the foundation of New England's Calvinist spirit, which Holmes acquired from his mother. He always contrasted his own philosophy with that of egoists, who shook their fists at the sky, and with that of William James, who, Holmes said, turned down the lights to give miracles a chance.[20]

All he knew was a material world, and so he was a materialist. There was no need to assume that matter had limits, however. Matter evidently could think; why imagine a mystery? Holmes evolved for himself or learned from his reading and talk something very like Spinoza's monism: the one Substance contained both matter and form, extension and thought. Holmes's address "The Use of Colleges" (11.10) is a rough paraphrase of Spinoza, and his lifelong affinity for the realist philosophers George Santayana and Morris R. Cohen shows the persistence of his views. After reading George Santayana's preface to Spinoza's *Ethics*, Holmes wrote that he felt, as he had in his youth, "how much nearer my view of the world is to Spinoza's than it is to, I don't know but I may say, any other—leaving the machinery and the would-be mathematically conceived reasoning out."[21]

3.3.2 Epistemology. To Holmes, personal consciousness was just an intersection of rays making white light where they crossed, phosphorescence on a wavelet in the sea, a crossroads with an electric light.[22] "The human mind is perfectly mechanical even when it feels most spontaneous. I have probably told you before, how, when I had a wound in my heel, I would see man after man, as he approached, irradiated with the same self-congratulative smile, and then would follow a reference to *Achilles.*"[23]

There was no difficulty about gaining knowledge of a kind. People had awareness that made them fit to survive. And this awareness told them the world was a coherent, evolving world with orderly laws. Holmes acquired from Chauncey Wright the idea that the primitive awareness of simple living things had evolved into the self-awareness of human beings, and finally the awareness-of-awareness that was consciousness.[24] The knowledge acquired by limited consciousness was no better than a guess or bet, however. "Chauncey Wright, a nearly forgotten philosopher of real merit, taught me when I was young I must not say *necessary* about the universe, that we don't know if anything is necessary or not. I believe we can *bet* on the behavior of the universe in its contact with us—so describe myself as a *bet*tabilitarian."[25]

Time, space, logic, and cause, were qualities of human thought, and you could not get outside them to see if they were absolute. "I surmise that our modes of consciousness [are] not fundamental to the universe, if there is one."[26] This was taken from Kant, from whom Holmes also took the phrase *ding an sich,* the thing in itself.[27] Holmes was constantly peering through the curtain, trying to get a glimpse of things as they were in themselves. He read compulsively to discover whether someone else had found the secret, heard a faint rustle: Maeterlinck, for instance, gave him the illusion of an "echo from behind phenomena." He was almost persuaded that he did hear the clang of the ultimate in Fabre's *Souvenirs Entomologiques.* After skimming those volumes in the summer of 1912, Holmes, when he wanted to express his faith in the ultimate purposes of evolution, would speak of the grub that blindly prepared a chamber for the winged thing it had never seen but was to be (11.20).

There was often a strong hint of rebellion in his writings, the struggle of his ambition against the weight of his sense of dutiful acceptance, of the same frustration with the inscrutable cosmos that he felt when Lord Davey silenced debate with "That is not the law of England."

> You have in England a type unknown to us, of men who sufficiently account for themselves by transmitting a name. I sometimes wonder, as I dare say I have said before now, whether the cosmos may not be like them, too great a swell to have significance, leaving that to the finite, and finding it enough to say "I'm ME," if it takes the trouble to say anything—which after all is not so remote from prevailing theological notions translated into other words.[28]

As he grew older, the "Great Swell" became the central metaphor in a highly compressed, frequently repeated summary of his philosophy:

> If I am in the universe, not it in me, I am in something that contains intellect, significance, ideals. True, I surmise, I bet, that these all are expressions of the finite, and that they are as unlikely to be cosmic categories as they are to apply to a prince with a genealogy of 1000 years. He doesn't live by his wits—He simply is—.[29]

Holmes always pictured the Great Swell as exercising the arbitrary power of a great king or the Old Testament's deity. The seeming regularity of causal laws in the natural world was simply one of the Great Swell's whims: the Cosmos was not bound by logic. Holmes adopted Mill's attack on Aristotelian logic, perhaps because he had a fundamental mistrust of deductive, syllogistic reasoning. Mill had argued that a syllogism did not produce new knowledge, because its conclusion was already contained in the premise; and Holmes made this one of the pillars of his thought. Especially in his early writings[30] he expressed the greatest contempt for purely deductive reasoning—the conclusion was always concealed in the premise. As he famously proclaimed, a judge's decision was hidden within the "inarticulate major premise" of his reasoning.[31] *The Common Law* is one long attack on purely deductive, logical systems of argument like the utilitarians' and modern Hegelians', and on the humbler rationalizations of the ordinary judges' opinions.

The thing to bet on was an induction, a conclusion from known particulars. Philosophy, which meant scientific thought, was just the accumulation of particulars, and the gradual development of more and more general statements about them. Holmes thought this accumulation of knowledge was progressive, so that the primitive thoughts of the Greeks had been thoroughly displaced by modern science,[32] but knowledge was never better than a probability. In Holmes's favorite paradox, the Great Swell, the arbitrary cosmos, was a "jumping spontaneity taking an irrational pleasure in a momentary rational sequence."[33]

Rational sequence was important. All experience showed, and all talk and argument about the world in general assumed, that its parts were related in an orderly causal way that could be summarized in scientific laws. Logic was a necessary but not a sufficient condition of truth. The cosmos was not limited by the rules of logic; it had thought, but perhaps more than thought, in it. Contradictory positions, logically derived from true premises, might both be true. As they were to his friends William James[34] and Louis Brandeis,[35] the antinomies of thought were familiar to Holmes. Perhaps he had encountered them originally in Kant—his favorite example was the infinity of consciousness, trapped within the finite limits of a skull. Antinomies, vividly pictured, became one of Holmes's conversational gambits: "I have often done my part to amuse a bored god by trying to imagine how many universes might be existing in the same space at the same time without conflicting. Where we are sitting now a tyrannosaurus may be locked in a death struggle with some unnamed creature of another sphere from ours."[36]

Truths in such a world were both personal and objective. One could know truths only from within the system of his own personal limitations, without external confirmation. This did not make them less true; they were only not absolute. One lived one's life—did one's job, in Holmes's frequent image—"without waiting for an angel to assure us that it is the jobbest job in jobdom."[37] Philosophy was a solitary and dangerous business, like life itself.

Holmes's philosophy rested on a demonstration of the inadequacy of reason, and indeed one of his frequently repeated paradoxes was that truth was just the system of his limitations, his famous "can't helps." He believed what he couldn't help believing, and his tastes and morals were what he couldn't help having. "All I mean by truth is the path I have to travel."[38]

This was not relativism; still less was it pragmatism. To Holmes, personal truths were true enough; a fact was part of the real, external world, and if you were wrong about one, it might kill you. In the process of surviving, you learned truths. Such truths were relative only in the sense that they were partial, and in a cosmos that insisted upon, but was not bound by, logic, there might be other true but contradictory systems of thought. "Everything seems an illusion relative to something else—as green relatively to vibrations—" and so on, until one came to the Great Swell, the unknowable cosmos. But "[t]he cell has its life as well as the larger organism in whose unity it has a part—and our subrealities are no doubt part of all the reality there is."[39]

Other people, with their own presumably different sets of personal limitations, allowed one to calibrate one's beliefs. As a judge, Holmes rarely dissented alone, because he thought it important to verify one's ideas by comparing them with other people's perceptions of the common, external reality.

> If I think that I am sitting at a table I find that the other persons present agree with me; so if I say that the sum of the angles of a triangle is equal to two right angles. If I am in a minority of one they send for a doctor or lock me up; and I am so far able to transcend the to me convincing testimony of my senses or my reason as to recognize that if I am alone probably something is wrong with my works. ("Natural Law," 10.23)

This is not the pragmatists' social test of truth by agreement. Holmes, the solitary observer, was simply checking or triangulating his observations by reference to other points of view in whose existence he could not help believing.

Kant is again visible here, as the common point of origin of both Holmes's realism and William James's pragmatism. To Holmes, complex ideas, like the sum of the angles of a triangle, were built into the structure of one's thought because evolution had taught the organism to make ideas that corresponded to qualities of the external world. "The condition of our thinking about the universe is that it is capable of being thought about rationally, or, in other words, that every part of it is effect and cause in the same sense in which those parts are with which we are most familiar" ("The Path of the Law," 10.9).

Complex ideas, like finite and infinite, could be mutually contradictory, and equally, objectively, true. Differences among sane observers were fundamentally matters of taste. "[T]wenty men of genius looking out the same window will paint twenty canvases, each unlike all the others, and every one great" (11.19). Moral, aesthetic, and practical values were all different aspects of national character at a particular time, each engaged with the ultimate in its own way, and equally expressed in art, or in law.[40]

The contradictions among perspectives were real and could not be resolved by discourse; one was obliged to choose,—or, where choice was not possible, to accept that one was helpless to get beyond one's own limitations.

> [P]roperty, friendship, and truth, have a common root in time. One cannot be wrenched from the rocky crevices into which one has grown for many years without feeling that one is attacked in one's life. . . . But while one's experience thus makes certain preferences dogmatic for oneself, recognition of how they came to be so leaves one able to see that others, poor souls, may be equally dogmatic about something else. ("Natural Law," 10.23)

Despite the need to gain objectivity by comparing one's ideas to others', there-fore, philosophy was a solitary activity. In the end there was no way to settle funda-mental disagreements short of killing the other fellow. And so the cosmos sorted out the greater truths from the lesser, in the only way that had any objective mean-ing, by extinguishing the lesser.

> I think that values like truth are largely personal. There is enough community for us to talk[,] not enough for anyone to command. . . . Whether you take sugar in your coffee or not you are equally up against an ultimate dogma, which as arbitrary you have no call to impose, unless indeed you care enough about it to kill the other man, which I admit is the logical outcome—you can't refute him.[41]

The chief claim of civilization was that it had substituted, however partially, an orderly process of peaceful discourse for this violent evolution. Politics and law, like the natural sciences, provided laboratories in which to test the correspondence of ideas to reality. But the laboratory was only a surrogate for reality; the test of civiliza-tion would ultimately be its success in subordinating itself to the Great Swell, the brutal and uncaring cosmos: "I do not believe that a shudder would go through the sky if our whole ant heap were kerosened."[42]

3.3.3 Ethics. As for ethics, Holmes insisted there was no such thing.

> I said to a lady at dinner the other night that morals were a contrivance of man to take himself seriously, which means that the philosophers instead of making them merely one of the conveniences of living to be talked about no more than money, make them an end in themselves, an absolute matter, and so an excuse for their pretention to be on the ground floor and personal friends of God.[43]

And so, in the end, Holmes reconciled science and morals by saying that there were no ethics, only manners.[44] Which is not to say that he took manners lightly; he always said that a gentleman was someone who would die for a point of honor. It was most gentlemanly, as in the Tennyson poem, to die for a *senseless* point of honor; this was the purest exhibition of an instinct implanted by nature for its own evolu-tionary purposes. Holmes felt that he could no more help having a sense of duty than he could help believing in an external, material world. His address "Memorial Day" (11.1), the first in the slim volume of speeches in which he encapsulated his philosophy, was a paean to the courage and idealism of young soldiers on both sides in the war, who had given their lives to their respective and mutually contradictory causes, both of which logically could not be worthy of sacrifice but which like the north and south poles of a magnet seemed to be part of some larger whole.

He closed the book, in 1913, on the eve of the world war, with "Law and the Court" (11.20), a declaration of faith in the unknowable future of evolution, to which duty required such sacrifices.

3.4
POLITICAL ECONOMY

Holmes was an evolutionist, what we now loosely call a Social Darwinist, but of a peculiar sort, explicable in a man who grew up in a world where evolution and chivalry were both taken for granted.

3.4.1 Evolutionism. Holmes called himself an evolutionist (see "The Path of the Law," 10.9) and believed that his ideas were derived from Darwin, but he had not read Darwin and his ideas reflected an older version of evolution, most strongly influenced by Hegel.[45]

I do not want to make too much of Hegel, and the reader may wish to use his name simply as a convenient summary of German idealism as it arrived in Boston in Holmes's youth. Even then, the name may be no more than a catchword for the mentality of his time. It is true that Holmes lived in a post-Cartesian, post-Kantian world, but it may be that Frederick the Great and Napoleon had as much to do as Descartes, Kant, or Hegel with the romantic picture of history as a clash of cultures, led by heroes, that Holmes absorbed. Whatever its source, this world view was certainly pervasive. It is interesting to compare Shelley's *Defence of Poetry*, which Holmes certainly knew, with Holmes's own idea of history, taking into account Shelley's special idea of the poet and its similarity to Holmes's special idea of the scientist. Shelley:

> It is impossible to read the compositions of the most celebrated writers of the present day without being startled with the electric life that burns within their words. They measure the circumference and sound the depths of human nature with a comprehensive and all-penetrating spirit. . . . Poets are the hierophants of an unapprehended inspiration; the mirrors of the gigantic shadows which futurity casts upon the present. . . . Poets are the unacknowledged legislators of the world.[46]

And Holmes:

> To one who lives in what may seem to him a solitude of thought . . . his unhelped meditation may someday mount a throne, and without armies, or even with them, may shoot across the world the electric despotism of an unresisted power. (11.17)

> If you want great examples, read Mr. Leslie Stephen's *History of English Thought in the Eighteenth Century*, and see how a hundred years after his death the abstract speculations of Descartes had become a practical force. . . . how much more the world is governed today by Kant than by Bonaparte. (10.9)

> [W]e should be grateful to all men like William Allen, whose ambition, if it can be called so, looks only to remote and mediated command; who do not ask to say to anyone, Go, and he goeth, so long as in truthful imagination they wield, according to their degree, that most subtle and intoxicating authority which controls the future from within by shaping the thoughts and speech of a later time. (11.11)

As to an evolutionary view of history, in any case, Hegel's ideas, transmitted through Spencer, Emerson, Carlyle, and the very air of Boston in the 1850s (Chauncey Wright called Herbert Spencer's philosophy "German Darwinism"),[47] coincided with British scientific rationalism.[48] It is not surprising that Holmes believed in a particular sort of evolution, an evolution that proceeded through the contest of nations or races, each representing a distinct principle or mode of life. This was a perfectly conventional pre-Darwinian view, embedded in the history and anthropology of the day,[49] and once Darwin's great work was published the notion of natural selection was assimilated very easily into it. Holmes and many of his contemporaries believed that natural selection operated on whole races or societies, determining which should survive,[50] rather than, as we should say now, affecting relative frequencies of genes.

Holmes also followed the conventional wisdom of his day (and ours) in believing that evolution had a direction, from the simple to the complex. His own society he thought more highly evolved, more advanced in some fundamental way, than any that had come before. Organisms became larger and more highly specialized, and so, he believed, did social institutions become larger and more specialized, over time; the "increasing organization of the world," the creation of monopolies and empires, with the concomitant organization of society into cadres of specialists, seemed to him patent and inevitable. He did not welcome the future this foretold. "Before the war it seemed to me that the trades unions and the trusts pointed to a more despotic regime. So long as efficiency is an ideal their tendency would seem to be enhanced by the war. I am not particularly in love with it."[51]

He was particularly dismayed at the increasing specialization this higher degree of organization entailed—not the specialization of knowledge, which he thought the route to truth, but the quasi-physiological specialization of social roles. The university professor was a favorite example: "those who have spared themselves this supreme trial [of battle], and have fostered a faculty at the expense of their total life" (11.14).

But it would not do to shake one's fist at the sky, and Holmes cheerfully accepted the inevitability of higher degrees of organization and specialization of social role. This once again is a view one finds in Herbert Spencer, but it was so much in the air that it would be wrong to attribute it to any particular influence; and to a large degree his observations were correct, although we would not now attribute them to "evolution" in any modern sense of the word.

One principal sign and mechanism of increasing complexity was the development of self-awareness, to which Holmes thought he had contributed importantly. Modern thinkers had learned to see themselves seeing, and modern philosophy was like a room with mirrors at both ends. Legal philosophy, through Holmes, had become self-aware, and he could announce that "[t]he time has gone by when law is only an unconscious embodiment of the common will. It has become a conscious reaction upon itself of organized society knowingly seeking to determine its own destinies" ("Privilege, Malice, and Intent," 10.5).

3.4.2 Malthusian Economics. It was universally assumed among Holmes's peers—wrongly, we should now say—that the mechanism of natural selection was violent competition among races for limited means of subsistence. The image was fundamentally that of Hegel's account of the battle of Salamis, a great clash of rival civilizations embodying competing principles; for Holmes, the image was the clash of North and South in the American Civil War. The motive for this rivalry was supposed to have been explained by Malthus, to whose books and ideas Holmes referred with increasing frequency as he grew older. It was an article of faith to Holmes, embedded in all the political economy of his day, that the growth of population would always exceed the increase in available resources.[52] The means of subsistence therefore would always be inadequate, and so the loser in the struggle for life must perish.

In considering his views, one should recall Holmes's three years in combat. One must also recall the brutal quality of life for the majority of people in Holmes's day. In Massachusetts, as late as 1890, the average life expectancy of a male at birth was forty-two years.[53] Women died in childbirth in what now seem incomprehensible numbers; perhaps 1 percent of all women of childbearing age died in childbirth each year.[54] There were few social services; working people depended on their health to a degree we have forgotten.

Infant mortality was nearly one in five, on the average, and still worse in working-class families. Every summer, epidemics of typhoid and diarrhea would sweep through the cities, so that the tremendous mortality among children was concentrated in a few weeks of August and September.[55] One is not surprised Holmes believed that, in peacetime as in war, the physically and mentally weak did perish, and that the resources available to society were simply not adequate to produce any other result. People were poor because there was not enough to maintain a decent average. The rich had no fund of luxuries large enough to alter the prevailing standard if it were redistributed. In a talk at Williams College as late as 1912, Holmes said, "I was informed that 85 percent of the total product here and in England was consumed by people with not over $1000 (£200) a year—the whole expenses of government and the moderate luxuries of the many coming out of the remaining 15 percent."[56]

The problem was particularly acute because the world was filling up, with the last unsettled regions becoming populated. "[T]here is so much forest, coal, etc. even so much atmosphere—and no more. I wonder if it might not be possible that those who are drawing nitrogen from the latter might in time be found to be doing a deadly thing."[57]

Holmes viewed life as a zero-sum game, as we should say now. The free market was not so much desirable as inevitable, and it was pointless and self-defeating to try to reverse the verdict of free competition. As fights always ended with a victor, so competition ended with monopoly. Although political regulation of the power of monopolies was justified and even necessary, prices reflected the intensity of the public's competing desires for different forms of consumption—what we would now call opportunity costs—rather than competition among producers.[58] Wages, similarly, were determined by competition between groups of workers, and any advantages achieved by trade unions were secured at the expense of unorganized workers;[59] there was no significant surplus accumulated by capital and withheld from the working class (see "Economic Elements," 10.14). National accounts had not yet been invented when Holmes began to preach his doctrine, and so he resorted to images, principally the image of a "stream of products," by which he meant roughly what we should now call the gross national product. He was quite certain that the stream of products was consumed by the large mass of people and that proportionately very little was diverted to the pleasures of the wealthy.

Proposals to undo the results of competition and redistribute wealth seemed to Holmes contemptible. With great relish he told his young socialist friend Harold

Laski, "When I read Malthus I thought he had ripped the guts out of some humbugs—but they are as alive as ever today. Humbugs have no guts—and live all the
better without them."[60] He told Frankfurter that he wished God would write in
letters of fire on the sky:

> The Crowd has all there is
> The Crowd pays for everything[61]

Life was a struggle over inadequate means, a struggle not so much among individuals as among races. "I incline to believe . . . that before our clamorers for 8
hours (with which clamor I sympathize) know it, the Chinese with their endless
gluttony for work, their honesty and imperturbable patience will cut the white races
out of the markets of the world."[62]

3.4.3 Race and Gender; Eugenics. A word must be said about both "race" and the
relations between the sexes, topics that were entwined with political economy in
Holmes's ideas.

As to race, we have to make an imaginative effort to recover the context of the
Victorian age. In Holmes's formative years the mechanism of genetics, revealed in
Brother Mendel's pea plants, had not yet been rediscovered. Nearly all scientists,
including Darwin, believed that acquired characteristics were inherited in some
way. Reinforcing this view were the huge disparities in nutrition and sunlight received by the different economic classes, so that the well-to-do and the poor were
physically quite different. The workman stunted with rickets looked as if he were
of a different race from his taller, healthier employer. The descriptions of "racial"
differences among the classes, so common in Henry James and other novelists of
the time, did not rest on prejudice but were realistic accounts. The candor with
which racial stereotypes were applied is shocking to us now, but in Holmes's generation study and discussion of "races" were not only acceptable but considered progressive and scientific. The premise of Progressive thinking was that better hygiene
and education would improve the racial stock of the "inferior" races.

The struggle for survival was understood to be a test of racial fitness, and here
we see brutal notions of racial hygiene coming into Holmes's ideas. He accepted
the validity of the "scientific anthropology" of his day, which promised to identify
inheritable criminal traits through measurements of skull dimensions and the like.
Referring to Cesare Lombroso's scientific anthropology,[63] which purported to show
that criminals were distinctive physiological types, a form of degeneration or ata-
vism, Holmes said: "The Italians have begun work upon the notion that the founda-
tions of the law ought to be scientific, and, if our civilization does not collapse, I
feel pretty sure that the regiment or division that follows us will carry that flag"
("Learning and Science," 11.13). Holmes concluded with relentless logic that a revival of extensive capital punishment for crime might be needed.

> If the typical criminal is a degenerate, bound to swindle or to murder by as deep seated
> an organic necessity as that which makes a rattlesnake bite, it is idle to talk of deterring
> him by the classical method of imprisonment. He must be got rid of; he cannot be
> improved or frightened out of his structural reaction. ("The Path of the Law," 10.9)[64]

Holmes did not view capital punishment as necessarily inhumane. The unfit were bound to perish by one means or another. "I always say that society is founded on the death of men—if you don't kill the weakest one way you kill them another."[65] Holmes never put any external limits on the power of a nation to seek its own survival, and he made no real distinction between law enforcement and war. "[C]lasses as well as nations that mean to be in the saddle have got to be ready to kill to keep their seat."[66] It followed that even violent eugenic measures were within the ordinary police powers.[67]

In addition to capital punishment, Holmes seems to have imagined, under a more advanced science, infanticide of those otherwise doomed to lingering misery and death: "I can imagine a future in which science shall have passed from the combative to the dogmatic stage, and should have gained such catholic acceptance that it shall take control of life, and condemn at once with instant execution what is now left for nature to destroy" ("The Soldier's Faith," 11.12).

He seemed to feel that this was the only real alternative to war, and was preferable. "I should be glad, to speak Hibernially, if it could be arranged that the death should precede life by provisions for a selected race, but we shall not live to see that."[68]

In retrospect, it is plain that the "scientific" anthropology and evolutionism on which Holmes rested his opinions were wrong, and indeed at this distance they seem dangerously foolish. Holmes was not to know that, but it is odd that this man, who prided himself on his skepticism of utopias and nostrums, and on his suspicion of purely logical arguments, accepted secondhand accounts of evolutionary science with so little question. While Holmes was not obsessed with the fears of racial degeneration common in his day and much written of lately, the ease with which he talked of capital punishment and infanticide is disturbing and seems to call for an explanation.

One passage is particularly striking. In a love letter to Lady Castletown, Holmes talked about reading a book by the socialist writer Edward Bellamy, and as always the mention of socialism set him off:

> The socialists so far as I know shut their eyes to matters of population or tell you in an airy way that Henry George has refuted Malthus and Darwin. I could discourse on this theme but won't. But until you substitute artificial selection for natural by putting to death the inadequate, or get the whole world to limit procreation to the visible means of support, I do not believe you will see socialism successful. Existing society is founded on the death of men. While I write in this abstract way I am thinking of you until you seem almost present—and I can hardly go on.[69]

Similarly brutal passages within very affectionate letters are not unusual for Holmes, and while they began in the 1890s they continued through much of his life. Twenty years after this letter to Lady Castletown, Holmes wrote in almost identical terms of his contempt "for all socialisms not prepared to begin with life rather than property and to kill everyone below the standard."[70]

There is an odd disconnectedness, an unexplained gap, between the brutal talk of killing and the warm expressions of affection that followed immediately after.

Without trying to delve too deeply into an unconscious mind that long ago escaped our questions, we can suggest a couple of thoughts.

As we have seen, Holmes's parents urged him to enlist and reenlist in the army at a time when he, and perhaps they as well, feared that meant death. His duty as an officer was principally to whip his men into standing up to being shot, and he came out of the Civil War persuaded that morality, honor, and duty all meant willingness to die in service to high principles. It always thereafter seemed to him understandable, even right, that people would be asked to die for society's inscrutable aims, and he was annoyed when they objected. His fantasies of scientific infanticide may also hint at an unconscious belief he had been sent to war by his parents to die.[71]

There is another strand to his feeling that is perhaps related to the first, coiled at its core. Holmes viewed all human relations as forms of power and combat. This was particularly marked in his feelings about women.

One of Holmes's chestnuts was that the moral quality of society was an "empirical mixture" of the masculine and feminine qualities. "Empirical mixture" was an image borrowed from his father's description of the atmosphere. Holmes used it to describe morality, "which is really a compromise between two irreconcilable sexes." Man's contribution to the mixture was "the ideal drawn from conflict—doing a stump, as the boys say."[72] The female contribution was not so clearly spelled out, but one gathers from his letters that if Holmes had to define the female ideal in equally simple and essential terms he would have defined it as the mother, infinitely accepting and reassuring.

The complete separation of two sexes into distinct roles, and the identification of the male role with combat and competition, led to a pretty bleak picture of life. Holmes opposed the vote for women, precisely because government was founded on force, and therefore politics was ultimately a business of the bludgeon and the bayonet to which women were not suited. The relation of men and women was itself a form of government founded ultimately on force. I think Holmes would have agreed with the modern, feminist assessment:

> We are not accustomed to associate patriarchy with force. So perfect is its system of socialization, so complete the general assent to its values, so long and universally has it prevailed in human society, that it scarcely seems to require violent implementation... And yet... control in patriarchal society would be imperfect, even inoperable, unless it had the rule of force to rely upon, both in emergencies and as an ever-present instrument of intimidation.[73]

If the ultimate *ratio regum* was force, it was all the more important to remember that in personal relations, as in law, the foundation of civility, and chivalry, was self-restraint. To Ellen Curtis he wrote: "In the matrimonial market virtue seems to be in the hands of the bears just now. It will come up again as most men like a naiveté which they rarely emulate. The talk of equality in such matters singularly fails to move my enthusiasm—I can't see any rights about it—but powers—and generosities."[74]

In this little fragment we see sexual relationships described in the same terms

Holmes used when speaking of law and government, and ending with the same result, that "rights" were only the consequence of self-restraint by the dominant power.

These were not unusual sentiments in a man of Holmes's time and place. Indeed, Holmes was the model for the conventional, chivalrous masculinity of Basil Ransome in Henry James's *The Bostonians*, and Holmes's relations with the opposite sex do not seem to have been unconventional in any way. Holmes preferred the company of women to that of men, by and large, and his letters to women were more open and more interesting than those addressed to men. There were few people that he treated as intellectual equals, but his letters to Alice Stopford Green, for instance, are far more revealing of his thought and feelings than his letters to, say, Felix Frankfurter.

Yet he had the conventional prejudices and blindness. He did not like women's writing to be sexually suggestive, "[p]erhaps because we know, though the older literary tradition is the other way, that they take less interest in the business than we do."[75] Noting the senseless brutality of the rule that a victim of rape must report the crime promptly, he nevertheless described the rule as a meaningless survival of the ancient hue and cry, without seeming to consider that it might reflect something worse (see "Law in Science and Science in Law," 10.10). Holmes and his wife had a vigorous if somewhat routinized sex life, as surviving letters between them make clear. Like Basil Ransome's marriage to Verena Tarrant at the conclusion of *The Bostonians*, it was a troubled, somewhat unequal relationship, profoundly conventional.

Holmes had a good deal of sexual energy, and the intensity and speed with which he worked—as a Massachusetts judge he tried to write opinions in the evening after oral arguments had been heard—was at least partly intended to keep his weekends and summers free for trips to New York and London, for the love affairs and the courtly flirtations that energized his work. Although one can never know what happens behind closed doors, it seems likely that, especially at times when Fanny was too ill to perform her conjugal duties—I think that is how both of them thought of it—he had affairs. Holmes's love letters to Lady Castletown, for instance, do not reveal the secrets of the bedroom, but they do not leave any doubt about the fundamental nature of the relationship.

There is no reason to think Holmes was promiscuous or exploitive in his relationships with women, however, he consciously made use of his abundant sexual energy by sublimating it in work. The traditions of chivalry, especially of courtly love, were particularly congenial to the Victorians on this score—see, for instance, the sustained imagery of his toast to "our mistress, the Law" (11.3)[76]—and much of the power of Holmes's writing is due to his ability to harness these energies consciously.

His relations with women therefore seem to have been simply conventional, and perhaps there is no need to look for reasons in his own history for his apparent feeling that the relations between the sexes, like all other human relationships, were ultimately a struggle for survival. Holmes's world was a rather bleak one; and after the Civil War, he was not a reformer. He was aware of the injustices of class and gender, if not acutely sensitive to them, and he accepted the existing order and did not blame anyone for it. He believed that the only hope for ameliorating the fundamental source of injustice, the lack of adequate means, was to limit the size of the population.

3.4.4 The Priority of Honor. We can now return to the difficult question of Holmes's views on eugenics. Holmes's relationships with women inevitably affected and to some degree explained his brutal approval of "artificial selection"; but a few words more are needed before we leave this topic. If in his views of class and gender he was simply a man of his time, his views on eugenics were a different matter. One cannot read Holmes's phrase "putting to death the inadequate," uttered so casually, without profound disquiet. This goes well beyond the conventional views on eugenics of his day, and it is worse than wrong; it is evil.

So I must explain why, in the end, I find Holmes better than his ideas. To do so I must lapse into biography.

It seems, although the evidence is limited, that Holmes faced the implications of his Social Darwinism in the early 1890s, in the years when his mother, brother, sister, and father died, leaving only a nephew and himself as the survivors of his name, and his wife sank back into the chronic illness that Holmes believed had left them childless.

Holmes was troubled at this time by the temptation to leave his childless marriage, and by the thought that it was his duty to do so, to ensure the survival of his line. There was a common feeling in his day that such duties were owed to the nation. The census of 1890 showed the relative decline of New Englanders of British origin, and there was much heated talk of "race suicide" of which Holmes was certainly aware. Theodore Roosevelt, for instance, made frequent references in speeches and letters to "race criminals," who refused to perform their duty to procreate: "The man . . . who has a heart so cold as to know no passion and a brain so shallow and selfish as to dislike having children, is in effect a criminal against the race and should be an object of contemptuous abhorrence by all healthy people."[77]

Holmes's letters show that he had indeed considered whether it was his duty to have children, but in the end he decided to stand by Fanny. This was both a duty to her and his personal inclination. The evidence on the subject is limited, however. Holmes, while open about his own feelings with friends, was very protective of his wife's privacy. His father's and his own papers relating to her illness were destroyed, and friends of the family seem to have cooperated. In one letter that has survived, however, Holmes discussed their childlessness:

> Once at dinner in England old Sir Fitzroy Kelly on hearing that we had no children said, "Le bon temps viendra." But I am so far abnormal that I am glad I have none. It might be said that to have them is part of the manifest destiny of man, as of other creatures, and that he should accept it as he accepts his destiny to strive—but the latter he can't help—and part of his destiny is to choose. I might say some sad things but I won't. Whatever I may think of life, the last years of mine have been happy and are so now. Of course, if I should break down before I die it would be awkward as there is no one to look after me as a child would—but I daresay my nephew and my friends would cook up something.[78]

Holmes seemed to be saying that he chose between duties and that in retrospect from the age of seventy-seven he was not sorry at the choice he had made.[79]

Holmes periodically reassured himself that his nephew, Ned, would carry on the Holmes name, but it gradually became apparent that Ned too had a childless marriage. From the 1890s onward, Holmes talked somewhat bleakly of the extinction of his family.

At the same time, the nation was going through a severe depression and the beginnings of violent class struggle. As a judge, Holmes was facing his first cases involving organized labor, which to him seemed an enemy not only of the existing order but of everything he found valuable in life.

Holmes extracted from all this the same lesson that he had with so much pain from the Civil War. He did not feel much personal sympathy for the trade unions and the new races that would displace his own, but still it was his duty to sacrifice himself, and for his race to perish, if that was what honor required. In the early 1890s, he began dissenting from the decisions of his court, on behalf of the right of the state legislature to conduct experiments in direct democracy and socialism.[80] This was a difficult step for him, as he did not like to dissent, especially to dissent alone; furthermore, although he did not like to admit this as a factor, his dissents were likely to cut off the prospect of eventual advancement to the Supreme Court, the only ambition that remained to him.

In 1894, he wrote "Privilege, Malice, and Intent" (10.5), in which he argued that it was the duty of judges to set aside their own personal interests, and even their fears of extinction, in order to preside fairly over the struggle for life.

From the depths of his worst time, Holmes extracted something admirable, if tragic. He turned to self-sacrifice as the fundamental moral principle. He wrote to Ellen Curtis describing a conversation with Fanny:

> [A] recent exposition I gave . . . with an excursus on suicide as the ideal expression of that illusory personal spontaneity or independence which exhibits itself in less marked forms as consideration for the weak, charity to the poor, drunkenness, going to the play, painting pictures, etc., in short, uneconomic expenditures of force—the final judgment on which by nature is death—but which in moderate doses is the consolation and glory of man.[81]

Holmes's sad and generous courage, his determination to perish in the fight rather than fight dishonorably; his determination to accept the inevitable, and, as Spinoza advised, to act well and joyously; these things, and not his conventional prejudices or his brutal talk of racial hygiene, are the core of the man and the inheritance we are entitled to receive from him.[82]

3.5
JURISPRUDENCE AND THE JUDICIAL FUNCTION

Holmes's thinking about fundamental legal questions developed in four clearly marked stages. In each, he added important elements to the structure already built.

The first stage was 1867–73, when Holmes was living with his parents, practicing law and writing dozens of brief essays for the *American Law Review* and his edition of Kent's *Commentaries* (chaps. 5–7). The second was the period of *The Common Law*, 1873–82 (chaps. 8,9, and 10.1–10.4). The third phase, the fruition of Holmes's work as a judge in Massachusetts, runs from roughly 1891 to 1902 and is marked by the publication of his last important theoretical work, "Privilege, Malice, and Intent" (10.5). Finally, there is the long period in which Holmes extended his ideas to federal law, in his opinions on the United States Supreme Court 1902–32 (see sections 8–10 of this chapter).

Most of what Holmes wrote in his later years, and nearly all of his judicial opinions, were parts of a single growing structure of theory. Holmes wrote for the "expert," by which he really meant someone familiar with his own previous writings, and so the isolated pieces are often difficult to understand until set in context.

In the very earliest works there is naturally a great deal of extraneous matter. Like his father, Holmes was a brilliant, nonstop talker. If there was no one nearby with whom to talk, he picked up a pen and wrote. From 1867, when he joined the staff of the newly formed *American Law Review*, until 1873, when he left the review for law practice, he had free access to print. He wrote a steady stream of anonymous articles, notes, digests, and essays. When he wanted law books, which were expensive, he reviewed them for the law review and got the books in payment. The result was a nearly continuous record of his thoughts, and his reactions to his reading, over a period of six years while his principal ideas about law were being formed.

He studied law in these early years as an activity rather than as a set of abstract ideas, and his earliest observations concerned lawyers and judges. As one might expect from someone still in his twenties, Holmes described the lawyer as someone very much like himself, engaged in a scholarly effort to understand the law. This advocate-scientist was rather like the soldier-scholar that Holmes aspired to be.

Lawyers collected the data of their science, which were the decisions of the courts. These were to be studied scientifically; to Holmes, as we have seen, science meant biological evolution. Holmes's very first publication on law, a review of a digest of cases on the law of evidence (6.2), stated his opinion that a law book should be arranged like a treatise on natural history. The object of such a work was to arrange the data—the individual specimens representing "species"—in such a way as to show the principle of their evolution (6.4 and 6.51), and ultimately to "extract philosophy from the history of law" (6.13).

Holmes himself was writing digests of cases for the *American Law Review* and trying to fit them into the somewhat arbitrary plan of arrangement devised by the editors (6.1). A digest or headnote summarizing a case, he concluded, above all must contain a statement of the facts. The judge's own words could safely be ignored, but what the court had *decided* should be clearly stated by the reporter himself (6.16, 16.32).

Law, in short, was what judges did in particular circumstances. This insight, which followed so naturally from Holmes's first investigations, was the beginning of a revolution in legal thinking.

What judges did, Holmes quickly observed, was pretty much what everyone did when faced with a decision. Holmes's first formal article on law began:

> It is the merit of the common law that it decides the case first and determines the principle afterwards. Looking at the forms of logic it might be inferred that when you

have a minor premise and a conclusion, there must be a major premise, which you are prepared then and there to assert. But in fact lawyers, like other men, frequently see well enough how they ought to decide on a given state of facts without being very clear as to the *ratio decidendi*. . . . It is only after a series of determinations on the same subject-matter, that it becomes necessary to "reconcile the cases," that is, by a true induction to state the principle which has until then been obscurely felt. ("Codes, and the Arrangement of Law," 6.20; see also 6.33)

Every judge's decision, in a case of first impression, accordingly, was based on an inarticulate major premise,[83] which consciously or unconsciously guided him to a decision on a state of facts.

Judges were the only source of law. Statutes, and even constitutions, from the lawyer's perspective were only additional "facts" that would provide the judge with a motive to decide in one way or the other. They did not become *law*, properly speaking, unless and until enforced by a court (6.82).[84]

The judge's decision itself was always a choice between contending principles of behavior.

Two widely different cases suggest a general distinction, which is a clear one when stated broadly. But as new cases cluster around the opposite poles, and begin to approach each other, the distinction becomes more difficult to trace; the determinations are made one way or the other on a very slight preponderance of feeling, rather than on articulate reason; and at last a mathematical line is arrived at by the contact of contrary decisions. (6.82)[85]

The area where the competing principles met and overlapped Holmes famously referred to as a "penumbra," a metaphor that has become part of the constitutional law of the United States.[86] Holmes later found that it was particularly important in constitutional cases to recognize this penumbral effect, apparently absolute principles shading off into uncertainty and leaving a margin of freedom and maneuver for the legislature (see section 9, below).

The contending principles were rules of behavior that judges found in customs, statutes, constitutions, or rules derived from earlier decisions. As early as 1870, Holmes was quite clear that the law's concern was with rules of external behavior rather than the subjective states of the persons affected: "The law addresses itself to the thing to be done" (6.20).

As Holmes continued his investigation of the work of judges, he eventually turned to the question of how judges made this intuitive choice between rival rules of conduct. His answer was that judges responded to the wishes of the power that they served. This power was not necessarily the parliament; judges might consult custom, or their own notions of policy, but ultimately the wishes of the dominant force in the community would have to be respected (6.53, 6.66, 6.81). "[T]he justification of a law. . . must be found in some help the law brings toward reaching a social end which the governing power of the community has made up its mind that it wants" ("Law in Science and Science in Law," 10.10).

Holmes thought that the contending sides in difficult cases represented conflicting social groups or classes, each with its own self-interest cloaked by a legal principle.

I think it most important to remember whenever a doubtful case arises, with certain analogies on one side and other analogies on the other, that what really is before us is a conflict between two social desires, each of which seeks to extend its domination over the case, and which cannot both have their way. . . . Where there is doubt the simple tool of logic does not suffice, and even if it is disguised and unconscious, judges are called on to exercise the sovereign prerogative of choice. (Ibid.)

Holmes sometimes was unclear as to how judges were to decide between competing class interests. In his earlier writings, and in the article just quoted, he seemed to be saying that judges should consciously choose the interest of the dominant force in society. But from the 1890s onward, as we shall see, he usually said that judges should choose in accordance with fundamental concepts of fairness in the fight.

3.6
THE COMMON LAW

Holmes's early work fell far short of his ambition. He had failed to find evolutionary principles in the rules of law. He had assembled some historical accounts of change, but these seemed to have no connection to his logical arrangement of law according to duties. When he finally did find an evolutionary account that satisfied him, the earlier arrangement of law seemed more than ever arbitrary; it was the persistence of the two lines of thought in *The Common Law* that made the structure of that book so puzzling.

3.6.1 The Arrangement of Law by Duties. When Holmes began his work, the British "analytical" school, founded by the utilitarian philosopher Jeremy Bentham and in Holmes's youth identified with the writings of John Austin, dominated legal scholarship. It was a Liberal, reformist doctrine, which the English liked to believe was founded on common sense, as contrasted with the idealist theories of continental jurisprudence. Austin's pronouncement, echoing Hobbes, was that law was the command of the sovereign (meaning the government). The proper purpose of government was to secure the greatest good of the greatest number, and laws therefore secured the "rights" of the community. The "analytical" school followed the quasi-mathematical logic of this scheme and divided the law into a taxonomy based on rights. Benthamite reformers wanted to replace the tangled mass of the common law with a clearly stated codification organized on these logical principles.

The principal rival school of jurisprudence was founded on German idealist philosophy and, following Kant and Hegel, purported to derive legal institutions from absolute principles.

The Common Law was partly an attack on these dominant philosophies, and more generally on the unreal rationalizations in which judges cloaked their decisions. Holmes's principal argument was that law was a system of partially outmoded precedents, evolving in response to changing conceptions of public policy. Ignorance was the great law reformer; judges, having forgotten why cases had been decided in earlier centuries, gave strained rationalizations for the old rules and gradually altered them to fit modern circumstances. "The life of the law has not been logic, it has been experience," Holmes famously declared, lumping together all existing theories and judicial rationalizations under the polite heading of "logic."[87]

But *The Common Law* was an assemblage of work done over a period of years, and the dominant insights were arrived at rather late. The form of organization of the book did not reflect this central argument.

Holmes's first law articles, as we have seen, emerged from his solitary effort at independent scholarship, before he had yet practiced law for any extended time. He had begun by accepting the terms of discussion in the scholarly literature. In his first efforts to bring order into the common law, a series of articles beginning with "Codes, and the Arrangement of Law" (1870) (6.20) and ending with "The Arrangement of Law—Privity" (1872) (6.75), he had prepared an analytical scheme based on duties, which he argued were prior to rights both logically and historically, but otherwise similar to the Benthamite taxonomy. His first attack on the analytical school, therefore, was hardly more than a mirror image of its system.[88]

In *The Common Law,* Holmes followed a logical taxonomy—visible in the chapter headings and the organization of material—based on duties. After the introductory chapter, which set out Holmes's general argument, the chapters that followed were organized on a continuum of duties and quasi-duties of declining force. First came criminal law, which Holmes called the realm of "true duties," the rules of conduct which must be followed at all times, on pain of punishment. (These corresponded roughly to the first category of duties in his earlier articles, the duties of citizens to the sovereign.)

The next two chapters, "Trespass and Negligence" and "Fraud, Malice, and Intent: The Theory of Torts," dealt with private wrongs, or "tort" law. These were the duties of each to all. Holmes had always argued (disagreeing with Austin) that torts were not violations of true duties—that is, the law did not require performance of prescribed conduct on pain of punishment—and in *The Common Law* even the rules of conduct had disappeared. The law only shifted to the defendant's shoulders the burden of harms that resulted from his or her behavior, whatever it had been, when in the circumstances it was found to be malicious or negligent.

The next chapters, "Bailment" and "Possession," dealt broadly with the concept of property and reflected the reciprocal duties of one in possession of something to and from all others.[89] Next, the three chapters on contract law dealt with voluntarily assumed duties between persons. In Holmes's (much criticized) view, the common law was indifferent to whether contracts were performed so long as damages were paid for any breach. Here, duty plainly had reached its most abstract and attenuated form.

Finally, the chapters on "Succession" attempted to show how duties, which arose in particular circumstances, might be passed on through sale or inheritance to persons in quite different circumstances. These final chapters also contained Holmes's most extended discussion of the manner in which the forms of the law, embedded in precedent, changed over the centuries.

3.6.2 The Attack on the Utilitarians. As we have seen, the dominant English view was that law was the command of a political superior. It seemed self-evident on grounds of common sense that law was simply an instrument for carrying out governmental purposes, and since Bentham's day it had been the Liberal view that the principal purpose of government was simply to secure the greatest good for the greatest number.

Holmes departed from this view in fundamental ways. First, he energetically denied the principle of utility. The various classes and races of which a nation was made were in conflict, and in a world of limited resources and unchecked population, not all would survive (6.81). There was no overall good of the community but only the conflicting interests of competing groups.

Holmes, as we have seen, also denied the Hobbesian premise that law was the command of the sovereign. He had learned in the Civil War that the ultimate source of power was not a nominal government but the force that lay behind it; and he argued that judges and courts responded, not to the government's edicts alone, but to the fundamental source of power—the dominant forces of the community, on which the ultimate sanction of force depended. (He later remarked that he had gone beyond the Hobbesian view to that of Jean Bodin, the French jurist now known for having drawn a sharp distinction between state and nation.)[90] Judges found the law not only in the commands of a political superior but also in customs and morals of the community, and even in ideas of public policy. Law was what the courts decided, and their decisions were backed by the sanction of force.

3.6.3 The Substance of Law. We return to the heart of Holmes's jurisprudence, his belief that the common law was the effect, and not the cause, of judicial action. Judges based their decisions on inarticulate grounds, ultimately reflecting the wishes of the community. In *The Common Law,* Holmes put this somewhat elliptically; he said that their grounds of decision were based on the "felt necessities" of their time.

> Every important principle which is developed by litigation is in fact and at bottom the result of more or less definitely understood views of public policy; most generally, to be sure, under our practice and traditions, the unconscious result of instinctive preferences and inarticulate convictions, but none the less traceable to views of public policy in the last analysis.

The Common Law was concerned almost entirely with form and method—it laid out structural principles which had guided the evolution of law. Holmes therefore had very little to say about the detailed content of law—the elements of a claim, say, or the defenses to a charge—or of the specific public policies it embodied. Holmes identified public policy broadly with "considerations of what is expedient for the community concerned" and described such policies only in the most general terms.

Consulting recent anthropological studies, Holmes said that the law of primitive societies had been based on a policy of satisfying the instinct of revenge peacefully, through the processes of law, instead of through personal violence. After centuries of evolution, the most highly evolved society, that of the English-speaking peoples, in addition to keeping the peace, had adopted a policy, suitable for a more complex culture, of allowing the greatest degree of personal freedom consistent with avoiding unjustified harm to others.[91]

The purpose of allowing such freedom was purely the expedience of the dominant force in the community, its collective sense that its welfare would be enhanced in this way.

If law was simply an instrument to accomplish certain material ends, it followed that the law should concern itself solely with external behavior; the merely moral or subjective would be stripped away by the process of evolution. Holmes argued that he could discern in the developing common law a trend toward complete reliance on "external standards" of behavior rather than on subjective states of mind or personal culpability. This was the principal conclusion of *The Common Law*.

3.6.4 The Meaning of the External Standard. The external standard accordingly became the central image, the metaphor for Holmes's whole theory up through the publication of *The Common Law* in 1881. It will be worthwhile to investigate its inner workings a bit, although that will require stepping back and reviewing some of Holmes's early writings again.

While preparing the lectures that became *The Common Law*, Holmes believed he had found a single principle at the heart of the whole immense tangle of the common law. A person would be held liable for any harms he or she had caused, that someone of ordinary prudence would have foreseen. This was the famous "external standard" of liability for foreseeable harm.

Holmes's first explicit statement of this as a general principle of law was in "Trespass and Negligence" (8.7), in 1880, during his final preparations for *The Common Law*. The idea had developed rather slowly in Holmes's thought, however. It first appeared, surprisingly, in Holmes's discussion of an English case concerning damages for the loss of "lateral support" for land.

In October, 1867, Holmes had used almost all of a brief book review (6.7), one of his first publications, to discuss lateral support cases. If a landowner had dug a ditch that undermined a neighboring property, and the neighbor's house had settled or fallen, the neighbor could recover for damages to his land by proving nothing more than that the ditch caused the damage to his land; but in order to recover for damages to his house, he would have to show either unusual carelessness ("want of due care") or actual misbehavior ("positive negligence") in the digging of the ditch. This, at least, was the conventional view of the law; it rested on ancient distinctions between direct invasion of land and more indirect harms. Holmes, in his review, argued that recent English cases had changed the traditional distinction between damages to land and to structures. Such distinctions no longer had any purpose, Holmes argued, and under the newer English cases a single rule should apply. According to Holmes, the only question now should be how closely connected the damages to land and buildings were to the defendant's behavior: "[H]ow shall the defendant infringe his neighbor's rights, and yet not be liable for the immediate consequences of his act?"

This was the germ of Holmes's external standard of liability. (This attention to the lateral support cases can be explained in a few words. Holmes's maternal grandfather, Judge Charles Jackson, had been the author of the leading American treatise on real actions; and in 1865, while still a student, Holmes himself had joined in a moot court exercise in which he had argued and lost on the precise question to which he now returned, apparently citing the same cases on which he had relied as a student.)[92]

When Holmes began to classify the law as a system of duties, he did not yet consider "negligence" or "torts" to be distinct subjects but dealt implicitly with negligence as among a person's several duties to neighboring landowners and others (6.20); in 1871, in a book review, he remarked that lawsuits for indirectly caused injuries—what we would now call negligence—had more in common with certain actions concerning damage to real estate than with other supposed "torts" like assault and battery (6.26; see also 6.27, 6.31).

By 1872, Holmes had fully worked out his classification scheme according to duties; negligence still did not appear separately but was assimilated to the category in which he included the "lateral support" real estate cases, a category governed by the duties of those in possession of land and other property (6.75).

In preparation for his edition of Kent's *Commentaries,* published in 1873, Holmes wrote a series of brief articles for the *American Law Review,* which he condensed and used as footnotes to the *Commentaries,* summarizing recent developments in the law. The very last of these was his article "The Theory of Torts" (6.82), in which Holmes grudgingly accepted what was by then the all but universal view that "torts" had become a distinct field of specialization in law which included the subtopic "negligence." Holmes gave a final elaboration to his categorization of law according to duties and subdivided the new topic of negligence into three tiers—negligence that depended on a culpable state of mind, negligence that was a violation of a rule of conduct, and negligence defined by particular circumstances.

Some of the substance of this article appeared in an essay-note Holmes added to Kent's commentary on the law of bailments (7.40, p. 561, n. 1). In this remarkable brief note, added when he had nearly completed his work on the *Commentaries,* Holmes stripped away the extraneous categorization of duties and for the first time[93] presented in highly compressed summary a functional theory of the common law as a whole:

Law was a set of rules of conduct, which judges drew from varying factual sources. The evolution of law was carried out by the gradual elaboration of these rules into philosophic species, as judges chose between competing principles and marked out their respective domains on an imaginary map.

Where there was no readily available, codified rule of conduct to fit a particular situation, the judge would fill the gap by relying on the behavior of an ordinary reasonable man in the circumstances; the jury's function was to supply this rule. Holmes drew on only a handful of English bailment cases to conclude that the standard of behavior at common law was said to be that of a "reasonable man," a generality that constantly was reduced to specific rules of behavior in particular cases.

Three years after completing Kent's *Commentaries,* in 1876, in the first article that would become a chapter of *The Common Law,* Holmes sketched a new synthesis, as we have seen. Holmes now argued that a judge's choice between conflicting principles was dictated by unconscious feelings or ideas of morality or public policy that he held in common with other members of the community. As these ideas evolved and changed, so did the rules of law. The qualities of mind common to judges, and not what was particular to any one judge, were the point of interest. Tracing the principles common to decisions would reveal the underlying elements or structures of thought, and their gradual evolution ("Primitive Notions in Modern Law," 8.1).

Holmes argued for his thesis with a series of examples.[94] The history of what had become tort law was used to reveal a central element of judges' thinking. Holmes returned once more to his student days and reargued the moot court case that he had lost. On one hand, Holmes said, there was an old rule based on strict liability for damages caused by trespass to land; on the other, there was a doctrine of liability for indirect harms. Each had been based on quasi-criminal violations of duty. Holmes said now that both rules should be swept aside; the proper question in every case was simply whether the harm was sufficiently closely related to the defendant's conduct for liability to attach ("Trespass and Negligence," 8.7). This was a standard based on prudential considerations rather than morality. In the table of contents of his own copy of *The Common Law*, Holmes marked beside the first summary lecture, "Progress from unconscious moral to external standards."

In the statement of this modern external standard, Holmes combined different elements of his earlier writing. From his note on the bailment cases he took the standard of the behavior of the reasonable man; from the lateral support cases (persons in possession of real estate), the standard of proximity of harm. The single test of liability was now that a defendant would be liable for harms sufficiently close to his actions that a reasonable man would have foreseen their happening.

This way of putting the rule, aside from uniting disparate cases with a common principle, allowed Holmes to fit tort law into a new overall scheme; not a codification of duties but more simply a restatement of the whole body of common law as an instrument of social purposes—in this case, to avoid needless harm.

Like a great poetic metaphor, the external standard condensed several important themes into a single statement. The principal themes were a structuralist theory of evolution, and the theory that law was concerned solely with material consequences.

3.6.5 The Mechanism of Evolution.

Having traced the development of Holmes's unifying principle, the external standard of liability, up to 1881, we can now return to his exposition of a comprehensive theory in *The Common Law*. That book, as we have seen, described the common law as evolving until it had achieved the external standard.

Holmes sketched the mechanism of evolution in his opening chapter, but he evidently realized soon after the book was published that this sketch was inadequate. He said only that judges departed from precedent because they forgot or never knew the true basis of older cases—""ignorance is the great law reformer." Holmes's notes on his own copy show that he planned to expand this discussion. Reliance on precedent itself required explanation; as to this point Holmes sketched out an argument: "Imagination of men limited. Can only think in terms of the language they have been taught. Conservative instinct" (8.Introduction, and 8.1). As society and its circumstances changed, the older forms of language and the law persisted. But ignorance of the past, and the process of rationalization, allowed judges slowly to infuse new ideas and purposes into the old forms, and these incremental departures from precedent compelled law to evolve, at every stage reflecting, within the limits of precedent, the judges' unconscious perceptions of public policy, of what was to the advantage of the community from which the judges were drawn. Holmes argued that these purposes were not necessarily conscious or rational, and that in early primitive societies (Holmes coolly referred to classical Greece as a primitive society), law expressed an irrational impulse to seek vengeance, even on inanimate objects.

As society evolved into higher and more complex forms, the purposes of the law became more rational, and the impulse to vengeance ultimately gave way to more refined and conscious purposes. Similarly, the territorial instinct gave rise to refined modern notions of property, and the unconscious identification of the son with his deceased father developed into modern forms of inheritance and succession.

This was not so much a completed system as a sketch of a method for restating the law in scientific terms. It was fundamentally what we would now call a structuralist method— Holmes sought to trace the development of unconscious elements implicit in the very language and institutions of the law, which he believed were evolving just as the bony skeleton of the mammal had evolved from the more primitive forms of the fish.

3.6.6 The Standard of Liability. To this general evolutionist argument of *The Common Law,* which was an extension of ideas already appearing in linguistic studies and in Herbert Spencer's *Sociology,* Holmes added a truly original insight. Law writers, including Holmes up through the very year of his Lowell Lectures, had tried and failed to make sense of the multitudinous rules of conduct that courts seemed to recognize and enforce. A landowner had a duty to guests but not to trespassers; railroad companies had complex duties to their passengers and the owners of their freight, still others to pedestrians crossing their tracks. Holmes had labored unsuccessfully, like his predecessors, to make sense of this tangled mass of duties and correlative rights.

In preparing for *The Common Law* in 1880, however, he seems to have seen a new organizing principle. The question in every case, Holmes realized, was whether liability would be imposed. He turned away from the rules themselves and gave his attention to the circumstances under which a breach of a rule would be punished. This was a natural enough extension of his thought; rules of conduct were drawn from various sources in ordinary life, and it was not until a rule was enforced by a court that it became law, properly speaking. By looking at the circumstances in which rules would be enforced and ignoring judges' rationalizations about rules of conduct that were duties and those that were not, Holmes for the first time was able to make general statements about law and its relation to society.

The external standard of liability, which had been evolving slowly in his thinking about tort law, fell into place, and like the shifting elements of a kaleidoscope the disparate elements of his theory arranged themselves around this central image. His general organizing principle had become clear: liability would be imposed for injuries that an ordinary person would have foreseen.

This statement of the theory seemed to reveal a fundamental policy determining the shape of modern law—to allow the greatest personal freedom while avoiding unjustified harms to others—and seemed to unify all the disparate branches of law around a single principle toward which the law had been evolving for centuries, the common ground of all law because it was the fundamental motive for enforcing rules.[95]

In *The Common Law*, Holmes argued that law had evolved from more primitive origins toward this still partly unconscious, "external standard" of liability, as a means of substituting the peaceful rule of law for the ancient regime of violence. In future, it would become a self-conscious instrument of the dominant forces in the community. Law would continue to evolve into consciousness, and lawyers of the future, like other scientists, would be part of the evolving social organism's self-awareness. Holmes's book itself, presumably, was an important step in this evolution toward self-awareness.

3.7
"PRIVILEGE, MALICE, AND INTENT"

As a judge of the Massachusetts Supreme Judicial Court from 1882 to 1902, Holmes had a chance to test the theory of *The Common Law*, and to some extent to fulfill its prophecies. But his respect for the work and for the precedents of his own court gradually required a considerable broadening of his views.

Holmes wrote opinions for the Massachusetts court in about thirteen hundred cases and joined in deliberations in thousands more. It is not practical to review these cases in detail. But his work as a judge forced him to consider a number of cases in which the external standard of foreseeable harm did not seem to apply, cases which forced him to broaden his theory to take into account, among other things, the limitations on the privilege accorded to free speech. It is worth examining these cases further.

3.7.1 The New Tort Cases. Holmes eventually divided these seemingly anomalous cases into two categories.

The first were cases in which some person had intervened between the defendant's act and the plaintiff's injury. In these cases, foreseeability seemed not to be at issue. In *Elmer v. Fessenden*,[96] for instance, a doctor falsely told one of his patients—who worked in a buggy-whip factory—that the silk used to make buggy-whip snaps was contaminated with arsenic. Other employees heard the story and quit work; the factory owner sued Dr. Fessenden. The doctor's defense was that his advice to his patient was privileged, and that the persons who repeated and spread the story, and not he, were the cause of the harm.

It was argued in rebuttal that the slander was bound to be repeated and that Fessenden was bound to foresee the injury. But Holmes, writing for the court, held that Fessenden could not be held liable for the repetitions: "The general rule, that a man is not liable for a third person's actionable and unauthorized repetition of his slander, is settled."[97] In this, and in a series of tort and contract cases, Holmes followed the long-established doctrine that liability would not be imposed on the defendant if the wrongful acts of a third party intervened between the defendant's conduct and the plaintiff's injury.[98]

To explain these cases and to reconcile them with his general scheme, Holmes enlarged upon the idea of "foreseeability." A person was not held by the common law to foresee wrongdoing by others: "When the third person's act was lawful, it stands like the workings of nature, and the question is whether it reasonably was to be anticipated or looked out for" ("Privilege, Malice, and Intent," 10.5). But intervening third-party wrongdoers were by definition unforeseeable, presumably because their behavior was unnatural in some sense.[99]

This may look arbitrary to a modern eye, but it was not so at the time. Holmes never had any knowledge of probability or statistics, and he did not think in quantitative terms. Furthermore, he was explaining precedents that had been decided in a still earlier age, an age of natural law thinking, when "rational" and "proper" were nearly synonymous.[100] One must bear in mind that to Holmes the common law was the fossil record of an earlier, unreflective, morality. Foresight, as it was known in the law, meant extending into the future the lines of orderly and proper behavior. If only lawful behavior "stands like the workings of nature," all else is an Act of God—fortuitous and "unforeseeable," even if perfectly unsurprising. It was in this old-fashioned sense that Holmes could say with a perfectly good conscience that one should not be held to "foresee" injuries caused by the independent wrongdoing of others.[101]

A puzzling aspect of these cases, however, was that the defendant's subjective expectations seemed important. The precedents were clear that a defendant could not shelter behind the wrongful behavior of a third party that he in fact expected (*The Common Law*, 9.4); but Holmes accepted this qualification without at first attempting to explain it.

With regard to these third-party wrongdoer cases, therefore, Holmes felt his scheme was preserved, although, as Frederick Pollock remarked, his analysis was too finely honed for everyday use.[102]

The second class of cases that had to be reconciled with the ""external standard" were those in which a defense of privilege had been raised. Holmes had addressed these briefly in *The Common Law*. In such cases, defendants admittedly could foresee that their conduct would cause injuries and yet still asked to be excused from liability. A privilege, if successfully asserted, could be defeated only by a showing of actual malice (9.4). In one case that interested Holmes, a couple had given advice to a married woman, as a consequence of which she had left her husband. The injured husband sued the interfering couple, but did not succeed, because despite his foreseeable injury the advice given was privileged. On appeal, the plaintiff took exception to the trial court's having admitted evidence of the defendants' motives. Holmes rejected the appeal, saying that the defendants "had a right to show their advice was given honestly, with a view to the welfare of both parties." On such a showing, the defendants' advice could have been held to be privileged and the couple would not be liable.[103] Similarly, Dr. Fessenden's advice to his patient, if honestly given, was privileged.[104] A newspaper report of corruption in office was privileged unless published with actual malice.[105]

Holmes, in *The Common Law*, had denied that "actual malice" referred to the subjective intentions of the defendant; indeed, he gave this as an example of law's having evolved from an earlier simple morality to an external standard based on behavior. In the earlier book, Holmes had interpreted the modern cases to say that "actual malice" meant no more than that by an external standard the defendant's statement was patently false and likely to cause harm: "The fact that the defendant foresaw and foresaw with pleasure the damage to the plaintiff, is of no . . . importance" (9.4). But as a judge, Holmes was obliged to concede that liability depended, not on an external standard alone, but also on evidence of the actual motives and feelings of the defendants. This was the same anomaly that had turned up in the third-party wrongdoer cases. Holmes set out to explain it.

He gave his answer in an article, "Privilege, Malice, and Intent," published in 1894 (10.5). The article began with bravado: "The law of torts as now administered has worked itself into substantial agreement with a general theory." This theory, which Holmes went on to summarize, was his own theory of the external standard, presented in the opening chapters of *The Common Law* and worked through in his opinions for the Massachusetts Supreme Judicial Court. But this theory was now only the "first part" of a more general synthesis. To complete the synthesis Holmes added his explanation of cases in which subjective intent was relevant to liability.

In every such case, Holmes insisted, one began with a *prima facie* demonstration of liability based on the external standard. "I assume that we have got past the question which is answered by the test of the external standard. There is no dispute that the manifest tendency of the defendant's act is to inflict temporal damage upon the plaintiff."

Holmes then turned to the defense of privilege. Repeating the analysis given in *The Common Law*, Holmes said that privileges were always based on tacit social policy, a judgment that the harms done by free speaking, for instance, were justified by the benefits to society. So far, the law was still in the realm of the external standard.

When a privilege was absolute—such as the privileges for petitions to the government and statements from the bench—the analysis went no farther. The defendant was privileged to do harm, regardless of motive.

But in the more usual case, the privilege was qualified. "Not only the existence but the extent or degree of privilege will vary with the case." A qualified privilege would be defeated if the defendant were shown to have acted on an expectation or a desire that damage would result. Similarly, defendants who would not otherwise be liable for harm caused through the intervention of third-party wrongdoers would be denied this defense if they had in fact foreseen or intended the wrongdoing.

The reason for this, Holmes said, was based in social policy. Privileges were granted for policy reasons—most generally, the policy of letting people do as they wished. But a malicious motive, by increasing the probability that harm would result from otherwise privileged behavior, would tip the balance of advantage the other way.

> There is no general policy in favor of allowing a man to do harm to his neighbor for the sole pleasure of doing harm. . . . If the privilege [extended to some useful behavior] is qualified, the policy in favor of the defendant's freedom generally will be found to be qualified only to the extent of forbidding him to use for the sake of harm what is allowed for the sake of good.

Holmes continued to insist that all liability at common law was based on "foreseeability" of harms that the dominant forces in society wished to prevent. This was still the old-fashioned sort of foreseeability: not a matter of mathematical probabilities but rather a projection into the future of the lines of lawful conduct and the usual course of natural events.

Holmes also continued to insist that certain behavior, like free speaking, was privileged as a matter of social policy, despite its manifest tendency to do harm. The new element in his theory was simply the recognition that actual intent to cause harm or induce unlawful conduct would defeat a claim of privilege. This new element, Holmes claimed, also was a matter of social policy, to discourage behavior that posed too great a risk of harm.

The doctrine of "clear and present danger" had been born.[106] Another twenty-five years would elapse before Holmes would apply the doctrine in First Amendment cases. In the intervening years, he tested it in his judicial laboratory.

3.7.2 Labor Unions. In the early 1890s, the courts were increasingly drawn into class conflict, as factory owners sought injunctions against strikes and boycotts. Holmes, expecting such cases to come before his court, prepared himself carefully. He began a systematic course of reading, beginning with Hobbes's *Leviathan* and continuing with Hegel, Karl Marx, Herbert Spencer, and William Morris on socialism.[107] He emerged from these studies confirmed in his belief in Malthus and natural selection. Population, unless controlled, would always press against the limits of the environment; in the struggle for scarce resources the weakest would perish. Human society, like other species, would evolve by natural selection of the fittest "races" and nations.[108]

As part of his program of studies, Holmes quietly called upon a labor leader—apparently Frank Foster, president of the Boston Typographers' Union.[109] Foster, it appeared, shared Holmes's Darwinist philosophy but hoped for the victory of labor in the struggle for existence; he argued simply for fair terms in the fight.[110]

Holmes, despite unswerving loyalty to his own class, heard Foster's plea with sympathy. The code of honor that Holmes had absorbed from earliest childhood, the code of a gentleman, required fairness. Chivalry and science, the two great themes of his time, fused in the idea of evolution through fair combat. His studies had persuaded him that law itself had evolved into a system of fair, peaceful competition.[111]

Holmes had argued that privileges to do harm were based on social policy. The question in labor cases therefore was whether such privileges should be extended to labor unions. The social policy in question was not whether labor unions were desirable—Holmes thought they were socialist humbug[112]—but whether the struggle for life should be carried on peacefully and fairly. This more fundamental principle, he thought, required that labor unions be accorded the same privilege as capital, to organize to inflict economic injuries on their opponents. But the trade unions' privilege did not go so far as to allow them to do damage simply for the sake of harm; the privilege would be defeated by a showing of malice ("Privilege, Malice, and Intent," 10.5).

The opportunity to test these ideas came in *Vegehlan v. Guntner,*[113] shortly after publication of "Privilege, Malice, and Intent." Sitting as a judge in the equity court in Boston, Holmes heard a petition from a factory owner for an order halting picketing and a boycott by striking factory workers. Holmes declined to enjoin peaceful picketing or acts of persuasion, on the ground that these were privileged; but he did grant an injunction against acts of violence.

He was reversed by the full Supreme Judicial Court, however, and entered a solitary, passionate dissent:

> I have seen the suggestion made that the conflict between employer and employed was not competition. But I venture to assume that none of my brethren would rely on that suggestion. If the policy on which our law is founded is too narrowly expressed in the term free competition, we may substitute free struggle for life. . . .
>
> One of the eternal conflicts out of which life is made up is that between the effort of every man to get the most he can for his services, and that of society, disguised under the name of capital, to get his services for the least possible return. Combination on the one side is patent and powerful. Combination on the other is the necessary and desirable counterpart, if the battle is to be carried on in a fair and equal way.[114]

Holmes's conception of law had undergone a profound deepening. The single standard of liability, foreseeability of harm, had imperceptibly become a more complex matter of privileges and states of mind, which required far more attention to individual defendants and their circumstances than the external standard of Holmes's youthful work. The judge, no longer the unconscious spokesman of the dominant forces in the community, became an arbiter of social conflict, somehow seated above the battle. The judge could not know which of the contending principles had the better claim for survival; he could only ensure that the conflict was carried out fairly, and the victor chosen by a neutral arbiter. On the eve of his retirement from the Massachusetts court, in 1902, Holmes spoke of his work as a judge:

> I have considered the present tendencies and desires of society and have tried to realize that its different portions want different things, and that my business was not to express my personal wish, but the resultant, as near as I could guess, of the pressure of the past and the conflicting wills of the present. ("Twenty Years in Retrospect," 12.20)

But this view, at which Holmes arrived in his fifties, seemed inconsistent with the theme of his earlier work, that a judge was necessarily spokesman for the dominant forces in the community. The difficulty was most obvious in cases like those involving organized labor, when judges decided what the rules would be and so decided who would win. While the outcome was still undecided, judges had to rely on some higher principle than those represented by the contending parties, in order to choose between them.

Now Holmes might have said—and if pressed on this point I think he would have said—that so far as his own loyalties went, a self-sacrificing sense of honor was part of the values of the class to which he was loyal. But this would not answer when the very question in the case was whether his class and the values they represented should continue in power, unless fairness were so important that his class and nation should perish rather than give it up.

This last conclusion was Holmes's own sense of duty. It was perhaps a shared value in the small circle of those he considered his peers, and in this sense it represented the values of his class. But Holmes sensed its paradoxical quality, and in speeches he gave in the late 1890s, he emphasized the self-sacrificing nature of moral and aesthetic ideals, which seemed to contradict the imperatives of natural selection (see 11.18, 12.17, 12.18).

Holmes did not at first try to reconcile the apparent contradiction, but eventually he said that his own determination to decide fairly, even when the survival of his class or nation was at stake, rested on faith in the evolutionary purposes of the cosmos rather than on the self-interest of any lawmaking power:

> Whatever else we learn from nature we learn from it a mystic faith. . . We all have cosmic destinies of which we cannot divine the end, if the unknown has ends. Our business is to commit ourselves to life, to accept at once our functions and our ignorance and to offer our heart to fate. (12.23)
>
> If I feel what are perhaps an old man's apprehensions, that competition from new races will cut deeper than working men's disputes and will test whether we can hang together and can fight; if I fear that we are running through the world's resources at a pace that we cannot keep; I do not lose my hopes. I do not pin my dreams for the future to my country or even to my race. I think it probable that civilization somehow will last as long as I care to look ahead—perhaps with smaller numbers, but perhaps also bred to greatness and splendor by science. I think it not improbable that man, like the grub that prepares a chamber for the winged thing it has never seen but is to be—that man may have cosmic destinies that he does not understand. And so beyond the vision of battling races and an impoverished earth I catch a dreaming glimpse of peace. ("Law and the Court," 11.20)

And so in ultimate questions Holmes, as a judge, finally seemed to abandon the premises of his jurisprudence. The mystical faith that as we have seen formed the core of his personal philosophy from the 1890s onward, and that was formed in the personal crisis of those years, seemed inconsistent with the ordinary judge's role in the system of law.

This question is discussed more fully in chapter 4. For the moment we note only that from the 1890s onward, the period in which Holmes wrote his well-known opinions, he treated judgeship as choosing between contending social policies, represented by privileges and their limitations, rather than as simply expressing the interests of the dominant class.

3.7.3 Criminal Conspiracies and Attempts. After the publication of "Privilege, Malice, and Intent," Holmes continued to serve on the Massachusetts Supreme Judicial Court for six more years, in which he continued to address common law questions, working his ideas out in practice. He applied the ideas in "Privilege, Malice, and Intent" to cases of criminal attempts and conspiracies, where the defendant's state of mind again was relevant. He eventually had the pleasure of seeing the majority of his court adopt his reasoning.

In criminal attempts, the problem for the court was similar to that in cases of privilege: the defendant's acts were not in themselves punishable but created a risk of harm in particular circumstances. A year after his dissent in *Vegehlan,* Holmes spoke for the court in a notorious case of attempted murder, *Commonwealth v. Kennedy.*[115] William Kennedy had taken an interest in the wife of his employer, Alfred T. Learoyd. When Learoyd fired him, Kennedy surreptitiously pasted rat poison under the bar of Learoyd's mustache cup.[116]

Kennedy had argued among other things that putting poison under the mustache bar, even if proven, was too remote from the completed crime to constitute an attempt at murder. Holmes seized the opportunity to deliver a little essay, with copious citations to English and American cases, on the law of attempts, extending the argument of "Privilege, Malice, and Intent" to this new class of cases.[117] "As the aim of the law is not to punish sins, but is to prevent certain external results, the act done must come pretty near to accomplishing that result before the law will take notice of it. . . . Every question of proximity must be determined by its own circumstances."[118]

In determining the degree of "proximity" to the completed crime, Holmes said, the court was to consider both an external standard and the defendant's subjective expectation or intent.[119] In this case, Kennedy expected and intended that Learoyd would drink poisoned tea from the cup and die, the expectation was reasonable in the circumstances, and so Kennedy was properly convicted of attempted murder.[120] As in the privilege and intervening-wrongdoer cases, behavior that was not in itself a crime, although dangerous in the circumstances, could not be punished unless a subjective intent to cause the harm could be proven.

Although Holmes did not say so, this departed dramatically from the doctrine stated in *The Common Law* (9.2), where the defendant's intent was said to be relevant only when his further acts, and his alone, were required to complete the crime. This, of course, was not the case in *Kennedy,* where the victim would have performed the remaining acts needed to accomplish his own murder.

Holmes extended and clarified the "Privilege, Malice, and Intent" analysis in a well-known case of attempted arson, *Commonwealth v. Peaslee.*[121] He repeated his foreseeability analysis in more detail: to prove an attempted crime, one first extended into the future lines of proper behavior and the course of natural events. Behavior that in and of itself foreseeably would lead to crime without further effort was not privileged, and no further showing was required.

Such behavior—like falsely shouting "fire!" in a theater[122]—was plainly punishable in and of itself. But the case was more difficult when future wrongdoing by the defendant or others was required to complete the crime. In such circumstances, the first preparations were privileged unless the further wrongdoing was actually foreseen or intended; then the combination of hazardous acts and specific intent brought the crime dangerously near completion (citing *Commonwealth v. Kennedy*).[123]

Conspiracy cases offered a modest extension of the same line of thought. Where the conspirators had not carried out a completed crime, the prosecutor was required to prove an overt act in furtherance of the conspiracy and the defendants' actual intent to carry it through. The overt act was not in itself criminal, and might be harmless or even privileged behavior. Acts wrongful because of their immediate consequences then would be required to complete the crime for which the conspiracy prepared. The defendants' actual expectation of such unlawful conduct made harm more likely and therefore would defeat any privilege that otherwise might be accorded ("Privilege, Malice, and Intent," 10.5).

The Massachusetts Supreme Judicial Court expressly adopted Holmes's reasoning as to conspiracies in 1902, citing "Privilege, Malice, and Intent";[124] and Holmes had the further triumph of seeing his theory of conspiracies, in opinions concerning labor unions, cited as precedent in the English Court of Appeal.[125] In 1905, soon after his appointment to the Supreme Court, Holmes wrote for the Court in *Swift and Co. v. United States*,[126] upholding an injunction issued against a conspiracy of meat-packers in violation of the Sherman Act. Repeatedly citing his own opinion in *Commonwealth v. Peaslee*, Holmes wrote into federal law the argument of "Privilege, Malice, and Intent": where individual acts charged were each lawful, an actual intent to accomplish a crime must be proved.[127]

Holmes accordingly saw the doctrines of "Privilege, Malice, and Intent" proven in practice, thoroughly assimilated into his general theory of the common law, and made a part of the common law of England and the United States.[128]

This was a fundamental transformation of the external standard, the central element of his theory and one that would increasingly bring Holmes into conflict with modern federal law. His argument in "Privilege, Malice, and Intent" concerned the circumstances under which the government could regulate risk from ordinarily privileged behavior. Just as the expanding federal government was beginning to create extensive regulatory programs, beginning with the mobilization for the First World War, Holmes began insisting that individuals could not be held liable for their privileged acts except on a showing that they intended harm.

3.7.4 "The Path of the Law." The later development in the central structure of his theory, reflected in "Privilege, Malice, and Intent," grew from his experiences as a judge and embodied his mature feeling of the judge's role. "Privilege, Malice, and Intent" was Holmes's last major addition to his theory of law. Henceforth his writings on law would be restricted to judicial opinions and occasional addresses to meetings of the bar—with one important exception. In the winter of 1896–97, he returned to a subject of his youth and wrote an address on the scientific study of law.

This was "The Path of the Law" (10.9), an address at the dedication of a new hall for Boston University School of Law, January 8, 1897. It was a remarkable piece of work in many ways. It was the only writing on law that Holmes did, other than his judicial opinions, which had a coherent form. When working on the address, he referred to it as "[m]y discourse on the Theory of Legal Study,"[129] and so it proved to be.

In the summer of 1896, as a respite from domestic cares, Holmes had gone to England; there he had fallen in love with Clare Castletown of Upper Ossory, the Anglo-Irish Lady Castletown. His letters to her have survived and show an extraordinary outpouring of enthusiastic feeling. The affair released a flood of creativity, in the letters themselves and in his discourse on the theory of legal study, "The Path of the Law."

The title is plainly a reference to Bushido, the way of the warrior, the Japanese chivalric code. Holmes had learned a good deal about Japan in the 1870s from Kaneko Kentaro and other Japanese students of the Samurai class when he tutored them for the Harvard Law School. The subject of the talk is the practice of law; Holmes's image of the gentleman soldier-scientist, which had appeared so often in his letters and speeches, now stepped into the center of his legal theory.

Implicit in *The Common Law* had been its assumption that scientific study of the law was itself law, that the rules to be derived from study of the decisions of the courts were of interest not only to the anthropologist but to the working lawyer.

Holmes himself had been a practicing lawyer when he wrote it, and he was as a common-law judge that he applied the principles of his book to the law of Massachusetts. He now made that assumption articulate and joined the halves of his life. The opening paragraph of "The Path of the Law" became as famous among lawyers as the opening sentences of *The Common Law:*

> When we study law we are not studying a mystery but a well-known profession. We are studying what we shall want in order to appear before judges, or to advise people in such a way as to keep them out of court. The reason why it is a profession, why people will pay lawyers to argue for them or to advise them, is that in societies like ours the command of the public force is intrusted to the judges in certain cases, and the whole power of the state will be put forth, if necessary, to carry out their judgments and decrees. People want to know under what circumstances and how far they will run the risk of coming against what is so much stronger than themselves, and hence it becomes a business to find out when this danger is to be feared. The object of our study, then, is prediction, the prediction of the incidence of the public force through the instrumentality of the courts. (10.9)

The elements of Holmes's early thought were now perfectly fused: this in a sense was the completion of *The Common Law.* The single standard of liability, the standard of foreseeable harm, was restated as Holmes had modified it in "Privilege, Malice, and Intent." The extraneous categorization of law into grades of duty was at last discarded, as irrelevant to the single principle of liability, and irrelevant, also, to the slow evolution of law as outdated forms slowly shifted under the pressure of changing ideas of social policy. A defendant was concerned, not with the myriad rules of duty, but with whether he would be punished for violating them. To make this point, Holmes used a very old device, traceable at least to Hobbes, the imaginary "bad man" who cared nothing for duty and therefore provided a sort of thought-experiment to see what was essential in the law.

The lawyer accordingly was transformed into a scientist, who predicted the imposition of liability by studying decisions of the courts and deriving principles of law by pure induction. Science opened the door to philosophy: the great lawyer was not a man tied to the narrow business of getting clients but one who reached out to the limits of his study, who devoted himself in true chivalric fashion to the pursuit of the ideal, the echo from behind phenomena, the smile of the Great Swell.

> The remoter and more general aspects of the law are those that give it universal interest. It is through them that you not only become a great master in your calling, but connect your subject with the universe and catch an echo of the infinite, a glimpse of its unfathomable process, a hint of the universal law. (10.9)

Holmes had not added anything to his formal legal thinking, but he had added a great poem to the literature of the law.

3.8
FEDERAL COMMON LAW

From 1902 until 1932, Holmes served on the United States Supreme Court. It is not surprising that at the age of sixty-one he no longer was struggling for new theoretical insights. He tried his well-formed ideas in the new fields of federal law, however, and in so doing, filled them out and strengthened the structure that supported his constitutional opinions.

The cases that most impressed Holmes with their intrinsic importance, during the years that he served on the Supreme Court, were those concerning conflicts among the states over natural resources. His own opinions on this subject were part of an overall approach adopted by the Court under Chief Justice Melville Fuller, who in 1901 had himself set out the outlines in an opinion suggesting that the proper approach was found in the common law of public nuisance. A state sufficiently injured by activities beyond its borders could bring suit in the original jurisdiction of the Supreme Court.[130] Holmes and David Brewer, who were usually on opposite sides of major questions, each delivered opinions on this theme, Fuller in characteristic self-effacing fashion having orchestrated an impressive performance by the Court as a whole. Holmes, in his opinion—*Georgia v. Tennessee Copper*[131]—set the case into the framework of his jurisprudence. The government of the State of Georgia had an interest in the air and soil of the state that gave it standing in the Court. This was not a property interest but a more fundamental interest inherent in government itself.

Holmes had explored the theoretical underpinnings of this scheme in cases from the new territory of Hawaii.[132] The fundamental notion was that the states fashioned private property rights in natural resources, and this was the fundamental source of wealth in the community. State power over natural resources was not based on any common law title but, like sovereign immunity, on the practical power of the lawmaker to define all rights.

The State of Georgia, as a "quasi-sovereign," accordingly could sue in public nuisance for an injunction to halt the air pollution (acid rain from a copper smelter) emanating from Tennessee that was damaging natural resources in Georgia. There was to be no balancing of equities as in a private nuisance suit; the sovereign's judgment as to how its natural resources were to be used was absolute. Holmes solemnly emphasized that a suit in the Supreme Court was the alternative to war between the states over scarce resources. (Brewer, in his opinion—*Kansas v. Colorado*[133]—somewhat dissipated the solemnity by pointing out that the states were prohibited from entering into agreements among themselves without congressional approval, and that a suit in the Supreme Court was accordingly the alternative not only to war but to peaceable treaty.)[134]

The following year, Holmes extended his reasoning a step. A private company was attempting to export river water from New Jersey for sale in New York City; a New Jersey statute forbidding construction of a needed pipeline was upheld, although on its face the statute seemed to interfere with interstate commerce.[135] Holmes's reasoning again was that the state had a prior interest in natural resources and could withhold them from commerce entirely; this was not a question of the state's title of ownership but of its power to prevent ownership of any kind. If a state could keep its resources out of commerce entirely, it followed that it could conserve those resources by putting a limit on their use or preserve them for use within a limited region. If that region had to be entirely within the state, there was still no interference with interstate commerce; the resources had never become articles of commerce, except within the limits defined by the state.

The conclusion was a little strained, and the Court declined to follow this reasoning when it came to deal with other resources. A majority struck down Oklahoma's effort to keep its natural gas within its own borders, distinguishing *Hudson County,* Holmes energetically dissenting.[136] In later years, a steady expansion of the federal commerce power pushed back the boundaries of the sovereignty Holmes would have reserved to the states, and the Court eventually reversed the substance of Holmes's argument without expressly overruling his decisions. In 1982, in *Sporhase v. Nebraska,*[137] Justice Stevens—complaining of the difficulty of understanding Holmes's opinions—held for a majority of the Court that the State of Nebraska could not withhold groundwater within its borders from interstate commerce, groundwater *per se* had become an article of commerce and a statute limiting exports necessarily was a burden on commerce between the states.

Nothing seems left of the doctrine of *Hudson County* after this. The principle of *Georgia v. Tennessee Copper* is untouched in principle, but federal common law in this area is preempted by federal legislation,[138] and interstate pollution disputes are so regulated by statute now that it is unlikely that anything practical remains.

Holmes's most enduring contribution to federal general common law, ironically, may be his assistance in its destruction.

In cases where the Court's jurisdiction is founded on diversity of citizenship, cases may be determined by state rather than federal law. The doctrine of *Swift v. Tyson*[139] was that, in matters of general jurisprudence, the federal courts were not obliged to accept the decisions of a state's courts as to what the state's law was, or should be. On questions of general common law, the federal courts were entitled to form their own judgment. The implicit assumption was that there were preexisting principles of general jurisprudence as to which state courts might be in error, a natural enough assumption in 1842 but an anathema to Holmes. He had founded his jurisprudence on the idea that all law was the result of court action and that there were no preexisting principles, other than the decisions of the state courts, in which a state's law might be found. "The common law is not a brooding omnipresence in the sky, but the articulate voice of some sovereign or quasi-sovereign that can be identified."[140] It followed that *Swift v. Tyson* had been wrongly decided, and the point was so fundamental that Holmes was willing to unseat nearly a century of precedents. In *Kuhn v. Fairmont Coal Co.,*[141] reluctant to overrule such a well-established precedent outright, Holmes suggested strongly that the efflorescence of the doctrine that had grown from *Swift v. Tyson* be cut back drastically.[142] He repeated the argument more clearly and forcefully in *Black and White Taxicab Co. v. Brown and Yellow Taxicab Co.,*[143] a particularly egregious case in which a company had changed the state of its incorporation to gain the protection of the federal courts in defying the law of the state in which it carried on all of its business. The Court, however, reaffirmed and enlarged the doctrine of *Swift v. Tyson,* and Holmes dissented:

> [I]n my opinion the prevailing doctrine has been accepted upon a subtle fallacy that has never been analyzed. If I am right the fallacy has resulted in an unconstitutional assumption of powers by the courts of the United States which no lapse of time or respectable array of opinion should make us hesitate to correct. . . .
>
> Books written about any branch of the common law treat it as a unit. . . . It is very hard to resist the impression that there is one august corpus. . . . But there is no such

body of law. The fallacy and illusion that I think exist consist in supposing that there is this outside thing to be found. Law is a word used with different meanings, but law in the sense in which courts speak of it today does not exist without some definite authority behind it. . . . In my opinion the authority and the only authority is the state, and if that be so, the voice adopted by the state as its own should utter the last word.[144]

This was written as a dissent, purposely to sting; Holmes plainly had no hope of carrying a majority. In 1938, after his death, however, the Court having narrowly survived an attack on its independence, and Congress then considering plans to reverse *Swift v. Tyson* by statute, Justice Brandeis could command a majority of the Court not only to prune the doctrine but to overrule *Swift v. Tyson* outright. Brandeis's opinion in *Erie Railroad v. Tompkins*[145] is one of the classics of legal literature, and it relies heavily for its concluding punch on long quotations from Holmes's dissent in *Black and White Taxicab Co.*

3.9
CONSTITUTIONAL LAW

In his first years of service on the Massachusetts Court, there were comparatively few opportunities to address constitutional questions, and at least until he became chief justice, Holmes did not seek the opportunities there were. He had little interest in constitutional law as such. One of his brother justices lampooned Holmes's preoccupation with the common law:

> When around this table we do sit
> And constitutions are discussed
> And 'tis inquired of what the Fathers writ
> Holmes says, says he, that he'll be cussed
> If for all that he cares a single bit—
>
> But when the topic's trover
> Or replevin as 'tis called
> Then like a bee among the clover
> From ancient flower to flower he flits
> That bloom upon the Year Book's pages
> And swears that here's the wisdom of the ages.[146]

Holmes addressed constitutional questions only when he thought duty required him to do so. In Massachusetts practice, for instance, the legislature requested advisory opinions on the constitutionality of statutes, and Holmes thought it his duty to give his own opinion.[147] And beginning in 1899, during the incapacity of Chief Justice Waldbridge Field, followed by Holmes's succession to his place, Holmes began his long career as spokesman for his courts on constitutional questions. As chief justice of Massachusetts, Holmes found it necessary, simply to clear the docket, to use his talents as an opinion writer in constitutional cases. In most of those few instances before 1899 in which he was obliged to give an opinion on questions of constitutional law, and many of those afterward, Holmes announced his consistent principle of deference to the legislature.

3.9.1 Deference to the Legislature. Holmes's doctrine was that, if the constitutionality of a statute were challenged, the court should uphold it unless reasonable people could not disagree that it violated the constitution.[148] Although he acknowledged the importance of the separation of powers and the deference due to an equal branch of government, Holmes's reason for deferring to the legislature in this way was more fundamental. As he said in a letter to a friend,

> [A] state legislature has the power of Parliament, i.e. absolute power, except insofar as expressly or by implication it is prohibited by the constitution—that the question always is where do you find the prohibition—not, where do you find the power—I think the contrary view [held by some of his fellow judges] dangerous and wrong.[149]

This was the reasoning of Thomas Cooley's influential book *Constitutional Limitations,* which Holmes had read, admiringly reviewed (6.51), and apparently used as a source for his lectures when teaching an undergraduate course in constitutional law at Harvard College; it was a line of argument that in any case was consistent with Holmes's common-law jurisprudence.

After his appointment to the Supreme Court, Holmes was rigorously consistent in deferring to the legislatures, especially when substantive rights were concerned. Indeed, a large part of his output for the first twenty years of his tenure on the Supreme Court was as its spokesman in constitutional cases, for the most part upholding challenged government action. Holmes and Chief Justice Melville Fuller formed a close collaboration, and Holmes was the chief author of constitutional opinions when they were both in the majority, as they generally were, from 1902 until Fuller's death in 1910. Chief Justice White, to a somewhat lesser degree, kept up this practice of assigning constitutional opinions to Holmes, and it was not until the 1920s, when Taft's majority began to resist progressive legislation, that Holmes was no longer the Court's constant spokesman.

From 1902 until 1918, although the Court decided about fifty challenges under the Fourteenth Amendment to state action each term, it only twice reversed socially progressive legislation in controversial opinions: *Lochner v. New York*[150] and *Coppage v. Kansas.*[151] Holmes dissented in both cases. Beginning in 1919, however, with the Red Scare cases (see section 10, below), Holmes was increasingly at odds with the Court. He held fast to his original position while the Court gradually changed its course until, in the late 1920s and early 1930s, it was overruling the precedents Holmes had written.[152]

Holmes's opinions for the Court and in dissent are stubbornly consistent with his opinions for the Court. The legislature's power was not to be doubted, except in the light of express and implied constitutional provisions. But even where there were explicit constraints on the legislature, these could not be taken to logical extremes. As Holmes had begun saying in his last years on the Massachusetts Supreme Judicial Court, constitutional restraints shaded off into a penumbra of discretion. This was Holmes's most puzzling doctrine of deference, allowing statutes to be upheld although they seemed contrary to the literal requirements of the constitution.

In Massachusetts, for instance, Holmes upheld with great reluctance a statute that extended the time for filing damage claims against a water company.[153] The statute operated retroactively, allowing claims to be filed that had already been barred under previous law. Holmes conceded that so far as logic went, the statute simply required the water company to pay money to people to whom, before the statute was passed, it did not owe anything and had never owed anything; the precedents of his own court suggested pretty strongly that the statute was unconstitutional. But "the prevailing judgment of the profession has revolted" against the merely logical argument that the statute took property from one person and gave it to another; and as to the precedents, "Perhaps the reasoning of the cases has not always been as sound as the instinct which directed the decisions."[154] Holmes continued with this remarkable passage:

> It may be that sometimes it would have been as well not to attempt to make out that the judgment of the court was consistent with constitutional rules, if such rules were to be taken to have the exactness of mathematics. It may be that it would have been better to say definitely that constitutional rules, like those of the common law, end in a penumbra where the legislature has a certain freedom in fixing the line.[155]

There are two points being made here. First, there is the familiar one, that the language of the Constitution cannot be understood in absolute terms. If there were to be *no* taking of private property interests, however slight, without a hearing beforehand and compensation afterward, government would halt.[156] "Some play must be allowed for the joints of the machine."[157]

But a second, distinct point was made here as well. Holmes did not suggest that in this case the subject matter of the case was insufficiently important to call constitutional guaranties into play. He was saying that even in important matters, the Constitution was often indeterminate.

Holmes had fallen back on his earliest jurisprudence, his first articles on the judicial function (see section 5, above). Constitutional principles rested on judgments that were not necessarily well or accurately expressed in judges' opinions. Constitutional rules of law, like those of the common law, were after-the-fact rationalizations of these judgments, giving them a logical coherence that might not hold beyond the cases themselves.

New cases represented a choice between competing principles, and as one moved away from the core of precedent the choice could not be determined by logic; it was based on some inarticulate premise. Eventually a series of choices would draw a line. Forty years after first stating this theory, Holmes speaking for the Supreme Court stated it as the fundamental law of the United States:

> Many laws which it would be vain to ask the Court to overthrow could be shown, easily enough, to transgress the great guarantees in the Bill of Rights. They more or less limit liberty of the individual or they diminish the property to a certain extent. We have few scientifically certain criteria of legislation. . . . With regard to the police power, as elsewhere in the law, lines are pricked out by the gradual approach and contact of decisions on the opposing sides.[158]

But in the zone of the penumbra that fell in the region between the poles of choice, the area where no rule yet predominated, where no instinct had yet prevailed, the legislature was not restrained by the Constitution and the court was obliged to defer to its choice. "But when it is seen that a line or point there must be, and that there is no mathematical or logical way of fixing it precisely, the decision of the legislature must be accepted unless we can say that it is very wide of any reasonable mark."[159] But this deference, wide as it seemed, did have some limits.

3.9.2 Substantive Due Process. The Court in these years looked for the content of constitutional provisions in principles thought to underlie the common law. In 1884, in *Hurtado v. California*,[160] one of its first important interpretations of the Fourteenth Amendment's requirement of due process of law, the Court set the foundation of this approach. The Court upheld a conviction for murder under a state statute that allowed trial on information rather than indictment (as the common law would have required). The due process clauses of the Fifth and Fourteenth Amendments, the Court held, did set substantive limits on legislation, but these were broad and were intended only to secure the individual from the arbitrary exercise of government power. Their content was defined by principles of natural justice, as expressed in the common law.

> It is more consonant to the true philosophy of our historical legal institutions to say that the spirit of personal liberty and individual right, which they embodied, was preserved and developed by a progressive growth and wise adaptation to new circumstances and situations of the forms and processes found fit to give, from time to time, new expression and greater effect to modern ideas of self-government. This flexibility and capacity for growth and adaptation is the peculiar boast and excellence of the common law.[161]

This view of what we now call substantive due process was widely accepted.[162] Even Ernst Freund, a severe contemporary critic of state courts' tendency to identify liberty with property rights, accepted the view that the due process clause set substantive limits on legislation.[163]

Beginning with his first opinion for the Court, Holmes solidified and made more rigorous the Court's reliance on fundamental principles of justice, identifying them solely with the common law. Cutting away the language of natural rights, Holmes sought these principles within the law itself. In *Otis v. Parker*, written less than a month after his appointment, Holmes announced the method he would employ for thirty years thereafter: the broad guarantees of the Fourteenth Amendment did have substantive as well as procedural content, Holmes wrote, but they contained only "relatively fundamental principles of right" that could be discovered in the common law.[164]

Soon afterward, Holmes wrote the opinion for the majority in *Aikens v. Wisconsin*.[165] A group of newspaper publishers had been convicted, under a Wisconsin malicious mischief statute, for conspiring to injure a competitor. The defendants challenged the statute under the Fourteenth Amendment, but Holmes declared that due process did not require more than the common law afforded and that at common law the privilege to do competitive harm might be defeated by a showing of actual malice.[166] The Wisconsin statute therefore could punish such malice without contravening the Constitution.[167] In *Gompers v. United States*[168] Holmes gave a famous statement of his method of construing the Constitution:

> The provisions of the Constitution are not mathematical formulas that have their essence in form; they are organic living institutions transplanted from English soil. Their

significance is vital, not formal; it is to be gathered not simply by taking the words and dictionary, but by considering their origin and the line of their growth.[169]

In these phrases Holmes managed to compress his view that constitutional restrictions were limited to the fundamental principles of the common law and that even these were not to be taken to logical extremes, along with his view that common-law principles themselves were evolving. It was a paraphrase of the famous opening sentence of *The Common Law:* "The life of the law has not been logic, it has been experience."

In dozens of opinions for the Court, reviewed in the preceding section, Holmes recited the homily of substantive due process while upholding most state statutes against statutory challenge.

3.9.3 The Bill of Rights. In a parallel line of cases, the Court had held the Bill of Rights generally to be merely declaratory of the common law. This was the view taken by Thomas Cooley in *Constitutional Limitations,* which had been cited approvingly by the Supreme Court in *Hurtado.*[170] Cooley argued that the First Amendment, for instance, although it abolished the English law of seditious libel, otherwise protected only existing rights at common law:

> [W]e understand liberty of speech and of the press to imply not only liberty to publish [free of prior restraints], but also complete immunity for the publication, so long as it is not harmful in its character, when tested by such standards as the law affords. For these standards we must look to the common-law rules which were in force when the constitutional guarantees were established.[171]

This approach was adopted by the Supreme Court in *Robertson v. Baldwin,*[172] holding that the Bill of Rights was subject to traditional common-law limitations:

> The law is perfectly well settled that the . . . Bill of Rights [was] not intended to lay down any novel principles of government, but simply to embody certain guaranties and immunities we had inherited from our English ancestors, and which had from time immemorial been subject to certain well-recognized exceptions arising from the necessities of the case.[173]

This is an attitude more familiar now in English constitutional law than American:

> When English statesmen have talked. . . of freedom, they have not been invoking a purely abstract idea, but have been appealing to specific traditions, which are enshrined in English history and in the Common Law tradition. Even the American Founding Fathers, in formulating their Bill of Rights, were unconsciously guided by what was intimated by the habits of behavior they had inherited from the English political tradition.[174]

When Holmes served on the Court, it was close enough to this tradition that it usually understood the broad guarantees of liberty in the Constitution to mean fundamental principles found in the common law, subject to traditional limitations.[175]

Holmes followed this approach consistently through his whole career as a judge.

In his Massachusetts opinions on constitutional law, he regularly referred to the common law for a standard; on the federal bench, his landmark opinions on the First Amendment were based on his common-law jurisprudence, as will be more fully shown in section 10, below.

In his few encounters with the Fourth Amendment, he expressed the view that the exclusionary rule, which in Holmes's day prohibited introduction in federal court of any evidence obtained through a violation of the Fourth Amendment, was a common-law rule.[176]

As to the Fifth Amendment and the corresponding provisions of the Fourteenth, Holmes's view that due process of law simply incorporated the principles of the common law has already been discussed. Probably the most frequently addressed provision of the Fifth Amendment during Holmes's tenure on the Massachusetts and federal courts, however, was not the guarantee of due process but the guarantee that private property would not be taken by the government without compensation. Holmes's opinions in these cases as well were based on his common-law jurisprudence. It takes a moment to see this, however.

One requirement of the Constitution was that a statute authorizing the taking of private property, like any other statute, be for a public purpose and meet the requirement of due process of law. Holmes held that a Vermont statute requiring a corporation to pay the debts of a predecessor in interest for which it had no legal obligation before the statute was passed was unconstitutional on this ground.[177]

The more serious question in most cases, however, was whether the state's action, admittedly for a public purpose, required compensation. Traditionally, the courts would discuss whether a statute authorizing a taking was within the "police power," the traditional authority of the state to protect the health and welfare of its citizens. If a statute were within the police power, it was said that no compensation was owed.

Holmes never failed to express irritation at this argument. There were no special "police powers" in his view; the legislature had all the power of parliament to do anything not forbidden by the Constitution. On the other hand, all the activities of government impinged on private rights and diminished liberty or property to some extent. The question in every case was the traditional one of Holmes's common-law jurisprudence—to choose between the government's power on one hand and the private individual's freedom on the other. In striking down a Massachusetts statute under which tidal flats in Boston were dredged so that they remained below the water line Holmes gave the following explanation:

It would be open to argument at least that an owner might be stripped of his rights so far as to amount to a taking without any physical interference with his land. On the other hand, we assume that even the carrying away or bodily destruction of property might be of such small importance that it would be justified under the police power without compensation. We assume that one of the uses of the convenient phrase, police power, is to justify those small diminutions of property rights, which, although within the letter of constitutional protection, are necessarily incident to the free play of the machinery of government. It may be that the extent to which such diminutions are lawful without compensation is larger when the harm is inflicted only as incident to some general requirement of public welfare. But whether the last mentioned element enters into the problem or not, the question is one of degree, and sooner or later we reach a point at which the Constitution applies, and forbids physical appropriation and legal restrictions alike unless they are paid for.[178]

Holmes consistently held that the expectation of profits lost through government action or competitive injuries caused by government entering a line of business were not compensable.[179] This was the origin of his famous dissent in *Truax v. Corrigan*,[180] on behalf of the states' rights to deny injunctive relief in labor disputes:

> By calling a business "property" you make it seem like land, and lead up to the conclusion that a statute cannot substantially cut down the advantages of ownership existing before the statute was passed. An established business no doubt may have pecuniary value and commonly is protected by law against various unjustified injuries. But you cannot give it definiteness of contour by calling it a thing. It is a course of conduct and like other conduct is subject to substantial modification according to time and circumstances both in itself and in regard to what shall justify doing it a harm.[181]

The pattern is once again drawn from Holmes's common-law jurisprudence. The judge's duty is to protect the core of liberty that lies within both civil and property rights, considered case by case, without attempting to insulate anyone from the injuries and accidents of free competition. Neither the injuries incidental to necessary government functioning nor the injuries caused by competition were "takings" which the Constitution required to be compensated.

3.9.4 Procedural Due Process of Law. Holmes's opinions on procedural due process, broadly defined, are in retrospect among the most important he gave, and are probably now the least controversial of his major opinions. They require little explication, but it is helpful to review them, as they provide an important part of the whole structure of his work.

As one might suppose from the preceding sections, Holmes made no explicit distinction between "substantive" and "procedural" due process of law. His ideas of due process were almost entirely what we would now call procedural. Substantive due process was simply a name for fundamental guarantees of the common law, and viewed from the perspective of centuries, no legislative policies were fundamental, not even the legal protections of private property or the right to vote. The truly fundamental guarantees of the common law revolved around the right to be heard in a fair, adversarial proceeding before being subject to the power of the state. In the next section, we will explore Holmes's First Amendment opinions, in which the common root of substantive and procedural guarantees in these fundamental principles was most fully explored. This section is concerned with the guarantees now considered purely procedural.

The outline of Holmes's approach appeared during his years in Massachusetts. From his first opinions, he was far less deferential to the legislature in procedural cases than in those where statutes were reviewed on substantive grounds. He was tolerant of innovations in matters of form,[182] but where fundamental principles were concerned, he freely reversed state action. A statute authorized local health officers to kill diseased horses, for instance, without any opportunity for the horse's owner to challenge the decision. Holmes—writing for a divided court—held the statute unconstitutional; although well within the traditional police power of the state, it allowed no opportunity for a hearing.[183] Holmes wrote that a hearing was required, if only after the fact, to allow claims for compensation in case of error to be presented. This case is particularly striking, since Holmes rarely wrote in constitutional cases before he became chief justice, and he wrote in this case for a narrow majority over three dissents.

A statute authorizing *ex parte* appointment of a guardian for an insane person was upheld only with difficulty, and Holmes construed it to apply only in cases where an emergency did not allow prior hearing, and added, although the statute was silent on this point, that in any case review in a court, with the ward represented by a separate guardian *ad litem*, would be available afterward.[184] The ward's request to deny payment of the temporary guardian's expenses was denied, however, Holmes rendering in characteristic form the formula he would repeat often later: "The great provisions [of the Constitution] intended to protect liberty and property cannot be read as extending with mathematical logic to every case where there is an unpaid for diminution of property rights or a temporary restraint of personal freedom without a hearing of both sides in court."[185]

His most frequent figure of speech again was the "penumbra" cast by constitutional provisions: as one moved farther from the area that lay directly in the shadow of a central principle and into its indistinct penumbra, there was more freedom to experiment.[186] But statutes that touched the core guarantees would be struck down.

This was the ground on which substantive and procedural cases met, for in the substantive cases, at least as Holmes viewed them, the question usually was whether the government's encroachment on protected liberties was serious enough to trigger the requirements of individualized hearings or compensation. The government's power to carry out its purposes by some means was rarely in question for Holmes, and so most constitutional issues reduced themselves to questions of procedure.

From Holmes's perspective, procedural questions in turn rested on the fundamental issue of whether persons subject to legislative commands had a right to have their own individual circumstances weighed before their interests were sacrificed to the general welfare.[187] In discussing the statutory power of the Interstate Commerce Commission to compel testimony as to railroad combinations, for instance, Holmes said the commission had no power to investigate individual dealings in railroad stock, except as those transactions themselves were relevant to an enforcement proceeding:

> [T]he power to require testimony is limited, as it usually is in English-speaking countries at least, to the only cases where the sacrifice of privacy is necessary—those where the investigations concern a specific breach of the law. . . .
>
> We could not believe on the strength of other than explicit and unmistakable words [in a statute] that such autocratic power [to compel testimony about private affairs] was given for any less specific object of inquiry than a breach of existing law, in which, and in which alone, as we have said, there is any need that personal matters should be revealed.[188]

Holmes, without mentioning any specific provision of the Constitution, said that the ICC statute would be subject to constitutional doubts unless construed in this way.[189] He plainly felt that fundamental questions were touched upon, for he asserted the unconstitutionality of the statute as the ICC had traditionally interpreted it, over three vigorous dissents. In letters, he said the ICC had made his blood boil, and he bemoaned the flabby state of the country, that there was no general revolt against this breach of what had been fundamental guarantees.[190]

He was even less deferential to the lower courts. In contempt cases, where no such prompt action was required to preserve the integrity of the judicial process, he chastised judges who imposed summary contempt penalties without affording a proper trial. The test for when the usual requirements of due process could be overridden was substantially the same as that for when free speech could be curtailed: there must be a clear and present danger of obstruction of justice.[191]

In a *habeas corpus* proceeding where the defendant charged that the state court had not afforded a fair trial, despite observance of most of the forms, Holmes insisted on a realistic assessment of whether fundamental fairness had been given:

> The argument for the appellee [State of Georgia] in substance is that the trial was in a court of competent jurisdiction, that it retains jurisdiction although, in fact, it may be dominated by a mob, and that the rulings of the state court as to the fact of such domination cannot be reviewed. But the argument seems to us inconclusive. Whatever disagreement there may be as to the scope of the phrase "due process of law," there can be no doubt that it embraces the fundamental conception of a fair trial, with opportunity to be heard. Mob law does not become due process of law by securing the assent of a terrorized jury. We are not speaking of mere disorder, or mere irregularities in procedure, but of a case where the processes of justice are actually subverted. In such a case, the Federal court has jurisdiction to issue the writ. The fact that the state court still has its general jurisdiction and is otherwise a competent court does not make it impossible to find that a jury has been subjected to intimidation in a particular case. . . .
>
> It would indeed be a most serious thing if this Court were so to hold, for we could not but regard it as a removal of what is perhaps the most important guaranty of the Federal Constitution. . . .
>
> And notwithstanding the principle of comity and convenience (for in our opinion it is nothing more . . .), that calls for a resort to the local appellate tribunal before coming to the courts of the United States for a writ of habeas corpus, when, as here, that resort has been had in vain, the power to secure fundamental rights that had existed at every stage becomes a duty and must be put forth.[192]

3.10
FREEDOM OF SPEECH

Holmes's principal legacy to modern constitutional law is his famous series of opinions and dissents on freedom of speech. These grow directly out of his common-law jurisprudence and are difficult to understand unless seen in that context. As some controversy has always surrounded these opinions, a few words of explication may be helpful.

There were essentially two groups of opinions. In a series of opinions for the

Court beginning with *Schenck v. United States*,[193] Holmes upheld criminal convictions of defendants who had attempted to obstruct the draft during the First World War. In the second group of opinions, beginning with an unpublished opinion in *Baltzer v. United States* (see section 10.2, below), Holmes dissented when the Court voted to uphold convictions that he thought were based on the defendants' opinions rather than on any efforts to obstruct the war effort. The two sets of cases, taken together, illuminate Holmes's application of common-law principles to the fundamental guarantees of the Constitution.

3.10.1 *Schenck*. Charles T. Schenck was general secretary of the Socialist Party of Philadelphia. Shortly after conscription began in August, 1917, the party arranged to print and mail 15,000 leaflets asserting that the Selective Service Act was unconstitutional and urging the reader to "wake up" and "assert your rights." The leaflets were to be mailed only to young men who had already been selected for induction by their draft boards. Schenck had personally joined in the decisions to print and mail the leaflets, and to send them only to draftees. Schenck and another officer, Elizabeth Baer, were convicted of violating the Espionage Act and sentenced to six months in jail.

The government had charged Schenck and Baer "in substance . . . with attempting to induce young men subject to the draft law to disobey the requirements of the law."[194] There was no evidence that the attempt had succeeded or that anyone who read the leaflet was moved to resist induction.

In an earlier round of appeals, *Goldman v. United States (The Selective Service Cases)*,[195] the Court had upheld prosecutions under the Selective Service Act for conspiracies and unsuccessful attempts to violate the draft laws.

In *Schenck*, in briefs and argument, both sides assumed that the statute required proof of specific intent to obstruct the draft. This was the federal law of conspiracies and attempts, as established by Holmes's opinion in *Swift*[196] and the Court's recent decision in *Goldman*.[197] The government treated the question of specific intent to obstruct the draft as the only seriously disputed question of fact in *Schenck*. The government's case on this point was simple: the circular was mailed only to young men awaiting induction. This was enough evidence to support the jury's verdict that the defendants intended to influence the conduct of persons subject to the draft.[198]

The government argued that this showing of specific intent, in itself, was sufficient to defeat a claim of privilege under the First Amendment.[199] The defendants insisted, however, that the evidence showed the leaflets were no more than an "expression . . . made with sincere purpose to communicate honest opinion or belief" protected by the First Amendment, apparently conceding that the convictions would stand if this seemingly innocent speech "masked a primary intent to incite to forbidden action."[200]

Arguing in the alternative, however, defendants claimed that even if specific intent were proven, the statute itself was unconstitutional to the extent it punished speech. This amounted to a claim for an absolute privilege for speech.[201]

On March 3, 1919, almost two months after arguments had been heard, Holmes announced the decision of the Court.[202] The first portion of his opinion was a recital of the charges in the indictment. Holmes quickly disposed of objections taken to evidence at trial and then summarized the admitted evidence that seemed crucial—the text of the leaflet and the fact that it was to be mailed only to draftees. To Holmes and to the Court, these facts were sufficient to establish the elements of a crime:

> Of course the document would not have been sent unless it had been intended to have some effect, and we do not see what effect it could be expected to have upon persons subject to the draft except to influence them to obstruct the carrying of it out. The defendants do not deny that the jury might find against them on this point.[203]

With the elements of a criminal conspiracy and an attempt to commit a crime—overt acts and specific intent—proven, the defendants had remaining only their constitutional claim, the claim of privilege under the First Amendment.

Holmes began his discussion with the defendants' claim of absolute privilege, which he disposed of quickly. There was no absolute privilege for speech in general: "The most stringent protection of free speech would not protect a man falsely shouting fire in a theater and causing a panic. It [the First Amendment] does not even protect a man from an injunction against uttering words that may have all the effect of force."[204]

Words may have all the effect of force by the very impact of their meaning, operating through the wrongdoing of others, and so they may be regulated as other acts are regulated, whenever they stand sufficiently close to the forbidden effect: "The question in every case is whether the words used are used in such circumstances and are of such a nature as to create a clear and present danger that they will bring about the substantive evils that Congress has a right to prevent. It is a question of proximity and degree."[205]

This was simply another restatement of Holmes's general principle of liability at the common law as applied to conspiracies and attempts. In other words, since the First Amendment did not extend an absolute privilege, Congress in some cases could provide for the punishment of speech that would have forbidden consequences. But the First Amendment did contain a qualified privilege: Congress could not go beyond the liability imposed by the common law. It could only authorize punishment for expressions when they lay sufficiently close to a forbidden result to pose a "clear and present danger."

The next question was whether these proven attempts to obstruct the draft posed such a danger. Congress plainly could outlaw speech that actually obstructed the draft.[206] If Congress had the right to punish otherwise privileged expressions that actually obstructed the war effort, then it only remained to be decided whether it might also forbid unsuccessful conspiracies and attempts by way of speech or publication. But the Court had already held, in *Goldman*,[207] that the Espionage Act applied to unsuccessful conspiracies and attempts.

In short, where Congress had the power to create a crime, and a speech or publication would constitute an attempt to commit such a crime, the First Amendment simply limited Congress to the standards of the common law. These standards Holmes then summarized in an unusually terse formula: in attempts by speech, as in other criminal attempts, the government was required to prove, first, an overt act that had a forbidden tendency and, second, that the defendant had the specific intent to bring about the forbidden result. "If the act (speaking, or circulating a paper), its tendency *and* the intent with which it is done are the same, we perceive no ground for saying that success alone warrants making the act a crime."[208]

In this final passage, Holmes said that when the alleged criminal act was speech, the Constitution required that both the objective standard of proximity and the specific intent to bring about the forbidden result must be proven.

What Holmes did not make quite clear in this opinion was whether the "specific intent" required by both the Constitution and the statute was a subjective intent, a conscious desire to bring about the result forbidden by Congress—as Holmes had argued since the 1890s—or was simply to be judged by an external standard. If the standard was solely external, then the terms "tendency" and "intent" were redundant. Holmes hinted, but did not plainly say, that the intent required by the Constitution was the same as that required by the common law: actual subjective intent to cause crime. Holmes's brethren probably did not agree on this last point in *Schenck,* and disagreement may have been the reason for avoiding facing the question squarely. It may also have accounted for the long delay (in Holmes's terms) in issuing the opinion. The question of the constitutional standard of intent could be avoided in *Schenck,* because the Court had already construed the *statute* to require, at least in attempt cases, actual intent. But in later cases, where a completed crime was charged, the question whether the Constitution required a two-branched test of danger plus intent was the point of dispute between Holmes and the majority.

Even without his hint of a need for proof of motive, Holmes's opinion was taken as a victory for freedom of speech. Some lower courts, and perhaps the majority of the Supreme Court, had been treating the Espionage Act of 1917 as if it created a category of forbidden expression—words of opposition to the war effort, whose meaning alone had a "bad tendency" to obstruct the law.[209] Holmes's accomplishment was to shift the focus of the courts' attention away from the proscribed category of expression to the narrower question of whether in the circumstances of the case the defendant's language posed a real threat.

Before the close of its term in June, 1919, the still-unanimous Court delivered two more opinions affirming convictions for attempts to obstruct the draft. Holmes wrote both opinions. In them he mentioned constitutional questions only in passing and to say that such questions had already been decided in *Schenck.*[210] In each, Holmes emphasized that under the statute the government had to prove both that the attempts to obstruct the draft had come dangerously close to success and that the defendants actually intended this result; but there was no need in these cases to decide whether that was also the requirement of the Constitution.

The seemingly cursory treatment of constitutional questions in these early cases did not stem from lack of interest but from the contrary; the Court had been embroiled in an internal controversy for months and was unable to agree on a more extensive statement.

3.10.2 Holmes's Dissents. Although it was not known outside the Court, Holmes had already written a dissenting opinion, in *Baltzer v. United States,*[211] before the *Schenck* line of cases had been decided; but the government had confessed error and the case had been withdrawn, even though a majority of the Court had already voted to uphold the convictions. In *Baltzer* the defendants were German socialists, and Holmes suspected they had been convicted for expressing their opinions rather than for any effort to obstruct the law. He wrote a stinging dissent:

> Real obstructions of the law, giving real aid and comfort to the enemy, I should have been glad to see punished more summarily and more severely than they sometimes were. But I think that our intention to put all our powers in aid of success in war should not hurry us into intolerance of opinions and speech that could not be imagined to do harm, although opposed to our own. It is better for those who have unquestioned and almost unlimited power in their hands to err on the side of freedom. We have enjoyed so much freedom for so long that perhaps we are in danger of forgetting that the bill of rights which cost so much blood to establish still is worth fighting for, and that no tittle of it should be abridged.[212]

The Court decided to defer action on the case, and during the delay, perhaps because it had learned of Holmes's dissent, the government withdrew.[213] It was undoubtedly because of this dissent, in which Brandeis joined, that Chief Justice White, anxious to secure a unanimous decision, assigned to Holmes the opinions in the *Schenck* line of cases.

In the next term of Court there was a new and, to Holmes, still more distasteful round of such cases to be decided. These cases arose under the Sedition Act of 1918, which among other things prohibited, during wartime, speech critical of the American form of government.

The first of these cases was *Abrams v. United States*.[214] Jacob Abrams was one of a group of recent Jewish immigrants from Russia, anarchists living in Manhattan. In the summer of 1918, the group met to plan protests against the sending of American troops into the Soviet Union, and soon afterward one of them threw copies of two leaflets from a window on lower Broadway. One leaflet was in English and the other in Yiddish. Each denounced the sending of troops to Russia and the "hypocritical" statements of the president on this subject. The Yiddish leaflet called for a general strike of all American workers.

A puzzled passerby turned the Yiddish leaflet in at a police station and within days, Abrams and four of his colleagues, three men and a woman, all in their twenties, were in custody. Tried in federal district court for violations of the Sedition Act, Abrams and the others were convicted and given brutal sentences of up to twenty years' imprisonment.[215]

When the defendants' appeals reached the Supreme Court, the government's brief emphasized strongly, even passionately, the inherent right of any government to protect itself from violent dissolution, seeming thereby to acknowledge that the defendants had been prosecuted, not for any perceived threat they may have posed to the war effort, but for fear of their threat to the system of government of the United States.

A majority of the Court evidently accepted the prosecutors' view of the case, and of the condition of the country. The eventual majority opinion, by Justice Clarke, held simply that it was a jury question whether these leaflets, on objective grounds, posed a clear and present danger of obstructing the war effort. A call for a general strike to halt the intervention in Russia would be understood by any reasonable person to result in an obstruction of the war effort as well. By an external standard the intent required for an attempt therefore was proven and the convictions sustained.[216]

Holmes dissented.[217] He began his opinion by reciting the charges of the indictment and reviewing the evidence as to each. The principal evidence was the two leaflets themselves, which the defendants did not deny printing and distributing.

Of the four counts of the indictment, Holmes focused on the fourth, the charge of advocating curtailment of production of war matériel, with intent to hinder prosecution of the war. This count alone charged a completed crime rather than an unsuccessful attempt.

The evidence of advocacy was principally in the second leaflet, which called (in Yiddish) for a general strike of American workers. The majority found that this pamphlet did "urge curtailment of production of things necessary to the prosecution of the war." But even assuming that this pathetic leaflet might have had some tendency in that direction, the statute also required proof of "intent . . . to cripple or hinder the United States in the prosecution of the war."

Holmes delivered a brief lecture on the subject of intent. Intent in a free speech case must be understood "in a strict and accurate sense" as encompassing both the external standard, so familiar from Holmes's own writings, and the subjective intent or motive to produce just those results forbidden by Congress. Holmes gave a brief example to show that unless specific intent in the sense of motive were part of the statute's requirement, it might be applied to honest criticism of the government's policies.

> A patriot might think we were wasting money on aeroplanes, or making more cannon of a certain kind than we needed, and might advocate curtailment with success, yet even if it turned out that the curtailment hindered and was thought by other minds to have been obviously likely to hinder the United States in the prosecution of the war, no one would hold such conduct a crime.[218]

As to completed crimes, therefore, as well as under the law of criminal attempts, the government was required to prove defendants had the specific, subjective intent to bring about harms that Congress had a right to forbid.[219]

The difference between Holmes and the Court was now plainly stated. As Professor Corwin observed, the majority had applied a purely external standard to determine intent.[220] Holmes believed that the Constitution required an added showing of actual malice or subjective intent.[221]

There was no evidence of such specific, subjective intent. Holmes thought the only evidence the government claimed was the publications themselves, and their words related solely to the intervention in Russia.[222] Specific intent was not proven, and conviction on the fourth count of the indictment should have been reversed. On the same reasoning and with even more force, the other counts should have been dismissed.

Up to this point, Holmes had only recapitulated the doctrine of *Schenck* and applied it in a mechanical way to the evidence against Abrams. But he went on to make a final point. Even if there had been sufficient evidence of intent and the jury had been properly instructed—"[e]ven if I am technically wrong and enough can be squeezed from these poor and puny anonymities to turn the color of legal litmus paper"—Holmes's outrage at the twenty-year sentences imposed could not be restrained. The brutal sentences and the government's insistence on pursuing the case were proof to Holmes that the prosecution had nothing to do with the war effort. "[T]he most nominal punishment seems to me all that possibly could be inflicted, unless the defendants are to be made to suffer not for what the indictment alleges but for the creed they avow."[223]

In *Baltzer*, Holmes had remarked that it was better for those who held unquestioned and almost unlimited power to err on the side of freedom. Now Holmes, plainly moved by genuine feeling, went on to explain more fully why the government should refrain from prosecuting people for their political beliefs, even when there might be nominal evidence of a crime.

> Persecution for the expression of opinion seems to me perfectly logical. . . But when men have realized that time has upset many fighting faiths, they may come to believe even more than they believe in the very foundations of their own conduct that the ultimate good desired is better reached by free trade in ideas—that the best test of truth is the power of the thought to get itself accepted in the competition of the market, and that truth is the only ground upon which their wishes can safely be carried out. That, at any rate, is the theory of our Constitution. It is an experiment, as all life is an experiment. Every year if not every day we have to wager our salvation upon some prophecy based upon imperfect knowledge. While that experiment is part of our system I think that we should be eternally vigilant against attempts to check the expression of opinions that we loathe and believe to be fraught with death, unless they so imminently threaten immediate interference with the lawful and pressing purposes of the law that an immediate check is required to save the country. . . Of course I am speaking only of expressions of opinion and exhortations, which were all that were uttered here, but I regret I cannot put into more impressive words my belief that in the conviction upon this indictment the defendants were deprived of their rights under the Constitution of the United States.[224]

3.10.3 The Rationale for Freedom of Speech. In *Abrams,* Holmes had made his one passionate effort to state the principle of social policy on which the First Amendment was based. Stripped of its poetry and restated in logical order, Holmes's argument was this: The "theory of our Constitution"[225] was that "truth" was the only ground on which the desires of men "safely" could be carried out. This "truth" that ensured safety, according to the Constitution, was to be determined by the victory of ideas in the peaceful competition of the marketplace, which Holmes said was to be preferred to "persecution" as a method of determining truth.

The premise, on which all the rest depends, is that the desires of men (presumably expressed in laws) can only be carried out "safely" if they are based on "truth." What can safety mean in this context, and why should it be the premise for constitutional safeguards?

One interpretation of this passage might be that the Framers feared violent revolution and tried to forestall it by allowing free expression of ideas.[226] This is part of the answer. Yet Holmes's dissent in *Abrams* shows the deepest contempt for the government's fear of revolution, and this interpretation does not quite match Holmes's always careful and precise syntax.

Another interpretation, more in accord with the words and with Holmes's general ideas, is that "safely" means "with assurance of success." In Holmes's jurisprudence, the purpose of statute law is to achieve the desires of the dominant class. To the extent the lawmaker understands his own self-interest well and designs his laws properly, his own survival and the survival of the system he has made will be ensured. The prevention of rebellion is only one of the prudent considerations that go into designing a legal system to ensure survival.

The competition of the marketplace is evidently to be preferred to violent persecution as a method of ascertaining truth in this limited and pragmatic sense. The marketplace may show whether the legal system is well designed for survival—at least that is the theory the Constitution requires to be tested by experiment. We are to test in the laboratory of experience—and ultimately in war—whether governments based on peaceful discourse are better equipped to survive than governments that rule by violence.[227]

It is fundamental to this view of freedom of speech that ideas attacking the very basis of government be allowed to flourish and to prevail, if they can, by peaceful discourse. Holmes repeatedly returned to this point. In 1919, the same year in which the Court affirmed Jacob Abrams's conviction, Benjamin Gitlow was tried in a New York courtroom and found guilty of criminal anarchism for publishing a Communist "manifesto." When the case reached his Court and the conviction was affirmed, Holmes said, "If in the long run the beliefs expressed in proletarian dictatorship are destined to be accepted by the dominant forces of the community, the only meaning of free speech is that they should be given their chance and have their way."[228] In 1928, he said—dissenting from the Court's decision that a pacifist, Rosika Schwimmer, because of her beliefs could not become a citizen of the United States—

> If there is any principle of the Constitution that more imperatively calls for attachment than any other it is the principle of free thought—not free thought for those who agree with us but freedom for the thought we hate.[229]

This was the lesson Holmes had learned in a lifetime of combat and study. The rule of law meant that the struggle for survival was to be carried on fairly and peacefully. A judge's duty was to ensure free and peaceful competition among political ideas, even if—especially if—his own survival, or the survival of the social order that held everything of value for him, was at stake.

Peaceful government under law ultimately rested, not upon the rights of the governed, but upon the honor and sense of fairness of the judges, upon their paradoxical willingness to risk everything, even survival itself, to see that fairness was preserved in the vast, chaotic struggle for life.

Editor's Notes

1. Holmes to Anna Lyman (Nina) Gray, December 2, 1910, Oliver Wendell Holmes, Jr., Papers, Harvard Law School Library (hereinafter "Holmes Papers"), B32 F5.

2. February 15, 1929, Holmes Papers, note 1 above, at B29 F12.

3. Holmes to Morris R. Cohen, August 31, 1920, reprinted in L. ROSENFIELD, PORTRAIT OF A PHILOSOPHER: MORRIS R. COHEN IN LIFE AND LETTERS (hereinafter "HOLMES-COHEN LETTERS") 327–28 (1962).

4. S. NOVICK, HONORABLE JUSTICE: THE LIFE OF OLIVER WENDELL HOLMES (1989) (hereinafter "HONORABLE JUSTICE").

5. Six years later, in 1864, Wendell, by then an infantry officer in the Union Army in winter quarters, triumphantly concluded the debate by showing that $1 + 1 = 2$ was *not* necessarily true in all imaginable worlds—and then characteristically refuting his own argument. Holmes to his father, April 8, 1864, and undated fragment of second letter, in O. HOLMES, TOUCHED WITH FIRE: CIVIL WAR DIARY AND LETTERS OF OLIVER WENDELL HOLMES, JR., 1861–1864, at 95 (M. DeW. Howe ed. 1946).

6. Holmes to Morris R. Cohen, February 5, 1919, in HOLMES-COHEN LETTERS, *supra* note 3, at 321. Holmes's diaries for the period 1864–72 show that he had read Spencer; see below.

Henry Thomas Buckle, whose HISTORY OF CIVILIZATION IN ENGLAND (1857–61) had an immense impact on English Liberal thought, attempted to frame a science of history, showing the development of civilization in response to "laws" of climate and geography. Compare the very similar statement, in less personal terms, by John Acton, Holmes's English contemporary: "Expressions like: the growth of language, physiology of the State, national psychology, the mind of the Church, the development of Platonism, the continuity of law—questions which occupy half the mental activity of our age—were incomprehensible to the eighteenth century—to Hume, Johnson, Smith, Diderot." Quoted in M. OAKESHOTT, RATIONALISM IN POLITICS AND OTHER ESSAYS 152 n.1 (1981 ed.). Oakeshott properly adds that these concepts have since become unintelligible again.

7. Hyland, *Hegel: A User's Manual*, 10 CARDOZO L. REV. 1746, 1763 (1989). I am indebted to Joanne Ertel for calling this article to my attention.

8. *The Times*, in THE COMPLETE WRITINGS OF RALPH WALDO EMERSON 80 (1929).

9. Holmes to Morris R. Cohen, August 31, 1920, HOLMES-COHEN LETTERS, note 3 above, at 327, 328.

10. *The Times*, note 9 above, at 90.

11. Holmes to Morris R. Cohen, February 5, 1919, in HOLMES-COHEN LETTERS, note 3 above, at 321.

12. Holmes to Canon Patrick A. Sheehan, October 27, 1912, in HOLMES-SHEEHAN CORRESPONDENCE: THE LETTERS OF JUSTICE OLIVER WENDELL HOLMES AND CANON PATRICK AUGUSTINE SHEEHAN (hereinafter "HOLMES-SHEEHAN LETTERS") 50, 51 (D. Burton ed. 1976).

13. Holmes to Ralph Waldo Emerson, Emerson Papers, Houghton Library, Harvard; copy, Holmes Papers, *supra* note 1, at B42 F20; quoted HONORABLE JUSTICE, note 4 above, at 149.

14. Holmes to Frederick Pollock, May 20, 1930, in 2 O. HOLMES, HOLMES-POLLOCK LETTERS: THE CORRESPONDENCE OF MR. JUSTICE HOLMES AND SIR FREDERICK POLLOCK 1874–1932 (hereinafter "HOLMES-POLLOCK LETTERS") 264 (M. DeW. Howe ed. 1941).

15. Published with very helpful annotations by Eleanor Little, *The Early Reading of Justice Oliver Wendell Holmes*, 8 HARV. LIBRARY BULL. 163 (1954).

16. *See* Wright, *Evolution of Self-Consciousness*, 116 N. AMER. REV. 245 (1873).

17. *See, generally,* N. ANNAN, LESLIE STEPHEN: THE GODLESS VICTORIAN (1984) (hereinafter "LESLIE STEPHEN"). Lord Annan's classic evocation of the intellectual world in which Stephen moved is immensely helpful for an understanding of Holmes.

18. Transcript of Holmes's conversation with a young law clerk, in D. ACHESON, MORNING AND NOON: A MEMOIR (hereinafter "MORNING AND NOON") 63 (1965).

19. Holmes to Lucy Clifford, November 17, 1924, Holmes Papers, note 1 above, at B39 F25. Holmes went on, as he often did when in this vein, to contrast himself with William James, who kept an open mind on spiritualism—miracles in the wrong place.

20. *Id.*

21. Holmes to Harold Laski, January 13, 1923, 1 O. HOLMES, HOLMES-LASKI LETTERS: THE CORRESPONDENCE OF MR. JUSTICE HOLMES AND HAROLD J. LASKI, 1916–1935 (hereinafter

"Holmes-Laski Letters") 473–74 (M. DeW. Howe ed. 1953); *see also,* to the same effect, February 5, 1923, *id.* at 477–78. Frederick Pollock, Holmes's dear friend, had written a commentary that was important in the Spinoza revival of his generation, and while Holmes seems not to have read Pollock's work until the 1890s, Spinoza, like the German idealists, was in the air.

22. Holmes to Lady Castletown, May 26, 1898, Holmes Papers, note 1 above, at B39 F12. Compare H. A. Wolfson, The Philosophy of Spinoza: Unfolding the Latent Processes of His Reasoning 523–24 (1934).

23. Holmes to Lady Castletown, January 18, 1898, Holmes Papers, note 1 above, B39 F12.

24. *See* Wright, *Evolution of Self-Consciousness,* note 19 above.

25. Holmes to Frederick Pollock, August 30, 1929, 2 Holmes-Pollock Letters, note 15 above, at 252.

26. Holmes to Anna Lyman Gray, August 26, 1905, Holmes Papers, note 1 above, at B31 F17.

27. Holmes seemed to identify his Great Swell with Kant's *ding an sich:* "[M]odes of consciousness [are] not fundamental to the universe, if there is one. I think there are grounds for the further surmise that Kant's *ding an sich* is not quite empty—that there is a somewhat, too closely predicated even by that phrase, as to which we can't talk." Holmes to Anna Lyman Gray, August 26, 1905, Holmes Papers, note 1 above, at B31 F17.

28. Holmes to Lady Castletown, October 17, 1896, Holmes Papers, note 1 above, B26 F9.

29. Holmes to Felix Frankfurter, February 16, 1912, Holmes Papers, note 1 above, B29 F2.

30. After twenty years as a judge, however, Holmes appears to have conceded that deductive reasoning could be creative in a modest way, by extending existing principles to new sets of facts and so developing new law. *See* Stack v. New York, N.H. & R. R. Co., 177 Mass., 155, 158–59 (1900). ("We do not forget the continuous process of developing the law that goes on through the courts, in the form of deduction.")

31. Lochner v. New York, 198 U.S. 45, 74 (1905) (Holmes, J., dissenting).

32. Holmes to Alice Stopford Green, October 1, 1901, Holmes papers, note 1 above, B43 F12.

33. *See, e.g.,* Holmes to Alice Stopford Green, March 29, 1908, Holmes Papers, note 1 above, B43 F12.

34. *See* 1 R. B. Perry, The Thought and Character of William James 719–20 (1935).

35. *See* Morning and Noon, note 19 above, at 83.

36. Part of a transcript of Holmes's conversation with a young law clerk, *id.* at 63.

37. Holmes to Morris R. Cohen, May 27, 1917, in Holmes-Cohen Letters, note 3 above, at 315, 316.

38. Holmes to Alice Stopford Green, October 1, 1901, Holmes Papers, note 1 above, B43 F12.

39. Holmes to Alice Stopford Green, October 14, 1911, Holmes papers, note 1 above, B43 F13.

40. This is the attitude of E. Auerbach, Mimesis: The Representation of Reality in Western Literature (1953), and also, I think, of Holmes's friend Henry James.

41. Holmes to Alice Stopford Green, August 20, 1909, Holmes Papers, note 1 above, at B43 F12.

42. Holmes to Morris R. Cohen, May 27, 1917, Holmes-Cohen Letters, note 3 above, at 315, 316. But this was too definite an assertion about the cosmos, so Holmes immediately added, "But then it might—in short my only belief is that I know nothing about it."

43. Holmes to Alice Stopford Green, February 7, 1909, Holmes Papers, note 1 above, at B43 F12.

44. *See* Shaffer, *Holmes's Honorable Style,* in Christian L. Soc'y Q., Fall 1990, p. 26. Holmes

did not believe in the reality of ethics in the Kantian or Christian sense of absolute standards. This, I think, is the central objection in some of the criticism of Holmes as a person and as a thinker. *See,* most recently, Kelley, *Book Review: The Life of Oliver Wendell Holmes, Jr.,* 68 WASH. U. L. Q. 429–82 (1990).

45. When Holmes got around to reading Hegel in the 1890s, with much muttering and complaint, he tacitly acknowledged the indirect influence: "The beast has insights but these are wrapped up in such a humbugging method and with so much that is unintelligible or unreal or both that you have to work your way. Such good as Hegel did I am inclined to think was mainly at second hand through his influence on people who wrote and talked outside his system and even then he has been a blight on juridical thoughts in Germany." Holmes to Lady Castletown, October 7, 1896, Holmes Papers, note 1 above, at B26 F9. *See also* Hoffheimer, *Holmes, L. Q. C. Lamar, and Natural Law,* 58 MISS. L. J. 71 (1988), citing Pound, *The Revival of Natural Law,* 17 NOTRE DAME L. REV. 287, 333 (1942).

46. *A Defence of Poetry,* in PEACOCK'S FOUR AGES OF POETRY 59 (H. F. B. Brett-Smith ed. 1921).

47. *German Darwinism,* 21 NATION 169 (1875).

48. *See* LESLIE STEPHEN, note 18 above, at 190.

49. *See, generally,* J. BURROW, EVOLUTION AND SOCIETY: A STUDY OF VICTORIAN SOCIAL THEORY (1966), for an account of evolutionist theories growing out of history and anthropology before Darwin.

50. *See, e.g.,* R. R. WALLACE, THE ORIGIN OF THE HUMAN RACE, quoted in J. W. BURROW, EVOLUTION AND SOCIETY: A STUDY IN VICTORIAN SOCIAL THEORY 114–15, n.2 (1966).

51. Holmes to Harold Laski, July 28, 1916, 1 HOLMES-LASKI LETTERS, note 22 above, at 8.

52. Leslie Stephen claimed that the whole school of classical economics was formed on Malthus, although the economists liked to give lip service to Adam Smith. 2 L. STEPHEN, THE BRITISH UTILITARIANS 239 (1900).

53. BUREAU OF THE CENSUS, UNITED STATES LIFE TABLES, 1890, 1901, 1910, AND 1901–1910, at 132 (1921).

54. BUREAU OF THE CENSUS, MORTALITY STATISTICS, 1900–1904, p. clxxxiv (1906) (mortality of women of child-bearing age is estimated from the proportion of all women dying).

55. *Id.* at xxii–xxxv. Doctor Holmes's household was more aware of these events than most. "The evenings grow cooler in August, but there is mischief abroad in the air. Heaven fills up fast with young angels in this month and in September." *The Seasons,* in O. W. HOLMES, PAGES FROM AN OLD VOLUME OF LIFE: A COLLECTION OF ESSAYS 1857–1881 (vol. 8 of Holmes's Collected Works) 156 (1892).

56. Holmes to Canon Sheehan, July 5, 1912, HOLMES-SHEEHAN LETTERS, note 13 above, at 45. The text of the talk has not survived.

57. Holmes to Harold Laski, February 28, 1919, in 1 HOLMES-LASKI LETTERS, note 22 above, at 187–88.

58. *See* Dr. Miles Medical Co. v. Park and Sons Co., 220 U.S. 373, 409 (1911) (Holmes, J., dissenting).

59. *See, e.g.,* Plant v. Woods, 176 Mass. 492, 504, 57 N.E. 1011, 1015 (1900) (Holmes, C.J., dissenting).

60. December 26, 1917, 1 HOLMES-LASKI LETTERS, note 22 above, at 121, 122.

61. Holmes to Felix Frankfurter, August 10, 1916, Holmes Papers, note 1 above, at B29 F4. Perhaps even letters of fire would not have been enough. In Frankfurter's thirty-page chapter *Property and Society,* in MR. JUSTICE HOLMES AND THE SUPREME COURT (2d. ed. 1961), he hinted heavily that Holmes was sympathetic to movements to redistribute the wealth of society. As to Holmes's stream-of-products argument, Frankfurter said only, obscurely, that Holmes subscribed to the "wage-fund" theory. He did not explain this reference to John Stuart Mill's contemptuous name for a doctrine supposedly held by classical economics, that

total wages were limited to a fixed share of the total product that could not be increased. Max Lerner, in his otherwise acute THE MIND AND FAITH OF JUSTICE HOLMES (1944), also muddled Holmes's straightforward image of the gross national product by calling it a "wage-fund" theory, and Samuel Konefsky, in his influential THE LEGACY OF HOLMES AND BRANDEIS (1956), devoted a full five pages to sneering at Holmes's supposed belief in the wage-fund theory, for which Konefsky thinks it a sufficient rebuttal to say, "Organized labor has always regarded this doctrine as both fallacious and reactionary." *Id.* at 23. These writers seem to have used "wage-fund" as a sneering reference to classical economics, which they assumed had been exploded.

62. Holmes to Canon Patrick Sheehan, September 17, 1907, HOLMES-SHEEHAN LETTERS, note 13 above, at 18.

63. For a brief summary of the Italian school of the 1890s, *see* R. HARRIS, MURDERS AND MADNESS: MEDICINE, LAW, AND SOCIETY IN THE FIN DE SIÈCLE 80–85 (1989). For a more extensive discussion of Lombroso's thought and its wide impact on views of social evolution, *see* D. PICK, FACES OF DEGENERATION: A EUROPEAN DISORDER, C. 1848–1918, at 109–52 (1989).

64. Holmes went on to note the contrary view of the French school, that the causes of crime were environmental, but concluded in either case that the criminal was organically malformed, and so could not be deterred or reformed.

65. Holmes to Frederick Pollock, February 26, 1922, 2 HOLMES-POLLOCK LETTERS, note 15 above, at 89, 90.

66. Holmes to Lewis Einstein, October 12, 1914, in O. HOLMES, THE HOLMES-EINSTEIN LETTERS: CORRESPONDENCE OF MR. JUSTICE HOLMES AND LEWIS EINSTEIN 1903–1935 (hereinafter "HOLMES-EINSTEIN LETTERS") 100, 101 (H. Peabody ed. 1964).

67. *See* Buck v. Bell, 274 U.S. 200 (1927) (Holmes, J.) (compulsory sterilization for "mental defectives" does not violate constitutional due process so long as procedural fairness is preserved).

68. Holmes to Frederick Pollock, February 1, 1920, 2 HOLMES-POLLOCK LETTERS, note 15 above, at 36.

69. Holmes to Lady Castletown, August 19, 1897, Holmes Papers, note 1 above, at B39 F2.

70. Holmes to Lewis Einstein, August 6, 1917, HOLMES-EINSTEIN LETTERS, note 67 above, at 144, 145. In this as in other ways, Holmes's letters to young men, when he was past seventy, were very much like his middle-aged letters to young women.

71. Holmes's Civil War experience may be the source of Michael Hoffheimer's intuition that Holmes's mother was absent. *See* Hoffheimer, *Justice Holmes: The Search for Control,* SUP. CT. HIST. SOC'Y YEARBOOK 58 (1989).

72. Holmes to Lady Castletown, April 10, 1897, Holmes Papers, note 1 above, at B39 F1.

73. Kate Millet, quoted by Jane Caputik, quoted by Susan Koppelman, in *Letter to Dear Friends,* AMER. VOICE, Winter, 1990, pp. 50, 58.

74. May 15, 1901, Holmes Papers, note 1 above.

75. Holmes to Frederick Pollock, June 20, 1928, HOLMES-POLLOCK LETTERS, note 15 above, at 222, 223.

76. *See also Courtly Love,* in HONORABLE JUSTICE, note 4 above, at 178; Hoffheimer, *Justice Holmes: Law and the Search for Control,* in SUP. CT. HIST. SOC'Y YEARBOOK 105–9 (1989). Hoffheimer's psychoanalytic study is marred by his unwarranted assumption that Holmes's references to chivalry were jokes.

77. T. DYER, THEODORE ROOSEVELT AND THE IDEA OF RACE 152 (1980).

78. Holmes to Lewis Einstein, August 31, 1928 (copy), Holmes Papers, note 1 above; quoted, with some alterations in punctuation, in HOLMES-EINSTEIN LETTERS, note 67 above, at 269; excerpted in M. HOWE, JUSTICE OLIVER WENDELL HOLMES: THE PROVING YEARS 8 n.17 (1963).

79. Mark DeWolfe Howe rather oddly read the letter quoted in the text to mean that Holmes had imposed a childless marriage on Fanny Dixwell in order to further his career (*see* note 78 above), but Howe was not aware of Fanny's illness.

80. *See* Opinions of the Justices (referendum, and votes for women), 160 Mass. 586, 593 (1894); Opinions of the Justices, 155 Mass. 598 (1892) (municipally owned coal yards); Commonwealth v. Perry, 155 Mass. 117, 123 (1892) (regulation of wage withholding).

81. January 7, 1901, Holmes Papers, note 1 above.

82. Since writing this, I have seen John Casey's PAGAN VIRTUE: AN ESSAY IN ETHICS (1990), the best of recent efforts to treat virtues like Holmes's, traced back to Classical roots, as an ethical system. I am much in sympathy with the effort, but I go no further here than to say that Holmes's code is a part of our Western tradition, a cautious respect for which is not a duty, as Holmes would say, but only a necessity.

83. Lochner v. New York, 198 U.S. 45, 74 (1905) (Holmes, J., dissenting). *See also* Danforth v. Groton Water Co., 176 Mass. 472, 59 N.E. 1033 (1901) (Holmes, C.J.) ("Perhaps the reasoning of the cases has not always been as sound as the instinct which directed the decisions").

84. The outlines of this argument were already visible in *Codes, and the Arrangement of the Law*, 6.18, published in 1870, where Holmes first clearly stated that legal principles were to be derived by induction from the decisions of the courts alone, and not from the opinions of the judges or the reasons that they gave.

85. *See, e.g.,* Commonwealth v. Rogers, 181 Mass. 184 (1902): "Here, as elsewhere, (it might be said especially in matters of constitutional law were the fact not universal,) it is vain to point out that the difference upon which a legal distinction is based . . . is one of degree, and to ask where you are going to draw the line, as is done by the defendants. Some legislation is permissible and necessary. A line between cases differing only in degree is worked out by the gradual approach of the decisions grouped about the opposite poles." *See also* Pennsylvania Coal Co. v. Mahon, 260 U.S. 393 (1922), and cases cited therein.

86. *See* Olmstead v. United States, 277 U.S. 438, 469 (1928) (Holmes, J., dissenting); Griswold v. Connecticut, 381 U.S. 479, 485–86 (1965); Henly, *"Penumbra": The Roots of a Legal Metaphor*, 15 HASTINGS CONST. L. Q. 81 (1987).

87. Opposite this opening passage, in the margin of his own copy of the book, Holmes wrote: "So parable & tale important & will remain so." (This was one of the notes he made in preparation for a new edition of *The Common Law* which was never completed; *see* 8.Introduction.) This seems to be intended to amplify the point that judicial opinions were to be treated as data showing the development of culture, equally exhibited in tales and parables of the time; the ordinary judge's logical reasoning accordingly was a rationalization to be ignored by the scientific student of law.

88. *See* M. DEW. HOWE, JUSTICE OLIVER WENDELL HOLMES: THE PROVING YEARS, 1870–1881 at 657–69 (1963).

89. In continental jurisprudence, following Roman law, property is traditionally treated as a combination of rights to possession, to disposition, and to inheritance. Savigny's classic essay *Possession*, to which Holmes devoted a separate chapter of his research notebook, in a characteristic Holmesian pattern, is both the inspiration of his ideas and the object of his attack.

90. Holmes to Harold Laski, February 4, 1927, 2 HOLMES-LASKI LETTERS, note 22 above, at 918.

91. This latter is similar both to Herbert Spencer's *Social Statics* and to J. S. Mill's *On Liberty*, but it should be borne in mind that Holmes did not advance this as a moral principle, or one he himself espoused, but only as the empirically derived policy he believed that he had observed operating in the modern common law.

92. Holmes's notes of the argument are in the Harvard Law School archives; a typescript

by Mark Howe is in the Holmes Papers, note 1 above, at B65 F6. *See also* HONORABLE JUSTICE, note 4 above, at 98, 423 n.14.

93. In *The Theory of Torts,* 6.82, Holmes had referred to the behavior of the "prudent man" as a general standard for negligence, where no rule of behavior had been taken from other sources, but he treated it as a rule of conduct, or duty, specific to negligence, and cited no cases.

94. In *Science in Law and Law in Science,* 10.10, Holmes described *The Common Law* as a study in the "development and transformation of ideas," and described this evolution with additional examples.

95. This new method of analyzing law by studying the circumstances under which liability was imposed would eventually make possible a detailed economic analysis of the common law, showing that many of its rules seemed to be aimed at the optimum allocation of resources. *See* R. POSNER, ECONOMIC ANALYSIS OF LAW (1972). But welfare economics had not yet been invented when Holmes wrote, and in any case Holmes denied that there was such a thing as an overall good of society. As we have seen, Holmes thought the parties in lawsuits embodied the inconsistent, competing demands of different sectors of society (*Law in Science and Science in Law,* 10.10). Holmes was concerned with survival of the fittest, rather than efficiency, and he disapproved of using either efficiency or average welfare as a criterion of social policy.

96. 151 Mass. 359 (1890).

97. *Id.* at 362.

98. *See* Graves v. Johnson, 156 Mass. 211, 212–13 (1892); Hayes v. Hyde Park, 153 Mass. 514 (1891); Clifford v. Atlantic Cotton Mills, 146 Mass. 47 (1888).

99. Note, *The Origin of the Modern Standard of Due Care in Negligence,* 1976 WASH. U. L. Q. 447 (1977).

100. *Id.*

101. *Privilege, Malice, and Intent,* 10.5 (citation omitted), and cases cited at n.21. Holmes extended the same analysis to cases in which the invalidity of a contract was asserted because on objective grounds it contemplated illegal behavior by third parties. Graves v. Johnson, 156 Mass. 211, 212–13 (1892).

102. Frederick Pollock to Holmes, March 30, 1898, 1 HOLMES-POLLOCK LETTERS, note 15 above, at 84. Pollock did not think the House of Lords had adopted Holmes's refined analysis of privilege and intent, but on the contrary had decided that competition was a matter of right and so not examinable as to motives. *Id.* Holmes replied to this point in *Law in Science and Science in Law,* 10.10, where he said the distinguished judges of the House of Lords were wrong to the extent they disagreed with him.

103. Tasker v. Stanley, 153 Mass. 148 (1891).

104. Elmer v. Fessenden, 151 Mass. 359 (1890).

105. Burt v. Advertiser Newspaper Co., 154 Mass. 238 (1891); *see also* Cowley v. Pulsifer, 137 Mass. 392 (1882).

106. *See* section 10 below. When a lifetime later he was asked about the origin of this doctrine, Holmes said, vaguely, that it was his work on the "common law," but his handwriting makes it difficult to say whether he was referring to the book or its subject, and by then he thought of *Privilege, Malice, and Intent* as an extension of the earlier book in any case. Holmes to Z. Chafee, June 12, 1922, Zechariah Chafee, Jr., Papers, Harvard Law School Library, B14 F12. As he also referred in this letter to his later criminal attempt and conspiracy opinions, see below, he must be taken to have meant the later, refined statement of his common-law doctrine. Failure to distinguish between the external standard as stated in *The Common Law* and the later formulation in *Privilege, Malice, and Intent* has bedeviled revisionist commentators, who take this letter to mean—against all other evidence—that Holmes was mechani-

cally applying an external standard in the early First Amendment cases. *See* Ragan, *Justice Oliver Wendell Holmes, Jr., Zechariah Chafee, Jr., and the Clear and Present Danger Test for Free Speech: The First Year, 1919,* 58 J. AM. HIST. 24, 26–27 (1971); Rabban, *The Emergence of Modern First Amendment Doctrine,* 50 UNIV. CHI. L. REV. 1205, 1265 (1983).

107. *See* HONORABLE JUSTICE, note 4 above, at 201–2.

108. *Id.* at 202.

109. *Id.* at 198–99.

110. *See The Labor Leader,* March 10, 1882, p. 2; HONORABLE JUSTICE, note 4 above, at 199.

111. HONORABLE JUSTICE, note 4 above, at 204.

112. *See* Plant v. Woods, 176 Mass. 492, 504 (1900) (Holmes, J., dissenting).

113. 167 Mass. 92 (1896).

114. Vegehlan v. Guntner, 167 Mass. 92, 104 (1896) (Holmes, J., dissenting). *See also* Plant v. Woods, 176 Mass. 492, 504 (1900) (Holmes, J., dissenting).

115. 170 Mass. 18 (1897).

116. Commonwealth v. Kennedy, 170 Mass. 18, 19 (1897).

117. In THE COMMON LAW, 66–68 (8.1, below), Holmes said that actual intent had to be proven only in cases where further acts of the defendant were necessary to complete the crime. The discussion in *Kennedy* used some of the language and examples from THE COMMON LAW, but the analysis was the more refined one of *Privilege, Malice, and Intent,* in which actual intent was to be proven in any case where the overt behavior was privileged or where the eventual harm depended on wrongdoing of the defendant or others.

118. 170 Mass. at 20–22.

119. 170 Mass. at 21.

120. 170 Mass. at 21, 24–25.

121. Commonwealth v. Peaslee, 177 Mass. 267 (1901).

122. Schenck v. United States, 249 U.S. 47 (1919).

123. Commonwealth v. Peaslee, 177 Mass. 267, 272 (1901) (citations omitted, including citation to Commonwealth v. Kennedy, 170 Mass. 18 [1897]).

124. Plant v. Woods, 176 Mass. 492 (1900).

125. Alan v. Flood (1898) A.C. 1.

126. 196 U.S. 375 (1905).

127. Swift and Co. v. United States, 196 U.S. 375, 396 (1905).

128. In Miller v. Milwaukee, 272 U.S. 713 (1927), writing for the Court, Holmes struck down a state statute because its evident intent was, by indirect means, to levy a tax on income from federal bonds exempt from direct taxation by the states. Holmes applied the doctrine of *Privilege, Malice, and Intent:* "It is a familiar principle that conduct which in usual situations the law protects may become unlawful when part of a scheme to reach a prohibited result." 272 U.S. at 715.

129. Holmes to Lady Castletown, October 17, 1896, Holmes Papers, note 1 above, at B26 F9.

130. Missouri v. Illinois, 180 U.S. 208 (1901) (Fuller, C.J.) (suit to enjoin Chicago Sanitary District from discharging untreated sewage into tributary of the Mississippi).

131. 206 U.S. 230 (1907).

132. Kawananakoa v. Polybank, 205 U.S. 349 (1907) (Holmes, J.); Damon v. Hawaii, 194 U.S. 154 (1904) (Holmes, J.).

133. 206 U.S. 46 (1907).

134. *Id.* at 98.

135. Hudson County Water Co. v. McCarter, 209 U.S. 349 (1908).

136. West v. Kansas Natural Gas Co., 221 U.S. 229 (1911).

137. 458 U.S. 941 (1982).

138. Milwaukee v. Illinois, 451 U.S. 304 (1981).

139. 41 U.S. 1 (1842).

140. Southern Pacific R. Co. v. Jensen, 244 U.S. 205, 222 (1917) (Holmes, J., dissenting).

141. 215 U.S. 349 (1910).

142. *Id.* at 370 (1910) (Holmes, J., dissenting).

143. 276 U.S. 518 (1928).

144. *Id.* at 532 (Holmes, J., dissenting).

145. 304 U.S. 64 (1938).

146. This was written by Justice James M. Barker—perhaps scribbled during a conference—and found in his locker when he died. The clerk of the court passed it on to Holmes, and it is now among his papers. Holmes Papers, note 1 above, at B45 F21.

147. *See, e.g.,* Opinion of the Justices, 160 Mass. 586, 593 (1894): "If the questions proposed to the justices came before us as a court and I found myself unable to agree with my brethren, I should defer to their opinion without any intimation of dissent. But the understanding always has been that questions like the present are addressed to us as individuals and require an individual answer."

148. *See, e.g.,* Coppage v. Kansas, 236 U.S. 1, 28 (1915) (Holmes, J., dissenting); Adair v. U.S., 208 U.S. 161, 190 (1908) (Holmes, J., dissenting); Lochner v. New York, 198 U.S. 45, 74 (1905) (Holmes, J., dissenting); Commonwealth v. Perry, 155 Mass. 117, 123 (1892) (Holmes, J., dissenting).

149. Holmes to James B. Thayer, November 2, 1893, Holmes Papers, note 1 above. *See* Opinions of the Justices, 160 Mass. 586, 593 (1894) (legislature may create referendum process); Opinions of the Justices, 155 Mass. 598 (1892) (state may authorize municipal coal yards); Commonwealth v. Perry, 155 Mass. 117, 123 (1892) (Holmes, J., dissenting) (state may regulate employers' practice of withholding charges from wages); *cf.* Commonwealth v. Davis, 162 Mass. 510 (1895) (state has absolute control over its property). Separation of powers and comity, Thayer's reasons for deference, although politely acknowledged in this letter, actually seemed to have very little weight with Holmes. *See, e.g.,* In re Janvrin, 174 Mass. 514 (1899) (Holmes, C.J.), upholding in an unusually tortured opinion a statute delegating to a panel of Supreme Judicial Court justices the duty to set water rates by legislative-style rules; Frank v. Mangum, 237 U.S. 309 (1915) (comity plays no role in habeas corpus challenge to fairness of state trial).

150. 198 U.S. 45 (1905).

151. 236 U.S. 1 (1915).

152. *See* HONORABLE JUSTICE, note 4 above, at 248–52, 456–57.

153. Danforth v. Groton Water Co., 176 Mass. 472 (1901) (Holmes, C.J.).

154. *Id.* at 476.

155. *Id.* at 476–77.

156. Springer v. Government of the Philippine Islands, 277 U.S. 189, 209–10 (1928) (Holmes, J., dissenting).

157. Missouri, Kan. & Tenn. R. Co. v. May, 194 U.S. 267 (1904).

158. Noble State Bank v. Haskell, 219 U.S. 104 (1911) (Holmes, J.). This opinion apparently said more than the other justices had realized, for after strong protests and petitions for rehearing, Holmes, again speaking for the Court, was obliged to say, "The analysis of the police power, whether correct or not, was intended to indicate an interpretation of what has taken place in the past, not to give a new or wider scope to the power." Noble State Bank v. Haskell, 219 U.S. 575 (1911) (petition for rehearing denied). That "correct or not" seems to withdraw the Court's approval for the broad statement of jurisprudence; one can almost hear Holmes muttering, "And yet it moves."

159. Louisville Gas Co. v. Coleman, 277 U.S. 32, 41 (1928).

160. 110 U.S. 516 (1884).

161. *Id.* at 530. *See* Alschuler, *Preventive Pretrial Detention and the Failure of Interest-Balancing Approaches to Due Process,* 85 MICH. L. REV. 510, 520–25 (1986). In an interesting opinion for the Massachusetts Supreme Judicial Court, Tyler v. Judges of the Court of Registration, 175 Mass. 71 (1900) (Holmes, C.J.), upholding a land title registration statute, Holmes cited *Hurtado* for the proposition that due process of law weighed government convenience against "substantial justice," 175 Mass. at 74, but immediately went on to say that he himself differed from the majority of his court and would have rested the decision solely on the common law, which allowed actions in rem without actual notice to affected individuals.

162. *See, e.g.,* Hough, *Due Process of Law Today,* 32 HARV. L. REV. 218 (1919).

163. *See* E. FREUND, AMERICAN STANDARDS OF LEGISLATION: AN ESTIMATE OF RESTRICTIVE AND CONSTRUCTIVE FACTORS 207 (1917).

164. Otis v. Parker, 187 U.S. 606 (1903).

165. 195 U.S. 194 (1904).

166. 195 U.S. at 206.

167. *Id.*

168. 233 U.S. 604 (1914).

169. *Id.* at 610.

170. Hurtado v. California, 110 U.S. 516, 525 (1884).

171. T. COOLEY, CONSTITUTIONAL LIMITATIONS 422 (1868).

172. 165 U.S. 275 (1897).

173. 165 U.S. at 281, cited as authority for limitations on the First Amendment in Frohwerk v. United States, 249 U.S. 204, 206 (1919) (Holmes, J.).

174. Casey, "Mankind in Conversation: The Philosophy of Michael Oakeshott and Its Misunderstandings," Times Literary Supplement, March 29, 1991, p.3, col. 1.

175. This is the meaning of Holmes's puzzling remark that there may be "exceptions" to the sweeping command of the First Amendment, Abrams v. United States, 250 U.S. 616, 631 (1919); *see* D. CURRIE, THE CONSTITUTION IN THE SUPREME COURT, THE SECOND CENTURY 1888–1986 123 n.206 (1990).

176. *See* Olmstead v. United States, 277 U.S. 438, 469 (1928) (Homes, J., dissenting).

177. Woodward v. Central Vt. R. Co., 180 Mass. 599 (1902) (Holmes, C.J.) (applying Vermont law). *See also* Dunbar v. Boston & Providence R. Co., 181 Mass. 383 (1902) (Holmes, C.J.), in which a statute reviving barred claims against a railroad was upheld only with great difficulty, and in deference to recent precedent; Danforth v. Groton Water Co., 176 Mass. 472 (1901) (Holmes, C.J.).

178. *Id. See also* Pennsylvania Coal Co. v. Mahon, 260 U.S. 393 (1922) (Holmes, J.); Block v. Hirsh, 256 U.S. 135 (1921) (Holmes, J.).

179. *See* Sawyer v. Commonwealth, 182 Mass. 245 (1902) (Holmes, C.J.); Earle v. Commonwealth, 180 Mass. 579 (1902) (Holmes, C.J.).

180. 257 U.S. 312, 343 (1921).

181. *Id.*

182. *See, e.g.,* Barry v. Lancy, 179 Mass. 112 (1901) (Holmes, C.J.) (statute protecting liens of mortgagee at tax sale upheld); Danforth v. Groton Water Co., 176 Mass. 472 (1901) (Holmes, C.J.) (statute requiring petitions for compensation to be filed first with county commissioners and extending time period for filing upheld); Aldrich v. Blatchford & Co., 175 Mass. 369 (1900) (Holmes, C.J.) (service on attorney representing foreign corporation in unrelated matter was adequate); Tyler v. Judges of the Court of Registration, 175 Mass. 71 (1900) (Holmes, C.J.) (procedure to cut off old claims of title valid despite lack of actual notice). In *Tyler* Holmes made his characteristic argument that procedures acceptable at common law would not violate the Constitution; *see also* Callahan v. City of Boston, 175 Mass.

201 (1900) (Holmes, C.J.) (statute making city responsible for its contractor's workmen upheld: "A compulsory relation of master and servant is not unknown even to the common law").

183. Miller v. Horton, 152 Mass. 540 (1890) (Holmes, C.J.).

184. Bumpus v. French, 179 Mass. 131 (1901) (Holmes, C.J.).

185. *Id.* at 133.

186. *See, e.g., Danforth v. Groton Water Co.,* 176 Mass. 472 (1901) (Holmes, C.J.); Henly, *"Penumbra": The Roots of a Legal Metaphor,* 15 HASTINGS CONST. L. Q. 81 (1987).

187. That people *could be* sacrificed to the general good—treated as means rather than ends—was to Holmes a fundamental distinction between law and morals. *See* THE COMMON LAW, 9.1; Buck v. Bell, 274 U.S. 200 (1927) (Holmes, J.).

188. Harriman v. ICC, 211 U.S. 407 (1908). This appears to be the first hint of a constitutional right of privacy in the opinions of the Court.

189. *Id.* at 422.

190. *See, e.g.,* Holmes to Harold Laski, September 25, 1916, 1 HOLMES-LASKI LETTERS, note 22 above, at 20, 21.

191. *See, e.g.,* Toledo Newspaper Co. v. United States, 247 U.S. 402, 422 (1917) (Holmes, J., dissenting). Holmes's view has since been adopted by the Court. *See* cases collected at L. Tribe, AMERICAN CONSTITUTIONAL LAW 856–57 (2d ed. 1988).

192. Frank v. Mangum, 237 U.S. 309, 347–49 (1915) (Holmes, J., dissenting) (citation omitted).

193. 249 U.S. 47 (1919).

194. Government's brief at 12, in LANDMARK BRIEFS AND ARGUMENTS OF THE SUPREME COURT 1021, 1037 (Kurland and Casper eds. 1975) (hereinafter "LANDMARK BRIEFS").

195. Goldman v. United States, 245 U.S. 474 (1918).

196. Swift and Co. v. United States, 196 U.S. 375 (1905).

197. Goldman v. United States, 245 U.S. 474 (1918).

198. *Id.* at 12–13; 18 LANDMARK BRIEFS, note 194 above, at 1037–38.

199. *Id.*

200. Defendants' brief at 14, 18 LANDMARK BRIEFS, note 194 above, at 989, 1002.

201. *Id.* at 7, 18, LANDMARK BRIEFS, note 194 above, at 985.

202. Schenck v. United States, 249 U.S. 47 (1919).

203. 249 U.S. at 51.

204. 249 U.S. at 52, citing Gompers v. Bucks Stove & Range Co., 245 U.S. 474, 477 (1917) (upholding an injunction to enforce a consent decree). This is one of the most famous passages in the law, and is often cited, and as often attacked. Professor Dershowitz has devoted a brief article to debunking the "shouting fire" image. Dershowitz, *Shouting "Fire!"* ATLANTIC MONTHLY, January, 1989, at p. 72. His attack rested on the assumption that Holmes was stating a reason for his holding in the case. But Holmes was just ticking off a subsidiary point in the argument—that the First Amendment does not protect all speech. *See* Texas v. Johnson, 491 U.S. 397, 421 (1989) (Rehnquist, C.J., dissenting).

205. *Id.*

206. 249 U.S. at 52.

207. 245 U.S. 474 (1917).

208. 249 U.S. at 52; emphasis added.

209. *See* Chafee, *Freedom of Speech in Wartime,* 32 HARV. L. REV. 932, 964–69 (1918).

210. Frohwerk v. United States, 249 U.S. 204 (1919); Debs v. United States, 249 U.S. 211 (1919).

211. 248 U.S. 593 (1918).

212. Holmes's dissenting opinion was never published, but it is preserved among his pa-

pers; Holmes Papers, note 1 above. The date and events surrounding preparation of the dissent are noted by him on a copy of the dissent.

213. The course of events is noted on Holmes's own copy of the dissent, which is bound with his opinions of that term in the Holmes Papers, note 1 above. *See also* HONORABLE JUSTICE, note 4 above, at 325.

214. 250 U.S. 616 (1919).

215. *Id.* at 629 (Holmes, J., dissenting).

216. 250 U.S. at 621.

217. Abrams v. United States, 250 U.S. 616, 624 (1919) (Holmes, J., dissenting).

218. 250 U.S. at 627. It is characteristic and amusing that Holmes turns to the First Amendment only *after* laying out these broad principles of freedom of speech.

219. 250 U.S. at 628. Holmes qualified his statement of the rule with the phrase "where private rights are not concerned." He plainly meant to limit the clear and present danger standard to cases of attempted crime, but it did not then follow that all other speech was afforded a higher degree of protection, as Professor Currie suggested. D. CURRIE, THE CONSTITUTION IN THE SUPREME COURT, THE SECOND CENTURY, 1886–1986, at 123 (1990). Evidently a different standard was to be applied where private rights are concerned, but Holmes probably just meant that the First Amendment did not disturb the common law of defamation.

220. Corwin, *Freedom of Speech and Press under the First Amendment,* 30 YALE L. J. 48 (1920).

221. There arguably was an "obscurity" in the opinion, however, as to whether the specific intent and the external standard "were alternative bases of criminal liability, or rather that both elements had to be shown." L. TRIBE, AMERICAN CONSTITUTIONAL LAW 843 n.16 (1988). I think the opinion is clear enough that, as to completed acts of advocacy, specific intent is an additional element that must be proven. But Holmes suggested that for attempts, the intent might make up for a lack of objective risk in the overt acts alone. The ambiguity was in the law of attempts, which imposed criminal liability for some acts that could not in themselves lead to harm unless part of a larger plan.

222. 250 U.S. at 628–29.

223. *Id.* at 629.

224. *Id.* at 630–31.

225. Not, evidently, Holmes's own theory. In letters he said he was not sure he believed in freedom of speech, although he hoped that he would be willing to die for it. *See, e.g.,* Holmes to Harold Laski, October 26, 1915, 1 HOLMES-LASKI LETTERS, note 22 above, at 217. He meant that he was loyal to the peaceful rule of law but had doubts whether it would prevail over regimes more frankly committed to the use of force.

226. Whitney v. California, 274 U.S. 352, 372 (1927) (Brandeis and Holmes, JJ., concurring).

227. *Cf.* Holmes's frequently quoted opinion, that the Constitution allows experiments in social policy to be carried out "in the insulated chambers of the states," in Truax v. Corrigan, 257 U.S. 312, 344 (1921). For the evolutionist interpretation of Holmes's theory of the First Amendment, *see also* M. LERNER, THE MIND AND FAITH OF JUSTICE HOLMES 306 (1944, reissued in 1990); Rabban, *The Emergence of First Amendment Doctrine,* 50 UNIV. CHI. L. REV. 1205, 1310–11 (1983).

228. Gitlow v. New York, 268 U.S. 652, 673 (1925) (Holmes, J., dissenting).

229. United States v. Schwimmer, 279 U.S. 644, 654 (1929) (Holmes, J., dissenting).

4

A Critical Appraisal

A recent study has shown that, more than fifty years after his death, law reviews still mentioned Holmes more than any other judge (except living Supreme Court justices).[1] References to his name show only a part of Holmes's presence. Holmes's opinions have entered not just legal literature but the fabric of legal language. A search in April, 1991, found the phrase "clear and present danger" cited in nearly one thousand opinions in the federal courts alone since 1919. Holmes's images—of the marketplace of ideas, of "no limit but the sky," of "shouting 'fire!' in a theater," and of the "penumbra" cast by provisions of the Constitution—are all equally pervasive.[2]

Frequent citations of his name by law professors do not necessarily indicate a high regard, however. Many of the articles on Holmes are attacks on his reputation, and more law review articles are at least mildly negative than are positive. One reason may be that Holmes did not cultivate the professors, and except for a rare mention of his friend John Chipman Gray he did not cite their articles in his opinions, as Brandeis and Cardozo did. When the details of his life began to emerge, it quickly became known that he had resigned a professorship at Harvard after only half a term, without stopping to say goodbye; that he had advised Felix Frankfurter to resign from teaching in favor of a judgeship; and that in well-known addresses he had referred contemptuously to professors who fostered intellectual ability "at the expense of their total life" (11.14): "But after all the place for a man who is complete in all his powers is in the fight. The professor, the man of letters, gives up one-half of life that his protected talent may grow and flower in peace" (10.10).

Such remarks were not calculated to endear Holmes to the gatekeepers of reputation. Furthermore, his conservative political views have long been out of fashion in the academy, and his most important opinions, those on freedom of speech, have been found offensive by many professors since the 1960s (see the case study which follows), as they did not give a clearly favored position in society to expressive behavior. Law students today, in their three years of law school, read only two or three of his opinions (and perhaps an excerpt from *The Common Law* in torts class), and, except for Holmes's dissent in *Lochner*, these are unfavorably contrasted with opinions by other judges. His essays and addresses have long been out of print.

Yet Holmes's name is better known to the general public than, I would venture, that of any other judge. His face adorns a postage stamp, and his reputation is very high among practicing lawyers and judges. For the American lawyer, "he is the beau ideal, and the lawyer quotes his aphorisms as the literate layman quotes Hamlet."[3] One cannot read very far in any area of law without encountering Holmes's name or his writings. Even his severe critics count him as the single most influential legal writer ("Holmes's name is uniquely weighty. To describe his commanding stature and influence apparently requires language both oracular and portentous")[4] and rate *The Common Law* as "the most important book on law ever written by an American."[5] His admirers call him the greatest judge in the English-speaking world.[6] His stature shows no signs of lessening and evidently does not depend on scholarly appraisal.

His is a popular reputation, and so one must account for the phenomenon of an Anglicized man of elitist tastes and inaccessible thoughts becoming America's "first citizen,"[7] a major public figure, rivaled in his sphere only by Chief Justice John Marshall. Holmes held no position of political power and worked no great changes in American institutions. Alone among American national heroes, he is celebrated for his intellectual achievements.

Holmes's extrajudicial writings plainly have very little to do with his modern reputation. *The Common Law*, because of the obscurity of its argument, was nearly forgotten in his lifetime and would be entirely forgotten now, I venture to say—the overheated praise and blame which Holmes seems to prompt notwithstanding—if it were not for his celebrity as a judge. The book itself now has little reputation of its own, except as a seminal work in the law of torts.

Nor is Holmes's work on the Massachusetts Supreme Judicial Court very well known. The obscurity of his opinions in his first twenty years as a judge is due partly to the narrowness of questions dealt with in a state court and partly to the relative difficulty of retrieving opinions published before 1890.[8] Holmes had not yet hit his stride in those years—most of the opinions we now quote, remarkably, were written after Holmes passed his seventieth year. His careful adherence to precedent and his reluctance to innovate deprive most of his Massachusetts opinions of anything very distinctive, except a highly individual style of expression. It is only when one follows the line of his thought through a sequence of cases that one sees his ideas at work. He did not, like Cardozo or Hand, write "leading cases."

Nor was he a public man. He did not usually give interviews, and after he joined the Supreme Court, with rare exceptions, he refused all invitations to speak or write outside the courtroom. He did not cultivate reporters or give anonymous assessments of the work of the Court, as some of his colleagues have always done. He declined all but one invitation to speak on the radio (12.24).

We therefore turn to Holmes's work as a justice of the Supreme Court of the United States, to understand his celebrity and his place in history. His reputation— and the continuing importance of many of his later opinions in widely scattered areas of law—owes something to chance. He was appointed to the Supreme Court on the strength of a personal acquaintance and an affinity of political views with Theodore Roosevelt. The assassination of President McKinley, which made Roosevelt president just as the "Massachusetts seat" on the Court fell vacant, was critical. Even the timing was fortunate. By Roosevelt's second term, Holmes would have been too old.

Holmes's success on the Court owes something to the good luck of his longevity and his steadying presence there during the turmoil of the 1920s. It also owes something to his knack for getting along with chief justices and his immense appetite for work, which together account for the unusually large number of cases assigned to him to write. He wrote 873 opinions for the Court, more than any other justice, even including justices with longer tenures.[9] He has been called the "workhorse" of the Court, but there is something more than good luck and the opportunity to write a lot of opinions behind Holmes's reputation.

The quality of his work has several components. There was the principal job that he did, which was to decide cases; and there was the ancillary task, to write opinions. Both Holmes's decisions and the opinions he wrote to explain them had special qualities which helped to account for the force of their impact. Holmes's decisions were consistent with each other and with a coherent body of jurisprudence, and were beautifully expressed in his opinions. But there was something more. Holmes made himself an embodiment of an ideal, and this ideal of the judge, although a limited one, was widely shared and deeply felt. Holmes projected it through the resistant medium of judicial opinions and across generations. This ideal, a vivid image of aristocratic American virtue, is still what draws us to him.

4.1

HOLMES'S JUDGMENTS—A CASE STUDY

It is difficult to get at the essence of a judge's work, his decisions. A vote is opaque, and there is little to distinguish it from the eight other votes. Only the pattern of votes discloses anything individual, and the pattern is hard to see without a thorough knowledge, not only of the cases that were decided, but of the aspects of the cases that in actual fact were important to the judges. But Holmes taught us that it was the judge's decisions, and not the reasons he gave, that mattered. And so we begin with Holmes's judgments, more than two thousand in all, or at least with an illuminating set of examples of them. Holmes's decisions on freedom of speech are among his best known and most important, and have a number of lessons to teach us concerning his work as a judge.

To begin at a little distance. Holmes wrote only a half-dozen opinions on copyright law, and this area of law has undergone substantial changes since his time. Yet several of his decisions are still cited. His opinion for the Court in *Bleistein v. Donaldson Lithographing Co.*[10] still defines the modicum of "originality" required for copyright. His prescient, concurring opinion in *White-Smith Music Co. v. Apollo Co.*[11] is more remarkable. The case concerned whether the manufacture of punched-paper music rolls for player pianos was a violation of a music composer's protection against the unauthorized copying of his songs. Seeing the case in its fundamental aspect, Holmes judged that copyright protection should extend to the making of copies in any medium, even when the copy was made by new technology and was not directly comprehensible to human readers. This opinion provided important arguments for securing copyright protection for electronic databases and computer programs in the 1970s. In *Bleistein* Holmes wrote for a divided Court, while in *White-Smith* he was alone,[12] but no one now doubts that Holmes had the better view in each case.

One hesitates to say that Holmes judged rightly, as if there were some general agreement on what right answers were. Yet Holmes's decisions for the Court and his dissents have a very high prestige among lawyers and judges at least in part because they are perceived as likely to be correct. They have a quality of intellectual authority that is difficult to explain. Certainly they are very intelligent. But Holmes's frequent opinions for the Court are no more or less prescient than, say, Melville Fuller's, with which he usually agreed.

Holmes's relatively infrequent dissents do occasionally seem clairvoyant; they have been followed more often than the majority opinions from which he differed. While on the Supreme Court, Holmes published 72 dissents, and his 30 concurring opinions were usually expressions of views that differed from the Court's. Roughly half of these 102 separate opinions concerned a single broad question, one that we might characterize as the content of the language of constitutional guarantees of liberty or perhaps as the degree of deference the Court owed to other branches and agencies of government.[13] In nearly all these cases, we would now accept Holmes's results rather than those of the changing Court majorities.

One aspect of this appearance of correctness is certainly Holmes's faithfulness to the principles he so often announced on behalf of the Court. His fundamental ideas had been formed before he joined the Court, and he rarely departed from them to secure a preferred result. Even his decisions which have not been followed, with occasional exceptions, are at least consistent. Holmes, for all his vindication of the judge's legislative power, was deeply respectful of precedent. He occasionally overturned statutes, but there are fewer instances of his voting to overrule settled precedent, even when he believed the precedent to have been decided wrongly. Holmes voted to reverse the precedents of his own Court that had allowed the post-master general to exercise prior restraint on the contents of letters,[14] but there he was reversing only his own earlier vote. Deeply as he disagreed with and campaigned against the doctrine of *Swift v. Tyson,* in his most stinging dissents he did not argue for overruling the case itself, but only for narrowing the interpretations which had been put upon it.[15] He expressed his Burkean respect for the past in characteristically skeptical terms:

> [W]e have a great body of law which has at least this sanction that it exists. If one does not affirm that it is intrinsically better than a different body of principles which one could imagine, one can see an advantage which, if not the greatest, at least, is very great—that we know what it is. For this reason I am slow to assent to overruling a decision. Precisely my skepticism, my doubt as to the absolute worth of a large part of what we administer, or of any other system, makes me very unwilling to increase the doubt as to what the court will do. ("Twenty Years in Retrospect," 12.20)

As we have seen, even where judges were obliged to apply substantive standards to legislation, Holmes believed that they should consult, not their own secular preferences, but the relatively fundamental principles discernible in the common law itself.[16] Deference and restraint were the common threads in Holmes's dissents. Accordingly, while Holmes argued that judges necessarily would consult views of social policy as well as precedent, he himself would do so only as a last resort. Judges' ignorance was the great law reformer; but the better and more learned the judge, the less frequently he would be thrown back on policy. Holmes regularly chastised his colleagues for relying on their views of social policy when principles of law might have been allowed to govern. And it is difficult to point to cases where Holmes himself was reduced to saying that precedent and legal principle did not supply a rule of decision. The only clear example is *Olmstead v. United States*,[17] in which Holmes, interestingly, chose as his principle of social policy that the government should not behave ignobly.

This relentless conservatism is visible in all Holmes's decisions, including some we may now think wrong. Perhaps the only important opinion that seems just plain wrong by Holmes's own criteria is *Giles v. Harris*,[18] in which he held for a divided Court that the Civil War amendments did not give federal courts authority to enforce what had been called "political" rights, including the right of African-Americans to vote on an equal footing with other citizens of the United States.[19]

But most of Holmes's opinions that now may be open to criticism were at least consistent with existing precedent and his own general views. In *United Zinc & Chemical Co. v. Britt*,[20] a case with distressing facts—a child had died in an unfenced pool of poisonous chemicals—Holmes maintained the old rule that a railroad company had no duty with regard to trespassers. In *Baltimore & Ohio R. Co. v. Goodman*,[21] Holmes repeated what he had said innumerable times on the Massachusetts bench, that a person at a grade crossing was obliged to stop and make sure that no train was approaching.[22] Both opinions were contributions to "sound learning," according to Frederick Pollock, Holmes's mentor in the common law.[23]

In *Bailey v. Alabama*,[24] Holmes voted to uphold an Alabama statute that authorized criminal penalties for violations of labor agreements of the sort that had been used to create a form of peonage for African-Americans. Holmes's argument was that the Thirteenth Amendment, prohibiting involuntary servitude, was, like other provisions of the Constitution, to be construed in light of the common law. In Massachusetts he had upheld the constitutionality of imprisonment for debt,[25] and he could see no basis for holding that the former slave states were subject to fundamental legal principles that did not apply in the northern states.

This conservatism poses a conundrum. What is greatness in a conservative judge? By definition a conservative makes no innovations. He holds himself bound by precedent, and so far as possible sets aside everything that is merely personal or temporary when making his decision. The passage of time will obliterate his decisions, bound as they are to the past. Judges like John Marshall and Benjamin Cardozo are known for their innovations, for their willingness to use legal materials to arrive at results dictated by social policy. Holmes in his writings certainly justified their work. But he set a different standard for himself. His devotion to his craft and his temperamental conservatism closed off his opportunity for greatness in this sense; in his opinions, he announced no new principles of tort or contract law, and even in constitutional law was as deferential to precedent and the legislatures as it was possible to be. This conservatism led Holmes's admirer Morris R. Cohen, himself a proponent of reform, and writing at the height of an era of reform, to make this assessment of Holmes's place in history:

> [H]e did not in his own lifetime exert any highly effective influence on the law and life of our country. . . . he has not, like Marshall or Taney, changed the current of our constitutional law, nor for that matter left any permanent impress on any other branch of law, as lesser men, like Story, did in admiralty, or conflict of laws. Holmes was a lone, though titanic, figure, and the currents of our national life have swept by and around him.[26]

There is nothing unusual in Holmes's conservatism itself, or even in his rigorous consistency. Justice Sanford, to take one example, was rigorously consistent and faithful to precedent, without being very much celebrated now. Yet lawyers and judges admire Holmes now, not for his character alone, but for his qualities as a judge.

In addition to all the other factors that contributed to Holmes's reputation, there is one that is fundamental, and that concerns the substance of the ideal to which he was faithful, and that I believe explains his celebrity.

By tracing out the later history of Holmes's decisions in the Court and the manner in which Holmes's influence was mediated by the opinions of other justices, one can gain a sense of what precisely it was that mattered about Holmes's decisions. This is a tedious process, plainly not practical in a large number of cases. But one illustrative case history of Holmes's influence should be illuminating.

In the following section, accordingly, the later history of Holmes's holdings on freedom of speech, arguably the most important of his judgments, will be traced in some detail.

4.1.1 The Case Study: The History of "Clear and Present Danger." As we saw in chapter 3, Holmes wrote a series of opinions on freedom of speech for the Court and then dissented from the decisions of the Court in nearly all First Amendment cases thereafter. The point that emerges from later cases is that, as to the issue on which they differed, Holmes touched on something fundamental, one to which the Court keeps returning.

But Holmes's dissents were narrowly drawn, and the precise issue dividing him from the majority of the Court hardly seems earthshaking on its surface. The issue was not simply whether speech should be protected, as some critics of the Court seemed to think. At least some contemporary commentators saw well enough that the point of difference between Holmes and the majority of his Court was on a narrow question, the precise intent required to be shown before speech could be punished.

As we saw in 3.10, Holmes, after circulating a strenuous dissenting memorandum on behalf of free speech in an unpublished case, *Baltzer v. United States,* was given the task in 1919 of writing the Court's unanimous opinion in *Schenck,* holding that attempts to obstruct the draft through speech and writings could be punished. Zechariah Chafee, in his pro-Holmes articles, and Day Kimball, a young critic (Kimball was about to begin his clerkship with Holmes), saw that *Schenck* was an extension of the common law of attempts.

Chafee noticed in *Schenck* the similarity in language and holding to Holmes's opinion in a Massachusetts attempted arson case, *Commonwealth v. Peaslee.*[27] Chafee and Kimball saw that a showing of intent was required by Holmes's opinion for the Court in *Schenck* and that the outcome in *Abrams,* where Holmes dissented, depended on the question, not clearly resolved in *Schenck,* whether the First Amendment allowed reliance on intent proven by an external standard or whether it also required the government to prove that defendants acted on a motive to bring about wrongdoing or harm of the kind specifically and lawfully prohibited by Congress.

In *Abrams,* the majority opinion by Justice Clarke also made it plain what issue divided the Court. According to Clarke, while there was evidence of the specific motive that Holmes demanded, the defendants might have been convicted on the external standard alone. The Espionage Act required that it be shown the defendants intended to injure the war effort; but by an external standard, as Holmes himself had once insisted, this "intent" did not refer to the defendants' actual state of mind; it was only a shorthand term for the general doctrine that one might be held liable for any harms that an ordinary person would have foreseen: "It will not do to say, as is now argued [in Holmes's dissent], that the only intent of these defendants was to prevent injury to the Russian cause. Men must be held to have intended, and to be accountable for, the effects which their acts were likely to produce."[28]

Clarke might have been quoting from *The Common Law*. But Holmes, as we have seen, had broadened his perspective in the 1890s and had come to think that, in addition to the external standard, the defendant's state of mind should be considered in cases of privilege, to determine whether a privilege to do foreseeable harm had been overcome by malice. He accordingly dissented in *Abrams*, as we have seen, and said that the Constitution required that a specific, subjective intent to bring about a forbidden result must be shown before a conviction could be sustained under the doctrine of *Schenck*.[29]

The first question for our case study, therefore, is why this narrow question should have had such enduring significance. To determine this, we will have to follow the later cases in some detail.

Three more cases of wartime dissent were decided after *Abrams*, the first two under the federal Espionage Act[30] and the third under a Minnesota statute.[31] Brandeis wrote dissents in the Espionage Act cases, asserting that the government's evidence was not adequate under the clear and present danger standard; and Holmes joined in these dissents.[32] In the second of the federal cases, *Pierce v. United States*,[33] evidence of intent was again critical and Mahlon Pitney for the majority stated the external standard once more: the government was required to prove only that the language of an antiwar pamphlet "itself furnished a ground for attributing to [the defendants] an intent to bring about . . . such consequences as reasonably might be anticipated from its distribution."[34]

Brandeis, with Holmes joining, argued in dissent that the standard established in *Schenck* required proof of subjective, specific intent, proof that was lacking in this case. The two justices expressly compared the standard to the actual malice required to defeat a claim of privilege in a libel action.[35]

In the third case, *Gilbert v. Minnesota*,[36] intent was not the issue, as there was enough evidence for a jury to find that the defendant actually intended to obstruct the draft. Prosecution had been under a state statute. The majority affirmed the conviction, and Holmes concurred in the result;[37] Brandeis alone dissented.[38]

In the whole line of cases from *Schenck* through *Gilbert*, Holmes's position remained stubbornly fixed. Because he rested his dissents on the narrowest available ground, his difference with the majority could be expressed in a single point of doctrine: the question of specific intent.

But the underlying difference between Holmes and the Court was deeper than this point of doctrine. Proof of subjective intent would have required attention to the unique defendants and the particular circumstances of individual cases. In Holmes's view, stated in all the criminal attempt and conspiracy cases from *Kennedy* to *Schenck*, it was only these particular circumstances that the Court had a right to consider in determining whether there had been a clear and present danger of harm.

The majority of the Court avoided such particularized deliberation by applying an external standard based on the defendants' words cut free from their immediate context. This allowed the majority to turn its attention to broader, quasi-legislative questions of policy.

In the realm of policy, there was no real dispute that civil unrest and dissent, if unchecked, might have hindered the war effort. Holmes himself was incensed by railroad strikes and threats of a general strike.[39] Holmes and the majority probably also agreed, although it is more difficult to be sure about this point, that the radical political movement that generally opposed the war, and of which Abrams and his fellow defendants were a small part, posed a threat—even a clear and present danger—of obstructing the war effort. Holmes in any case would have deferred to the factual determination of a judge or legislature on such a question.

In *Schenck* and *Pierce,* the pamphlets distributed by the defendants were copies of literature being distributed in large numbers by national organizations. In *Abrams* the leaflets were filled with familiar, stereotyped harangues, and the defendants plainly considered themselves part of a larger revolutionary movement. By looking at the language of the pamphlets alone in these cases, cut free from the defendants' motives and circumstances, the Court majority allowed itself to consider the danger posed by the political movement as a whole. It treated the stereotyped vocabulary of the political left as a forbidden category or form of expression and held the defendants strictly liable for using it.

Justice Clarke, speaking for the *Abrams* Court, for instance, quoted liberally from articles written by others but found in the defendants' possession. These articles may have been relevant to the defendants' intent, but by quoting from them at length, Clarke seemed to treat the defendants as representatives of a movement and to affirm their guilt simply for using that movement's language. To the majority it did not seem that the defendants were held guilty for expressing ideas but for lending their support, however small, to a criminal enterprise.

In contrast to Clarke's method, Holmes's insistence on proof both of the defendants' subjective intent to cause wrongdoing or harm and of proof that on objective grounds the forbidden result was dangerously likely *in the circumstances of the case* would have required the Court to focus on the liberty of the individual defendants rather than on form or manner of expression.

The underlying tension between the majority's approach, of applying strict liability for any use of an expression that fell into a dangerous category, and Holmes's individualized consideration of motive and circumstance in particular cases, remained submerged beneath points of doctrine in the Espionage Act cases, in part because no one on the Court was able to force Holmes off his moorings in the common law.

Within a year after *Gilbert,* however, there had been a profound change in the makeup of the Court. Former president William Howard Taft had been appointed chief justice in 1921, and he energetically assisted the president in filling seats on the Court that had become vacant. Taft, together with Peirce Butler, Arthur Sutherland, Edward T. Sanford, and Willis Van DeVanter—the latter appointed by Taft himself—constituted a comfortable majority of like-minded, able justices. They were an unusually powerful group, including as they did both a former president and Sutherland, a former chairman of the Senate judiciary committee. Taft masterfully managed the Court's dealings with Congress and the executive branch, and by 1925 the chief justice was at the head of a unified federal judiciary.[40] The Court was in control of its docket through the newly authorized expansion of the writ of certiorari and could choose the questions of policy on which it would focus. Through Taft's efforts, the Court soon would have a new building, and the justices each would have offices and a staff; the Court would be an equal branch of government in practice as well as theory.[41]

The prosecution of dissidents had continued through the 1920s. Twenty states had adopted peacetime statutes prohibiting sedition, criminal anarchy, or "syndicalism," a radical creed identified with the Industrial Workers of the World.[42] The first appeals from peacetime prosecutions under these statutes came to the Supreme Court in 1925, when Taft's new majority was securely in place. The Taft Court quickly put the categorization approach to sedition cases on a firmer footing than its predecessors had succeeded in doing.

Benjamin Gitlow, an officer of the tiny, nascent Communist party, was convicted of advocating criminal anarchism in violation of a New York statute. The violation consisted of the publication of a "Left Wing Manifesto" and other documents that in plain if turgid Leninist language called for the forceful overthrow of the United States government.

Justice Sanford, writing for the seven members of the Court who had voted to affirm Gitlow's conviction, now made powerfully explicit what had been submerged in *Abrams*. Gitlow had been convicted, not because he had been shown to threaten or even to desire an immediate insurrection, but because the New York legislature had determined that the forms of language he had used posed a danger to the state. Assuming that freedom of speech was protected against state action by the due process clause of the Fourteenth Amendment, as it was protected against federal action by the First, the Court nevertheless upheld the constitutionality of the convictions.[43]

Justice Sanford emphasized that the New York statute was not construed to prohibit the expression of ideas or opinions as such, but was directed only against "advocacy," which the Court took to be equivalent to incitement of crime.[44] By an external standard, the language of the Left Wing Manifesto was shown to contain language of "direct incitement,"[45] and as so construed both the statute and the prosecution under it would pass muster under the standard of the First Amendment, even if it were made applicable to the states by the Fourteenth.

> That utterances inciting to the overthrow of organized government by unlawful means, present a sufficient danger of substantive evil to bring their punishment within the range of legislative discretion, is clear. Such utterances, *by their very nature*, involve danger to the public peace and to the security of the State. They threaten breaches of the peace and ultimate revolution. And the immediate danger is none the less real and

substantial, because the effect of a given utterance cannot be accurately foreseen. The State cannot reasonably be required to measure the danger from every such utterance in the nice balance of a jeweler's scale. A single revolutionary spark may kindle a fire that, smoldering for a time, may burst into a sweeping and destructive conflagration. It cannot be said that the State is acting arbitrarily or unreasonably when in the exercise of its judgment as to the measures necessary to protect the public peace and safety, it seeks to extinguish the spark without waiting until it has enkindled the flame or blazed into the conflagration.

. . . And the general statement in the *Schenck Case* that the "question in every case is whether the words are used in such circumstances and are of such a nature as to create a clear and present danger" . . . has no application to [cases] like the present, where the legislative body itself has previously determined the danger of substantive evil arising from utterances of a specified character.[46]

At least in cases of very grave hazards, such as the risk of revolution, the legislature need not wait until the harm itself was imminent—and remedy impossible—but could act whenever the *risk* of harm was clearly present.[47]

When *Gitlow* was decided, in 1925, Holmes was eighty-four years old. More than forty years before, he himself had called attention to the fundamentally legislative character of privileges and had repeatedly counseled deference to the legislature on such questions of policy. He agreed that the fundamental principles of free speech taken from the evolving common law were incorporated in both the First Amendment and the due process clause of the Fourteenth. He dissented from the majority's conclusion as to what those principles required, but he had no adequate response to Sanford's argument and was reduced to reiterating—in moving, memorable language to be sure—his doctrine of clear and present danger.[48]

As to the external standard submitted to the jury in this case, which allowed it to find that the language of the publication considered alone was an "incitement," Holmes had only his famous but unhelpful dictum, "[E]very idea is an incitement."[49] But surely some forms of expressions were greater incitements than others, and Holmes was a lifelong enemy of the argument, "Where will you draw the line?"[50] He insisted without explanation that the only permissible way of distinguishing true incitements to crime from other expressions of ideas was to consider the circumstances of the particular case in isolation. "[W]hatever may be thought of the redundant discourse before us it had no chance of starting a present conflagration."[51] If the whole category of expression was dangerous—well, that was the sort of danger the First Amendment required us to tolerate. "If in the long run the beliefs expressed in proletarian dictatorship are destined to be accepted by the dominant forces of the community, the only meaning of free speech is that they should be given their chance and have their way."[52]

This was nobly and memorably said. But Holmes neither addressed nor answered the argument that the legislature had the power to identify categories of peculiarly hazardous forms of speech that threatened to cause, not peaceful political change, but crime.

4.1.2 The Case Study—Brandeis's Role. Two years later, in *Whitney v. California*,[53] Justice Brandeis attempted a different form of reply to Sanford. Whitney had been convicted of violating the California Criminal Syndicalism Act, which was closely

similar to New York's Criminal Anarchy statute. The opinion for the majority upholding the conviction was again written by Justice Sanford. He repeated the argument that speech that fell within a reasonable legislative category could be
punished in and of itself, with no showing of clear and present danger in the circumstances.[54]

There had been evidence, on which the conviction might have rested, that activities of the Communist Labor party posed a danger of violence, and Whitney failed
to argue that her own activities in themselves did not pose a clear and present danger. Brandeis and Holmes concurred in upholding the conviction. But Justice Brandeis wrote a concurring opinion, in which Holmes joined, to answer Sanford's argument and to insist on the application of the *Schenck* doctrine.

> It is said to be the function of the legislature to determine whether at a particular time
> and under the particular circumstances the formation of, or assembly with, a society
> organized to advocate criminal syndicalism constitutes a clear and present danger of
> substantive evil; and that by enacting the law here in question the legislature of Califor-
> nia determined that question in the affirmative. Compare *Gitlow v. New York*.[55]

Brandeis said that the Court alone should determine whether the danger in the
circumstances would justify the curtailment of the defendant's right of free speech.
The basis of his argument was that freedom of expression had a fundamental value
which had not yet been mentioned in the opinions of the Court. True, the contest
of ideas was a method for shaping practical legislation, but this was not the only
value of free expression.

> Those who won our independence believed that the final end of the State was to make
> men free to develop their faculties . . . . They valued liberty both as an end and as a
> means. They believed liberty to be the secret of happiness and courage to be the secret
> of liberty. They believed that freedom to think as you will and to speak as you think
> are means indispensable to the discovery and spread of political truth . . . [but also]
> that the greatest menace to freedom is an inert people; that public discussion is a
> political duty; and that this should be a fundamental principle of the American gov-
> ernment.[56]

Freedom of speech was not only a means but an end in itself: it was a form of the
self-realization that was a fundamental purpose of the American state. This freedom
could not be restricted simply on ordinary legislative grounds; it could only be restricted in a particular case after weighing the individual liberty it was designed
to protect.[57]

This argument touched for the first time on the fundamental importance of the
individualized nature of the clear and present danger standard, and Holmes joined
in Brandeis's opinion—which he did not do lightly, even at this late stage in his
career.[58] But Brandeis's answer was not entirely Holmes's.

The question had come up between the two justices before. Holmes had relentlessly ridiculed the antitrust statutes, considered as economic measures, as both
foolish and futile; the Sherman Act, Holmes remarked, commanded everyone to
fight but forbade anyone from being victorious.[59]

Brandeis's answer had always been that the antitrust laws (which he had in part
written) were not solely economic measures; they were also political measures de-

signed to preserve the freedom and autonomy of a modern yeomanry—artisans, union members, and small business people—against the power of the trusts. Brandeis thought it was a part of the task of government to foster the virtues of citizens of the republic, a class of independent freeholders who might be poor but would stand up like men against the swollen institutions of big government and big business.[60]

Holmes thought Brandeis's vision of small-scale republican institutions attractive, but he did not agree that the Constitution had in it any program of social reform.[61] So the case can be made that Holmes did not entirely accept Brandeis's argument in *Whitney*. But Brandeis had at last touched the core of Holmes's decisions.

4.1.3 The Case Study—Sanford's Doctrine in Ascendancy. Holmes's views fell into neglect for a time. Sanford's doctrine was not simply a rationale to approve convictions; the Court applied it to invalidate state statutes that sought to enjoin or criminalize classes of language that were not incitements to crime,[62] and neither Holmes nor Brandeis dissented in these cases. In 1932, Holmes retired from the Court.

Taft's majority was gone by 1937, but their New Deal replacements gratefully inherited the strong, policy-oriented Court Taft had built. In opinions on the First Amendment they continued to use Sanford's categorization approach and occasionally used it affirmatively to protect at least some favored categories of speech.

A famous footnote in the 1938 case *United States v. Carolene Products*[63] hinted that statutes which affected access to the political process—including those limiting First Amendment rights—were subject to a higher standard of judicial review than other legislation.[64] By 1942, the Court, in *Chaplinsky v. New Hampshire*,[65] had erected an explicit scheme of categorization. Certain "well-defined and narrowly limited classes of speech" including "the lewd and obscene, the profane, the libelous, and the insulting or 'fighting' words" fell outside the protection of the First Amendment and so were within the legislative power of the states.[66] Advocacy of sedition, of course, also fell into an unprotected category.[67] As in *Abrams* and *Whitney*, the Court's role was limited in each case to seeing that the legislative category was reasonably drawn and that the defendant's speech fell within the statute.

Chaplinsky was also quickly understood to mean, on the other hand, that political speech and other expressions of opinions and ideas that were not direct incitements to wrongdoing fell into a specially protected category. The Court seemed finally to have abandoned the clear and present danger standard in favor of this categorization approach when, in *West Virginia Board of Education v. Barnette*, it struck down a state statute requiring school children to salute the flag, on the grounds that states could not regulate expressions of opinion and belief except when a "grave danger" required regulation of an otherwise protected category of expression.[68] In *Terminiello v. Chicago*, striking down as overbroad a disorderly conduct ordinance, the Court ruled that legislation could not infringe a protected category of speech except under a clear and present danger of "serious substantive evil" posed by speech of that kind.[69] The rule was thereafter said to be that a rarely met standard of "compelling state interest" must be met before punishment could be authorized for speech that fell within a protected category—apparently without regard for the danger posed in particular circumstances.[70]

The Court's rationale for the favored-category approach was never clearly spelled out. In *Barnette,* the majority did not reply to Felix Frankfurter's assertion that freedom of speech was on the same footing, in the Constitution, as the right to be compensated for property taken by the government.[71]

The Court nevertheless continued to give favored status to certain exercises of constitutional privilege. In *First National Bank of Boston v. Bellotti,*[72] the Court struck down a statute that limited the participation of banking corporations in a Massachusetts referendum. In doing so, it squarely held that expressions falling in the category of political speech—"indispensable to decision-making in a democracy"[73]—had near-absolute protection, regardless of their source and apparently without much regard to their consequences.

The Court did not say that the First Amendment gave favored status only to political speech, which would have been consistent with Brandeis's rationale,[74] but neither did it say this favored status for free speech was just part of a larger system of favored rights, as the *Carolene Products* footnote had hinted.

Whatever their source, the categories of expression that the Court established were based on external standards applied to the words or forms of expression themselves, and left little room for consideration of particular circumstances in each case. Congress and the state legislatures appeared to be free to apply strict liability for any use of expressions in the prohibited categories. In upholding a statute that punished "fighting words," in *Chaplinsky,* the Court said the category consisted of words that would have an inflammatory effect on the "man of average intelligence."[75] No evidence was required that the words were intended to cause a disturbance or that in the circumstances of the case they were likely to do so. When it came to defining the category "obscenity," the Court adopted an external standard based on community values.[76] Once again, no evidence of risk of harm in the particular circumstances was required. In *Bellotti,* the Court separated the speech from the speaker entirely and concluded that political speech—apparently any speech in connection with the governmental process—was protected in and of itself.[77] Justice Sanford's doctrine, coupled with a still somewhat mysterious favored status for certain categories of speech, was in the ascendant.

4.1.4 The Case Study—Clear and Present Danger Revived. The clear and present danger doctrine had its own line of development, however, in parallel with the system of legislative categories of protected speech, despite the apparent inconsistency of the two.

In the 1930s, the Hughes Court, while extending the categorical approach to speech, also confirmed Holmes's doctrine and repeated the formula words "clear and present danger." In *Herndon v. Lowry,*[78] reversing a conviction for criminal syndicalism, the Court held that the state statute violated the Constitution because it did not require adequate appraisal of the circumstances of an utterance and allowed criminal convictions of defendants who lacked the actual intent to cause violence.[79] *Schenck* was expressly relied upon during the Second World War in *Hartzel v. United States,*[80] which reversed a conviction under the Espionage Act of 1917 for causing insubordination in the military. The Court applied to the facts of the case both an external standard and a statutory requirement of subjective intent.[81]

The most spectacular and controversial revival of Holmes's doctrine occurred in

1951, however, in *Dennis v. United States*,[82] affirming the conviction of the leaders of the American Communist party for violations of the Smith Act,[83] a federal statute patterned after the state laws in *Whitney* and *Gilbert* forbidding the organizing of a conspiracy and the advocacy of revolution. Although no opinion commanded a majority of the Court in that case, all the justices except Frankfurter and Black assumed that the outcome depended upon whether the defendants' conduct in the circumstances posed a clear and present danger of some harm that Congress had power to prohibit. Chief Justice Vinson, with whom three other justices joined, said that the convictions could be affirmed on Holmes's original understanding of the standard in *Schenck*.[84]

Specific intent was taken as proved, since the defendants were the leaders of the Communist party and their actual intent to carry out its expressed purposes by organizing the party and advocating its aims was not seriously at issue. The difficulty in the case concerned the external branch of the standard—there was no evidence in the trial record that the violent revolution which the Communist leaders advocated and presumably desired was at all likely to occur.[85]

In addressing this point, the chief justice adopted reasoning that had first turned up in Holmes's Massachusetts criminal attempt cases:[86] the serious nature of the harm that was feared compensated for the smallness of the probability that it would occur in the near future. In cases where violent insurrection was threatened, Vinson held, the government was not required to wait until the event was upon it but could act as soon as a significant *risk*—in the form of a well-organized and active conspiracy—was clear and present.[87]

There was little evidence in the trial record of immediate danger posed by the Communist party's activities; the government, however, had proven to a jury's satisfaction that the party was a well-organized conspiracy whose plan was to act when the circumstances should be propitious, and that it therefore posed an unacceptable risk of grave harm.[88]

It would seem, therefore, that in *Dennis* the Court reaffirmed Holmes's doctrine, requiring proof of a clear and present danger posed by the particular acts of the defendants and the specific intent to cause the harm that was threatened. The plurality added the gloss that the magnitude of the harm might be used to balance the probability of its coming to pass. As Professor Currie noted, "[C]lear and present danger had become the test of convictions even under statutes specifically directed to subversive speech."[89] And as Yosal Rogat pointed out, by "modifying" the standard of clear and present danger in accordance with Learned Hand's opinion in the court below, the Court had "reconstituted its original elements."[90]

Six years later, the Court reaffirmed these aspects of the reasoning of *Dennis* in *Yates v. United States*,[91] reversing the convictions of lower-echelon Communist party functionaries. In *Yates*, the charge of organizing a conspiracy was barred by the statute of limitations[92] and the Court was obliged to deal with the purported crime of advocacy alone. Justice Harlan's opinion for the Court took specific intent as proven, and the only remaining question was whether the defendants themselves had contributed culpably to the risk posed by the party. But the jury had been asked to find only that the defendants advocated revolution, not that their advocacy had added to the risk of resulting wrongdoing. The Court accordingly reversed the convictions, relying in part on *Schenck*,[93] and said that it must be proven the individual defendants had advocated action in a manner that might have brought it about, and had not merely preached belief in a doctrine.[94] Expressly reaffirming *Schenck* and *Dennis,* the Court required the lower courts to consider the danger posed in the circumstances by the defendants' overt acts in furtherance of the conspiracy.[95]

The Supreme Court reaffirmed this approach in 1969, in *Brandenburg v. Ohio*,[96] when it expressly overruled the majority holding in *Whitney v. California*,[97] while citing and reaffirming *Dennis*.[98] One could not ask for a clearer rejection of Sanford's legislative-category approach and a clearer adoption of Holmes's common-law approach. The heated dissent by Justice Douglas in *Brandenburg,* vigorously denying that the Court was thereby also adopting clear and present danger, rather confirms this impression than otherwise.

In *Brandenburg,* the Court restated the rule of *Dennis* and *Yates,* which to an innocent eye is also the rule of *Schenck,* of Holmes's dissent in *Abrams,* and of Brandeis's concurrence in *Whitney:*

> These later decisions have fashioned the principle that the constitutional guarantees of free speech and free press do not permit a State to forbid or proscribe advocacy of the use of force or of law violation except where such advocacy is directed to inciting or producing imminent lawless action and is likely to produce such action.[99]

That is, a state may not proscribe a category of speech as such but may punish speech of a particular kind only where it poses a specific threat. The words "directed to" clearly seem in this context to mean "aimed at" or "actually intended," and so understood this was the standard announced by Holmes in 1919 and revived in *Dennis*.[100]

Finally, in 1978, a unanimous Court calmly restated "Mr. Justice Holmes's test," giving it as it had been applied in *Dennis:* "Properly applied, the test requires a court to make its own inquiry into the imminence and magnitude of the danger said to flow from the particular utterance and then to balance the character of the evil, as well as its likelihood, against the need for free and unfettered expression."[101]

Chief Justice Burger's opinion went on to demonstrate at some length the proposition that, "before a state may punish expression, it must prove by 'actual facts' the existence of a clear and present danger."[102] The court must "go behind the legislative determination and examine for itself the particular utteranc[e] here in question and the circumstances of [its] publication."[103] If there is anything of the categorization approach still here, it is difficult to detect. But in its careful restatement of the standard, the Court failed to mention the defendant's intent.

In short, Holmes's standard, so far as it was firmly tied to the particular circumstances of the case, seemed to have prevailed. The Burger Court, at least, seemed to feel that the link to the particular circumstances of the case was decisive; perhaps specific intent was only one aspect or indicator of that more fundamental principle.

4.1.5 The Case Study—Justice Brennan Completes the Revival. It was Justice William O. Brennan who revived the importance of subjective intent; and then he too turned from this narrow issue to the more general principle of liability based on particular circumstances, in the context that gives meaning to a particular utterance. The landmarks, early and late in Justice Brennan's career, were *New York Times v. Sullivan*[104] and *Texas v. Johnson*.[105]

In *Sullivan*, the newspaper had carried an ad complaining of a police "wave of terror" against students who were conducting civil rights protests in Montgomery, Alabama. The county commissioner responsible for supervising the police sued for libel. The ad contained a number of admitted false statements, and an Alabama court awarded general and punitive damages.[106]

The Supreme Court reversed. Justice Brennan's opinion for the Court in some respects paralleled Holmes's opinions in *Abrams* and *Schenck*, and cited the gloss put on them by Justice Brandeis in *Whitney v. California*.[107]

Brennan's premise was that the people, not the government, were sovereign. The purpose of the First Amendment (made applicable to Alabama by the Fourteenth) was to ensure free and open criticism by the people of the government and its officials.[108]

This was a new rationale for the First Amendment. Holmes had imagined a battlefield or a marketplace, and Brandeis a solitary freeholder, master in his own house; but Brennan's vision was of a community of equals: a town meeting.[109]

The protection afforded by the First Amendment was not absolute, Brennan continued; there were many well-recognized exceptions. But the state could not take a case out of the protection of the Constitution just by putting a label on it. State charges of "libel" were no more insulated from constitutional restraint than claims of "insurrection," advocacy of unlawful acts, or contempts of court. Drawing the now-familiar analogy between liability for criticism of public officials and contempts of court that had originated in Holmes's opinions in contempt cases, Brennan said that "such repression can be justified, if at all, only by a clear and present danger of obstruction of justice" in the circumstances of the case itself.[110] The method of imposing strict liability for all speech that fell within a legislative category, in other words, was firmly rejected.[111]

A critical question in setting constitutional limits was the defendant's state of mind. Even false statements about public figures were privileged unless made with actual malice—knowledge of falsity or reckless disregard for the truth.[112]

The similarity to the clear and present danger standard is striking. Holmes probably would have accepted Brennan's formulation as consistent with the common law. Errors would not defeat the privilege accorded to the press at common law so long as a publication was made in good faith; but actual malice—in the sense of a knowingly uttering a falsehood for the purpose of doing harm—would overcome the privilege.[113]

Justice Brennan did not explicitly rest the requirement of actual malice on the common law. He did cite the general trend of state libel law, without explaining its relevance;[114] but later, he sharply distinguished the constitutional requirement of "actual malice" from a supposed common-law "malice," mere spite or ill will.[115] But his doctrine was substantially the same as Holmes's common law.

Which is not meant to suggest that Holmes necessarily anticipated the holding of *New York Times v. Sullivan* or that Justice Brennan was simply following Holmes's reasoning. But it is striking that the two justices, beginning from such different places, should have arrived at results that differed so little.

The parallels in *Texas v. Johnson,* the flag-burning case, were also marked. When this case came to the Court, in 1989, Justice Brennan, writing for the majority, adopted the *Schenck* analysis.[116] Protestors had burned an American flag and were convicted of violating a Texas statute that prohibited desecration of a "venerated object."[117] The protest occurred during the Republican National Convention in 1984. Republican television advertising had relied heavily on images of the flag. The protestors, by publicly burning a flag, forcefully expressed their dislike for the message of the Republican campaign, the Reagan administration, and the Republican party's supposed corporate backers, and secured extensive free television coverage for their countermessage.

Writing for a bare majority and without referring expressly to *Schenck,* Brennan said that flag burning, although a form of expression, was not necessarily protected under the Fourteenth and First Amendments. In some circumstances Texas might punish flag burning—if the burning threatened to trigger "imminent" disorder, for instance.[118] No such harms were threatened in this case, however, and the prosecution could not be sustained. Rather, Justice Brennan concluded, the facts were very like the situation in *Abrams:* the protestors, whatever their intent, could not have achieved the kind of harm that the government had a right to forbid.[119]

4.1.6 The Case Study—Why Did Holmes's Doctrine Persist? These seventy years of development of the "clear and present danger" concept in the Supreme Court suggest a number of things. One curious point is that, while the Court seemed to recur to the clear and present danger doctrine, it never repeated Holmes's own rationale. Recall there were two strands of Holmes's thought. First, there was Holmes's theory of the social policy on which he believed the privilege accorded to free speech to be based. Second, there was the justification Holmes gave for restraints on the privilege.

As to the first, Holmes's theory of the First Amendment was that among the "relatively fundamental" principles of the common law, embedded in the evolving Constitution, were freedom of speech and freedom of the press. It was Holmes's conviction that legal protection for individual freedom was not based upon supralegal rights of man, but was logically and historically derived from the self-restraint of the governing power. Self-restraint, Holmes believed, could be based only on self-interest; the relentless operation of natural selection would extinguish any other motive.

But on grounds of self-interest alone, the governing power ought not to allow experiments with ideas and laws designed and intended to ensure its destruction. From the perspective of the governing power's self-interest, there should never be freedom for the thought we hate, for the opinion that is fraught with death. Government is not a chess game that one resigns without playing out the final moves. Holmes believed that peaceful competition would prepare the nation for international conflict, but this was not a reason for the government to capitulate without a struggle.

This, indeed, has always been the difficult question about free speech. Holmes's contemporaries on the Court, more consistent Darwinists than he, accepted the government's argument in *Abrams*, that the State had a right—even a duty—to ensure its own survival by repressing expressions of dangerous ideas.

Holmes, as we have seen, was perfectly aware of the difficulty. He felt that his own sense of duty, and the duties of his class, often called for self-sacrifice. His definition of a gentleman was someone who would die for a point of honor[120] or for a feather.[121] The willingness of the soldier to die, and of the scholar, scientist, and judge to sacrifice themselves to truth, Holmes believed, must have an evolutionary basis. As we have seen, he compared these instincts with the behavior of the grub, which prepared a chamber for the winged thing that it was to be.[122] Evolution, Holmes came to believe, had purposes beyond the merely human, and the instinct of self-sacrifice somehow played its part in the larger design of the cosmos; but a soldier's duty was to do and die, without understanding the plan of battle.[123]

This philosophy Holmes called "mystical materialism"; to an observer who does not share his faith, Holmes's mysticism looks to be just his recognition of a dilemma in his thought and an expression of trust that the logical difficulty doesn't matter.

There is a similar problem in the second strand of Holmes's thinking, his explanation for the limitations placed on free speech and all other rights. In *The Common Law*, Holmes had argued that privileges to do harm were extended for the sake of the social benefit of the behavior that was thereby encouraged. Competition in the marketplace was privileged even when it was carried on maliciously and for the sake of causing damage. In a zero-sum world, the injury to the loser is as much the object of competition as the benefit to the winner.

Later in life, however, he changed his mind about this and after a decade as a judge began to accept the reality behind the language of "actual malice": a privilege would be withdrawn if it were used for a malicious motive.[124]

Holmes was careful to find an instrumental rather than a moral justification for this concern with subjective motive, and so preserved the overall framework of his philosophy. He said the common law had judged the risk of harm from malicious motives to tip the balance of social advantage back against the privilege. "It seems to me hard," Holmes said, "for the law to recognize a privilege to induce unlawful conduct." Hard, indeed, but was the difficulty really a practical one? Judges often held that even lives might be sacrificed in the competition of the marketplace.[125] Indeed, tort law in Holmes's day seemed to be built around just this principle.[126] Why then should not the law accept the added increment of harm, if such there was, that came with more fierce competition, or even a malicious pleasure in victory? Were the judges' unconscious judgments of empirical advantage really so finely drawn?

Holmes's insistence that actual intent or malice would always defeat a privilege separated him from his own Court. It was at the heart, as we have seen, of what was distinctive in his approach; and once again we find difficulties as we approach the heart of Holmes's theory.

It seems to me that the difficulties on both lines of Holmes's thought were related and that he answered them in the same way, and it is this reply that begins to explain the durability of his judgments. Holmes's answer was given in the Massachusetts labor cases and in his other writings on the judge's role: the true justification for the freedom accorded to ideas lay in the judge's duty to deal fairly with the parties before him.

Freedom of speech was judge-made law. There were no statutes encouraging attacks on the government, no federal agencies devoted to protecting unpopular ideas. And Holmes was a judge above all. When the freedom of speech cases were decided, he had been on the bench for nearly forty years. He had spent those years subordinating himself to his task. The judge's devotion to fairness was something fundamental to Holmes, an instinct to be accepted like the other data of natural history. Whatever he might have thought or said about the legislative policy that lay behind the common law, in the end he could do no other than to perform his fundamental function as a judge, to decide each case fairly—without regard to his own interests—whatever the ultimate consequences might be.

If freedom of speech rested on the duty of the judge to deal fairly, then it was easier to see why the privilege was particularly important in cases where the defendant's beliefs were freighted with death. It was then that the judge's sense of honor and duty was called upon. Frank Foster's plea for fair treatment for trade unions counted most with Holmes, counted more than all the Spencers and Darwins in the world. This is why Holmes's words are so powerful; we see looming behind them, overshadowing all calculations of self-interest, a man who was prepared to die for freedom of speech, not because of its practical importance, but because that was his duty.

One can see, if freedom of speech is based on fairness, why the privilege would be destroyed by bad intent. The malicious party had sacrificed his claim to fair treatment; he came with unclean hands. And one can see why Holmes insisted on attention to the particular circumstances of the defendant's behavior. Twenty years as a judge in Massachusetts had taught him that fairness was not a question to be decided by abstract forms but only in the concrete circumstances of particular cases. Legislative categories in themselves necessarily disregarded fairness in some individual cases,[127] and the question was where the Constitution required one to draw the line. "Clear and present danger" was just one of many shorthand expressions for this central idea.

Holmes insisted not only that trials be conducted fairly but that politics be conducted fairly, in the sense that the power of the state to do violence should not intrude on peaceful debate. The government must not sweep the pieces from the board and decide public policy questions by force.

This was a position to which the Court regularly returned, and it shows that Holmes's greatness was also in a sense a judge's narrowness, his unwillingness to adopt exclusively legislative considerations or to adopt the attitude of the executive.[128] To Holmes, law was what judges decided and the rule of law meant a system of peaceful debate ultimately regulated by judges. Anyone who violated the rules of honest discourse for the purpose of doing harm could be punished as a lawbreaker; but the expression of ideas as such could not be punished, except in the most extraordinary circumstances.

This may not be the only correct view of freedom of speech. But it is a uniquely judicial view; it reflects the long tradition of the common law in a practical way. The question Holmes asked was whether a particular person should be punished, and the answer was tailored to the circumstances of his or her case.

This study of the free-speech cases has shown that the actual influence of Holmes's opinions is difficult to define. The further one enters into the details, the harder it is to say precisely how Holmes's judgments affected later decisions of the Court. His early dissents undoubtedly forced the Court to articulate an opposing principle that received eloquent statement in Sanford's opinions. The justices thereafter had available to them at all times two clearly expressed attitudes, the legislative and the judicial, both of which had deep roots in precedent.

But Holmes's opinions did have a magnetic attraction for the justices. The case study shows this cannot be attributed solely to the force of his language (which is discussed in the next section), since the Court seemed to revive the substance of his doctrine even when it avoided his controversial language. It seems that, in 1919, in his freedom of speech decisions, Holmes touched on a fundamental attitude that judges may adopt in such cases, so that versions of his doctrine keep reappearing in the opinions of justices as different from him and from each other as Brandeis and Brennan.

A great judge, it appears, is one who touches on a fundamental insight to which later judges will recur, not necessarily for doctrine, but for reassurance.

4.2
HOLMES'S OPINIONS

However high the quality of Holmes's judgments, we should have known nothing about them if they had not been embedded in memorable opinions. In this sense, Holmes's place in history depends on his qualities as a writer of opinions.

4.2.1 Holmes's Literary Style. Indeed, it is sometimes said that Holmes's opinions are so often cited simply because they are well written. This is a somewhat belittling explanation. As a prose stylist, Holmes's accomplishment seems to me modest, hardly adequate to account for his reputation. Edmund Wilson in 1961 gave the judgment that the power of Holmes's opinions owes more to their implicit philosophy than to their prose style:

> The younger Holmes was not, like his father, a fluently felicitous writer; but his literary sense was developed in a remarkable, if limited way. . . . he developed for his occasional pieces, a literary style of his own which conforms to the same austere ideal as his professional legal papers. He worked very hard over writing, and he gave to these short pieces a crystalline form as hard and bright as Pater's flame. They are perfect, and they are undoubtedly enduring—since their value lies not merely in their style, by means of which he "makes every word tell": it is almost impossible for Holmes to touch upon any problem of legal interpretation or to compose a brief memorial for some old colleague of the Boston bench or bar without assigning it or him to a place in a larger scheme.
>
> It is Holmes's special distinction—which perhaps makes him unique among judges—that he never dissociates himself from the great world of thought and art, and that all his decisions are written with awareness of their wider implications and the

importance of their literary form. He was not merely a cultivated judge who enjoyed dipping into belles lettres or amusing himself with speculation: he was a real concentrator of thought who had specialized in the law but who was trying to determine man's place, to define his satisfactions and his duties, to try to understand what humanity is.[129]

Holmes's style is certainly worth attending to. He brought the precision of classical forms to the rhythms of American speech. Speaking of the "dirty business" of illegal wiretapping by government agents, for instance, Holmes said that evidence obtained by this means should not be allowed in court:

> If it [the Government] pays its officers for having got evidence by crime I do not see why it may not as well pay them for getting it in the same way, and I can attach no importance to protestations of disapproval if it knowingly accepts and pays and announces that in future it will pay for the fruits. We have to choose, and for my part I think it a less evil that some criminals should escape than that the Government should play an ignoble part.[130]

The precise contrast of verb tenses—"for having got . . . for getting," "pays . . . will pay"—combined with the informality of "dirty business," "I do not see," "it may as well," "I can attach no importance," "I think . . . "—makes for easy, personal, and frank talk of high precision, a style that is Holmes's own, a synthesis of table talk and the oral opinions of English judges. It is not an easy style, and Holmes's opinions, dense and aphoristic, are difficult to follow, but in their own way they are perfect.

To have an original style, and to write as well as Walter Pater, is something; no other American judge has merited appraisal by a critic of Wilson's stature, let alone merited ranking among even the minor Victorian writers. Still, as Wilson says, it is for the larger perspective his writings open, and not for his style, that we remember Holmes. This is as Holmes would have wished. As he wrote to a close friend in 1911, when he felt at the peak of his form:

> [T]he thing to aim at is to see and feel as much as one can the great forces behind every detail—a wavelet of the Atlantic Ocean is different from one of Buzzard's Bay. Therefore after a man has a working knowledge of his job—at least if he is a judge— I would advise him not to be eternally reading late cases but to let in the streams of philosophy, sociology, history, economics, etc. etc. I guess it tells. I was more pleased than I can say by a letter on my 70th birthday from our leading law writer quoting a French remark . . . and applying it to my decision—that he had one foot on the finite and the other on the infinite. It pleased me that anyone should see my intent—to look at the particular in the light of the universal.[131]

4.2.2 Holmes's Opinions as an Art Form. When people praise Holmes's style, I think they sometimes have a quite different thing than style in mind. Holmes's medium was not really English prose; it was legal thought itself. Holmes's opinions, with their special form and style, were contrived to present with special force Holmes's own thought, alive and wriggling.

Holmes conceived of an opinion, not as a printed document, but as talk delivered from the bench. He paid careful attention both to the writing and to his style of delivery, to ensure their impact. When Justice Sanford submitted one of his first opinions for approval, Holmes, with the freedom of an elder, gave him some advice: "Non obstant the effective and powerful example of Brandeis to the contrary I don't think opinions should be written in the form of essays with notes—they are theoretically spoken."[132]

The model for this form was the English judge, a gentleman rather than a professional. "I don't believe in the long opinions which have been almost the rule here [on the Supreme Court]. I think that to state the case shortly and the ground of decision as concisely and delicately as you can is the real way. That is the English fashion and I think it civilized."[133]

Holmes's opinions accordingly were brief and well written enough to be read aloud, and they were written so quickly, and with so little revision, as to seem, like the opinions of English judges, to have been extemporized from the bench. They were fundamentally *dramatic;* their impact was almost physical. This was the quality for which Holmes strove in all his opinions but often was able to achieve only in dissent. In a letter to Alice Stopford Green, the historian, Holmes talked about this aspect of his writing:

> [I have finished] two dissents that I wrote with gaiety of heart, in a railroad and a telegraph case[134] that I was pleased to have decided as they were, but in which I couldn't swallow the pretense at logic of Harlan and White. If they'd just brusqué the thing and said: Logic for law-school—this is business—and when a railroad has a right to come into a state it comes in with all its roots, I probably should have grinned and shut up. My form of expression evidently is modelled on what I heard an actress saying—that if she should recommend a play to Mr. Frohman he would read it politely and return it and say "That is literachoor—what we want is drayma."[135]

Holmes's opinions often swept his colleagues into agreement, and they continue to carry us along. His opinions seem to defy logical analysis; they move us at quite another level of thought and feeling. They convey, not just Holmes's ideas, but the force of his personality.

The ideas and the man himself were fused by the same principle that had led him to his form of expression from the outset: his ideas and attitudes were those of a gentleman, what we should now call an aristocrat. There is nothing so attractive to Americans, so in keeping with our picture of ourselves, as a native aristocrat, a Yankee from Olympus, in Elizabeth Sargent's inspired image. The late George Olshausen, in a perceptive article, called Holmes's appeal that of a "medieval knight," and used de Tocqueville's famous account of the aristocratic virtues to describe him: "[F]eudal honor . . . imperiously commanded men to subdue themselves; it decreed forgetfulness of self. It prescribed neither humanity nor gentleness. . . . Foremost among virtues the nobles of the Middle Ages put military valor. . . . the aristocracy dealt in the grand manner with abstract ideas and theories."[136]

But one more element must be mentioned. Holmes was no mere clotheshorse for traditional forms; he was an intensely energetic, passionate man who, like other popular figures—one thinks of Presidents Kennedy and Reagan in their different ways—managed to convey the ambition, optimism, and energy of youth. Richard

Rovere summed it up nicely: "The chivalrous assumptions, the pleasure he took in the stuff of life, and the reaching for high C combined to give us a great jurist, a great sage, and a gay and gallant and cheerful companion."[137] This is the personality Holmes constructed for himself and managed to put right through his opinions; the persona of a young chevalier. His ideas were embodied in this persona as much as in the specific words.

Which is not to say that the opinions are not also logical; with patience and knowledge of the context one can always parse the opinions out in logical sequence. But it is not the logic that persuades; it is the fundamental insight transmitted in dramatic form.

Holmes, in other words, was an artist of a high order. The careful, logical arguments were there in the underpainting, as it were; in the surface they were reduced to essentials. As he described his own work:

> Did I ever tell you of Corot—the painter—that I heard once that he began as most careful draughtsman working out every detail and came to his magisterial summaries at the end? I have thought of that in writing opinions latterly. Whether the brethren like it I don't know. Of course—the eternal effort of art even the art of writing legal decisions is to omit all but the essentials—'The point of contact' is the formula. The place where the boy got his fingers pinched—the rest of the machinery doesn't matter. So the Jap. master puts five dots for a hand—knowing they are in the right place.[138]

His opinions indeed remind one of the paintings of Matisse or the poems of Wallace Stevens. They are often criticized for undue brevity, for lack of the stepwise exposition one finds in ordinary opinions. But Holmes's opinions transmit conviction as by an electric current. One might apply to Holmes what Matisse said of his own work: "When a master works simply, with broad relationships—it is because his feeling rejects complicated things that do not come to him directly and do not go directly to the feelings of others. What is sometimes mistaken for a defect, for a lack, thus becomes an essential quality."[139]

Holmes is not important to us now as a great originator of ideas but because he expressed the spirit of his time in vivid form: in a country that generally does not honor poets and philosophers, Holmes is our Tennyson, our Hugo, our Gorky, and our Schopenhauer. There is something great in this spirit that we fear to lose.

4.3
HOLMES'S THOUGHT

A great work of art harmonizes disparate, even contradictory, elements. But we demand something more of law than that it be high art; and so we return to the seeming contradictions in Holmes's thought.

4.3.1 Philosophy. In 1867, wrangling with William James, Holmes took the materialist position he had formulated for himself while in winter quarters with the Union Army in 1863–64; James, who had stayed at home during the war, was at the time a doubting idealist. (There was always a hint of condescension to weakness in Holmes's letters and a certain defensiveness in James's.) Holmes tended to lump together William James's idealism and William's father Henry James, Sr.'s religion so that, when Holmes had difficulty answering one of William's objections to materialism, he said, "What a passion your father has in writing and talking his religion! Almost he persuadeth me to be a Swedenborgian, but I can't go it so far—will see whether the other scheme [materialism] busts up first, I think."[140]

As we saw in chapter 3, the other scheme never did bust up. Holmes came to think that materialism could encompass all of the phenomena of life and thought. One could not speak of "brute" matter; "a certain complex of energies can wag its tail and another can make syllogisms."[141]

James, on the other hand, eventually abandoned idealism for a new doctrine, pragmatism, his effort to get beyond the terms of the debate with Holmes on the one side and his father on the other. But Holmes never saw anything more in pragmatism than the old weakness for subjectivity he despised.

> I now see . . . that the aim and the end of the whole business [James's pragmatism] is religious. . . . just as an automatic sweetheart wouldn't work (the illustration is his) an automatic universe won't—or not so well as one that has a warm God behind it, that loves and admires us. But for that conclusion I don't think we would ever have heard from him on the subject, taking that as the significance of the whole business I make it my bow.[142]

William James's pragmatism might have been an effort to reconcile himself to his father's religion without surrendering to it. Be that as it may, Holmes was very plain about his own position. He was a realist, equally opposed to James's early idealism and James's later effort through pragmatism to get above the debate.

Richard Rorty suggests that the terms of the philosophical discussion in English-speaking countries have not much changed since Holmes and William James debated: "Philosophers in the English-speaking world seem fated to end the century discussing the same topic—realism—which they were discussing in 1900. In that year, the opposite of realism was still idealism. But by now language has replaced mind as that which, supposedly, stands over and against 'reality.'"[143]

Holmes is on the realist side of the debate, and so we should probably assess him in relation to modern antirealism and pragmatism. But first, we must rescue Holmes from the embrace of the pragmatists.

Despite Holmes's own evident realism, which he endlessly insisted upon, and his contempt for William James's pragmatism, there has been a persistent effort to portray Holmes himself as a pragmatist.

4.3.2 Pragmatism and Liberalism. There were two sources of the mistaken effort to portray Holmes as a philosophic pragmatist. The first was a simple misunderstanding about his place in the development of law.

Although the English sociologists of law count Holmes among their predecessors, he is usually treated as a purely American figure. In our own provincial history the most common judgment is that he was one of the leaders of the supposed "revolt against formalism"—a shift from the systematic natural law of the eighteenth century to the empirical science of the twentieth.

Holmes himself viewed the law in which he was educated as unsystematic and informal to the last degree. Blackstone had long been forgotten, and the reality of law in the mid-nineteenth century was that it was a trade. Even the best of the scholarly judges had little interest in systematic thought. Holmes's predecessor on the Supreme Court, Horace Gray, was in his day considered one of the great judges. Yet here is Mark Howe's description, from Holmes's perspective:

> In cast of mind he was not unlike Chancellor Kent and Joseph Story, learned, in the traditional fashion of lawyers, clearheaded, after the manner of able judges, he was a man of considerable force and capacity. Yet his most ardent admirers admitted that his intelligence was not philosophical and that his inclination to write opinions of inordinate length deprived them of any semblance of artistry.[144]

The opinions of the courts lacked formality of thought or expression. The law itself was a miscellaneous collection of unrelated details, justified by judges and commentators alike as expressing an unsystematic sense of natural justice. In American legal history, Holmes would be more properly described as one who assisted in the rise of formalism in judicial opinions, an insistence on neutral principles and systematic thought.

The confusion seems to have begun with Holmes's famous attack on "logic": "The life of the law has not been logic, it has been experience."

Chancellor Kent's *Commentaries* (chap. 7) and the state court cases of the 1850s and 1860s, which provided Holmes's education in the common law were not especially logical in the sense of being systematic or deductive systems. While there was a good deal of talk about natural law and the principles of justice in it, this law was a mass of unrelated details, and rested on nothing more formal than common sense and familiar custom. Blackstone's quasi-scientific systematization of the common law had long since vanished from American awareness; one rarely saw even a reference to Blackstone in Holmes's day, unless it was an attack. When Holmes launched his famous aphorism, he was criticizing English and German commentaries (and Dean C. C. Langdell of the Harvard Law School), not American law. More importantly, he was criticizing the judges' habit of rationalization, of finding seemingly logical but unsystematic reasons for rules whose true explanation was historical and legislative.

In 1944, Felix Frankfurter's brief biography of Holmes was published in the *Dictionary of National Biography,* and for fifteen years this remained the only authoritative account of Holmes's early work. Frankfurter said of Holmes's writings that Holmes rejected "a view of the law which regarded it as a merely logical unfolding."[145] Frankfurter's statement is easily misunderstood. Catherine Drinker Bowen in her fictionalized group biography of Holmes and his family, also published in 1944, gave a similar account, emphasizing the clash of progressive, modern social criticism with the supposed dry logic of the past.[146]

It was therefore natural enough that, when Morton White published *Social Thought in America: The Revolt against Formalism* in 1947, Holmes appeared as a major protagonist, somewhat improbably linked with Thorstein Veblen in a supposed attack on classical economics and formal systems of legal thought. Works based on secondary materials continue to repeat this judgment.[147] Holmes is imagined in these works to be a sort of Woodrow Wilson of the law, smashing the highly formal-

ized study of written constitutions and natural law, and replacing it with an empirical, fundamentally progressive study of social policy.

This confusion was nourished by a parallel development, what one must call a
conscious effort to portray Holmes as a political liberal. The keynote was struck by
John Dewey, in a remarkable article, "Justice Holmes and the Liberal Mind,"[148] in
which Dewey seemingly played on the ambiguity of the word "liberal" to hint that
Holmes's tolerance for intellectual experiments was actually political liberalism, or
at least a sanction for it. This article was reprinted in the April, 1931, issue of the
Harvard Law Review largely given over to a ninetieth-birthday celebration for Justice
Holmes, in which Cardozo and Frankfurter also referred to Holmes as a "liberal."
Frankfurter went to some trouble in his article to portray Holmes as a pragmatist,
quoting from then-unpublished papers of pragmatist Charles S. Peirce and listing
Holmes's publications after 1870, but omitting the earlier works, and so conveying
the impression that Holmes's first original work was influenced by William James
and Charles Peirce in the early 1870s.[149]

Felix Frankfurter after Holmes's death continued the effort to portray Holmes
as a pragmatic liberal. In 1938, then-Professor Frankfurter gave a series of public
lectures on Holmes at Harvard and published them as a slim book.[150] Frankfurter,
shortly to join the Supreme Court himself, combined great forensic abilities and
high stature as a legal scholar with a well-known twenty-year intimate friendship
with Holmes. Frankfurter's word was taken as authoritative. In his lectures, he
gave a selective view of Holmes; he portrayed Holmes's tenure as a period of class
struggle in which the Court principally regulated the relations of government and
business. He barely mentioned any of Holmes's opinions for the Court and dwelt
at length on Holmes's dissents in cases where the majority had struck down progressive legislation. He skipped past Holmes's own conservative views on politics and
economics,[151] hinted heavily that Holmes favored the "redistribution of wealth,"
and concluded that in 1937, when the Court began upholding New Deal legislation
more regularly, "the old views of Mr. Justice Holmes began to be the new Constitutional direction of the Court."[152]

In 1941, with the Court now dominated by Roosevelt appointees, Robert H. Jackson wrote, "Justices such as Holmes and Brandeis have not only furnished the highest expression but they have been the very source and the intellectual leaders of
recent liberalism in the United States."[153]

The picture of Holmes as a politically liberal pragmatist, hinted at by Frankfurter
and Jackson, was drawn in full colors by Philip P. Weiner, whose well-received 1949
book *Evolution and the Founders of Pragmatism* devoted a chapter to Holmes, whom
Weiner described as one of the founders of philosophic pragmatism. He said that
Holmes's "liberal hope for reform" made him a sort of godfather to the New Deal.
This portrait was again reinforced by Catherine Drinker Bowen's best-selling
book,[154] in which she simply invented conversations between Holmes and the actual
founders of pragmatism, Charles Peirce and William James, complete with direct
quotes.[155]

The political effort to portray Holmes as a pragmatic liberal, in the sense of a
social democrat, collapsed in the 1940s. A backlash from liberals themselves began
soon after the first volumes of Holmes's letters were published, in 1943, in which

Holmes's true views of politics and economics began to appear. Another heavy blow was dealt in 1951 by the Supreme Court's decision in *Dennis v. United States*[156] affirming the convictions of the leaders of the Communist party of the United States and seeming to ratify the Red Scare of the 1940s and 1950s with all its excesses. As we have seen, the Court relied on Holmes's opinion in *Schenck v. United States*.[157] It became increasingly difficult to carry Holmes at the head of the New Deal parade.

Holmes's liberal credentials were finally withdrawn, as it were, by Samuel Konefsky, in an influential book, *The Legacy of Holmes and Brandeis,* published in 1956. Konefsky took it for granted that Holmes and Brandeis were responsible for the new thinking in the Supreme Court after 1937, "the Constitutional ideology to which the Supreme Court as reorganized by Franklin D. Roosevelt was heir."[158]

But, Konefsky easily showed, Holmes's private views were very much at odds with the policies of the New Deal and Holmes's influence on the later Court, as in the First Amendment cases, at times was mediated by Brandeis's opinions. Konefsky argued that Holmes had no real ideas of his own, only unreflective prejudices— Holmes's views on economics were just unexamined prejudices carried forward from his youth; "clear and present danger" was just a casual remark, a rationalization to uphold criminal convictions, that did not become a rationale for protecting freedom of speech until Brandeis lent his "powerful support."[159]

There was a heavy air of suggestion about the study, a suggestion that Brandeis was the true source of the ideas and the dissents from which Frankfurter had fashioned his portrait of Holmes.[160]

The criticism of Holmes continued. Judge Learned Hand, who gave the Holmes Lectures at Harvard in 1958,[161] devoted part of one lecture to attacking Holmes's version of clear and present danger, comparing it unfavorably with his own objective test of incitement.[162] Justice William O. Douglas, in a separate opinion, objecting to the majority's revival of clear and present danger, in *Brandenburg v. Ohio,* approvingly cited Hand's lectures as authority for the violent attack on Holmes's standard that has continued to this day.[163]

The effort to make Holmes a pragmatic liberal therefore seems to have self-destructed, the original puffery and the later revisionism having pretty well canceled each other out.

There has been a more authentic effort in recent years, without any apparent political agenda, to show that Holmes's jurisprudence rather than his overall philosophy is consistent with some forms of pragmatism. The emphasis of this effort is on Holmes's idea that law is an instrument of social purposes, that lawyers like scientists predict behavior (of judges), and on Holmes's insistence that judges necessarily look outside the law itself for useful grounds of decision. These aspects of Holmes's thought are certainly consistent with some forms of pragmatism, and one can hardly argue with the proposition that Holmes is one of the founders of legal pragmatism in this limited sense.[164]

Henry Steele Commager in *The American Mind* gave a very clear account of Holmes's approval of legal "pragmatism," in the sense of social experimentation, emphasizing that Holmes's personal philosophy was quite different from the one he saw working itself out in the law.[165] Perry Miller and Edmund Wilson both categorized Holmes as one of those who introduced "scientific" or evolutionary thinking into what came to be called the social sciences; and this seems a fair enough appraisal, consistent with the view that Holmes fostered legal pragmatism.

Richard A. Posner also sees Holmes as a founder of modern legal pragmatism. By legal pragmatism, Judge Posner means "a future-oriented instrumentalism that tries to deploy thought as a weapon to enable more effective action,"[166] which is not unlike what Holmes said a judge went through when deciding a case. This milder, eclectic pragmatism has replaced notions of hard science, as something law can aspire to, in the thinking of those who believe that law is or should be an instrument of social purpose, and to this extent is in accord with Holmes's views and can legitimately claim him as a forbear.

But Holmes was not a philosophic pragmatist. The pragmatism he attributed to law was a product of social evolution, not a metaphysical necessity. Yet Thomas C. Grey in an important long article[167] has argued that Holmes's philosophy was like John Dewey's pragmatism. Grey's direct evidence consists principally of the qualities which Holmes attributed to the common law and some vague, if admiring, remarks Holmes made about Dewey's *Experience and Nature* after much prompting by mutual friends.[168]

But Grey makes an interesting argument. He notes the contradiction between Holmes's view that law was only an instrument of social policy and the uneconomic idealism that Holmes recommended in his addresses to young lawyers. Grey calls this a conflict between the "actor" and the "witness" in Holmes, echoing Rogat's criticism of Holmes as a "spectator."

Grey says that Holmes tried to reconcile these qualities—and ended with a weak anticipation of John Dewey's philosophy. And this may be so; it is a question of how one understands Dewey.[169]

Dewey, unlike more recent pragmatists, advanced a metaphysics in which there was a suggestion of objective reality in experience, and Holmes heard in this an echo of his old friend the cosmos. As Holmes wrote to Frederick Pollock,

> But although Dewey's book [*Experience and Nature*] is incredibly ill written, it seemed to me after several rereadings to have a feeling of intimacy with the inside of the cosmos that I found unequaled. So methought God would have spoken had He been inarticulate but keenly desirous to tell you how it was.[170]

To Holmes, as we have seen, the methods of natural science give us our only truthful knowledge and behind them we hear a hint of the ultimate. He seems to have seen similar views in Dewey's book. But Grey wants us to understand Dewey as he and Richard Rorty do, as denying to natural science any favored position and as rejecting its claim to have a preferred method for arriving at truth. Rorty puts the position this way:

> [P]ragmatists would like to drop the idea that human beings are responsible to a non-human power. We hope for a culture in which questions about the "objectivity of value" or the "rationality of science" would seem equally unintelligible. Pragmatists would like to replace the desire for objectivity—the desire to be in touch with a reality which is more than some community with which we identify ourselves—with the desire for solidarity with that community. They think that the habits of relying on persuasion rather than force, of respect for the opinions of colleagues, of curiosity and eagerness for

new data and ideas, are the *only* virtues which scientists have. They do not think that there is an intellectual virtue called 'rationality' over and above these moral virtues.[171]

There is nothing in Holmes's writings that supports such a view. The following is more characteristic: "When the . . . man said Europe has given us the steam engine, Asia every religion that ever commanded the reverence of mankind—I answered I bet on the steam engine. For the steam engine means science and science is the root from which comes the flower of our thought."[172] Taken overall, I cannot imagine a more direct and violent contrast than that between Holmes's philosophy of scientific realism, his utter acceptance of the nonhuman power of the material world, and Rorty's pragmatism, the gentle pragmatism Professor Grey has found in John Dewey. However one feels about this pragmatism, Holmes did not share it.

4.3.3 Holmes's Place in Intellectual History. Holmes, like Leslie Stephen, was a principal figure in the Victorian attempt to invent a rationalist morality, a scientific replacement for religion.[173]

Holmes believed that "science"—by which he meant inductive reasoning, as opposed to revelation—was the only route to truth. But Holmes's project, like Stephen's, was to find a scientific explanation for duty. In Holmes's earliest writings he said that was the task of his generation (5.5, 5.6), and he said later that his transition to adult thinking was marked by reading R. A. Vaughan's *Hours with the Mystics,* an evolutionary account of religion.[174] From the time of his Civil War notebooks, he believed that moral principles were only another aspect of the fundamental laws of the material world:

> Of course when I thought I was dying the reflection that the majority vote of the civilized world declared that with my opinions I was *en route* for Hell came up with painful distinctness—Perhaps the first impulse was tremulous—but then I said—by Jove, I die like a soldier anyhow—I was shot in the breast doing my duty up to the hub—afraid? No, I am proud—. . . . Then came in my Philosophy—I am to take a leap in the dark— but now as ever I believe that whatever shall happen is best—for it is in accordance with a general law—and *good & universal* (or *general law*) are synonymous terms in the universe.[175]

Emerson provided inspiration for this quest after the good and universal. Holmes's whole career of study of the common law, which he believed was the record of evolving morality, was a search for the underlying principles of history and hence of the good. Holmes was proudest of his thinking when it arrived at results substantially the same, he imagined, as "prevailing theological notions." He regularly described his own views as a sort of advanced religion,[176] and he admired the Japanese, in part, because he thought that Shinto and Bushido were moral codes, like his own, freed from belief in a personal god. He gave his eschatology in a memorial for his friend and mentor George O. Shattuck. In the memorial he also spoke of himself:

> Sooner or later the race of men will die; but we demand an eternal record. We have it. What we have done is woven forever into the great vibrating web of the world. The eye that can read the import of its motion can decipher the story of all our deeds, of

all our thoughts. To that eye I am content to leave the recognition and the memory of this great head and heart. (11.14)

This is the Calvinism of a rationalist, a sort of scientific Buddhism. Holmes felt that he had found fundamental principles that would explain and reconcile him to duty. Henry Adams, in his similar quest for the fundamental principles of human life, looked to physics for analogies and tried to work through a calculus of energies that would explain the pattern of history. Holmes, like Leslie Stephen, looked to evolution. Stephen had studied the history of philosophy itself, and the biographies of the great thinkers, in a vain search for the deeper principles of the universal. Holmes used the data of the law, the decisions of the judges, in the same way, to expose the evolution of language and thought. But unlike Adams or Stephen, Holmes felt that he had succeeded in finding principles that, if not ultimate, were true, and as nearly universal as the thought of his own time was capable of achieving.

Holmes, in short, because of the nature of his quest, was an important spokes-man for the realist side in the great philosophical debate of his age. He hoped that philosophical investigation would ultimately justify his faith in the material world and the purposes of the cosmos, but he tried to set aside his merely personal needs while the investigation was going on. He stuck as rigorously as possible to the evi-dence and tried to see arguments in a dry light. We accordingly can still find in Holmes's abstract thought the fundamental impulse of realist philosophy, the "hu-man need to stand outside all needs," the need for "transcendence" that Richard Rorty quite properly said was the enemy of pragmatism.[177] It was a chivalric quest that in itself, as Holmes was perfectly aware, represented a deep European tradition.

Holmes's philosophy required him to try to escape the limits of subjectivity, to escape the "illusion" of self, and to assume the perspective of the cosmos so far as possible. This pursuit involved him in the same problems and paradoxes as did his effort, as a judge, to stand outside the evolution of the law.

Let us examine this double perspective a little more closely. Holmes believed there were two sorts of duty: the duties imposed on everyone, even on the "bad man," by the power of the state; and the self-imposed duties of a gentleman. He did not like to use terms like "duty" in discussing law because he did not want to confuse these two senses of the word. (See "The Path of the Law," 10.9, where he recom-mended to his audience of presumed gentlemen the higher path of autonomous duty.)

When we put this division of duties in such a blunt way, we see that it correctly states Holmes's view, and at the same time we understand that he himself could not have spoken in the same terms. To a gentleman, personal morals, like money, were not to be spoken of, and it would hardly have been polite or tactful to contrast his own standards with those of the "crowd." The point had to be made gracefully, as it was in nearly every one of his speeches.

Addressing Harvard seniors, Holmes described the dominant forces in the com-munity of his day, the makers of law, and contrasted their code with the idealism of the gentleman:

The society for which many philanthropists, labor reformers, and men of fashion unite in longing is one in which they may be comfortable and may shine without much

trouble or any danger. . . Most of my hearers would rather that their daughters or
sisters should marry a son of one of the great rich families than a regular army officer,
were he as beautiful, brave, and gifted as Sir William Napier. . . .

Who is there who would not like to be thought a gentleman? Yet what has that name
been built on but the soldier's choice of honor rather than life? . . . who of us could
endure a world, although cut up into five-acre lots and having no man upon it who
was not well fed and well housed, without the divine folly of honor, without the senseless passion for knowledge out-reaching the flaming bounds of the possible, without
ideals the essence of which is that they never can be achieved? ("The Soldier's Faith,"
11.12)

Law was the expression of an evolving morality, imposed by the dominant forces
in society on all. The records of the law showed that this mass morality had pro-
gressed from such unconscious, subjective impulses as the territorial instinct and
the impulse to take revenge for injuries, to a more highly evolved, conscious instrumentalism that sought for the survival of "racial" values within the limits imposed
by precedent and enlightened sympathy. This evolutionist morality was different in
detail but not in spirit from the other scientific morality of Holmes's day, utilitarian-
ism, which also tried to discover the mechanism that had translated private self-
seeking into public codes of behavior.

The gentleman's duty evidently was of a higher order than the minimal standards
meant to apply to all. The gentleman's duty was to advance his ideals through
frankly uneconomic expenditures, to risk death or failure in warfare, science, art,
or jurisprudence. If the judge was a gentleman, he sat above the struggle for life,
setting aside his own loyalties, and helped in small ways to advance the purposes of
cosmic evolution. This self-sacrificing idealism was implanted by the evolutionary
process itself, of course, just as the humbler, prudential sort of duty had been, although Holmes could not divine its purpose.

To put these ideas in more modern terms, we can compare them to Michael
Oakeshott's, which are similar in some ways. Oakeshott also describes two distinct
moral systems, reflected in two distinct ideas of the state, each embedded in European language and thought. Modern European states resemble one of these forms,
which Oakeshott calls an "enterprise association." The enterprise association is a
voluntary association of persons who agree to submit themselves to the power of
the state. Its purpose is to achieve some common goal of the persons who form it.
In its British, and I suppose American, version it somewhat resembles a corporation
organized to exploit the natural resources within its territory for the common benefit of its members. The state as enterprise association educates and commands its
citizens to follow rules of behavior whose purpose is to attain their common goal.

The second idea of the state is the civic association. In Oakeshott's view it does
not now exist anywhere; it is an ideal based to some extent on qualities of the old
regimes. It too is a voluntary association. The persons who form a civic association,
however, do not agree to surrender their freedom. The purpose of this state is to
maintain a different sort of law, a set of rules that mediate the dealings among its
citizens in such a way as to resolve disputes and facilitate "conversation," the complex interaction of free persons, without depriving them of autonomy.

The two forms of association correspond to the two conflicting themes in
Holmes's writings. The enterprise association looks very much like Holmes's realm

of ordinary law, the society of prudent "bad men," and the instrumental rules through which enterprise associations exercise their power are like the instrumental common law that Holmes described. Oakeshott expressly criticizes Holmes's view that judges make law,[178] which I venture to say is an error on Oakeshott's part, as he seems to think that judges need do no more than interpret the words of a statute in a new setting. But with that qualification, which does not alter anything that is central to Oakeshott's ideas,[179] Holmes's view of the rules of behavior created by the common law appears to be Oakeshott's view of the enterprise association.

On the other hand, Holmes's fundamental principles of the federal Constitution are a set of essentially moral rules that require fair adjudication of disputes and that protect open discourse among free individuals. This looks remarkably like an example of Oakeshott's civic association, his idealized "rule of law."

Holmes's view of his own duty as a judge also is like Oakeshott's description of a judge in the idealized civic association, who resolves disputes in accordance with enacted law,[180] without regard to himself or the practical interests of the parties.[181]

In his most comprehensive presentation of these ideas,[182] Oakeshott repeatedly insists that the two systems are incompatible: membership in an enterprise association is inconsistent with membership in a civic association. The qualities which lead a person to join one association or the other, and the purposes of the two types of association, are incompatible. This may be so, but Oakeshott's earlier writings, which are more detailed in this area, hint at how the two systems might coexist, and indeed might depend on each other.

The most interesting for a student of Holmes is Oakeshott's account of Thomas Hobbes's writings.[183] The Leviathan is the prototypical enterprise association. People associate themselves out of weakness, to end the state of perpetual war and to achieve their common purposes. The association is prudent, and while it deprives citizens of the excitement of victory it provides the more moderate pleasures supplied by peace. Leviathan is based on "the morality of the tame man, the man who has settled for safety and has not need of nobility, generosity, magnanimity, or an endeavor for glory to move him to behave justly. And, in so far as this was Hobbes's view, he has been recognized as the philosopher of a so-called 'bourgeois' morality."[184] This is very much like Holmes's description of bourgeois society, which he contrasted with the gentleman's idealism, in "The Soldier's Faith" (11.12), quoted above. Oakeshott too goes on to contrast the morality of the tame man to an "aristocratic"[185] morality. Quoting Hobbes, he says that this latter is the morality of the "just" man, who subscribes to law, not out of weakness, but out of disdain for personal consequences. "'That which gives to human actions the relish of justice,'" as opposed to mere prudence, "'is a certain Nobleness or Gallantness of courage (rarely found), by which a man scorns to be beholden for the contentment of life, to fraud or breach of promise. This justice of Manners, is that which is meant, where justice is called a virtue.'"[186]

Hobbes's just man, the man of pride, is plainly also Oakshott's free individual, who knows how to be his own friend, who joins in a civic association to preserve his autonomy. His laws are the higher-order "rule of law" that so much resembles Holmes's own code.

Oakeshott believes that the citizen of aristocratic virtue is Hobbes's own ideal.

And he shows the apparent contradiction between Hobbes's private morality and his prescriptions for the state,[187] as we must face the similar conflict in Holmes.

Although Oakeshott says the two codes of morality are fundamentally inconsistent and cannot be held by the same person, he gives some hints on how they might coexist in the same society. In his essay on the rule of law, for instance, he seems to accept that a national or federal state might be a civic association governed by the rule of law, while smaller units or local "governments" might be enterprise associations devoted to specific purposes.[188]

Another, still more interesting, hint is the suggestion Oakeshott makes that the just man is needed to form any kind of voluntary association.[189] If the social contract is to have legitimate authority, it must be possible at least to imagine its coming into being through voluntary agreement, and it is hard to imagine the weak, fearful, ordinary man for whom it is created voluntarily undertaking the risks necessary to bring it into being. Oakeshott hints that the just man, the man of pride rather than fear, is needed to make the enterprise association conceivable.[190]

Now, it is plain that Holmes's federal Constitution is a great deal like Oakeshott's rule of law. I do not mean that the actual federal government in Holmes's day resembled Oakeshott's ideal civic association, only that the fundamental principles which Holmes thought were embodied in the Constitution were themselves an ideal order like the one Oakeshott describes.

State and local governments, with their instrumental purposes, are like Oakeshott's local authorities. The flourishing of all these lower levels of society, with their prudent concerns and their striving for the mediocre, depends on protection of their freedom by a higher order of government in which freedom and autonomy are valued more than all the other aims of legislation, more than the existence of the federal government itself.

Holmes was not quite clear how or why evolution should have produced this higher standard of morality; he simply accepted that, like everything else, it was a product of the natural world. In the end, Holmes simply accepted his own morality, as well as the prudence of his "bad man," as a necessary part of the world, no more to be explained or accounted for than a taste for beer, but no less real.

The conflict in his thought, which he resolved with a faith in the cosmos that he could not justify, was created solely by the machinery of the evolutionary process as he understood it. If laws were made by a dominant power, considered as an entity, a sort of collective organism or "race," natural selection would favor the power whose laws were best calculated to ensure survival. Laws, and lawmakers, that did not ensure the survival of the fittest would be swept away. There was no place in this system for a judge who *decided* which power would prevail and so sat outside the struggle for life.

But we now believe that biological evolution does not proceed in this way, as a contest between races. If there is an analogous evolution of competing cultures, we have no hint as yet of how it operates, and there is no particular reason to think it works as Holmes imagined. He was unable to get outside his own picture of the struggle for survival, because this conventional view was seared into fabric of his being by the Civil War.

We are now more familiar with arguments showing that altruistic traits might have evolved through natural selection. Modern genetics suggests that an individual might very well sacrifice himself for the sake of others who carry the same gene; a sacrifice on behalf of others might increase the frequency of a particular gene in the population. Indeed, even in Holmes's day, if he had not been so blinded by the picture of warring races, it might have occurred even to this lonely, childless man that a self-sacrificing sense of duty was simply the instinct of a parent.

We therefore need not be too greatly troubled by the apparent contradiction in Holmes's thought and may evaluate his system of duties for what it was, a moral code based on a life devoted to duty. It was an elitist, paternalistic morality, but Holmes was no snob. He thought that only the poverty caused by the excess of population over resources kept the majority of people from attaining to the same heights as the fortunate minority. But the minority's good fortune did allow them to rise to heights of idealism on which, paradoxically, the whole of society depended. He did not believe in the institutions of peerage and monarchy, and showed in his later opinions that he thought America's open, democratic society, with its complex federal system, its political experiments in the insulated chambers provided by the states, was the most highly evolved social organism yet to appear, and an elite corps was an essential part of it. "I have read Plato's *Laws*—unreal atmosphere with some real flashes of lightening. They had clear notions of what a gentleman should be."[191]

4.3.4 Holmes's Jurisprudence—The Common Law. Like his philosophy, Holmes's jurisprudence can be divided into two segments, one pertaining to the ordinary law of society and one pertaining to the judge's duty.

His principal writings on law concern the jurisprudence of the "enterprise association": ordinary private law, the rules of behavior in the common law that the bad man and the good were equally obliged to observe. Holmes expected that fifty years after his death his ideas about this law, however original at the time, would seem either commonplace or wrong, and I suppose that is the overall judgment one must render. Holmes's idea that the common law was the result rather than the cause of judicial decisions was epochal; in law it was comparable (and in some ways similar) to the impact of relativity on physics. Holmes's insight is accepted as correct and now seems almost too obvious to mention.

It is also a commonplace to say that law is evolving; as soon as one admits that judges make law, then it is plain that the law changes. But few now share Holmes's idea that changes in law reflect natural selection among competing groups in society, much less his notion that legal evolution exhibits the particular direction toward greater objectivity and self-awareness that he thought he had detected.

These fundamental insights earned Holmes a place in the history of ideas, but they have less immediate importance today. The lawmaking role of courts, except in constitutional law, has been overshadowed by the immense growth of the administrative state, in any case, and one can hardly say now, as Holmes did, that what courts do is the only law. Legislation and regulation are now such a pervasive presence, often directly enforced by administrative agencies without court intervention, that it just marks one as quaint to say that statutes and regulations are not law, properly speaking, but facts to be consulted by the courts when they make law.

As to Holmes's substantive description of the common law, it is deeply flawed by his scientism, his insistence on finding one, unifying principle for all of law. The dominant image in all Holmes's work on the common law was the single standard of liability, by which all judges were to measure all their decisions.

At the very beginning, in his first synthetic work, the notes to Kent's *Commentaries*, Holmes said this central pillar of law was the conduct of the prudent man. In *The Common Law*, there was a fundamental shift in his view, like the "paradigm shift" in physics that followed the theories of relativity: the fundamental question was not the rule of conduct but the circumstances under which the judge would impose liability. The focus of Holmes's investigation shifted away from political society as a whole and narrowed to the judge's courtroom. The judge was the sole arbiter of when liability should be imposed, and the single criterion for his choice was embedded in a complex metaphor, the "external standard," that encapsulated Holmes's philosophy of advancing materialism and the need for the individual to accept and submit himself to the larger purposes of society and life. The imagery is bleak and linear, a landscape of solitude and combat. It is the imagery of Hobbes's *Leviathan*.

Later in his career, Holmes embedded this image of an external standard in a more complex matrix. The central question of when the defendant's conduct was too threatening of harm, in his later view, required investigation into the circumstances of the individual defendant, his motives and intentions. The metaphor of the external standard became a complex image of fairness. The supposed single standard proliferated into a complex set of privileges and defenses based on judgments of social policy; the judge sat above the conflicts of society, ensuring that competing principles of social organization were each given their chance to prevail peacefully in the struggle for life.

We will turn to the judge's role in this system in a moment; for now, we must note that the shift in the meaning of the supposed single standard of liability made hash of the whole original scheme. In Holmes's later writings, the organizing principle of law, which allowed one to predict the actions of the courts, was not "foreseeable harm" but the patchwork of policies and exceptions that under some circumstances imposed liability on behavior that resulted in foreseeable harm and in other situations granted it a privilege.

Holmes was only forty years old when *The Common Law* was published. His account there of law, and the society it reflected, was oddly impoverished. The effort to cram the whole variegated mass of the common law into the philosophy of his youth obliged him to reduce large areas of law to abstract, rather theoretical, principles. This tendency was most marked in the areas of law where he had least personal experience. It is now and was then surprising for Holmes to assert that the common law was indifferent as to whether or not contracts were performed. It must have seemed even more surprising in Holmes's day than it does now when he asserted that criminal law no longer had a moral component and did not seek retribution, only deterrence. He himself was obliged to abandon the dogma that subjective intent played no significant role in tort liability or criminal law.[192] One cannot help concluding that in *The Common Law*, Holmes simply filled in large areas previously left blank in his writings with extensions of his general principles. His evolutionary scheme allowed him to argue the general tendency of the law of the future, and to disregard much of the law of the past as an anachronism. In this way he dismissed the large number of cases in tort and criminal law in which the defendant's subjective state of mind was not only relevant but decisive to the outcome.

But the deeper failure was inherent in the design. There *was* no single principle to which judges and lawyers could recur in deciding particular cases. Holmes, because at bottom he had no real conception of empirical science, or rather an odd scholastic conception of it, was asking the wrong questions. Even if it were true that in a sense the task of the lawyer was scientific—to predict the action of judges from study of past decisions—and even if there were undiscovered laws of motion of human society, there was no reason at all to think that judges' law could be derived from those more general principles.

Holmes was like a carpenter trying to deduce a mortise and tenon joint from Newton's laws of motion. The things that concern people in particular cases, and even in the law as a whole, are local and historical. The good lawyer knows the judges in his own courts and the precedents they are likely to find persuasive. He has no more need for scientific jurisprudence than for cosmology. Holmes's "The Path of the Law," where his aspirations to law as a science are most clearly spelled out, has always been popular with law professors, but it is rarely cited by the courts.

The most that we can now say about the quasi-scientific jurisprudence embedded in Holmes's early writings on the law, culminating in *The Common Law,* is that it provides a reassuring precedent for later ideas linking law to social policy.

4.3.5 Holmes's Jurisprudence—Constitutional Law. *The Common Law,* then, for all its being a remarkable personal accomplishment, and despite its fascinating insights into structuralist thought, is now a museum-piece of Victorian scientism. But Holmes's opinions for the Supreme Court, which take their character from his later writings, exemplify a still lively, if not universally shared, moral philosophy.

It may be easier to see this by imagining Holmes's rules of constitutional law in isolation, as if there were no statutes or private law in existence. In isolation one sees the structures of government and only a very few rules of law—the relatively fundamental principles of the common law, as modified in some respects by specific language in the Constitution. These rules are that all persons are privileged to act and speak freely; that they may not use violence without the authority of the state and may not inflict injuries maliciously; that when joined in subordinate, local governments to accomplish their common purposes, they may use force, but they may not significantly infringe an individual's constitutional privileges except in the face of imminent harm or grave risk of harm to values that in themselves meet the requirements of law.

The courts are responsible for interpreting these laws in particular situations, and hence for setting the limits on the use of force by others and for directing the use of force by the state. The courts must decide each case without regard to the interests of the parties or the judges in the outcome, but solely in accordance with the few fundamental principles of law adopted through constitutional procedures.

There is nothing instrumental here (except as Holmes supposed, on principle, that these rules must serve some purpose of evolution, without knowing what that might be). These are fundamentally moral principles, setting relations of fairness and freedom in discourse among autonomous individuals, and limiting the role of the state to what is necessary to maintain the rule of law.

As we have seen, this federal Constitution is an example of a civic association governed by the rule of law, which Michael Oakeshott discerned in European tradition, most notably explicated in the writings of Bodin, Hobbes, Kant, and Hegel. Holmes was in good company as a thinker, and he was able to carry this ideal, in some degree, into practice.

It is an ideal that one draws from the older regimes of Europe and from their values of pride, honor, temperance, and justice. This ideal lies behind Holmes's great opinions and constitutes his principal legacy.

4.4

HOLMES'S LEGACY

Holmes was of the Victorian age. Bleak as was his vision of personal significance, his view of the world was fundamentally optimistic. Indeed, he was a leading figure, perhaps for Americans the paradigm, of an optimistic age sure of its values.

Henry James saw what the Great War meant for such a view. In an often-quoted letter to Howard Sturgis, on August 5, 1914, he said,

> The taper went out last night, and I am afraid I kindle it again to a very feeble ray— for it's vain to try to talk as if one weren't living in a nightmare of the deepest dye. How can what is going on not be to one as a huge horror of blackness? . . . The plunge of civilization into this abyss of blood and darkness by the wanton feat of those two infamous autocrats is a thing that so gives away the whole long age during which we have supposed the world to be, with whatever abatement, gradually bettering, that to have to take it all now for what the treacherous years were all the while really making for and *meaning* is too tragic for any words.[193]

Not until seventy-five years later, with the withdrawal of Soviet troops from Eastern Europe and the reunification of Germany, did the long war end. The violent effort to erase history had been put down, and it was again possible to open the old books and resume the old discussions of the rule of law.

Holmes is valuable and fascinating as a representative of the old regime, who lived long enough to remind us of what is in danger of being entirely lost.

In his childhood, Holmes saw a parade in which white-haired veterans of the Revolution were carried in a barge, and he conceived an ambition to be such a survivor, to be carried in processions as a symbol of dimly understood ideals.[194] It is touching to reflect that he achieved this childhood ambition.

Edmund Wilson guessed that to his later audiences Holmes represented rectitude, courage, and patriotism.[195] I suppose it is difficult to say how he was perceived. The ideals to which Holmes devoted himself, and which perhaps continue to shine from his portrait, were honor, and devotion to duty.

Honor was not easily won. Holmes was a highly self-aware, intellectualized man, and it was difficult for him to accept the duty that he felt, to give his life for principles that he could not justify logically. It was the special quality of his thought that he tried to reconstruct a code of honor from within a self-reflexive, ironical philosophy. There is something noble and very modern in this effort to wrest honor from meaningless chaos.

What, then, is the heritage of Holmes's code of honor?

The best of Holmes's philosophy was shown in his work as a judge, most clearly as we have seen in his opinions on freedom of speech.

Let us return once more to those cases. Holmes said in his opinions that the foundation of freedom was self-restraint by the wielders of power and that freedom of speech should not be abridged by them, short of grave risk of harm to lawful values.

It is true that Holmes said that speech as such could be punished when it was used for the purpose of causing harm of a kind the government could lawfully forbid. This has been objected to as reflecting a fundamental deficiency in Holmes's ideas; the objection seems to be that Holmes treated speech as a form of activity that had practical consequences and so was entitled to protection no greater than that afforded to other types of behavior.

The late Harry Kalven, Jr., for instance, complained that Holmes washed out the political element of speech entirely: he put the speech of Eugene Debs, a national party candidate for president, on the same footing as a cry of "fire!" in a theater.[196] One encounters the same difficulty, if it is one, in many of Holmes's opinions. He resolutely refused to consider the political context. It seemed extraordinary to Ernst Freund, Harry Kalven, and other revisionists that Holmes should insist on treating Eugene Debs as if he were the defendant in an attempted robbery case, just as it had seemed incredible to other critics that Holmes would treat the Northern Securities Company as if it were a small exporting grocer.[197] But that is what Holmes deeply believed his duty as a judge required of him.

The premise of the objection, Yosal Rogat's carefully supported argument that Holmes was indifferent to the results in particular cases,[198] is plainly correct; but it is oddly ambiguous. Indifference to consequences, after all, is one of the traditional qualities we demand of a judge: *fiat justitia, ruat coelum*. In more modern, cooler language, we expect judges to decide cases on neutral principles that are not contrived or distorted to achieve particular results.

The distinctive quality of Holmes's thought is its acceptance of the givens of life. Holmes liked to say that he didn't believe in very much that was, but he believed a damn sight less in anything that *wasn't*. He did not believe in utopias or sudden ruin, and took life as he found it, without blaming anyone for its evident injustices. He accepted the chaotic nature of ordinary life, the vast extinctions of the natural world, the similar upheavals and creative destruction of the free market. His evolutionism was just a hopeful gloss on this clear-eyed view of the world around him. He set as the highest aim of which law was capable a certain modest conception of fairness: equality of treatment, not equality of result.

It was this that eventually divided him from the liberal tradition. In his earlier writings, it is true, well into his middle age, he thought and said that the Progressives of his day were the men of the future, and that the chaotic workings of the natural world and the marketplace might yet be put under the orderly regime of science; that the world of struggle might give way to a sort of scientific Athens.

But as Holmes grew older, he grew more skeptical, and in his later opinions—

those for which he is now famous—it is remarkable how rarely he asserted any particular view of social policy as the basis of his opinions. In these later cases one saw nothing but his Olympian skepticism and a determination nevertheless to see that the government conduct itself honorably: that the struggle of competing ideas and principles, of classes and races, be carried out fairly and peacefully, in accordance with the rule of law, come what might.

This is what we expect of a judge.

There is nevertheless something troubling here. Holmes, for all his remarkable abilities and admirable qualities, was too single-minded, too correct. He was better than his worst ideas, but in one respect he fell short of his best understanding.

A judge is subject to two mutually inconsistent duties. They correspond to the two senses in which we say that a judge's duty is to decide fairly. To be "fair" in one sense is to render judgment with a sympathetic understanding of the individual who stands before the court. But to be "fair" also means to be blind: to decide on the basis of neutral principles, without regard for the result in a particular case.

Holmes was no stranger to the harmony of conflicting principles. As he wrote to Lady Castletown,

> Life is an art not a thing which one can work out successfully by abstract rules. It is like painting a picture. At every moment one has to use one's tact and pigments in the right proportions between inconsistent desirables—between reading and writing—saving and spending—work and play etc. The trouble with many moralists as with many men of business is that they give too absolute a right of way to one interest.[199]

And Holmes understood well enough that a judge was required to unite the conflicting principles of detachment and compassion. Purportedly describing Judge William Endicott, he set down his image of the ideal:

> [H]e sat without a thought of self, without even the unconscious pride or aloofness which seemed, nay, was, his right, serenely absorbed in the matters at hand, impersonal yet human, the living image of justice, weighing as if the elements in the balance were dead matter, but discerning and collecting those elements by the help of a noble and tender heart. (12.15)

Holmes was always correct and dispassionate; the impersonal law of honor and duty spoke through him. He was Hobbes's just man: he had that "certain Nobleness or Gallantness of courage (rarely found)," "which gives to human actions the relish of justice." This is quite enough to justify our keeping his memory green.

Holmes showed few signs of a tender heart. But, when vindicating the right of free speech and other fundamental principles of the Constitution, or when insisting on fairness in the procedures of the courts, he did unite his respect for the law with, if not sympathy, detached respect and a noble regard for the freedom of the individual. These opinions accordingly rise higher than all the rest.

Editor's Notes

1. R. Posner, Cardozo: A Study in Reputation 76 (1990). Table 1 of this book shows the number of times judges' names are mentioned in law reviews in the Lexis database 1982–89. Holmes is listed third, after Chief Justice Rehnquist and Justice Brennan, then just com-

pleting his career. (If Posner had included his own name in the rankings, however, his name would have appeared above Holmes's.) Judge Posner makes various adjustments in tables 2 and 3, to take account of names that are also common words (Black) or otherwise used (Brandeis University), that do not seem relevant to the first three names on the list, but which he applied to all the names. On all three lists Holmes is in the first half dozen, and is still ranked with the living.

2. And have their own subliterature of commentary. *See, e.g.,* Henly, *"Penumbra": The Roots of a Legal Metaphor,* 15 HASTINGS CONST. L. Q. 81 (1987).

3. Kalven and Zeisel, *Law, Science, and Humanism,* in THE HUMANIST FRAME 329, 331 (J. Huxley ed. 1961), quoted Rogat, *Mr. Justice Holmes: A Dissenting Opinion,* 15 STANF. L. REV. 3, 5 n.7 (1962).

4. Rogat, *Mr. Justice Holmes: A Dissenting Opinion,* 15 STANF. L. REV. 3, 4–5 (1962).

5. Rogat, *The Judge as Spectator,* 31 U. CHI. L. REV. 213, 214 (1964); Rabban, *The Emergence of Modern First Amendment Doctrine,* 50 U. CHI. L. REV. 1205, 1267 (1983).

6. *See, e.g.,* A. BICKEL, THE UNPUBLISHED OPINIONS OF MR. JUSTICE BRANDEIS 241 (1957); *cf.* Cardozo, *Mr. Justice Holmes,* 44 HARV. L. REV. 682, 691 (1931) ("the great overlord of the law and its philosophy"). A page of such effusions was collected by Rogat, *Mr. Justice Holmes: A Dissenting Opinion,* 15 STANF. L. REV. 3, 4 n.4 (1962) ("he is the summit of hundreds of years of civilization, the inspiration of ages yet to come").

7. From an anonymous sketch of Holmes on his retirement in 1932, reprinted in VANITY FAIR: SELECTIONS FROM AMERICA'S MOST MEMORABLE MAGAZINE (Amory & Bradlee eds. 1960); *see also* Llewellyn, *Holmes,* 35 COLUM. L. REV. 485, 490 (1935) ("America's most distinguished citizen").

8. West Publishing Company's Northeast Reports, and the Westlaw and Lexis databases, all begin with 1890.

9. *See* P. BLAUSTEIN AND R. MERSKY, THE FIRST ONE HUNDRED JUSTICES 102 (1978). Holmes also published thirty concurring opinions and seventy-two dissents while on the Supreme Court, and wrote many of the per curiam opinions toward the end of Melville Fuller's term as chief justice, 1909–10, and when Holmes himself was acting chief in 1929.

10. 188 U.S. 239 (1903).

11. 209 U.S. 1, 18 (1908) (Holmes, J., "concurring specially").

12. And accordingly concurred, although his reasoning pointed to a dissent.

13. The remainder range from tax to admiralty and are difficult to characterize as a group, but I should say that the majority would be accepted as good law today, in some cases almost a century after they were written. This is partly because Holmes was reluctant to dissent and chose his moments. Although he wrote more opinions for the Court than any other justice, at least ten other justices wrote more dissents. *See* P. BLAUSTEIN AND R. MERSKY, THE FIRST ONE HUNDRED JUSTICES 102 (1978).

14. Milwaukee Social Democrat Pub. Co. v. Burleson, 255 U.S. 407, 437 (1921).

15. *See* 3.8, above.

16. *See* 3.9. There is a similarity in Holmes's view to Ronald Dworkin's argument that judges apply principles internal to law, even when deciding hard cases. R. DWORKIN, LAW'S EMPIRE (1986); A MATTER OF PRINCIPLE (1985); TAKING RIGHTS SERIOUSLY (1977). Holmes would have agreed with Dworkin that such principles, discernible in the prior decisions of the courts, are themselves law. But Dworkin believes that such principles make a self-enclosed system, so that there is always a right answer to any legal question. Holmes, in contrast, famously insisted that general propositions did not decide concrete cases and that a judge in hard cases would have to choose between conflicting principles, each with a logical claim; to do so, she would have to consult principles outside the law itself. The difference is fundamental, for if Holmes is correct, Dworkin's system smuggles in a version of natural law, of supposedly objectively correct principles, that actually reflects some underlying social policy. Like

any other natural law scheme, Dworkin's would allow the overruling of precedents that were wrongly decided, to which Holmes most strongly objected.

17. 277 U.S. 438, 469 (1928).

18. 189 U.S. 475 (1903) (Holmes, J.).

19. *See also* Nixon v. Herndon, 273 U.S. 536 (1927), striking down a statute that barred African-Americans from voting in Democratic primary elections, as a violation of the Fourteenth Amendment's guarantee of equal protection, and awkwardly avoiding consideration of the Fifteenth. The Court may have been hoping to avoid the question of whether the Fifteenth Amendment guaranteed a right to vote, which it has never squarely held, and which would have jeopardized the *Giles v. Harris* holding and many state laws setting up qualifications for voters. If the Fifteenth Amendment simply prohibited discriminating against African-Americans whenever a right to vote was granted to others by the states, it would seem to have been redundant, as the Fourteenth Amendment already prohibited any denial of equal protection of the laws. We see again the Court's and Holmes's reluctance to enforce the Civil War amendments.

20. 258 U.S. 268 (1922).

21. 275 U.S. 66 (1927).

22. *See, e.g.,* Merrigan v. Boston & Albany R. Co., 154 Mass. 189 (1891) (Holmes, J.); Johanson v. Boston & Maine R. Co., 151 Mass. 57 (1891) (Holmes, J.); Donnelly v. Boston & Maine R. Co., 151 Mass. 210 (1890) (Holmes, J.). The facts in the 1927 "Stop, look, and listen" case were compelling from the plaintiff's side, but the rule was not based on preference for the railroad: Holmes had applied his rule on plaintiffs' behalf in Massachusetts. In *Johanson*, Holmes held that evidence that the injured children had stopped to look for a train was sufficient to overturn a directed verdict for the defendant; and in *Merrigan* he held for the plaintiff.

23. Pollock, *Mr. Justice Holmes,* 44 HARV. L. REV. 693, 695 (1931).

24. 219 U.S. 219, 245 (1910).

25. Brown's Case, 173 Mass. 498 (1899) (Holmes, J.).

26. *Justice Holmes,* 82 NEW REPUBLIC 206 (1935).

27. Chafee, *Freedom of Speech in Wartime,* 32 HARV. L. REV. 932, 963 (1919). Not everyone agreed; *see* Corwin, *Constitutional Law in 1919–1920,* 14 AM. POL. SCI. REV. 635, 637 (1920) (clear and present danger "made up out of whole cloth").

28. Abrams v. United Sates, 250 U.S. 616, 621 (1919). Day Kimball's note defending the position of the majority of the Court argued that the common law of attempts met the constitutional standard established in *Schenck* and that this required no more than a showing of intent by an external standard. Note, *The Espionage Act and the Limits of Legal Toleration,* 33 HARV. L. REV. 442, 444–45 (1920).

29. 250 U.S. at 627–28; Chafee, *A Contemporary State Trial: The United States versus Jacob Abrams, et al.,* 33 HARV. L. REV. 747, 751–54 (1920). Chafee noted pointedly that Learned Hand was cited approvingly by the majority in favor of their strict liability standard; *id.* at 752 n.7. Chafee's first article, on the *Schenck* case, was approvingly cited shortly thereafter, in Justice Brandeis's dissent in which Holmes concurred, in Schaefer v. United States, 251 U.S. 466, 486 (1920).

30. Pierce v. United States, 252 U.S. 239 (1920); Schaefer v. United States, 251 U.S. 466 (1920).

31. Gilbert v. Minnesota, 254 U.S. 325 (1921).

32. 252 U.S. at 253; 251 U.S. at 482.

33. 252 U.S. 239 (1920).

34. *Id.* at 249.

35. *Id.* at 269–72.

36. 254 U.S. 325 (1921).

37. 254 U.S. at 334.

38. *Id.* at 341. Brandeis argued for a more stringent limitation on state action in peacetime—based on the privileges and immunities of United Sates citizens, which Brandeis suggested for the first time created a zone of privacy into which no government could intrude in peacetime—than the Court had established in *Schenck* for the federal government at war. Brandeis abandoned this line of argument after this dissent, and returned to Holmes's clear and present danger standard for state as well as federal law; but Brandeis advanced a similar privacy notion based on the Fourth and Fifth Amendments in Olmstead v. United States, 277 U.S. 438, 470 (1928), where Holmes again declined to accept Brandeis's expansive doctrine.

39. Holmes to Lewis Einstein, October 12, 1914, HOLMES-EINSTEIN LETTERS 100 (Peabody ed. 1964); Holmes to Felix Frankfurter, March 27, 1917, Oliver Wendell Holmes, Jr., Papers, Harvard Law School Library.

40. F. FRANKFURTER AND J. LANDIS, THE BUSINESS OF THE SUPREME COURT (1925).

41. A. MASON, WILLIAM HOWARD TAFT, CHIEF JUSTICE (1965).

42. *See* Brandenburg v. Ohio, 395 U.S. 444, 447 (1969).

43. 268 U.S. at 670.

44. *Id.* at 664–65.

45. *Id.* at 665.

46. *Id.* at 669 (emphasis added).

47. Interestingly, this is the premise for Brandeis's later suggestion that the probability and the magnitude of the harm be considered separately. *See* his concurrence in Whitney v. California, 274 U.S. 352, 372 (1927), discussed below.

48. Gitlow v. New York, 268 U.S. 652, 673 (1925) (Holmes, J., dissenting).

49. 268 U.S. 652, 673 (Holmes, J., dissenting).

50. *See, e.g.,* Holmes to Herbert J. Croly, May 12, 1919, 1 HOLMES-LASKI LETTERS 202, 203 (M. DeW. Howe ed. 1953): "[F]or thirty years I have made my brethren smile by insisting [the law] to be everywhere a matter of degree."

51. 268 U.S. at 673.

52. *Id.*

53. 274 U.S. 357 (1927).

54. *Id.* at 371–72.

55. *Id.* at 374.

56. *Id.* at 375 (Brandeis, J., concurring).

57. The last link in Brandeis's argument—the reason why his rationale for free speech requires individualized adjudication and forbids Justice Sanford's strict liability—is not explicitly made, and I have interpolated what seems to me implicit. Brandeis's dissents in *Gilbert* and *Olmstead* seem to support this reading, but Brandeis plainly was still uncomfortable with clear and present danger and I suppose would have preferred a more straightforward approach to a right of privacy or self-realization, if he had been able to secure Holmes's support. Professor, later Judge, Bork denied on related grounds that Brandeis had given any adequate answer to Sanford; Bork denied that speech had any special role, more than other forms of behavior, in self-realization. *See* Bork, *Neutral Principles and Some First Amendment Problems,* 47 IND. L. J. 1, 25 (1971).

58. Holmes did not join Brandeis's dissenting opinions in Gilbert v. Minnesota, 254 U.S. 325 (1921), and Olmstead v. United States, 277 U.S. 438 (1928), in both of which Brandeis argued for a right of personal freedom or "privacy" that was not anchored in specific provisions of the Constitution.

59. Quoted by Holmes's former law clerk Francis Biddle. F. BIDDLE, JUSTICE HOLMES, NATURAL LAW, AND THE SUPREME COURT 9 (1961).

60. *See* Holmes to Harold J. Laski, January 1, 1923, 1 HOLMES-LASKI LETTERS 469 (M.

DeW. Howe ed. 1953) (quoting Brandeis); *see* T. McCRAW, PROPHETS OF REGULATION 103–42 (1984).

61. *See* Freund, *Holmes and Brandeis in Retrospect*, BOSTON BAR J., Sept.–Oct. 1984, p.7.

62. *See* Near v. Minnesota *ex rel.* Olsen, 238 U.S. 697 (1931); Stromberg v. California, 283 U.S. 359 (1931).

63. 304 U.S. 144, 152 n. 4 (1938).

64. *Id. See, generally,* J. ELY, DEMOCRACY AND DISTRUST (1980), the influential book that developed this germ into a fully leafed constitutional jurisprudence. Professor Ely's distinction between "specific threat" and categorization approaches was most helpful in preparing this section. His approach was quite similar to that sketched out more briefly by Judge Bork a decade earlier, in *Neutral Principles and Some First Amendment Problems*, 47 IND. L. J. 1 (1971). Both Bork and Ely argue for a categorization approach like Sanford's (Ely doesn't remark on the similarity), differing on the rationale and on the question of whether speech advocating crime is properly an unprotected category. Both are critical of Holmes.

65. 315 U.S. 568 (1942).

66. *Id.* at 571–72.

67. Whitney v. California, 274 U.S. 352 (1927).

68. 319 U.S. 624 (1943).

69. 337 U.S. 1, 4–5 (1949).

70. *See* Elrod v. Burns, 427 U.S. 347 (1976); Buckley v. Valeo, 424 U.S. 1 (1976); J. ELY, DEMOCRACY AND DISTRUST 113–15, 233–34 n.27 (1980); L. TRIBE, AMERICAN CONSTITUTIONAL LAW 829–36 (2d ed. 1988). Tribe treats clear and present danger as if the Court in each case determined whether expressions of the kind at issue posed a threat, making it a special, ad hoc, category of speech.

71. West Virginia State Bd. of Ed. v. Barnette, 319 U.S. 624 (1943).

72. 435 U.S. 765 (1978).

73. 435 U.S. 765, 777 (1978).

74. *See* Bork, *Neutral Principles and Some First Amendment Problems*, 47 IND. L. J. 1, 26 (1971); Meiklejohn, *The First Amendment Is an Absolute*, 1961 SUP. CT. REV. 245, 255.

75. 315 U.S. 568, 574 (1942). *Cf.* Terminiello v. City of Chicago, 337 U.S. 1 (1949), where a statute was held invalid on its face because it incorrectly defined the category of fighting words.

76. *See* Paris Adult Theater v. Slaton, 413 U.S. 49 (1973); Roth v. United States, 354 U.S. 476, 485 (1957, rejecting a clear and present danger analysis offered in the court below, 237 F. 2d 766, 801–2 (2d Cir. 1956) (Frank, J., concurring); *see* L. TRIBE, AMERICAN CONSTITUTIONAL LAW 908 (2d ed. 1988).

77. 435 U.S. at 777.

78. 301 U.S. 242 (1937).

79. *Id.* at 261–62.

80. 322 U.S. 680, 687 (1944).

81. The Court emphasized the two-branched standard of hazard and intent under the Espionage Act and cited *Schenck* for the external standard of risk, 322 U.S. at 687, but emphasized in its holding the lack of evidence for the subjective element of intent; *id.* at 687–90. Justice Reed for the four dissenters argued that *Schenck*, whose facts were similar, was based on a finding of actual intent. *Id.* at 693. *Cf.* Watts v. United States, 394 U.S. 705 (1968) (reversing conviction for threatening the president's life where there was no actual danger).

82. 341 U.S. 494 (1951).

83. 54 Stat. 671 (1940).

84. 341 U.S. at 505–10.

85. *Id.* at 588 (Douglas, J., dissenting).

86. *See* 3.7, above. This risk analysis had been applied to freedom of speech cases by both Sanford and Brandeis. *See* Whitney v. California, 274 U.S. 352, 372 (1927) (Brandeis and Holmes, JJ., concurring), 3.10, above, and adopted by Learned Hand in the court below in United States v. Dennis, 183 F. 2d 201, 212 (2d Cir. 1951) (Hand, J.).

87. 341 U.S. at 510. Risk analysis is now a generalized method of approaching government regulation. Holmes thought it better that judges should only truncate due process when harm itself, and not only the risk of harm, was imminent, but he was willing to accept that the constitution allowed regulation of risk alone. *See* Toledo Newspaper Co. v. United States, 247 U.S. 402 (1917); *cf.* Commonwealth v. Peaslee, 177 Mass. 267 (1901) (Holmes, J.), and Commonwealth v. Kennedy, 170 Mass. 18 (1892) (Holmes, J.) (the degree of risk that will justify a conviction for criminal attempts is a function of factors such as the defendant's intent and the gravity of the crime). In regulatory programs it is now a commonplace that the government may act when a risk appears, without waiting until the evil itself is imminent, although private rights will be abridged by regulation. *See, e.g.,* Ethyl Corp. v. EPA, 541 F. 2d 1, 15 (D.C. Cir. 1976) (en banc) (Wright, J.). In environmental law it is now held that statutory language authorizing enforcement in cases of "imminent and substantial endangerment" authorizes suit when the risk of harm, rather than the harm itself, is imminent. *See* United States v. Price, 688 F. 2d 204, 213–14 (3d Cir. 1982), and cases cited therein. And while risk itself may be regulated, it appears to be a general principle of law, perhaps of constitutional dimension, that only significant risks may be controlled. Indus. Union Dept., AFL-CIO v. Amer. Petr. Inst., 448 U.S. 607 (1980) (OSH Act regulation). In determining whether the regulated activity poses a risk meriting control, the probability of the harm and the magnitude and nature of the harm if it occurs are to be separately weighed. *Id.; see also* Ethyl Corp. v. EPA, 541 F. 2d at 18 n. 32 (air pollution); Carolina Envtl. Study Group v. United States, 510 F. 2d 796 (D.C. Cir. 1975) (risk of nuclear accident); S. NOVICK, D. STEVER, AND M. MELLON, LAW OF ENVIRONMENTAL PROTECTION §§ 2.03, 2.05 (1986); *cf.* Bork, *Neutral Principles and Some First Amendment Problems,* 47 IND. L. J. 1, 29 (1971) ("pornography is . . . a problem of pollution of the moral and aesthetic atmosphere . . . on a par with . . . smoke pollution"). Federal courts are slowly working out a general framework for analyzing the limits of government regulation in terms of a continuum of risk; "clear and present danger" in retrospect may be seen as the beginning of this effort. At some point on the continuum of risk, regulation is justified in particular circumstances. Risks below that point are insignificant and do not justify infringement of liberty, while risks above it are clear and present dangers.

88. 342 U.S. at 510–11. Justice Jackson, concurring in the result, appears to have accepted this reasoning but rejected the language of "clear and present danger." Jackson, fresh from the prosecutions at Nuremburg, had no difficulty accepting that a political party might in fact be a criminal conspiracy. He would simply have held that organizing the conspiracy, and not the advocacy, was a crime. *Id.* at 561. With his vote, a majority appeared to approve the reasoning if not the label attached to it in Vinson's opinion. Justice Douglas, dissenting, also assumed that *Schenck* would govern the result but declined to accept the plurality's view that an imminent risk of distant future harm met the *Schenck* standard, even in cases of very great potential harm. *Id.* at 581. Only Justices Frankfurter and Black, from their different perspectives, argued over the power of Congress to prohibit a category of speech—advocacy of revolution—on legislative grounds. Justice Frankfurter concurred in the result but relied on the majority opinions in *Gitlow* and *Whitney* and rejected Holmes's clear and present danger standard; *id.* at 542–46. Justice Black dissented, insisting that advocacy of revolt falls within the category of protected speech; *id.* at 579.

89. D. CURRIE, THE CONSTITUTION IN THE SUPREME COURT, THE SECOND CENTURY — 1888 TO 1986, at 354 (1990).

90. Rogat, *The Judge as Spectator,* 31 UNIV. CHI. L. REV. 213, 215 n.11 (1964). Rogat was not claiming Holmes had been vindicated; he was heaping the coals of *Dennis* on Holmes's head. *See,* to the same effect, Bork, *Neutral Principles and Some First Amendment Problems,* 47 IND. L. J. 1, 23 (1971) ("The great Smith Act cases of the 1950's . . . mark the triumph of Holmes and Brandeis").

91. 354 U.S. 298 (1957).

92. *Id.* at 312.

93. *Id.* at 318.

94. *Id.* at 318–19.

95. *Id.* at 319–27, 334. Justice Harlan spoke of the need to find incitement to action in particular words used by the defendants, and Professor Harry Kalven therefore argued that in *Yates* the Court had implicitly rejected the clear and present danger standard in favor of Hand's categorization scheme—Kalven apparently assuming that only words of "direct incitement" would show the kind of advocacy called for by the Court—and thereby worked a sort of revolution in First Amendment jurisprudence. H. KALVEN, JR., A WORTHY TRADITION: FREEDOM OF SPEECH IN AMERICA 211–222 (1988). With the greatest deference and respect to the late Professor Kalven, I do not find this view tenable. The Court, although never doctrinaire, certainly seemed to act in *Yates* as if it had adopted the Holmes-Brandeis standard, remanding some of the defendants for new trials to determine whether in the circumstances their advocacy was an incitement to crime or only exhortation to belief, which hardly sounds like a per se standard based on the words alone. 354 U.S. at 331–33.

96. 395 U.S. 444 (1969) (*per curiam*).

97. 395 U.S. at 449.

98. *Id.* at 447–48.

99. 395 U.S. at 444.

100. Professor Gunther insists, however, that under *Brandenburg,* a class of language, the language of "direct incitement," may be prohibited so long as an external threat in the circumstances is shown. In other words, Gunther argues, the Court had at last adopted Learned Hand's external standard, coupling it with a version of *Schenck.* Gunther, *Learned Hand and the Origins of Modern First Amendment Doctrine,* 27 STANF. L. REV. 719, 722, 754 (1975). For the life of me, I cannot see why the Court's phrase "directed to inciting" should be taken to mean "words literally demanding the performance of a crime." The only natural interpretation of this phrase seems to be that it refers to the defendant's intent. Ely argues that *Brandenburg* created a more general form of categorization, not tied to specific forms of words, of which he approves. J. ELY, DEMOCRACY AND DISTRUST 110 (1980). He doesn't explain how one can decide whether a particular expression is an incitement to wrongdoing without examining the circumstances in which it is given.

101. Landmark Communications, Inc. v. Virginia, 435 U.S. 829, 843 (1978). The "balancing" language is drawn from the contempt cases, which also began with Holmes's opinions. The notion is implicit in Holmes's idea that proximity of punishable harm is a continuum, and liability is fixed at some point on the continuum by weighing factors such as the gravity of the risk and the nature of the behavior. *See* Commonwealth v. Kennedy, 170 Mass. 18 (1897) (Holmes, J.); 3.7, above.

102. 435 U.S. at 843.

103. 435 U.S. at 844.

104. 376 U.S. 254 (1964).

105. 491 U.S. 397 (1989).

106. 376 U.S. at 256.

107. *Id.* at 270.

108. *Id.* at 269–70.

109. *Id.; see also* Brennan, *Address,* 32 RUTGERS L. REV. 173 (1979).

110. 376 U.S. at 273.

111. It is worth noting that Brennan at about this time began dissenting from the Court's categorization approach to obscenity. *See* Paris Adult Theater v. Slaton, 413 U.S. 49, 97 (1973) (Brennan, J., dissenting).

112. 376 U.S. at 279–83.

113. *See id.* at 279; 3.7, above.

114. 376 U.S. at 279–80. Justice Brennan believed that the Due Process Clause of the Fourteenth Amendment incorporated the Bill of Rights, as such, rather than any fundamental common-law principles underlying the amendments, and so it is not at all clear why tort law should have any relevance here except on pure policy grounds. *See id.* at 295–96 (Black, J., dissenting), arguing that the Fourteenth Amendment contains the literal terms of the First, without any common-law limitations.

115. *See* Rosenbloom v. Metromedia, Inc., 403 U.S. 29, 52 n.18 (1971) (Brennan, J., plurality opinion).

116. Texas v. Johnson, 491 U.S. 397 (1989).

117. *Id.* at 400.

118. *Id.* at 409.

119. *Id.* at 418–19. Because of the lack of evidence of any specific threat, Brennan had no need to discuss the defendant's intent.

120. Endlessly repeated in letters and speeches: e.g., "But if . . . the gentleman and the soldier is a survival, still it is a joy to some of us to see embodied in a lively picture man's most peculiar power—the power to deny the actual and to perish." *Paul Bourget,* 12.4.

121. "[A] bit of red ribbon that a man would die to win." *Harvard College in the War,* 11.2. (In England the winner of a race or contest traditionally receives a red ribbon.)

122. "Law and the Court," 11.20.

123. "The Soldier's Faith," 11.12; "Memorial Day," 11.1.

124. *See* 3.7, above.

125. As Holmes liked to repeat, a ship's officer was justified in closing a hatch to contain a fire although a carpenter was smothered as a result. Pierce v. Cunard Steamship Co., 151 Mass. 87 (1891).

126. *See* United Zinc & Chem. Co. v. Britt, 258 U.S. 268 (1922) (Holmes, J.).

127. *See* Smith v. Mayor and Alderman of Worcester, 182 Mass. 232 (1902); Sears v. Street Commissioners, 180 Mass. 274 (1902); Lincoln v. Board of Street Commissioners, 176 Mass. 210 (1900); Carson v. Sewerage Commissions of Boston, 175 Mass. 242 (1900). In these cases, the constitutional question was whether a street or sewer assessment was reasonably related to the benefits conferred and hence did not constitute a taking of private property without compensation. Holmes's general rule was that legislative categories necessarily created some disproportion of costs and benefits in particular cases, but that these were acceptable so long as the disproportion was not too great. The parallel to free-speech cases seems clear—the government may set up legislative categories to regulate speech so long as the limitation on rights in particular cases is not too severe.

128. This is one criticism of clear and present danger. *See* Linde, *"Clear and Present Danger" Reexamined: Dissonance in the Brandenburg Concerto,* 22 STANF. L. REV. 1163, 1175 (1970).

129. *Justice Holmes,* in E. WILSON, PATRIOTIC GORE 781 (1962).

130. Olmstead v. United States, 277 U.S. 438, 469 (1927) (Holmes, J., dissenting).

131. Holmes to Alice Stopford Green, June 18, 1911, Oliver Wendell Holmes, Jr., Papers, Harvard Law School Library.

132. Holmes to Justice Edward T. Sanford, January 1, 1925, Sanford Papers, MS-204, Uni-

versity of Tennessee, Knoxville. I am indebted to Liva Baker for placing a copy of this letter among the Holmes Papers at Harvard.

133. Holmes to Anna Lyman (Nina) Gray, March 2, 1903, Holmes Papers, quoted in S. NOVICK, HONORABLE JUSTICE: THE LIFE OF OLIVER WENDELL HOLMES 256 (1989).

134. Western Union Telegraph Co. v. Kansas, 216 U.S. 1, 52 (1909) (Holmes, J., dissenting), and Pullman Co. v. Kansas, 216 U.S. 56, 75 (1909) (Holmes, J., dissenting). The Court invalidated, as an unconstitutional burden on interstate commerce, fees imposed on the companies for the privilege of doing business in the state, because the fees were based on the total capital of the companies, including their out-of-state facilities, and were not related directly to the intrastate business within Kansas. Holmes said a fee based on the size of the company was perfectly reasonable.

135. Holmes to Alice S. Green, February 8, 1910, Oliver Wendell Holmes, Jr., Papers, Harvard Law School Library.

136. G. Olshausen, *Oliver Wendell Holmes: Aristocratic Critic of Capitalism,* AMERICAN SOCIALIST, July 1956; reprinted in THE [NATIONAL LAWYERS' GUILD] PRACTITIONER 16 (1980).

137. Rovere, *Sage,* THE NEW YORKER, April 6, 1957, p. 145.

138. Holmes to Felix Frankfurter, December 19, 1915, Oliver Wendell Holmes, Jr., Papers, Harvard Law School Library, B29 F3; quoted in E. Chadbourn, *Touched with Fire: Justice Oliver Wendell Holmes* (catalog of a retrospective exhibit at the Harvard Law School Library, February 15–June 15, 1975), at 18 (1975).

139. Matisse to André Rouveyre, "Sur les arbres," no date given, quoted in P. SCHNEIDER, MATISSE 59 (1984).

140. Holmes to William James, December 15, 1867, James Papers, Houghton Library; reprinted in 1 R. B. PERRY, THE THOUGHT AND CHARACTER OF WILLIAM JAMES 507 (1935). The difficulty Holmes had was with *vis viva,* the then mysterious quality of mechanical force. The recently discovered principle of conservation of energy had increased the impression that force was not explicable in materialist terms but had independent existence; this is rather like the mystery that absorbed the previous generation, of the manner in which gravity seemed to act at a distance with no material agency. Holmes was well aware of both debates and frequently compared the concepts of "rights" to the then mysterious "force" of gravitation, words which did no more than reify an imagined explanation for the behavior of the data. *See, e.g.,* Holmes to Frederick Pollock, January 19, 1928, 2 HOLMES-POLLOCK LETTERS 212–13 (M. DeW. Howe ed. 1941).

141. *Natural Law,* 10.23.

142. Holmes to Frederick Pollock, July 6, 1908, 1 HOLMES-POLLOCK LETTERS 140 (M. DeW. Howe ed. 1941).

143. R. RORTY, OBJECTIVITY, RELATIVISM, AND TRUTH 2 (1991).

144. M. DEW. HOWE, JUSTICE OLIVER WENDELL HOLMES: THE PROVING YEARS, 1870–1882, at 116–17 (1963).

145. F. Frankfurter, "Oliver Wendell Holmes, Jr.," in DICTIONARY OF NATIONAL BIOGRAPHY, reprinted in MR. JUSTICE HOLMES AND THE SUPREME COURT 11 (2d ed. 1961).

146. C. BOWEN, YANKEE FROM OLYMPUS 280–83 (1944).

147. *See, e.g.,* G. AICHELE, OLIVER WENDELL HOLMES, JR. 112–23 (1989); G. WHITE, PATTERNS OF AMERICAN LEGAL THOUGHT 223 (1978).

148. 53 NEW REPUBLIC 210 (1928), reprinted in MR. JUSTICE HOLMES (F. Frankfurter ed. 1931).

149. *See* note 165 below.

150. F. FRANKFURTER, MR. JUSTICE HOLMES AND THE SUPREME COURT (1938).

151. Except for a single sentence: Frankfurter said that Holmes "personally 'disbelieved

all the popular conceptions of socialism,' and came dangerously close to believing in the simplicities of the wage-fund theory." *Id.* at 72. This hardly seems an adequate exposition of Holmes's views.

152. *Id.* at 44.

153. R. JACKSON, THE STRUGGLE FOR JUDICIAL SUPREMACY 312 (1941); *see also* M. LERNER, IDEAS FOR THE ICE AGE 100–101 (1941); quoted in S. KONEFSKY, THE LEGACY OF HOLMES AND BRANDEIS 7–10 (1956).

154. YANKEE FROM OLYMPUS (1944).

155. The shred of fact on which all these accounts were based, which Frankfurter had exhumed from the Peirce papers in 1930, was Charles S. Peirce's description, late in his unhappy life, of a "Metaphysical Club," at one of the regular meetings of which Peirce claimed to have read a paper introducing pragmatism for the first time to William James, Holmes, and other lesser lights who thereafter followed up on the central idea. Max Fisch accepted this account and counted Holmes among the founders of pragmatism, on the theory that he had been present at the early meetings of the Metaphysical Club. Fisch, *Justice Holmes, the Prediction Theory of Law, and Pragmatism,* 39 J. PHIL. 85 (1942). Bowen then dramatized these supposed meetings in her book in 1944. Finally, Philip P. Weiner organized his influential book EVOLUTION AND THE FOUNDERS OF PRAGMATISM (1949) around the image of the meetings of the Metaphysical Club. As Wiener himself noted, however, there is no evidence in the voluminous papers of the others involved that there was such a club or that Peirce read such a paper. There were occasional meetings of friends in William James's house in Cambridge, beginning in the spring of 1870, but Holmes stopped visiting James very shortly thereafter, and the others had not yet in fact developed any of the ideas which later came to be called pragmatism. Holmes himself first encountered pragmatism in William James's writings of the 1890s, when he thought very little of it. The facts are not in dispute: *see* P. WIENER, EVOLUTION AND THE FOUNDERS OF PRAGMATISM 18–25 (1972 ed.); S. NOVICK, HONORABLE JUSTICE 426–27 (1989); Grey, *Holmes and Legal Pragmatism,* 41 Stanf. L. Rev. 787 (Appendix) (1989). Morton White, Wiener, Grey, and most other commentators do not rest any of their weight on the historical accuracy of Peirce's story but use it as a convenient image: "The most significant fact for the historian of thought is that Peirce brought together in his account of the genesis of pragmatism a historically important group of persons who really lived in the same place and time, moved in the same intellectual atmosphere, and influenced each other in ways that shaped the growth of certain pervasive ideas current in our thinking today." Wiener, above, at 25–26. I should have thought the most significant fact about Peirce's story, for any sort of historian, was that it was substantially untrue.

156. 341 U.S. 494 (1951).

157. 249 U.S. 47 (1919).

158. S. KONEFSKY, THE LEGACY OF HOLMES AND BRANDEIS 9 (1956).

159. *Id.* at 201.

160. David Rabban has amplified this suggestion into a fully developed theory that a cabal of liberal law professors manipulated Holmes, consciously misrepresenting his ideas and their own, in order to achieve a compromised doctrine of the First Amendment that was nevertheless more liberal than Holmes first intended, an effort that Rabban calls "heroic but often disingenuous." In this theory, Brandeis became converted to the effort to put a spin on Holmes's opinions in the 1920s, when his dissents and concurrences added a libertarian gloss to Holmes's unreflective aphorisms. Rabban, *The Emergence of First Amendment Doctrine,* 50 UNIV. CHI. L. REV. 1205, 1210–11 (1983).

161. Published as L. HAND, THE BILL OF RIGHTS (1958).

162. *Id.* at 57–59. There was a certain irony in this—the *Dennis* Court had relied on Hand's

own statement of the clear and present danger standard to affirm the convictions of the Communist leaders. Dennis v. United States, 341 U.S. 494, 510 (1951).

163. Brandenburg v. Ohio, 395 U.S. 444, 454 (1969).

164. *See* R. POSNER, THE PROBLEMS OF JURISPRUDENCE 26–30, 221–25 (1990).

165. H. S. COMMAGER, THE AMERICAN MIND 359 (1950).

166. *See* R. POSNER, THE PROBLEMS OF JURISPRUDENCE 25 (1990), quoting West's description of philosophic pragmatism in C. WEST, THE AMERICAN EVASION OF PHILOSOPHY: A GENEALOGY OF PRAGMATISM 5 (1989).

167. Grey, *Holmes and Legal Pragmatism,* 41 STANF. L. REV. 787 (1989).

168. Grey says that when Holmes read Dewey's EXPERIENCE AND NATURE, he reacted with "unmediated enthusiasm" and "wrote at once to Laski, 'I thought [it] a great book.'" Grey, *Holmes and Legal Pragmatism,* 41 STANF. L. REV. 787, 868–70 (1989). As the letter to Pollock quoted in the text shows, this somewhat exaggerates Holmes's reaction.

169. *Id.* at 804. Dewey's followers differ radically among themselves as to what Dewey meant to say. Grey, for instance, adopts a representational theory of truth, which Rorty—another follower of Dewey—claims is the antithesis of his own philosophy (and which I would have thought inconsistent with any sort of pragmatism). Rorty says that he and his teacher Sidney Hook differed fundamentally in their reading of Dewey; and Rorty rejects the "scientistic, method-worshipping side" of Dewey that Grey admires. R. RORTY, OBJECTIVITY, RELATIVISM, AND TRUTH 17 n.30 (1991).

170. Holmes to Frederick Pollock, May 15, 1931, 2 HOLMES-POLLOCK LETTERS 286, 287 (M. DeW. Howe ed. 1941).

171. R. RORTY, OBJECTIVITY, RELATIVISM, AND TRUTH 39 (1991). This is plainly Grey's version of pragmatism as well; *see* Grey at 789–91. But I quote the Rorty passage, which was published after Grey's article, as a succinct and authoritative statement of the school to which he seeks to assimilate Holmes.

172. Holmes to Laski, June 1, 1919, 1 HOLMES-LASKI LETTERS 210 (M. DeW. Howe ed. 1953). Of course, it is possible to take "science" to mean only what Rorty means, but the steam engine is like Samuel Johnson's kick at a stone: "I refute him *thus.*"

173. *See* N. ANNAN, LESLIE STEPHEN: THE GODLESS VICTORIAN (1984).

174. S. NOVICK, HONORABLE JUSTICE: THE LIFE OF OLIVER WENDELL HOLMES 28 (1989).

175. O. W. HOLMES, TOUCHED WITH FIRE: CIVIL WAR LETTERS AND DIARY OF OLIVER WENDELL HOLMES, JR., 1861–1864, 27–28 (M. DeW. Howe ed. 1943). This is an account of Holmes's injury at the battle of Ball's Bluff in October, 1861. It was written in one of Holmes's pocket diaries, probably during the time when he had become an aide-de-camp and was at leisure in winter quarters, in the winter of 1863–64, and was trying to extract philosophy from the experiences of the war. *See* 2.2, 3.2, above. He added after the quoted passage: "I can now add that our phrase *good* only means certain general truths seen through the heart & will instead of being merely contemplated intellectually."

176. "I felt ashamed of my own egotisms—not too much, because I [am] too sincerely skeptical not to see them as a bait with which nature gets work out of men. Real skepticism builds all its arrogance on humility and I think with only a seeming paradox might be said to be the most religious of attitudes." Holmes to Alice Stopford Green, February 7, 1909, Oliver Wendell Holmes, Jr., Papers, Harvard Law School Library, B43 F12. "No doubt I have said before that I think a real skeptic ([Holmes himself,] who hasn't got a little Godhead for himself) may come nearer to what I call religion than most if not all who go to church." Holmes to Frederick Pollock, December 7, 1927, 2 HOLMES-POLLOCK LETTERS 207–8 (M. DeW. Howe ed. 1943).

177. R. RORTY, OBJECTIVITY, RELATIVISM, AND TRUTH 8 (1991).

178. *The Rules of Law,* in ON HISTORY AND OTHER ESSAYS 147 (1983), misquoting Holmes's *Law in Science and Science in Law* (10.10): "[J]udges are called upon to exercise the sovereign prerogative of choice"; Oakeshott has "arbitrary choice."

179. It is essential to Oakeshott that in the rule of law, judges only interpret law that has been enacted by a process agreed upon among the members of the civic association beforehand, and therefore may not make law in the sense that judges do in the enterprise association, by choosing in accordance with social policies. In the civic association, as in Holmes's federal Constitution, however, it seems perfectly reasonable that judges would build up a body of precedent interpreting the fundamental principles of enacted law, as well as the enactments themselves, which would be making law but still in accordance with the agreed-upon principles of the Constitution and hence with Oakeshott's requirements.

180. We see here again the question of whether judges may make law. In the civic association, unlike the enterprise association, the rule of law is a system of moral principles. In my view, the fundamental principles Holmes found in the common law and the Constitution are such a system. While Oakeshott's judge makes law only in the sense of establishing rules for new situations, he need not go outside the system of principles found in previously enacted law; and Holmes rarely if ever did.

181. This brief summary does not do justice to the richness of Oakeshott's ideas or to the many points of similarity with Holmes's writings. It is interesting to note that Oakeshott, certainly no stranger himself to the common-law tradition, also says that the "civic association" is most clearly described by "Bodin, Hobbes, Spinoza, Kant, Fichte, and Hegel," *id.* at 252, the same writers, except Fichte, whose direct or indirect influence, as we have seen, were most important to Holmes.

182. ON HUMAN CONDUCT (1975).

183. *The Moral Life in the Writings of Thomas Hobbes,* in RATIONALISM IN POLITICS; AND OTHER ESSAYS 248 (1981 ed., first published 1962).

184. *Id.* at 293.

185. *Id.* at 294.

186. *Id.* at 290, quoting Hobbes's *Leviathan.*

187. Oakeshott really gives two answers to the apparent contradiction (rejecting as unlikely a third, that Hobbes was simply careless in his thinking). The first is that Hobbes advanced two doctrines, only one of which he thought was true. Hobbes was a propagandist for the existing order of his day, and *Leviathan* was written in an idiom likely to be familiar to his intended audience. But Hobbes had a second purpose, to explore the implications of his own philosophy; and the result was a set of writings that embodied two doctrines, one open and the other purposely hidden from all but the initiated. *Id.* at 289–90. Oakeshott notes that some will have difficulty accepting that Hobbes had an esoteric doctrine inconsistent with his open meaning, and I pass this question by, for Oakeshott also hints that the two may not be in conflict, as discussed in the text, in which case there is no reason, other perhaps than tact, for one to be hidden.

188. *See The Rule of Law,* in ON HISTORY; AND OTHER ESSAYS 163 (1983). Oakeshott insists that local authorities should not be called "governments" at all and that local "rates" proportioned to the benefit provided should not be confused with "taxes" to support a general government.

189. Oakshott, like Hobbes and Holmes, uses the masculine gender, not as a neutral term for humanity, but to designate the male sex, and it was part of their idea that the "just man" was a man.

190. *The Moral Life in the Writings of Thomas Hobbes,* note 195 above, at 294–300.

191. Holmes to Frederick Pollock, September 27, 1931, 2 HOLMES-POLLOCK LETTERS 292, 293 (M. DeW. Howe ed. 1941).

192. *See* 3.7, above.

193. Quoted in H. JAMES, THE PORTABLE HENRY JAMES 672 (M. D. Zabel ed. 1951; revised ed. 1968).

194. S. NOVICK, HONORABLE JUSTICE: THE LIFE OF OLIVER WENDELL HOLMES 11 (1989).

195. E. WILSON, PATRIOTIC GORE 795 (1962).

196. H. KALVEN, JR., A WORTHY TRADITION (1988); Kalven, *Professor Ernst Freund and Debs v. United States,* 40 U. CHI. L. REV. 235 (1973).

197. Northern Securities Co. v. United States, 193 U.S. 197, 401 (1904) (Holmes, J., dissenting).

198. Rogat, *The Judge as Spectator,* 31 U. CHI. L. REV. 213 (1964).

199. Holmes to Lady Castletown, June 18, 1897, Oliver Wendell Holmes, Jr., Papers, Harvard Law School Library, B26 F11, quoted in S. NOVICK, HONORABLE JUSTICE: THE LIFE OF OLIVER WENDELL HOLMES 217 (1989).

NONJUDICIAL WORKS

5

Youthful Works

This chapter includes Holmes's undergraduate essays, addresses, and poems, and his Civil War writings. Most of them were published anonymously; in most cases, I have followed Mark DeWolfe Howe in attributing to Holmes the undergraduate works identified as his in the Harvard Archives's "Hackett Index," a "List of Authors of Articles in Harvard Magazine: 1859–61," by Holmes's classmate Frank Warren Hackett. Holmes's translation of the *Apology of Socrates* (5.7) and his Bowdion Prize essay (5.11) have not been published before, but are identified as his in college records, as noted. The Civil War pieces are preserved with other war memorabilia in a scrapbook that is now among Holmes's papers at the Harvard Law School Library. He marked with his initials, and sometimes corrected, clippings of notices or poems that he had written. I have followed his hand-corrected text in this edition, noting changes from the newspaper version in each case.

The last four items, newspaper obituary notices for former comrades of his regiment, the Twentieth Massachusetts Volunteer Infantry, were written between 1889 and 1910, and are not works of Holmes's youth, but they are included here as they belong to the Civil War poetry more than to the later writings on law.

5.1
BOOKS

From *Harvard Magazine* 4:408 (1858).

The highest conversation is the statement of conclusions, or of such facts as enable us to arrive at conclusions, on the great questions of right and wrong, and on the relations of man to God. And so we all know well enough the difference, in our various associates, between him who lives only in events, and can relish nothing but the College gossip for the day, and him who feels that this is well enough, but that he can find higher food for thought, and who, while still young, passes restless hours longing to find some one who will talk to him of better things. Those, then, who have somewhat higher aspirations than the mass of their companions, and who in the ranks of boyish insipidity find none who meet or satisfy their desires, must as an alternative take to books.

And, again, many even of the somewhat unthinking will resolve every day to "read," (a phrase of slightly indefinite meaning, even to those who use it,) but, every day discouraged by the idea of the enormous quantity of books pronounced "indispensable," end by reading nothing. But this is very unnecessary trouble. Books are now almost innumerable, and most of them have been written within three hundred years. Regarding, then, what has been done already by mighty minds, and looking forward on the futurity we may reasonably suppose to be still remaining for this world, we see that the time is not inconceivably distant when a bookworm's life shall be spent in perusing a literature of Shakespeares and Prophets. This view, it is evident, will very materially contract the importance to be attached to any single volume, and will show two or three rules to be all that can be laid down with any real certainty.

First, then, we must read for ideas, not for authors. And we shall find that every grand book carries with it and implies ten thousand lesser ones; just as, when a huge tree is torn from the ground, it carries along with its roots an entire body of weeds and flowers and saplings. We read the Bible, and do not feel the need of Doctor Johnson's instructions in morality; and after studying the works of William Shakespeare, we find that Addison's Cato can teach us nothing. The first two contain all the last, and a great deal to spare; as I said in the beginning, they imply them.

Secondly, I cannot get beyond the belief that it is best to read what we like; there must be some book or books not absolutely vicious which would be interesting to any reader of this Magazine, and these, whatever they be, will necessitate a certain degree of thought, which of itself is sufficient cause for a better choice in the second instance. Of course a certain number selecting simply by preference would choose certain yellow-clad volumes and newspapers not of the best; but they are capable of higher things, and the rule is good. A great reader said, "As soon as you forget the color of the heroine's hair, lay down the book." We must read no longer—of course I speak of such reading as fills the intervals of other study, and does not itself form our labor—we must read no longer than we are perfectly engrossed in our subject.

Thirdly, for the description of books. After what has been said, it is sufficiently evident that but few rules can be laid down when we start by leaving all to individual judgment; but this may be suggested. First, as for the great books of other tongues, there are in each language one, or perhaps two or three geniuses, that have, as it were, originated the very literature of that state and period from which they sprung; that, like the loadstone mountain of the Arabian Nights, have drawn to their own mighty bulk the nails and strength of the time, and, while everything around them has fallen to pieces, stand only in increased power and majesty. These we must know; but for the Antoninuses and Thomas à Kempises, the reflectors and commentators, their spirit is the same in one language as in another, our native English furnishes enough of them, and, moreover, all the fine ideas that were their *end* are in the books of the present day the assumed axioms from which we start. But more important than all this, we must at once in some shape understand the questions of the day. Just as one man implies humanity, so the history of the struggles of one period implies eternity. And though there always is a fight and crisis, yet are we not in a peculiarly solemn position? Books and papers, within a century or two only accessible to the common people, have had their effect. A hundred years ago we burnt men's bodies for not agreeing with our religious tenets; we still burn their souls. And now some begin to say, Why is this so? Is it true that such ideas as this come from God? Do men own other men by God's law? And when these questions are asked around us,—when we, almost the first of young men who have been brought up in an atmosphere of investigation, instead of having every doubt answered, It is written,—when we begin to enter the fight, can we help feeling it is a tragedy? Can we help going to our rooms and crying that we might not think? And we whistle or beat on our piano, and some—God help 'em!—smoke and drink to drive it all away, and others find their resting-place in some creed which defines all their possibilities, and says, Thus far shall ye think, and no farther. No, no; it will not do to say, I am not of a melancholic temperament, and mean to have my good time. It will not do for Ruskin to say, Read no books of an agitating tendency; you will have enough by and by to distress you. We *must*, will we or no, have every train of thought brought before us while we are young, and may as well at once prepare for it.

History should be the finest, in fact, the all-comprehending study. But we do not find it so. The cause, as it seems to me, being that facts and dates are mistakenly supposed to constitute its chief part. Yet, if we think, we shall know that these are not what impress us with the realities of past time. Little things—anecdotes—will often display the whole manners and customs of a period, when we should have laid down the statistics as ignorant as we took them up. What is most pleasant about Herodotus is, that, in a history of the great nations of the earth, he tells us such facts as that the mares that gained three races are buried by the side of their master in the road that runs through the Hollow. This history, which we can by no possibility get, except by fragments from contemporary plays and poems, with regard to past days, at present we can have, or almost have forced upon us by the daily newspapers, reading in them details about each day enough to fill a volume of Grote or Macaulay. And so I say again, we must study the present to know the past. Emerson, who probably takes about as large a view of men and events as any one we could point out now living in America, gains much of this breadth by the peculiar direction of his studies. Look into his article on Books,—never was a stranger list of indispensables, will be our first impression. But we shall soon see the plan that regulates him. *We* read principally, more even than we do Shakespeare or any great man who lived as many as fifty years ago, the ephemeral productions of the day,—a very different thing from studying the progress or regress of the day in politics and religion. We encourage a hot-bed operatic taste that requires a strong stimulus to excite it, and consequently the delicacy of the noblest and calmest books is to us insipidity. The great secret of all delight in literature is preserving this fineness of taste, and Emerson understands it, and not only reads the great works of our own tongue, but he studies all the great inspired books of all the great literatures. He knows and reverences Shakespeare, Montaigne, and Goethe; but he has also penetrated into Plato and Confucius, into the Buddhist and Zoroastrian sacred books, which we contemn on the authority of others, without ever having looked into them ourselves, and some of which, written five hundred years before our Christian Scriptures, teach us lessons of love and forbearance, that, after eighteen hundred years have gone by, we have not yet granted the New Testament to inculcate. It seems to me that there is nothing in literature so elevating as these volumes; and we cannot help feeling how infinitely better were our time spent in really learning these, than in reading book after book of puzzling and involved commentary on a book which bears on its face that it was written for all if for any. Yet books are but little seeds after all, seeming insignificant enough before the merest weed of real life; but they lie soaking in our minds, and when we least expect it, they will spring up, not weeds, but supporters that will be our aid in the sorest struggles of our life.

5.2
SELECTION FROM THE APOLOGY OF SOCRATES

An original translation from the Greek, from a manuscript in *Exhibition and Commencement Performances 1859–1860*, Item 33, Harvard University Archives. Delivered orally May 1, 1860.

(XXIX) As you are unwilling to wait a very little while, Athenians, you will soon have the reproach cast upon you by those who like to speak ill of our city, of having put to death Socrates, a wise man; for they will call me wise, though I am not, from the wish to throw shame upon you. Now if you had only shown a little patience, the thing you desire would have come to pass of itself; for you see my age; that I am now far advanced in years and that death is near at hand.—This I do not say to all of you but to those only who have voted for my condemnation. (XXXI) With those of you on the other hand who have voted for my acquittal I would gladly speak of what has just taken place, while the officers are not yet ready, and the time has not quite come for me to go to the place where I must die.—For these few moments then, I beg of you to stay by me, since nothing hinders our talking with one another, while there is yet time, and I should like to tell you as my friends the meaning of what has happened. . . . [1] The prophetic voice of my spiritual guide has heretofore never failed to oppose me, and in the most trifling matters too, if I were about in any way to do otherwise than well. But now there has happened to me what by popular opinion is judged the greatest of all evils. Yet neither this morning, as I left my house, nor as I was coming before the court, nor in any part of my speech did the spirit offer me the least opposition, and that too though it has often restrained me when speaking on other occasions. In this matter it has not restrained me in anything I have either said or done. What then is the reason of this? I will tell you. It proves that this is a good thing which has happened to me and that those who think that death is an evil do not judge at all rightly.[2] You then, my judges, should feel high hopes with regard to death and hold this one thing firm in your convictions: that to a good man no event, whether he lives or dies, is evil, nor are his concerns ever neglected by the gods. My present condition is not the result of chance, but I plainly see that it was better for me to die and be freed from earthly cares. On this account it is that no warning has turned me from my course and that I feel no anger either towards those who have condemned me or towards my accusers.[3]—But I beg this of you, when my sons grow up, do you punish them and discipline them just as I have troubled you, should they seem to care for riches or any thing else more than virtue; and if they being of no real account should think themselves something, rebuke them, as I too have you, for not attending to their proper business and for their too great self-esteem. If you do this, both I and my sons will have secured the proper treatment at your hands. But now it is time for us to separate, for me to die and for you to live. Which is the better fate is unknown to all but God.

O. W. Holmes, Jr.

Editor's Notes

1. The ellipses replace "xxx," indicating that Holmes omitted a sentence at this point.
2. Holmes omitted a long passage here without indicating the omission.
3. Holmes omitted the balance of this sentence.

5.3
EDITORS' TABLE

From *Harvard Magazine* 7:26 (1860).

We read in the papers, that at the Alumni dinner Mr. T. W. HIGGINSON gave as a sentiment, "*The Harvard Magazine:* May it have new usefulness, long life, and *almost* as many subscribers as the Atlantic."

For this kind wish, coming just as the new debutantes are making their first and naturally timid bow, they feel, of course, a gratitude as real as this demonstration of good-will, from one not immediately and personally interested in the support of the Magazine, was unexpected. And yet the very unexpected nature of the toast suggests to the editors a wish that it were not quite so tacitly assumed that a College periodical could have no interest outside of the College walls. The common assumption, that nothing but matters connected with students, as such, have here a fitting place, contributes to this impression; whereas the true statement should rather be, that the preponderance of such subjects gives the *Harvard* its distinctive tone as a College magazine, just as the opening offered to every student to speak *any* sincere opinion imparts to it its greatest value. If it were our rule never to let anything, however slight, escape from our hand into print but what was the result of our life and experience *so far,* the lightest pieces, as well as the most solid, would still find equal place; but the detestable flippancy of College slang would be avoided, while all the real wit and peculiar humor of youth would appear the more evident by the destruction of its disguises. If this were done, though new *results* would not probably be displayed to the world, *tendencies,* which, in almost every man, are more important, would be shown, and we should be free from the dread of a future shame at these productions, which no one would rightly feel as the true exponent of a certain stage of development. Moreover, an increased sincerity in fun, as well as in more serious productions, would not fail to excite that degree of attention in the surrounding world, that seems to us but the *Harvard's* proper due;—not great, of course, but merely a proper respect for the expressions of our thought and sentiment, instead of the contempt which youthful flippancy is so sure to inspire. In offering these remarks, however, the editors would not be understood as finding proofs of what unearnest people like to call "earnestness" in a heavy subject; there is not even much presumption in favor of the superiority of an essay so mounted, but evidence is to be drawn only from the matter of the piece, and the question is, Did the author write with an intention?

To do their utmost in conducing to such writing, in place of articles only intended to fill a vacancy, the editors wish, once for all, to solicit *voluntary* contributions from *all the classes,* to prevent, as far as possible, that compulsory, hurried, and, probably, therefore bad writing, which is too apt to be the result of a promise hastily made and ill kept. As assurance, moreover, of an unbiassed judgment on the contributions that may be offered, the editors have determined that each number shall be published under the care and supervision of the whole board; thinking, also, that by this means there will be prevented that limitation of the contributions to a single class—alternating as the editor for the month was Senior or Junior—that ensued under a different method. Finally, as the editors on their part promise a diligent care (for which, observe, they gain literally no remuneration), the least that the students can do, if they choose to elect editors for the continuance of the Magazine, is to contribute their annual two dollars to its support; and we would also signify to those now Alumni, that they too, as they praise, may well drop their mite into the coffers of the *Harvard.*

<h2 style="text-align:center">5.4</h2>
<h3 style="text-align:center">EDITORS' TABLE</h3>

From *Harvard Magazine* 7:37 (1860).

In this number will be found recorded the annual victory of the Harvard boats in the College Union Regatta of last July. For two beautiful days Worcester was overflowing with the student life that filled its hotels and streets; confident Cambridge men and more doubtful Yale, with the rarer few from other colleges. In the soul of one from Cambridge everything was calculated to inspire satisfaction and delight. The enthusiastic bets, somewhat wild in the eyes of the more prudent, that on the first day Harvard won every race, brought in to the adventurous that solid assurance of the right direction things were taking that opened the hearts of the happy ones to extraneous joys; for such, the song did not unrequited woo, with nocturnal blandishments, sleep from their embrace. Such even the harmless but expensive pleasures of Worcesterian cabbage-leaf did not in vain allure; the Cantabrigians were happy;—nor were all others sad, but rather each after his kind, whether on the winning or the losing side, shared in the general jollity.

We cannot here detail the events that then took place,—the chess, the billiards, the songs of the Glee Club, the feats of individual prowess, nor even the meeting of sad-eyed editors, though we may mention the fact that the resolutions of their general conclave as to the University Quarterly will be printed on a separate sheet for distribution; and though we might become critical on some minor points, as for instance at the too easy down-heartedness of the Yale Sophs, on the second day, for men of real pluck, at the accidental impeding of their course by our Sophomore boat, still it is not worth while so to disturb the pleasant retrospect offered in those two days.

One matter, however, not set down in the record, yet as justly to be catalogued against us as our better parts to be noted in our favor, needs a mention here. We refer, of course, to the general rowdyism of demeanor shown by the students. We can but say *general,* for the most public demonstrations of this sort were participated in by a large majority of the collegians present; and that their conduct was only to be characterized as *rowdyism,* any one who was there, and will forget the special fact of who was concerned in it, will grant. Now, without undertaking to express a belief that when many young men meet together all will or should be members of the

Temperance Society, and not forgetting that to the natural ebullition of animal spirits on such an occasion some license may be allowed, as it certainly will be taken, still we cannot but protest against such behavior as was shown at Worcester, on the two grounds of the advantage and the honor of the students; *the advantage,* for outsiders, not ever inclined to be over-lenient to such a class, and experiencing a personal offence in such proceedings, are led to form their opinion of college manners and morality from this single exhibition; and when once this opinion is formed they do not hesitate to publicly express it, to the great injury of the reputation of the college, and to the great diminution of the possible repetition of such gatherings as were the cause of the offence. Moreover, this lawless behavior is to the dishonor of the students, as it directly casts upon them the imputation that public drunkenness is a necessary concomitant of public enjoyment, and a neglect of a decent respect for the comfort and the laws of the city that receives them the consequence of a permitted increase of their freedom of intercourse. In brief, while we believe that these troubles were the result of thoughtlessness rather than of deliberate malice, and consequently have perhaps received too harsh a treatment in some of the papers, it is clear, on the other hand, that, if the gentlemanly feeling and the morality of the collegians does not suffice to stop a repetition of the trouble, expediency tells them that continuance in such ways insures inevitably the interference of the authorities and the speedy stopping of the cause of the offence.

5.5

PLATO

From *University Quarterly* 2:205 (1860).[1]

Socrates, who is continually before our eyes as forming the nucleus of the Platonic dialogues, and as the foundation which furnished them their stability and weight, is known to us chiefly through the colored medium of those writings; and when we also include the humbler memoirs of his other pupil, Xenophon, we have the chief authorities for his life and teachings. In connection with Plato, then, he stands like one of the Blue Hills: the roots and base of the unyielding rock, but covered with the growth of forests and the accumulations of centuries, clothing and softening the contours of its rough ribs and only here and there the stern lines of the massive core showing unmistakably to the sky. As far as possible let us first settle the character and relation of this nucleus to the later growth which has enveloped it.

Socrates does not appear to have been a systematic philosopher; the dogmas he enunciated were few and uncertain. He was a rough old citizen with a big brain, who, belonging at Athens, and exceeding even his countrymen in his making man the proper centre of human thought, occupied himself in asking all sorts of questions of everybody with regard to matters practically interesting to men. Here is a condensed translation from the Theaetetus of a passage wherein he speaks of himself and his province:—"Have you not then heard that I am the son of the very noble and reverend midwife, Phaenarete, and that I follow the same profession? Consider all the relations of midwifery and you will more easily see what I mean. For you know that no one at the time of conception and pregnancy delivers others, but those who are past that period; and is it not evident that midwives more than others have the power to distinguish those really pregnant and those who are not?—Now in other respects my art of midwifery resembles theirs, but it differs in that it delivers men not women, and has regard to pregnant souls, not bodies; *and in this point I am like the midwives; I am barren of wisdom, and that which many have taunted me with, that I question others but give no answer myself on any subject, is a true reproach.* The cause being that the Diety compels me to act the part of midwife, but has prevented me from myself bringing forth. *I am not, therefore, at all wise, nor have I any discovery that is the offspring of my own mind.* But of those who associate with me, some appear at first very ignorant, but all, as our intimacy advances, if the Deity grants it, show such a wonderful proficiency that it is evident to all. And this clearly without learning anything from me, but of themselves discovering and becoming possessed of many beautiful and noble thoughts."

Though Socrates often uses these statements of his as a sly cover for an impending confutation, he still was perfectly in earnest as to the fact. His peculiar power lay not so much in a profound perception of truth as in a natural spirit of argumentative questioning, which he developed into his system of dialectics, demanding the initiatory definition, which it is also his claim to have introduced, as the necessary first step. He had a bent not too speculative and ideal to prevent his avowing the amelioration of present institutions as the ultimate purpose of his questions, rather than any more remote love of truth as such. Taking a subject bearing on the education of youth, perhaps, or, as in the Theaetetus, propounding a question on the nature of science, he would easily obtain from his companion some definition, loosely thought out, as might be expected from the unscientific use of language and lax thought of that time, and then would proceed with fatal effect to apply the proffered garment to the form it was to fit, and prove it here too short, there too full, and in another place again too tight to meet its destined end.

Many of the dialogues most representative of the real Socrates come to an end, having only indicated by negations a positive opinion, and others give us no clue to his idea of the truth; and indeed very likely he had no clear idea of it, but was working after his obstetric fashion to see if he could not elicit it from some other mind. But when Socrates did undertake to arrive at the truth constructively, his chief means was by the fallacious argument drawn from single analogies; a plausible analogy furnished to his mind proof all-sufficient and conviction to every doubt, and when it was once in his grasp he held on to it until he had pressed from it every germ of possible suggestion. The resemblance of principal ratios being settled, he would unhesitatingly assume the same likeness in all minor points without being startled by any result that might be induced by the process. It is thus in an example from the same part of the Theaetetus that I have previously quoted from, which I use merely as it happens to be the nearest at hand, though in other cases results far more illogical and in some instances even shocking to sound morality occur. In this instance he merely trivially argues from a recognized similarity between the midwife and the reaper of grain that, because, as he assumes, the reaper should also know the proper seed to be sown in various soil, therefore the midwife should know as part of her business the becoming mates in marriage for the various temperaments.[2] It is not an important point, nor does Socrates make it so, but it will illustrate the fact.

"*Socr.*—Didn't you know this about them, that they are most skillful matchmakers, as being competent to distinguish from what unions will spring the finest children?

Theaet.—I did not altogether know that.

Socr.—* * * Consider; do you think that the cultivation and gathering of the fruits of the earth, and again the knowledge of the proper soil for the various plants and seeds, belong to the same or a different art?

Theaet.—Certainly to the same." (In the first part of this analogy, even, we have a fallacy, for a reaper may clearly be competent for his business and know nothing of planting or cultivation.[3])

"*Socr.*—But with regard to women, my friend, do you think there is one art of adapting the seed to the soil and another of gathering the fruit?

Theaet.—It is not reasonable to suppose so."

Just as personally he was a wonder of physical endurance, able to walk barefoot through the snow at a temperature which his fellow-soldiers could hardly bear, wrapt in their warm fur coverings, and undergoing all hardships without a complaint, or even the appearance of suffering, so was Socrates characterized mentally by an enormous vitality. This did not fail him in his latest hours, but gave him that confidence which enabled him to face his death with such calm dignity; and the same activity of mind which led to his questions and his public cross-examinations must have imparted to his conversations a vigor that, with the sense of his moral strength, probably did much to gain over and retain for him the many pupils who attended his daily steps.

Having now seen, as well as the brief space allows, the philosophical position of Socrates, as a man rather of a keen and caustic spirit of enquiry, than of great constructive power, and naturally therefore the one to introduce definition and logical induction from more or less accurate premises; as a man whose more practical turn of mind and unflinching moral courage, as well as physical daring, seem to have been a foundation that was needed for the speculative superstructure reared by his chief pupil; let us, without undertaking the uncertain task of settling the distinctive dogmas of the master's creed, turn our attention to Plato, who, being apparently more devoted to purely abstract speculation, seems to have embraced all the positive opinions of Socrates, aiding them by new arguments and illustrations, and who has certainly also added new ones peculiar to himself;[4] Plato, moreover, who was fully in our sense of the word a philosopher, has arranged and perfected the conversational method of Socrates into a delicate and powerful instrument of exact written thought, and has obtained the best results possible to be gained by its means. In addition to all this, he gives life and breath to all his dialectics by the animation of his dramatic power and the grandeur of his poetic allegory.

In speaking of Socrates, I have briefly explained the peculiar logical method which Plato received from his master, and aided and enlarged by the addition of a more rigid analysis. Now with the first of the two the method was all in all, as it gave a systematic order to his daily conversations; and though by its means truth was brought to light, yet still it was with the delivering of the person in labor, not with the child when fairly in the world, that he was especially concerned. Plato, however, the scientific lecturer, (though he too set a value on dialectic skirmishing merely as such,) had aspirations also to positive theories; among these the most prominent is the famous but sometimes misinterpreted Theory of Ideas, and this, as the basis of his system, I will now endeavor to explain.

Everything material has of course certain qualities by which it is characterized; as for instance, that of beauty—a deer, a landscape, and a man, might all, though very unlike, be rightly called beautiful—moreover, there is the higher beauty of the soul, and still higher, one of science.

What is it that makes it right to apply the same adjective to all of these? It is, answers Plato, generalizing, because in an ascending scale all of these partake and more and more nearly approach the abstract *idea of beauty;* 'which is eternal, being neither produced nor destroyed, and suffering neither increase nor decay, which is not beautiful at one point or at one time only and not at another, nor beautiful in the eyes of some but not so to others; nor is this beauty an outward appearance merely, like a face or a hand or anything corporeal, nor is it any discourse or science, nor does it exist anywhere in any being, nor in any point in space; but it subsists by and with itself in eternal unity. And all other things are beautiful in so far as they partake of this, and in such a way that while everything else is subject to birth and decay, it suffers no change and is liable to no casualty.'

Man is man, again Plato also says, just so far as he partakes of humanity, and a table a table so far as it partakes of the tabular idea. But here, as it seems to me, there is a serious confusion introduced into the system, owing to the admitting equally, without distinction, the simple ideas like those on which mathematical truth is dependent, or, perhaps, like beauty, which alone are recognized by our intuitive faculty, (and which, with Plato, we may suppose necessary ideas permanently existing in the mind of the Creator,) and the *complex* conceptions of table and chair, which are evidently mere arbitrary combinations effected by man; or still further, those like *humanity,* which is a purely general statement, drawn from observation, of a *present* fact, equally, as far as we know, dependent on the arbitrary will of the Deity. In other words, more briefly, as long as we have faith in reason we must believe in the truths of mathematics and the like existing as absolute necessities in the nature of things, while we see, at least, no such necessary existence for the ideas humanity, table, &c.; and Plato was wrong, therefore, in characterizing both the classes as absolute and as equally ὄυτως ὄντα.*

A convenient illustration of the above theory might be offered in the shape of a diagram.

Let us suppose from a common focus the principal axes of many ellipses to radi-

---

* The above is meant to be so stated as to be true in outline to sensationalist and idealist alike; for, without entering into the distinctions of necessary and contingent truth, it is evident that mathematics express the simplest relations of all created things, whereas creation might conceivably have stopped short of man or man not have invented a table. But it is especially the including of the idea table, which no sensationalists of the present time would call of the same order, in the same category with those connected with mathematical truth or beauty that stamps the unscientific character of his theory.

Since the above words were written and the whole essay finished and put into other hands, a new volume by Whewell, on the 'Philosophy of Discovery,' has appeared, in which the same criticism is made, in language so nearly similar that I insert the passage here; "But Plato seems, in many of his writings, to extend this doctrine much further; and he assumed not only Ideas of Space and its properties, from

ate in all directions; the various nature of the different ellipses depends entirely on the relation of the separate foci, (which to our view may represent the centres of individuality,) to the common central focus which stands for the Platonic abstraction, and which, although the essential point common to all the ellipses, is, nevertheless, only a geometrical idea destitute of extension or any predicable qualities. The ratio of the focus of individuality to this central point is, I say, the essential matter; and the ellipse, a figure having extension, yet depending for its character on an idea, precisely represents the relation, according to the theory of Plato, of a beautiful object to the abstract quality, beauty. Now beauty, Plato likewise holds, is the most sensible presentation of the Good, which is the definition, so to speak, of God, and which embraces all the other permanent representative ideas. The Good is the end of all philosophy, and as this is attained to by the study of the various ideas which represent it and which it comprehends, such study is philosophy, is Science *par excellence.*

Dialectic, therefore, or Logic, as concerned with these immutable ideas, which alone, as he holds, owing to their immutability, admit of definition, is exalted to this position, and science founded on observation, as concerned with mutable matters, must take an entirely secondary place. But Logic is, in fact, merely an instrument which works with data previously obtained, whether from this very physical science or from intuition; and the unhappy fallacy in connection with this point, that is, with regard to its functions, which runs all through Plato, is that he confounds this drawing of conclusions already contained in the premise, by Logic, which can only develop a pre-existing statement, with the finding of new data or statements, for which we must look to consciousness or to generalizations from experience. Moreover* all logical investigation into the nature of the subject of a statement or definition, is only good so far as the definition may be supposed absolutely and not only relatively true; and yet Plato, in common with others of the ancients, assuming a definition which will only stand in the capacity of showing the meaning *he attaches* to a word to be the true expression of the actual fact referred to by it, proceeds thence to deduce consequences relative to the essential nature of the fact.

As I have made use of this prominent example of beauty in illustrating Plato's Ideal Theory, it may be worth while to try to explain, before leaving the subject, the real nature of the famous Platonic Love, which is connected with this idea of the beautiful.

Love is the faculty by which we immediately apprehend the Good, of which, as has been said, beauty is the most sensible presentation. Every being that is mortal desires and earnestly strives to partake of these verities which are alone immortal;

---

which geometrical truths are derived; but of Relations, as the Relations of Like and Unlike, Greater and Less; and of mere material objects, as Tables and Chairs. Now to assume Ideas of such things as these solves no difficulty and is supported by no argument. In this respect the Ideal Theory is of no value in Science." pp. 12, 13. It is pleasant to find one's self sustained by such high authority.

*This latter point I first found noticed in Lewes' Biogr. Hist. of Philosophy; (library ed. London, p. 130.) See also Devey's Logic, Bohn 'Nominal Definition mistaken, &c.' p. 73; Lewes also was the first, as far as I know, to point out the difference of the Socratic and Baconian induction; I have used these points as aiding in establishing conclusions originally founded on the study of Plato himself.

and this striving after immortality, in the lowest organisms, takes the forms of mere animal desire for procreation. Those, however, who feel desire in their souls, have as their proper offspring intellect and every other excellence, of which poets and inventors are the chief generators. Now when any one of a really divine soul arrives at maturity, he longs earnestly to beget an offspring; and, being unwilling to generate upon what is ugly, seeks ardently for a beautiful object. And if he meets another beautiful and noble soul, especially if it have also a finely moulded body to match, he rushes to embrace this combination, and, discoursing much on virtue, he, acting as teacher, endeavors to direct his pupil in the path of his duty, and to bring up those immortal children, (beautiful and noble thoughts,) which any one who might choose would prefer to those of mortal birth. Platonic Love is, in more modern language, the association of two noble souls, master and pupil, in the bonds of affection, for the purpose of encouraging a higher morality, a profounder perception of truth and a more real inward beauty.

I have spoken thus at length about this Theory of Ideas and the matters connected with it, because these ideas are the pillars on which Plato's system stands, and because by discovering, as far as possible, the strength and weakness of his foundation, we can infer the soundness of the whole structure. What has been the result of our investigation? We have seen that the fundamental classification of the ideas was loose and unscientific; that Plato's conception of the true method of investigating their nature was vague and incorrect; and, to cap the climax, we need only to have studied his works to know the extreme difficulty of fixing on any exact and consistent opinion as steadily held to by him. I believe that his notion of the relation of the material individual form to the ειδος, the type or species, varied at different times; he even left room for dispute as to exactly what he thought with regard to the central matter, and has furnished texts for the extremest realists, as well as to those of more moderate views. And after the best pains that we take to find him out, there are many ready to inform us that our labor is quite vain, for all that we can gather from these writings is but exoteric doctrine, whereas his esoteric opinion was transmitted only by word of mouth to his disciples: in this latter statement, however, founded chiefly on an equivocal expression of Aristotle, I do not put the least faith, since that which we have offered us in the dialogues is exactly such as we should have expected from one of Plato's natural constitution, reacting on the method and teachings received from his masters, and since there is only too great a willingness to give credit to all remote persons and times for unattainable and hidden superiorities.

From the above results we may fairly conclude, I think, that the constructive system of Plato, confused and doubtful as it is, though a vast step as introducing more accurate and well defined thought than had previously existed, has for us no scientific value whatsoever. It needed a complete remodelling before it would suffice as a consistent cosmology. This point, which will be briefly explained in another place, we must, I think, concede, and I wish especially to insist upon it, because there is a continual unscientific neglect of the history of the progress of thought in our ordinary way of looking back upon past time; in which we seem like infants grasping vaguely at remote objects, with no power to distinguish them from those near at hand. Swedenborgianism, admirable as it is in its philosophy of human life, is peculiarly guilty in this point, looking back and quoting Pythagoras, and relying much on esoteric doctrine, not seeing that from the entire absence of the central idea of science, it was impossible for the people of that time to have held secrets that the world has not yet caught up with, or rather has entirely fallen away from. Our chemists do know really more than the best of the alchymists, and it is not worth troubling ourselves now much about their elixirs and their philosopher's stone,* and so with the ancient metaphysicians, we may spend much time in looking for what they never had, and for what the whole order of things forbade their having; but more of this further on. But now, abandoning that exactness of science which Plato lived too early to attain, let us wonder at the profound insight into all nature, the instinct for great truth, which he displays. His allegorical presentation of the soul, in the Phaedrus, as a charioteer driving two horses, the one of noble birth and beautiful, the other base and struggling with the reins, and the charioteer, as long as he can command the latter, remaining in the contemplation of the eternal verities and of God; but, losing that control, being forced to sink to an earthly body, while the twelve gods drive calmly on forever; and the rest: how sublimely does it set forth the conditions of human life! Indeed, as has just been noticed of Swedenborg, where Plato is supernatural, and deals with demons and with other states of being, he is most supremely natural; as the "Heaven and Hell," though we may not accept it as revelation, is not less wonderful if we are content to apply it to this world for its explanation of relations here.

Moreover, in separating man the idea, from man the concrete, how completely Plato has anticipated the best art by dividing the accidental from the real. How deeply would he have felt the difference of the plodder, who, professing nature as his model, puts before him a flower, and copies every corrosion and chance stain upon its leaves, (not that such art may not have its place,) and the great artist, who, seizing the type of the plant, paints that upon his canvass, and leaves the rest in the subordination in which it belongs.[5] When the admirable artist of the *White Captive* said that in every man and woman he tried to see their face and form as it would have been if it had descended from Adam, still characteristic, but free from the marks of sin and sickness, he was talking pure Platonism and true art.

What, again, is more profound than his perception of the fatality attaching to matter? With it the law of cause and effect is absolute; if we know the data, the results are inevitable; only self-determining vital centres are free from this necessary consequence and fix on this or that for no cause except that such was their will. Matter represents the limits of our thoughts, and is the evil necessity which the free soul, inclined to virtue so far as it is free and still wise, must over come. Heaven, the world of the absolute ideas and the pure spirits, cannot, consistently with the goodness of God, contain evil, and its existence is consequently found to be in this gross matter, veiling the ideas and deadening the perception of the spirit. Hence the

---

*As an example on the other side might be offered the splendid structures of Egypt and of Baalbec, but these very structures owed their magnificence to a semi-barbarian disregard of the life of the lower classes on the part of those in power.

philosopher's is, in Plato's estimation, the highest pursuit among mortals; for what is philosophy but a preparation for death, or the anticipation of the time when we shall be rid of those blinds of the flesh which interpose between us and wisdom.

If we could see to-day the telescope constructed by Galileo, with its clumsy tube and simple lenses, ground, perhaps, by his own hand, with what reverence should we handle that primitive instrument, with what feelings should we gaze up through it at the satellites of Jupiter first discovered by its means! But if we desired to study the mysteries which perplex the astronomer of to-day, we should very certainly seek an instrument which the latest perfections of science had best adapted to our needs. We should not, therefore, detract from the glory of him who first revealed the mighty powers hidden in what previously had been known only as an amusing toy; nor would he be less great because his successors, following in his footsteps, had attained results which he could never have anticipated by means of instruments which had superseded his own.[6] We are too apt to forget those accumulations of new material, and consequent correction or annulling of old results and methods in every branch of knowledge, which, with the steady advances of civilization, each eager generation continually makes.[7]

Galileo's telescope, doubled, is our opera-glass; and as it has been with the astronomer so also has it been with Plato, the explorer in different realms. While he remains the original interpreter of certain primary facts and relations of the human spirit to the central and eternal ideas, he still bears to us the same relation that a self-made man does to one who has been bred in the midst of riches, and educated from his earliest youth; the circumstances of the former may even have aided to display and develop his natural powers, (and genius at any rate needs but few materials to work with,) but certainly the latter starts with an advantage which can never be annulled, whatever may be his inferiority in natural parts.

We start far beyond the place where Plato rested. He lived too early to be able to avail himself of the history of the fluctuations in philosophy, to aid in shaping his own conceptions of philosophical truth; and far more important, and what should continually be taken into account in estimating his views, it is only in these last days that anything like an all-comprehending science has embraced the universe, showing unerring law prevailing in every department, generalizing and systematizing every phenomenon of physics, and every vagary of the human mind.[8] Plato, having raised to an exquisite perfection the instrument of dialectics which he received from his master, was led thereby to the most noble and remote of his discoveries, though scientifically imperfect as we have seen—the Theory of Ideas. When he had laid this result before the world he had done all that with his facilities was possible, and was of necessity compelled to wait for a more extended experience, and more perfect instruments to exceed his farthest vision and embrace in a wider science his boldest generalizations; and when he undertook the construction of a Republic from the few data which he could attain, he was laboring as vainly as one who should endeavor to find the successive actual positions of the moon from his mathematical knowledge, being ignorant of the solar perturbations, and the motion of the nodes and apsides; and yet, owing to the comparative obscurity of the subject, we see his crudest ideas discussed to-day with a gravity of which the Ptolemaic system is now equally worthy.

In quitting this subject, on which free criticism as well as praise has been used, I should wish my last words to be those of the reverence and love with which this great man and his master always fill me; it seems to me that on the subjects that are the highest, and also the most difficult, few final *results* are yet attained;[9] I do not feel sure that each man's own experience is not always to be that which must ultimately settle his belief, but to see a really great and humane spirit fighting the same fights with ourselves, and always preserving an ideal faith and a manly and heroic conduct; doubly recommended, moreover, to our hearts by the fact of his having only himself to rely on, and no accepted faith that killed a doubt it did not answer; the spectacle, I say, of these two grand old heathen, the master the inspired fighter, the scholar the inspired thinker, fills my heart with love and reverence at one of the grandest sights the world can boast.[10]

Editor's Notes

1. All marginalia are from Holmes's copy: OWH papers, Paige Box 18, Item 4.
OWH note at top: took the prize for the year 1860. Written in the summer vacation 1860. [The prize referred to was one awarded by the *University Quarterly*.]
2. OWH correction to: . . . sown in various soils. . . .
3. OWH correction to: . . . competent to his business. . . .
4. OWH correction to: . . . himself. Plato. . . .
5. OWH correction to: . . . professing to take nature as his. . . .
6. OWH insertion of comma after "anticipated."
7. OWH correction to: . . . and the consequent correction. . . .
8. OWH correction to: . . . and which is far more important, and should continually. . . .
9. OWH correction to: . . . it seems to me on the subjects which are the highest. . . .
10. OWH corrects "heathen" to "heathens."

5.6

NOTES ON ALBERT DURER

From *Harvard Magazine* 7:41 (1860).

If we regard any of the modern finished woodcuts, we shall find them conceived primarily in *tints* expressed by delicate lines, sometimes confused, sometimes systematic, which are individually insignificant, but collectively effect just and fine pictorial gradations. The same fact is further shown by the drawing on the block, which in the most characteristically modern cuts, as in the case of nearly all the illustrations of the popular periodicals, is almost entirely washed in with the brush; the reproduction of the smooth *tints* by systems of *lines,* being left to the discretion and technical skill of the engraver. Even when the drawing is made entirely with the pen by the artist, and the engraver merely cuts its fac-simile upon the block, we shall still find the fundamental conception to be the same, only in this case the draughtsman has endeavored in the first place to express those tints by careful shading with the pen, which in the other he left to the methods of the cutter. Albert Durer, on the other hand, contrary to the moderns, made a pen-drawing upon the block, bold and rudimentary, in which the finest gradations are not attempted, and all elaboration of tints is quite secondary to the thoughtful meaning of the individual *line*. The reason for the difference evidently lies in the improved methods and increased understanding of the material in our time. Thus, the introduction of the use of the graver on cross-cut blocks, instead of the old knife-cutting on blocks sawed along the grain, has revolutionized the technical methods of treatment; and the substitution of lines of differing thickness and varying proximity, instead of the old cross-hatchings, as a means of expressing shades, renders a thousand effects possible or easy that were once unattempted. Hence, our woodcuts are comparatively finished works of light and shade, in place of the sketches, perfect as they are as such, which are the utmost results of the old art. Ruskin, who has noticed the value of Durer's line, attributes it to his profound knowledge of drawing, using the simplest means to express the most possible truth, with a material inadequate for perfect work; but if this were all, it is evident, according to Ruskin's own principles of finish, that these means ought to give all the truth consistently attainable with the material in question, whereas quite the reverse appears to be the case. In short, it is vain to deny that the reduced prominence of the single line in our cuts is the natural accompaniment of more perfectly gradated tints of color. To be sure, there were good effects from the old limitations, and indeed it was chiefly to show these that this whole comparison has been made. When each additional pen-stroke was an additional labor to the engraver, the draughtsman would take care that every line should tell as much as possible, and, giving up the delicacy to be gained by a fuller treatment, would put upon the block a severe and thoughtful drawing. Thus it is, that, as I have said, we find with Durer every line is keen and searching as the stroke of a surgeon's knife, not one superfluous, not one to be changed but with a corresponding change of effect; so that, besides the care and thoughtfulness thus gained, there is the advantage in these old works, that finally a man shows just what he knows, and when he is ignorant must needs confess it without any of our possible disguises of uncertainty in mystery or vagueness.

Having seen the technical relations of the woodcuts of Durer to those of our own time, a matter which will be useful when we come to look at the work of three hundred years ago, let us now endeavor to determine his position as an artist.

The men of the fifteenth and sixteenth centuries, it seems to me, had one advantage not likely to be soon possessed again. Without stirring the dogmas of the Church, it is clear that a noble philosophy will suffice to teach us our duties to ourselves and our neighbors, and some may think also to our God. Some may take satisfaction in basing their moral obligations on this foundation, and in contemplating the future construction of an abstract religion on the same general ground; it is certainly now true, however, that the weaker faith of the majority of mankind prefers for these pure abstractions a clothing of more concrete fact, and demands the stimulus of a story and a life to excite their souls, sluggish to receive the highest truth; and that this demand will not remain to the end of time is by no means sure. But however this may be, certainly the growth of civilization increases our faith in the natural man, and must accordingly detract from the intense and paramount importance attached in darker times to the form of the story embodying the popular religion. Thus, while it has come to pass, that nowadays we see that duty is not less binding had the Bible never been written, or if we were to perish utterly to-morrow; on the other hand, the story that once made corporeal, and fit subject for the painter, man's highest religious conceptions,—that dramatized philosophy,—is now regarded in so far a different light, that those scenes, once wrought out with such loving faith, have now, I fear, passed from the province of art. This is something that civilization cannot restore; and neither the drooping sickliness of the modern religious painting in Germany, nor the feverish strength of all the Pre-Raphaelite religious work that I have seen, can compare with the unconscious work three centuries old and more, full of the life of the artist: thoughtful, for it came from the soul of a reformer, yet faithful, with the simple and childlike faith of early times.

But, however much be lost to art when the religious stories become matter for reasoning and scholarly dispute, in place of the old reverence for the letter, art does not finally depend for inspiration on religious form. The ideal spirit may be influenced by circumstances, but it is the great gift of humanity, not of a sect; it inspired the philosopher Plato, the artist among thinkers, as well as the Christian Durer, a thinker among artists. This it is that sees the eternal disguised in the visible form, in the particular event; and I notice that its highest results with Durer, after all, are not found in even the profound pathos and grand tenderness of the *Passion* and the *Life of Christ*, but in conceptions more remote from the contact of history. The mortal figures there portrayed were personal and ephemeral, but the MELANCOLIA sits forever, an undecaying and immortal thought.

If we study this last-named print, we shall find it more illustrative of Durer's power, and more characteristic of his tone of thought, than perhaps any other of his works. In the anatomy of that figure there is the mass and grandeur of Michael Angelo's Night, but it is hidden under the curiously crumpling folds of the enveloping garment, elaborated with a touch of German realism; this corresponds to and illustrates the peculiar power of the artist: like that form, massive and imposing, but like it, hiding its naked strength under the thousand folds of a disguising fancy; and if we turn to the idea of this great work, we find in it set down the history of Durer's inner life. It is full of a symbolism that we neither can entirely understand, nor wish to treat with too rude a curiosity; whatever was in Durer's mind when he wrought out the engraving, we feel, instinctively, as I have said, that into it he has thrown his life. That solitary woman is the true picture of his soul, in its strength and in its weakness; powerful, but half overcome by the many objects of its universal study; crowned with the wreath of the elect and beautiful with ideal genius, but grave with thought and marked with the care of the world; winged, yet resting sadly on the earth. Durer's genius was thoroughly German; to all its ideality there was added a realizing tendency, that makes positive his most remote and mystical fancies, in this respect recalling the criticism of Coleridge on George Herbert and the elder English poets, as "conveying the most fantastic thoughts in the most correct and natural language;" while the antithesis of the modern school, by the same author, may be quoted as also applicable to a degree in art. Of this Coleridge speaks, as "in the most fantastic language, conveying the most trivial thoughts. The latter is a riddle of words; the former, an enigma of thoughts." But this last is only true of those hangers-on to a great school, who catch the mannerisms without possessing the genius of its founders.

If I have now succeeded in making plain the character of Durer's mind, it will be easy to see that in his works we may expect a wide range between those of profound imaginative thought on the one hand, and on the other, those which his love of the simplest every-day truth has prompted; and his prints and pictures may be classified according to their position between these poles. Highest would come such poems as the MELANCOLIA, which is as preferable to any scene or representation of a momentary fact as existence is higher than incident; even the *Knight and Death,* though often called the greatest of his engravings, would, strictly, have to give place to this by just so much as, in the figure of the knight, it becomes lowered to the personal and individual; but there is, on the other hand, to this latter that active strength which almost forbids us to place it second to anything. The next division would contain those works which conveyed a great idea, through the medium of a person, either actually or conceivably historical; as in the almost awed expression, as of man rising from the experience of the other world, and yet the look of Godlike benignity, portrayed in the face of Christ (strangely contrasting with the animal immobility of the sleeping guards), in the woodcut of the Resurrection in the *Lesser Passion.* A different example of the same class is the *War-Horse,* of which a good copy on wood was published by Charles Blanc, in the *History of the Painters of all Nations,* the same cut being republished in the Illustrated Magazine of Art, for January, 1854. Only lower than the just mentioned Resurrection in the capacity of the subject, perhaps greater in power of treatment, is the larger woodcut of Christ sinking under the cross; to judge of Raphael's similar picture by engravings, the older print is as far superior in sincerity, in sentiment, and in grandeur, as it is in vivid reality, and this though Raphael had probably seen either it, or the similar one of the smaller series, before he began his painting. Thus, through the second division there would be a gradual descent, marked by the decrease of the higher qualities, through the works containing appeals to the nobler human feelings but approaching nearer to every-day life, such as many of the cuts in the *Life of the Virgin,* down, finally, to purely unimaginative statement of fact.

The above classification is the best one, I believe, of so general a nature, and though, of course, not absolute, points out a principle applicable in ranking the works and in settling the position of all artists. There are various considerations, however, which act as drawbacks; thus, we have already seen that certain qualities in the *Knight and Death* caused us to value it as little inferior to the MELANCOLIA, nay, in some respects superior, though the presumption was in favor of the superiority of the latter. We can, again, easily fancy it possible that the magnificent vitality of Titian might be worth more than any less healthy, though more aspiring work; and, in the same way, the majestic grace of Raphael might very probably outweigh profounder thought expressed in the coarser forms of Durer. To speak about such different qualities relatively is as hard as to compare the commanding power of a great statesman with the more abstract ability of the philosopher; the one conveys the greater sense of power, yet in the other we recognize the higher range of thought; the best we can do is to fix on an intermediate point, where the keen eye and directing brain of the man of the world keep more abstract reflection from falling into weakness. One thing I think we can say; just as the lowest form of good art is the mere portraiture of the single, unconnected fact, with no further view beyond,—like the painting of a nosegay, for instance, with the decay, the worm, and the dew-drop set down with equal faithfulness,—so art is great in proportion as it rises above this, and the presumption is always in favor of that picture being greatest in which the lower truth of the individual is made subservient (notice, I do not say falsified or even neglected, but made subservient) to the profounder truth of the idea. Knowledge of the stains of the earth, and of the decay that accompanies all earthly life, doubtless the painter needs, but higher than this is the sight which beholds the type distinguished beneath the wasting form, and higher than anything connected with the individual is the conception of the harmonious whole of a great work, and this again is great, just as its idea partakes of what is eternal. And this striving to look on types and eternal ideas, is that highest gift of the artist, which is called the ideal tendency.

I had hoped finally to have devoted a few words to Durer in his wider relations, as a man who resumed in himself and represents in his works the great tendencies of his age and country, but the limited space forbids. As it is, all that I have attempted, has been to hint at that combination of noble powers, coming at a thoughtful time, that have made his works dearer to me, and more valued instructors than any book and than any other art.

5.7
ALMA MATER

(READ AT THE SOPHOMORE SUPPER OF THE CLASS OF '61.)

From *Harvard Magazine* 7:48 (1860).

> Two years have passed since fair Harvard received us,—
> Two years touched the face of our smiling young earth,—
> She, who with many a pang has conceived us,
> Two years from now will give some of us birth;
> And we shall love her,
> Our bountiful mother,
> We shall all love her, wherever we go;
> Both for her motherhood,
> And for our brotherhood,
> We shall all love her, wherever we go.
>
> Babies in life, we shall play with its roses,
> Boys, see their opening; men, watch their decay;
> But the beauty departing a higher discloses,
> And we find the fruit just as the flower drops away.
> Then drink to our mother,
> Our bountiful mother,
> For we shall love her, wherever we go;
> Both for her motherhood
> And for our brotherhood
> We shall all love her, wherever we go.

5.8
BOOK NOTICES

From *Harvard Magazine* 7:111 (1860).

1. *The History of England, from the Accession of James II.* By THOMAS BABINGTON MA-CAULAY. 4 vols. Small 8vo.

2. *The Works of* CHARLES LAMB. A New Edition. 4 vols. Small 8vo.

3. *The Lives of Dr. John Donne, Sir Henry Wotton, Richard Hooker, George Herbert, and Dr. Robert Sanderson.* By IZAAK WALTON; with some Account of the Author and his Writings, by THOMAS ZOUCH, D.D., F.L.S., Prebendary of Durham. New Edition, with Illustrative Notes, complete in One Volume. Small 8vo. Boston: Crosby, Nichols, Lee, & Co. For sale by Sever and Francis.

The first of the above-mentioned works is offered in a most respectable library form; four volumes, well bound, and legibly printed on good paper; and thus makes decidedly the most attractive edition of the History yet published in America, and almost the only one worthy of Lord Macaulay's fame. Of the work itself, so often criticised, and surviving criticism so well, there is nothing to be said here, except that it is one of those books which maturity admires, and even youth finds attractive, in spite of the early imbibed and righteous horror of history-books as such.

But while these volumes preserve in their aspect a kind of middle-aged sobriety, becoming to the gravity of their matter, the next quaternity appears with somewhat gayer air; here there is a more open and larger type, a certain rambling generosity befitting the kind-hearted author. Leaving out of question some private leanings, and a silent preference to have Charles Lamb in a more tatterdemalion guise than the usual full-dress suit; just as he affected old copies of his favorite authors, with the odor of a dead century in their pages; we welcome this new edition as one of that order of publications which have done so much, within a few years, toward putting the better products of our press more nearly on a level with the best English work. The Life and Letters and Talfourd's Final Memorials, combined with the more familiar Essays of Elia, the Poems, and Lamb's Miscellaneous Works, are here brought together to make an edition most satisfactorily complete.

If we may say so, *Lamb* is rather a pungent flavor than solid food; he has that unmistakable individual *smack* which is a sure mark of genius, even when its existence in excess points, as in his case, to consequent limitations of scope. His criticisms, so frequently praised with too general a commendation, though always that of a connoisseur and lover of picturesque antiquity, are often biassed by his strong idiosyncrasies and personal preferences, for the very reason that he was so individual a man. Yet this, as well as his more creative work, is dear to us, for all belonged to one who had not only wit, but humor,—wit and love,—to a lovely spirit and a courageous heart.

But we must pass to the last volume of our list, the "Lives" of Izaak Walton.

This is the best edition of the book, and of the form in which it is issued we need only say it is of a size and appearance uniform with that of Lamb's Works, published by the same well-known firm. These "Lives," less known than Walton's charming pastoral, "The Complete Angler," make a book most opportune for our times; if, in an age of fast living, of hurrying business, and of unrepose, where the general taste is for condiments and dishes unnaturally stimulant, we had constantly on hand some works of this stamp, it might prove a wholesome corrective and a useful change of diet. There is here such a delightful old-world calm, a leisure so grave and saintly, that we feel on each page the effects of the holy life that fitted Walton for his task. Though it is vain enough to attempt to transplant the habits or modes of thought belonging to another period into this, still we may learn some purity of heart, and some tranquillity of spirit from these lives, which were first published, and found "passable, in an eloquent and captious age."

5.9
BOOK NOTICES

From *Harvard Magazine* 7:235 (1861).

Marion Graham; or, "Higher than Happiness." By META LANDER. Small 8vo. Boston: Crosby, Nichols, Lee, & Co.

We are sorry that the publishers, whose well-known names appear on the title-page of this book, should have so far fallen away from their usually careful selection as to have undertaken its publication. It belongs to that class of vulgar novels, and, what is worse, vulgar novels written by women, which are one of the afflictions of our day. Not that this story is of the worst or weakest order, but simply that it is irretrievably vulgar without displaying ability enough to excuse its printing. The plot is poor and unpleasing, and you cannot help feeling all the time about the characters that you know them better than the authoress does, and that they are neither handsome nor wise, in spite of her assurance to the contrary. The heroine, Marion, is introduced, at first, under the influence of a sort of preliminary passion for a Mr. Maynard, a minister (ministers are as thick throughout the book as salamanders after a rain; a new one creeps out from under every leaf we turn over). But Maynard, having foolishly preferred her friend, who is more spooney than herself, Marion gives up No. 1. Then enter a dark man, black hair, glittering teeth, eyes, voice, brain, everything, and Marion proceeds to increase the size of the volume that tells her life, with her passion for him, and extracts from the more familiar writings of Carlyle. But, alas! he is an unbeliever, and she "renounces" him. So after knavish scenes with another handsome man, Mr. Perley, and other interesting by-play, she espouses No. 3 (Mr. Sunderland, a minister). Briefly after marriage enter No. 2 (who is now converted and a minister). Tableau. Marion gets over it, however, loves her husband well enough; husband and previous lover swear eternal friendship, and then the lover goes among the heathen. Now in all this there is a certain purity of tone that is really much better than the hot, bad atmosphere of some books of more ability, but *three* times are rather too many for a heroine to love, and there is through the whole this tainting vulgarity. There is no better example of this than the scene between Maurice and Julia Whipple in the arbor (p. 60) which is simply insufferable.

5.10
FRANCIS LOWELL GARDNER

From the Records of the Porcellian Club.[1]

Francis Lowell Gardner, our late Secretary, and beloved Brother and friend, died on the 10th of February, 1861.[2]

Endowed with virtues which made him the delight of his domestic circle, he also possessed those manly qualities and lighter graces which compelled the respect while they won the love of his companions.

An only son, he was brought up with a tender solicitude which served to make more refined and thoughtful his naturally fine and considerate disposition; this those who knew him best most deeply appreciated, for they saw it working in every action of his life; but it needed not intimacy to feel the courage and courtesy which never deserted him, even when most tried, but which always walked hand in hand; his high breeding restraining all needless display of his bravery, and that, in turn, giving to his manner dignity and weight.

His graceful bearing and the beauty of his features harmonized singularly with the rare qualities of his spirit, and combined with them to make and signalize him among his fellows.

But he is gone from us whom, as a man, we honored, as a brother we loved. In the social circle, and in the walks of friendship we shall feel the void which he has left unfilled, yet we shall recall his memory rather with pleasure than with pain, and one who did honor to his College, his Class, and his Club, as a truly chivalrous gentleman.

Editor's Notes

1. The copy text of this obituary was a transcript of a transcript, with many obvious typographical errors which I have silently corrected.
2. Gardner died during a hunting trip.

5.11
SUBMISSION FOR THE BOWDOIN PRIZE, 1861

From a manuscript in *Bowdoin Prize Dissertations* 15: 1860–1861, at the Harvard University Archives. Submitted May 1, 1861.[1]

Σκυτάλη ἐπέμφθη ὑπὸ τῶν ἐν Λακε-
δαιμονίᾳ τελῶν (Thuc. 4. 15.) πρὸς Λύσανδρον
ἐν Ἀσίᾳ ἐπιτάξουσα αὐτῷ διαπράξαι
ὥστε Ἀλκιβιάδην ἀποθανεῖν. ὁ δ᾽ ἀνδρα
τοίνυν τοῦτο τὸ ἐπίταγμα (Plut. Alc. 21.) πρὸ
τὸν Φαρνάβαζον ἐφράσατο — ἐτύγχανε
γὰρ ὁ Ἀλκιβιάδης ἐν τῇ ἐκείνου σατραπ
είᾳ διατρίβων — καὶ ἐδεῖτο αὐτοῦ τοῦτ
τελεῖν. Ἐκ παντὸς τοῦ(τοῦ) Φαρναβάζου
τρόπου δῆλόν ἐστιν ὅτι τοιοῦτο ἔργον
οὔποτ᾽ ἂν εἰργάσατο ἄνδρα αὐτῷ ξενωθέντα
εἰ μὴ ἀληθῶς ἄκων ὑπ᾽ ἄλλων ἠναγκάσθη,
καὶ μάλα ἐπεὶ ἀποφεύγοντα ῥᾳδίως ἂν
κρυφῇ παρεῖδε τὸν μέλλοντα ἀποθανεῖν.
Ἐκ τούτων οὖν πάρεστιν ἡμῖν σαφῶς
εἰδέναι ὅτι ὁ Κῦρος πυθόμενος ἃ Ἀλκι
βιάδης ἔμελλεν μηνύειν ἠξίωσε Φαρνά
βαζον πράττειν ἃ ἐδεῖτο Λύσανδρος· καὶ
ὅτι ἃ αὐτὼ συνεκελευσάτην δεινότερα
ἦν ἢ (ὑπ᾽ αὐτοῦ) ἀναδύεσθαι· πολὺ δ᾽
ἧττον φανερῶς ἀμελεῖσθαι. Φαρνάβαζος
τοίνυν τὸν ἀδελφὸν ἀπέστειλε Μαγαῖον
καὶ τὸν θεῖον Σισαμίθρην σὺν τάξει ὁπ
λιτῶν τὸν Ἀλκιβιάδην κτενοῦντας ἐν τῇ
κώμῃ τῆς Φρυγίας ἐν ᾗ διέτριβεν. Οὗτοι
οἱ ἄνθρωποι, οὐ τολμῶντες βίᾳ εἰσωθεῖσθαι

2.

εἰς τὴν αὐτοῦ οἰκίαν, περιέστησαν καὶ ἀνεπύρωσαν αὐτήν. Ἀλλ' ὁ Ἀλκιβιάδης μεμηχανημένος {Παρ. Ξεν. Ἑλλ. 1.5.11} τὴν φλόγα κατα- σβεννύναι, ὥρμησεν ἐπὶ τοὺς ἐπιβάλλον- τας ἐγχειρίδιον ἐν τῇ δεξιᾷ ἔχων καὶ τῇ ἀρισ- τερᾷ ἱμάτιον περιβαλόμενος ὡς ἀσπίδα. Οὐδεὶς ἐτόλμα προσιέναι αὐτῷ, ἀλλ' ἀμή- χανον παλτῶν πλῆθος καὶ βελῶν ἔβαλλον ἕως ἀπέθανεν οὔτε ἀσπίδα ἔχων πρόβλημα οὔτε ὅπλισιν (Plato, Sim.24.B. ἐχ κειν.) οὐδεμίαν. Ἑταίρα ᾗ συνῴκησεν - Τιμάνδρα - ἑαυτῆς ἱμάτια τὸ σῶμα ἠμφίεσε καὶ πάντα τὰ νομιζόμενα ἐποίησεν.

II. Τοιοῦτο ἦν τὸ ἔργον ὃ οὔτε ὁ Κῦρος καὶ οἱ Λακεδαιμόνιοι ὤκνησαν ἐπισκήπτειν, οὔτε ὁ δῆος καὶ ὁ ἀδελφὸς σατράπου Περσικοῦ ποιεῖν, καὶ ᾧ ἀπέθανεν οὗτος ὁ φανερὸς Ἀθη- ναῖος πρὶν εἰς ἔτος πεντηκοστὸν ἥκειν. Εἰ περιεγένετο (Thuc. 4.27.) οὐκ ἀμφίλογόν ἐστιν ὅτι φανερόν τι ἂν διέπραξεν — οὔτε γὰρ ἡ φύσις οὔτε ἡ θειότης εἴασαν ἂν αὐτὸν μένειν ἐπὶ ἡσυχία — ἀλλὰ πότερον συμφερόντως ταῖς Ἀθήναις ἢ οὔ, μᾶλλόν ἐστιν ἀμφίλογον. Σαφές ἐστιν ὅτι ἐὰν ἅπαντα σκοπῶμεν τὸν τοῦ Ἀλκιβιάδου βίον οὐ φανήσεται ἀγαθὸν αὐτὰς πεποιηκὼς κατὰ λόγον (Xen. Symp. 8.c.11.) τοῦ πολὺ μείζονος κακοῦ. Τοῦ ἀτυχοῦς Σικελίαν στόλου μᾶλλον ἢ ἄλλος τις ἰδιώτης αἴτιος αὐ- τός, καίπερ ἐκεῖνος ὁ στόλος ἔργον ἰδιώτου

τιτὸς οὐκ ὀρθῶς ἂν λέγοιτο ἀλλὰ μᾶλ
λον ἀφ' ὁρμῆς κοινῆς γεγενῆσθαι. Πρῶτον
μὲν σύμβουλος πλέον ἢ ἄλλος τις συμ-
βεβλημένος πρὸς τὸ προκαλέσαι τοὺς
Ἀθηναίους εἰς τοῦτο τὸ ἀλόγιστον τόλμη
μα (Thuc. VI.31.) ἔπειτα δὲ φυγὰς πλέον ἢ ἄλλος
τις, πλὴν τοῦ Νικίου, συνεβάλετο πρὸς τὸ
διαφθείρειν τὸν στόλον καὶ πρὸς τὸ τὰ
ἀπ' αὐτοῦ συμβαίνοντα μεταστρέφειν καὶ
εἰς μείζονα φθοράν. Εἰ μὴ δι' αὐτοῦ, ὁ
Γύλιππος οὔποτ' ἂν εἰς Συρακούσας ἐ-
πέμφθη, Δεκέλεια οὐκ ἂν ἐτειχίσθη, Χίος
καὶ Μίλητος οὐκ ἂν ἀπέστησαν, ἡ συνωμο
σία τῶν ὀλιγαρχικῶν ἀρχὴν οὐκ ἂν ἔλαβεν·
Οὔτε δύναιτο ἂν τις λέγειν ὅτι συνέβη τὰ
τρία ἔτη τὰ πρότερα ἐν οἷς Ἀλκιβιάδης
τὰ πολιτικὰ ἔπραττεν ὡς προεστηκὼς
τῶν Ἀθηναίων συμφερόντως τῇ πατρίδι·
καὶ ταῦτα ἐν χρήμασιν ὑπ' αὐτοῦ πεπραγ
μένοις· ἐν τῇ σὺν Ἄργῳ συμμαχίᾳ καὶ ἐν
ταῖς ἐν Πελοποννήσῳ στρατείαις. Τοὐναν-
τίον δὲ τούτου, ἐπιὼν πρὸς τοὺς πολεμίους
ὅτε μόλις ἱκανῶς παρεσκευάσθη ὡς ἀμυ-
νόμενος αὐτούς, ἐξουσίαν παρέσχε τοῖς
Λακεδαιμονίοις τὴν βλαβεῖσαν δόξαν ἀνα
λαμβάνειν καὶ τὴν ἡγεμονίαν; διὰ τῆς με
λης νίκης τῆς Μαντινείας. Ἡ μοῖρα τοῦ
βίου τοῦ Ἀλκιβιάδου ὅπως τῇ πατρίδι
ὠφέλιμος καὶ αὐτῷ ὅπως δόξαν φέρουσα

‖ * or τὸ κῦρος - the ἡγεμονία was not theirs till 404-3 B.C. ? julpion

τὰ τρία ἐγένετο ἔτη τελευτήσαντα εἰς τὴν
αὐτοῦ κάθοδον   Ἀθήναζε ἐν τῷ δευτέ-
ρῳ τῆς τρίτης καὶ ἐννενηκοστῆς Ὀλυμπάδος.
Ἃ ἂν ἀπέβη ἐκ τούτων τῶν τριῶν εὐτυ-
χῶν ἐτῶν ἐσφάλη τῇ τοῦ Κύρου ἀπροσδο=
κήτῳ καταβάσει σατράπου· ἀλλ' αὐτῷ
ἐκείνῳ τῷ καιρῷ ᾧ ἐξῆν τὸν Ἀλκιβιάδην
μείζονα προσέδεσθαι ἀνδραγαθίαν (Thuc.2.42)
ἵνα, ἐναντίον τούτου τοῦ καιροῦ κωλύματος, ἃ
ὑπέσχετο ἐπετέλει - ἐκείνῳ τῷ καιρῷ εὑρίσκο-
μεν αὐτὸν διατριβὴν ὑπὸ (Xen.Mem.1.2.24-5.) τῶν
Ἀθηναίων ἐξ ἀπροσδοκήτου αὐτὸν νεωστὶ ἀσ-
πασαμένων, καὶ ἀθλίως (Sen.142.10.) ἐνδέοντα καὶ
τῆς προτέρης ἀρετῆς ἢ ἀσπάζεσθαι ἐφράσαι

III. Ἐὰν ἐκ τῶν ὑπ' αὐτοῦ πραχθέντων τραπ-
ώμεθα πρὸς τοὺς τρόπους, τὰ τέλη, τὰς
μηχανάς, ἡ συγγραφὴ τῶν Ἑλληνικῶν ὀλί-
ους ἀποδείξει ἐλάττορος ἀξίους λόγου, ἐάν τε
ὡς τὰ πολιτικὰ ἐάν τε ὡς τὰ ἑαυτοῦ
πράττοντα σκοπῶμεν. Τὰ τέλη ἐστὶ τὰ
τῆς ὑπερμέτρου φιλοτιμίας καὶ λαυρότητο!
αἱ μηχαναὶ ἅρπαγές τε εἰσὶ καὶ ἱταμαί, ἐκ
τῶν πραγμάτων ἃ πρῶτον αὐτῷ πρὸς Λακε=
δαιμονίαν ἦν καὶ πρὸς τοὺς πρέσβεις τοὺς
Λακεδαιμονίους, εἰς τὸ τέλος τοῦ βίου. Αἱ τέ.
ραι αἷς οἱ τὰ πολιτικὰ ἐναντίοι αὐτοῦ τῇ
φυγῇ ἐπράσαντο μάλα αἰσχραὶ ἦσαν, ὡς ἀληθῶ!

καὶ ἄδικοι· ἀλλὰ χρὴ μεμνῆσθαι ὅτι εἰ οἱ
ἐναντίοι πλείονες ἦσαν καὶ δεινότεροι ἢ οἱ ἄλ-
λου τινὸς τὰ πολιτικὰ πράττοντος Ἀθήνῃσι(?)
τὸ σπέρμα ἐσπάρη ὑπὸ τῆς αὐτοῦ ὑπερηφανίας
καὶ τῆς ὀλιγωρίας τῶν τοῦ τε νόμου καὶ τῆς
ὁμιλίας ὅρων.   (Ἀλκιβιάδης)

IV. Ἀλλ' ὅμως οὐδεπώποτε ἐνικήθη οὔτε κατὰ
γῆν οὔτε κατὰ θάλατταν. Θάρσους, δεινότητος,
τόλμης, δυνάμεως εὖ χρῆσθαι καιροῖς ἀνθρώ-
ποις καὶ καιροῖς τύχαις οὔποτ' οὐδὲν ἐνέλιπεν·
ἃ φύσει ἐνόντα αὐτῷ, καὶ πρὸς τούτοις ἡ
εὐγένεια καὶ ὁ πλοῦτος καὶ ἡ εὐμουσία
ἤρκεσαν πρῶτον αὐτὸν ποιεῖν (τέως) ἐν τῇ ἀεὶ
προαιρέσει ἧς εἴχετο: ἢ Ἀθηναίων ἢ Λακεδαι-
μονίων ἢ Περσῶν· ἢ ὀλιγαρχίας· ἢ δημοκρα-
τίας. Ἀλλ' οὐδεμιᾷ αὐτῶν πίστιν βεβαίαν
οὔποτ' ἐνέθηκεν· πᾶσαι ἐν μέρει ἀφῆκαν
αὐτόν. Καθόλου ὀλίγους εὑρήσομεν ἀνθρώ-
πους ἐν οἷς μεγάλη δύναμις τοῦ τε δρᾶν καὶ κελεύ-
ειν βλάπτεται οὕτω παντακῶς ὑπὸ κακῶν
ἠθῶν ὥσπερ ἐν Ἀλκιβιάδῃ.

[Translation; citations in English have been omitted]

A coded message was sent by the authorities in Sparta to Lysander in Asia Minor to instruct him to bring about the death of Alcibiades. Lysander accordingly related this order to Pharnabazus—for Alcibiades happened to be staying in Pharnabazus' province—and asked him to execute it. From the whole character of Pharnabazus it is clear that he would never have done such a deed to a man who was his guest and friend unless he was actually compelled to do so by others against his will, and especially when he could easily have disregarded the escape of the man who was supposed to be killed.

Thus it is possible for us to know with certainty that Cyrus, after learning what information Alcibiades was going to reveal, thought it best for Pharnabazus to do what Lysander asked, and that, while the actions that the two of them were urging upon Pharnabazus were more terrible than inaction on his part, still it was far worse that they be neglected.

Accordingly Pharnabazus sent his brother Magaeus and his uncle Susamithres with a detachment of hoplites to kill Alcibiades in the Phrygian village in which he was staying. These men, not daring to force their way into his house, surrounded it and set it on fire. But Alcibiades, having managed to put out the fire, rushed at his attackers with his dagger in his right hand and with his cloak thrown over his left arm to serve as a shield. No one dared to approach him, but they hurled an overwhelming number of javelins and arrows at him until he was killed, with neither a shield as protection nor any armor at all. The courtesan with whom he lived—Timandra—put her own clothes about his body and performed all the customary rites.

II. Such was the deed that neither Cyrus and the Spartans hesitated to order nor did the uncle and the brother of the Persian governor hesitate to carry out, and by which this eminent Athenian died before reaching his fiftieth year. If he had survived, there is no question that he would have accomplished something remarkable—for neither his character nor his cleverness would have allowed him to remain quiet—but whether or not his actions would have proved profitable for Athens is more debatable. It is evident that if we examine Alcibiades' life in its entirety, it will be clear that he did not benefit Athens when we consider the much greater harm he did. He himself is responsible for the unfortunate expedition to Sicily more than any other individual, although that expedition could not rightly be said to have been the work of any individual, but rather to have risen from public impulse. First as a counselor, by contributing more than any one else to plunging the Athenians into this unconsidered act of daring, and then as an exile, he contributed more than any one except Nicias to destroying the expedition and to turning the events that he had brought about into an even greater disaster. If not for him, Gylippus would never have been sent to Syracuse, Decelea would not have been fortified, Chios and Miletus would not have revolted, and the oligarchic conspiracy would not have seized power. Nor could any one say that the three earlier years in which Alcibiades was handling state affairs as leader of the Athenians had turned out in any way advantageously for the country, and that too in undertakings carried out by him—in the alliance with Argos and the campaigns in the Peloponnese. On the contrary, in attacking the enemy when he was barely adequately prepared to defend against them, he provided the Spartans with the opportunity to repair their damaged reputation and assume the supremacy, through the great victory at Mantinea. The way Alcibiades' life turned out was actually helpful to his country and brought glory to him for the three years preceding his return from exile to Athens in the second year of the 93rd Olympiad.[2] What would have resulted from these three fortunate years was frustrated by the unexpected return of the Persian governor Cyrus. But at that very moment at which it was necessary for Alcibiades to display greater valor so as, in the face of this new obstacle, to fulfill his promises—at that moment we find him pampered by the Athenians, who had just now unexpectedly welcomed him back, and miserably lacking the former excellence with which he had earned the welcome.

III. If we turn from his deeds to his character, his goals, and his methods, the history of Greek affairs will show few less worthy of consideration whether we consider him in his handling of state affairs or of his own. His goals are those of excessive ambition and empty conceit. His methods are rapacious and reckless, from the dealings he first had with Sparta and the Spartan envoys till the end of his life. The methods by which his political opponents first brought about his exile were disgraceful and actually dishonest, but one must remember that if his opponents were more numerous and clever than those of any one else engaged in public affairs in Athens, the seed was sown by his arrogance and his contempt for the limits of the law and society.

IV. Alcibiades, however, was never defeated, either on land or on sea. He never had any lack of courage, shrewdness, daring or the power to make good use of new people and new chances. His innate qualities and in addition his nobility of birth and wealth and feeling for the arts were sufficient to make him for the time first in whatever form of state he was associated with, whether Athenian or Spartan or Persian, oligarchy or democracy. But he put no sure trust in any of these, and all in turn sent him away. In all, we shall find few people in whom great power of action and of command is as completely spoiled by bad character as in the case of Alcibiades.

Editor's Notes

1. This is an original essay in classical Greek by Holmes, submitted under the initials R. L. S.—the last letter of each of Holmes's names. Underlining in the original is probably the Prize judges'. The English translation which appears here was done by Mr. Alexander Sens and Professor David Coffin. The staff of the Harvard Archives was able to verify the deadline for submission of Prize essays at the President's office.

2. I.e. A.D. 407

5.12

PRE-RAPHAELITISM

From *Harvard Magazine* 7:345 (1861).

Within a few years a body of young men have stood forth in direct hostility to almost all the principles of modern art, and have attempted to restore by revolution the aims and motives of the painters of four hundred years ago. As if eager to provoke the contest which they challenge, they have signified their ambitious purpose by the name which they have themselves adopted,—the Pre-Raphaelites,—and hinted also at the principles which must insure their ultimate victory or defeat.

The belief on which the school founds its name is, that there exists a difference in kind between the spirit of the earlier painters, down to the time of Raphael, and those who have come after him. The difference consists in nothing less than this: that the first painted sincere and simple pictures,—the combined result of their limited technical knowledge, and their childlike religious faith,—whereas their successors painted pictures that were very often neither simple nor sincere. That such should have been the fact is quite conceivable, without imputing a personal responsibility to the later schools. Painting had advanced from its earliest stages of ignorance and conventionality, and consequently composition, drawing, and the other technical excellences of the art, as such, had acquired an undue preponderance over the spirit by which that art was prompted. In religion, too, the stage of infancy, which takes for granted all which it is told, had given way to the inquiring doubts of youth, and thus again the simplicity of the childlike work was gone forever.

The object of the Pre-Raphaelites is a reform in the spirit of their art, and a restoring of that spirit to its proper supremacy over the academic rules. The simplicity which comes from ignorance of the capacities of an art, or the religious credulity belonging to semi-barbarism, of course cannot be restored; but religious devotion after the different light of our time may be, and still more is that deep sincerity which forms the only possible basis for noble work possible for all ages and for all religions. Pre-Raphaelitism, then, though to a degree a religious movement, professes chiefly to reform the spirit of art by making it more sincere.

As the proper means of attaining their object, the men of this school adopted, as their sole principle, *truth*. Truth, literal and uncompromising, in everything, from the first general conception down to the minutest detail of the finished work. When a Pre-Raphaelite conceives a composition, his aim is to think what would most probably have happened in fact, not what might have happened most picturesquely; and when he has his general plan clearly in his mind, he strives to work it out with the most faithful portraiture of which he is capable. The trees in the distance are drawn in the open air from real trees, the flowers of the foreground are painted from real flowers, the man is a friend of the painter, the woman may be his wife, and the infant his child.

Knowing what is the principle which the Pre-Raphaelites profess, we are naturally led to ask whether they have carried out their theory in their works. The answer is doubtful, to say the least. While their keen study of minute details gives them a nearly unequalled power in the delineation of delicate shades of expression and human feeling, they are, as a body, guilty of absurdities which it is equally hard to palliate or deny. We could excuse awkwardness and want of grace in a school which began by seeking truth and leaving beauty to come after as best it might. But when one of them makes the head of a man standing on the ground to be nearly level with that of a woman upon the top of a stile three feet high, we cannot call it awkwardness, but simply gross bad drawing,—deficiency in the very point where these artists should be strong. Whether the Pre-Raphaelite designs in general *are* probable, as they certainly are far from graceful, may well be questioned; certainly an attempt to imitate the position of the figures in the Huguenots, which is one of their best and most widely known productions,will show how nearly impossible it is. Yet the pale, beseeching face of the woman in that picture shows a power unequalled in its way by the artists of any other modern school.

The brief statement of Pre-Raphaelitism is, that it is a reaction from the artificiality of earlier schools, and professedly a return to the simple copying of Nature. But as Art involves in its very nature *selection,* and as this school does not recognize that principle, the nature of its excellence and its failings becomes evident at once. Its pictures continually touch our hearts by their artless directness of appeal, and yet they are wanting in all those excellences of composition and arrangement which are the fair and rightful field for the painter's genius. As painting had before this revival degenerated into merely academical study, so we may doubt whether the present works have a right to bc called the fruits of art in its highest sense at all; but they are a step towards the truth; and when, in part by their means, a more careful study of Nature shall have become universal, we may hope that a later and maturer race of painters shall combine the highest art with the noblest truth, in works of worthy brotherhood with the greatest of all time.

5.13
CLASS BOOK 1861—ENTRY

From *Class Book 1861,* pp. 329–331. Harvard Archives.[1]

I, Oliver Wendell Holmes, Jr., was born Mar. 8, 1841, in Boston. My father was born in Cambridge, graduated at Harvard, studied medicine in Paris and returning to Boston practised as a physician there a number of years. Giving this up, however, he has since supported himself by acting as a professor of the Medical School of Harvard Coll., by lecturing, and by writing a number of books.* In 1840 he married Amelia Lee Jackson, daughter of Judge Jackson, of Boston, where he has since resided.—All my three names designate families from which I am descended. A long pedigree of Olivers & Wendells may be found in the books called "Memorials of the Dead in Boston.—King's Chapel Burying Ground." p.p. 144. & 234-5-6-7-8. Of my grandfather Abiel Holmes, an account may be found in the Biogr. dictionaries, (He was the author of the *Annals* of *America* &c.) as also of my other grandfather Charles Jackson. (See, for instance, Appleton's *New American Cyclopedia* where the account of Judge Jackson was written by my father.) I think it better thus to give a few satisfactory references than to write an account which is half so. Some of my ancestors have fought in the Revolution; among the great grandmothers of the family were Dorothy Quincy & Ann [[sic]] Bradstreet ("the tenth Muse"); and so on; but these things can be picked up from other sources I have indicated. My Grandfather A. Holmes was graduated at Yale in 1783 & in 1792 was "gradu honoraris donatus" at Harvard. Various Wendells & Olivers will be found in the triennial, as also various Jacksons; including my grandfather. Our family has been in the habit of

---

* { "Autocrat at the Breakfast Table"
  "Professor at the do.   do."   } First appeared in the
  "Elsie Venner"   } Atlantic Monthly.
  "Currents & Counter Currents"—[[broken]]

receiving a College education and I came of course in my turn, as my grandfathers father & uncles had been before me. I've always lived in Boston, and went first to a woman's school there, then to Rev. T. R. Sullivan's, then to E. S. Dixwell's (Private Latin School) & thence to College. I never had any business but that of a student before coming to College; wh. I did with the majority of our class in July, entering without conditions. I was, while in College, a member and editor of the Institute, (had somewhat to do with one or two private clubs,) of the Hasty Pudding, the Porcellian, the Φ.B.K. and the "Christian Union"; not that I considered my life justi- fied my belonging to the latter, but because I wished to bear testimony in favor of a Religious society founded on liberal principles in distinction to the more "ortho- dox" & sectarian platform of the "Xtian Brethren." I was editor in the Senior Year of the Harvard Magazine. (the chief piece I wrote in it being on "Albert Durer.") I was author of an article on Plato wh. took the prize as the best article by an under- graduate (for the first year of its existence) in the "University Quarterly". The only College prize I have tried for was the Greek wh. was divided between one of the Juniors & me. When the war broke out I joined the "4th Battalion of Infantry" & went down to Fort Independence expecting when drilled to go south. (as a private.) While at the Fort & after we were ordered up I had to patch up a Class Poem as quickly & as well as I could under the circumstances, since I had been elected to that office shortly before going (2nd term Senior). We stayed about a month at the Fort & then came to Boston & on Class day (a week & a half ago) I delivered my poem side by side with my friend Hallowell who was orator and who had also been at the fort. The tendencies of the family & of myself have a strong natural bent to literature &c. at present I am trying for a commission in one of the Massachusetts Regiments, however, and hope to go South before very long. If I survive the war I expect to study Law as my profession or at least for a starting point.

(in haste) O. W. Holmes Jr. July 2nd. 1861.

(N.B. I may say I don't much believe in gushing much in these College Biog's and think a dry statement much fitter. Also I am too busy now to say more if I would.)

Editor's Note

1. This is handwritten, evidently in haste. I have allowed the errors of punctuation and capitalization to stand.

5.14
LETTER TO COLONEL WILLIAM RAYMOND LEE

From an initialed newspaper clipping in the OWH Papers, Paige Box 22, Item 1.[1]

HEADQUARTERS 20TH MASS. VOLS.
CAMP NEAR FALMOUTH, VA. DEC. 21, 1862.

The officers of the Twentieth here present, in behalf of themselves and their absent brothers, earnestly desire to express to their Colonel, who is now retiring from the post he has so long held with such honor to himself and his regiment, their affection and appreciation, and their regret for the necessity which compels him to leave them.

Entering the regiment as strangers, your constant and truly parental kindness begot in us an almost filial love. Your example taught us more perfectly than we could learn elsewhere to strive not only to acquire the discipline of soldiers but the high feelings and self-sacrifice of chivalrous gentlemen. How could we, young, and with comparatively little to leave behind, repine at any self-denial, when we saw our colonel leaving wife and children, constantly endure, without a thought of self, hardships which tested the strength of the strongest, and face, without shrinking dangers which tried the courage of the bravest hearts.

It moved us at once to admiration and to sadness to see you defying with indomitable will the sickness and exhaustion to which any other would have yielded, and returning again and again in spite of failing strength to lead your regiment or command the brigade through every hard fought action.

And now, sir, that the ill-health against which you have so nobly borne up compels you to resign the command of the regiment, whose fame is identified with your own, you will not be less present to our hearts and remembrance, as tender friend and gallant commander, than when you were present to lead us forward in the field.

> GEO. N. MACY, Actg. Major Commanding.
> NATHAN HAYWARD, Surgeon.
> C. W. FOLSOM, Quartermaster.
> O. W. HOLMES, JR., Capt. Co. G.
> H. L. ABBOTT, Capt. Co. I.
> C. L. TILDEN, Capt. Co. C.
> C. A. WHITTIER, 1st Lt. and A.D.C.
> W. F. MILTON, 1st Lt. and A.D.C.
> JAMES MURPHY, 1st Lt. Commanding Co. A.
> H. C. MASON, 1st Lt. Commanding Co. H.
> H. L. PATTEN, 1st Lt. and Adjutant.
> HENRY ROPES, 1st Lt. Commanding Co. K.
> WM. F. PERKINS, 2d Lt. Commanding Co. E.
> SAML. WILLARD, 2d Lt. Commanding Co. D.

To COL. WM. RAYMOND LEE.

Editor's Note

1. There is, in *Reports, Letters & Papers Appertaining to the 20th Massachusetts Volunteer Infantry*, Volume II, in the 20th Massachusetts Regiment Collection in the Rare Book Department of the Boston Public Library, a handwritten transcript of this letter. The copy text used, however, was the version printed in the newspaper and preserved by Holmes in his "Civil War Notebook."

5.15
HOW FOUGHT OUR BROTHERS

Harvard College Class of 1861, *First Triennial Report* (Cambridge: privately printed, 1864), p. 64.

How fought our brothers, and how died, the story
  You bid me tell, who shared with them the praise,
Who sought with them the martyr's crown of glory,
  The bloody birthright of heroic days!

But, all untuned amid the din of battle,
  Not to our lyres the inspiring strains belong;
The cannon's roar, the musket's deadly rattle,
  Have drowned the music, and have stilled the song.

Let others celebrate our high endeavor,
  When peace once more her starry flag shall fling
Wide o'er the land our arms made free forever,
  We do in silence what the world shall sing!

5.16
H.L.A.[1]

Twentieth Massachusetts Volunteers

From an initialed newspaper clipping (October 17, 1864) in the OWH Papers, Paige Box 4.

He steered unquestioning, nor turning back
Into the darkness and the unknown sea,
He vanished in the starless night, and we
Saw but the shining of his luminous wake.
Thou sawest light, but ah! our sky seemed black,
And all too hard the inscrutable decree,
Yet, noble heart, full soon we follow thee
Lit by the deeds that flamed along thy track.
Nay, art thou hid in darkness, shall we say,
Or rather whisper with untrembling lips,
We see thee not, yet trust thou art not far,
But passing onward from this life's eclipse,
Hast vanished only as the morning star
Into the glory of the perfect day!

Editor's Note

1. H. L. A. is Henry L. "Little" Abbott, who was a friend of Holmes's. He was killed during the Wilderness Campaign.

5.17
ARTHUR DEHON

Second Lieutenant 12th Mass. Vols. (Infantry), January 16, 1862;
First Lieutenant, May 13, 1862;
killed at Fredricksburg, Va., December 13, 1862.

In *Harvard Memorial Biographies*, ed. T. W. Higginson (Cambridge, Mass: Sever and Francis, 1866), Vol. 2, p. 233.

Arthur Dehon was born January 24, 1841, the son of William and Caroline (Inches) Dehon of Boston. He was prepared for college at Mr. Tower's school in Boston; at the boarding-school of Mr. T. P. Allen in Sterling, Mass. (afterwards removed to New Bedford); and finally at the Boston Latin School. When he was sixteen years old he entered college as a Freshman in the Class of 1861, and he continued with it for nearly two years. He then went to New York and entered the office of his uncle, Mr. Theodore Dehon, where he was doing excellently until his health, which was always delicate, gave way. He was accordingly led, in February, 1861, to try the rough medicine of a voyage around Cape Horn, and the beginning of the war found him in California. He soon returned, however, and at once showed his eagerness to join the troops already in the field. At first it seemed that he might be unable to follow out his wishes immediately, and in a letter to a friend dated October 13, 1861, he wrote, "I mean to be reconciled and do what I can to live *sans peur et sans reproche*." Later, after Ball's Bluff, in the same spirit he wrote again: "The more reverses the more I wish to go. But at present my duty keeps me here, and I mean to try to be cheerful and keep up my spirits." He had not long to wait before his wishes were fulfilled. On the 16th of January, 1862, he was commissioned Second Lieutenant in the Twelfth Regiment Massachusetts Volunteers, Colonel Webster.

His letters from the field began the same month, and in February he was already so pleased with his new profession as to write: "I wish to see one fight as a line officer, and I should not desire to change were it not that I wish to get into the Regular service." On the 13th of May, 1862, he was promoted First Lieutenant. In a letter of the 16th of the same month, dated near Fredericksburg, he thus mentions one of his first experiences of the hardships of the march:—

"We arrived here at twelve, A.M., on Wednesday, in a pouring rain, after a march of thirty-four miles. We started on Monday at twelve, A.M.,—just forty-eight hours. Tuesday we marched eighteen miles under the hottest sun, in the heat of the day, and did it at a rate of two miles per hour. Every step seemed to be the last; but I was bound to go in with the regiment. Only two companies brought in more men than I did.

Meanwhile he had learned the true feeling of an officer towards his men. He says:—

"I do this to show the boys I take an interest in their sending their money home, and so encourage it. I want them to feel I am interested in them, and will do what I can to assist them."

At Cedar Mountain he had his first taste of battle. He writes:—

"I was ordered to mount 'Joe,' and take an order to the wagon-train. When I returned the regiment had moved toward the firing. The firing commenced about two . . . I caught the regiment about six, and dismounted and took my place in the company. We reached the field about half past seven. About eight o'clock we were in first position, and a shell came and exploded over us. We moved quickly, supposing the Rebels were at least a mile or two off. When we reached the second position, what was our surprise to receive a volley of rifle-balls; for a moment I feared the regiment would break. We were marching by the flank, and the men started a little for the right. Every officer promptly stopped them, brought them to the front, and ordered them to lie down on their bellies. We delivered one volley, the Rebel battery opening with shell and grapeshot all the time. The rifle firing lasted from fifteen to twenty minutes, and the enemy were within fifty yards. . . We were under fire about two hours and a half, and only about five men left the ranks, none from our company. . . The time we were under fire seemed to me about half an hour. I did not feel frightened or want to run, but I could not help stooping to avoid the shells, though they were not half so bad as the rifle-balls. The crack of the rifles made me feel a little nervous, but I was too much taken up with the company to be scared. . . I believe the Rebels have skedaddled; but the papers will tell you more than I know. I am waiting for them to find out about the battle."

A little later he served as Adjutant of his regiment, and was consequently a good deal in the society of Colonel Webster, for whom all his letters show the warmest affection and the most soldierly loyalty. That the feeling was not only on his part is manifested by a passage in one of the Colonel's letters: "There sits by my side Arthur,—a hero in the conflict, cool, calm, and brave." Unfortunately, Arthur was only too soon to prove his faithfulness to his commander and his father's friend, and to deserve and win once more the praise which he had already earned.

Colonel Webster was killed at the second Bull Run; and Lieutenant Dehon, when the fight was over, obtained permission to go outside the lines of our army to search for his body, although he was informed that the intention of the Confederates was to retain all officers. He was detained, in fact; but Dr. Guild, General Lee's Medical Director, on hearing the circumstances from Dr. McFarland, the Medical Director of General Pope's army, very courteously gave him a pass for the desired purpose. Then for several hours he searched in vain, but having at last found the remains, he buried them himself on the spot. Subsequently, however, having obtained an ambulance, he returned, disinterred the body from its deep grave with his naked hands for want of any instrument, and succeeded by his untiring energy in having it sent home to Massachusetts, where, but for his efforts, it would have never arrived.

He wrote: "Every one I have met feels and deplores the loss of the Colonel; he was so brave and gentle. The regiment feels it most, and mourns him as a friend and commander." How he had fared in the engagement may be judged from his own words:—

"The Rebels stole my sword, pistols, and belt. I had a bullet through my coat and pantaloons in the fight, which ruined them, and in the stampede of the wagon-train most of my baggage was lost, which leaves me nearly destitute... Williams says I look ten years older since I returned from Rebeldom; but I am well and hearty, though this work is enough to make the youngest old."

At South Mountain the writer met him, and he expressed a modest satisfaction that, joining the regiment as he did in the field, very young, and being at the outset unknown to most of the officers, he had succeeded in gaining their respect. A boy fresh from college, he might well be pleased to have successfully endured the severest scrutiny of older men; but his gallantry was already known beyond the limits of his regiment.

Three days later, at Antietam, he had another chance to prove his manhood, and he showed himself equal to the need. Most of the men of his regiment were killed or wounded, and hardly an officer remained unhurt.

"Then," he says, "they seemed to come to me for orders, as I was the only field or staff officer left. After the color-sergeant was shot, I ordered three different men to take the colors up, and saw one after another wounded; and when the last fell, I had not the heart to order another up, so I picked them up and brought them off myself, till we were out of danger, and then gave them to one of the men."

For this he was honorably mentioned in the report of his brigade commander. But his labors did not end here. As soon as his regiment was sent to the rear, he rode to Colonel Coulter, now commanding the brigade in the absence of General Hartsuff, wounded, and offered his services, which were accepted. For the rest of that day, and for several days afterwards, he accordingly did double duty, as Adjutant of his regiment and as Acting Assistant Adjutant-General of the brigade.

In the same month of September, Lieutenant Dehon was detailed as Acting Aide-de-Camp to Major-General Meade, then temporarily commanding the Twelfth Army Corps. He was present in his new position at the review when the President visited the army, shortly after the battle of Antietam, and it seems to have suggested a contrast to his mind. "I notice these reviews in the field are not so well conducted as the militia reviews. No collation, no champagne, etc., but hard work and no dinner. I give my vote for the militia."

There is little to tell from this time until the day of his death. In his last letter he writes as follows:—

"December 9.

"It seems quite funny to be sitting in one's tent, just as comfortable as can be, and with the consciousness that there will be an action to-morrow. Generally the night before an action we have been so busy or so tired that rest and sleep were most sought after. But now one has a perfect opportunity to sit down comfortably and contemplate it. We shall cross, I think, without a serious fight, and shall not have one till we get near Richmond; but I can't tell. I hope we shall thrash them severely, and then there will be a satisfactory peace. I shall try to do my duty to-morrow, and be of what assistance I can to the General, and endeavor to repay by well-doing his uniform kindness."

"December 10, 9 A.M.

"P.S.—No orders for us yet, though some of the artillery has been put in motion. Good by. The batteries are moving."

The rest of the story is told by General Meade's letter to Mr. Dehon:—

"Camp Opposite Fredricksburg, Va., December 16, 1862.

"Dear Sir,—It was my painful duty to telegraph you yesterday of the loss of your son Arthur. He fell on the morning of the 13th instant, while endeavoring to carry an important order to one of my brigade commanders. He was seen to fall from his horse, and was immediately approached by an officer in the vicinity, who, finding life extinct, removed his watch from his person. The ground on which he fell remaining at the close of the action in the possession of the enemy, his fate was involved in uncertainty until yesterday afternoon, when, under a flag of truce, a search was made for our dead and wounded, and Arthur's body was found where he was seen to fall.

"My experience of the unnecessary suffering occasioned to relations and friends by the premature announcement of the loss of officers, and the hope I would not abandon till forced by positive evidence, that it might please God in his infinite mercy to spare Arthur, induced me to make no effort to telegraph you till the result of yesterday's examination proved he was no more. His body was immediately taken charge of by the officers of my staff, and every respect paid. This morning my aide-de-camp, Captain Coxe, has taken him to Washington, with his servant, horse, and his personal effects, and was directed to telegraph you of this fact, and make such arrangements as you might desire.

"In addition to the pain which always accompanies the duty I am now discharging, I now have to mourn the loss, not only of a faithful and efficient officer, but that of a valued and cherished friend. During the brief space that Arthur and myself have been officially connected, I had time to learn his many good qualities, his high sense of duty, his amiability of disposition, and that which most particularly charmed me, his earnest desire to promote by every means in his power the happiness of yourself and the other members of your family.

"I am aware, my dear sir, of the impossibility of offering consolation to one afflicted as you are. All I can offer is sympathy and condolence, in which I am joined by the whole division, to whom Arthur had become endeared by his manly character and the exhibition of his personal gallantry. In the army your son is truly and sincerely mourned; and if it were possible to be reconciled to the sacrifice you have been called on to make, the reputation he had acquired, the love that was borne him, and the grief his death has occasioned, might in a measure soften the severity of the blow.

"Believe me, I feel most deeply for you, and earnestly pray God will give you strength to support the affliction which He, for some good purpose, has visited you with.

"Most truly and sincerely yours,
"Geo. G. Meade.
"Wm. Dehon, Esq."

In his report, which forms part of his testimony before the Committee on the Conduct of the War, General Meade pays this further tribute to the memory of his young aid: "The loss of Lieutenant Dehon (Twelfth Massachusetts Regiment), my aid, is greatly to be deplored, as he was a young man of high promise, and endeared to all who knew him for his manly virtues and amiable qualities."

There are delicacies of youthful character which it is as hard to portray in words as for the sculptor to fix in marble the changing beauty and evanescent grace of youthful features. To say that Arthur Dehon was one of the bravest and most chivalrous of soldiers, the truest of friends, the most affectionate of sons and brothers, is still to miss the secret of his virtue and his charm. His short story has been told as far as possible in his own words, but his deepest and most sacred feelings cannot appear in any public record. The writer saw him a day or two before his death, and he then spoke with a most touching humility and tenderness of his aspiration to prove himself worthy of the confidence reposed in him, and of the affection of which he was the centre. But these things cannot be told. It is enough to say here that, unselfish and devoted, he lived for others and he died for his country.

5.18
FRANCIS W. PALFREY

From an annotated newspaper clipping (*Boston Post*, December 24, 1889) in the OWH Papers, Paige Box 18, Item 4.[1]

The survivors of the Twentieth Massachusetts Regiment have learned that their former fellow soldier and Commander Colonel Francis W. Palfrey died at Cannes, France, on the   [2]day of December, 1889.

The courage and fortitude with which he faced and bore up against illness could only prolong the suffering and put off the final effect of his death wound. At last the shot which struck him upon the field of Antietam has done its work and he suffers no more. His name is added to the glorious list of those whom he loved and who loved him—Revere, Bartlett, Abbott, Lowell, Ropes, Putnam and so many more—who, like him and no more than he, fell in battle, although the end was less delayed. The few soldiers who served with him and who remain alive wish his family to know the appreciation and honor which they felt for him in the field and which later years have only enhanced. In time of war they saw his good sense, his equanimity, his courage, and they profited by his discipline. In time of peace he would not have had them see, but they knew his generosity and the great-heartedness beneath his reserve. They offer their respectful sympathy to those who have lost him. But for him their regret is swallowed up in the glory of a good soldier's death.

Copy of resolution drawn by me as Chairman of Committee & sent to Mrs. Palfrey. Printed in Boston Post, December 24, 1889.

Editor's Notes

1. The clipping begins "The courage . . ." and ends with " . . . good soldier's death." The contextual notes at the top and bottom are added in Holmes's hand.

2. There is a blank space here; apparently Holmes meant to complete the date, but never did.

5.19

TRIBUTE TO A BRAVE SOLDIER

Resolutions on the Death of General W. Raymond Lee

From a corrected newspaper clipping (*Boston Evening Transcript,* January 6, 1892) in the OWH Papers, Paige Box 19, Item 5.

The survivors of the Twentieth Massachusetts Regiment desire to express to the family of their former colonel, William Raymond Lee, the love and veneration which every man of the Twentieth felt for him from the moment when he came under his command.

His appointment as colonel at the beginning of the war put the breath of life into the regiment. He took to himself Palfrey and Paul Revere, and those three brought in Bartlett and John Putnam and Tremlett and Macy and Abbott, and so many more whom we all remember, and together they shaped the body in the form it was to keep. At Ball's Bluff the regiment's experience began. Its training continued at Yorktown, at Fair Oaks, at Glendale and the other battles of the seven days on the peninsula, at Antietam. So that when it reached Fredricksburg, already it was a veteran corps, and the colonel's task was achieved when his body gave way under the exhaustion of the campaign.

Others had contributed knowledge of tactics, knowledge of the world, good sense, bravery, and a noble feeling of duty, but the old chief had given the regiment its soul. He was the example of careless, generous gallantry. His "Forward Twentieth" stirred us more than trumpets. From him too the rest learned to be silent when their work was done. The Twentieth in its day was what a great regiment should be. It was in the thickest part of all the famous battles of the Army of the Potomac. It was known to all soldiers and to not many others. Now for a quarter of a century it has ceased to exist, and that it ever was is remembered only by a few gray-haired men. We believe that the colonel would not have had it otherwise, and would have asked no other memory for himself. It is enough one's self to remember great deeds, to have felt the passion of life to its top, to have for companions the living and the dead who shared the incommunicable experience of war. Colonel Lee might have remembered also that he had lifted the hearts of a thousand men to heights which, but for him, they would never have reached.

For the regiment,
Oliver Wendell Holmes, Jr.
Gustave Magnitzky

Boston, Dec. 29, 1891.

5.20

CHARLES C. BEAMAN

From a corrected newspaper clipping (*Boston Evening Transcript,* December 18, 1900) in the OWH Papers, Paige Box 19, Item 5.

Mr. Charles C. Beaman, who will be buried tomorrow at Windsor, had one of those crowd-compelling temperaments which so many remember in Richardson, the architect, and older men in Professor Agassiz. It made him a social as well as a business force, and he was equally wanted to make a great dinner a success or to carry through work which was to be done. From the Harvard Law School, where he began his upward course by writing a prize essay which attracted the attention of Charles Sumner and which led to his going to Geneva to take part in the case of the Alabama arbitration, to the brilliant and premature close of his career, his life was the same story of triumphant and single-hearted power. At the same time he was a man of unbounded generosity and a most tender heart. No friend appealed to him in vain for any kind of help. He seemed to live in those he loved. As a natural consequence he was not only the very heart of those who were nearest to him, but a large figure to those who knew him less. It is impossible to believe that such a centre of radiant energy is gone. He lives, and will live as long as memory remains to the very, very many who knew and loved him even at a distance, and who got new heart for life from his great cheer. O. W. H.

5.21
CAPTAIN MAGNITZKY

From an annotated newspaper clipping (*Boston Evening Transcript,* September 20, 1910) in the OWH Papers, Paige Box 19, Item 5.

To the Editor of the Transcript:

I was expecting to stop and see Captain Magnitzky on going to town this week, when the telephone told me that he was dead. Our friendship has lasted for nearly fifty years. He was my First Sergeant when I commanded Company G. of the Twentieth Massachusetts in the Civil War, he having recently come to this country from Polish Prussia and having gone into the army upon principle and because of his sympathy with the cause. We made many a heart-breaking march and were in many a battle together and his gallantry and efficiency gained him a commission in a regiment in which a sergeant had to be a fighting man to keep his chevrons and an unusual man to gain the shoulder-straps. He became a captain and in some of the fierce days at the end of the war had the regiment under his command. After the war he attained the same rank in the regular army. When somewhat later I joined Shattuck & Munroe in the practice of the law he was already the managing man of the firm. In those days things were simpler than now. We had no typewriters or stenographers, but the captain did everything that we did not do in person. There as in the army he was invaluable and he became one of the best-known figures in legal Boston. He remained with Shattuck & Munroe and then with Munroe after Mr. Shattuck's death and since that time has been with gentlemen who were with Munroe when he died. The Twentieth was a regiment that never talked much about itself but that stood in the first half dozen of all the regiments of the North for the number of killed and wounded in its ranks. Quiet and steady under fire, quiet and effective in camp, modest, distinguished in bearing and soul, Captain Magnitzky was a type of the great regiment in which he served. He merits a larger memorial than this little wreath which one who loved him lays upon his grave.

O. W. Holmes

Boston, Sept. 20. 1910

CORRECTIONS AND VARIANT TEXTS

5.5   p. 149, l. 23: "which can only develop" corrected from "which can only develope."

5.10   p. 160, l. 21: "we shall recall his memory" corrected from "we shall recall him memory."

5.21   p. 179, l. 28: "shoulder-straps" hyphenated at line end.

6

The American Law Review 1867–1873

Holmes was a member of the staff of *The American Law Review* from January 1867 (midway through its first year of publication) until June 1873, when he left to devote himself full time to law practice. The review had been founded by its first editors, Holmes's friends John Ropes and John Chipman Gray, who also founded the Boston law firm that still bears their name. Holmes and Arthur Sedgwick succeeded Ropes and Gray as editors with the October 1870 issue; in June 1872, Holmes became sole editor.

There were few law journals at that time, the system of law school-based reviews not yet having begun, and there were no American law journals concerned with wide questions of theory or history. *The American Law Review* accordingly became the vehicle of publication for speculative articles and scholarly studies by a circle of young men, including Holmes, Sedgwick, Gray, Nicholas St. John Green, and others. Many of the shorter pieces were unsigned.

Digests. Holmes's early work on these "digests" was an important part of his development, but the digests themselves are too mechanical to merit republication. A description of the form will convey the signficance they had to Holmes.

Digests of English and American cases were a regular feature of the quarterly *American Law Review*. Beginning with its first issue in October, 1866, the review had published digests of the reported English cases, and these remained the most prominent feature. In the second issue, the editors added digests of United States Supreme Court and state court decisions. The digests usually were no more than a sentence or two, and consisted of a brief statement of the facts and a terse holding stated in narrow terms. These digests were placed under one- or two-word subject headings arranged alphabetically, with very general headings ("Admiralty") and specific topics ("Bottomry Bonds") treated on the same level. Apparently cases that bore on several issues were given a more general heading, and cross-references were entered under the more specific topics. The topics were not chosen by any discernible system; "Steamboats" was a heading, as was "Delivery." The digests in short were the rawest of data.

The *Review* included digests of all the cases included in the uniform system of English Law Reports (adopted by the English bar in 1864 to replace the scattered and conflicting independent reporters), and all of the cases in the official reports of the United States Supreme Court. Selections of state cases were taken from the state reporters, usually the reports of the highest court. On a less regular basis the *Review* reported the opinions of the United States District Court of the District of

Massachusetts, principally admiralty decisions by Judge John Amory Lowell; and occasionally a digest of bankruptcy decisions from the district courts.

From the October 1868 number[1] through October 1869 Holmes wrote the digests of state cases. For each quarterly digest he reviewed roughly a dozen volumes of state reports, apparently in the order they were received, and selected perhaps a hundred cases for each issue. Each of the quarterly state digests covered from 20 to 40 printed pages.

Holmes also wrote the digests of English cases in October 1868, and October 1869, a total of seventy printed pages. He wrote the digests of United States Supreme Court cases in January, 1869 (26 pages).

The digests of English cases are longer than the American digests, principally because the facts are stated in more detail and with more care. The digests in 6.1, below, are selected from Holmes's digests for the October 1868 number. The copy text was taken from a bound set of the journal in the Library of Congress, but not Holmes's copy. There are marginal notations in Holmes's copy, of citations to later cases, not noted here. (See "Editorial Principles," above.)

Articles, Comments, and Book Notices. Many of these brief works were identified as Holmes's for the first time in 1989,[2] and most are republished here for the first time in more than a century. Included are all those Holmes marked as his in his bound set of *The American Law Review,* now in the Library of Congress. These notices and essays show Holmes's first efforts to make a naturalistic or scientific study of the law, by classifying the decisions of courts; they show his belief that law was an evolving system that could be studied like botany or zoology. He made his first descriptions of the judges' work, and his first sketches of the external standard of liability that would be the central image of *The Common Law* here (see chap. 3), and drew a sharp distinction between an evolutionist theory, which showed classes in conflict, and utilitarian thinking, which assumed that there was some common good that bridged the differences among groups (6.81).

As in all of his work of which he kept copies, Holmes made marginal notations of later research. His notes on current topics, for instance, are often annotated with citations to theoretical or historical works of an earlier day—Bentham, Austin, Savigny, and others—as well as of later decisions of the courts on pertinent points. These articles plainly formed a kind of filing cabinet in which he kept track of his reading. I have not transcribed these research notes; but where Holmes marked corrections of the text, and where he added to or clarified his thought, I have recorded these annotations in end notes.

Editor's Notes

1. In John Chipman Gray's copy of the bound volumes for 1868 and 1869 in the Harvard Law Library, he marked the authors of various articles and digests and attributed the state digests in April and July 1868 to Holmes. Mark DeWolfe Howe accordingly reported that Holmes had written the state digests in those numbers. *See* M. DeW. Howe, *Justice Oliver Wendell Holmes: The Shaping Years,* 315 n. 99 (1957). However, in Holmes's own bound volumes,

now in the Library of Congress, in which Holmes seems to have carefully listed all of his own work, he takes credit only for the state digests beginning in October 1868.

2. See bibliography, Sheldon Novick, *Honorable Justice: The Life of Oliver Wendell Holmes*. Boston: Little, Brown and Co., 1989. A list of Holmes's early works published by Felix Frankfurter, "The Early Writings of Oliver Wendell Holmes, Jr.," 44 *Harv. L. Rev.* 717 (1931), omitted all of those published before 1870; see Chapter 1, above.

6.1
DIGEST OF THE ENGLISH LAW REPORTS
FOR MAY, JUNE, AND JULY 1868[1]

From *American Law Review* 3:87 (1868)

. . . .

Copyright.

1. By the International Copyright Act, 7 Vict. c. 12, § 6, no author or his assigns of any musical composition first published abroad, shall be entitled to the benefit of the act, unless the name and place of abode of the author or composer of said composition are registered in England. N. composed and published an opera in full score at Berlin, and, after his death, B. arranged the score of the whole opera for the piano-forte; in registering this arrangement, N.'s name was inserted as composer. *Held*, that the entry was invalid, and gave no title to the assignee of the registered composition. The said arrangement was an independent musical composition, of which B., not N., was the composer (Exch. Ch.).—*Wood v. Boosey*, Law Rep. 3 Q.B. 223; s.c. Law Rep. 2 Q.B. 340 (*ante*, 2 Am. Law Rev. 110).

. . . .

Exoneration.

In the will of one dying before 30 & 31 Vict. c. 69 came into operation, a direction, that all his debts should be paid "out of his estate," does not entitle a devisee of mortgaged land to have the mortgage debt discharged out of the residuary real estate, under Locke King's Act (17 & 18 Vict. c. 113).

But a specific devise of one of two estates comprised in the same mortgage, the other being left to pass by a residuary clause, will make the latter first liable in exoneration of the former.—*Brownson v. Lawrance*, Law Rep. 6 Eq. 1.

Factor.

By the Factor's Act, 5 & 6 Vict. c. 39, § 1, "Any agent who shall thereafter be intrusted with the possession of goods" may make a valid pledge of the same, although the pledgee know of the agency. A party, to whom the plaintiffs had sent wine for sale, pledged the same to the defendants after his authority had been revoked and the wine demanded of him by the plaintiffs, but wrongfully detained by him. The *bona fides* of the defendants was not questioned. *Held*, that the pledgor was not "an *agent*, nor *entrusted*, within the meaning of the act."—*Fuentes v. Montis*, Law Rep. 3 C.P. 268.

. . . .

Negligence.

1. The defendants provided gangways from the shore to ships lying in their dock, the gangways being made of materials belonging to defendants, and managed by their servants. The plaintiff went on board a ship in said dock on business, at the invitation of one of the ship's officers; and, while he was there, defendants' servants moved the gangway, and negligently left it insecure, so that it gave way, and the plaintiff was injured on his return, without negligence on his part. *Held* (by BOVILL, C.J. and BYLES, J.; KEATING, J. *dubitante*), that there was a duty on the defendants toward the plaintiff not to let the gangway be insecure without warning him, and that he could recover damages for his injuries.—*Smith v. London & Saint Katharine Dock Co.*, Law Rep. 3 C.P. 326.

2. The plaintiff, while travelling by the defendants' railway, was injured by the fall of an iron girder, which workmen, not under the defendants' control, were employed in placing across the walls of the railway. It was proved that the work was very dangerous; that the defendants knew of the danger; that it was usual, when such work was going on, for the company to place a man to signal to the workmen the approach of a train; and that this precaution was not adopted. *Held*, sufficient evidence to warrant a jury in finding that the defendants were guilty of negligence and liable, even though the workmen were so also.—*Daniel v. Metropolitan Railway Co.*, Law Rep. 3 C.P. 216.

. . . .

SELECTED DIGEST OF STATE REPORTS.

From *American Law Review* 3:116 (1868).

. . . .

Bills and Notes.

1. An instrument promising to pay "five hundred" to A. or order, but having "$500" on its face, *held,* a promissory note.

In this case, the assignee had obtained judgment against the maker; but, that not having been satisfied, he sued the assignor. The note drew ten per cent interest after due. *Held,* that the measure of damages was the amount of the judgment, with six percent interest from the time it was rendered, and costs in obtaining the same.—*Corgan v. Frew,* 39 Ill. 31.

2. The maker of an accommodation note, not restricted as to the mode of its use, is liable to one who has received it to pay or secure a precedent debt; otherwise, *it seems,* where the note is obtained by fraud, or was given for a specific purpose, or is void in the hands of the payee on grounds of public policy.—*Schepp v. Carpenter,* 49 Barb. 542.

. . . .

Criminal Law.

It is error in a judge to give any charge to the jury in the absence of the prisoner.—*State v. Blackwelder,* 1 Phillips, N.C. 38.

See INDICTMENT; LIQUOR LAW; PROSTITUTION; ROBBERY; SLAVE, 4.

. . . .

Notice.

The agents of one claiming title to land put up on the premises a board, on which was printed, "For sale by S. H. Kerfoot & Co., 48 Clark Street." K. & Co. were the above agents. The party claiming title had also laid down a sidewalk on the premises. *Held,* that these facts amounted to notice of the claim to a creditor whose judgment lien attached while the above notice was posted on the premises.—*Hatch v. Bigelow,* 39 Ill. 546.

. . . .

Principal and Agent.

1. A cashier received at his bank a sum of money from the plaintiff, with the order to apply it to a note of the latter, then not due. He did apply it to another note signed by the plaintiff as surety, which was overdue, both of said notes being payable to said bank. The plaintiff never acquiesced in said application. *Held,* that the cashier was personally liable for said money, with interest from the time when received, whether he applied it to his own use or that of the bank.—*Norton v. Kidder,* 54 Me. 189.

. . . .

Slave.

1. A partition of an intestate's estate, consisting of land and slaves, which was made and confirmed, without objections then taken, by decree of the Court of Equity in 1864, allowed only slaves to complainants, but no land. *Held,* valid. Slaves did not become free, either *de jure* or *de facto,* by the Emancipation Proclamation in 1862.—*Pickett v. Wilkins,* 13 Rich. S.C. Eq. 366. See *Mitchell v. De Schamps, ib.* 9.

. . . .

Editor's Note

1. See pp. 181–82 above.

6.2

From *American Law Review* 1:375 (1867).

Roscoe's Digest of the Law of Evidence in Criminal Cases. By DAVID POWER, Esq., one of Her Majesty's Counsel, and late Recorder of Ipswich. Sixth American from the sixth London Edition. With Notes and References to American cases, by GEORGE SHARSWOOD. Philadelphia: T. & J. W. Johnson. 1866.

Mr. Roscoe's able treatise has long established its reputation, as the number of editions published in England and America sufficiently shows.

The method of its arrangement is not unlike that which is pursued in treatises on Natural History, and which has been followed with advantage in some psychological works, as well as in this digest of a branch of law. The subject is divided into two parts. The first states general properties, or, in this case, general principles, and sets forth a system of classification. These principles are in turn discussed, and instances are given of their various modes of operation. The second part treats of the different species in detail; in this case, the species being the various crimes known to the law. As the scientific analogy only holds in part, we have in this portion, instead of a classification adopted to exemplify a theory, a simple alphabetical arrangement, with a view to convenience which is here the only thing to be considered. But the law of each crime is laid down upon a constant system, so that it presents itself to the student as an organic whole, while, at the same time, it affords the greatest facilities for reference to one who seeks the authorities upon a special point. The book deserves its name of Digest, for the matter is not given in crude form, but digested and combined.

The differences which exist between a criminal trial at common law, and the corresponding process before the courts of Continental Europe, have led to an equal difference in the canons of evidence obtaining in the two systems. At common law, the trial of a man indicted for a crime is substantially a litigation between the sovereign power and the accused. Except in so far as the counsel for the government is held to a more than common nicety in using no unsound arguments to obtain a conviction, the opposing advocates encounter each other with the same efforts for victory, the same objections, the same mutual scrutiny, as are witnessed in civil actions. In France, on the other hand, the duties of the Procureur-Général, who is a sort of judge advocate, are to make a detailed investigation into the circumstances of the crime, and to use every means in his power to discover the guilty party. In the latter country, therefore, any evidence is admitted which will enable trained experts to form a theory; and a latitude is allowed co-extensive with the circumstances which may furnish hints to minds alert to take them, and subtle in imaging their existence. In the English and American courts, the object is very different. It is, in a word, to enable ordinary men to arrive at a working belief,—to come to a conclusion such as they would feel justified in acting on in a business matter of their own. It has accordingly been remarked, that the rules concerning the admission of evidence are determined, in the long run, by the average intelligence of juries. However that may be, as the object to be attained is not hypothesis but belief, the general laws of evidence in our criminal courts are wholly similar to the rules familiar in civil tribunals. A student would derive an almost equal benefit from reading the first part of Roscoe's treatise or the first volume of Greenleaf.

In the American notes, a Massachusetts lawyer occasionally misses a reference to some familiar cases; as, for instance, on p. 12, n. (1), on the admissibility of letterpress copies, *Commonwealth v. Jeffries*, 7 Allen, 548: under the general head of murder, p. 663, n. (1), on the presumption of malice, the leading case of *Commonwealth v. York*, 9 Met. 93; and also *Commonwealth v. Webster*, 5 Cush. 295, and *Commonwealth v. Hawkins*, 3 Gray, 463: and under the general head of insanity, p. 900, n. (1), *Baxter v. Abbott*, 7 Gray, 71, which contains important principles of evidence just as applicable to criminal as to civil cases.

We might suggest also that a work intended as a *vade mecum* would admit of fuller statements of the points settled by American cases.

When we have noticed the absence of the American references from the table of cases cited, our fault-finding is done.

Judge Sharswood, although his labors as an annotator are of a less extensive character in this than in some of the works which he has illustrated and enriched with his comments, sufficiently guarantees the general faithfulness of their performance by giving them the sanction of his name.

Finally, we are pleased to observe in the late publications of the Philadelphia house which issues this volume, an accession of care in the proof-reading, of which we have, at times, felt the want.

6.3

From *American Law Review* 1:377 (1867).

A Manual of Medical Jurisprudence. By ALFRED SWAINE TAYLOR, M.D., F.R.S., & c. Sixth American from the Eighth and Revised London Edition. With Notes and References to American Decisions, by CLEMENT B. PENROSE, of the Philadelphia Bar. Philadelphia: Henry C. Lea. 1866.

Every one remembers Mr. Pott's answer to Mr. Pickwick as to the sources of the erudition displayed by his critic in reviewing a work on Chinese metaphysics, "He read up for the subject, at my desire, in the 'Encyclopedia Britannica.' . . . He read, sir," said Mr. Pott, . . . "he read for metaphysics under the letter M, and for China under the letter C; and combined his information, sir!" Without venturing to hint any application to such books as that before us, we may express a doubt whether doctors would regard a work on "medical jurisprudence" as a sufficient hand-book of science; and we are very confident that few lawyers would feel strongly bound by its opinions on a point of law. Dr. Taylor's manual stands high among the works on this subject; but the question arises whether "Medical Jurisprudence" is, in fact, a legitimate title, either in law or medicine. We do not make any objection to the empirical and accidental character of the connection between the different matters discussed. If it is useful to have these topics treated together, that is enough, although it may destroy the unity of the treatise. But take a single one of the subjects: insanity, for example. A lawyer wants to know under what circumstances the courts have admitted this defence in a criminal action. If he looks at *Commonwealth v. Rogers,* and the following note, in Bennett and Heard's "Leading Criminal Cases," he gets the law, the whole law, and nothing but the law, concisely stated in a legal way. If, on the other hand, he consults a medical work, he can neither rely on finding the statement of it exhaustive nor accurate. A doctor is not trained to that business. In the book before us, the law which is given is melodramatic with exclamation points, and is interspersed with medical views, not tending to elucidate the legal bearing of the question; and when a case is cited, the author, instead of referring to the volume and page of the report, contents himself with giving the month and year and the court. Thus (p. 670), "*Monckton v. Cameraux* (Exchequer, June, 1848)," which is cited on the same page in the American note *sub nom. Molton v. Cameraux* from 2 Exch. R. 502, &c., and which ought to be cited *Molton v. Camroux*. With regard to the use of such a work to medical men, it becomes us to speak with more modesty. It seems clear, that a man must be familiar with a range of scientific facts found there, before using the book, or he will not be fit to use it. What its value as a *vade mecum* may be to the practitioner, like a volume on *nisi prius*, we cannot say, though possibly it is greater than we are aware. But, if so, why insert the law? You cannot make a physician look at a question in a legal way by such a short hand process, even if it were of much importance to do so. And scientific memoranda could be confined to the points likely to be needed at a trial, without a parade of cases. There is, moreover, this objection to the course pursued, that, by such a union of law with medicine, the physician is very apt to be misled as to his duties in the court room. He goes there with a theory about the law as well as the facts, and is in danger of usurping the place of the judge as well as of the special juror, which he thinks, perhaps rightly, that he ought to be. We do not, however, mean to deny the value of practical hints, such as those at the beginning and in other parts of the book before us. If "medical jurisprudence" requires a volume for its treatment, we should suppose the present one to be satisfactory. Indeed, as we have already said, it ranks among the very best of its kind. The American notes add to the value of the work, and to the statements of law in them our criticisms on those of the author do not apply.

6.4

From *American Law Review* 1:554 (1867).

Commentaries on Equity Jurisprudence, as administered in England and America. By JOSEPH STORY, LL.D. Ninth edition. Carefully revised, with extensive additions, by ISAAC F. REDFIELD, LL.D. In two volumes. Boston: Little, Brown, & Co. 1866.

Even as we were beginning this notice, we had occasion to consult the work before us, and found the information of which we stood in need in one of Judge Redfield's notes. It would be ungrateful, therefore, not to tender him our thanks at the outset.

Chief Justice Redfield is an experienced equity judge; and, in this edition of Judge Story's book, we listen with renewed respect to many of those *responsa prudentum* which, elsewhere and at an earlier time, he has uttered with all the weight of judicial authority. But while most of the added paragraphs justify their presence by the new riches which they bring, a few of them hardly bribe us to forget the boundaries which interpolations into another's labor should not pass. It might be well hereafter to commit to foot-notes some passages which are now spread at large in the text.

There are certain faults of execution which are common to all of Judge Redfield's works, though less prominent here than elsewhere. One of them is a habit of moralizing, which is notably out of place among the rules and precedents of courts. The following remarks as to *Riemers v. Druce* are still less in keeping with the character of the subject (§ 1584): "We can only say, that such decisions, although they may have the appearance of doing justice in the particular case, always tend to bring the administration of justice into discredit with those whose instincts are in favor of the firm adherence to principle, and trusting consequences to Him with whom are all the issues of life." When the learned editor calls in the authority of religion to make weight against the authority of the Master of the Rolls, by doing so he only renders the want of legal authority more conspicuous.

Again, would it not have been well to imitate the example of Story and of Kent, in severing the personality of the text-writer from that of the chief justice? As a matter of taste, it may be doubted whether an editor should tell a reader that "*We have discussed the question in all its bearings, in a case in Vermont.*"

These are only faults of execution, it is true. If the book were a new one, it would not be just to touch upon them before carefully considering its substantial merits. But we are dealing with a classic which all lawyers must buy, and of which they will buy the latest edition. It comes from the hands of an eminent and able man, and our demands are in proportion to what we have a right to expect. But for these defects, which can be easily cured, the treatise has materially gained in value. Judge Redfield's additions, though they may be condensed, will always be retained.

Of the original work, or its subject, little remains to be said at this late day. The ecclesiastical conception of a right supplementary to the law, and at times transcending it, was an embryo of vague and doubtful figure. By an organic necessity, however, it has slowly developed into a stable body of principles. Centuries have firmly knit its tissues, and have shaped its exact contours. Many portions of its structure have even ossified so far as to have united with the rigid skeleton of legal doctrines. The rest may do so in time. Meanwhile, legislation, gaining in flexibility as the courts lose it, supplies many of the aids for which, four centuries ago, the suitor must have looked to the churchman who administered the conscience of the king.

6.5

From *American Law Review* 2:159 (1867).

A Treatise on the American Law of Easements and Servitudes. By EMORY WASHBURN, LL.D., &c. Second edition. Boston: Little, Brown, & Company. 1867.

No work of Judge Washburn can be otherwise than faithfully done. In the duties of his professorship at the Cambridge Law School, and in his books, he is alike untiring, laborious, enthusiastic. The treatise before us has already become an authority. It is a very useful book: in it we find, not only a thorough collection of cases, but a discussion of principles at once able and judicious. A hundred added pages in this second edition bear witness to the author's watchful fidelity. There are, however, one or two of the *apices juris,* which we were disappointed not to see brought to a finer point by the aid of recent decisions.

Thus, the law of lateral support of land has received important modifications in late cases, and there is hardly consistency in the language employed. *Foley v. Wyeth,* 2 Allen, 131, 133, is cited at some length. There it is laid down, that, for injury to the soil resulting from the removal of the natural support of the adjoining tract, the owner has a remedy, on the ground that a right of property is violated. The court (MERRICK, J.) then goes on to say, "This unqualified rule is limited to injuries caused to the land itself. . . . For an injury to buildings which is unavoidably incident to the . . . slide of the soil on which they stand . . . an action can only be maintained when a want of due care or skill, or positive negligence, has contributed to produce it." Under the inspiration of the above language, the author lays down the principle which he does on page 526 [*444]. But, in this connection, the English cases of *Brown v. Robins*, 4 H. & Norm. 186, and *Stroyan v. Knowles*, 6 H. & Norm. 454, 465, did not, we think, receive the attention they deserve. To our apprehension, they put a new face on the English law.

In *Brown v. Robins*, it was shown that the land would have fallen in consequence of neighboring excavations, even if no house had been upon it. It was thereupon *held*, that the plaintiff could recover for the damage to the house as well as for that to the land: and this seems reasonable, for it cannot be pretended that, by any analogies, the damage is too remote; and, if not, how shall the defendant infringe his neighbor's rights, and yet not be liable for the immediate consequences of his act? This doctrine was upheld in the other case mentioned, and seems inconsistent with the opinion expressed in *Foley v. Wyeth*. Indeed, in the latter case, the court emulate the jury's function, and seek to divide losses as seems fair on the whole, rather than to follow the strict logic of the law to its conclusions.

Smith v. Thackerah, Law Rep. 1 C.P. 564, which is not referred to in this treatise, gives us an additional refinement. A. dug a well near B.'s land, which sank in consequence, and a building, erected on it within twenty years, fell. It was proved, as in *Brown v. Robins*, that, if the building had not been there, the land would still have sunk; but it was also shown in this case that the damage would then have been inappreciable. *Held*, that B. had no cause of action against A.

Erle, C. J., "For a man to dig a hole in his own land is in itself a perfectly lawful act of ownership, and it only becomes a wrong if it injures his neighbor; and since it is the injury itself which gives rise to the right of action, there can be no right of action unless the damage is of appreciable amount."

Witty diversities, as Yelverton says, but apparently sound.

A consideration of them might have modified the rule laid down by Judge Washburn.

6.6

From *American Law Review* 2:328 (1868).

A Treatise on the Law of Bills of Exchange, Promissory Notes, Bank-Notes, and Checks. By Sir JOHN BARNARD BYLES, Queen's Sergeant, now one of the Judges of Her Majesty's Court of Common Pleas. Fifth American, from the Ninth London Edition. With Notes from the Fourth American Edition; with Additional Notes, illustrating the law and practice in the United States, by GEORGE SHARSWOOD. Philadelphia: T. & J. W. Johnson & Co. 1867.

If there should ever be an attempt to codify the whole body of the law, which, we suppose, would amount in substance to the publication of a series of government text-books, the work of Mr. Justice Byles would furnish an admirable model. The arrangement is so lucid, the statements of the law are so concise, there is such an entire absence of the loose talk in which inferior writers abound, that the book might well be enacted entire by Act of Parliament. Text-books are of growing importance now-a-days in the multitude of reports; and, without any conferred authority, a work so honest and able as the present of itself commands respect. This edition contains nearly a hundred more pages than the last. Most of these are filled with American notes of late cases, and with additions to the original text, which show the minute care and watchfulness of the author. Mr. Justice Byles, we notice, compliments his learned editor in this country, and makes some use of his labors. When the cosmopolitan character of commercial law, and especially of this branch of it, is considered, and in view of the ability and learning of some of the American courts, it is only remarkable that this has not been done to a greater extent.

The only criticism we have to make,—and it is a grave one,—is on the omission to insert the American cases in the index—a serious deficiency in this otherwise complete edition.

6.7
SUMMARY OF EVENTS: IMPEACHMENT

From *American Law Review* 2:547 (1868).

We propose to give, first, a very brief diary of events up to the time of going to press; secondly, to set forth some of the most important documents bearing upon the case; and then to offer a summary of the leading arguments which have been urged on the principal questions involved, and on one or two collateral points.

. . . .[1]

The principal questions raised by the above articles of impeachment are as follows:—

1. Is the Tenure of Office Act constitutional? As to this, it will be found to have been thought, (*a*) That the President had the right of removal under the general grant of executive powers in the Constitution, either exclusively, which would make the act unconstitutional, or in the absence of legislation, which would make it constitutional: (*b*) That the power to remove was incident to the power to appoint, and that the power to appoint was in the President, which would make the act unconstitutional; or that the power to appoint was in the President and Senate jointly, which would make the act constitutional: (*c*) That the power to remove is impliedly given exclusively to the President, along with and as incident to the power to nominate.

2. The second question is, Has the Tenure of Office Act been infringed, and, if not, was the appointment of General Thomas *ad interim* lawful?

3. Another question, raised by the tenth article, is, whether the President can be impeached except for an offence against the Constitution or the statutes of the United States.

4. The last question on the merits is whether, if the act violated should be held unconstitutional by the Supreme Court, the Senate could still convict on articles charging that violation.

I. (*a*) Has the President an indefeasible right, under the Constitution, to remove officers which that instrument gives him the power to nominate, and, by and with the advice and consent of the Senate, to appoint? The debates of 1789 (1 Annals of Congress, 456–485, especially 461) have been cited as sanctioning this conclusion.

On the other hand, it has been said that—

"The question involved in that debate was not whether the President had the power of removing an officer, the tenure of whose office was fixed by law, but whether he had such power when the law was silent as to the tenure." (Lawrence *arguendo.—Unites States v. Guthrie*, 17 Howard, 284, 298; Congr. Globe, Feb. 1, 1867, Mr. Hale's Speech.)

Mr. Madison's argument in those debates, in favor of the President's power, as put by Mr. Webster,* is as follows:—

"The executive power is vested in the President: this is the general rule of the Constitution. The association of the Senate with the President, in exercising a particular function belonging to the executive power, is an exception to this general rule, and exceptions to general rules are to be taken strictly; therefore, though the Senate partakes of the appointing powers, by express provision, yet, as nothing is said of its participation in the removing power, such participation is to be excluded."

Mr. Webster replied to this, that the power of removal did not vest in the President under the general grant of executive power, but it was incident to the power to appoint, and the power to appoint was in the President and Senate jointly. His conclusion was, that, by a true interpretation of the Constitution, the President had not the power of removal, without the advice and consent of the Senate,—a view which is sanctioned by Mr. Justice McLean, in his opinion in *United States v. Guthrie*, 17 *How.* 306, and in which, he says, the Supreme Court, in the time of Chief Justice Marshall, concurred. Mr. Webster went on to say, in the speech above referred to, that, without admitting that Congress might not hereafter, if necessity should require it, reverse the decision of 1789, yet as that decision had been sanctioned by practice, and recognized by subsequent laws, Congress should act upon it for the present. Whereupon he voted for a law recognizing the power of the President to remove, but requiring a statement of reasons to be laid before the Senate when the power was exercised. It seems, therefore, that Mr. Webster did not consider that the decision of 1789 went farther than it did in the opinion of Mr. Lawrence. Indeed, he says, "If Congress were to declare by law that the Attorney General or the Secretary of State should hold his office during good behavior, I am not aware of any ground on which such a law could be held unconstitutional" (p. 196); and again (p. 197), "If a law were to pass, declaring that district attorneys or collectors of customs should hold their offices four years, unless removed on conviction for misbehavior, no one could doubt its constitutional validity; because the legislature is

*Speech in the Senate, Feb. 16, 1835. (Webster's Works, vol. iv.)

naturally competent to prescribe the tenure of office. And is a reasonable check on the power of removal any thing more than a qualification of the tenure of office?"

(*b*) A different view has been taken by some, who stand on the premises that the power to remove was incident to the power to appoint; viz., that the President alone appointed, after submitting his nomination to the Senate, and therefore had the power to remove. That the President alone appoints, seems to have been the opinion of Congress when they passed the Act of Feb. 20, 1863, section 1 of which speaks of the heads of executive departments, "or other officer in either of said departments, whose appointment is vested in the President." This seems to have been thought by the Supreme Court also, when they decided *Marbury v. Madison,* 1 Cranch, 137, 159. The Chief Justice there says, "The appointment being, under the Constitution, to be made by the President *personally.*" (The italics are his. See, also, p. 167.) But it is not probable that Congress would have accepted the conclusion; and it appears, from the rest of the case first cited, that the Supreme Court certainly did not. This suggestion is so little pressed now-a-days, that we pass it over with a mention.

The great case of *Marbury v. Madison,* just cited, certainly seems to be authority for the constitutionality of the Tenure of Office Act. Mr. Marbury was a justice of the peace for the District of Columbia, appointed by the President by and with the advice and consent of the Senate, but by act of Congress having a tenure of five years. It is very clearly resolved in that case that the President could not dismiss him before that time. See pp. 167, 168: "It is, then, in the opinion of the court, . . . that the appointment conferred on him a legal right to the office for the space of five years."

Page 172: "It has already been stated that the applicant has to that commission a vested legal right, of which the executive cannot deprive him. He has been appointed to an office from which he is not removable at the will of the executive."

Ex parte Hennen, 13 Peters, 230, has been cited on the other side; but Thompson, J., who gave the decision in that case, appears to have been contemplating only the right of removal in the absence of statutory regulations, and asserting the authority of the President in that case. Indeed, he seems clearly to admit the power of Congress to pass a law regulating the tenure of office. He says, p. 259, "All offices, the tenure of which is not fixed by the Constitution *or limited by law,* must be held at the will and discretion of some department of the Government,"—"*In the absence of all constitutional provision or statutory regulation,* it would seem to be a sound and necessary rule to consider the power of removal as incident to the power of appointment."

(*c*) An argument has been made, from the use of the word *nominate,* in the Constitution. It is said this power is in the President alone. Otherwise the word would be synonymous with *appoint,* and superfluous. Now, if the President is dependent on the Senate for his power of removal, what becomes of his undoubted right to nominate? He has no opportunity to nominate, except by their permission. Reference is also made to the second half of the clause of the Constitution, just alluded to, by which the President may fill vacancies occurring during the recess of the Senate, by granting commissions which shall expire at the end of the next session.

The last words, clearly, only mark the farthest time of expiration, and do not prescribe that the office shall continue until that time. The President, after filling a vacancy, might remove the officer of his own creation, and put in another in his place. May he not do the same while the Senate is in session? Does not the power to nominate include the power to make a vacancy? it is asked; or, rather, does not nomination create a vacancy of itself, *proprio vigore?*

The practice, however, is said to be the other way (Webster's Works, vol. iv, p. 189); and that an officer in possession of the office at the time of nomination should be held to continue in possession until the appointment of his successor, only seems to deprive the President of the power of subjecting the Senate to duress in cases where they do not concur in the appointment of a new incumbent,—a power they unquestionably possess.[2]

II. Has the Tenure of Office Act been infringed?

It is urged, on the part of the President, that the removal of Mr. Stanton and the appointment of General Thomas do not constitute a breach of the Tenure of Office Act. The first part of the first section of that act enacts generally that every person holding any civil office to which he has been appointed by and with the advice and consent of the Senate, shall be entitled to hold such office until a successor shall have been in like manner appointed and duly qualified. This, by a slight circuity, deprives the President of the power of removal from any office, without the consent of the Senate. But by a proviso attached to the said first section, the Secretaries of State, of the Treasury, of War, &c., shall hold their offices respectively for and during the term of the President by whom they may have been appointed, and for one month thereafter. The insertion of this proviso must be taken as limiting the generality of the preceding clause, which, without this, would have covered the chiefs of departments. These officers are, by the proviso, only entitled to hold for a month after the term of the President by whom they are appointed. But, says Mr. Johnson, I never appointed Mr. Stanton. His only appointment was from my predecessor, and this act confers no rights on him. I am at liberty, therefore, to remove him, as I could have before the Tenure of Office Act was passed.

Assuming, then, that the removal was lawful, was the appointment of General Thomas *ad interim* so? The President, after referring to section 2 of the Act of Aug. 7, 1789, creating the War Department, to show that removal was then contemplated as one of the causes through which a vacancy might occur, cites as the authority for his action section 1 of the Act of Feb. 13, 1795. By this section, in case of vacancy in the office of Secretary of War (among others), it shall be lawful for the President of the United States to authorize any person or persons, at his discretion, to perform the duties of the said respective offices until a successor be appointed or such vacancy be filled. It is admitted that the Act of Feb. 20, 1863, § 1, makes provision for the vacancies occurring in certain specified ways, and does not include one caused by removal; but this section only repeats, in substance, section 8 of an Act of May 8, 1792, and so cannot be taken as repealing an act subsequent to the one last mentioned, by implication merely.[3]

We have observed that in the standard edition of the Statutes at Large, the Act of Feb. 13, 1795 is marked obsolete; but we are not aware that this is authoritative, and it is immaterial in view of the answer to the other branch of the argument. It is said in reply, To be sure, Mr. Stanton was not appointed by Mr. Johnson; but he was by Mr. Lincoln, and the term of the latter has not yet expired. To this it is rejoined, and with great force, if the fact is as alleged, True it is, that Mr. Lincoln's second term had not expired, but Mr. Stanton was not recommissioned at the beginning of Mr. Lincoln's second term. Supposing, then, any other person than Mr. Lincoln had been elected for that second term, and Mr. Stanton had held over in like manner, he would have been a mere tenant by sufferance under this act;[4] for he was only entitled, under the proviso in section one, to hold a month after the term of the President, by whom he was appointed, had expired.

Can the construction of the word *term,* in the act which the President is charged with violating, be changed, because an individual, after filling one term, was chosen for another?

We do not undertake to discuss the moral aspects of the case; but it certainly seems to us, that, of the legal defences, this is the strongest, as to all the articles reached by it.

III. Mr. Butler's article suggests another question: Can the President be impeached except for a crime? On this point we can do no more than refer to two or three sources of information. An able article by Professor Theodore W. Dwight, in 6 Am. Law Reg. N.S. 257, since published in pamphlet form, strenuously maintains that "the Constitution only adopts (impeachment) as a mode of procedure, leaving the crimes to which it is to be applied to be settled by the general rules of criminal law." He further argues that, as there are no common law crimes under the United States, "there can be no impeachment, except for a violation of a law of Congress, or for the commission of a crime named in the Constitution." In a subsequent number of this same periodical (*Ibid.* 641) Judge W. Lawrence, of Ohio, upholds a contrary doctrine in an interesting article.

The clause in the Constitution that the President, &c., shall be removed from office on impeachment for and conviction of treason, bribery, or other high crimes and misdemeanors, Art. 2, § 4, certainly seems, on its face, to express the intended limit of impeachable offences, as well as to prescribe a punishment. That clause clearly excludes removal from office as a penalty for a conviction of any other offence than those named; and it would be a strange sight to see the Senate sitting to decide whether the President was liable to a pecuniary mulct or to imprisonment while his tenure of office was secure.

Perhaps so much as this will be conceded. But, it is said, the words "high crime and misdemeanor" leave the whole question open. They must be interpreted by parliamentary usage; and, by the parliamentary law, an impeachable offence and an indictable offence are not synonymous.

But though a previous impeachment be no answer to an indictment, and even admitting, what the authorities seem to settle otherwise, that an indictable offence is not a necessary element in one which is impeachable, still the fact remains that impeachment was only a method of punishing what the common law or statutes recognized as a crime, (1 Story on Const. § 798). So much was this so, that the opinion of the judges might be asked as to what the law was. This being so, we are not aware of any reasoning which suffices to destroy the common law jurisdiction of the United States courts over crimes that does not equally apply to impeachment.

Indeed, this seems to be admitted by those whose opinions are the strongest in support of the jurisdiction of the Senate independently of statute. Story says (1 Com. on Const., § 798), "Those who denounce the common law, as having any application or existence in regard to the national government, must be necessarily driven to maintain that the power of impeachment is, until Congress shall legislate, a mere nullity, or that it is despotic both in its reach and in its proceedings." Rawle, in his work on the Constitution, is stronger to the same effect (ch. xxviii., *ad finem*).

But that the courts of the United States have no common law jurisdiction seems to be settled against Judge Story's opinion; and the conclusion which he deprecated, but admitted as logical, seems to follow.

It may be worthy of note by those who are inclined to cite early English precedents to show that impeachment extended to offences not indictable, that, from the beginning of the reign of Edward IV till the 17th year of James I, this jurisdiction was supplanted by bills of attainder and the Star Chamber (4 Hatsell, 72, 73). Neither of the last-named institutions have a good name now-a-days, yet the reasons offered for the latter are much the same as those now put forth for impeachment at common law. Bacon said of the Star Chamber, "This court is one of the sagest, and noblest institutions of this kingdom; . . . there was always reserved a high and pre-eminent power to the king's council in causes that might, in example or consequence, concern the state of the commonwealth." Lord Somers said, "It was set up as a formal court in the 3d year of Henry VIIth, in very soft words,—'To punish great riots, to restrain offenders too big for ordinary justice, or, in modern phrase, to preserve the public peace.' But in a little time it made this nation tremble." Cited 4 Hatsell, 73, n.

IV. There is one other principal question raised in this matter which must be mentioned. Supposing the act is unconstitutional, can the President still be impeached for its violation? That a law which is unconstitutional is void *ab initio,* and can impose no obligation, seems too clear for argument. The newspaper suggestion, that, if this be so, any one may violate a law, conceiving it to be void, is obviously futile. Of course any one may disregard a law under those circumstances, but at his own peril; for, if he wilfully violates a valid law, his having acted conscientiously will not relieve him from one tittle of his punishment. There is some language of Chief Justice Chase, however, in *Mississippi v. Johnson,* 4 Wall. 475, which looks as if it were his opinion that each of the three great divisions of government must determine the constitutionality of laws for themselves, irrespective of a contrary determination elsewhere. He says, "Suppose the bill filed, and the injunction prayed for allowed. If . . . the President complies with the order of the court, and refuses to execute the acts of Congress, . . . may not the House of Representatives impeach the President for such refusal?" It certainly would have seemed, but for this language, that, when the Supreme Court of the United States had once declared an act unconstitutional, every department of government was bound to respect their decision.

On the other hand, if the act in question is constitutional, and the President has wilfully violated it, whatever may have been his duty, and whatever may be the policy of impeachment, it seems too clear for argument that he is legally punishable, in spite of any conscientious motives which he may have had.

Two or three questions have already arisen as to the nature and proceedings of a court of impeachment. The Chief Justice has been sustained, as was noted in our diary, in his position that the Senate did not become a court of impeachment capable of making rules, until he had taken his place as presiding officer. Had it not been for this decision, it might, perhaps, have been doubted—interpreting the Constitution in light of the English precedents—whether this were so. In Foster's Crown Law, a resolution of the Lords is cited that "The High Steward is but a speaker or chairman *pro tempore* for the more orderly proceeding at the trial; the appointment of him doth not alter the nature of the court, which still remaineth the Court of the Peers in Parliament." The force of this may be impaired by the fact that it was alleged that an impeachment might proceed without the appointment of a High Steward at all. But this seems to have been because the king, from whom the special commission issued, might otherwise have been able to suspend proceedings indefinitely (*Ibid.* 142–145). This difficulty was avoided by nominating the officer who should preside.[5] In the same clause of the Constitution which required that the Senate should have a president other than the usual one, and whether any other object than this was proposed in that clause, would seem to admit of a reasonable doubt. At any rate, as we have said, it seems to be undeniable that the peers felt no scruples in acting judicially before the appointment of a High Steward. Yet it is to be noted that the High Steward was often the Lord Chancellor, or other person learned in the law, and fulfilled functions similar to those of the Chief Justice with us. As to the right of the Chief Justice to vote, the authorities cited by Mr. Conkling, in his speech of March 4, seem conclusive against it, unless there should be put forward other grounds besides precedent. Speaking of impeachment, Foster says (Crown Law, 143), "The High Steward, himself voting merely as a peer and member of that court, in common with the rest of the peers, and in no other right."

With regard to Mr. Wade's right to be sworn of the court, it would seem that the decision of the Senate, that any objection to him was premature, was correct, and that the proper time for considering his right was when he should be challenged by the accused.

Editor's Notes

1. The ellipsis replaces a summary of events; excerpts from the Tenure of Office Act (March 2, 1867); "Articles exhibited by the House of Representatives of the United States, in the name of Themselves and all the People of the United States, against Andrew Johnson, President of the United States, in Maintenance and Support of their Impeachment against him for High Crimes and Misdemeanors"; the text of a letter from Chief Justice Chase to the Senate; and the "Rules of Procedure and Practice in the Senate when Sitting on the Trial of Impeachments."

2. Substitution for "a power they unquestionably possess" in Holmes's copy (Library of Congress): as they unquestionably may refuse to do by the express provision of the Constitution.

3. In his copy, OWH adds here: Note also the Act of March 2, 1867 § 6 (ante p. 550) only applies to letters of authority for employment not "contrary to the provisions of this act."

4. OWH alters this last phrase to: his tenure of office would not have been strengthened.

5. OWH note to merge this sentence with the one following, joining them with a comma.

6.8

From *American Law Review* 3:141 (1868).

Reports of Cases heard and decided in the Supreme Court of Michigan, from July 11, 1867, to April 28, 1868. WILLIAM JENNISON, Reporter. Vol. III., being Vol. XVI. of the series. Detroit: Wm. A. Throop & Co. 1868.

It is our fortune, good or bad, to be called upon to examine pretty carefully nearly all the new volumes which appear in the different series of State Reports. In doing so, we have been much struck by the unaccountable diversity of merit which they manifest. We say unaccountable, for the distribution of excellence is according to no principle which we can ascertain; contiguous States sometimes offering the most striking examples of learning and ability on one side, and of the want of those qualifications on the other side, of their dividing boundary.

We are most happy that in the present case our only duty is to praise. The Michigan Reports are among the best in the country at the present time. The reporter is better than the average, and the judges are candid, able, and well-informed. We shall here refer to but three cases, as the American Digest of our next number will glean the field which we have partially reaped before. (See 2 Am. Law Rev. 352, 573, 775.) As to the point on which the court were divided in *McMillan v. Mich. S. & N.I. R.R. Co.*, p. 79 (*ante,* 2 Am. Law Rev. 352), we feel a strong leaning to the view of *Campbell,* J., and the Chief Justice, that notice to the consignee of the arrival of goods at the end of their transit is not necessary to terminate the liability of a railroad company as common carriers. The adverse argument seems based upon the assumption that the undertaking of the railroad is to deliver the goods to the consignee at his house or store, from which it is excused, to be sure, on showing its inability to run its cars beyond the end of its track, but excused only on accepting the substituted duty of giving notice. We should have thought, on the other hand, that when goods have reached the consignees' end of the road, the contract of carriage, which was made with knowledge of and with reference to the nature of the road, was fulfilled. (See *Norway Plains Co. v. B. & M. R.R. Co.*, 1 Gray, 263, 272.) As a question of expediency, too, while there is an obvious reason for holding carriers to be insurers of goods *in transitu,* in the difficulty, in case of loss, of ascertaining their whereabouts or circumstances, this reason loses its force when the goods are housed and at the end of the transit.

The second case we would mention is *Hyatt v. Adams, p.* 180 (*ante,* 2 Am. Law Rev. 352). We question whether there should not be a civil remedy for causing the death of a human being, just as for any other felony. So far as we know, the only authority which even hints at such a distinction in the English cases is a somewhat broad remark of Lord *Ellenborough,* at *nisi prius,* in *Baker v. Bolton,* Camp. 493. The other cases, and especially the argument of *Bosanquet,* Sergt., in *Stone v. Marsh,* 6 B. & C. 551, which was approved by the court, look the other way. If there is no difference, it is hard to see why an action might not have been brought against one who had been convicted of manslaughter, had his benefit of clergy, and been burnt in the hand (6 B. & C. 558), unless the analogy of the appeal of death was followed (4 Bl. Com. 315). Had we room, we should like to discuss the allowing of damages for loss of service before the death, but not for the death. The death having taken place within a year and a day, we should have thought, that, just as thereby the act which caused it became felonious, that act (in this case, malpractice) would have received its character from the same fact, in like manner, when made the foundation of a civil suit. The cause of action was not simply malpractice sufficient to cause loss of service; it was malpractice grave enough to cause death. If damages were allowed, how could that element of the case be left out? If the death had taken place after a year and a day, we suppose there would have been no more legal connection for civil than for criminal purposes between it and the unlawful act, its supposed cause. In that case, therefore, the fact of death would have been immaterial.

In *People v. Cicott*, p. 283 *(ante,* 2 Am. Law Rev. 574), ballots giving the initials only of the candidate's Christian name were rejected with some hesitation, and, apparently, chiefly on the authority of earlier cases. The House of Representatives in Massachusetts arrived at a different conclusion in a similar case, in 1867, in spite of a strong argument by ex-Governor Andrew, who relied a good deal on the earlier Michigan decisions. Six votes for *Jonas Champney* and one for *J. Champney* were admitted, although the candidate's name was *Jonas A. Champney,* and although he had a father living and eligible, whose name was *Jonas C. Champney.* House Documents, 1867, No. 64. See *Peabody v. Brown,* 10 Gray, 45. See notice (p. 150) of 3 Ellis & Ellis, *ad finem.*

6.9

From *American Law Review* 3:144 (1868).

Reports of Cases in Law and Equity, argued and determined in the Supreme Court of Georgia, at Milledgeville, December Term, 1866. With an Appendix, containing Several Cases decided by the Honorable John Erskine, in the Circuit and District Courts of the United States for Georgia. To which is prefixed a Table of Cases reported in the first thirty-one volumes of the Georgia Reports, and afterwards cited in one or more of said volumes. Volume XXXV. By LOGAN E. BLECKLEY, Reporter. Atlanta, Ga. 1868.

Mr. Bleckley ends his labors as reporter with this volume, and has shown his conscientious industry by prefixing to it the table mentioned in the titlepage. This is most useful; and it is only to be regretted that, whenever new reports appear, a similar index to the cases cited in them is not added as a matter of course. The index to the present volume also is remarkably complete.

The Georgia Reports are equal to the average of our State reports. If they are not above that mark, we think it is in part owing to the small number of judges; a matter which is alluded to in connection with another State (Nevada) in this number. When it is considered under what interruptions and difficulties the law must have been practised for the last few years in several of the Southern States, it is matter of surprise that their courts should have maintained so high an excellence as is to be observed. It is still more gratifying to notice that in these pages there is little, if any, of the misplaced and turgid rhetoric to which some American judges are too prone. There is a touch of bathos in *Heard v. State,* pp. 169, 170, and a doubtful figure in *Riley v. Martin,* p. 139, where the abolition of slavery is likened to "the flaming sword placed at the east of the garden of Eden, at Adam's expulsion, turning every way towards the community." But these, we believe, are all.

We have only space to refer to one or two cases here; the next Digest will contain all of general interest.

Ansley v. Anderson, p. 8, was as follows: A. sold goods for Confederate money, for and at the request of B., who, mistaking his legal rights, refused to accept the proceeds when tendered him. A. thereupon deposited the amount to his own credit in his general bank account, and notified B. that it was subject to his order at any time. Confederate money became worthless, and B. now ratifies the sale and demands the value of the proceeds at the time of the sale. *Held,* that he could not recover. The loss was not owing to negligence of A., but to the nature of the proceeds themselves. *Fulton Bank v. Marine Bank,* 2 Wallace, 252, was distinguished. *Harris,* J., dissented, on the ground that A., by mixing the specific proceeds with his general balance, had converted them to his own use; that the proceeds were not really subject to B.'s order, and so not at his risk. This is a close case, and the reasoning of the dissenting judge is hard to answer. But look at it this way: A. was ordered to barter goods for a certain other commodity, of a kind known to be in the market and circulating at fixed valuations. Before tender, A. surely was only bound to furnish B. the amount and kind of the commodity ordered, not any specific bills. B. surely could not have objected to the tender on the ground that the bills were not those received, though of the same kind. Now, A. always had in his storehouse, in this case his bank, the commodity of the amount and kind he was directed by his principal to procure, and was always ready to deliver the same to him. The commodity, not being called for, perished by inherent defect. Why should the agent be liable? He was ordered to procure, not specific bills, but bills to a certain amount, and this he did.

To put contracts made during the war on a fair basis, an ordinance of the Convention of 1865 wisely provided that either party to such a contract, which was not yet executed, might give in evidence, in any suit for the enforcement of the same, the consideration and value thereof at any time, and the intention of the parties as to the particular currency in which payment was to be made, and the value of such currency at any time; and that the verdict and judgment should be on principles of equity. *Held* (waiving discussion of the legislative power of the Convention), that said ordinance did not impair the obligation of contracts. *Slaughter v. Culpepper,* p. 25. It is certainly desirable that such an ordinance should be upheld, if possible. The results of some of the decisions noted in a late number of our Digest—Title "Confederate Money" (*ante,* Vol. II pp. 694, 695)—must be distressing and unjust in the extreme. See, also, *Baily v. Milner,* p. 330. *Adams v. Brooks,* p. 63, wisely upholds the principle of *stare decisis,* in the face of doubts of the correctness of the original decision. Our courts are not apt to err on the side of too much respect for precedent.

The opinions of the circuit and district judge, *Erskine,* in the Appendix, are all on questions of great moment and interest. *Ex parte Law,* p. 285, decided before *Ex parte Garland,* 4 Wallace, 333, *held,* that the test oath required from attorneys of the national courts was unconstitutional.

State of Georgia v. Atkins, p. 315: A State may sue in a circuit court; and it is not a "corporation," within the United States Internal Revenue laws.

Baily v. Milner, p. 330: A note given in consideration of Confederate money is void. See *Scudder v. Thomas,* p. 364.

United States v. Athens Armory, p. 344: A full pardon granted and accepted prior to the seizure of property or the institution of any proceeding to condemn it, is a bar to a judgment of condemnation under the Confiscation Acts.

Such are some of the points which Judge Erskine discusses with learning and industry. Altogether, this little volume contains more interesting matter than many of twice its size.

6.10

From *American Law Review* 3:147 (1868).

Reports of Cases argued and determined in the Supreme Court of the State of Wisconsin. With Tables of the Cases and Principal Matters. By O. M. CONOVER, Official Reporter. Volume XXI. Containing all the cases decided before the September Term, 1867, and not previously reported. Madison, Wis. 1868.

This is quite an interesting volume, in a good series. There is more of a legal atmosphere about the Supreme Court of Wisconsin, we should judge, than in some longer established tribunals.

We give two or three cases, taken somewhat at random, as there is more matter of interest than we have room to refer to here.

In *Klauber v. American Express Co.,* p. 21, plaintiff's goods, not being secured in cases or by any waterproof covering, were injured by rain in their transfer from the cars to the wagon of the defendant, a common carrier, and thence to defendant's office. *Held,* that defendant was liable for the damage.

In *Boorman v. American Express Co.,* p. 152, a receipt for goods exempted the carrier from all liability for loss or damage of any package for over fifty dollars, unless the just and true value thereof was stated in the receipt. It seems to have been *held,* that this would exempt him in the specified cases from losses by his own negligence. But see, on this point, *Prentice v. Decker,* 49 Barb. 21; *Limburger v. Westcott,* 49 Barb. 283; American Digest for present number, title "Carrier," 2,3.

Pfeil v. Higby, p. 248, does justice, at the expense, perhaps, of logic; though, on this, opinions are much divided. See *Bush v. Baldrey,* 11 Allen, 367, and other Massachusetts cases. It was *held,* that, defendants being bound to pay a foreign debt of plaintiff, and to indemnify him from liability thereon, and plaintiff, on their default, having paid it in exchange purchased at the current rate with legal tender notes, defendants were liable to him in the full amount paid for such exchange.

In *Stephenson v. United States Express Co.,* p. 66, a question analogous to that in *McMillan v. M.S. & N.I. R.R. Co.* is moved. (See notice of 16 Michigan Reports.) But it is to be observed, that, in this case, the defendants are an express company, not a railroad. See, however, *Hermann v. Goodrich,* p. 536. *Druecker v. Salomon,* p. 621, *held,* that the rules and regulations for enrolling and drafting the militia, adopted by the President and promulgated by the War Department, under which the draft of 1863 took place, were constitutional and valid, and that the Governor, while engaged in enforcing the draft pursuant to those rules, and the draft commissioners appointed by him, were officers of the United States. The decision of the President as to calling forth the militia was binding on all, and resisting the draft was levying war on the United States. Defendant, being governor in 1863, arrested plaintiff for resisting the draft, and kept him twelve days in custody. *Held,* that he was not liable, as he had not exceeded the discretionary power which was his by virtue of his office.

In *Candee v. Pennsylvania R.R. Co.,* p. 582, there is a *semble* by *Cole,* J., that a railroad, selling a through ticket over lines connecting with its own, undertakes to transport, or cause to be transported, the passenger and his baggage to the place of destination. *Downer,* J., expressed no opinion.

The reporter's work seems to be unusually well done. We have expressed our views as to the bad effect of the small number of judges, in our notice of the Nevada Reports. It is fair to say that this court, from its greater experience or some other cause, is more unanimous than the other.

6.11

From *American Law Review* 3:148 (1868).

Reports of Cases determined in the Supreme Court of the State of Nevada, during the year 1867. Reported by ALFRED HELM, Clerk of the Court. Volume III. San Francisco. 1868.

We cannot but think that the small number of judges (three) which constitute the Supreme Court in this as in several other States is to be regretted. It detracts from the weight of a united decision, and almost destroys the authority of one from which a member of the court dissents. Moreover, it may be doubted whether it does not make differences of opinion more likely. A wise judge would have to feel very clear before expressing a view adverse to that of five of his brethren, when he might well be less solicitous if he were barely outweighed by one. This conclusion is confirmed by an examination of the volume before us. There are, if we have counted right, seven opinions in the whole book fully concurred in by the three judges; five opinions fully concurred in by two, in which the third concurs specially; six opinions concurred in by two, from which the third dissents; three opinions (one a murder case, in which the judgment of death was affirmed) delivered by one, a second judge concurring only in the result, and a third dissenting; two opinions delivered by one judge, and one other concurring only in the result; and all the residue, about twenty-five, decided by two judges, the third being absent. This, to use no stronger language, is not as it should be; and it is not to be expected that such decisions should be treated with much deference beyond the jurisdiction of the court by which they are made.

We have not had time, since receiving these reports, to do more than glance over them; and the head-notes to the cases are so long and rambling that they afford no aid in ascertaining the points really decided. *Beatty v. Rhodes,* p. 240, is the singular case of one of the judges arguing before the other two that an act of the legislature making his salary payable in legal tender notes, it having been previously payable in gold, was contrary to a section of the State Constitution, ordaining that the salary of the judges should not be increased or diminished during their term of office. *Held,* that the law was constitutional.

The Constitution of Nevada provides that no person holding a lucrative office under the United States shall be eligible to any civil office of profit under that State. Defendant, being United States District Attorney, mailed a letter of resignation, November fifth, and was elected Attorney General of the State the next day. *Held,* that "eligible" meant both "capable of being legally chosen" and "capable of legally holding," but that the resignation was complete when the letter was mailed. *State ex rel. Nourse v. Clarke,* p. 566.

The judges seem to be faithful and hard working. One would think that trouble might be saved, and a fairer chance given to change the first impression of the court, by having a case re-argued, when thought necessary, before, instead of after, one opinion had been written.

6.12

From *American Law Review* 3:150 (1868).

Reports of Cases argued and determined in the Court of Queen's Bench and the Court of Exchequer Chamber on appeal from the Court of Queen's Bench. With Tables of the Names of the Cases reported and cited, and the Principal Matters. By THOMAS FLOWER ELLIS, of the Middle Temple, and FRANCIS ELLIS, of the Inner Temple, Esqs., Barristers at Law. Vol. III. Containing the Cases of Trinity Term and Vacation, and Michaelmas Term and Vacation, 1860, and Hilary Term and Vacation, 1861. XXIII. & XXIV. Victoria. With References to Decisions in the American Courts. JAMES PARSONS, Esq., Editor. Philadelphia: T. & J. W. Johnson & Co. 1868.

There is much force in Chancellor Kent's objection to making the reporters the vehicle of dissertations; and, unless this is attempted, it seems to us that the best course for an editor is to give only a note of such analogous cases as have not yet found their way into the text-books and digests. The industry of Mr. Parsons has led him somewhat beyond this limit, but he has, in the main, been guided by such a principle, as in the brief but useful notes to *Regina v. Saddlers' Co.,* pp. 42, 88, on the power of a club to expel a member; to *Embleton v. Brown,* pp. 234, 237, on the common law jurisdiction to low water mark; and to *Dixon v. Fawcus,* pp. 537, 548, on trade marks. (See, on the last point of this note, *Newman v. Alvord,* 49 Barb. 588; American Digest of present number, title "Trade Mark," 1.)

There are a number of cases of general interest in this volume, though very many turn in the main on statutes. In *Smith v. Mundy,* p. 22, it was *held,* that when halves of bank notes had been sent in payment of a debt due to the receiver from a third person, with an intention on the part both of sender and receiver that the other halves were to follow, the property remained in the sender until the second halves had been sent; the transfer and payment being until then inchoate. The sender could therefore disaffirm the transaction before sending the second halves, and demand the first halves of the receiver.

Regina v. Herford, p. 115, is pleasantly redolent of the old law. *Held,* that a coroner cannot hold an inquest as to the origin of a fire by which no death has been occasioned. He has no jurisdiction to hold any other inquest than one on death, *super visum corporis. Held,* also, that a writ of prohibition lies to a court of criminal as well as to one of civil jurisdiction.

Embleton v. Brown, p. 234: The justices of a county have jurisdiction over offences committed in the part of the sea adjoining their county, comprised between high and low water mark.

In *Regina v. Howes,* p. 332, a girl between fifteen and sixteen was given into custody of her father on *habeas corpus,* although contrary to her desire.

In *Sinclair v. Maritime Passengers' Ass. Co.,* p. 478, it was *held,* that sunstroke was not an "accident," within the terms of a policy insuring against any accident which should happen to the assured upon any ocean, sea, river, or lake, excepting injuries by wounds in battle, or by the act of the Queen's enemies, or to which the assured should knowingly and without some adequate motive expose himself.

In *Dixon v. Fawcus,* p. 537, defendant having wrongfully directed plaintiff to mark bricks (which the latter was to make, and which he had agreed to mark as defendant should direct) with the trade mark of R., a third party, and the plaintiff having so done in ignorance of R.'s rights; and R. having thereupon filed a bill in chancery against plaintiff for an injunction and an account, and plaintiff having compromised the suit, and having subsequently brought his action against the defendant to recover the amount paid R. in settlement of the equity suit: *Held,* that plaintiff had a good cause of action, inasmuch as, though innocent of fraud, he was yet liable in equity to R. *Semble,* also, that he could recover of defendant the costs of the equity suit, on the ground that the same was the natural consequence of defendant's acts, whether the plaintiff was liable in such suit or not.

Regina v. Bradley, p. 634: A statute required a voting paper to contain, *inter alia,* the Christian name and surname of the candidate. *Held,* that papers inscribed "Wm. Bradley," and "Willm. Bradley," were admissible as votes for William Bradley. (See the notice of 16 Michigan R., in this number.)

Ashworth v. Stanwix, p. 701: A member of a firm took part in the work of a servant of the firm, and injured him by his negligence. *Held,* that the firm were liable. The case was not within the rule, that a master is not liable for an injury caused his servant by the negligence of a fellow-servant while engaged in the common employment.

Such are some of the cases that have attracted our attention; for other matters of interest we must refer to the volume itself.

6.13

From *American Law Review* 3:357 (1869).

Reports of Cases in Law and Equity, determined in the Supreme Court of the State of Iowa. By EDWARD H. STILES, Reporter. Vol. II., being Vol. XXIII. of the series. Ottumwa: Published by the Reporter. Sold by Miles & Co., Desmoines. 1868.

The Reports of several of the Western States are noticeably good. One does not, perhaps, find in the opinions of the judges much of that flavor of legal learning which is so pleasant in the decisions of some longer established courts. While conservative New Jersey furnishes a quiet Southern exposure for the ripening of lawyers of the Old School, in the busy West, justice is administered by men more intent on adapting the law to modern requirements than on standing in the ancient ways. And it is well that this is so. No branch of knowledge affords more instances than the law, of what a blessing to mankind it is that men begin life ignorant. Every one knows that it often happens, that, from historical cases, analogous cases are governed by dissimilar rules, and that forms which have lost their significance by lapse of time remain as technicalities. One who is familiar with these nice distinctions has no interest in their reform, even if he does not become prejudiced in their favor. But when, after barely three years' study, a young man finds himself at once in active practice, to simplify rules, to destroy anomalies, to make partial analogies complete, is his only safeguard. We might point to Judge Walker's admirable work on American Law as a typical Western book. It goes at once to the root of the matter. What is the practical use of all these traditions and forms? is the question it asks; and those which cannot show such a use in their favor are dismissed from consideration. While one would not expect from the West a second Maine, to extract philosophy from the history of the law, it has produced the best book we know of to explain to the student the actual bearing of legal principles upon the daily affairs of men. The Western Reports manifest similar characteristics, and few of them are marked by a more business-like common sense than those of Iowa. The present volume does not happen to contain very many decisions of other than local interest, but there are several that deserve attention. In *Blackwell v. Denie,* p. 63, it was *held,* that the fact that a note was not stamped until after it was issued was not a defence as against a *bona fide* holder for value. *Brown v. Crandal,* p. 112, also arose under the Internal Revenue Act. A deputy collector stamped an appeal bond after the same was filed, without leave of the court. The act was not authenticated by the collector's seal, nor were his inability to act and the deputy's authority proved. The appeal was dismissed. A third case is *McBride v. Doty,* p. 122, which decides that the record of an insufficiently stamped chattel mortgage is not notice to a purchaser of the chattels, and that his rights are not affected by the collector's restamping the mortgage after his purchase. Also, that evidence that when such mortgage was executed, the mortgagor received only such a part of the amount secured as the stamp would cover, and that it was agreed, that, on payment of the rest, a new stamp should be affixed, and that the rest was never paid, is inadmissible as against the purchaser. In *Hubbard v. Board of Supervisors,* p. 130, it was *held,* that a tax on shares in national banks was illegal, when the laws allowing the incorporation of other banks taxed only the capital of the latter, although there were no such banks in existence; COLE, J., *dissenting,* on the ground that, by the State laws, the shares of such other banks were taxable. *Wilson v. Triblecock,* p. 331, affirms the constitutionality of the Legal Tender Law as to debts contracted before its passage. *Cole v. Cole,* p. 433, bears on the same points as the cases referred to in the American Digest of this number, DIVORCE, 5.

6.14

From *American Law Review* 3:541 (1869).

A Treatise on the Law of Sale of Personal Property; with References to the American Decisions and to the French Code and Civil Law. By J. P. BENJAMIN, Esq., of Lincoln's Inn, Barrister-at-Law. London: Henry Sweet. 1868.

On most of the branches of commercial law there have long been numerous and able works. Mr. Benjamin gives us for the first time a book on Sales, worthy to take its place by the side of Collyer and Lindley on Partnership, Byles on Bills, and the treatises of Mr. Justice Story. "This," the author says in his preface, "is an attempt to develop the principles applicable to all branches of the subject, while following Blackburn on Sale as a model for guidance in the treatment of such topics as are embraced in that work." Any one now dealing with the subject certainly must follow in the steps of that very acute writer as far as he has gone. Had he undertaken more than a discussion of some questions peculiar to the law of Sale, the work could not have been done a second time so well. What Mr. Blackburn did not do, however, Mr. Benjamin has supplied, in such a way as to leave little to be desired.

The arrangement adopted is simple and good. Book I., somewhat inexactly entitled "Formation of the Contract," contains two parts. The first treats of the elements essential to the contract of sale at common law, and has successive chapters on the parties, mutual assent, the thing sold, and the price. The second part is on the effect of the Statute of Frauds. Book II. is on the effect of the contract in passing property. Book III. treats of avoidance of the contract for mistake, failure of consideration, fraud, or illegality. Book IV., under the head of performance of the contract, contains chapters on conditions, the vendor's duties, including warranty and delivery, and the buyer's duties, acceptance, and payment and tender. The last book has two parts on breach of the contract, one treating of the rights and remedies of the vendor both of action against the buyer, and of resale, lien, and stoppage *in transitu* against the goods: the other on the rights and remedies of the buyer.

The second part of the first book, the second book, and part of the fifth book, especially that relating to stoppage *in transitu,* seem to be modelled on Mr. Blackburn's treatise, but for the other portions Mr. Benjamin was left to his independent research. We have spoken of Mr. Blackburn's treatment of the subject as partial only, and of Mr. Benjamin's as complete. Yet it is worthy of notice that the earlier writer has considered almost all the law peculiar to the contract of sale. Were the law philosophically arranged, there would be little to be added to what he has said. As it is, a book of reference on any subdivision of the law, in order to be satisfactory, must set forth at length, not only the principles constituting the specific difference of the subject-matter, but also those common to it and to many other classes of the same genus. Thus, it may be doubted, whether, in a comprehensive summary of our law, *fraud* would not more properly be treated under the general title *contract,* or possibly under some still wider head, rather than repeated in every text-book dealing with every one of the different sorts of contract known to modern commerce. At present, we must put up with the latter alternative.

Take again the chapter on Conditions, in which Mr. Benjamin has presented many cases at considerable length. The rules laid down are not peculiar to the law of sales, and many of the examples introduced seem to turn simply on general principles of construction. Still, this is not the author's fault, but is the necessary result of the state of the law.

Singularly enough, the least valuable portions of the work before us seem to be those professing to give the result of American authorities. These appear to be meagre, and the discussions of cases not quite satisfactory. We notice that in the English Law Magazine and Law Review for November, 1868, the disapproval of the case of *Cook v. Oxley*, 3 T.R. 653, expressed by some American text writers, cited by Mr. Benjamin, p. 45, *et seq.*, is maintained to be sound, contrary to his opinion. See also Met. on Contr. 19.

On the vexed question of what is a contract of sale within the statute, and what only a contract for work and labor requiring no memorandum, a distinction taken by Chief Justice Shaw, between a contract for the future sale of articles which a party is habitually making, although not made or finished at the time, and cases where the article is made pursuant to the agreement, is declared unsatisfactory. It certainly is open to question. Yet it is difficult to deny that in the latter case the contract has a double aspect,—as an agreement that the manufacturer shall perform certain labor, and that the employer shall purchase the result of his labor when complete. For it is to be observed that in many, if not all, of such agreements, the labor of the particular person employed is contemplated as an essential term. It does not seem to be going very far to refuse to discharge a party from liability for labor undertaken and performed at his request, because he chooses to avail himself of his right to refuse to purchase the result of such labor.

We observe that the author repeats Mr. Blackburn's second rule, that, when any thing remains to be done to goods for the purpose of ascertaining the price, the performance of these things shall be a condition precedent to the transfer of the property, without repeating his objections to it. Those objections seem to us the least sound of the speculations of that able writer. In the absence of evidence of a contrary intent, a vendor can hardly be supposed to mean to part with his property in goods under circumstances in which, if they were destroyed, he would have no indemnity. While they were his, he could insure them; afterwards he has only a right of action for the price. The purchaser is only liable on his contract, and it has, in the case supposed, become impossible to ascertain his liability in accordance with its terms.

We should have liked a fuller discussion of what facts are admissible as evidence of a preconceived design on the part of a purchaser not to pay for goods, as well as a clear statement of the grounds on which it is held that this is fraud entitling the vendor to avoid the sale, a principle which we believe has been questioned in at least one American case.

6.15

From *American Law Review* 3:550 (1869).

Reports of Cases Determined in the Supreme Court of the State of California, at the October Term, 1867, *and January Term,* 1868. J. E. HALE, Reporter. Vol. 34. San Francisco: Sumner Whitney. 1868.

This volume of reports, which we have just received, contains several interesting cases, of which we indicate a few below.

An action for libel will lie against a corporation. *Maynard v. Firemen's Fund Ins. Co.,* p. 48.

A demurrer will not lie to a complaint, declaring on a promissory note, which fails to show or aver that the note was duly stamped. *Hallock v. Jaudin,* p. 167; following *Trull v. Moulton,* 12 All. 396, and *Hitchcock v. Sawyer,* 39 Vt. 412.

In *Arrington v. Liscom,* p. 365, it is *held,* that adverse possession of land for a sufficient length of time, under the Statute of Limitations, does not merely bar the party against whom the possession is adverse of his remedy, but gives an absolute right of possession, so that one so in possession is entitled to all the remedies given by the law to quiet his possession, and may therefore maintain an action against one having the record title, to have the claim under such title declared null and void as against him.

In *Hahn v. Kelly,* p. 391, is an interesting discussion on the distinction between courts of superior and inferior jurisdiction.

Turner v. North Beach & Mission R.R. Co., p. 594. The plaintiff, a colored woman, was put off a car of the defendants by the conductor. It was *held,* that the plaintiff could recover against the defendants only for the damage she had actually received; that, to render them liable for punitive or exemplary damages, it must be shown that the conductor's conduct was authorized or ratified by the defendants, and this not being shown, a verdict for the plaintiff for $750 was set aside as excessive. The case of *Pleasants v. Same,* p. 586, is to a similar effect.

Where a party seeks to have a conveyance made by him, which is absolute on its face, declared a mortgage, to secure the performance of an oral agreement by him to pay an amount in gold coin, he cannot be allowed to redeem without tendering the amount in gold coin; and this not under what is known as the "Specific Contract Act," legalizing contracts in writing for the payment of gold, but on the ground, that he who seeks equity must do equity. *Cowing v. Rogers,* p. 648.

It is competent for the State legislature to enact, that all tolls, dockage, and wharfage charges, payable into the public treasury, shall be due and collectible exclusively in gold and silver money of the United States. *People v. Steamer Africa,* p. 676.

The Constitution of California provides that, "Taxation shall be equal and uniform throughout the State. All property in this State shall be taxed in proportion to its value, to be ascertained as directed by law, except such property as two-thirds of both houses of the legislature may think proper to exempt from taxation." A tax was imposed, by statute, on all property in the State, with the exception of certain classes. *Held,* that the exception was void, and the tax must be levied on all the property in the State. *People v. McCreery,* p. 432. This overrules the case of *People v. Coleman,* 4 Cal. 46.

A State statute, requiring stamps of a certain value to be placed on all passenger tickets, and on all contracts for passage on vessels leaving the State, is unconstitutional, as violating the provision in the Constitution of the United States, empowering Congress to regulate commerce. *People v. Raymond,* p. 492.

The cases are accurately reported, but the head-notes are not what they should be; they consist mainly of extracts from the opinion of the court, touching often merely collateral matters, and, though very long, they fail sometimes to present the points decided.

6.16

From *American Law Review* 3:556 (1869).

Reports of Cases at Law and in Chancery Argued and Determined in the Supreme Court of Illinois. By NORMAN L. FREEMAN, Counsellor-at-Law. Vol. XLI. Containing a part of the Cases decided at the April Term, 1866. Chicago: Eugene B. Myers, 1868.

There are several cases of interest in this volume, besides those for which we could find room in our Digest. In *Dickey v. McDonnell,* p. 62, the question was whether if plaintiff, after suspecting that defendant's intention was to have sexual connection with her, still rode with him to a secluded spot, voluntarily alighted, and then resisted his advances for the purpose of extorting money, until he threatened and violently assaulted her, when she assented, she could recover. A verdict for the defendant was set aside. Mr. Justice *Breese* dissented from the opinion of the court, which was neatly put by *Lawrence,* J., thus: "It certainly cannot be contended, because a woman would sell her person for one hundred dollars, and would resist with all her physical force any attempt to take possession of her, except upon these terms, that, therefore, violence may be lawfully used to overcome her."

In *Henchey v. City of Chicago,* p. 136, it was *held,* that an attorney's lien for his fees did not attach to a claim for unliquidated damages prior to the judgment, so as to deprive his client of the power to settle the case as she might see fit.

In *Bowen v. Schuler,* it is intimated *obiter,* p. 196, that, in case of a purchase of goods, with a fraudulent intent not to pay for them, the title to the property does not pass. Mr. Benjamin, in his book on Sales, p. 325, has deduced a contrary conclusion from the English cases, though affirming, of course, the vendor's right of rescission.

In *People v. Harvey, Same v. Miller,* p. 277, two hostile lawyers seem to have attempted each to have the other removed from a sphere too narrow to contain both. Neither succeeded; but each received a sound lecture, with an intimation of his fate in case of future misconduct.

In *Reeder v. Purdy,* p. 279, Mr. Justice *Lawrence* gives an interesting opinion, adverse to the right of the owner of land who is wrongfully kept out of possession, to enter forcibly against the will of the occupant.

Dole v. Olmstead, p. 344, affirms the decision in the same case, 36 Ill. 150, *ante,* 2 Am. Law Rev. 528.

Morgan v. Peet, p. 347, affirms a point about which there has been expressed an unaccountable doubt, that when an indorser, with knowledge of facts discharging him from liability, makes a new promise, he will be liable, although he is ignorant that by the rules of law he is discharged.

On pp. 425, 441, 444, Mr. Justice Breese, an able judge, lets his rhetoric get a little the better of him, beginning thus: "Observe the generosity, the loving-kindness, philanthropy, and benevolence of this good Samaritan, the complainant!" He arrives on p. 444 at the oratorical climax: "Which of these parties, both with unclean hands, should a court of equity assist? Justice and those pure principles which are the ornament of such a court,—its brightest jewels,—answer, neither."

The most important cases are in this number of our Digest, and we do not repeat them. The opinions of the judges are short, strong, and business-like.

The reporter's work seems to be well done, except the head-notes. These are better than those in some American reports, which consist of slices cut at random from the body of the opinion, but are not so good as they might be. A head-note ought above all things to contain a statement of the facts of the case put categorically, not hypothetically, and what was held on those facts. Then, if a clean principle of law can be extracted as the *ratio decidendi*, it may well be allowed a short, separate paragraph; and important principles deliberately approved by the court, but not necessary to the case, may be sparingly introduced under a *semble*.

6.17

From *American Law Review* 3:757 (1869).

Michigan Reports. Reports of Cases heard and decided in the Supreme Court of Michigan from April 28, 1868, to January 11, 1869. WILLIAM JENNISON, Reporter. Volume IV., being Volume XVII. of the Series. Detroit: Wm. A. Throop & Co. 1869.

We have spoken of the excellence of the Michigan Reports in former numbers of this review. It will do no harm, however, to repeat that this court sets an example of judicial gravity and decorum which one could wish were more widely followed. The volume before us does not happen to be a particularly interesting one; but, as it arrived too late for the digest of this number, the most important cases are inserted here.

In *Perrott v. Shearer,* p. 48, it was *held* that a wrongful taker of goods is liable for their whole value, if destroyed in his possession, although the owner had insured them, and has been paid in full. The case of *Hart v. Western R.R. Co.,* 13 Met. 99, which does not seem to have been cited, would perhaps have aided the discussion.

By a contract for the carriage of live stock, the owner took the risk of damage "in loading, unloading, conveyance, and otherwise, whether arising from . . . negligence . . . or otherwise." The bottom of the car dropped out. *Held,* that, if the car was unfit, the carrier was liable.—*Hawkins v. Great Western R.R. Co.,* p. 57.

A specific tax on express companies on the gross receipts of their current business within the State, was *held* constitutional. CAMPBELL, J., *dissenting.*—*Walcott v. The People,* 17 Mich. 68.

We have noticed *Hobart v. Detroit* before (*ante,* p. 170). The city of Detroit had power by its charter to pave its streets, but all contracts were to be made with the lowest bidder. It contracted for the Nicholson pavement, the only bidder being the patentee, who had a monopoly. *Held,* that the contract was legal. CAMPBELL, J., *dissenting,* p. 246.

In *Hogsett v. Ellis,* p. 351, it was *held,* that, after the determination of a tenancy at will by notice to quit, assumpsit for use and occupation lies against the tenant if he holds over. Were the question a new one, there might perhaps be a doubt whether any distinction could be properly taken between the position of a tenant at will, after the expiration of the time required to be allowed by a notice to quit, and that of a tenant for years after expiration of his term. We suppose it is settled, however, that the tenant at will holding over after notice becomes a trespasser, and it would appear from such cases as *Ibbs v. Richardson,* 9 Ad. & El. 849, that the landlord may waive the tort and sue on an implied contract.

We may further mention *Detroit & Milwaukee R.R. Co. v. Van Steinburg,* p. 99, as containing a discussion as to when negligence is a question of law and when of fact.

Probably the case of the most local interest is *The People v. The Auditor General,* p. 161, arising out of an act of the legislature providing for the appointment of a Professor of Homoeopathy in Michigan University, with which one is led to suppose the learned regents of that institution did not fancy compliance beyond the letter of the law.

For other cases, see 3 Am. Law Rev., pp. 381, 581.

The custom of citing cases by the volume and page of the reports only, and not by name, in this series, is to be regretted.

6.18

From *American Law Review* 4:752 (1870).

The History of the Law of Tenures of Land in England and Ireland. With particular reference to Inheritable Tenancy; Leasehold Tenure; Tenancy at Will; and Tenant Right. By W. F. FINLASON, Esq. London: Stevens & Haynes. 1870.

It is equally hard to say either that this is a work of some originality, or that it is not. One who is already versed in the law will probably find suggestions in the earlier chapters for which he will be grateful. The law of fixtures, of way-going crops, and the like, the doctrines of tenures, the Statutes of *Quia Emptores* and of Frauds, are seen in these pages more nearly in their practical bearing on life than they are in the abstract and logical form of the text-books. Perhaps it is this fact, as much as the more enlightened and comprehensive views of modern criticism, that make the author's notes to Reeves's history better reading than the text. We are inclined to say that this book is worth looking over. On the other hand, there is something in Mr. Finlason's writing that excites distrust. He seems to work too much in a hurry. We are assured that he is learned, and believe it, from a certain ease with which he moves in dark places. Yet in his notes to Reeves he seems to rely too much on the Mirror, even if he is right against Palgrave and the rest of the world in thinking it not apocryphal. This book, again, does not seem to be thought out. One reads each chapter with a general sense of learning something, but at the end finds no clear idea remaining detached in memory. We must add, that one cannot feel entire confidence in an author who allows such shamefully slovenly work as the printing of the notes to Reeves and his Martial Law to be published under his name. The former are fuller of gross misprints than any book we ever laid eyes on. It is fair to say, however, that, with different publishers, this volume is better in that way.

6.19
SUMMARY OF EVENTS: THE LEGAL TENDER CASES[1]

From *American Law Review* 4:768 (1870).

To the Editors of the American Law Review.

Gentlemen:—

It is easy to admit that some powers, as to which the Constitution is silent, may be claimed as a necessary means of exercising other powers expressly given. But it is hard to understand, when a power *is* expressly given, which does not come up to a required height, how this express power can be enlarged as an incident to some other express power.

The power to "coin money" means, I take it, both by the true construction and as interpreted by practice, (1.) to strike off metallic medals (*coin*), and (2.) to make those medals legal tender (*money*). I cannot, therefore, see how the right to make paper legal tender can be claimed for Congress when the Constitution virtually contains the words "Congress shall have the power to make metals legal tender."

It is to be remembered that those who deny the power have only to maintain that it is not granted by implication. They are not called on to find a constitutional prohibition.

It is perfectly consistent with this argument that the power to issue bills not legal tender may be claimed under the borrowing clause, and of this opinion was Mr. Madison. Mad. Pap. Aug. 16, 1787. Vol. 3, p. 1346, note. H.

Editor's Note

1. This letter is Holmes's response to a Comment in the April 1870 issue of the *American Law Review* on the first of the so-called legal tender cases, Hepburn v. Griswold, 8 Wall. 603 (1870), in which the Supreme Court decided that it was unconstitutional for Congress to pass a law making paper money legal tender for pre-existing debts. The writer of the Comment agreed with the decision but felt that it was on weak ground, in that if the Court admitted that Congress could issue notes as currency, it could go further and make its notes legal tender for its existing debts. 4 Am. L. Rev. 604 (1870).

6.20
CODES, AND THE ARRANGEMENT OF THE LAW

From *American Law Review* 5:1 (1870).

It is the merit of the common law that it decides the case first and determines the principle afterwards. Looking at the forms of logic it might be inferred that when you have a minor premise and a conclusion, there must be a major, which you are also prepared then and there to assert. But in fact lawyers, like other men, frequently see well enough how they ought to decide on a given state of facts without being very clear as to the *ratio decidendi*. In cases of first impression Lord Mansfield's often-quoted advice to the business man who was suddenly appointed judge, that he should state his conclusions and not give his reasons, as his judgment would probably be right and the reasons certainly wrong, is not without its application to more educated courts. It is only after a series of determinations on the same subject-matter, that it becomes necessary to "reconcile the cases," as it is called, that is, by a true induction to state the principle which has until then been obscurely felt.[1] And this statement is often modified more than once by new decisions before the abstracted general rule takes its final shape. A well settled legal doctrine embodies the work of many minds, and has been tested in form as well as substance by trained critics whose practical interest it is to resist it at every step. These are advantages the want of which cannot be supplied by any faculty of generalization, however brilliant, and it is noticeable that those books on which an ideal code might best be modelled avowedly when possible lay down the law in the very words of the court. When, then, it is said to be one of the advantages of a code that principles are clearly enunciated and not left to be extricated from cases, either the definiteness of well settled law is underrated, or it is intended to anticipate the growing process we have described, and to develop by legislation doctrines of which the germs may be found in isolated decisions. We need not dwell on the latter alternative, as its possible importance is obviously small.

Suppose that a code were made and expressed in language sanctioned by the assent of courts, or tested by the scrutiny of a committee of lawyers. New cases will arise which will elude the most carefully constructed formula. The common law, proceeding, as we have pointed out, by a series of successive approximations—by a continual reconciliation of cases—is prepared for this, and simply modifies the form of its rule. But what will the court do with a code? If the code is truly law, the court is confined to a verbal construction of the rule as expressed, and must decide the case wrong.* If the court, on the other hand, is at liberty to decide *ex ratione legis,*—that is, if it may take into account that the code is only intended to declare the judicial rule, and has done so defectively, and may then go on and supply the defect,—the code is not law, but a mere text-book recommended by the government as containing all at present known on the subject.

Another mistake, as we cannot but think, is that a code is to be short. This probably springs from the thoroughly exploded notion that it is to make every man his own lawyer, and would hardly be worth mentioning did not the makers of both the New York and Canada Civil Codes seem to entertain it. A code will not get rid of lawyers, and should be written for them much more than for the laity. It should therefore contain the whole body of the law in an authentic form. When the ablest text writers in the competition of the open market exhaust volumes on subdivisions, what inspiration is there in government patronage to produce a different result?

We are inclined to believe that the most considerable advantage which might be reaped from a code is this: that being executed at the expense of government and not at the risk of the writer, and the whole work being under the control of one head, it will make a philosophically arranged *corpus juris* possible. If such a code were achieved, its component treatises would not have to be loaded with matter belonging elsewhere, as is necessarily the case with text-books written to sell. Take up a book on sales, or one on bills and notes, or a more general treatise on con-

*But see *post* pp. [223–24].

tracts, or one on the domestic relations, or one on real property, and in each you find chapters devoted to the discussion of the incapacities of infants and married women. A code would treat the subject once and in the right place. Even this argument does not go much further than to show the advantage of a connected publication of the whole body of the law. But the task, if executed *in extenso,* is perhaps beyond the powers of one man, and if more than one were employed upon it, the proper subordination would be more likely to be secured in a government work. We are speaking now of more serious labors than the little rudimentary text-books in short sentences, which their authors by a happy artifice have called codes instead of manuals. Indeed we are not aware that any of the existing attempts are remarkable for arrangement. The importance of it, if it could be obtained, cannot be overrated. In the first place it points out at once the leading analogy between groups. Of course cross-divisions will be possible on other principles than the one adopted, and text-books arranged by these subordinate analogies, like Mr. Joshua Williams's two volumes, are instructive and valuable. The perfect lawyer is he who commands all the ties between a given case and all others. But few lawyers are perfect, and all have to learn their business. A well-arranged body of the law would not only train the mind of the student to a sound legal habit of thought, but would remove obstacles from his path which he now only overcomes after years of experience and reflection.

As to what the method of arrangement should be, of course there is room for infinite argument.[2] Our own impression is pretty strong that it should be based on *duties* and not on *rights,* and we suspect the fact that the custom has been the other way to be at the bottom of some difficulties which have been felt. Duties precede rights logically and chronologically. Even those laws which in form create a right directly, in fact either tacitly impose a duty on the rest of the world, as, in the case of patents, to abstain from selling the patented article, or confer an immunity from a duty previously or generally imposed, like taxation. The logical priority of the duty in such instances is clear when we consider that in its absence any man might make and sell what he pleased and abstain from paying for ever, without assistance from law. Another illustration is, that, while there are in some cases legal duties without corresponding rights, we never see a legal right without either a corresponding duty or a compulsion stronger than duty. It is to be understood that these are the principles of the general scheme only. From what point of view the several topics should be treated in detail is a mere question of convenience. And this suggests a further remark. Law is not a science, but is essentially empirical. Hence, although the general arrangement should be philosophical, even at the expense of disturbing prejudices, compromises with practical convenience are highly proper. There are certain legal units which must be preserved although they lie on both sides of a great natural dividing line; *e.g.,* contract. Some subjects have acquired a unity in practice that it might be unprofitable to analyze, *e.g., dominium* or ownership. Other conceptions again, although complex, if we break them up into the ideas out of which modern law is built, lie, historically speaking, at its foundation, and have acquired cohesion from their very antiquity; *e.g.,* parts of the *jus personarum.* We shall refer to some of these examples again.

We proceed to illustrate our views of arrangement a little more in detail, although, of course, only in a fragmentary way.

A word in the first place as to the subject-matter. What is law? We doubt whether Austin did not exaggerate the importance of the distinctions he drew. A law, we understand him to say, is a command (of a definite political superior, enforced by a sanction), which obliges (intelligent human beings) to acts or forbearances of a class. This as a definition of what lawyers call law is doubtless accurate enough. But it seems to be of practical rather than philosophical value. If names are to mark substantial distinctions, one hesitates to admit that only a definite body of political superiors can make what is properly called a law. In the first place, who has the sovereign power, and whether such a power exists at all, are questions of fact and of degree. But waiving this, by whom a duty is imposed must be of less importance than the definiteness of its expression and the Certainty of its being enforced. In the nature of things, which is most truly a law, the rule that if I am invited to a dinner party in London I must appear in evening dress under the penalty of not being asked to similar entertainments if I disobey; or the statute against usury in New York, which juries do not decline to carry out simply because they are never asked to do so? If it be said that an indefinite body cannot directly signify a command, it is to be remembered that the rules of judge-made law are never authentically promulgated as rules, but are left to be inferred from cases. Certainly some social requirements are to be inferred as easily from social penalties explained by common discourse. The difference which might be insisted on with most effect is in the definiteness of the sanction, and the sanction of some laws improperly so called according to Austin is quite as definite as the uncertain chance of a jury's inflicting an uncertain amount of damages. A sovereign or political superior secures obedience to his commands by his courts. But how is this material, except as enhancing the likelihood that they will be obeyed? Courts, however, give rise to lawyers, whose only concern is with such rules as the courts enforce. Rules not enforced by them, although equally imperative, are the study of no profession. It is on this account that the province of jurisprudence has to be so carefully determined. The further difficulty which might be suggested, of fixing the line when the desires of indefinite bodies become so certain in form and sanction as to come within the category of laws (philosophically speaking), is no greater than that which a court encounters in deciding whether a custom has been established.

The importance of these considerations, in spite of the fact that lawyers have little to do professionally with rules falling outside of Austin's division, lies in their application to international law. This is a subject which lawyers do practically study, while according to Austin it is not law at all, but a branch of positive morality. But if, as we have tried to show, his definition can only be supported on grounds of practical convenience, and if they fail in this case, the ancient name may properly be retained. Is not that law which is certain in form and in sanction? Here are rules of conduct so definite as to be written in text-books, and sanctioned in many cases by the certainty that a breach will be followed by war; why does it so much matter that they are not prescribed by a sovereign to a political inferior?[3] If on these grounds it is admitted not to be an anomaly to include international law in the law-student's curriculum, we are content to stand by the lines as now drawn, and to omit ethics until the coming of a second Grotius.

Our first division then contains duties of sovereign powers to each other. For although the doctrines of this branch are copied in great measure from municipal law, convenience requires that they receive a separate treatment.

The second division would probably be duties without corresponding rights, or duties to the sovereign. Here belongs, for instance, the duty to pay taxes, often mentioned as an implied contract, a phrase to which we shall refer again. Another example is the law of treason. Perhaps under this head, also, should come the great body of criminal law, as administered in this country. For, not only is the sovereign the formal plaintiff, and for an offence against the sovereign well-being, but the private person injured has not any voice, in theory, as to whether the public prosecuting officer shall or shall not push a case to trial. How can a man be said to have a right to his life, in a legal sense, when he can in no wise affect or dispense with the duty on which the alleged right depends? Whether this part of the law falls on one side of the line or the other, however, it connects the second division with the third, which contains duties from all the world to all the world. Under this would clearly come assault and battery, libel, slander, false imprisonment, and the like, considered as causes of actions *civiliter.*

To the fourth division belong duties of all the world to persons in certain particular positions or relations. Here we should first consider the situation known as absolute ownership of a specific thing. Property in this restricted sense, or title, as the word is often used by English lawyers, although not an ultimate legal conception, is one of those practical units to which we have referred, and which should be discussed in one place. Although this division is devoted to duties of all the world, it would probably even be found convenient to deal here with the restrictions on the use of property by its owner, (*sic utere tuo,* etc.), rather than to place them in the separate division of duties of persons in particular positions or relations. *Dominium,* ownership, or property, are phrases expressing the aggregate of rights corresponding to the duties of all the world to persons in a certain situation. Laying out of the case special doctrines like tenure, or the prerogative of the sovereign in cases of treasure trove and the like, which only complicate the subject, and duration, which is not material to our purposes, the primitive elements are possession, which is a fact or situation outside of the law, and a duty imposed on the rest of the world to respect it. This duty is absolute only toward the earliest of immediately successive possessors, or his representative.[4] We say earliest, for, without raising any harder question, if the possessor be not the earliest or his representative, but a disseizor, for instance, or a finder, there is one person as against whom his possession is not protected. And possession is not called ownership unless it is protected against all. The words "immediately successive" are inserted to meet the case of abandonment. The common law as to animals ferae naturae, illustrates the fact that the essential elements of ownership are what we have stated. The so-called right of user in the owner is not derived from the law. Any man, unless restrained, may use any thing he can lay his hands on, in any way he can devise. But the analysis is not yet complete. The law adds to the primary constituents the possibility of substitution in the objects of the duties in question. When this is accomplished by delivery, there occurs only a repetition of the previous case; that is, we have a protected possession as before, though the possessor is changed. But the same result may be obtained while the possession remains with a third person, *e.g.*, by conveyance or descent. The rest of the world will owe a duty to the purchaser or heir in this case, in most respects the same as that owed to the actual possessor before. This gives to title a more extensive signification than protected possession, and makes of it that metaphysical entity which a lawyer gets to regard as a positive thing, changing hands from time to time, like coin or other tangibles. It would be possible indeed to postpone title by conveyance, etc., without possession, to the subdivision next to be suggested, but perhaps with more inconvenience than advantage. The text-books commonly treat, under the head of sale, title by delivery, in which case sale is analogous to gift, title by conveyance, and title by contract which turns into a conveyance on the occurrence of some event. While on the subject of successions it might be desirable to point out the extent of the conception.[5] Thus agency resembles conveyance and descent in so far that in each case there is an aggregate of rights and duties analogous to a *persona* which remains unchanged in spite of the substitution of successive natural persons as the object of such duties, and as entitled to such rights. When the agent assumes a part of his principal's *persona*, the latter is not necessarily excluded from it to a corresponding degree, as is the case between grantor and grantee, or decedent and executor or heir, but this does not seem to affect the resemblance, any more than the fact that the duty is still in form owed only to the principal. It is to be observed that the various means of succeeding to the position of object of the duties explained, or as it is commonly expressed, of transferring title, are considered in the text-books from the point of view of right. The same is equally true of the learning of estates, involving the duration of such position, and the occupation of it by one or more. These two subjects, moreover, constitute much the most considerable part of the law of property. But as we have said already, the side of the shield contemplated is unimportant, if it is not suffered to become a source of delusion.

Without pausing to discuss the exact place of duties to judges, and other law arising out of what might be called a status independent of a relation (*e.g.*, the law of contempts), which, on practical considerations, might belong elsewhere, we come to a class of relations which belong in the general division we are now considering, and which, like ownership of a specific thing, are correlative to a duty from all the world, but which, unlike it, are peculiarly burdensome on a particular individual. Here we are in the midst of very difficult questions, as to which we can only offer a few suggestions *de bene*. If we are right, this subdivision should include or refer to easements, contracts, and some other obligations, and status so far as involving a personal relation, domestic or other, if this be a proper title at all. To explain. It is pretty decidedly to be inferred from *Lumley v. Gye*, 2 El. & Bl. 216, that an action would lie against a stranger to a contract for forcibly and maliciously preventing its performance, with intent to cause a loss to the plaintiff, the contractor, which the defendant knew would follow his act.[6] If this be so, it would seem that the distinction between *jura in rem*, in the sense of rights against all the world, and obligations, which are also called *jura in personam*, and supposed to be rights against a particular individual only, is not absolute as Austin supposed it, but that the latter are simply a class of *jura in rem*, which are more likely to be infringed by a certain person, (*i.e.,* the party obliged) than by the rest of the world, and the parties to which are subject to more extensive liabilities than others.[7] Other reasons for this belief will appear shortly. Assuming it to be well founded, it will nevertheless be observed that if contract were approached from the side of duty, the duties of strangers only would fall on this side of the dividing line, and those of parties would be considered in a new division, duties of persons in particular relations. But the right may be thought of as a single right, more or less qualified, against A., B., C., and all the rest of the alphabet, that A. shall do a particular thing. Whether on this ground both classes of duties should be kept together, in one division or the other, with a cross reference to point out that a distinction exists, is a question of detail.

An easement, like a contract, is a right as against all the world,* but imposes a particular burden on the servient owner. But it may be said, the duties imposed on the parties to contracts are often positive, whereas, as Austin lays it down in a different connection, that of a servient owner is always negative. If there be any ground for a legal distinction between duties to do and to forbear, it is sufficient to observe that some easements impose positive duties; *e.g.,* to repair fences. There is perhaps one minor difference which should be adverted to. Easements being rights of qualified enjoyment or possession of a particular thing, are more nearly connected with the complex conception property, which we have just explained. Again, the duty of a servient owner is without doubt generally negative, and that of a party to an ordinary contract is generally positive. In contracts, therefore, the duty of the party obliged is all in all, and that of third persons is so rarely called in question, that it is hardly supposed to exist. Hence there is a fair question to which we have just alluded, whether contracts should not be kept for a fifth division. It is true again that although an easement may be created as well by way of covenant as by grant (a fact which marks in an interesting way the relationship we are insisting upon), and is presumably binding on a *bonâ fide* purchaser, without notice, other executory (true) contracts touching a specific thing would not have this effect. At law, such a contract (*e.g.,* to sell) would not bind a subsequent purchaser, even with notice, but the remedy would have to be sought in equity. But it is immaterial, for the purposes of classification, whether equity or law gives the remedy, so long as a remedy is given. That equity would afford one in the latter case, is another evidence that contracts impose duties on all the world.

As a matter of speculation our inference from *Lumley v. Gye* does not want reason or analogy. It is proper to say, however, that the doctrine that a party to a contract may be sued upon it for non-performance, although caused by *vis major,* looks the other way, and as the subject is not yet exhausted it may be held that the only remedy in the case we supposed is by action against the contractor, leaving him to his remedy over if he has one. Should this ever be so determined, it would perhaps justify the absolute distinction drawn between *jura in rem* and *obligationes* in existing schemes, and would certainly throw the latter into the fifth division we have spoken of.

---

*This is not likely to be denied, and is very clearly implied by *Saxby v. Manchester, Sheffield, &c., Railway Co.,* L.R. 4 C.P. 198.

But at all events it remains the law that if the contracting party may be called the plaintiff's servant, the master has an action *per quod servitium amisit,* although his only right to those services in our times arises out of contract. Were the contrary determination reached in the case of an ordinary contract, it would afford a reason beside those usually given for retaining the *jus personarum* or law of status, so far as involving a personal relation, as a distinct title. It is not material to our point whether the action is given to the master by the Statute of Laborers or whether it arises from the fact that the duties incident to a well recognized status were settled before a contract was ever heard of; as would seem to be shown by the fact that an action by a parent for enticing away his daughter has been sustained on the ground of loss of service, although there was no pregnancy and of course no actual contract of service.* So long as anomalous duties exist it may be well to keep the ancient classification and put them under a separate head, either where they are provisionally placed above or in the fifth division. At the same time it is very clear that many of the component elements of a status or *persona, e.g.,* the capacity of an infant to contract, his liability for crime, the immunities and disabilities of a slave and the like, might as well be noted under strictly legal divisions such as we have suggested. Mr. Maine has noticed the transition from status to contract as a mark of progressive societies. To consider the relations of master and servant, and husband and wife, as originating in contract, is an innovation which may be a step towards treating them as dependent on contract throughout, and so toward the disappearance of the conception of status from the law. As things are now, we venture to say that more than one intelligent student, reading Kent's chapters on master and servant, and on principal and agent, has wondered why they were separated by half a volume, and where the one subject ended and the other began.

We go back a little to make one or two more suggestions. There are several titles now in use which we believe it would be well to give up, and others which required explanation. Thus Austin, if we remember rightly, has shown the absurdity of the phrase incorporeal hereditaments. Bailment seems to us objectionable for other reasons. At the time the term was originated, delivery, like the conveyance of the legal title to land at the present day, so far passed the property to the bailee that a sale and delivery by him was good as against his principal.** This may have been that spacial property in the bailee which has left its impress on later law. It may be conjectured and would rather seem from the abridgments that, in those early days at least, there were few cases turning on other points than that of title in which the delivery of a chattel was the essential fact. But in modern times under bailments are collected matters not only of title but contract, and of a kind which would be equally possible in the nature of things if there were no delivery or bailment at all. Not to mention the unsuccessful attempt to get in telegraphs, we find thrust into this omnium gatherum the duty of innkeepers, which certainly never depended either on delivery or contract, but on the custom of the realm which compelled them to receive all travellers (with unimportant exceptions), and to be responsible for the safety of their goods and chattels *infra hospitia.* It is said in Calye's case that

---

**Evans v. Walton,* L.R. 2 C.P. 615.
**Y.B. 21 H. 7, 39; See 2 E. 4, 4.

"although the guest doth not deliver his goods to the innholder to keep, nor acquaint him with them, yet if they be carried away or stolen the innkeeper shall be charged." We must add with regard to the usual subdivisions taken from the civil law that very generally where we find that law retaining its original form in the body of our own, it seems to us to be a source of anomalies and confusion.

As an instance of a subdivision requiring explanation, we have already mentioned implied contracts. Under this head we find included both contracts which are truly express, and cases which are not contracts at all. If A. requests B., his grocer, to send him home a barrel of flour, and says nothing more, and B. does as requested, there is a true contract on A.'s part to pay for it. It is called implied, and is so if that only means that A. does not put his promise into words or state the terms of it, but leaves B. to infer both from his acts. But that distinction is unimportant, for A.'s acts are intended to lead to the inference drawn, and therefore express a promise as well as words would have done. On the other hand, under the same head of implied contracts are often included another totally distinct class of cases which in fact are not contracts, but which are analogous to the *obligationes quasi ex contractu* of the civil law. Thus in some states, the law recognizes as a duty to be enforced by action the duty to pay taxes, which has been already alluded to as one of those called by the name in question. But the law is confined to certain definite forms of action, and cannot proceed on a simple statement of the actual facts to enforce performance or award damages for non-performance. The forms of action available for the recovery of money are or are supposed to be based upon a contract. Hence the law by a fiction supplies such elements as are wanting to make this duty into one. But a legal fiction does not change the nature of things. And a fiction which is only invented to conceal the fact that the common law does not afford a remedy in a case where one must be had, and which would be needless with another system of pleading and practice, like that of equity, cannot be allowed to affect a classification on the principles proposed.

We return to our main subject. A duty, strictly so called, is only created by commands which may be broken at the expense of incurring a penalty. That which the law directly compels, although it may onerously affect an individual, cannot be said to impose a duty upon him. The law addresses itself to the thing to be done, not to the person affected, and does not punish his failure to co-operate. In the classification of principal rights,—that is, of the great body of jurisprudence, this distinction is less important than the considerations which induce us to neglect it. Thus, on account of the practical cohesion of the conception property, we bring together under it not only the true duty to respect possession which is enforced by the action of trover, but likewise the *quasi* duty, the performance of which is compelled by the officers of the law when they give possession to the successful plaintiff in a real action. So again we do not distinguish between nuisances which the sheriff is ordered to abate, and those which the court persuades the defendant to put an end to by inflicting damages. When we come to what Austin calls sanctioning rights, these reasons cease. In a classification by duties we cannot but doubt whether they would find an independent place. Take the case of a successful plaintiff in trover. He has undoubtedly a right to his damages, which he may discharge or assign. But when the law seizes and sells the defendant's goods to satisfy the judgment, can the latter be said to be performing a duty? It would seem to be more proper that the sanctions should follow the duties to which they are attached. Having decided on this, we should put in the same class (with proper cross-references) equitable remedies like decrees for specific performance; although these may fairly be said to impose duties, sanctioned by liability to process for contempt.

The place for pleading and practice presents some difficulties. In the time of the common-law forms of action the question was partly solved by placing rights under the remedies by which they were enforced. This, however imperfect, was a legal arrangement; for the distinctions between the different remedies were legal distinctions, and embodied a kind of philosophy of the law. If forms of action and the distinctions between law and equity are to wholly pass away, and the courts are by and by to enforce duties on a plain statement of the facts out of which they arise, the little of pleading that remains beside the name will come in with sanctions under the duty to which it applies. In an intermediate condition, such as most of the United States are now in, pleading retains an arbitrary element, which makes it more convenient to treat it separately. Practice does not seem to be a part of the law in any other sense than parliamentary law, or the by-laws of certain corporations. If it goes into the *corpus juris* it is for the practical convenience of lawyers, and it will, of course, have a separate place.

Editor's Notes

1. In the margin, opposite "It is only . . . " in Holmes's copy of the *ALR* (Library of Congress): This is wonderfully illustrated by hard cases on contract where the chronological growth of [[illeg.]] is shown.

2. In the bottom margin, below the fifth sentence in this paragraph, in Holmes's library copy of the *ALR:* My coincidence is so striking that it is proper to say that the book was received at the Athenaeum (where I first saw it) Aug. 24/70 at which time this was in print. I had noted the idea on the fly leaf of Austin long before and I never saw the passage in Comte.

3. In margin of OWH library copy of *ALR*, opposite "war; why": Take the case of a confederat[[ion]] of sovereign sta[[tes]] is an act of the c[[on]]federation law or not? Federalist [[Illeg.]].

4. In OWH library copy, an asterisk after "possessors," and in margin: * recognized by the sovereign—There may have been earl[[y]] ones' dispossessed conquest.

5. OWH library copy has an asterisk after "successions" and in the bottom margin: * Succession is one of the great fundamental legal ideas—and must very likely be treated in a separate discussion outside the corpus of duties.

Added later: *Corporations* are to be added to the instances mentioned. Universal successors have a persona or status as such—at the same time the succession is [[illeg.]] and object of a right *in rem*. Austin 954, 5. Same thing applies to property owners and property.

6. Note in Holmes's copy (OWH Papers, Paige Box 18, Item 4), dated November 25, 1877: the disscussion of p. 8 is very old [[presumably referring to *Lumley v. Gye*]]. It arose in the middle ages—or at least one nearly akin to it did, on the questions of possession—It was settled that rights of a real nature such as easement, tithes, &c. could be quasi-possessed and protected by the possessory remedies—and the controversy was whether the same was true of purely personal obligations—in practice it was was [[sic]] admitted—.

7. OWH margin note opposite this sentence in Library copy: A right to make a contract might conceivably be a right *in rem* and right *ex contractu* is only *in personam* and see Austin 401 on franchises—.

6.21

From *American Law Review* 5:113 (1870).

A Treatise on the Law of the Domestic Relations: Embracing Husband and Wife, Parent and Child, Guardian and Ward, Infancy, and Master and Servant. By JAMES SCHOULER, of the Boston Bar. Boston: Little, Brown, & Company. 1870. 8vo.

The authors of volumes like the present have great difficulties to overcome. They must have satisfied themselves on the first of these, to be sure: we mean the propriety of retaining the *jus personarum* as a separate title of the law. But then comes the question, what *personae, status,* or aggregates of rights and duties shall be allowed within it? If you give a chapter to infants, why not divide another between idiots and lunatics? The position of judge confers a status which is as well defined as any. Why exclude executor or heirs?

Our author takes the domestic relations. In doing so he stands on what seems nowadays to be the strongest ground. The family is one of the roots of modern society, as it was the precursor of ancient law. It does, moreover, give rise to certain peculiar aggregates of rights and duties, which, at least in the case of parent and child, it might be hard to refer to any general legal conception. Indeed the relation of husband and wife, although both parties enter it voluntarily, and although admitted to begin in contract, is always considered from the point of view of status. However it may be as to the title infants, we are inclined to believe that the domestic relations, properly so called, are, for the present at least, entitled to a separate treatment.

No one will doubt that we needed a new American law book on some of the subjects of this volume. Whether on all, is more questionable. It is hard to glean where Mr. Bishop has reaped, and that author has made the subjects of marriage and divorce, and perhaps of husband and wife, generally, his own. On the other hand, the relation of guardian and ward is one as to which it is next to impossible to get information, and it is dealt with at large here.

We have made extensive and careful comparisons of the book before us with the authorities, and have found that the cases are pretty fully but not quite exhaustively collected, and that principles are clearly stated in well-ordered divisions. We should doubt whether the author had been as great a reader of cases as of the text-books. Hence he does not seem to us to cite with great discrimination, nor to get as much new law from the new decisions as he might: as it is the one merit of Josiah W. Smith's little hand-books to get, for instance. He has hardly produced a very learned work, nor does he aspire to anticipate principles still *in gremio legis*. He has rather given us a serviceable manual, such as our generation so well knows how to make, and which will be at the right hand of many American practising lawyers for the next ten or twenty years. It will not remain a classic, but it will be bought and used more than we have ever been able to use some undoubted classics.

6.22

From *American Law Review* 5:114 (1870).

Essays upon the Form of the Law. By THOMAS ERSKINE HOLLAND, M.A., Fellow of Exeter College, Oxford, and of Lincoln's Inn, Barrister-at-Law. Author of "An Essay upon Composition Deeds, etc., under 24 & 25 Vict. c. 134." London: Butterworths. 1870. 8vo. pp. 187.

Such books as Mr. Holland's interesting little collection of essays and the papers of the Juridical Society, show us how different is the English lawyer of to-day from those of fifty years ago; we fear we must add from too many American lawyers of our own time. As our author happily puts it, "the old-fashioned English lawyer's idea of a satisfactory body of law was a chaos with a full index." Now reformers and conservatives seem to agree in the desire to deal philosophically with the questions of jurisprudence. The most distinguished of recent chancellors advocates a code. The present occupant of the woolsack proposes a comprehensive scheme for re-modelling the English courts. Whatever may be the merit of particular opinions, there is an atmosphere in which great results are possible; in which originality is not suffocated at its birth.

The most considerable of the essays in the book now before us, and the one which will most repay the general reader, is that on Codification, reprinted from the Edinburgh Review. The shorter papers from the Saturday Review, although we have read them with pleasure and profit, are more local, and of less general bearing. The specimen digest does not strike us as particularly good. We would call particular attention to the author's intelligent remark, that the defects of the law at the present day are chiefly defects of form, and that the consideration of these ought to be kept distinct from the discussion of defects of matter (p. 26).

Perhaps the question on which the desirableness of a code depends is whether it is desirable to put an end to the function of the judges as law-makers. We confess we doubt it. At the same time one of the objections suggested in the article at the beginning of this number of our Review, might be obviated by a law commission, with authority somewhat similar to that attributed by Austin to the Prussian. Then, if the courts should find themselves required by the letter of the code to decide a case contrary to principle, the letter might be at once amended so as to express the principle more accurately thereafter. Possibly this power might be confided to the court itself. If such a scheme were practicable, we should have fewer of those decisions which lay down a sound rule for the future at the expense of retrospectively declaring a course of conduct illegal, although it may have been guided by the best attainable advice.

The codification of the statutes is a simple matter, and the only wonder of an American is why this has not been done in England already. However we must remember that our present commission have hardly begun their labors on the statutes of the United States. They, by the by, may find some useful hints in this book.[1]

Editor's Note

1. At bottom of page in OWH Library copy: Holland's talk about principle of dichotomy pp 19–118 is nothing but the first sentence of Bentham's View of Completed Code—Works Vol. 3 p. 157.

6.23

From *American Law Review* 5:115 (1870).

Commentaries on Equity Jurisprudence, as administered in England and America. By JOSEPH STORY, LL.D. Tenth Edition, carefully revised, with extensive additions. By ISAAC F. REDFIELD, LL.D. In Two Volumes. Boston: Little, Brown, & Company. 1870. 8vo. pp. lxxxvi, 810; viii, 896.

"About one hundred new sections have been added to the text," Judge Redfield tells us in the advertisement to this edition, and nearly "five hundred cases in the notes." In the ninth edition it was stated that one hundred and twenty-five, and in the eighth that two hundred sections had been inserted in like manner. From an examination of the whole work, section by section, and pen in hand, we feel justified in saying that a great deal of what was thus put into the text might, at the cost of a little more trouble but with greater propriety, have found a place in notes to the original work. The editor is not free from another fault most incident to note writers, we mean the desire to insert useful information, irrespective of its connection with what goes before or comes after. This is carried to the farthest point in the notes added to Kent's Commentaries since the death of the Chancellor. There is a chaos of cases, which are collected with really faithful labor, but which lie in a tangled mass across the current of the text, and too often obstruct where they should enlarge. We not rarely find a similar difficulty here and although one gets much assistance from the admirable head-notes to chapters which have been introduced, we are not even guided through the labyrinth of new matter by a good index. Of course, the additions which have been made are valuable, and derive an additional authority from the implied assent of Judge Redfield. But in spite of our respect for his learning and ability, we doubt if the work would be considered very well done if it came from an unknown hand.

We will take up, quite at random, a point or two in detail.

There are few recently developed doctrines of more interest than that of the voluntary assignment of equitable *choses in action*. Whether this was not a contract, and so void for want of consideration: how there could be a gift when no delivery was possible; whether there must not be a delivery of the *indicia*, or an instrument under seal, or notice to the debtor or to the assignee,—these were some of the questions which were raised and passed upon. Judge Story returns to the subject more than once. But it is only recently that the rule has been satisfactorily stated, in such cases as *Richardson v. Richardson*, L.R. 3 Eq. 686, and *Penfold v. Mould*. L.R. 4 Eq. 562. Neither of these cases is cited, nor have we found any new discussion except that in § 793 c, which is confined to a statement of *Donaldson v. Donaldson*, decided in 1854, and a reference to the earlier case of *Kekewich v. Manning*.

If the last matter was apt to interest lawyers of a speculative turn, *Ultra Vires* is a subject of practical importance. There are innumerable recent decisions of the English equity courts upon it, which are yet to be reduced to order by the extraction of principles. Not trusting the blank of the index, we turned to the table of cases, and found there some of the earlier and better known. But on verifying the citations we found that they were but relics of the submerged labors of earlier editors. The sections in which *East Anglican v. Eastern Counties Railway, Eastern Counties Railway v. Hawkes,* and *McGregor v. Deal and Dover Railway* were said to be given, had been replaced by others in which those cases were not found.

We might go on with this most disagreeable business of pointing out shortcomings, but we will not. We have stated our impression, which we leave to our readers to verify or contradict by their own investigations.

The present edition, we are very glad to see, restores the integrity of Story's text which was mutilated in the last.

6.24

From *American Law Review* 5:116 (1870).

The House of Lords Cases: on Appeals and Writs of Error, and Claims of Peerage, during the Sessions 1852, 1853, and 1854. By CHARLES CLARK, ESQ. Vol. IV. Boston: Little, Brown, & Company. 1870. 8vo. pp.

We think that this reprint is very much to the credit of the publishers. It is handsome, accurate, and cheap, and of vastly greater value to the profession than is likely to be indicated by the amount of the sales, although we hope they may be large. The present volume contains several very leading cases. It begins with *Egerton v. Earl Brownlow,* p. 1, in which, after an elaborate discussion, a condition subsequent attached to a contingent interest was held void as against public policy, contrary to the opinion of the majority of the judges and of the Lord Chancellor. On p. 353 is the well-known case of *Gibson v. Small,* which decided that by the law of England, in a time policy effected on a vessel then at sea, there is no implied condition that the ship should be seaworthy on the day when the policy is intended to attach. In *Anderson v. Fitzgerald,* p. 484, it was *held* a misdirection to leave to the jury whether answers in a proposal for a life-policy which was conditioned on the truth of such answers, were material as well as true.

Passing by less important cases, we come, on p. 815, to *Jefferys v. Boosey,* which has filled as large a place in the law of copyright, as *Gibson v. Small* in insurance, although it must now be read with the qualifications put upon it by *Routledge v. Low,* L.R. 3, H.L. 100. The discussions are of great length (*Gibson v. Small* covers two hundred and fifty-six pages, and *Jefferys v. Boosey* one hundred and eighty-two), and they exhaust their subjects. We are glad to see in this volume the customary abbreviated method of citation. We may add that we believe the citations to have been so carefully corrected and purged of the many errors of the English edition, as to make this copy more valuable than the original.

6.25
ULTRA VIRES:
HOW FAR ARE CORPORATIONS LIABLE FOR ACTS
NOT AUTHORIZED BY THEIR CHARTERS?

From *American Law Review* 5:272 (1871).

*THE EAST ANGLIAN RAILWAYS CO. v. THE EASTERN COUNTIES RAILWAY CO.**

. . . .[1]

There are three classes of cases which may be ranged under the head of *Ultra Vires*, using that phrase with a certain latitude. First come those in which a corporation, created by a special statute, is alleged not to be bound by its acts on the ground that they are contrary to such statute. The second class, which is peculiar to England, is of acts unauthorized by the deed of settlement of a company. The third includes transactions which are possibly within the powers of the corporation, but which are beyond the powers of the directors who have undertaken them. We shall consider each class in turn.

1. In England and in some of the United States, acts of incorporation are public acts, which are supposed to be known to all, and it is clear that contracts, expressly or by necessary implication prohibited by such acts as being against public policy, are void like other illegal contracts.[2] It is very well settled, moreover, that in the above class of cases the corporation is not estopped to set up the defence of *ultra vires* to a suit brought by a third person.** The difficulty has been to determine what acts charters are to be construed as prohibiting, and prohibiting on the above ground.

The two views which have been taken are well shown by *Taylor v. Chichester & Midhurst Railway Co.**** in the Exchequer Chamber. The case, as shortly stated by Mr. Justice Blackburn, was a suit on a covenant by a railway company, by which they bound themselves, in the event of a bill then pending in parliament being passed into an act to pay to the plaintiff, within the space of three months next after the passing of the bill, the sum of £2,000. It was admitted that the covenant was not in itself illegal, and that it might have been enforced against any private persons, who, being promoters of a railway bill, had executed a deed containing similar stipulations on their part (p. 376). But the defendants were a railway company, who, at the time they executed the deed, were incorporated by a public act. The act which

---

*We print this case rather than any later one, because it is short, and yet very clear, is one of the earliest and most constantly cited of the many cases on the subject, and after being much criticised, has been followed in the latest English adjudications. It is reported 11 C.B. 775; 21 L.J. n.s. C.P. 23; 16 Jur. 249.

** *MacGregor v. Dover & Deal Railway,* 18 Q.B. 618; *Chambers v. Manchester & Milford R. Co.,* 5 Best & S. 588; *In re National Permanent Bl'dg. Soc.,* L.R. 5 Ch. 309; *Earl of Shrewsbury v. North Staffordshire R. Co.,* L.R. 1 Eq. 593; *Hood v. N.Y. & N.H. R.R.,* 22 Conn. 502; *Pearce v. Madison & Indianapolis R.R.,* 21 How. 441; and cases sited hereafter. Even those courts whose indignation is moved at the defence, *Brown v. Winnissimmet Co.,* 11 Allen, 326, 331, would unquestionably sustain it, *East Boston Freight R.R. Co. v. Hubbard,* 10 Allen, 459; *East Boston F. R.R. Co. v. Eastern R.R. Co.,* 13 Allen, 422; *Whittenton Mills v. Upton,* 10 Gray, 582.

***L.R. 2 Ex. 356.

they obtained after the making of the agreement in question was also a public act, and contained no provision sanctioning the agreement; and both of the acts contained the clauses usual in such acts naming certain purposes to which "only" the funds of the company were to be applied. The covenant sued upon was not for any of the purposes specified. The majority of the court held that the covenant was *ultra vires* and void, but Blackburn and Willes, JJ., dissented, and the former delivered an opinion marked by his usual ability. He admits not only, "that a contract to do an act forbidden by a public statute, as contrary to public policy, is illegal and void,—a doctrine in which I completely concur,—but also that the provisions relating to the appropriations of the capital to the purpose of the statutes authorizing it to be raised, are not merely for the benefit of the shareholders, which, therefore, they may waive, but are for the public benefit, making the appropriation of the funds to other purposes *malum prohibitum.*" But he doubts the soundness of the last doctrine, and he is very clear in his opinion "that the position to be inferred from the language of the judgment in the *East Anglian Railway Company v. Eastern Counties Railway Company,** that every appropriation of the funds that is not so far authorized by the statutes as to be binding on a dissenting minority of shareholders, is therefore forbidden and illegal," (p. 383), or as he elsewhere, (p. 382), puts it, "that every thing not expressly or implicitly authorized as against the shareholders is forbidden as against public policy, and void," is not the law. He cites Baron Parke as stating the proposition correctly, thus: "if it appears by the express provisions of the statute creating the corporation, or by necessary or reasonable inference from its enactments, that the deed was *ultra vires,*—that is that the legislature meant that such a deed should not be made"—then the deed will not bind it;** and after referring to the cases which have adopted that statement, he says, "I think, therefore, we are entitled to consider the question to be, not whether the present defendants had, by virtue of their act of incorporation, authority to make the contract, but whether they are by those statutes forbidden to make it." (p. 384.) His arguments did not prevail however, and the majority of the court not only refer to the *East Anglian* case above cited as good law, but seem indisposed to limit the inferences to be drawn from the language there used, and apparently deny that there is any distinction between transactions *ultra vires* under the act of incorporation, as between the corporation and its members, and those which are void as between it and third persons on the ground that they are against public policy. In other words, we understand the court to be of opinion that acts *ultra vires* in the first connection are void in the other, and that the consent of all the stockholders would not suffice to make them valid. In this case, four judges in the Exchequer Chamber reversed the opinion of four in the Exchequer in addition to the two who dissented above (See s.c. 4 H. & C. 409). But the case does not seem to have been so carefully considered in the court below.

* *Supra.*
**This was referred to by the majority as if it substantially agreed with the *East Anglian* case. It was considered by the Lord Chancellor in *Shrewsbury & Birmingham R. Co. v. Northwestern R. Co.,* 6 H.L.C. 113, a more correct way of enunciating the doctrine; but he seems to think that the difference is unimportant, and it may be doubted whether the other cases referred to by Mr. Justice Blackburn, treat Baron Parke's statement as materially modifying the language of previous cases.

An important American case on the same subject is *Bissell v. The Michigan South-ern & Northern Indiana R.R. Co.*[*] This was an action to recover damages for injuries negligently inflicted on the plaintiff while travelling on a road in Illinois, alleged to be part of the defendants' line. The defence was that the defendants were two corporations, one of Michigan the other of Indiana; that they had connected their roads, and had mingled their funds and were doing a joint business; that this was beyond the powers conferred on them by their respective charters, and so that the contract of carriage along the consolidated line in a third State was void. But this defence did not prevail. Most of the judges gave no reasons for their decision, and may have held, as Clerke and Selden, JJ., thought, that the action could be main-tained for the tort, irrespective of the contract of carriage; but Comstock, Ch. J., thought otherwise, and so the whole matter was discussed between him and Judge Selden. The former begins his very able opinion by a powerful assault on the notion that acts *ultra vires* cannot be acts of the corporation. There is undoubtedly an air of logical consistency in the argument, that the law creates a corporation, and only calls it into being *quoad* the legitimate objects of its creation; that it only exists in the exercise of those functions which the law has endowed it with, and that it is unlike a natural person who exists and acts independent of and outside the law, and consequently may transgress it. But to this Judge Comstock replies, not only by pointing out the great inducements to fraud which it would hold out, but by asking, "Why does the law provide the remedy by *quo warranto* against corporations for usur-pation and abuse of power? Is it not the very foundation of that proceeding, that corporations can and do perform acts and usurp franchises beyond the rightful authority conferred by their charter?" "The privileges and franchises granted are not the whole of a corporation. Every trading corporation aggregate includes an association of persons having a collective will, and a board of directors or other agency in which that will is embodied, and through which it may be exerted in modes of action not expressed in the organic law. Thus, like moral and sentient beings, they may and do act in opposition to the intention of their creator, and they ought to be accountable for such acts." We suppose then that we may take it to be the law, on considerations of at least practical weight, that corporations have a gen-eral and not a qualified existence; and that when they escape liability for acts be-yond their powers, it is not on the ground that such acts are not to be attributed to them, but that they are illegal or at least unauthorized and void, as acts of natural persons would have been under the same circumstances. It is with this doctrine that Judge Comstock next deals, and takes ground not unlike that of Mr. Justice Black-burn. He says (p. 269), "The words *ultra vires* and illegality represent totally different and distinct ideas. It is true that a contract may have both those defects, but it may also have one without the other. For example, a bank has no authority to engage, and usually does not engage, in benevolent enterprises. A subscription, made by authority of the board of directors and under the corporate seal, for the building of a church or college or an almshouse, would be clearly *ultra vires,* but it would not be illegal. If every corporator should expressly assent to such an application of the funds, it would still be *ultra vires,* but no wrong would be committed and no public

[*]22 N.Y. 258.

interest violated." It is very manifest that this instance, and others which the learned judge goes on to give, are contrary to the prevailing English doctrine as already explained. He and those who agree with him endeavor to sustain their view by treating corporations as chartered partnerships, and the franchise, &c., as merely convenient methods of effecting the partnership purposes (p. 270). Hence, they say, just as the objects of association are stated in the articles of an unincorporated company, they are also set forth in the act of the legislature. But they are no more binding on third persons in the latter case than in the former. For the managers of the company to disregard them may be a breach of trust or of contract, but does not constitute a "public wrong." Even a *quo warranto*, Judge Comstock continues, "is a civil and not a criminal proceeding, and its object is purely and solely to try a civil right."

The last position which he takes is, that conceding the contract to be illegal, it does not follow that it is void. But it is noticeable that the only examples by which he sustains this, are of acts *intra vires* in their external aspect, and only beyond the corporate powers because done with a secret unlawful intent; a class of cases which form a clear exception to the general rule, and with which we shall deal directly.

The opinion of Judge Selden, upholding as it does what we have given as the result of the English cases, may be more shortly stated. He admits that the defence *ultra vires* does not rest on the ground that the contract sought to be enforced is not the act of the Corporation (p. 283), but on the ground that it is illegal. He then goes on to show more elaborately and perspicuously than has been done elsewhere, that incorporated bodies have important franchises and privileges which are not possessed by unincorporated partnerships, and that the public have very great interest in requiring that they do not exceed the powers conferred upon them. He says that a *quo warranto* "is not only public and *quasi* criminal in form, but is not in its nature adapted to the enforcement of any mere private right." The stockholders have their appropriate remedies by injunction and otherwise. He considers the English cases, and shows that the doctrine uniformly established by them and by the American authorities is, that contracts of a corporation prohibited by its charter, whether expressly or by implication, are void and cannot be enforced (pp. 303, 304); and he seems to agree with the language of Lord Langdale which he cites to the effect that any dealing with the funds of a company by its managers, "in any manner *not distinctly authorized* by the act of parliament, is, in my opinion, an *illegal* application or dealing" (pp. 294, 295). Having come to the conclusion that the contract of carriage was void, however, he gives his opinion, as has been stated, that the defendants were liable for the tort irrespective of any contract, and that the plaintiff was entitled to judgment on that ground.* The only other fact to be noted in this remarkable case is the dissent of Mr. Justice Denio, which would seem to imply that in his opinion the contract of carriage was the only foundation of the action, and that being *ultra vires* it would not sustain one.

We gather from the cases which have been cited, and from others, that when a corporation is created by a public statute for definite and limited objects to which its funds are to be applied, a contract which is entirely unconnected with those purposes, or which, on its face, will cause the funds to be applied to other objects,

---

* *Brown v. Winnissimmet Co.*, 11 Allen 326, 334.

is illegal and void.[*] And, according to Lord Cranworth, it does not make much difference whether we say that the company has no authority given to it by its incorporation to enter into contracts as to matters not connected with its corporate duties, which he seems to consider the preferable statement, and substantially that of Baron Parke, or that it is impliedly prohibited from so doing, because, by necessary inference, the legislature must be considered to have intended that no such contracts should be entered into.[**] The question whether a particular contract is binding on a particular corporation or not, is to be answered by determining whether on a fair construction of the charter it relates to matters connected with the corporate duties and purposes. It will not be out of place to cite here, as a rule of construction midway between the opposite extremes of Lord Langdale and Mr. Justice Blackburn, the language of Bigelow, C.J., in a case[***] in which it was held not beyond the power of a ferry company, authorized to own vessels, &c., up to a certain value, to let one of its steamboats at a certain rate *per diem* for no specified time or place, it not being proved that the vessel was not proper to be used in connection with the business of the ferry, or was owned in excess of the lawful amount of corporate property. He says: "We know of no rule or principle by which an act creating a corporation for certain specific objects, or to carry on a particular trade or business, is to be strictly construed as prohibitory of all other dealings or transactions, not coming within the exact scope of those designated."[****] The decision in the case shows how far the court were prepared to go, while, on the other hand, it is admitted, in the course of the opinion, that a street railway corporation, for instance, could not lawfully engage extensively in the transportation of passengers and merchandise on land or sea by steam.

We do not undertake in this note to go at large into the examples in which these principles have been applied. But we may mention that it seems to be a reasonable inference from the late cases, that a railway company is authorized to provide such carriage by land or water on the line of its road as may fairly be considered incident to the due employment of the railway;[*****] although it cannot engage in a new and distinct enterprise, such as running a line of steamboats beyond and entirely outside of the line of transportation contemplated in its act.[******]

In the English courts it has been thought to be a deduction from the general

---

[*] *Taylor v. Chichester & Midhurst R. Co.*, L.R. 2 Ex. 356, 369, 373; *Bateman v. Mid-Wales R. Co.*, L.R. 1 C.P. 499, 508; *Eastern Counties R. Co. v. Hawkes*, 5 H.L.C. 331, 348; *East Anglian R. Co. v. Eastern Counties R. Co.*, *supra*; *Pearce v. Madison & Ind. R.R.*, 21 How. 441; *Buffett v. Troy & Boston R.R. Co.*, 40 N.Y. 168, 172; *Pennsylvania, Del. & Md. Steam Nav. Co. v. Dandridge*, 8 Gill & J. 248; *Orr v. Lacey*, 2 Dougl. Mich. 230; *Abbott v. Baltimore & R. Steam Packet Co.*, 1 Md. Ch. 542; *Downing v. Mount Washington Road Co.*, 40 N.H. 230; *Straus v. Eagle Ins. Co.*, 5 Ohio State, 59; *Morris & Essex R.R. Co. v. Sussex R.R. Co.*, 5 C.E. Green, N.J. 542.

[**] *Shrewsbury & Birmingham Railway Co. v. Northwestern Railway Co.*, 6 H.L.C. 113, 137. See 10 C.B. N.S. 682.

[***] *Brown v. Winnissimmet Co.*, 11 Allen, 326, 334.

[****] See also *Colman v. Eastern Counties Railway*, 10 Beav. 1, 18.

[*****] *South Wales Railway Co. v. Redmond*, 10 C.B. N.S. 675, 687; *Buffett v. Troy & Boston R.R. Co.*, 40 N.Y. 168.

[******] *Pearce v. Madison & Ind. R.R. Co.*, 21 How. 441; *Coleman v. Eastern Counties Railway*, 10 Beav. 1. See 10 C.B. N.S. 685.

principle, that a railway company incorporated in the usual way for the formation and working of a railway, could not bind itself by accepting a bill of exchange.* The argument being that it would be contrary to the principles governing negotiable paper to allow an inquiry to be gone into between the company and *a bonâ fide* holder for value and without notice, whether the bill in question was issued for a legitimate purpose or not. But the contrary doctrine prevails in America.** In *Bissell's* case, above stated, Judge Selden deduced from the same premises that if a corporation were authorized to give notes for any purpose, it could not set up, as against a *bonâ fide* indorsee of a note in fact issued by it, that it was given for other purposes than that authorized.*** If, on the other hand, it was prohibited to give them at all, its notes would be voidable (qu. void?) in whosever hands they might be.

This leads us to consider an important exception to the rule which we have laid down as established by authority; an exception which has been supposed by some, Judge Comstock among the rest, to throw doubt upon the rule, but which in fact is perfectly consistent with it. When an act in its external aspect is within the general powers of a company, and is only unauthorized because it is done with a secret unauthorized intent, the defence of *ultra vires* will not prevail against a stranger who dealt with the company without notice of such intent.****

The reason of this we take to be the converse of the principle which confers immunity upon a married woman for her representations that she is capable of contracting, as a corollary from her incapacity to contract. The law authorizes third persons to enter into some transactions with the corporation, of a class indicated by certain external acts on the part of the latter, for example, to sell rails to it for the purposes of its railway but not for the purpose of a resale on speculation. The external acts (*e.g.* in the case put, the offer to buy), are alike in the authorized and unauthorized cases, and it is only by the representations of the company that a third person can ascertain whether the proposed transaction falls within the authority of the charter. The charter contemplates his acting, and yet he cannot act if he is not at liberty to rely on representations by the corporation of matters which are of necessity solely within its knowledge, and yet upon which, as between the company and its members, the legality of the transaction depends.***** The exception which

*Bateman v. Mid-Wales R. Co., L.R. 1 C.P. 499.

**Frye v. Tucker, 24 Ill. 180; Smith v. Law, 21 N.Y. 296, 299; Mechanics Banking Ass. v. N.Y. & S. White Lead Co., 35 N.Y. 505; Curtis v. Leavitt, 15 N.Y. 9, 62; Olcott v. Tioga R.R., 40 Barb. 179; 27 N.Y. 546, 557; Rockwell v. Elkhorn Bank, 13 Wis. 653; Hardy v. Merriweather, 14 Ind. 203; Clarke v. School District No. 7, 3 R.I. 199; 2 Kent, 278 n (c).

***Monument National Bank v. Globe Works, 101 Mass. 57; Supervisors v. Schenck, 5 Wall. 772, 784; Gelpcke v. Dubuque, 1 Wall. 175, 203; Madison & Indianapolis R.R. Co. v. Norwich Savings Soc., 24 Ind. 457, stated post. pp. 287, 288.

****Miners Ditch Co. v. Zellerbach, 37 Cal. 543. This case contains a very interesting discussion. See also the remarks of Lord Campbell cited there from Norwich v. Norfolk Railway Co., 4 El. & Bl. 397, 443; those of Comstock, Ch. J., in 22 N.Y. 273; and the cases of promissory notes just mentioned.

*****However, a shade of doubt is thrown on this explanation by the language used by Lord Romilly in the case of a corporation formed by articles. The claim was for rails alleged to have been purchased for other than authorized purposes, with the knowledge of the *Ebbw Vale Company,* the vendor. The judge went so far as to say: "I think that one company is not bound to know what the other is doing, and that the most perfect notice would not entitle them to say any thing on the subject." *In re Contract Corporation; Claim of Ebbw Vale Co.,* L.R. 8 Eq. 14. We believe an appeal is pending in this case. If the Master of the

has now been stated is perhaps the only case in which acts may be illegal as towards the members of a company, because in excess of statutory powers, and yet bind the company to strangers. For it remains to be noted that in these cases a dissenting stockholder would have his remedy in equity against the company.[*]

When the transaction which is *ultra vires* is only an incident and the principal matter is within the company's powers, the latter may sometimes be upheld. Thus, in a case where the directors of a company were prohibited giving bills of exchange, but had power to borrow on mortgage, and gave bills to secure an existing debt, and also a mortgage under the seal of the company, subject to redemption on payment of the bills, the Master of the Rolls construed the mortgage to be security for the debt and not for the bills, and held that it was not affected by the invalidity of the latter.[**]

There is another class of cases of some interest. Although when a company issues bonds for the mere purpose of raising money under circumstances in which a penalty is imposed on them for so doing, such bonds will be void within the decision of *Chambers v. The Manchester & Milford Railway Co.*,[***] yet, when a party has lent money which has gone to pay debts of the borrower, the lender may be subrogated to the rights of the paid-off creditors, although he could not have maintained an action directly; just as a husband who has deserted his wife is liable in equity for money lent to her for the purchase of necessaries and so applied, although he would not be at law. In *Jenner v. Morris*,[****] a case of this sort, Lord Campbell suggests that it may be "that equity considers that the tradespeople have, for valuable consideration, assigned to the party who advanced the money the legal debt which would be due to them from the husband on furnishing the necessaries, and that, although a *chose in action* cannot be assigned at law, a court of equity recognizes the right of the assignee." In a later case, in which *Jenner v. Morris* was cited, *Lloyd's* bonds had been given by the directors of a company with the knowledge of the shareholders, acknowledging sums of money to be due from the company for work, &c., and conditioned for the payment of the same. The company had at the time expended the whole of its capital, and reached the extent of its borrowing powers, and was in

---

Rolls is right we may put the explanation higher still, and say that it is similar to that of allowing money paid to a stakeholder with the intent to have it applied to an unlawful wager, to be recovered back before it is paid over. The act of paying in the one case, or the making of the contract in the other, are *per se* lawful when taken apart from the accompanying intent. And the intent may change in either case before it is executed in an illegal act. At the moment the contract to furnish the rails, for instance, became binding, if ever, there was nothing to prevent their being applied to the authorized purposes of the company. But this opens up a subject which cannot be handled at large, and on which it may be hard to reconcile different parts of the law; viz., how far the legal character and consequences of an act *per se* indifferent may be affected by the intent with which it is done.

We have not found any cases on the point whether if the corporation were trying to enforce a contract of this class the party dealing with it could defend successfully on the above ground. We may conjecture that the liabilities would be reciprocal, although the answer might depend on which of the suggested explanations is the correct one. See *South Wales R. Co. v. Redmond*, 10 C.B. N.S. 675.

[*]*Forrest v. Manchester S. & L.R. Co.*, 30 Beav. 40; S.C. 7 Jur. N.S. 887; 749; *Shrewsbury & Birmingham R. Co. v. Northwestern Railway Co.*, 6 H.L.C. 113, 137.

[**] *Scott v. Colburn*, 26 Beav. 276.

[****]5 B. & S. 588.

[*****]3 De G., F. & J. 45, 52.

addition heavily embarrassed with lawful debts to contractors and the like.[*] The bonds, if issued for the mere purpose of raising money, would have been void within *Chambers v. Manchester, &c., R. Co., supra.* But the obligee in some instances, and in others the company, had applied the money raised to the payment of the above debts. The case arose between the company and parties from whom the obligee had raised the money by the deposit of the bonds. The Lord Chancellor says: "The proper course to be taken seems to me to be this: that, so far as the company have adopted the proceedings of their directors by allowing these moneys to be raised on the issue of these debentures, and so far as the money raised by the issue of the debentures has been applied in paying off debts which would not otherwise have been paid off, those who have advanced the moneys ought to stand in the place of those whose debts have been so paid off. It is not simply that the bondholders stand as assignees of the debts, which, no doubt, have not actually been assigned, but it has been represented by the directors that the persons who lent their money on these acknowledgments were lending their money for the purpose of clearing off the debts; in fact, that they were to be put in the position of assignees of the debts."[**]

In a still later case the Lord-Justice Giffard, who took part in the last judgment, says: "I have no hesitation in saying that those cases have gone quite far enough, and that I am not disposed to extend them. They were decided upon a principle recognized in old cases, beginning with *Marlow v. Pitfield*,[***] where there was a loan to an infant, and the money was spent in paying for necessaries, and in another case of a more modern date, where there was money actually lent to a lunatic, and it went in paying expenses which were necessary for the lunatic. In such cases it has been held, that although the party lending the money could maintain no action, yet, inasmuch as his money had gone to pay debts which would be recoverable at law, he could come into a court of equity and stand in the place of those creditors whose debts had been paid. That is the principle of those cases. It is a very clear and definite principle, and a principle which ought not to be departed from."[****]

2. The second class of cases, which, as we have said, are peculiarly English, are those of transactions unauthorized by the deed of settlement of a company. In England companies are authorized to be formed by executing and registering a deed under the hand and seal of the members, and the deed is to determine the objects of the company, and the extent of its powers, and of the members' liability. Athough the distinction between these companies and those incorporated by a public act of the legislature seems often to have been overlooked, that it exists is very clear. The consent of every member of a corporation cannot make lawful what has been made unlawful by statute, and we have seen that in general whatever the latter class of corporations are not authorized to do as against their members, is also held to be unlawful or unauthorized as toward the public. But where the company is formed by deed, what the members are competent to do, they are competent to undo. The question is no longer of illegality but of contract. An act unauthorized by the deed

---

[*] The Lord Chancellor cited *White v. Carmarthen R. Co.*, 1 H. & M. 786, as showing that debts to contractors for services might be lawful under such circumstances.

[**] *In re Cork & Youghal Railway Co.*, L.R. 4 Ch. 748, 761.

[***] 1 P. Wms. 558.

[****] *In re National Permanent Benefit Bl'dg Soc., Ex parte Williamson*, L.R. 5 Ch. 309, 313.

is of course invalid as against a dissenting shareholder, whether entered into by the directors or by the vote of a general meeting, because each one has a right to hold the rest to the terms of the original undertaking. But if all assent the act is legal, and therefore it may become binding from tacit acquiescence and lapse of time. Thus in *Brotherhood's Case*,[*] a company was in difficulty, and it was resolved at a general meeting to wholly remodel it, and to allow dissentient members to retire upon terms which were said not to be authorized by the deed of settlement. All the members were informed of these terms, and some retired, of which the others were, as far as possible, notified. After twelve years, during which the transaction had not been impeached by members or creditors of the company, it was held too late for shareholders who had had notice to impeach the transaction.

The same principle was applied in *Evans v. Smallcombe*.[**] But it is to be noted that the opinions of the Lords seem to have stood only three to two, and the other cases cited in the note limit the doctrine pretty narrowly. There may be circumstances under which an act *ultra vires* in this sense would be held to bind the company, and yet to be invalid so far as it would affect the security of a previous creditor, just as one who has been induced to become a stockholder by fraud may be relieved as against the company,[***] when as towards creditors his name would be retained on the register.[****]

That persons dealing with these companies are bound to look to the terms of the deed of settlement is well established law in England.[*****] And this leads us to the consideration of the third class of cases which we mentioned in the beginning of this note. Taking what has just been laid down as settled, it is clear that a company is not bound by transactions of the directors, which are on their face beyond the powers conferred on such directors by the registered articles of association. Thus in *Balfour v. Ernest*[******] directors, who had power by the deed to accept bills for the purposes of the company issued a bill to the plaintiff in satisfaction of a debt due him from another company, and it was held that he could not recover, and the principle of this case is approved in the others cited. But notwithstanding this, and although in England they have been thought to be special rather than general agents, "if," in the language of the present Lord Chancellor, "as in the case of *Royal British Bank v. Turquand*[*******] the directors have power and authority to bind the company, but certain preliminaries are required to be gone through on the part of the company before that power can be duly exercised, then the person contracting with the directors is not bound to see that all these preliminaries have been observed. He is entitled to presume that the directors are acting lawfully in what

---

[*] 31 Beav. 365.

[**] L.R. 3 H.L. 249. But see *Spackman v. Evans*, ib. 171; *Houldsworth v. Evans*, ib. 263.

[***] *Central R. Co. of Venezuela v. Kisch*, L.R. 2 H.L. 99.

[****] *Oakes v. Turquand*, L.R. 2 H.L. 325, 367.

[*****] *Kearns v. Leaf*, 1 H. & M. 681, 706.

[******] 5 C.B. N.S. 601. See further, *Kearns v. Leaf, supra; In re German Mining Co.*, 4 De G. M. & G. 19, 40, 51; *Ex parte Eagle Ins. Co.*, 4 K. & J. 549; *In re London, Hamburg & Continental Exch. Bank*, L.R. 9 Eq. 270; *Ernest v. Nicholls*, 6 H.L.C. 401, 419.

[*******] 6 E. & B. 327.

they do. That is the result of Lord Campbell's judgment in *Royal British Bank v. Turquand.*[*]

Again, it has been laid down in an Indiana case, that "the general agent of a corporation, clothed with a certain power by the charter, or the lawful act of the corporation, may use the power for an unauthorized, or even a prohibited purpose, in his dealings with an innocent third party, and yet render the corporation liable for his acts."[**] In that case a railway company, within whose corporate powers it was to sell and guarantee bonds held in the usual course of business, was sued on a guaranty alleged by it to have been made for the accommodation of another road, and so *ultra vires;* but the court considered that as the contract was on its face of a class within their powers, this defence was not open as against a *bonâ fide* holder without notice.[***] Take again the well-known case of the Schuyler frauds. There Schuyler, who was the president, one of the directors, and transfer agent at New York, of a company, had acted pretty generally as its financial agent, and had authority in many instances to issue certificates of its stock; of the stock, for instance, not taken by the original subscribers; of certain forfeited shares; of shares transferred to him on behalf of the company, &c. He fraudulently over-issued certificates of stock of the same form with those he was authorized to issue, and continued doing so through a series of years, when ordinary care on the part of the company, it was found, would at any time have disclosed the frauds, and when on the other hand, in accordance with the custom in New York, the books of the corporation were not open to dealers. Considerable sums raised indiscriminately from the fraudulent and from genuine stock of the company were applied upon its construction account, but the principle of *In re Cork & Youghal Railway Co.,* and the other cases before cited of that class, does not seem to have been referred to. The Court of Errors and Appeals, after great discussion, held that the company was liable on the false certificates to parties who had paid or advanced money on the strength of the transfer of such stock to them on the books of the company from others in whose names it had previously stood. The question principally discussed, and on which alone we cite the case, was a question of agency, and the judge expresses the *ratio decidendi* as follows (p. 73): "Where the principal has clothed his agent with power to do an act upon the existence of some extrinsic fact necessarily and peculiarly within the knowledge of the agent, and of the existence of which the act of executing the power is itself a representation, a third person dealing with such agent in entire good faith pursuant to the apparent power, may rely upon the representation, and the principal is estopped from denying its truth to his prejudice."[****]

The reason of this rule, which seems to be more extensive than cases of agency, we have already tried to state in one form, when considering how a corporation could be bound in any case by acts beyond the powers conferred on it by the legisla-

---

[*] *Fountaine v. Carmarthen R. Co.* L.R. 5 Eq. 316, 322; *In re Land Credit Co. of Ireland,* L.R. 4 Ch. 460, 469; *Totterdell v. Fareham Brick Co.,* L.R. 1 C.P. 674 (where the agreement was not under seal); *Zabriskie v. Cleveland, C. & C. R.R.,* 23 How. 381; *De Voss v. Richmond,* 18 Gratt. 338, 347.

[**] *Madison & Indianapolis R.R. v. Norwich Saving Society,* 24 Ind. 447.

[***] *Bird v. Daggett,* 97 Mass. 494, *ante* p. 282.

[****] *New York & N.H. R.R. v. Schuyler,* 34 N.Y. 30.

ture. The principal clearly contemplates and gives it to be understood that he con-templates his agent's acting. Moreover he contemplates his agent's acting in his absence, or there would be no object in appointing the agent. But the agent cannot act in his principal's absence if the party dealing with him is bound to recur to the principal for information about a fact necessarily resting solely in the knowledge of the agent and his principal. Therefore it must be taken to follow from the authority expressly conferred, that the principal holds out to the rest of the world that they may rely on the agent's representations under the circumstances set forth in the rule. *Ubi aliquid conceditur, conceditur et id sine quo res ipsa esse non potest.*[4]

In this connection, however, we must call attention to the decision in *D'Arcy v. Tamar, Kit Hill & Callington R. Co.*[*] There a company was held not to be liable on a bond to which its corporate seal had been affixed by the secretary, who was admit-ted to be the proper person to do so, and by the authority of three directors, who were admitted to be the proper number to give such authority, on the ground that they had acted separately and not at a meeting as required by law. It may be im-portant in this case that the secretary does not appear to have had any general authority from the company to affix the seal of the company on certain preliminar-ies being gone through with, but seems to have received it from the directors spe-cially in each instance. Otherwise it might be hard to reconcile it with *In re Land Credit Co. of Ireland, supra,* where it was cited, and seemingly thought distinguishable. See *Torrey v. Dustin Monument Association,* 5 Allen, 327, 329.

We conclude with an extreme case decided by the Lord-Justice Giffard, affirming the decision of the Master of the Rolls. A life assurance company was formed and registered in January, 1863, under the *Companies Act,* 1862, and one Preston was named as the managing director in the articles of association. In June, directors who were named in the articles, and had signed the memorandum, held a meeting and resolved that no shares should be allotted, and no further steps taken toward the formation of the company. They gave notice of this resolution to Preston and to the other subscribers. Preston, however, and one shareholder proceeded there-upon to choose other directors and to allot shares and thereafter business was car-ried on at the *registered office* of the company. On the winding up of the company it was held liable to a *bonâ fide* holder of a policy issued from its office, sealed with what purported to be the company's seal, and signed by three of the new directors.[**]

The court says that "a stranger must be taken to have read the general act under which the company is incorporated, and also to have read the articles of association; but he is not to be taken to have read any thing more, and if he knows nothing to the contrary, he has a right to assume as against the company that all matters of internal management have been duly complied with.

"The company is bound by what takes place in the usual course of business with a third party where that third party deals *bonâ fide* with persons who may be termed *de facto* directors, and who might, so far as he could tell, have been directors *de jure.*"

---

[*]L.R. 2 Ex. 158.
[**]*In re County Life Assurance Co.,* L.R. 5 Ch. 288.

Editor's Notes

1. The ellipsis replaces the text of the case. See Holmes's first note for the citation.
2. Note in OWH Library copy: I suppose the same wd apply to private acts.
3. OWH addition to the text of this note in Library copy: & of course it is here assumed that the agent or officer issuing the note has all the powers of the corporation—See *Clark v. Desmoines*, 19 Iowa 199—here the question was as to the powers of an agent to bind a municipal corp. without a vote of the council required by law to appear on the public records.
4. OWH note in Library copy: But this argument if sound must probably be confined to general agent.

6.26

From *American Law Review* 5:340 (1871).

The Law of Torts. By C. G. ADDISON, Esq. Abridged for use in the Law School of Harvard University. Boston: Little, Brown, & Company, 1870.

This book is best explained by the preface. "When it was determined that special instruction should be given at the Harvard Law School in this branch the law, Addison's Law of Torts appeared to the person appointed to give such instruction to be the work best adapted for a text-book; but its cost was high, and a large portion of the matter which it contained (as for instance the chapters upon bailments, easements, patents, and copyrights, and much of the text relating to evidence, pleading, and practice) seemed to fall more properly within branches of instruction taught by others, while the full citation of English Statutes, and the special adjudications upon them, appeared to be almost valueless to the American student."

This indicates quite accurately what has been left out, and may convince the practising lawyer, as a comparison has convinced us, that he, as well as the students, will do better to buy this cheap little book than the bulky and costly volume from which it is abridged. All that has been omitted will be found better done in other common books.

We are inclined to think that Torts is not a proper subject for a law book. Under this title we expect to find some or all of the wrongs remedied by the actions of trespass, trespass on the case, and trover. But we cannot help believing that the cohesion or legal relationship, say, of trespass *quare clausum*, is closer with the duties to him in possession enforced by real actions, than with assault and battery. So, to give another example, the law of actions for deceit seems to us to be properly presented in connection with that of estoppel *in pais* as two forms of sanction for the same duty,—not to defraud one's neighbor, to put it broadly. Seduction, which we find in the next chapter of this book, belongs at the other end of the *corpus juris*.

We long for the day when we may see these subjects treated by a writer capable of dealing with them philosophically, and self-sacrificing enough to write a treatise as if it were an integral part of a commentary on the entire body of the law. Such a result might be anticipated if the able lecturer for whose use this abridgement was prepared, and who is achieving so deserved a success at Cambridge, should apply his subtle and patient intellect to the task.

6.27

From *American Law Review* 5:343 (1871).

A Treatise on the Law of Negligence. THOMAS G. SHEARMAN and AMASA A. REDFIELD. Second Edition. New York: Baker, Voorhis, & Co. 1870.

This book has achieved a practical success in eight months. Before it had done so, we expressed our opinion of it at some length (4 Am. Law Rev. 350), and we observe that such of our suggestions as could not fairly be called matters of opinion have been acted on in the second edition.

As a matter of opinion, we still think that the merit of this work is practical, not philosophical. The authors were philosophical in their first step, to be sure, when they planted themselves upon a legal conception instead of a branch of trade, as is too often the case now-a-days. *Negligence* is a better subject for a law book than *telegraphs*. But when we look further than the title-page, the discussions and arrangements are altogether those of a working manual. Viewed in this light the book is a credit to its authors. There is a great deal of hard work and of new law in it, and we do not wonder that so many lawyers buy it.

In this edition, besides those improvements which have been referred to, others, which experience has shown to be possible, have been added.

6.28

From *American Law Review* 5:346 (1871).

The House of Lords Cases on Appeals and Writs of Error and Claims of Peerage. By CHARLES CLARK, ESQ. Vols. V. and VI. Boston: Little, Brown, & Company. 1870.

We have received two more volumes of this invaluable reprint, in which every other case is famous wherever the common law is studied. Among the interesting decisions are the often cited *Mayor of Southmolton v. Attorney-General,* 5 H.L.C. 1, and *Mayor of Beverley v. Attorney-General,* 6 H.L.C. 310, on the subject of charities. On page 72 of the former volume, we have *Ranger v. Great Western R. Co.,* an important case bearing, *inter alia,* on the liability of corporations for the fraud of their agents, more or less explained in the later case of *Western Bank of Scotland v. Addie,* L.R. 1 H.L. Sc. 145, which the editors have cited, and to be read with *Barwick v. English Joint Stock Bank,* L.R. 2 Ex. 259, which they have not, following the mistaken plan of only citing subsequent decisions of the House of Lords. *Jordan v. Money,* p. 185, is on the principle of equitable estoppel. But perhaps there are more well-known decisions involving the defence of *ultra vires* than on any other single subject. In the fifth volume are *Bargate v. Shortridge,* p. 297, and *Eastern Counties Railway v. Hawkes,* p. 331; in the sixth, are the equally important *Shrewsbury v. Birmingham R. Co. v. Northwestern R. Co.,* p. 113; and *Ernest v. Nicholls,* p. 401.

Passing by others of only less interest we find at page 811, *Scott v. Avery,* on the extent to which it is possible to oust the jurisdiction of the courts by contract. This is always referred to, we believe, as the leading case on this subject. The fifth volume also contains the *Wensleydale Peerage,* that decision which is to us in America only matter of historical curiosity, but which made such a profound sensation and has given rise to such endless discussion in England.

The sixth volume contains fewer cases of broad principles than the fifth. But besides those already mentioned, there are many which are of value, on charities, wills, commercial law, &c., &c. We must not omit to mention the case of *Hooper v. Lane*, p. 443, as an instance of the elaborate discussions contained in these volumes. A hundred pages are occupied by the Judges and Lord Chancellor in determining against the right of the sheriff who has arrested a party on an invalid writ to arrest him on a good writ while unlawfully in custody.

6.29

From *American Law Review* 5:359 (1871).[1]

The Code of Procedure of the State of New York, as Amended to 1870. With Notes on Pleading and Practice, Rules of the Courts, and a full Index. Tenth Edition. By JOHN TOWNSHEND. New York: Baker, Voorhis, & Co.

To say that the latest edition of the Code is a necessity to every New York lawyer is to say very little, and yet it is difficult to say more. Long use only can test the exact value of Mr. Townshend's annotations, which occupy by far the greater part of the volume before us. He has been the editor of all the editions, and his notes show an industry which is as unusual as it is necessary in the preparation of books of this kind. The present edition, Mr. Townshend says in his preface, contains references to all the reports issued to June, 1870, and includes 40 New York, 54 Barbour, 39 Howard, part 1; 7 Abbott, N.S., 1 Lansing, and some cases from advance sheets of 2 Daly, and 55 Barbour; also references to such of the statutes of 1870 as pertain to practice and pleading; some of these, not having been received in time to fill their appropriate place, have been placed in the appendix.

The fundamental difference between the New York and the Massachusetts system of pleading consists in the abolition under the former of all the forms of action and the substitution of a "plain and concise statement of the facts constituting a cause of action, without unnecessary repetition." As to facility of amendment, there is very little difference; speaking generally, amendments are allowed under either system, whenever they are really needed to advance justice.

Whatever may be the defects in the New York Code of which we have lately been reminded so forcibly, and whether these defects are in the system or in the way it is practically administered, we believe that it is clearly right in giving up the common-law forms of action. If those forms had been based upon a comprehensive survey of the field of rights and duties, so that they embodied in a practical shape a classification of the law, with a form of action to correspond to every substantial duty, the question would be other than it is. But they are in fact so arbitrary in character, and owe their origin to such purely historical causes, that nothing keeps them but our respect for the sources of our jurisprudence. It is very clear that in some cases they are a positive hindrance to sound legal conceptions. Of course it would not be intended to change our rights, by a change in the forms of pleading. Accordingly where the present existing law gives alternative remedies,—say, the specific recovery of a thing or damages,—the plaintiff's election, signified at the common law by the action brought, would be one of the facts to be stated in the case. The fusion of law and equity, which is daily becoming more complete, points to such a system, which, for the rest, need not be less skilfully administered than the old, but would allow less skill to be wasted on immaterial points of form.

Editor's Note

1. A note in the margin of Holmes's copy, at the Library of Congress, indicates that he wrote only the last paragraph of this book notice; the rest was written by Arthur Sedgwick.

6.30

From *American Law Review* 5:534 (1871).

A Treatise on the Rules for the Selection of the Parties to an Action. By A. V. DICEY, Esq., of the Inner Temple, Barrister-at-Law, and Fellow of Trinity College, Oxford. London: William Maxwell & Son. 1870.

The form of this book recalls Stephen on Pleading, and still more Macaulay's Penal Code for India, which it resembles so far as to suggest that the author meant to forward by example the long talked of codification of English law. It is arranged in a series of rules, numbered consecutively up to 118, each expressing a general principle. Each rule is illustrated by concisely stated cases, making its application and extent clear, and is qualified by exceptions arranged and numbered in the form of subordinate rules. Thus: "RULE 54.—An agent who, without having authority, enters into a contract on behalf of a principal, cannot himself be held *on the contract;* but is otherwise liable." Then among other cases: "A. fraudulently represents to T. that he has authority to contract for P. with intent to deceive. A., when he has no authority from P., and knows it, nevertheless makes a contract with T. as having such authority. A., though not having in fact any authority to contract as agent of P. with T., yet does so under the *bona fide* belief that he has authority; *e.g.,* from having received a forged power of attorney. T. can, in the first and second of these cases, sue A. for false representation, and in all of them for a breach of the implied contract, that he has authority to contract as agent of P. *Thomson v. Davenport,* 2 Smith, L.C. 6th ed. 327." . . . "*Exception.* —Where the authority of the agent has without his knowledge expired at the time of his making the contracts." We may question by the by whether this last is not too broadly stated. It is undoubtedly true in the case of the death of the principal, which is said to be a public fact, *Marlett v. Jackman,* 3 Allen, 287, 293; but in what other cases the doctrine will be applied remains to be decided.

We call attention to the form of this work because it is precisely that in which most of our law books fail; and although we are not fully convinced that the method of rules, cases, and exceptions is better than that of continuous exposition with a sound and accurate arrangement, yet Mr. Dicey has applied it so happily that the question becomes at least doubtful.

The principle divisions are 1. Rules common to all Actions. 2. Rules in Actions of Contract. (*a*) Plaintiffs, with chapters containing general rules, and on Principal and Agent, Partners, Corporations, Husband and Wife, Bankrupt and Trustee, Executors and Administrators. (*b*) Defendants, with similar chapters. 3. Rules in Actions for Tort. (*a*) Plaintiffs. (*b*) Defendants. Each of these being subdivided as before. 4. Ejectment. 5. Effect of Errors.

In all of these the reader will find new law, and old law put so that it seems new,— two tests of a clever book. The only difficulty which we have is with the subject. So far as the law has the philosophical consistency which every one now wishes to give it, the parties to an action depend on the questions what is the duty sought to be enforced, to whom is it owed, who owes it? In other words, the law of parties is logically only the corollary of certain rights and duties, and it seems undesirable to separate the one part from the other. This is made very apparent by the book before us, thanks often, no doubt, to the talent of the author. However, such a rule as the following can hardly be distinguished from substantive law. "RULE 63.—An infant cannot be sued on any contract made by him." "*Exception* 1.—Contracts for necessaries." We cannot help saying that useful as books often are which gather under a remedy or class of remedies, such an injunction or action, the rights which it protects, the day for such an arrangement is passed. Forms of procedure come earlier in the history of jurisprudence than rules of conduct, and it is very natural that the latter should as first be classified under the forms through and by means of which they are developed. Later we find the two side by side; but now we want principles as they are related to each other, not according to the accidental differences in the way of enforcing them.

6.31

From *American Law Review* 5:536 (1871).

The Law of Negligence; being the first of a series of Practical Law Tracts. By ROBERT CAMPBELL, M.A., Advocate (Scotch Bar), and of Lincoln's Inn, Barrister at Law, Late Fellow of Trinity Hall, Cambridge. London: Stevens & Haynes. 1871.

This is not likely to have a great sale in this country. For practical purposes it cannot compete with a work giving the American cases, and we should hardly recommend it to a student as a philosophical discussion. In the first place, the subject is open to observation, notwithstanding what we said to the contrary in noticing Mr. Shearman's last edition. A culpable state of mind is an element in most wrongs; and negligence and wilfulness, into which negligence shades away, express the more common of these states. In this point of view the conception is too general to found a classification upon. Then, although the divisions of the civil law may be very well adapted to a system where the same person is to decide facts and law, they are of doubtful use with us. If the question is one of negligence in the modern sense, if negligence must be alleged in the pleadings, we suppose it is wholly for the jury to say whether the party has used such care as a reasonable and prudent man would have used under the circumstances of the particular case whatever they may be. On the other hand, when there is no question for the jury, when negligence is not alleged, but only, for instance, that the defendant kept an animal, knowing its vicious propensities, and allowed it to escape and do mischief; or that defendant broke and entered my close; then all that can be said is that there is a positive rule of law that when facts A., B., and C. concur, and no qualifying fact is shown or presumable, the defendant is liable. It may or may not be true that when the judges made the rule they did so on the ground that certain conduct was clearly negligent. It is certainly not illogical for them to take cognizance of facts so notorious as that prudent men do not do certain things. But by the present form of the rule certain acts or omissions are prohibited irrespective of the state of mind of the party guilty of them. If, then, we confine negligence to the cases when it must be alleged in pleading, it is as much too narrow to found upon as in the other aspect it was too broad. It is an ultimate fact to be found by the jury, and should be left to them equally at large whether the cause of action arises from *depositum* or *commodatum;* whether the subject of a loss be diamonds or coal dust. After all is said, however, negligence although not the proper subject for a treatise in a series intended to exhaust the law, is a legal conception, and it is therefore instructive to trace the relationship of different classes of cases by this test. We should not think this an altogether safe book for a student, but we can promise that maturer lovers of their profession will find it so interesting as to repay their reading, and that the author's knowledge of Roman and Scotch law makes it the fuller and the more suggestive without cumbering the text.

6.32

From *American Law Review* 5:539 (1871).

A Digest of the Decisions of the Federal Courts, from the organization of the Government to the present time. By FREDERICK C. BRIGHTLY, Esq., of the Philadelphia Bar; Author of "The United States Digest;" "A Digest of the Laws of Pennsylvania;" "A Treatise on Equity," etc. Vol. II. Philadelphia: Kay & Brother. 1870.

We do not have to say of this as critics so often do, that a digest can only be tested by experience. The profession already know the character of Mr. Brightly's work and would be prepared to assume without inquiry that this, like the volume to which it is a supplement, is the result of honest labor, that it gathers cases from all quarters, from Wallace's Reports and from those of Washington Territory, from periodicals which every reader knows, and from those which few lawyers have ever opened; that it is marked by the same conciseness and general accuracy of statement. We can say as much as this from practical use of the book. The want of cross references was the greatest defect which we discovered in the first volume, and probably may be found so in this; but one so easily becomes accustomed to the author's arrangement of his matter that he will hardly be long at a loss where to find what he wants.

It should be added that the author, in a very prepossessing preface, vindicates his plan of extracting principles from cases instead of giving an abridgment of the facts with the judgment of the court upon them. We believe that he is wrong; and that just in proportion as a case is new and therefore valuable, no one, not even the judges, can be trusted to state the *ratio decidendi.* We believe that the very essence of a digest, apart from its alphabetical arrangement, is that it should state cases and not principles. But when the other course is deliberately taken, we go no further than to differ, and to be thankful that if generalizing was to be done it should be done so well.

6.33

From *American Law Review* 5:539 (1871).

A Selection of Cases on the Law of Contracts. With References and Citations. By C. C. LANGDELL, Dane Professor of Law in Harvard University. Prepared for use as a text-book in Harvard Law School. Boston: Little, Brown, & Company. 1870. (Part I.)

Mr. Langdell's scheme is to present without comment the series of cases by which an important principle has been developed, arranged in order of time, and after indicating by the heading of the chapter and section the topic to be illustrated, to leave the rest to the student. Even head-notes are wisely omitted, although for the sake of the profession we shall hope for a full index at the end of the volume. The first chapter, for instance, which is on Mutual Consent, contains *inter alia* the line of cases from *Payne v. Cave, Cooke v. Oxley, Adams v. Lindsell* to *Dunlop v. Higgins,* with parallel American decisions, and with valuable discussions drawn from the Scotch reports and from Merlin. Thus the important and difficult question as to the *punc-tum temporis* when parties at a distance, and attempting to contract with each other, become bound, is seen from the time when it was hardly well enough understood to be asked, up to its final answer upon the maturest deliberation, and by the highest tribunals. The chronological arrangement, although it may sometimes add to the labor of a beginner, we have found to be most instructive and interesting. Tracing the growth of a doctrine in this way not only fixes it in the mind, but shows its meaning, extent, and limits as nothing else can. We must mention that we have been struck with the confirmation here afforded to a remark made on the first page of this volume of the *Law Review,* that judges know how to decide a good deal sooner than they know why.

Without going into the contents of the volume in detail, it may be said to have in it the whole law of contracts proper; of contracts, that is, considered as imposing an obligation upon the parties to them. The only criticism that has occurred to us is that the cases on *Forbearance,* in Section 4 of the chapter on Consideration, are collected with an over-scrupulous minuteness. It seems as if the desire to give the whole history of the doctrine had led to putting in some contradictory and unrea-soned determinations which could have been spared. Indeed, one surmises that a skeptical vein in the editor is sometimes answerable for the prominence given to the other side of what is now settled. But very likely he had deeper reasons and is right. At all events we advise every student of the law to buy and study the book. If he does not find that the plan of it is both original and instructive we shall be mistaken.

6.34

From *American Law Review* 5:540 (1871).

Law and Practice in Bankruptcy. The Practice in Bankruptcy, with the Bankrupt Law of the United States as amended, and the rules and forms; together with notes referring to all decisions reported to December 1, 1870, to which the Rules of the District Court of the United States for the Southern District of New York. By OR-LANDO F. BUMP, Register in Bankruptcy. New York: Baker, Voorhis, & Co., 1871. pp. xx. 610.

We do not perceive the excuse for making this book so expensive. It is intended only to be used as a practical manual for a year or two at most, and then to be superseded by later editions or newer digests as it supersedes others now. Take out the forms, the rules, and the act, which may be had for the asking, and we pay our money for the digest, or rather for that part of it which we do not already possess in other forms, and for the treatise on practice; good honest work both of them, but they ought to be sold cheap like other transitory hand-books. Such practical use as we have made of this edition leads us to believe it to be decidedly the best of the works to which the present Bankrupt Act has given rise.

6.35

From *American Law Review* 5:541 (1871).

The Law Magazine and Law Review; or Quarterly Journal of Jurisprudence. September, 1870, to February, 1871. Volume XXX. London: Butterworths. 1871.

The book notices in this number are intelligent, and it contains some interesting articles. One of these is not that entitled "American Legal Notes." We have often wondered why it is that Englishmen allow themselves to write on American law and literature with so little knowledge; but the editors have not bettered matters by their selection of an American contributor. "Early English Codes" restates the general opinion as to the Mirror and Leges Henrici I., which Mr. Finlason so disregards in his notes to Reeves.

"New Books on Roman Law" gives us a glimpse on the present state of the English mind on that subject. The writings of the English civilians do not lead us to anticipate much from the second revival which seems to be going on. The legal historian or philosophical jurist cannot afford to be ignorant of the works of some continental writers; but we have yet to see any evidence that such studies will make better practitioners, which is all that most lawyers aspire to be. In fact we surmise that the civil law is rather talked about than studied even now in England, and it is hardly even talked about here. We think it can well be left to those who will study it notwithstanding its not being included in the regular curriculum.

6.36

From *American Law Review* 5:542 (1871).

Treatise on the Law of Private Corporations Aggregate. By JOSEPH K. ANGELL and SAMUEL AMES. Ninth edition. Revised, corrected, and enlarged. By JOHN LATHROP, of the Boston Bar. Boston: Little, Brown, & Company. 1870.

Mr. Lathrop's reputation as an editor is established. He collects his authorities with fulness and care, and then—rarest of virtues—he cites them in the right places.

But he is so overscrupulous in abstaining from discussion that we can hardly judge of his power in dealing with difficult questions. This is a pleasing contrast to the opposite vice which more prevails, but we could wish he allowed himself greater latitude. While we repeat that we find the cases to have been carefully gathered, we note an occasional omission to show that the editor is human. For instance, *Barwick v. English Joint Stock Bank*, L.R. 2 Ex. 259, ought to be cited as a decision of the Exchequer Chamber almost directly contradicting the *obiter* remarks cited § 387, from *Western Bank of Scotland v. Addie*, L.R., 1 H.L. Sc. 145. So we miss *Bateman v. Mid-Wales Railway Co.*, L.R. 1 C.P. 499, which gives the narrow English rule as to the power of corporations to accept bills; *Baltimore and Ohio R.R. v. Glenn*, 28 Md. 287, on the effect in Maryland of a conveyance made by a corporation in Virginia where it was incorporated; *Gue v. Tide Water Canal Co.* 24 How. 257; *Steward v. Jones*, 40 Mo. 140, against the liability of the franchise to be sold on execution; *Butts v. Wood*, 37 N.Y. 317, where a contract between a corporation and one of the directors made at a meeting of directors where there was a bare quorum including the one interested, was held void; and *Buell v. Buckingham*, 16 Iowa, 284, *contra*.

Over three hundred and fifty cases have been added.

6.37

From *American Law Review* 5:542 (1871).

A Digest of all the reported Cases decided in the Supreme Court of Errors and the Superior Court of the State of Connecticut, and in the United States Courts for the District of Connecticut, down to those contained in Vol. XXXV. Connecticut Reports, and Vol. V. Blatchford's Circuit Court Reports, inclusive. By SIMEON E. BALDWIN, of the New Haven County Bar; Lecturer on Constitutional and Commercial Law in Yale College. Boston: Little, Brown, & Company. 1871.

A digest can to a great extent defy criticism, as about the same number of people will buy it whether it is well or ill done. It is the tool which every workman must have, and which none but workmen care to possess. The features which we most notice in this one are the excellence of the mechanical device by which the key word or words of each statement are double-leaded so as to catch the eye at once; the usual want of sufficient cross references; and as it seems to us the satisfactory character of the digesting. In speaking of Mr. Brightly's new volume we have expressed our conviction that a digest like a head-note should state facts categorically, and give the judgment under a *"Held."* Mr. Baldwin leans to this form of statement, although he often allows himself an introductory "Where," which is superfluous.

6.38

From *American Law Review* 5:543 (1871).

A Treatise on the Statutes of Elizabeth against Fraudulent Conveyances; The Bills of Sale Registration Acts and the Law of Voluntary Dispositions of Property independently of those Statutes; with an Appendix containing the above Acts and the Married

Women's Property Act, 1870; also some unpublished cases (1700–1733) from the Coxe and Melmoth MS. Reports. By HENRY W. MAY, B.A., &c. London: Stevens & Haynes. 1870.

In the preface of this book the author expresses "his surprise that the labors of some far abler pen than his own have not been attracted by a subject so full of interest," and says that he has aimed at attaining originality by working almost entirely from the reports of decided cases. The subject and the work are both very good. The former is well chosen, new, and interesting. The latter has the quality which always distinguishes original research from borrowed labors. There are six parts to the work: the first on the General Operation of the Statute of Elizabeth against Fraudulent Conveyances, and the general distinctions between them; the second on the Rights of Creditors under 13 Eliz. c. 5, this part being subdivided into chapters and very well arranged; the third on the Rights of Purchasers under the 27 Eliz. c. 4; the fourth on What is a Valuable Consideration under the Statutes of Elizabeth; the fifth on Voluntary Dispositions of Property independently of the Statutes of Elizabeth; How validly made, and when liable to be set aside; the sixth on Points of Practice and Costs under the Statutes of Elizabeth. We cannot go at length into the merits of the different parts, but we may refer to the discussion in the fifth of the question of equitable gifts by way of a voluntary declaration of trust, where for the first time the whole matter is laid out in an orderly manner in the light of recent cases. When Spence wrote, the decisions were in a confusion which he did little to clear up, and as we have had occasion to remark, the last editor of Story did not take the chance which offered of being first in the field.

In the third chapter of the fourth part we are not quite sure that the author does not fall into a confusion under the head of *Ex post facto* considerations, p. 296 *et seq.* The principle of *Prodgers v. Langham* that a voluntary settlement may be made valid as against purchasers by a subsequent marriage entered into by the husband on the faith of that provision, seems to come in here properly enough, because the settlement must be taken to have been made with intent to induce the marriage, and therefore the marriage, when it occurs, may be called the consideration of the settlement. But it seems to be overrefining to say that a conveyance by a voluntary grantee to a *bona fide* purchaser for value, retroactively imparts a consideration to the former conveyance. The true ground would seem to be that the title passed, notwithstanding the fraud or want of consideration, which only gave certain persons the election to avoid that title if they saw fit. Before they have avoided it, it passes into the hands of a third person who, as he takes *bona fide* and for value, has an equity equal to theirs, and whose legal title is therefore allowed to prevail.

6.39

From *American Law Review* 5:544 (1871).

The House of Lords Cases on Appeals and Writs of Error, and Claims of Peerage, during the sessions 1858–1864. By CHARLES CLARK, Esq., of the Middle Temple, Barrister-at-Law. By appointment of the House of Lords. Vols. VII. VIII. IX. and X. Boston: Little, Brown, & Company, 1871.

Among the interesting cases in these volumes are *Whicker v. Hume,* vol. 7, p. 124, and the still more important one of *Moorehouse v. Lord,* vol. 10, p. 272, on domicile; the latter a very leading case as modified by *Udny v. Udny,* L.R. 1 H.L. Sc. 441. In vol. 7 we also find *Chasemore v. Richards,* p. 349, on subterranean waters, and *Dolphin v. Robins,* p. 390, one of the series of cases on the effect of Scotch divorces on English marriages. In vol. 8 are *Wing v. Angrave,* denying that among persons whose death is occasioned by one and the same cause, there is any presumption, either of survivorship or that they died at the same time; and *Cox v. Hickman,* the case which changed the complexion of the English law about partnership as to third persons. In vol. 9 is *Brook v. Brook,* p. 193, which held void a marriage between domiciled British subjects within the prohibited degrees, celebrated while they were temporarily in a country whose laws allowed such marriages. *Beamish v. Beamish,* p. 274, follows *The Queen v. Millis,* and holds that a clergyman cannot perform his own marriage ceremony. *Stuart v. Bute,* p. 440, is important on the jurisdiction of chancery over infants, and amusing for a lecture to the Scotch Judges which it contains. *Backhouse v. Bonomi,* p. 503, is one of the great cases on the right of lateral support. In *Lynch v. Knight,* p. 577, a wife, joining her husband for conformity, brought slander for saying that she had been almost seduced by B. before her marriage, etc.; *per quod* her husband put her away from him and she lost his *consortium,* but the action was not maintained. *New Brunswick & Canada R. & L. Co. v. Conybeare,* p. 711, is one of the line of cases on the liability of companies for the fraud of their directors. *Enohin v. Wylie,* vol. 10, p. 1, is very strong in favor of the courts of the domicile of a testator, as against other courts within whose jurisdiction personalty is found. *The Queen v. Saddlers' Company,* p. 404, relates to the power of corporations to make bylaws, and *Di Sora v. Phillipps,* p. 624, to the principles to be applied when contracts made in a foreign country and foreign language come before the Court.

Every one of the decisions we have mentioned will be recognized by our readers as of the very first importance on the subject to which it relates, and there are many others almost equally valuable side by side with them. We are delighted to hear that vol. 11, which came out too late for notice, is to be followed by a reprint of Clark & Finnelly. There could not be a more meritorious enterprise. But we shall hope for substantial notes.

6.40

From *American Law Review* 5:546 (1871).

The Law of Wills: Parts II. and III. Devises, Legacies, and Testamentary Trusts; Their Construction, Discharge, and Mode of Enforcement; The Probate of Wills; The Duties of Executors, Administrators, and other Testamentary Trustees; and the Settlement and Distribution of Estates, with the Law of Trusts. By ISAAC F. REDFIELD, LL.D. Second edition. Boston: Little, Brown, & Company. 1870.

"That portion of the work upon the Law of Trust," the author says, "is so brief, that it is necessarily very incomplete; but it has been prepared with great care, and contains the outline of a complete treatise, so far as not already fully presented in other portions of the work." If this only means that care has been used, and not that Judge Redfield used it, it is probably true, for we have always understood that Mr. Lewin's treatise on that subject was a careful and laborious performance. But when the author continues, "We venture to trust to the same indulgence, etc. . . for its acceptance in this imperfect form, and to hope, etc., etc.; and that, when completed, it may form what is much needed,—a complete American Treatise upon the Law of Trusts;" and when on page 517, § 72*a*, we read, "The American cases profess in the main to follow the English law upon the subject of Trusts, even more implicitly than upon some others. It is for this reason that, in this brief outline of the law on that topic, we have not alluded more to the decisions of the American Courts," we should suppose, did not the known character of the writer make such an interpretation impossible, that he meant to intimate that the labor of the preparation was his. He will thank us for calling attention to the ambiguity, for the care of abridging and paraphrasing Lewin can hardly have been great, and the sections 72*a*–72*d*, 90*a*, and 118*a*–118*i*, in all about seven pages, and the two or three scattering American notes, including a portion of the head-note to *Walker v. Walker,* 9 Wall. 743, on page 544, and the solution of the woman's rights question on page 475, we take to be thrown in for the love of the thing.

Some parts of the second and third volumes which we have examined with care we think better than the first. They contain a great mass of American and English law not wholly accessible elsewhere.

6.41

From *American Law Review* 5:549 (1871).

The American Reports. Containing all Decisions of general interest decided in Courts of Last Resort of the several States, with Notes and References. By Isaac Grant Thompson. Vol. I. Including Cases decided in the Courts of Maryland, Massachusetts, Wisconsin, Iowa, Vermont, Pennsylvania, and New York. Albany: John D. Parsons, Jr., 1871.

This is an attempt to enable American lawyers to possess all the important and valuable cases decided during the year in the courts of last resort throughout the United States, at a comparatively small expense. Is it likely to succeed? Let us see. We are told in the preface that "the volumes of these reports will be issued at intervals of four or six months, thus giving two or three volumes a year." The number of reports from which selections are to be made, is estimated pretty correctly by the editors at about fifty per annum. Seven volumes, and two cases from an eighth, inserted to complete a term, are represented in the book before us. At the same rate it will be doing well to compress thirty of the fifty into three. But this is not the most striking form of the difficulty. The selections here have been made with judgment, but they do not begin to exhaust the cases of general interest. Lay on one side all decisions on points of construction of wills, statutes, and the like, a most important class in modern times, and there are still many omitted which are as deserving of a place as others which are reprinted. *Dingley v. Boston,* 100 Mass. 544, for instance, is an elaborate argument on the right of the legislature to declare the existence of a nuisance, and authorize a city to take the fee of a large tract of land for the purpose of abating it. A collection is not satisfactory which has to leave out a case like that.

The truth is, the publishers are between the horns of a dilemma, either to limit their market by much increasing the frequency of their issues, or else to choose cases arbitrarily to a certain extent, and so to more or less dissatisfy everybody. Some justification is always necessary for printing elsewhere decisions which appear in the regular reports. They may be anticipated in ephemeral publications, they may be arranged for the instruction of the student, as in Mr. Langdell's most valuable book, or those which relate to a particular subject may be gathered for the library of the specialist, as in Mr. Bigelow's forthcoming volume of fire and life insurance cases. But we do not think that this publication makes good its claim for a place.

The work of the editors is not ill done. They have shown judgment as we have said, and the head-notes are fair, although in the Massachusetts cases they are not as good as the originals, and it is hard to look kindly on an attempt to rewrite the careful statements of facts without reference to the original papers.

If the work is continued it is to be hoped that a new series of unauthorized citations of "Amer. R." will not take their place side by side with the detestable "E.L. & Eq." and "E.C.L."

6.42
SUMMARY OF EVENTS
PALMER v. De WITT

From *American Law Review* 5:567 (1871).

COPY BEFORE PUBLICATION.—*Superior Court of the City of New York. Palmer v. De Witt. (Pamphlet. Diossy & Co.)* This was a suit for an injunction to restrain the defendant from printing or publishing a drama called "Play." Before it had ever been acted or published, its author, T. W. Robertson, a British subject, residing in London, sold to the plaintiff the exclusive right of printing, publishing, and performing the same, together with all his rights therein and thereto as the author thereof, throughout the United States. After the plaintiff's purchase, "Play" was publicly performed at the Prince of Wales Theatre in London for a great number of times, with the sanction of the author. The defendant received the words of the comedy, and a description of the arrangement, stage directions, &c., &c., from persons who had seen these public performances in England; and he had printed and sold, and he still openly offered for sale copies of said comedy identical in all respects with the plaintiff's copy. An elaborate opinion was delivered by MONNELL, J., to the effect that the plaintiff, as assignee of the British authors rights in this country, had a right of property at common law which would continue until the work was published. That our copyright acts were only intended to originate a right after publication, and do not affect, but are rather ancillary to the common law ownership of literary compositions before that event. That the only publication contemplated in the copyright laws is a publication in print. That apart from those acts public representations are not such a publication as to destroy the property of the author or his assignee, inasmuch as the whole value of this kind of property lies in the using it for such representations. That as it did not expressly appear that the parties from whom the defendant obtained the comedy had carried it away in their memory only, they could not be presumed to have done so, as the burden was on the defendant to show that he had come by his copy lawfully; (and there was a pretty decided intimation of the opinion of the court, that if the play had been carried away in memory only, it would not better the defendant's case). And finally that it did not matter that there was no notice to the spectators of the London performance not to carry away or use the comedy.

The decision may or may not be right, but the argument drawn from the author's "property" in his composition, is a conclusion *a dicto secundum quid, ad dictum simpliciter,* and is not the first example of the danger of using a word of such flexible meaning in one's premises.

6.43

From *American Law Review* 5:715 (1871).

The Academical Study of the Civil Law. An Inaugural Lecture, delivered at Oxford, February 25, 1871, by JAMES BRYCE, D.C.L., of Lincoln's Inn, Barrister at Law, and Fellow of Oriel College; Regius Professor of Civil Law in the University of Oxford. London and New York: Macmillan & Company. 1871. Pamphlet.

This is an able and well written argument for the study of the Roman law; a statement of the utilities "which connect it with the liberal studies of this place (Oxford), and specially with classical philology, with history, and with ethics; and those which belong rather to the faculty of law, and entitle it to a place in a strictly professional *curriculum.*" With regard to the latter class we do not think that the author's recommendations would be sound for students of the law in this country. The temptation in our practice is rather to content oneself too easily with general principles than to "become absolutely averse to them," which we are told is the tendency of an English practitioner. Nor do we think that it is true that "the characteristic type of excellence, which the profession" in America "has delighted to honor, is the so-called 'case lawyer.'" Our practice is too general and unspecialized for that. The common law begins and ends with the solution of a particular case. To effect that result we believe the best training is found in our moot courts and the offices of older lawyers. It should be said, however, that Mr. Bryce is speaking rather of the advantages of the study to the jurist than to the practitioner. But even here we cannot help surmising that he has in mind the merits of Savigny and Von Vangerow, quite as much as those of the Roman lawyers. We quite agree that it would be well if every student could be made to study law philosophically from the beginning. But we should send him for that purpose to Maine and to Austin, to the history of our own law in Spence's first volume, and the invaluable little book just published by Mr. Stubbs,* and even to text-books which might be named. We should hesitate to send him to Ulpian. That every lawyer who aims at being more than a prac-

---

*Documents illustrative of English History. Clarendon Press Series. Oxford, 1870.

titioner should know, at least, so much of the Roman law as to intelligently estimate its influence on our own, we not only admit but confidently assert; but we think that the knowledge is best acquired after our own is pretty well mastered. Having said so much it is only right to give Mr. Bryce full credit for the candor and force with which he states his opinion, and for a sense of the proportion of things which has been sadly wanting in some English writers who have trod the same paths before him.

6.44

From *American Law Review* 5:717 (1871).

Curiosities of the Law Reporters. By FRANKLIN FISKE HEARD. Boston: Lee & Shepard. New York: Lee, Shepard, & Dillingham. 1871.

There are few more generally amusing subjects for a collection than the *facetiae* of the law, and we can safely say that this little volume will be found entertaining by laymen as well as lawyers. The latter will find in it a good many old friends and some new acquaintances, and will be glad to have them all gathered where they can get at them. But there are plenty more curiosities where these came from, and we shall hope for a second series.

Cunningham's Reports, which have been lately republished, will give the editor this:—

> In the year 1598, Sir Edward Coke, then Attorney-General, married the lady Hatton, according to the book of Common Prayer, but without banns or license; and in a private house. Several great men were there present,—as Lord Burleigh, Lord Chancellor Egerton, &c. They all, by their proctor, submitted to the censure of the Archbishop, who granted them an absolution from the excommunication which they had incurred. The act of absolution set forth, that it was granted by reason of penitence, *and the act seeming to have been done through ignorance of the law. Middleton v. Croft,* pp. 55, 61, of the original edition.

We may also refer him for his private reading to L.R. 1 P. & D. 405, 406, 407. Meanwhile, we thank Mr. Heard for a very pleasant hour.

6.45

From *American Law Review* 5:720 (1871).

Leading and Select American Cases in the Law of Bills of Exchange, Promissory Notes, and Checks; arranged according to subjects, with Notes and References. By ISAAC F. REDFIELD and MELVILLE M. BIGELOW. Boston: Little, Brown, & Company. 1871. 8vo.

"The editors have first endeavored to present the history of commercial paper throughout its usual stages; and then to illustrate such collateral branches of the general subject as are of practical importance." They begin with the form and requisites of negotiable paper, pass in order to the maker's liability, drawer's liability, acceptance, indorsement, holder for value, presentment and demand for payment, payment, proceedings on non-payment, excuses of presentment and notice, actions and evidence; and then finish with a number of matters, such as suretyship, forgery, lost bills and notes, checks, and so forth, which cannot be classed exactly, but of which a knowledge is useful. The cases under each head are numerous, and seem to be well chosen; the notes are short, but show hard work and acuteness. We may refer, for instance, to that which follows *Hortsman v. Henshaw*, p. 59 *et seq.* Mr. Bigelow has already shown himself so honest and useful a writer that he does not need the aid of an eminent name to commend him to the public. Of course it has not been possible to compare this book with the text-writers, and to find out exactly how much of what is contained in Parsons or Byles is not contained here; indeed we should probably be told that this volume was intended to supplement those authors, not to supplant them. Looking at it in this way, there seems to be room for it in the libraries of lawyers who want the important cases on some leading subjects, and who cannot (as who can?) afford the reports.

6.46

From *American Law Review* 5:725 (1871).

Cases decided in the District and Circuit Courts of the United States for the Pennsylvania District; and also a case decided in the District Court of Massachusetts, relative to the employment of British licenses on board of vessels of the United States. Philadelphia: Published by Redwood Fisher, 1813. Reprinted by Bourguin & Welsh, Philadelphia. 1871.

Those who have the ambition so common among our admiralty lawyers of possessing a complete collection of the United States Court reports will have to buy this interesting little pamphlet. The cases arose out of the war of 1812, and we read in them of the nature and effect of a *Foster*, and a *Sawyer* (as the licenses of the British Minister and Admiral were called), and find allusions to the "unpleasant period of Mr. Genet's transactions," which have a pleasant smack of the past. The decisions are rather a matter of curiosity than of law; for the point, that sailing under an enemy's license does not constitute of itself an act of illegality which subjects the property to confiscation, was overruled by the Supreme Court on appeal in some of these very cases. But Judge Peters's reasoning is strong, and he speaks with the tone of one having authority.

6.47

From *American Law Review* 5:742 (1871).[1]

The Journal of Psychological Medicine. For April, 1871. New York.

The current number of this excellent Review contains an interesting article by the editor, Dr. William A. Hammond, on "The medico-legal value of confession as an evidence of guilt." Dr. Hammond objects to the doctrine that confession has any value as evidence of guilt, for, he says: "We know that not very many years ago, thousands of individuals confessed to being witches, and to having intercourse with the devil, and this with the full knowledge that such admissions consigned them to torture and death. Many cases are on record in which persons have confessed to crimes for the purpose of saving the really guilty person from punishment. Many others have voluntarily come forward, in times of great public excitement in regard to some crime, and have apparently courted punishment and death by acknowledging themselves to be the criminals, when very slight investigation has shown that they were liars; and physicians constantly meet with patients not obviously suffering from mental derangement, who confess to having perpetrated offences, which, if really committed, would send them to the prison or the gallows."

The article is mainly occupied with an account of the English case of Constance Kent, who was sentenced to death on her own confession to the murder of her brother, five years after the commission of the act. It is not a fortunate case for Dr. Hammond, as there is no evidence which makes it clear that the confession was not true. Moreover, it is not enough to show that confessions are often false. The only ground on which they could be objected to as evidence, would be that they are false in the great majority of cases, and even so improbable a statement as that would go to their weight, and not to their admissibility, in connection with other facts. But if three-quarters of the confessions made are true, a confession, although uncorroborated, has a corresponding presumption in its favor. We certainly agree with Dr. Hammond, that confession, unsupported by collateral evidence, is not very trustworthy; but the question is one of degree, and depends on the proportion of false to true confessions, as a matter of statistics; and it is to be remembered that men may be hanged, and rightly, on a presumption of fact. For example, all convictions grounded on circumstantial evidence are instances of this. Indeed, in the last resort, all verdicts involve presumptions of facts; as, for example, that men in general speak the truth under oath.

Editor's Note

1. A note in the margin of Holmes's copy, at the Library of Congress, indicates that he wrote only the conclusion of this book notice, beginning "The only ground. . . ." He did not specify his coauthor.

6.48
SUMMARY OF EVENTS: THE KU-KLUX BILL

From *American Law Review* 5:749 (1871).

So much has been said against the constitutionality of this act, and the argument has been put with so much force, notably in some articles in *The Nation*, by one of our ablest writers on such subjects, that we must state in a few words some arguments which may be adduced on the other side; premising, however, that we express no opinion on the policy of the law, or on the general question of its constitutionality. It is of much more importance that the act should be discussed in an impartial and professional spirit, than that any particular conclusion should be reached.

We have in mind particularly the third and fourth sections, which authorize the

President to employ the army and navy, and to suspend the privileges of the writ of *habeas corpus* in certain cases. These sections are as follows:—

SECTION 3. That in all cases where insurrection, domestic violence, unlawful combinations, or conspiracies, in any State, shall so obstruct or hinder the execution of the laws thereof and of the United States as to deprive any portion or class of the people of such State of any of the rights, privileges, or immunities, or protection, named in the Constitution, and secured by this act, aud the constituted authorities of such State shall either be unable to protect, or shall from any cause fail in or refuse protection of the people in such rights, such facts shall be deemed a denial by such State of the equal protection of the laws to which they are entitled under the Constitution of the United States, and in all such cases or whenever any such insurrection, violence, unlawful combination or conspiracy shall oppose or obstruct the laws of the United States, or the due execution thereof, or impede or obstruct the due course of justice under the same, it shall be lawful for the President and it shall be his duty to take such measures, by the employment of the militia or the land and naval forces of the United States, or of either or by other means, as he may deem necessary for the suppression of such insurrection, domestic violence, or combinations; and any person who shall be arrested under the provisions of this and the preceding section shall be delivered to the marshal of the proper district, to be dealt with according to law.

SECTION 4. That whenever in any State or part of a State the unlawful combinations named in the preceding section of this act shall be organized and armed and so numerous and powerful as to be able, by violence, to either overthrow or set at defiance the constituted authorities of such State, and of the United States within such State, or when the constituted authorities are in complicity with, or shall connive at the unlawful purposes of, such powerful and armed combinations; and whenever by reason of either or all of the causes aforesaid, the conviction of such offenders and the preservation of the public safety shall become in such district impracticable, in every such case such combinations shall be deemed a rebellion against the government of the United States; and during the continuance of such rebellion and within the limits of the district which shall be so under the sway thereof, such limits to be prescribed by proclamation, it shall be lawful for the President of the United States, when in his judgment the public safety shall require it, to suspend the privileges of the writ of *habeas corpus,* to the end that such rebellion may be overthrown. *Provided,* That all the provisions of the second section of an act entitled "An act relating to *habeas corpus,* and regulating judicial proceedings in certain cases," approved March third, eighteen hundred and sixty-three, which relate to the discharge of prisoners other than prisoners of war, and to the penalty of refusing to obey the order of the court, shall be in full force so far as the same are applicable to the provisions of this section; *provided,* further, that the President shall first have made proclamation, as now provided by law, commanding such insurgents to disperse; and *provided,* also, that the provisions of this section shall not be in force after the end of the next regular session of Congress.

The third section, it has been assumed, empowers the President to use the army and navy and the militia to suppress "insurrection, domestic violence, unlawful combinations, or conspiracies" against a State, and color is given to the notion by the language of the act itself, perhaps intentionally. Nevertheless, that is not what the act says. The words are "in all cases where insurrection, &c., in any State shall so obstruct, &c., the execution of the laws thereof, *and of the United States,* as to deprive, &c.," it shall be lawful for the President to use the powers granted. It is true the section continues, "and the constituted authorities of such State shall be unable to protect, &c., the people in such rights, such facts shall be deemed a denial by such State of the equal protection of the laws," &c. But the condition precedent to the whole grant of power is an obstruction not only of State, but United States law. It would undoubtedly be argued on the other side that "and" must be read "or." But as the section must stand, if at all, not on the fourteenth amendment, but on the authority to enforce the laws of the United States, and as a law is to be construed so as to be constitutional if possible, should not the act be taken as meaning what it says? Then can it be denied that, when opposition to the United States authority is organized, it is lawful for Congress, instead of addressing itself to enforcing the particular judgments of its courts, to go at once to the root of the matter and extirpate the unlawful organization? Perhaps, on this construction, even the references to the obstructions of State law are not wholly without meaning. They may have been intended to give an impression that the act accomplishes more than it does, but they may have been added as an additional proof or test of the reality and magnitude of the danger.

Much the same reasoning may be applied to the fourth section, for by that, before the combination is to be "deemed a rebellion against the United States," and the privilege of *habeas corpus* may be suspended, it must "be organized and armed, and so numerous and powerful as to be able by violence to either overthrow or set at defiance the constituted authorities of such State, *and of the United States.*"

Were that all there could hardly be a doubt; for we suppose, that it will be admitted that "to be able to overthrow" refers to an ability manifested by overt acts. But the section continues in the alternative thus: "*or* when the constituted authorities (*i.e.,* of the State, we suppose) are in complicity with, or shall connive at, the unlawful purposes of such powerful and armed combinations." At this point one might begin to hesitate, although it might perhaps be argued that the only unlawful purposes in question were, overthrowing or setting at defiance the United States authorities. But it is not left to doubtful conjecture. The next clause is, "*and* whenever by reason of either or all of the causes aforesaid, the conviction of such offenders and the preservation of the public safety shall become impracticable." Conviction where? Surely in those courts for which Congress has power to legislate. Is it going very far to say that when an armed organization sets at defiance the United States authorities, or intends to do so and is abetted by the State officers, and in consequence prevents the United States from convicting offenders and preserving public safety, there exists a state of rebellion?

The second section seems to us more questionable in some of its parts. But the examination of it in detail would take more space than we can give.

6.49
CORRESPONDENCE:
THE RIGHTS OF CHINAMEN

From *American Law Review* 5:780 (1871).

We gladly take the opportunity afforded us by our correspondent, a very intelligent French gentleman, to say a few words on the interesting questions he propounds.[1] It will be observed that the fourteenth amendment is less carefully worded than the Civil Rights Bill. The latter only declared those persons to be citizens who were born within the United States, "and *not subject to any foreign power.*" The amendment was "born within the United States, and *subject to the jurisdiction thereof.*" It of course overrides the earlier enactment, and makes the place of birth alone determine the duties of citizenship. The great weight of modern opinion, and we believe the practice of most nations, is in favor of making parentage and not place the test of nationality by birth. In our days, when citizenship and allegiance are a matter of choice and not of compulsion, if a party is too young to choose, it seems most proper to fix his nationality *pro tempore,* either by the wishes of those having authority over him, or else by what it may be presumed would have been his own wishes, if he had been capable of having any. By such criteria the country of the child would, in general, be that to which the parents acknowledge their allegiance to be due, rather than that in which the child happened to be born. The Civil Rights Bill seems to have had all this in mind, and would not have applied, for instance, to a child born of French or English parents temporarily travelling in America. The fourteenth amendment, though framed *alio intuitu,* would cover that case and most others. For all persons, excepting children of ambassadors, persons born within the lines of an invading army, and a few others, including probably Indians, are "subject to the jurisdiction" of the country within which they are born while they remain upon its territory. The evils of this principle, now made part of the Constitution, would be very great were it still held, that *nemo potest exuere patriam.* For on the one hand, a man might find himself perforce a traitor to one of two warring governments which claimed him, or on the other, a government might find itself unable to refuse protection to its citizens, whom another government was punishing as its own subjects. But they are in great measure done away with by the congressional assertion of the liberty of expatriation. For this, though directed at citizens of other States, applies, we suppose, to our own, and allows them to throw off the duties which are arbitrarily imposed on them, and which are inconsistent with those which they owe to the country of their fathers. Perhaps the worst that can be said is, that it is a pity to incorporate an exploded theory in our organic law.

While this is the law, however, we do not see any ground for denying that Chinese born in this country are as much citizens as negroes.

2. We see no reason to question our correspondent's conclusion, that the naturalization acts do not apply to Chinamen.

3. In the absence of the act disqualifying them as witnesses, the question would be, whether their religious belief disqualified them, a matter which is regulated by statute in most States. In California a man is not disqualified by his religious belief.

4. The effect of the fourteenth amendment on the statute disqualifying China-men we leave to the tribunal before which it has been carried.

Editor's Note

1. Holmes is replying to a long letter asking the status of persons born in China, or born in the United States of parents born in China, under the newly adopted Fourteenth Amendment.

6.50
MISUNDERSTANDINGS OF THE CIVIL LAW

From *American Law Review* 6:37 (1871).

Chancellor Kent, in his Commentaries, after mentioning several cases of incapacity to contract, and showing that imbecility of mind is not always sufficient to set aside an agreement, continues: "Nor is a person born deaf and dumb to be deemed abso-lutely *non compos mentis,* though by some of the ancient authorities he was deemed incompetent to contract. The proposition would seem to be a reasonable one, that every such person was *primâ facie* incompetent, inasmuch as the want of hearing and speech must exceedingly cramp the powers and limit the range of the human mind. But it is well known by numerous and affecting examples, that persons de-prived of the faculty of speech and the sense of hearing possess sharp and strong intellects, susceptible of extensive acquirements in morals and science."[*]

The modern authority cited by the author is *Brower v. Fisher.*[**] In this case the plaintiff had purchased real and personal property of the defendant, who was deaf and dumb from birth, and he had given a bond for the purchase-money, on which the defendant had recovered judgment and taken out execution. The plaintiff filed his bill to stay the execution, on the ground that he was advised that the conveyance to him was void for want of legal capacity in the defendant to contract, and that, if the title should prove defective, he would be without redress against the defendant, who had become intemperate, and was wasting his property. On the petition of the plaintiff, a commission of lunacy was issued, to inquire whether the defendant was *compos mentis* or not. It was found that he was not a lunatic, unless the fact of his having been born deaf and dumb made him so in judgment of law, and that he had conveyed his title to said property for a fair consideration. Thereupon the injunc-tion was dissolved, and the plaintiff paid the judgment with costs. The question now was whether the bill should be dismissed with or without costs. The Chancellor cited Bracton, Fleta, and others, and said: "The bill does not appear to have been filed vexatiously, but rather to obtain, for greater caution, the opinion of the court on a point which has been left quite doubtful in many of the books, and which had never received any discussion here. . . . Perhaps, after all, the presumption, in the first instance, is, that every such person is incompetent. It is a reasonable presumption, in order to insure protection and prevent fraud. . . . A special examination to repel

[*]Vol. 2, p. [453]. Compare Shelford on Lunatics, p. 3.
[**]4 Johns. Ch. 441, 443.

the inference of mental imbecility seems always to have been required; and this presumption was all that was intended by the civil law, according to the construction of the ecclesiastical courts. . . . I am satisfied that the plaintiff is justly to be exempted from the charge of a groundless and vexatious inquiry; and the course is not to punish the prosecutor of a charge of lunacy with costs, if the prosecution has been conducted in good faith, and upon probable grounds. I shall therefore dismiss the bill without costs." It was held, in short, that the inquiry whether one born deaf and dumb was not a lunatic was so proper to be directed that he who set it in motion should not be required to pay the cost of conducting it. If a man not versed in the law were told that, as a matter of fact, there was a strong presumption that persons who had been deaf and dumb from birth were idiots, he would probably be a good deal astonished, and say that that had not been his experience. Indeed, the statement is so contrary to common observation that we should find it hard to accept it as law, by whatever authorities repeated. There can be no policy in making such a presumption if it is not sustained by the facts; but, on the contrary, it may be the source of such great injustice, that an investigation into the sources of this supposed rule will have more than an antiquarian interest.* The fact is, that the above passages show in a curious way the illicit relationship of the common and civil law, and would never have been written, had not texts of the latter been adopted into the former, and at first misunderstood and later wholly perverted from their meaning and from reason. In the language of the Institutes of Justinian, 3, 20, 7, repeating Gaii Inst. 3, 105, *mutum neque stipulari neque promittere posse palam est, quod et in surdo receptum est.* The usual and one of the earliest forms of contract known to the Roman law, after the primitive *nexum,* was made by stipulation and promise; that is, by an oral interrogation in certain formal words by the promisee (*stipulator*) and an equally formal answer by the promisor (*promissor*). The oral pronunciation of these formulae was as much of the essence of that kind of contract as a seal is of the essence of a deed, which is our archaic form. We now regard a consideration and a mutual understanding, no matter how arrived at, as the essential in ordinary cases; but both of these might have existed without creating an obligation, at least of this sort, just as they might have in Glanville's time without imposing any liability outside of the ecclesiastical courts. The form was every thing. It therefore stood to reason that one who could not pronounce the words could not make the contract; and it was about equally clear that one who could not hear the question could not answer it, or, if he were the *stipulator,* could not accept an answer which he did not understand. Gaius says: *Mutum nihil pertinere ad obligationem verborum, natura manifestum est. Sed et de surdo idem dicitur; quia etiam si loqui possit, sive promittit, verba stipulantis exaudire debet; sive stipuletur, debet exaudire verba promittentis: unde apparet non de eo nos loqui qui tardius exaudit, sed qui omnino non exaudit.**

Another text of the Institutes (2, 12, 3) is explained in a similar way: *Item surdus et mutus non semper testamentum facere possunt,* &c. This, as Vinnius remarks, citing

---

*It is proper to say that in *Harrod v. Harrod,* 1 K. & J. 4, 9, Wood, V.C., without referring to the ancient authorities, lays it down that "there is no exception to the rule" that the presumption is always in favor of sanity, "in the case of a deaf and dumb person."

**D. 44, 7, 1, § 14 *et seq.*

Pauli Sent. (*lib.* 3, *sent.* 4), was because a dumb person could not call upon the witnesses nor a deaf person hear them *testimonium perhibentes.*

Bracton, as is well known, copied largely from the civilians, and the passage first cited from the Institutes is to be found in his text very little changed.* But he shows that he either did not know or disregarded the strictly technical meaning of *stipulari* and *promittere* in the original, by adding, *nisi sit qui dicat quod hoc facere possunt per nutus vel per scripturam* (unless it should be suggested that they can do this by nods or writing). On page 12 also, after throwing out that dumb persons *possunt consentire secundum quosdam per signa et nutum,* he adds, *generaliter tenendum est quod mutus donationem facere non potest quia donationi consentire non potest sicut nec furiosus,* &c., using the word *consentire* to signify "express assent," a source of subsequent error. Again, on page 421, we find the beginning of another misapprehension in a distinction then taken between those deaf and dumb *naturaliter, hoc est a nativitate,* and those who have become so by accident. This may have been suggested by the word *natura* in the passage cited above from Gaius.

After Bracton came Fleta, who copied him as Bracton had copied Azo. Fleta says:** *Competit autem exceptio tenenti propter defectum naturae petentis, vel si naturaliter a nativitate surdus fuerit aut mutus, tales enim adquirere non poterunt nec alienare, quia non consentire, quod non est de tarde mutis vel surdis,* &c. Here *consentire* seems to be used in a broader sense than by Bracton, and to mean that persons born deaf or dumb are incapable of the consenting mind, a further aberration from the original doctrine. At the same time, the first proviso of the Latin law, that the disqualification does not attach to one who is only slow of hearing (*qui tardius exaudit*), has assumed the form of an antithesis suggested by the misplaced acuteness of Bracton, between those *born* deaf or dumb and those who have become so later in life; for so we suppose we are to translate *tarde mutis.**** Of course, from the Latin point of view, it did not matter how a man became unable to utter or hear the words of the formulae; the only question was whether he could do so or not.

Britton briefly alludes to "those who neither know how nor have the ability (*ne sevent ne ne poent*) to consent, as the deaf and the mad, and mere idiots."****

That this is based upon the earlier treatises is clear enough without the aid of Selden's observation "that the name of Henry de Bracton or Breton, in the book commonly called Britton and Breton, is to be understood as of that of the primary author of the work, though enlarged with some matters of a later date than his time."*****

Some two centuries later the ingenious Perkins, in his Profitable Book, presented further improvements upon the ancients; and, although he got farther away from them, he got nearer to the facts of life by doing so. He says: "A man that is born dumb and deaf may make a gift, if he have understanding; but it is hard that such

*L. 3, f. 100; cf. L. 5, c. 18, f. 415, and c. 20, f. 421.

**L. 6, c. 40, § 2; cf. L. 3, c. 3, § 10. Bracton (*De Exceptionibus*), f. 421.

***The English authors stick blindly to the catchwords of the ancient texts, but only to be led astray by them.

****L. 1, c. 29, f. 62; cf. L. 6, c. 5, f. 279.

*****Diss. ad Fletam, § 3, p. 457; Kelham's Tr. p. 16. The case in Y.B. 2 H. 4, 8, Bro. Eschete, 4, does not call for notice.

a person should have understanding. For a man ought to have his perfect under-standing by his hearing, yet divers persons have understanding by their sight, &c. And a man born dumb and blind may have understanding. But a man that is born blind, deaf, and dumb can have no understanding; so that he cannot make a gift or a grant."* Lord Coke follows Perkins in laying down that a man deaf, dumb, *and* blind from his nativity is disabled to enfeoff, &c. But he adds that "a man deaf dumb *or* blind, so that he hath understanding and sound memory, albeit he express his intention by signs, . . . may enfeoff,"** &c.

The same idea, together with Fleta's antithesis, is repeated about this time by Wakering, reader of Lincoln's Inn: "A man deaf and dumb *a nativitate* is *non compos,* but otherwise if *by accident.* But deaf, dumb, and blind, by accident, is *non compos.*"*** We have only one other citation to add to the foregoing. Lord Hale puts the crimi-nal liability of the deaf and dumb in such a moderate and reasonable way, that one is inclined not to follow too closely the steps by which he got to his result:—

"A man that is *surdus et mutus a nativitate* is in presumption of law an idiot, and the rather, because he hath no possibility to understand what is forbidden by law to be done, or under what penalties: but if it can appear, that he hath the use of understanding, which many of that condition discover by signs to a very great meas-ure, then he may be tried, and suffer judgment and execution, though great cau-tion is to be used therein."****

We doubt the wisdom of making the civil law part of the course to be studied by beginners who intend to practise at a common-law bar. There is ground for suspi-cion that it tends to encourage a dangerous reliance on what Mr. Choate would have called glittering generalities, and a distaste for the exhaustive analysis of a particular case, with which the common law begins and ends. But does not the above instance show that it would be well for older lawyers to give it some thought in their leisure hours? Nobody doubts, nowadays, that a large part at least of the common law is founded on that of Rome. Bracton made no secret of what he owed to it. But Coke, when he used Bracton, did not go behind his text; and Coke is the modern starting-point. The consequence must be that in other cases, as in this, doctrines get swerved from their true meaning and extent, because we do not re-member their history and origin. A rule of law that has been gradually developed can only be understood by knowing the course of its development; and that is more or less known by good lawyers, if the rule took its rise in England. So far as our jurisprudence reaches back to an earlier date, there are the same reasons for trac-ing it to its source. Again, not only would it be hard to name any one who has thrown new light on such general problems of jurisprudence as the arrangement of the law, who has not known something of the labors of the civilians; but we shall try to show that an ignorant misunderstanding of the Roman classification has led to confusion in our own in another instance beside those already pointed out by Austin and others.

The reasons for making bailment a title in our law are not obvious, if we consider

*Pl. 25.
**Co. Lit. 42*b.*
***Vin. Abr. Deaf, Dumb, and Blind, pl. 8; Dyer, 56*a,* pl. 12, note.
****1 P.C. 34.

the matter on principle. If we trace the history of the classification under that head, we shall perhaps be convinced that it consists of fragments of the Roman structure, which have been built into the body of the common law in such a place and manner as to entirely miss the ends which they originally answered, while at the same time they are equally ill adapted to any new purpose.

The Roman law, like our own, did not treat every agreement (*pactum*) as binding, but required it to be clothed with one of several solemnities. Just as we should say that a writing under seal or a consideration is necessary to make a promise legally binding, the civil law said that an obligation *ex contractu* was made effectual, *aut re aut verbis aut litteris aut consensu* (Inst. III. 13, 2), or as Bracton (16*b*) puts it, with modern additions which may be disregarded,

> Re, verbis, scripto, consensu, traditione,
> Junctura, vestes sumere pacta solent.

The obligation contracted *verbis* was the *stipulation* already mentioned, in which the formal question and answer were the operative fact creating the duty.

An obligation was contracted *litteris* by the entry of a debt in the creditor's ledger with the assent of the debtor, or in some cases on by an acknowledgment of indebtedness signed by him. This entry, like a bond with us, was said not to be merely evidence of the obligation, but to itself impose it.[*]

Our present concern, however, is with obligations contracted *re*. We may say in a general way that these embraced the duties properly generated by one person's having lawfully acquired the possession of a thing belonging to another. As this does not usually happen except by consent of the parties, such obligations may be treated in most cases as arising *ex contractu;* and although this is not true of all, yet, as the same form of action applied indifferently, it was not necessary to distinguish between them. In all of them the delivery or possession of a specific thing was the fact of legal significance, and the obligation was said to arise from the thing itself. This does not at all imply the modern doctrine of consideration, even in those cases where a contract could properly be said to exist. That doctrine had no more place in the civil law than it had in our own in Glanville's time, or than it has now in the law of instruments under seal. What it did signify, we take it, was this: At the time the Roman treatises were written, in which the various obligations were classified, a stipulation was in general the proper and formal method of contracting; but there were certain well-marked cases of frequent recurrence which were not governed by the same rule. Without investigating the historical origin or date of the exceptions, we can see that people in any society would be very apt to borrow money, corn, or implements of each other, or, on the other hand, to leave similar articles in one another's charge without much thought of formal ceremony. And it is not surprising that in such simple transactions, and under a mature system of law, the delivery of a thing was held sufficient to create an obligation in respect of that thing. It would be very unjust to allow the party to whom it was delivered to refuse to return it, or its equivalent, because some formality had been omitted. The law, therefore, gave certain actions to compel him to do so. But this was about the extent of the

---

[*]Gaius, 3, 131, *et seq.*

obligation which arose *re,* and which was enforced by the actions *depositi, commodati, pigneratitia,* and the rest. The possession of a thing owned by another, to which the owner had never parted with his title, imposed a duty to return it or to show a good excuse for not doing so, as that it had been destroyed under circumstances for which the party in possession was not responsible. The receipt of a thing which the bailor was expected to use up imposed a duty to return another thing of the same kind. So far as this, delivery took the place of stipulation, and no farther. So far as this, indeed, the duty might be said to exist independent of contract. If it had been wished to modify the legal liability, or to add new terms or a collateral undertaking to the obligation, we understand that generally a stipulation would have been as necessary as if nothing had been delivered.*

It will now be seen that the reason why the civil law put *depositum, commodatum,* and *pignus* into one group, was that in each of those cases the obligation discussed derived its legal force from the fact of delivery or possession, instead of the stipulation which was the usual form.**

For the same reason there was placed side by side with them a fourth transaction, which no definition of bailments can be made to include. We mean of course *mutuum.* Here the thing delivered was not to be returned *in specie,* but only *in genere.* The bargain contemplated that the title in the thing delivered should pass to the party receiving it, and only held him to a return of other articles of the same sort, generally without, but sometimes with, interest. These were articles dealt with by weight, number, or measure, including not only such matters as wine and oil and corn, when the *mutuum* might be called by us a sale (L.R. 3 P.C. 101), but also the important commodity of money. An ordinary loan, without security or writing, would have created an obligation *ex mutui datione;* and it may be mentioned that even if afterwards the borrower assented to an entry in the lender's books, still, as a rule, the writing was only evidence, like a memorandum under the Statute of Frauds, and did not substitute an obligation *litteris* by novation for the former one contracted *re.**** On the one side, bailments do not include this most considerable subdivision; on the other, however, the industry of Lord Holt added two, *locatio* and *mandatum,* which belonged to a different class of obligations in the civil law. His original, Bracont, had followed the civilians in this instance; but Lord Holt, when he caught at the general notion of obligations imposed *re* for aid in deciding the great case of *Coggs v. Bernard,* and thought to embody the same principles in his discourse on bailments, found that neither of the species enumerated under the genus in question included his case. But as he probably did not understand the technical reasons which fixed the limits of the group, and as he found allusions to other contracts which must, or at least might, involve a delivery, and one of which answered his needs, he completed his classification with them. The case before him

---

*See, however, D. 17, 1, 39.

**We are aware that the obligation contracted *re* has been considered an earlier modification of the primitive transaction *nexum* than the stipulation; and we do not undertake to give reasons for thinking otherwise. But it is clear that the stipulation was the general form at the time when the institutes of Roman law were written; and therefore, taking the law as it was then, the other obligations were properly grouped together as an exception to the general rule, whichever came first in point of time.

***Gaius, 3, 131.

came in very well under *mandatum,* so he added that; and as it was said to be a contract *bonae fidei,* he laid it down that the consideration of the defendant's undertaking was being "trusted" with the plaintiff's goods.* The list was then finished with *locatio,* which was found in the next line to mandate.

Many of our readers are aware that in the Latin system *mandatum* meant gratuitous agency, not gratuitous bailment, and that the ground of distinguishing it from other binding contracts was not the absence of consideration, but that it was allowed to be effected without either stipulation or delivery.[1] There were four contracts *quae consensu fiunt* which were recognized and enforced by the later law,—sale, letting and hiring, partnership, and mandate,—and these were grouped together on the ground that in them the obligation arose neither *stipulatu* nor *re,* but that it was enough that the minds of the parties had met.** Gaius lays it down that no form of words or writing is necessary; and we might infer, *a fortiori,* that delivery was not necessary in those cases where there was any thing to be delivered, even if Justinian had not added that *nec dari quidquam necesse est.****

It must be admitted that a classification which has grown up in the way we have described has a certain presumption against it. We do not propose to elaborately consider what may be said about it on general principles; but we may ask, what is the specific difference on which the classification is based? The ground cannot be that the *consideration* is the delivery of a chattel; for if there is a consideration for simple contracts, it does not matter what it is. Besides, it has been shown there are many cases of such consideration which, although they would have imposed an obligation *re,* do not constitute bailment; for example, a common loan of money, or the delivery of grain for use upon a promise to return an equal amount of the same quality. Again, there is not any philosophical propriety in making a class out of all contracts, irrespective of their consideration, which relate to a chattel belonging to the contractee, but in the possession of the contractor. Is a tailor's undertaking to mend my coat enlarged or diminished according to whether I send the coat to his shop, or he is to do the work at my house as one of my household? The classification for which most could be said would follow the general idea of the obligations *re* rightly understood, and would include all duties generated by the mere receipt or possession of another man's chattel. But this would not be bailment, for a breach of such duties cannot always be remedied by an action *ex contractu.* The difference was unimportant in the civil law which gave the *actio depositi* equally, whether the defendant had received an article willingly or by accident, whether he had voluntarily taken charge of it, or it had been left upon his hands by a shipwreck; and perhaps Mr. Joshua Williams had a leaning in the same direction when he put bailment and trover together as the title of one of his chapters. But bailment, as commonly understood, is a subdivision of the title contract. If the title should be enlarged as suggested, however, we should still feel some doubts of its propriety. Does not the duty of the possessor to return the thing to the owner

---

*We think it will appear from the whole passage in Lord Holt's judgment that it was the trust, not the delivery, which was regarded as the consideration; and there is at least color for attributing the origin of this idea to the words *bonae fidei.*

**Gaius, 3, 135, 136, *et seq.*

***Inst. 3, 22 (23, § 1 in some ed.)

seem to be only one aspect of the general right of the owner to the possession of his property, and to belong side by side with the duty not to take it away from him? And is the liability for its injury or destruction any thing more than a branch of the general liability of all men for negligent damage to the property of another? So, again, are the duties and responsibilities of the bailor peculiar to cases of bailment?[*] If bailment should be confined to liabilities *ex contractu* arising from the mere possession of the thing, the classification would be open to one of the most serious objections possible in our day,—that of sacrificing the character and true origin of the duty to the form of the remedy, besides the more general difficulties just stated. For these liabilities ought in most instances to be enforced by an action of tort if there were no contract in the case. The heads of the civil law which have been so arbitrarily brought together, have been kept, we suppose, because they contain the civil law rules as to degrees of negligence. But, apart from the prevailing doubts whether those rules are applicable to our system, it is to be remembered that the Roman law did not confine them to cases of bailment, and no more could ours. Different writers have tried to resolve the doubts which induced Lord Holt to resort to the doctrine of *mandatum* in *Coggs v. Bernard,* in two different ways. The first is that the action was case for a tort, for negligently staving the plaintiff's cask and spilling his brandy while carrying it, and that the argument arose on a motion in arrest of judgment after verdict for the plaintiff. If a man negligently staves my cask to my damage, it certainly would seem that he is guilty of a breach of his duty to me, although no special relation subsists between us, and that I ought to recover, irrespective of contract. It is hard to see why possession, either under or without a contract, if the contract does not expressly refer to the point, should exonerate the defendant from a duty he would have owed had he merely passed my goods in the street. If the modern English cases throw doubt on this, we venture to think them wrong; but we pass to the views of those who consider the action to have been a somewhat anomalous form of assumpsit. It has been said that there was sufficient consideration for the promise laid. Carrying the cask would have been called a gratuitous service by the civilians, as it would be by laymen, because they did not have the technical doctrine of consideration, and because the defendant had no benift or reward. But the delivery of the cask might have sufficed for a consideration under our system, as a detriment to the plaintiff. It is true that, looking forward to the time when the whole business is over, if all ends as I expect, the delivery will have redounded to my advantage; but that is not the question. The question is whether I have suffered no detriment at the moment when the alleged consideration is executed, by putting my goods out of my possession, and into that of another. It cannot be denied that I have. The objection to this view, which we cannot easily get over, is that it is highly improbable that the detriment in question was contemplated by the promisor as the inducement of his promise, or as any thing more than a necessary condition precedent to his performance of it; and we do not see how it can be taken to have been the consideratu, without an averment that it was. The declaration did not, in fact, allege any consideration; and Lord Holt, as

---

[*] *Blakemore v. Bristol & E.R. Co.,* 8 E. & B. 1035; *George v. Skivington,* L.R. 5 Ex. 1; *Francis v. Cockrell,* L.R. 5 Q.B. 501, 515.

we have seen, alludes [*] to the *trust,* not to the *delivery,* as making the promise binding. It may at times be a matter of some nicety to distinguish between a detriment precedent and a consideration; but it must be admitted that the seeming tendency of the cases is to construe any such detriment as sufficient, when possible, and to discourage refined inquiries upon the point. Lord Holt's notion** that Bernard would not have been liable for nonfeasance (although after delivery, as we understand the opinion), may have been suggested either by the Roman rule that a mandatary could renounce the mandate *re integra,* but not afterward, unless excused by illness, &c., or by the early history of the action of assumpsit, as a branch of the action on the case. The former reason is unsound, as inconsistent with our theory of contracts, apart from other objections. If there was a sufficient consideration for any part of the contract, there was for the whole of it, and one part was as binding as another. The other point is more interesting. The real difficulty which was felt in the earliest cases in the year-books, as we read them, was not on any question of consideration, for that doctrine was very properly not deemed applicable, but how an action of *trespass* on the case, *i.e.,* an action for a tort analogous to a trespass, but wanting some of its formal elements, could be brought for a nonfeasance. This difficulty was as great when there was a consideration as when there was none. The earliest examples suggested by the judges of actions on the case arising out of a contractual relation are those in which, as in *Coggs v. Bernard,* the agreement concerned property, and the defendant, while performing his agreement, damages the property. The contract at once sinks out of sight, and the action is case for a tort, as it would have been had no agreement been made. The next step, logically speaking, in the enlargement of the jurisdiction of the court, was to hold the defendant liable for a tort, when he merely let in a natural source of damage by his omission or nonfeasance. This was clearly right in cases where the unperformed duty was not imposed by contract, and the same was thought to be true, still independent of consideration, when the damage was caused by the defendant not keeping his promise. Thus it is put as a tort if one agrees to cover my house within a certain time, and does not, so that for want of the covering the roof of the house is rotted by the rain. After it had been recognized that a nonfeasance might be a tort, the doubt was introduced whether the traverse should be on the undertaking or the negligence, where both are alleged; and when the issue *non assumpsit* was settled as the proper one in such cases, it is no wonder that the notion of a tort as the gist of the action became enfeebled and disappeared, that of contract taking its place, and introducing the averment of consideration into the declaration. The declaration, however, in *Coggs v. Bernard* more resembled that in Y.B. 19 H. VI. 49*** than the then well-settled form of assumpsit; it alleged an undertaking rather by way of inducement, and then set forth a negligent injury to property, and the issue was *not guilty.* This ancient mode of declaring evidently revived in Lord Holt's mind the

---

* *Bainbridge v. Firmstone,* 8 Ad. & El. 743. [There is no footnote indicator for this note in the original.]

** See also 2 Kent, 570 *et seq.*

*** Where we see assumpsit just beginning to distinguish itself from case. It was alleged that defendant *undertook* to cure plaintiff's horse, but applied medicine so *negligently* that the horse died. A traverse of the assumpsit was held good on the ground that the negligence might have been a mere nonfeasance. Consideration was neither alleged nor spoken of.

doubt which had preceded the earlier cases of assumpsit, and which has just been explained. "Assumpsit," he says, "in such a case as this signifies an actual entry upon the thing; . . . and if a man will do that, and miscarries in the performance of his trust, an action will lie against him for that, though nobody could have compelled him to do the thing." Compare with this the language in 11 H. IV. 33, which was case for not building a house within an agreed time. It was objected that the action sounded in covenant, without showing a specialty. To this Norton replies, "Sir, if he had made my house ill, and had thrown my timber into confusion, I should have an action on my case well enough without deed;" but Thirning, Chief Justice of the Common Pleas, answers the case put by saying, "I grant well that you should in your case, because he shall answer to the tort which he has committed, *quia negligenter fecit;* but when a man makes a covenant, and will not perform any part of such covenant, how shall you have your action against him without speciality?" If this view had prevailed, the action of assumpsit would never have grown out of the action on the case, for it would have been stifled in the beginning by the suggestion that miscarriage in performing a promise might be a tort, but that a failure to perform it could not be. That suggestion, as we have seen, was yielded to at first, but had ceased to prevail long before Lord Holt's time, and his remark, which would have applied with equal force to any action of assumpsit for nonfeasance, was contradicted by the practise of at least a century.

Editor's Note

1. Marginal note in Holmes's copy (OWH Papers, Paige Box 18, Item 4), opposite "*mandatum* meant gratuitous agency . . . ": Wrong. The mandatary acted in his own name. ?

6.51

From *American Law Review* 6:134 (1871).

The Science of Legal Judgment. A Treatise designed to show the Materials whereof, and the Process by which, Courts construct their Judgments; and adapted to practical and general Use in the Discussion and Determination of Questions of Law. By JAMES RAM, of the Inner Temple, Barrister-at-Law. With extensive Additions and Annotations, by JOHN TOWNSHEND, of the New York Bar. New York: Baker, Voorhis & Co. 1871.

A treatise on the sources of the law which shall strike half way between the somewhat latitudinary theorizing of Savigny and the too narrow exclusiveness of Austin, will form a chapter of jurisprudence which is not yet written, and which it is worthy of the ambition of an aspiring mind to write. Mr. Ram flew lower, and was content to pick up the fragments let fall here and there by the judges. His book, however, is not without its value, for some of the theories which it belongs to jurisprudence to unfold must be more or less expressly taken for granted, and acted upon in the body of the law. In fact, such questions as what constitutes possession, what is the meaning of property or of status, or what is the relation of custom to law, have not often been considered by common lawyers, until lately, apart from their bearing on a special case. It is true that broad and general views are not likely to be reached in this way, but we sometimes find a practical wisdom and soundness in particular conclusions not always shown by the German professors, attained by men to whose general notions they would show but little deference. Savigny, if we remember rightly, thinks that a custom may repeal a statute.

We should say that the volume before us would be instructive to those who are already instructed, and entertaining to all. The author was neither unlearned, nor without ideas, and certainly wrote a very readable book. The American editor makes large interpolations in the text, which one always resents a little, as destroying the proportions, and, to a certain degree, the identity of an original work. We notice, too, signs of haste in the editing, and suspect some of the less obvious citations to have been got at second-hand. Still, the additions are also quite readable, and we find throughout the whole contents much valuable matter not elsewhere collected.

We refer the reader to the chapters on precedents, distinguishing a present case from a former case, deciding on particular circumstances, and deciding new cases (c. 14–17), for a good deal of most interesting and instructive judicial discourse. On page 324 the editor makes merry over a Wisconsin judge for thinking this syllogism correctly framed, although false in fact: "A felony is an offence punishable by imprisonment in the state prison; but the crime of adultery is punishable by imprisonment in the state prison; therefore, adultery is felony." The following is offered as parallel: "Vegetables grow; animals grow; therefore, animals are vegetables."

We back the judge, although his major premise is obscurely expressed. The first proposition is a definition, not the subsumption of a species under a genus; Chief Justice Marshall says, "A contract is an agreement in which a party undertakes to do, or not to do a particular thing." The meaning is not that "a felony is (a case of) an offence," &c., but "is (defined as) an offence," &c.

6.52

From *American Law Review* 6:137 (1871).

Law and Practice in Bankruptcy. The Practice in Bankruptcy, with the Bankrupt Law of the United States as amended, and the Rules and Forms; together with Notes referring to all decisions reported to July 1, 1871, to which is added the Rules of Practice for the Courts of Equity of the United States. By ORLANDO F. BUMP, Register in Bankruptcy. Fourth Edition. New York: Baker, Voorhis & Co. 1871. 8vo.

Already a fourth edition supersedes that which was noticed in our last number but one, and illustrates the impropriety of making works which are necessarily so short-lived, and of which so large a part can be had for nothing, so expensive. We are glad to see that the bankruptcy rules of a particular district are now omitted. They are a kind of padding to which too many authors resort. In place of them the rules of practice for the courts of equity of the United States are introduced. These take up more room, and account for fourteen of the fifty-four pages which are added. The preliminary treatise does not seem to be much changed. The book has gained in value by thirty-five pages of new matter in the notes of decisions. The digesting seems to be done with care, and the cases are inserted interstitially, where they belong. In this, as in his other works, Mr. Bump shows himself very accurate and painstaking; and we retain the impression that it is the best of the books on the Bankrupt Law.

6.53

From *American Law Review* 6:140 (1871).

A Treatise on the Constitutional Limitations which rest upon the legislative power of the States of the American Union. By THOMAS M. COOLEY, one of the Justices of the Supreme Court of Michigan, and Jay Professor of Law in the University of Michigan. Second Edition, with considerable additions, giving the results of the recent cases. Boston: Little, Brown, & Co. 1871. 8vo.

We have recently had an illustration of the general interest of state constitutional law, in the discussion which has agitated North Carolina. A constitution prescribes certain rules as to the manner of amending it; can it be amended without the required preliminaries? We must suppose the question to be argued before a court established under the old constitution, for the obvious reason that the new instrument could hardly be effectively and peaceably assailed except from a *point d'appui* outside of it. On the one side it would be said, perhaps conclusively, that the people of the state are *quoad hoc* sovereign, and that the sovereign power is incapable of limitation; that, therefore, any expression of the will of the majority must be obeyed in spite of the trammels which a previous majority has attempted to impose; just as the power of a legislature cannot in general be limited by the act of its predecessor. On the other hand it might be replied, there is not the same difficulty in discerning an authentic expression of the will of the legislature for the time being, that there is in attributing a popular act to the people in its sovereign capacity. We are hampered in the latter case by tradition if not by law. Suppose the women, taking advantage of the majority which they are said to have in Massachusetts, should call a convention, and enact a new constitution by a clear majority of adults, but against the will of nearly every man in the Commonwealth: would the men obey it, or the courts regard it? Would the English courts regard the will of a majority of the male inhabitants of Great Britain expressed outside of Parliament? It is true that if the will of the majority is unmistakable, and the majority is strong enough to have a clear power to enforce its will, and intends to do so, the courts must yield, as must everybody else, because the foundation of sovereignty is power, real or supposed. But so long as there is a reasonable doubt of that power and intent, and the officers holding appointments under the old instrument refuse to yield, the question is in substance the question of recognition, which so often perplexes foreign governments. Where the sovereign power resides at any time, and what is the sovereign will, are questions of fact. But the old constitution is an admitted expression of the sovereign will, and that assures us that no other is authentic which does not come through certain channels. The courts may properly abide by that until they see that the new manifestation is not only unmistakable, but irresistible.

Judge Cooley does not discuss this question, although by comparing p. [34], n.

2, and p. [598], we are led to suppose that he holds the opinion towards which we incline.

On p. [74] *et seq.*, he has some good remarks on the distinction between directory and mandatory laws. After very justly observing that courts have sometimes, in their anxiety to sustain the proceedings of careless or incompetent officers, gone very far in substituting a judicial view of what was essential for that declared by the legislature, he adds: "But the courts tread upon very dangerous ground when they venture to apply the rules which distinguish directory and mandatory statutes to the provisions of a constitution." We would call attention to the whole section in which this opinion is justified for its good law and good sense. When we consider the unparalleled powers conferred on the judiciary in America, and as it sometimes seems to us the diminution of the sense of responsibility on the part of the judges in disregarding the legislative will, and if we take into account the questionable nature of the distinction referred to, a few words of caution seem very proper.

Since taking part in the decision of the *People v. Salem,* and delivering the able opinion printed in our last volume, we may presume the author to have arrived at a pretty settled conviction that towns cannot be authorized to lay and collect taxes for the purpose of subscribing to the stock of railroad companies or otherwise aiding them with money. We notice, however, that this does not blind him to the state of the authorities, and that he hardly refers to his own distinguished part in the discussion. Indeed, we may almost reproach the author for over-modesty, and for not giving the case of *People v. Salem* the prominence it deserves. Another interesting topic on which we find an instructive chapter is the police power. We suppose this phrase was invented to cover certain acts of the legislature which are seen to be unconstitutional, but which are believed to be necessary; or as Judge Christiancy puts it, powers of which "the framers of the Constitution could not, as men of ordinary prudence and foresight, have intended to prohibit the exercise in the particular case, notwithstanding the language of the prohibition would otherwise include it." We do not know in what other book the subject is so well discussed.

The only criticism which we feel at all inclined to make,—and we make this with hesitation,—is on the absence of historical explanation of the famous "except by the judgment of his peers or the law of the land." Mr. Hallam says: "Perhaps the best sense of the disjunctive will be perceived by remembering that *judicium parium* was generally opposed to the combat or the ordeal, which are equally *lex terrae.*"

Whether this is accurate or not, it is pretty certain that meanings undreamed of by the framers of *Magna Charta* have been imported into it. As Judge Cooley devotes a chapter to the subject, it might not have been out of place to trace the growth of the modern interpretations.

We have made a good deal of use of this book, and have carefully compared the text with the authorities in many places. We consider it a very laborious, clear, and valuable work upon a subject equally new and well chosen.

6.54

From *American Law Review* 6:149 (1871).

A Treatise upon the United States Courts, and their Practice: Explaining the Enactments by which they are controlled; their Organization and Powers; their peculiar Jurisdiction; and the Modes of Pleading and Procedure in them. With numerous Practical Forms. By Benjamin Vaughan Abbott. Vol. II. Original Suits; Review; Forms. New York: Diossy & Co. 1871. 8vo.

We welcome the second volume of this valuable work. The first volume contains statutes of practical utility, rules of court (more properly inserted in this than in the many other books which they help to fill), an elaborate exposition of the organization and jurisdiction of the courts of the United States, and a convenient summary of the principles by which they are governed. The present volume is devoted to procedure in the exercise of original and appellate jurisdiction, and to forms. Such use as we have had occasion to make of the former has satisfied us that it may be safely purchased by that large number of lawyers who need a trustworthy guide through the labyrinth of statutes and rules upon the subject. The Messrs. Abbott do not aspire to mould opinion by original thinking and writing, nor to do more than to make useful tools. But when we consider the large number of books that have been turned out under their name, we must give them credit for understanding what is wanted, for many devices which aid the practitioner at his daily work, and certainly, in this instance, for a care which is not shown by all professional book-makers.

6.55

From *American Law Review* 6:349 (1871).

English Chancery Reports. Macnaghten & Gordon, 3 vols. De Gex, Macnaghten, & Gordon. Vols. I. II. Boston: Little, Brown, & Co. 1871.

The publishers of the late edition of the House of Lords' Cases are conferring another benefit on the profession, by reprinting the most expensive and inaccessible of the Chancery Reports. The doctrine and procedure of equity are perhaps the most important part of the law in a great business community, and we have to learn them almost entirely from England.

With the exception of New Jersey, which still keeps up the ancient traditions with scholarly ability, we do not recall a single state which has retained a separate chancery court, and, with all the advantages of the fusion, we think it might be admitted that the nicety of equity practice suffers from the absence of a special chancery bar.

The decisions in the volumes before us, and those which follow them, furnish a body of precedents for which no substitute can be found in our own reports and yet which are of a daily increasing importance. Macnaghten and Gordon are rather dull. But the volumes which follow of De Gex, Macnaghten, and Gordon, and those of their successors, down to the Law Reports, are perhaps as well worth buying as any equal number which could be selected.

6.56

From *American Law Review* 6:350 (1871).

Massachusetts Reports 103—Cases argued and determined in the Supreme Judicial Court of Massachusetts, October 1869—January 1870. ALBERT G. BROWNE, JR., Reporter. Boston: H. O. Houghton & Co. 1872.

Mr. Browne is a model reporter, and his assistant, Mr. Gray, is well known for his learning, accuracy, and ability. We have sometimes noticed a tendency to make the head-notes too long for clearness, out of anxiety to omit no material facts, but we do not observe it in this volume. The principal cases will be found in our American Digest; we shall therefore only mention one or two. The head-note of *Williams v. Merritt*, p. 184, is as follows: "By an adjudication of bankruptcy under the bankrupt act (U.S. St. 1867, c. 176), even when the proceedings were begun on the debtor's voluntary petition, his property becomes exempt from subsequent attachment on mesne process."

Bradley v. Rea, p. 188, we venture to think wrongly decided. This was an action on an account annexed for the price of pigs. The answer set up a breach of warranty, and that the sale was made on the Lord's day. The parties made an agreement for the sale and purchase of hogs on Sunday, at a certain price, and the vendor, the plaintiff (according to the defendants' evidence), specially warranted them to be healthy. The pigs were marked the same day. "One of the defendants came on Monday, and at his request one of the marked pigs was changed for one not marked, out of the drove. No price was named on Monday; and the parties were not agreed as to whether any thing was then said about the terms of payment." They were afterwards delivered on Monday, by a servant of the plaintiff.

The jury were instructed *inter alia* "that neither a price fixed on Sunday, nor a warranty made on that day, would form part of *any contract which could support an action;* but that they were to consider whether *the facts in proof* satisfied them that a sale was made on Monday, and for that purpose they were to consider *all the circumstances,* including the delivery of the pigs by the plaintiff and the acceptance of them by the defendants, and would determine whether such delivery and acceptance were understood by the parties as a delivery and acceptance of goods sold, and which were to be paid for. If they found *that it was understood by the parties that the pigs were bought,* then the plaintiff was entitled to recover the actual market value of the pigs at the time of such sale, without any reference to the price named or fixed on Sunday." As we read these instructions, the jury were not forbidden to consider the conversation on Sunday for the purpose of arriving at the conclusion that the parties intended a sale on Monday; and were told in ambiguous language that if they found that the parties understood that there was a sale, even on the terms mentioned on Sunday, then they would find that there was a sale on other terms, viz.: without a warranty and for a different price! The conversation on Sunday was only excluded as a ground of defence. But it was one of the "facts in proof," and the one which most powerfully led to the conclusion "that it was understood by the parties that the pigs were bought."

There were three instructions possible for which something could be said, either that the jury could not consider the evidence for any purpose; or, if they were allowed to consider it, that they might consider it as incorporated into the Monday's bargain; or that they might consider it as rebutting the inference of an undertaking to pay a reasonable price without warranty which might otherwise be drawn from the delivery on Monday. We think nothing can be said in favor of allowing them to consider it for the purpose of finding that a bargain was intended, but not for the purpose of finding what that bargain was.

In delivering the opinion of the court, overruling exceptions taken by the defendant, Chapman, C.J., says: "the jury must have found that on Monday the pigs were delivered by the plaintiff, and accepted by the defendants, with the purpose that they should be sold and paid for. This would constitute a sale; and if nothing was said about the price, the law would imply a fair price. . . The contract derived all its validity from the transactions of Monday; and if the defendants, on that day, omitted to make stipulations that they would otherwise have made, because they relied on the illegal acts of the preceding day, it was their own folly to do so. The jury were correctly instructed that no valid sale could be made on Sunday; nor could any contract made on Sunday be ratified on Monday so as to be valid or effectual; and that neither a price fixed on Sunday nor a warranty made on that day would form any part of a contract which would support an action."

The court seem to us to err in considering the transaction of Monday as an attempted ratification of a void contract.

It has another aspect. Assuming the defendant's evidence to be true, as we must for purposes of argument, the sale on Monday was made on certain terms on which the minds of the parties *then* met. The defendant did not, and was not understood to promise to pay absolutely, but only on condition the hogs were sound. If the parties had agreed in their testimony, the plaintiff would have admitted that he so understood the defendant's promise. There was a continuing intention manifested by a conversation on Sunday, it is true, and not binding then, as it would probably not have been on any other day, on account of the Statute of Frauds, but which the parties still entertained and carried out on Monday, as they lawfully might. It surely would not have been necessary for the parties to repeat the conversation of the preceding day if it had been expressly referred to as the basis of the sale, any more than to repeat the terms of an offer made on Sunday and accepted the next day; and they might refer to and incorporate the conversation as well by acts as by words. This, which seems to us the true view of the case, was excluded by the instructions to the jury. But if it is wrong, it seems monstrous to make a man perform a contract which he never made and never was understood to make, and that unless the Sunday conversation was entirely excluded from the consideration of the jury, and in the alternative of the conversation not being admissible to show what the contract *was*, it was at least admissible to show what it *was not*, and that for this purpose unless the evidence was excluded altogether, or allowed its full effect, an instruction asked for should have been given, to the effect that if the jury believed that the delivery and acceptance on Monday were made only in pursuance of the terms agreed on on Sunday, such delivery and acceptance would not be evidence of a sale on Monday. In other words, if the jury believed that, they should have been told either that there was a sale on the terms of Sunday, or no sale at all. In fact, as we have said, they must have considered the evidence in finding that a bargain was intended, and then were forbidden to consider it in finding *what* bargain was intended.

Donnell v. The Starlight, p. 227, upholds the jurisdiction of the Courts of a state to enforce liens created by its laws, for labor and materials furnished in constructing or repairing domestic vessels, citing *The Belfast,* 7 Wall. 624, where a dictum to that effect will be found on p. 645. This dictum has recently been confined in New York to cases where the *contract* as well as the lien is not maritime. *Brookman v. Hamill,* 43 N.Y. 554, 560; *Sheppard v. Steele, ib.* 52.

In *Kyle v. Kavanagh,* p. 356, it was held that under an agreement to sell and convey land with a good title, the purchaser is not entitled to a warranty deed; a point which has been a good deal mooted. In *Simonds v. Simonds,* p. 572, a special statute of the state of Maine, authorizing the Supreme Judicial Court of that state, in its discretion, to decree a divorce between individuals named was held unconstitutional, as granting a special indulgence by way of exemption from the general law.

We have taken these cases almost at random, as there are too many of interest for us to be able to notice all.

6.57

From *American Law Review* 6:353 (1871).

A Selection of Cases on the Law of Contracts. With References and Citations. By C. C. LANGDELL, Dane Professor of Law in Harvard University. Prepared for use as a text-book in Harvard Law School. Boston: Little, Brown, & Co. 1871. 8vo. pp. xvi, 1022.

We have already expressed our very high opinion of this selection in noticing the first part (5 Am. Law Rev. 539). Further reflection and examination have confirmed us in our estimate. It must be remembered that the work is intended for use as a text-book, as is stated on the title-page; and that, therefore, head-notes and other conveniences in a book for general reference are purposely omitted, in order to make the student find out the principle and trace the connection between case and case for himself. Even the index is very different from that to which the profession are accustomed. There is nothing of what the codifiers of the United States Statutes call the "manual method." A contract concerning coal is not indexed under the head Coal, nor even under the popular name of the contract, as Charter-party or Insurance. The cases are referred to under the general principle of the law of contracts, which they illustrate, and this ought to be enough for lawyers. As is observed in the preface, "the number of fundamental legal doctrines is much less than is commonly supposed; the many different guises in which the same doctrine is constantly making its appearance, and the great extent to which legal treatises are a repetition of each other, being the cause of much misapprehension." If the present generation is to improve upon the text-books of the last, as it easily may, it must work in the direction followed by Mr. Langdell by discarding popular and adopting legal distinctions.

We do not agree with him, however, in his seemingly exclusive belief in the study of cases. We should not shut our eyes to a rapid and continuous view of the principles deduced from them. And this can only be got in the text-books. The popular prejudice that a case lawyer is apt to want breadth, has something in it, although it is certain that the opposite danger is more to be feared now-a-days in America. Moreover, to put a beginner upon the cases without aid or introduction, seems to unnecessarily increase difficulties which he is sure to find great enough, however assisted. We think he would find the present work a pretty tough *pièce de résistance* without a text-book or the assistance of an instructor. The students of the Harvard Law School are to be congratulated that they have the aid of Mr. Langdell's learning and remarkable powers in their task.

6.58
CORRESPONDENCE

From *American Law Review* 6:392 (1872).[1]

RICHMOND, IND. Oct. 26, 1871.

TO THE EDITORS OF THE AMERICAN LAW REVIEW: —

In the last number of the Review, under the caption "Suits against Government, Government Officers, &c.," you approach, but do not quite reach, a question on which I have for some time wanted to see a review of the law; namely, how far are government, State, county, or city officers liable, on general principles, for *interest* made by them, in the use of public funds while in their hands? For instance, an officer collecting revenues lends them while in his hands, makes large gains, and puts these gains into his own pocket. Is he liable on his bond, or for money had and received, like an agent or trustee holding funds in a fiduciary capacity? Officers are using public funds in this way to an astonishing extent. The tendency is corrupting. If there is a legal liability, the law ought to be enforced. Your readers here would like to hear from you.

Yours, &c., J. Y.

This letter was received too late for us to attempt to consider it at length. We shall be glad to receive suggestions upon the subject, Why could not the money be followed into the trade, and the extra profits demanded in equity, on the same principle as in the case of a trust fund improperly invested? *Robinson v. Robinson,* 1 De G., M. & G. 247, 257; Story Eq. Redfield, §§ 462, 462*a*; *Makepiece v. Rogers,* 11 Jur. N.S. 314, per Turner, L.J.

Editor's Note

1. The reply in this exchange was written by Holmes. The first letter has been reproduced to supply the necessary context. The piece referred to by J. Y. appeared in the "Summary of Events," *ALR* 6:153.

6.59
GRAIN ELEVATORS:
ON THE TITLE TO GRAIN IN PUBLIC WAREHOUSES

From *American Law Review* 6:450 (1872).

HARRY CHASE AND OTHERS V. JOSEPH C. WASHBURN.[*]

. . . .[1]

Preliminary. Confusion of goods.—With respect to the state of a confusion of goods, Chancellor Kent writes,[**] that where those of two persons are so intermixed that they can no longer be distinguished, each of them has an equal interest in the subject as tenant in common, if the intermixture was by consent. But if it was made wilfully, the common law gave the entire property, without any account, to him whose property was originally invaded, and its distinct character destroyed. But this rule, he says, is carried no farther than necessity requires, and he gives Lord Eldon's construction of the old cases in *Lupton v. White*[***] with seeming approval. His lordship says, "What are the cases in the old law of a mixture of corn or flour? If one man mixes his corn or flour with that of another, and they were of equal value, *the latter must have the given quantity;*[****] but if articles of different value are mixed producing a third value, the aggregate of both, and through the fault of the person mixing them, the other party cannot tell what was the original value of his property, he must have the whole." The same principle, that each owner retains a proportional interest in the mass, obtains when the mixture is brought about by accident. The case of *Spence v. Union Marine Ins. Co.*[*****] shows this. The facts as stated in the head-note were that cotton belonging to different owners was shipped at Mobile for Liverpool. Forty-three bales belonged to the plaintiffs, and were insured by the defendants against the usual perils. The ship was wrecked near Key West; some of the cotton was lost, and all was damaged, some so much so that it had to be sold at Key West. The rest was brought in another vessel to Liverpool. The marks on many of the bales were so obliterated by sea-water that none of the cotton lost or sold at Key West, and a part only of that brought to Liverpool, could be identified. Two only of the plaintiffs' forty-three bales were identified, and these were delivered to them. The court held that in respect to the cotton lost and that sold at Key West, there was a total loss of a part of each owner's cotton, and that all the owners had a proportional interest in the cotton which arrived at Liverpool and could not be identified; the share of each owner's loss in the cotton totally lost or sold, and his

---

[*]Reported 1 Ohio N.S. 244. This case is selected as presenting the ablest exposition of the opposite opinion to that which will be maintained in the note.

[**]2 Comm. 364, 365.

[***]15 Vesey, 432, 442.

[****]This seems hardly borne out by the old cases, but would perhaps be followed, as there seems to be no substantial reason for depriving the wrong-doer of his whole property in such a case. *Hesseltine v. Stockwell,* 30 Me. 237; *Moore v. Bowman,* 47 N.H. 494, 502; Story, Bailm. § 40; *Ryder v. Hathaway,* 21 Pick. 298; but see *Spence v. Union Marine Ins. Co.* L.R. 3 C.P. 427, 437, bottom. It may be observed also that it is hardly probable that Lord Eldon thought legal proceedings necessary for a partition in this instance.

[*****]L.R. 3 C.P. 427.

share in the remainder which arrived at Liverpool being in the proportion that the quantity shipped by him bore to the whole quantity shipped; and therefore that there was neither an actual nor constructive total loss of the plaintiffs' forty-one bales. Whether the proximate cause of the loss was a peril of the seas was not decided. The same rule applies when the mixture was made by the mistake of one owner[*] or by the wrongful act of a stranger.[**] These general principles have become important, and have been applied in questions as to the property in timber cut either purposely or by mistake from the land of different owners in the great forests of the United States, or mingled while being cut into boards at saw-mills.[***]

Grain.—The same is true with regard to grain. In *Inglebright v. Hammond*,[****] wheat was delivered by Hammond to a miller to be ground, and by the terms of a written contract between the parties the grinding was "to be made out of the wheat furnished . . . and the flour made therefrom" was to be delivered to Hammond. The parties however mingled the corn with other corn belonging to the miller. Evidence of a custom that when a person took wheat to a mill, and consented to its being mingled with the miller's, the property in the wheat passed to the miller, was held rightly rejected. It will be observed that nothing is said of any custom which would have authorized the miller to make any further additions to the mixture beyond those expressly assented to. By the written contract the wheat was to be ground into flour and returned.[*****] This was waived to the extent of the mixture assented to by Hammond, and thereafter the contract would have been satisfied by the return of the proper number of barrels made from the mixed wheat. But it was only so far that Hammond had changed the character of his interest. It is perfectly clear on the authorities and the reason of the thing that when the same identical wheat is to be returned in the shape of flour, the property remains in the bailor.[******]

Nature of legal interests in the mass.—So far as we have gone there is no difficulty. But a question has been raised on the legal nature of the different owners' interests in the mass. In *Morgan v. Gregg*,[*******] a case of intermixture by consent of specific parcels of grain belonging to the plaintiff and a third person, in the warehouse of the defendant, trover was brought for the refusal of the warehouseman to allow the plaintiff to remove his proportion, and the plaintiff was held entitled to maintain the action. The court thought that as the defendant was the other owner's bailee there could be no recovery if there was a tenancy in common, and therefore expressed an opinion that although there was a loss of identity each owner somehow remained a tenant in severalty, with a right to take and sell or destroy his share without being liable to the owner of the other part. The same opinion is half intimated by one of the ablest of modern judges (Comstock, J.) in the leading case of

---

[*] *Pratt v. Bryant,* 20 Vt. 333; *Ryder v. Hathaway,* 21 Pick. 298, 305; *Moore v. Bowman,* 47 N.H. 494, 501.

[**] *Bryant v. Ware,* 30 Me. 295.

[***] *Ryder v. Hathaway; Hesseltine v. Stockwell, sup.; Jenkins v. Steanka,* 19 Wisc. 126.

[****] 19 Ohio, 337.

[*****] See *Pribble v. Kent,* 10 Ind. 325.

[******] *Chase v. Washburn,* 1 Ohio St. 244, 251, *sup.* p. 454; 2 Kent, 589; *Foster v. Pettibone,* 3 Seld. 433; *Mallory v. Willis,* 4 Comst. 76, 85; *Hyde v. Cookson,* 21 Barb. 92.

[*******] 46 Barb. 183.

Kimberly v. Patchin,[*] which was the case of an executed sale of 6000 bushels of wheat, parcel of a large quantity.[2] On the other hand the language of the most authoritative courts and text writers is that there is a tenancy in common,[**] and we think it will appear that it must be so considered. The difficulty which is felt is that ordinarily a tenant in common has not the right of severing the tenancy by his own act. But the mode of severance is an executive detail which must be modelled to suit the requirements of justice,—the essential features of such a tenancy are severalty of title and unity of physical possession; because, as Blackstone says,[***] "None knoweth his own severalty, and therefore they all occupy promiscuously." There is certainly such a unity of possession in the case of the grain, and its incidents are similar to those of a tenancy in common. If a portion of the mass was destroyed, one owner clearly could not take out an amount equal to that put in by him and throw the whole loss on the other party.[****] All that the New York cases can mean to assert is that each owner has a right to take out his share from the mass without the consent of the other and without legal process. For before such separation it is absolutely impossible that he should have any more claim upon one part than another, and therefore he falls within the definition of a tenant in common, which is based upon that very circumstance.

Means of severance.—Now with regard to the means of severance. In *Spence v. Union Marine Ins. Co.,*[*****] Bovill, C.J., puts the case of one shipper owning ninety-nine bales, and another, one, of the same description, and of all being transshipped with the loss of the marks, by reason of the stranding of the vessel, after which the cargo arrives safe. "Practically," he says, "in such a case, the owner of the one bale would receive one of the bales, *either by the delivery of the ship-owner or* by agreement, and probably be content, *and this ought to operate as a partition, so as to vest the residue in the owner of the larger share.*" This seems to contemplate a partition *in pais,* without consulting the other owner, as sufficient; and this is excellently stated in another New York case, by Johnson, J.: "I apprehend the right of severance, amongst tenants in common, by one tenant of his share, always existed at common law as to all property in its nature severable. I do not find the point anywhere expressly adjudged, and no case is referred to. But it seems to me that when personal property severable in its nature, in common bulk, and of the same quality, is owned by several as tenants in common, each tenant may go and sever and appropriate his share, if it can be determined by measurement or weight, without the consent of the others, and sell or destroy it, without being liable to them in an action for the conversion of the common property. And when one tenant in common takes from the common property, under such circumstances, if he does not take beyond his proportion or share,

---

[*]19 N.Y. 330.

[**] *Cushing v. Breed,* 14 Allen, 376, 380; *Channon v. Lusk,* 2 Lansing, 211; *Tripp v. Riley,* 15 Barb. 333, 335; *Fobes v. Shattuck,* 22 Barb. 568; *Dole v. Olmstead,* 36 Ill. 150, 154; *Spence v. Union Marine Ins. Co., sup.; Jones v. Moore,* 4 Younge & Coll. 351, 357, 358; *Buckley v. Gross,* 3 Best & S. 566, 575; *South Australian Ins. Co. v. Randell,* L.R. 3 P.C. 101, 113; *Wood v. Fales,* 24 Penn. St. 246, 248.

[***]2 Comm. 191.

[****] *Spence v. Union Marine Ins. Co., sup.; Dole v. Olmstead,* 36 Ill. 150, 154; 41 Ill. 344.

[*****]L.R. 3 C.P. 427, 437.

he will be presumed in law to have severed and taken his own, merely. The rule would be different in the case of property not severable in its nature. . . . In such cases the partition must necessarily be by agreement or proceedings in equity."* In other words, the mode of partition is not of the essence of tenancy in common, and the law is not so idle as to put persons to a legal process when the result can be accomplished without it and without the possibility of doing injustice. This is fully recognized by the late New York decision of *Channon v. Lusk,*** where it was held that the owner of part of an undivided heap of oats could maintain trover against the owner of the rest for refusing to allow him to separate and remove his share, although the plaintiff and defendant were admitted to be tenants in common. And the general rule that there is no remedy between tenants in common in such a case*** which embarrassed the judges in *Morgan v. Gregg, supra,* was considered inapplicable to articles like grain or fluids in bulk, which are not adapted to common use amongst several owners. The same principle was also decided in the very similar case of *Lobdell v. Stowell.*****

Depositors in public warehouses.—We are now approaching the real difficulty with which we have to deal. In *Kimberly v. Patchin,***** the transaction related to six thousand bushels out of a specified heap of grain, and it did not appear that the warehouseman had any authority to add other wheat to the pile. Neither did it in *Russell v. Carrington,****** a case like the last; nor in *Morgan v. Gregg,******* nor in *Inglebright v. Hammond,******** stated *supra,* nor in *Hall v. Boston & Worcester R.R.,********* although *Cushing v. Breed, infra,* was relied on by the court, nor in *Channon v. Lusk,* stated *supra,* &c. In each of these cases there was a specific mass in which the parties had a vested right of property. Their rights could have been changed from a tenancy in common of the whole to a tenancy in severalty of a part by the act of either, on the principles stated above, but their title could not be divested, and a substitution or addition of other grain of the same quality, so far as appears or can reasonably be conjectured, would have been unlawful. In the grain elevators and public warehouses, which are now everywhere in use, however, the custom which we believe is universal throughout the West, and perhaps throughout the country, is to mingle all the grain of a given quality which is received, in a single bin, and to give a receipt which entitles the first holder, or one to whom he has transferred it with the assent of the warehouseman, to call for an equal amount at any time, but not to demand

---

* *Tripp v. Riley,* 15 Barb. 333, 335. The same principle is asserted in *Fobes v. Shattuck,* 22 Barb. 568, 570; *Channon v. Lusk,* 2 Lansing, 211; *Fiquet v. Allison,* 12 Mich. 328; *South Australian Ins. Co. v. Randell,* L.R. 3 P.C. 101, 113; *Wilson v. Nason,* 4 Bosw. 155, head-note (4); *Horr v. Barker,* 6 Cal. 489; *Young v. Miles,* 20 Wisc. 615, 623; Sup. p. 455 n. (3).

** 2 Lansing, 211.

*** Co. Lit. 199*b.*

**** 37 How. Pr. 88. In *Clark v. Griffith,* 24 N.Y. 595, it was held that trover could be maintained under similar circumstances without intimating what the nature of the parties' interest was. See also *Fiquet v. Allison,* 12 Mich. 328. .

***** 19 N.Y. 330.

****** 42 N.Y. 118.

******* 46 Barb. 183.

******** 19 Ohio, 337.

********* 14 Allen, 439.

the very grain which was delivered. It is much easier to consider such a transaction as this a sale than a bailment. The warehouseman has unlimited control over the grain on hand at any moment. He may have emptied and refilled his bin a dozen times since putting a certain parcel of grain into it and before the amount is demanded of him. There seems to be that unlimited right of dealing with the grain in store, at any moment, which is the most characteristic mark of ownership. The doctrine is very clearly stated by Bartley, J., in the case printed at the head of this note: "When the owners of wheat consent to have their wheat, when delivered at a mill or warehouse, mixed with a common mass, each becomes the owner in common with others of his respective share in the common stock. And this would not give the bailee any control over the property which he would not have if the wheat of each one was kept separate and apart. If the wheat, thus thrown into a common mass be delivered for the purpose of being converted into flour, each owner will be entitled to the flour manufactured from his proper quantity or proportion in the common stock. If a part of the wheat held in common belong to the bailee himself, he could not abstract from the common stock any more than his own appropriate share without a violation of the terms of the bailment; and such a breach of his engagement could not be cured by his procuring other wheat, to be delivered to supply the place of that thus wrongfully taken. But if the wheat be thrown into the common heap, with the understanding or agreement that the person receiving it may take from it at pleasure and appropriate the same to the use of himself or others, on the condition of his procuring other wheat to supply its place, the dominion over the property passes to the depositary, and the transaction is a sale, and not a bailment."*

In *Wilson v. Cooper,*** the plaintiff delivered wheat without special directions at a grist and flouring mill advertised as a merchant and exchange mill. "The custom of the mill was that when any one brought wheat and did not specially direct that the same be ground into a grist for the person so bringing the wheat, it was thrown into a general pile or bin belonging to the mill, and a receipt given to the person so leaving the wheat, which entitled the party holding it to call for flour, bran, or wheat again, as he should prefer." The wheat in question was thrown into the general pile and had been ground and a part of the flour sold to a third person, when the contents of the mill were attached. It was held that an action of trover, against the sheriff and an attaching creditor, for the conversion of wheat, flour, bran, and middlings, could not be maintained, if the delivery was under and with knowledge of the custom, on the ground that the title would have vested in the mill owners. A very similar question has recently been decided by the Privy Council in England. *The South Australian Ins. Co. v. Randell*** was an action on a policy of insurance against fire upon the stock of wheat, &c., in a mill, which contained the following clause: "Goods held in trust or on commission must be insured as such, otherwise the policy will not extend to them." Part of the wheat destroyed was received from farmers, and mixed in large hutches with other wheat received in the same way,

---

* *Chase v. Washburn,* 1 Ohio St. 244, 281, *sup.* p. 454.
** 10 Iowa, 565.
*** L.R. 3 P.C. 101; 6 Moore, P.C. N.S. 341.

and was either sold by the millers, or ground in their mill; the millers could do what they liked with it. It never was intended by the parties that the identical wheat delivered by the farmers, should be returned to them. Storage receipts were given to the farmers, and they had the right at any time to demand the price of the same quantity of wheat of equal quality, according to the market price of the day on which they claimed payment. It was also assumed by the court for the purposes of decision, although the evidence was somewhat obscure, that the farmers had the option to claim as of right an equal quantity of wheat of the like quality, instead of the price, if they preferred. If no demand was made within a certain time a charge was made for storage. The wheat in question, which was received from farmers in the manner just described, was not insured as goods held in trust or on commission, but it was held to be covered by the policy on the ground that the transaction amounted to a sale to the millers. The court observed, "Supposing that there was an implied option to claim an equal quantity of the like quality at any time after delivery, there could be no right of claiming an aliquot part of the identical bulk with which his wheat was mixed up at the time of delivery, for this was consumable at the will and pleasure of the miller, as part of the current stock, liable to fluctuation, from time to time, both in quantity and quality. Moreover, it appears to their Lordships, that there is no sound distinction in principle between this and the case of money deposited with a banker on a deposit receipt. . . By the deposit it is placed in the disposing power of the banker; and surely he who has acquired the disposing power over property for his own benefit without the control of another, has the beneficial ownership," citing *Foley v. Hill,* 2 H.L.C. 28.

*Ives v. Hartley** must be mentioned, but does not raise any difficulty. The receipts were in the following form: "Received of M. Hartley, to be stored, 150 bushels wheat, to take market price when he sees fit to sell.—H. & E. Ives." The court adverted to the fact that the warehouse was a private one in connection with a mill, not a public warehouse, and were inclined to consider that Hartley had no right to demand wheat or flour instead of money, and that the transaction was a sale.**

There are, however, some cases which cannot be reconciled with those which have just been cited, and which seem to need further argument before they can be accepted as law. The first which we shall consider is *Cushing v. Breed.**** This was an action for goods sold and delivered to recover the price of 500 bushels of oats. "The plaintiffs were owners of a cargo of black oats received by the schooner *Seven Brothers,* which on being weighed was found to contain 6695 bushels, and was elevated and stored" in a grain elevator in Boston belonging to third persons. "The cargo was put into two bins, and the plaintiffs thereafter agreed to sell to the defendants 500 bushels thereof at ninety-one cents a bushel," and gave them an order on the warehouseman for "500 bushels black oats from cargo per schooner *Seven Brothers,* storage commencing, to the person or persons in whose favor this order is drawn, June 29, 1864." This order was presented to the warehousemen and accepted by them. "Before July 5, 1864, the whole cargo had been sold and delivered and re-

*51 Ill., 520.
**See further 2 Kent, 589, 590.
***14 Allen, 376.

moved from the elevator except 1274 bushels; and this amount which remained in the elevator included 305 bushels of the quantity agreed to be sold to the defendants." On the 5th of July the oats remaining in the elevator were rendered nearly worthless by fire without the fault of either of the parties to the action. By the usage of grain dealers in Boston, after an order was accepted by the proprietors of an elevator under the above circumstances, the grain covered thereby was treated by them in all respects as the property of the purchaser. The vendor had no further control over it, and did no act in reference to separating it from the rest, or removing it from the elevator; but the proprietors held the same subject to the order of the purchaser in like manner as they had before held it subject to the order of the vendor. "They made no charge to the purchaser except for storage. *Different cargoes of the same quality, belonging to different owners, were sometimes mingled in the bins.* Parcels of grain, bought as above, were paid for according to contract, and without regard to whether or not they had been separated and removed from the elevator, and all damage to grain so sold, from internal causes occurring after the delivery of the order, was borne by the purchaser. All the above usages were known to the defendants; but they objected to the evidence to prove the same." On these facts it was held that the property in the whole 500 bushels had passed to the purchaser. To reach this conclusion two steps are necessary: first, to hold that the depositor retained his title to oats in the elevator; and second, that a sale of a portion *ex* a larger quantity would pass the title. We are only considering the first point here. Taking the form of the order in connection with the fact, of which we are informed but which does not appear in the printed report, that the cargo in question had not been mixed with any other, it may be that the decision could have been put upon the ground that the warehousemen by their acceptance undertook to hold 500 bushels out of a specific heap for the defendants, in which case there would have been less difficulty. But we do not understand the court to confine its opinion so narrowly. Supposing then that the order had no other effect than if it had been drawn for so many bushels of such a quality in the elevator, it is obvious the case would be different from *Kimberly v. Patchin* and others of that class to which we have referred. The usage is cautiously stated, that "different cargoes of the same quality, belonging to different owners, were *sometimes* mingled in the bins." But we understand the usage to be a general one in most of the elevators in Boston and elsewhere. Then the question would be whether the warehouseman was any thing more than a debtor for a parcel of grain to the original depositor, not to speak of his assignees. We suppose that the court would have said that taking the case that way, still the depositor remained owner, and was therefore able to pass a title by his sale. Chapman, C.J., says, "When several parties have stored various parcels of grain in the elevator, and it is put into one mass, according to a usage to which they must be deemed to have assented, they are tenants in common of the grain." The usage is here stated as if it only authorized the addition of a specific parcel, C, to other parcels, A and B, already on hand, and if this were so it is clear on the principles cited from Kent at the beginning of this note, that the owners of the three would become tenants in common. But the usage goes farther. It equally authorizes the subsequent addition of parcels D, E, &c. Moreover, it, or the law, authorizes deliveries to the receipt holders in the order in which receipts may be presented. It follows, that, after the given deposit, other grain might be put in and corresponding amounts drawn out, until ten times the contents of the bin had passed through it before the first depositor drew on the elevator, so that he could no longer found his claim to a share of the contents on the fact that his grain formed a part of them; and this raises our question how a man can be said to have a title to property in the hands of another when the other is not held to deliver any specific article, but on the contrary may deal with any specific quantity on hand as he chooses. There must be a specific thing owned or there cannot be ownership. Assuming that the oats were delivered to the warehouse under the usage stated, and laying the form of the acceptance out of the case, the question whether the delivery to the warehouse was a sale or a bailment would not be affected by the fact that the oats had not, as it happened, been mixed with others. It is enough that the warehouseman was at liberty to do so if he chose.

We next come to a later case in Maine, in which *Cushing v. Breed* was cited. *Warren v. Milliken** was trover against a third person for preventing delivery of grain from an elevator by an unfounded claim of title. The plaintiffs were holders of an order drawn on the owner of the elevator for 3170 $^{55}/_{56}$ bushels of corn by persons who had delivered a larger amount to the elevator where it had been mixed with various parcels belonging to others; the order had been accepted by the warehousemen and partial deliveries made under it. The plaintiffs recovered. This case is imperfectly reported, and we have to gather the facts from the opinion. Nothing is said of a custom to mix parcels of the same quality. But taking the statement of the court that the corn "was stored . . . in common with various parcels of grain belonging to others" in connection with the notorious custom of elevators, we may, perhaps, assume that it was understood that further additions might be made by the warehousemen.

*Dole v. Olmstead*** is a very important case, but the facts are somewhat obscure. We believe we state them correctly. Warehousemen engaged in the business of buying, selling, and storing grain, received certain grain for storage, gave a receipt, and stored the grain with that of other parties and with their own, in a common mass. This was according to custom, and was not objected to by the owners. The warehousemen afterwards assigned the corn in their warehouse, and certain contracts for the purchase of other corn, as security for debts, giving the assignee notice of the outstanding receipts. The corn turned out to be insufficient to satisfy all the grain receipts. It was held that the common mass of corn was to be distributed in the proportion in which the holders of receipts and the warehousemen had contributed to the same. The corn to be received under the contracts went of course to the assignee.

In *Young v. Miles,**** it is said that the agreement was that the plaintiff's wheat should be stored with other grain received at the warehouse for other owners, about the same time, of the same quality by inspection. The grain was mixed accordingly, and afterwards the warehouseman delivered so much from the warehouse that

*57 Me. 97.
**36 Ill. 150; 41 Ill. 344.
***20 Wisc. 615; 23 Wisc. 643.

there was hardly enough left to cover the plaintiff's receipts. This remainder was consigned to the defendants in the course of dealings of the warehouseman with them, but the plaintiff seems to have given them notice that he claimed it before it was delivered to them; he brought replevin and recovered. The court, after laying down that the plaintiff did not lose his title by the mixture, say, "The plaintiff being owner of so many bushels of the wheat, a proper construction of the receipt required (the warehouseman) to keep that number of bushels always on hand to answer the receipt; and if at any time he sold or took from the common quantity, so as to leave only enough or less than enough of the same quality of wheat in the warehouse to satisfy the receipt, it follows that, as between him and the plaintiff, the wheat so remaining became the absolute and exclusive property of the plaintiff. . . . So far as (the warehouseman) invaded the quantity of wheat belonging to the plaintiff, first or last, it was a wrong and a conversion, and the plaintiff might follow his wheat wherever it could be identified."

In the cases which we have now gone over the argument is very strong that there is a sale to the owners of the elevator, and it has already been fully stated. At the same time it cannot be denied that if the law is so, it will be followed by injustice and inconvenience. Undoubtedly those who deliver grain to an elevator think they have something more than the personal liability of the warehouseman, and regard him as their bailee in charge of their property. The holders of accepted orders look upon them as representing property in like manner.* If the transaction is regarded as a sale, the safety of receipt-holders depends upon the warehouseman's solvency; if the doctrine which will be advocated here prevails, they run no risk unless he is both insolvent and dishonest. Of course, the opinion of merchants as to the nature of the transaction is not conclusive. As is observed by the Lord Justice James in a late case, "there is no magic in the word 'agency.' It is often used in commercial matters, when the real relation is that of vendor and purchaser."** But it is undoubtedly desirable to work out the expectations and intentions of the parties if the machinery of the law admits it. Suppose that warehousemen became insolvent, having always been careful to keep a quantity of grain in store corresponding to the amount for which they had receipts out, would not the holders of the receipts have a right to feel that they were unjustly treated, unless they were preferred to the general creditors in their claim upon that grain? Let us look at it a little more exactly.

Suppose I deliver a copy of the General Statutes of Massachusetts, or other book easily purchasable in the market, to an agent to keep, telling him, however, that he may sell it at any time, provided that he will immediately appropriate another copy to me upon doing so, and give him like power of sale and substitution as to all succeeding copies. The title in the copy for the time being appropriated to me, to be vested in me. Is not that a perfectly possible transaction? The analogies of the law show that the title to a substituted volume would vest in me as soon as it was definitely appropriated to me.***

---

*The evidence which has been held insufficient to make out a custom shows that it is the general opinion of merchants that they get a right of property before separation of the specific article. *Southwestern Freight & Cotton Press Co. v. Stanard*, 44 Mo. 71, 82.

**Ex parte White. In re Nevill*, L.R. 6 Ch. 397, 399.

***Aldridge v. Johnson*, 7 El. & Bl. 885, 898, per Lord Campbell, C.J.; *Langton v. Higgins*, 4 H. & N. 402.

Would it make any difference if the agent also had power to mix the volume with others belonging to third persons, from which it was not distinguishable, each owner being at liberty to call for one at any time? Would it make any difference that he was at liberty to add others of his own, if he was only at liberty to withdraw as many as he put in?

The owners of grain elevators are subject to a duty to keep on hand an amount of grain equal to their outstanding receipts.[*] And this is recognized by the charge for storage which they are in the habit of making. Is there any legal difficulty in considering them as bailees to keep, with power to change the bailor's tenancy in severalty into a tenancy in common of a proportionately larger mass, and back again, and also with a continuous power of sale, substitution, and resale? At any given moment holders of receipts are tenants in common of the amount in store in the proportion of their receipts. If it is wholly destroyed by accident, the warehouseman will not be liable further on his receipts; if it is injured, or a part destroyed, the loss should be borne proportionally, as in *Spence v. Union Marine Ins. Co., ante* pp. 455, 456. If the warehouseman is honest there will always be a sufficient amount on hand; and when all have drawn out their shares but one, that one will be owner of what is left. Suppose, however, the warehouseman is dishonest, and sells and delivers to a third person grain which is covered by an outstanding receipt. This would be wrongful as between himself and his principal; but would it be effectual to pass the title? The Wisconsin court seems to think not;[**] but it is questionable whether its opinion can be sustained. It is in the general course of a warehouseman's business to sell grain, and those who deal with him have no means of knowing whether any particular grain is covered by an elevator order or not, except his word. It would seem that the delivery of grain from the mass in store was one of those acts within the apparent scope of an agent's authority, of which the principal must bear the consequences. The argument is much stronger when, as we have seen in *Dole v. Olmstead* (*sup.* p. 463), the custom authorizes the warehousemen to mix their own grain in the common mass, which is probably always the case. It has recently been settled in England that when a set of three bills of lading are signed, the person to whom one of them is first indorsed gets a better title than a subsequent indorsee of another of the set, although the latter first gets possession of the goods;[***] but the analogy does not seem to hold in the present case. The person to whom the first receipt was issued covering all the available grain in store would have a good title, it is true, and the warehouseman would hold the grain as his agent; but as it is according to known usage to deliver any grain in the common store on any order for that quality, a delivery to the holder of a later order or receipt, which is a binding contract to deliver grain from that warehouse, would seem to be within the apparent powers of the proprietors of the elevator. No doubt is thrown on this by cases where such a delivery by ordinary warehousemen has been held not to bind the true owner, because it is not within the scope of an ordinary

[*] *Young v. Miles,* 20 Wisc. 615; 23 Wisc. 643; *sup.* p. 464. See L.R. 3 P.C. 111.

[**] *Young v. Miles, sup.* p. 464; 20 Wisc. 615; 23 Wisc. 643. Where however it would seem that there was no delivery to the defendants until they had notice. In *Gardiner v. Suydam,* as explained in *Kimberly v. Patchin,* 19 N.Y. 330, 339, the flour was delivered to the holder of the earlier receipt.

[***] *Barber v. Meyerstein,* L.R. 4 H.L. 317.

bailee's powers to substitute another article of like value for the identical thing delivered, and this perhaps explains the language used in *Burton v. Curyea.*[*] The reporter's note at the beginning of that case shows that the peculiar nature of grain receipts has been recognized by the legislature of Illinois, and that they have gone the extreme length of making all receipts for grain issued by any warehouse negotiable.[**]

If the general views here indicated are right, it is important to fix the moment when grain received by the warehouseman becomes appropriated to his warehouse receipts. Suppose the warehouseman wrongfully misappropriated grain belonging to another in his warehouse, that would not give the injured party any title to other grain of the same quality in a different city merely because it belonged to the wrong-doer, and it would make no difference that the latter entertained an unexecuted intention of making good the deficiency out of his own grain.[***] Suppose that by the waste attending delivery on other orders the amount on hand had become reduced below what would satisfy the last outstanding receipt under circumstances in which the warehouseman was responsible; that would not, we suppose, give the holder any title to grain in an adjoining warehouse, or which might be delivered to the warehouseman elsewhere on a contract with him.[****] The foundation of the claim of property in part of a specific mass is that the claimant's property was originally mixed with that mass; that is, with the mass in a certain receptacle. He is tenant in common with others of a mass which is continually being added to and subtracted from, but which always contains enough to satisfy his claim, as well as those of the other tenants in common for the time being. Strictly it would seem that his right of property depended on the continuous existence of a pile of grain in the bin, into which his own was shot. Suppose, however, the warehouseman having a large order to fill, and having grain enough on hand to answer that and satisfy all outstanding receipts, for convenience of loading empties the bin into the purchaser's car, and immediately refills it with the amount for which his receipts are out. It seems pretty clear that the law ought not to say that the receipt-holders have no longer a right of property; but that it could with advantage presume from the ordinary course of business that the refilling of the bin amounted to an appropriation of grain to the receipts, and that it was assented to by the receipt-holders. There has been in strictness a breach of duty on the part of the warehouseman in emptying the bin for a single moment; but if the amount is replaced, it is the reasonable presumption that it is done with the assent of parties, to whom it is a matter of indifference what grain they receive, if it is of the right quantity and quality. As has been said, the bin may be filled from the top and emptied from the bottom, and may have had ten times its contents pass through it since a particular deposit was made, so that even if it is kept full the depositor's right of property does not depend on the presumption that any of his original grain was there. We think therefore that assent to the substitution may be presumed, even as against a creditor attaching

[*]40 Ill. 320, 329. See *Second National Bank v. Walbridge,* 19 Ohio St. 419.
[**]See also *McPherson v. Gale,* 40 Ill. 368.
[***]*Wood v. Fales,* 24 Penn. St. 246.
[****]*Dole v. Olmstead,* 36 Ill. 150, 154; 41 Ill. 344.

before the receipt-holder has had notice and ratified the transaction,* notwithstanding the general rule which has been laid down,** that the act of ratification must take place at a time, and under circumstances, when the ratifying party might himself have lawfully done the act which he ratifies. It has been laid down in New York in a somewhat similar case that the title would enure by way of estoppel.***

It is a somewhat perplexing question whether the doctrine can be pressed farther than this without legislation, and yet if it cannot it would seem that legislation is necessary. It is quite possible that an elevator should contain more than one bin for grain of a certain kind and quality; it is at the same time probable that the depositor does not inquire into which bin his grain is shot, and that the warehouseman conceives that he is doing his whole duty, and is doing all that is practicable, if he keeps enough grain on hand anywhere in the warehouse to cover the receipt. It may often happen that he has emptied the bin A, in which a certain parcel was placed, considering his receipt for the amount to be covered by the contents of bin B. If the theory that the transaction is a bailment rather than a sale depends on the mixture of the original parcel with a continuing heap, the difficulty just adverted to in the case of a breach of continuity in the heap becomes greater when we allow the title of the bailor to be shifted from bin to bin at the option of the bailee. If emptying the bin A is wrongful as against one whose wheat was placed there, and the warehouseman has no authority to appropriate part of the contents of bin B to that receipt, it might be hard to say that he could ratify afterwards as against the general creditors on the principle just laid down, although according to *Grove v. Brien,* just cited, his assent might perhaps be presumed. But if the act can be regarded as within the scope of the warehouseman's original authority, it would be somewhat analogous to the case of a vendor who is authorized by the buyer to appropriate a specific article to the contract so as to pass the title, which it is settled that he may do.**** It seems reasonable to presume an authority to this extent from the fact, if, as we suppose, it be a fact, that a depositor does not look further than the warehouse, and regards the grain of a certain quality in that warehouse as actually or possibly mixed in one common mass.

We are led by this to distinguish the case of grain in a warehouse from the case of the banker which it was thought to resemble by the Privy Council. The case in which that observation was made, as well as the case of *Wilson v. Cooper,******* and possibly *Chase v. Washburn,* printed above, are distinguishable from the elevator cases by the fact that the person delivering the grain had no more than an option to take grain or something else, such as money. That circumstance may well be held to create a presumption that the title to the grain was parted with, and that the miller assumed an alternative liability *ex contractu.* Moreover, in the case in the Privy Council, the evidence of an option to take grain was thought doubtful, and it is to be noted that the storehouse was connected with a private mill, and that the power

---

* *Grove v. Brien,* 8 How. 429, 440.
** *Bird v. Brown,* 4 Exch. 786, 799.
*** *Gardiner v. Suydam,* 3 Seld. 357, 363, explained in *Kimberly v. Patchin,* 19 N.Y. 330, 339.
**** *Aldridge v. Johnson,* 7 El. & Bl. 885, 898; *Langton v. Horton,* 4 H. & N. 402.
***** *Sup.* p. [279]; 10 Iowa, 560.

of the millers was stated by the court in terms hardly consistent with the possibility of their not having the title. The duty of owners of an elevator is not alternative, but single. It is to deliver the amount receipted for, and nothing else. It is further to keep that amount on hand in that elevator and to deliver from that elevator. This is wholly different from the undertaking of bankers. They do not assume any duty to keep on hand a pile of dollars or sovereigns, out of which a delivery may be demanded by their customer. They are guilty of no breach of duty to him if they part with their last coin, provided that when he draws on them they find means to honor his check. In the other case there is a specific fund at every moment, determined by locality, either the bin or the elevator as may hereafter be held, to the whole or a part of which the receipt-holder may look.

Buyers from public warehouses.—We have pretty much confined our discussion to the relation between warehousemen and depositors; but it has been incidentally mentioned that proprietors of elevators are often themselves buyers and sellers of grain, and that they mix their own stock with the general mass in store. This not only complicates the question already considered, but raises a new one as to the rights of purchasers holding orders before delivery. The same policy, however, which leads to the treatment of depositors as bailors retaining a right of property would seem to apply to buyers from the warehouseman with nearly equal force. There is a preliminary difficulty that while the bailor may be able to follow his property into a particular bin, supposing his claim not to extend to all grain of the kind in the elevator, the buyer on the other hand gets only an order on the elevator generally. But assuming this to be got over in both cases, as we have suggested, there remains a general principle of the English law of sales to be encountered. The rule is that when a contract is made for a part of a specific mass, no title passes to the buyer until appropriation of a certain portion to that contract.* This has led to nice distinctions of which perhaps the most remarkable is the latest. The defendant had sold A. eighty quarters of barley, parcel of a large amount in his granary. A. gave the plaintiff an order on the defendant for sixty quarters out of the eighty. The plaintiff paid A., and afterwards asked the defendant to confirm this transfer." Defendant said, "All right, when you get the forwarding note I will put the barley on the line," and sent samples. A. became bankrupt, and the defendant, whom he had not paid, was held liable to the plaintiff in trover for refusing to deliver sixty quarters, on the ground that although the title had not passed, the defendant was estopped to set that up, having (it was presumed), induced the plaintiff to take no steps by his statement that it was all right.**

It may be observed in this case that there does not seem to have been any evidence that the plaintiff was induced to abstain from active measures by the defendant's representations, and that seems to have been presumed by the court to found the estoppel. Moreover, there seems to be room for doubt whether the representa-

---

* *Campbell v. Mersey Docks and Harbor Board,* 14 C.B. N.S. 412, and many other cases. As Bayley, B., says, "If I agree to deliver a certain quantity of oil, as ten out of eighteen tons, no one can say which part of the whole quantity I have agreed to deliver until a selection is made. There is no individuality until it has been divided." *Gillett v. Hill,* 2 Cr. & Mees. 530, 535.

** *Knights v. Wiffen,* L.R. 5 Q.B. 660. See *Woodley v. Coventry,* 2 Hurlst. & C. 164.

tions of the defendant necessarily implied any thing more than an undertaking to deliver the specified amount of barley, on which he might be liable *ex contractu,* but which did not import a passing of property.

The New York cases tend in an opposite direction. *Kimberly v. Patchin,** was a sale of six thousand bushels out of what was in fact a larger quantity; but the parties thought that the specific heap contained either just the amount or less, and used words importing a present transfer, and the seller afterwards signed an acknowledgment that he had received the amount in store. There was no doubt as to the intention of the parties, and it was held that the property passed. The court intimated that when the quantity and the general mass from which an article sold by weight, measure, or count is to be taken are specified, the title might pass if the sale was complete in all its other circumstances, and the parties so intended.

So in *Cushing v. Breed,* which has been already discussed with reference to the rights of the original depositor, it will be remembered that the plaintiff was purchaser of part of a larger quantity deposited; and in *Hall v. Boston & Worcester R.R.,*** where there had been an appropriation, the court say that even without that, "the effect of the vendor's order, when accepted by the parties who had the custody of the whole property, and were to select out of the whole the portion to be delivered, under the circumstances and according to the usual course of business, would have transferred the property in twenty-eight barrels to the plaintiffs, as against the creditors of the vendor, so as to subject the vendees to the loss in case of fire."****

However, it is not intended to criticise the general rule of the English and most of the American cases. It is enough to say that we are now considering a peculiar transaction, and the question is what the intention of the parties may fairly be presumed to be. There is no doubt that buyer and seller can become tenants in common in certain proportions of a certain mass, if they want to. There is, we presume, equally little doubt that they do want to in this case. In ordinary purchases the buyer contemplates carrying off his purchase as a preliminary to dealing with it. But grain in bulk is habitually stored in elevators, and cannot well be kept elsewhere. A great part of the dealings in it are by the simple transfer of warehouse receipts.**** The buyer very probably does not desire to withdraw the grain, but only to acquire property as the basis of future dealings of his own. He may not draw on the elevator for six months. He may not draw on it at all. The grain may not be called for until the order has changed hands a dozen times.

The subsequent power of substitution on the part of the warehouseman stands on the same ground as in the case of a deposit previously discussed.

In reviewing what has been suggested in this note, it is impossible not to think of Lord Abinger's language in a case of another sort; "that is a very elaborate kind

---

*19 N.Y. 330. See *Russell v. Carrington,* 42 N.Y. 118; *Waldron v. Chase,* 37 Me. 414. *Young v. Miles,* 20 Wisc. 615, which prefers the doctrine of *Kimberly v. Patchin* to that of *Scudder v. Worster,* 11 Cush. 573, was not a case of a sale *ex* a mass, but a deposit to be mingled with the mass according to the ordinary usage of elevators.

**14 Allen, 439, 443.

***See also *Warren v. Milliken,* 57 Me. 97.

****They have ever been thought a sufficient tender in Chicago to satisfy a contract to deliver grain, unless the purchaser should insist on seeing it. *McPherson v. Gale,* 40 Ill. 368.

of contract;" but if "it might be true that the contract is such as that suggested,"* we think that, in the absence of evidence of a contrary intent, it should be presumed. Business men who deal with elevators can hardly be supposed to have in view the legal machinery by which the result is worked out; but if as we suppose they have in view that result, it is the business of the law to carry out their intentions, if it can. If the common law is inadequate to the task we conceive that legislation is needed.

Editor's Notes

1. The ellipsis replaces the text of the case. See Holmes's note for a complete citation.
2. Correction, in Holmes's copy (OWH Papers, Paige Box 18, Item 4): . . . parcel of a larger quantity.

6.60

From *American Law Review* 6:549 (1872).

Principles of the Law of Real Property. Intended as a first book for the use of students in conveyancing. By JOSHUA WILLIAMS, Esq., of Lincoln's Inn, one of Her Majesty's Counsel. Fourth American from the Ninth English edition, with the notes and references to the previous American editions by WILLIAM HENRY RAWLE, Author of "A Treatise on Covenants for Title;" and additional notes and references by JAMES T. MITCHELL. Philadelphia: T. & J. W. Johnson & Co. 1872.

This is a reprint of the last English edition of Mr. Williams's treatise, and has the advantage of containing the author's latest corrections. The present American editor has confined himself in the main to making a few additions, some of them quite interesting and important, however, to Mr. Rawle's notes. The latter we always read with renewed pleasure whenever we take up the book. Instead of spoiling the proportions of the text, as American notes to English works are apt to do, they elucidate and explain it with an ability fully equal to that of the author. They are always apposite, always well written, and everywhere show the hand of a master who moves easily through his work. There is little which needs to be said as to the merits of Mr. Williams's text, for its excellence is attested by its popularity. American beginners will be troubled by the frequent reference to late English statutes. But they will do well to read it notwithstanding. Indeed the statutes are not the least instructive part, as they indicate the weak points of the common-law system more accurately than our sweeping changes do.

The author's definition of a vested remainder seems to us open to criticism. He says, p. 243, "if any estate . . . is always ready from its commencement to its end, to come into possession the moment the prior estates, be they what they may, happen to determine,—it is then a *vested remainder*, and recognized by law as an estate grantable by deed." Suppose that land is devised to A. for life, and at his death then to be divided among such of the children of B. as shall outlive A., and that B. has died leaving children before the will goes into effect; that, we take it, is a contingent

*8 M. & W. 426, 427.

remainder, according to *Olney v. Hull,* 21 Pick. 311; a case which is not in the least impaired by *Blanchard v. Blanchard,* 1 Allen, 223, and similar English cases where a different intent was manifested.—See *Thomson v. Ludington* in notice of 104 Mass.

We do not see but this answers all the requirements of the definition however. The children of B., who will take at any given moment should the estate determine then, are ascertained, and the remainder is always ready to come into possession at that moment. But the instant which fixes the right to possession also fixes the title of the remainder-men for the first time; and when the contingency goes not only to the enjoyment, but to the title, the remainder is contingent. It is not enough that the estate is ready to come into possession whenever the prior estate determines, but the remainder-man must have a title before it determines, in order to have a vested interest. Perhaps it would complete the definition to add, "and if there is a remainder-man now answering the description under which he is to take" before, "it is then a vested remainder."

Those who are interested in the discussion (Appendix C.) of the common law rights of the tenants of a manor—a discussion which goes to the roots of the notion of individual property in land—should compare the very learned monograph of M. Nasse, on the Land Community of the Middle Ages, recently translated for the Cobden Club, and published by Macmillan.

6.61

From *American Law Review* 6:550 (1827).

American Leading Cases; being select decisions of American Courts in several departments of law, with especial reference to Mercantile Law. With Notes. By J. I. CLARK HARE and H. B. WALLACE. Fifth edition, enlarged and improved, with additional notes and references to American decisions, by J. I. CLARK HARE and J. W. WALLACE. 2 vols. Philadelphia: T. & J. W. Johnson & Co. 1871.

New editions of good books seem to be dangerous things for the reputation of their authors. The cases which accumulate on any subject in ten years are too numerous to be collected, compared, distinguished, explained, and generalized, without more labor than a successful lawyer is willing to give. Yet, however able a man may be, nothing will take the place of drudgery, and a book by a second-rate man, who has searched the reports and read the cases he cites, is better than one by a first-rate man who has not taken that trouble. The American Leading Cases have an established reputation. The broad handling of Mr. Wallace and the acuteness of Mr. Hare have each had their share of well-deserved praise. It is to be regretted if a new edition of such good work does not accomplish for the last decade what has already been done for the law up to that time. We must say that the book before us falls short of that mark. The place of the late Mr. H. B. Wallace, who wrote the notes to the first volume, is taken by the learned reporter of the Supreme Court. But his labors in other departments have prevented his doing justice to this. We have not space for a detailed examination. An example taken at random here and there must suffice. According to our count there have been added to the first note in the book, an elaborate discussion of voluntary conveyances, just eight cases. Not to speak of others, we find no notice of *Spirett v. Willows*, 3 De G., J. & S. 293, in which Lord Westbury goes nearly the whole length of *Reade v. Livingston;* nor of *Freeman v. Pope*, L.R. 5 Ch. 538, in which the language of the former Chancellor is qualified by Lord Hatherley and the Lord Justice Giffard. Other notes which we have looked into seem to give equally discouraging results. Under the head "power of one partner to bind the firm," we find four or five new cases cited on the power of one partner to make an assignment of all the partnership property, including *Robinson v. Gregory*, 29 Barb. 560, but do not see *Welles v. March*, 30 N.Y. 344, on the same point, in which it appears that *Robinson v. Gregory* was reversed by the Court of Appeals. The half dozen lines in which the result of the cases referred to is given, are the main addition to the note in question. Not more than ten cases are added to the very valuable note on partnership real estate; and among those ten we do not observe *Darby v. Darby*, 3 Drew. 495, and *Essex v. Essex*, 20 Beav. 442, in favor of conversion into personalty out and out; nor the equally important *Wilcox v. Wilcox*, 13 Allen, 252 and *Shearer v. Shearer*, 98 Mass. 107, in which Mr. Justice Welles maintains the contrary doctrine with remarkable ability. So in the note on Domicile, we do not see *Udny v. Udny*, L.R. 1 H.L. Sc. 441, perhaps the most important case on the subject.

When we turn to Mr. Hare's volume we must speak with more reserve. It is much harder to form an opinion of the value of considerable additions than to detect their absence. We have missed some cases where we should have expected to find them, but we have found too many to draw a general conclusion from the absence of a few. If there is ground for complaint, we do not forget the excellence of the original work, and we remember with respect that Mr. Hare, like Mr. Rawle, to whom we have referred in another notice, has in these days of slopwork and ignorant makeshifts written on legal subjects with the knowledge and style of an accomplished scholar.

There is no table of cases cited in either volume, which is inexcusable, and the proof-reading and verification of citations seem to have been carelessly done.

6.62

From *American Law Review* 6:553 (1872).

American Trade-Mark Cases. A compilation of all the reported Trade-mark Cases decided in the American Courts prior to the year 1871, with an Appendix containing the leading English Cases, and the United States Act in relation to the registration of Trade-marks, with Constructions of the Commissioners of Patents affecting the same. Edited by ROWLAND COX, &c. Cincinnati: Robert Clarke & Co. 1871.

This "is arranged as a compilation of cases" we are told, "from a conviction that the nature of the subject is such that in no other manner can it be as safely and satisfactorily treated." We do not perceive any thing in the nature of the subject that should make the exercise of intelligence less satisfactory in this than in other branches of the law. The justification for the collection is that trademarks form a distinct head of the law, and that the authorities are comprised in such small bulk that they can be given *in extenso* in a single volume. A mere republication, without more, has its value to those lawyers who are especially interested in the questions to which the cases relate, and we have already found this one useful. But a reprint of reported cases in chronological order, with occasionally one not to be found in the reports, is not a treatment of the subject, for that requires comparison, analysis, and criticism. Whether the editor has not done wisely in abstaining from it in the present stage of the law, is another question. We are inclined to think that he has, and to say that in gathering the *disjecta membra* of the law of trade-marks into a *corpus* contained in one handy volume, he has done a very good thing for the profession, without much trouble to himself.

6.63

From *American Law Review* 6:554 (1872).

Reports of all the published Life and Accident Insurance Cases determined in the American courts prior to January, 1871.

Reports of the Life and Accident Insurance Cases determined in the Courts of America, England, and Ireland, between January, 1871, and January, 1872 together with most of the prior English Cases. With Notes and References By MELVILLE M. BIGELOW, of the Boston Bar. New York: Hurd & Houghton. 1872.

This is another series of cases on a special subject which it is convenient to have separate from the reports at large. The decisions are arranged by states, and subordinately in order of time. We see the care of the editor in the footnotes and cross-references which abound, and in the accuracy of the citations. These show that he has performed the thankless task of verifying references, a duty so easily shirked and yet so essential with our American reports, where the grossest carelessness is rather the rule than the exception. We observe that the second volume contains the case of *Miller v. Brooklyn Life Ins. Co.,* in the Baltimore *Law Transcript,* to which we called attention in our last volume, as well as the still unpublished decision of the Supreme Court of the United States, affirming that below. There are also several unreported decisions of some value.

6.64

From *American Law Review* 6:556 (1872).

Massachusetts Reports, 104. Cases argued and determined in the Supreme Judicial Court of Massachusetts, January to September, 1870. ALBERT G. BROWNE, Jr., Reporter. Boston: H. O. Houghton & Co. 1872.

This volume contains among other interesting decisions the Boston Theatre cases and that on the exemption of Harvard College from assessments for betterments on some of its lands. These and others will be found in our Digest, and we shall only call attention to one or two.

The case of *Jones v. Boston,* p. 75, which decided that a city is not liable on the Gen. Sts. c. 44, § 22, for an injury received by a traveller on a sidewalk which it is bound to keep in repair, through the falling on him of a sign which the proprietor of an adjoining building had suspended over the sidewalk on an iron rod insecurely fastened to the building, although the city had notice of the position and insecurity of the sign and its fastening, should be compared with *Hewison v. New Haven,* 34 Conn. 136, which does not seem to have been cited. There a city subject to a somewhat similar duty was held not liable for an injury occasioned to the plaintiff, while in the use of due care, by the falling of an iron weight attached to a flag which was suspended across the street by third parties. Both cases follow *Hixon v. Lowell,* 13 Gray, 59 in preference to *Drake v. Lowell,* 13 Met. 292, and state the distinction which in *Hixon v. Lowell* the court thought it easier to feel than to express.

In *Hill Manufacturing Co. v. Boston & Lowell R.R. Co.,* p. 122, upon facts which were considered to warrant the inference that the defendants were liable as common carriers beyond their own route, it was held that the Act of Congress of March 3, 1851, c. 43, 9 U.S. St. at L. 635, limiting the liability of ship-owners, &c., does not relieve a common carrier, who ships goods over part of his route on a vessel which he does not own or charter, from liability for the destruction of such goods by an accidental fire on the vessel.

In *Independent Ins. Co. v. Thomas,* p. 192, the court considered themselves bound by *Bronson v. Rhodes,* 7 Wall. 229, and *Butler v. Horwitz, ib.* 258, to order a specific judgment for gold coin upon a debt payable in gold—a point upon which some doubt has been felt, we believe.

In *Thomson v. Ludington,* p. 193, a devise to testator's widow during her life or widowhood, and at her decease or marriage "to such of my children as shall then be living, share and share alike; the names of my said children are A., B., C., D. and E., to them and to their heirs and assigns forever," was said to create a contingent remainder, following *Olney v. Hull,* 21 Pick. 311. On the other hand a devise to a wife for life, remainder to A., B., C., D., and E., "provided that if any of the last five named children die before my wife, then the property to be equally divided between the survivors," has been held by the same court to create a vested remainder, defeasible on a condition subsequent. *Blanchard v. Blanchard,* 1 Allen, 223. Both decisions are clearly right, and *Blanchard v. Blanchard,* which has been somewhat questioned at the bar, is not unsupported by authority,—*Hervey v. M'Laughlin,* 1 Price, 264; *Price v. Hall,* L.R. 5 Eq. 399, 402; *Poor v. Considine,* 6 Wall. 458, 476.

The distinction lies in the intent manifested by the testator. The moment that effect is allowed to an expression of intention, that an estate should vest at one moment rather than another, so that the same future interest may be made vested or contingent, at the will of the person creating it, as it clearly may be, the slightest difference of phraseology may suffice to establish a difference of intent, and may give a vested remainder by one set of words and a contingent remainder by another, although the same conditions are prefixed to the enjoyment by the one and the other. A remainder to A., B., C., D., and E., shows a present intent to confer a benefit on A., B., C., D., and E., although there is a divesting clause. One to such of my children as shall survive a certain future event manifests no intention to benefit all my children, but only those who survive the event in question.

There are some important insurance cases in the volume.

6.65

From *American Law Review* 6:558 (1872).

The Law of Contracts. By FRANCIS HILLIARD, Author of "The Law of Torts," "The Law of Injunctions," &c. In two volumes. Philadelphia: Kay & Brother. 1872.

This, we are told in the preface, "has been prepared upon the same plan as the author's work upon the law of torts, and the idea of adding another to the already numerous treatises upon contracts was in part suggested by a pardonable desire to illustrate this other comprehensive department of civil jurisprudence." It is a feature of the work, as the author says, that "the decided cases, of which a brief abstract is attempted, are to a great extent recent." There are collected a large number of decisions that will not be found elsewhere out of the digests. The collection is not exhaustive, nor is the handling of them able, but the difficulties to be overcome are great, and the practitioner may find the book convenient. We have before remarked on the objectionable habit of citing the English Law Reports according to the parts, instead of the volumes in which they are bound; thus, *"Appleby v. Myers,* Law Rep. (Eng.) September, 1866 p. 614;" instead of "L.R. 1 C.P. 615;" and we may add, L.R. 2 C.P. 651, where the earlier decision was reversed. We must add another objection to this sort of thing, *"Warburton v. Great,"* for *Warburton v. Great Western R. Co.;* a method of abbreviation much used by the author.

6.66

From *American Law Review* 6:723 (1872).

The Law Magazine and Review. New Series. No. 3, April 1, 1872. London: Butterworths.

In the third article of this interesting number Mr. Frederick Pollock discusses Austin's definition of law. As his results more or less coincide with opinions which were expressed more at length at the beginning of a course of lectures on jurisprudence, delivered at Harvard College while his article was going through the press, it may be interesting to briefly state some of the points developed by the lecturer, as we hope to present them more at length at some future time.

The general opinion that Austin's definition was not satisfactory from a philosophical point of view has been already expressed in our pages. According to him, law, properly so called, is defined as a command of a definite political superior, or sovereign, which obliges political inferiors or subjects to acts or forbearances of a class, by the imposition of a penalty in case of disobedience; and all sovereign commands which purport to do that are laws. Now it is admitted by every one that who is the sovereign is a question of fact equivalent to the question who has the sum of the political powers of a state in his hands. That is to say, sovereignty is a form of power, and the will of the sovereign is law, because he has power to compel obedience or to punish disobedience, and for no other reason. The limits within which his will is law, then, are those within which he has, or is believed to have, power to compel or punish. It was shown by many instances that this power of the sovereign was limited not only without, by the liability to war (which it was shown might be a true sanction), but within, as by conflicting principles of sovereignty (the territorial and the tribal), by organizations of persons not sharing in the sovereign power, and by unorganized public opinion. It was shown that there might be law without sovereignty, and that where there is a sovereign, properly so called, other bodies not sovereign, and even opinion, might generate law in a philosophical sense against the will of the sovereign. For it is to be remembered that in most states there has been a large number, and in many a numerical majority of males, who have had no share in the political power; while at the same time their physical power, and consequently their desires, were not to be ignored, and in some cases were not to be disobeyed.

In the lectures referred to, it was doubted whether law, in the more limited meaning which lawyers give to the word, possessed any other common attribute than of being enforced by the procedure of the courts, and therefore of practical importance to lawyers. It was shown that the rules enforced in that way did not always depend on the courts for their efficacy in governing conduct, and that it was a mere fiction to say that, either philosophically or legally, they necessarily emanated from the will of the sovereign *as law.*

Austin said, following Heineccius (*Recitationes,* § 72), that custom only became law by the tacit consent of the sovereign manifested by its adoption by the courts; and that before its adoption it was only a motive for decision, as a doctrine of political economy, or the political aspirations of the judge, or his gout, or the blandishments of the emperor's wife might have been. But it is clear that in many cases custom and mercantile usage have had as much compulsory power as law could have, in spite of prohibitory statutes; and as to their being only motives for decision until adopted, what more is the decision which adopts them as to any future decision? What more indeed is a statute; and in what other sense law, than that we believe that the motive which we think that it offers to the judges will prevail, and will induce them to decide a certain case in a certain way, and so shape our conduct on that anticipation? A precedent may not be followed; a statute may be emptied of its contents by construction, or may be repealed without a saving clause after we have acted on it; but we expect the reverse, and if our expectations come true, we say that we have been subject to law in the matter in hand. It must be remembered, as is clear from numerous instances of judicial interpretation of statutes in England and of constitutions in this country, that in a civilized state it is not the will of the sovereign that makes lawyers' law, even when that is its source, but what a body of subjects, namely the judges, by whom it is enforced, *say* is his will. The judges have other motives for decision, outside their own arbitrary will, beside the commands of their sovereign. And whether those other motives are, or are not, equally compulsory, is immaterial, if they are sufficiently likely to prevail to afford a ground for prediction. The only question for the lawyer is, how will the judges act? Any motive for their action, be it constitution, statute, custom, or precedent, which can be relied upon as likely in the generality of cases to prevail, is worthy of consideration as one of the sources of law, in a treatise on jurisprudence. Singular motives, like the blandishments of the emperor's wife, are not a ground of prediction, and are therefore not considered.

Passing to the sufficiency of Austin's definition for determining what sovereign commands are to be called law, it was thought, in the lectures referred to, that the specific penalty or sanction which Austin seemed to tacitly assume as the final test, could not always be relied on.

The notion of duty involves something more than a tax on a certain course of conduct. A protective tariff on iron does not create a duty not to bring it into the country. The word imports the existence of an absolute wish on the part of the power imposing it to bring about a certain course of conduct, and to prevent the contrary. A legal duty cannot be said to exist if the law intends to allow the person supposed to be subject to it an option at a certain price. The test of a legal duty is the absolute nature of the command. If a statute subjects a person to a penal action in case of certain conduct on his part, but such conduct is protected and treated as lawful in all the other connections in which it may come before the court, an option is in fact allowed. A very striking illustration will be found in the well known case of the *Creole,* 2 Wall. Jr. 485, where a statute providing that certain vessels should be "obliged" to employ a pilot or "forfeit and pay" a sum spoken of as "a penalty," was held to leave the employment optional, subject to a tax,—whether rightly or not is immaterial. The imposition of a penalty is therefore only evidence tending to show that an absolute command was intended (a rule of construction). But an absolute command does not exist—penalty or no penalty—unless a breach of it is deprived of the protection of the law, which is shown by a number of consequences not accurately determinable in a general definition, such as the invalidity of contracts to do the forbidden act;—the rule *in pari delicto potior est conditio defendentis,*—the denial of relief when the illegal act is part of the plaintiff's case, &c.

A fortiori in those cases where there is no penalty directly attached to a given act, the existence of a legal duty to abstain from or to perform it, must be determined by these collateral consequences. Liability to pay the fair price or value of an enjoyment, or to be compelled to restore or give up property belonging to another, is not a penalty; and this is the extent of the ordinary liability to a civil action at common law. In a case of this sort, where there are no collateral consequences attached, (which is perhaps the fact with regard to some contracts, to pay money, for instance), it is hard to say that there is a duty in strictness, and the rule is inserted in law books for the empirical reason above referred to, that it is applied by the courts and must therefore be known by professional men.

As liability to a civil action is not a penalty or sanction of itself creating a duty, so, on the other hand, it does not necessarily imply culpability, or a breach of duty, as Austin thought, who looked at the law too much as a criminal lawyer. The object of the law is to accomplish an external result. When it can best accomplish that result by operating on men's wills, or when it is secure of what it desires in the absence of wilfulness or negligence, then it may very properly make wilfulness or negligence the gist of the action,—one of the necessary elements of liability. But in other instances it may be thought that this is too narrow a limit; it may be thought that titles should be protected against even innocent conversion; that persons should be indemnified, at all events, for injuries from extra-hazardous sources, in which case negligence is not an element. Public policy must determine where the line is to be drawn. The rule of the common law, requiring the owner of cattle to keep them on his land at his peril, has been very properly abandoned in some of the western states, where the enclosure of their vast prairies is necessarily for a long time out of the question.

6.67

From *American Law Review* 6:728 (1872).[1]

A Treatise on the Law and Practice of Injunctions in Equity. By WILLIAM WILLIAMSON KERR, of Lincoln's Inn, Barrister-at-Law. Edited with notes and references to American cases, by WILLIAM A. HERRICK. Boston: Little, Brown, & Co. 1871.

A Treatise on the Law of Fraud and Mistake. By WILLIAM WILLIAMSON KERR, &c. With notes to American cases, by ORLANDO F. BUMP, Counsellor-at-Law. New York: Baker, Voorhis, & Co. 1872.

A Treatise on the Law and Practice as to Receivers appointed by the Court of Chancery. By WILLIAM WILLIAMSON KERR, &c. With notes and references to American authorities, by GEORGE TUCKER BISPHAM. Philadelphia: Kay & Brother. 1872.

The best testimony to Mr. Kerr's merits is the simultaneous reprinting by different American publishers of so many of his works. The most important of them is the first named, and it is really a very useful book. The chapters on patents and copyrights, for instance, are excellent; and we have got aid from him in a partnership question which we did not find elsewhere.

The second of the volumes on our list is concerned mainly with the principles which govern equitable interference in cases of fraud and mistake. But Mr. Kerr's treatise is not confined to a statement of these principles. His task is a different one, and a more useful one than this. The principles which regulate the action of a court of chancery, even if stated as ably and as clearly as they are by Mr. Adams, do not afford much help to the ordinary practitioner. When you are considering whether you have any remedy in equity, and, if you have, what the court will probably do under the peculiar circumstances in which your client finds himself, you want some case in point. The equity reports, with their formidable masses of facts, which the nature of a chancery suit renders it impossible to boil down into the convenient catchwords of the common law, are too much for most men. To one, therefore, who, like Mr. Kerr, has gone through the books with especial reference to only one or two topics of chancery jurisdiction, and has, therefore not been compelled either to reduce the number of the divisions of his subject, or to compress his illustrations beyond the point of intelligibility, one may well feel grateful.

The work on receivers deals less with general principles, and has, perhaps, rather more of peculiarly local law than the others. But the extensive and minute character of British legislation makes a considerable portion of all modern English text-books useless in this country, while it is impossible to present the results of the American cases in the form of foot-notes. What is needed, as Mr. Bump says in his preface, is a book which shall combine both the English and American law in one text; and that is not likely to be done, except on this side of the water.

None of the three American editors above named attempt to present the American law *in extenso*. Mr. Herrick puts in a few cases here and there as flying buttresses to the original structure, without much affecting it one way or the other. Mr. Bispham's notes seem to be very good as far as they go, and have the merit of being largely drawn from late cases, but they are not a back-breaking labor. Mr. Bump seems to have done the most, and we know him to be a man of industry and skill. But the value of all three volumes lies mainly in the text.

All of them are well indexed, well arranged, well printed, and give the American as well as the English cases in the tables.

Editor's Note

1. According to Holmes's copy in the Library of Congress this book notice was coauthored with John Ropes. There is no indication of which portion was written by Holmes.

6.68

From *American Law Review* 6:731 (1872).

Fire Insurance Cases: being a collection of all the reported cases on Fire Insurance, in England, Ireland, Scotland, and America, from the earliest period to the present time, chronologically arranged. Vol. I. Covering the period from 1729 to 1839. With notes and references. By EDMUND H. BENNETT. New York: Hurd & Houghton. 1872.

This is a companion volume to those of Mr. Bigelow, and like them is handsomely printed and carefully edited. Little more than care was required for the work to be done, but to collect "all the reported cases upon fire insurance or land, gleaned from the English, Scotch, Irish, and American reports, including the British Provinces," from 1729 to 1839, to rewrite head-notes, abridge diffuse statements of facts and arguments, not to speak of the occasional notes which Judge Bennett has added, is a matter of considerable and rather thankless labor.

We suppose there is a limit to the business of reprinting the reports by topics, which just now seems to be having a run. The original series and an index will suffice with regard to most subjects of the law. And where are we to draw the line? If we do not want a collection of all the cases on contracts, or on shipping, or on whatever other subjects or subdivisions the conflicting fancies of different editors may lead them to redistribute the reports under, what is the excuse for any? There is none, perhaps, other than the practical reason to be found in the subjects selected. Insurance is a distinct business, and the lawyers and business men who are concerned in its several branches are very glad to be able to lay their hands on all the cases relating to their specialty. Judge Bennett's book, like Mr. Bigelow's, will probably have a great sale among those who want a perfect library on this subject, but not on others; and if there is a class in the community who will buy a book, that is a tolerably fair proof that it is needed.

6.69

From *American Law Review* 6:732 (1872).

Index to Precedents in Conveyancing, and to Common and Commercial Forms, arranged in alphabetical order, with subdivisions of an analytical nature; together with an Appendix containing an Abstract of the Stamp Act, 1870, with a Schedule of Duties; the Regulations relative to, and the Stamp Duties payable on, Probates of Wills, Letters of Administration, Legacies, and Successions. By WALTER ARTHUR COPINGER, Esq., of the Middle Temple, Barrister-at-Law, author of "The Law of Copyright in Works of Literature and Art." London: Stevens & Haynes. 1872.

This index to above ten thousand precedents and forms must, we should think, prove most useful in England. But a considerable portion of its contents is of only local value, and so many of the books referred to are only to be found in large libraries, that it is not likely to be much used in this country. We wish that the author's plan could be followed in this country, but we fear that it could hardly be done to advantage.

6.70

From *American Law Review* 6:732 (1872).

Notes on Common Forms. A Book of Massachusetts Law. By URIEL H. CROCKER. Second Edition, revised and enlarged. Boston: Little, Brown, & Company. 1872.

This is one of the first books which a lawyer practising in Massachusetts needs to buy. Indeed, it needs no recommendation to the profession in this state, for its merits are already known. Unpretending as it is, it could not have been produced without a great deal of patient industry, a familiarity with the reports and statutes, and a union of ability and experience, which have enabled the author in the first place to discern and then to answer the questions which arise in practice. It is one of those excellent books to which you can go in a hurry and find what you want. The local character of the work, and our limited space, make it impossible to go into a detailed examination of the new edition. It is considerably enlarged and added to, and some of the errors which we had noted in the first edition have been corrected. We still observe one or two, mostly slight. The most important is the definition of dower, which is obviously too inaccurate, even for a rough statement.

Some of the innovations suggested we do not like; for instance, the advice to omit the seal from a will. A seal may be necessary to make the will a valid execution of a power to appoint by an instrument under seal. More important is the omission of the mention of heirs in the devise of a fee, which is all very well if there are no lands outside of Massachusetts, but which, we think, cautious scriveners would always insert. We must say that we also dislike the similar omission in the granting clause of Mr. Crocker's form of a deed, but perhaps with less reason.

6.71

From *American Law Review* 6:733 (1872).

The Massachusetts Digest; being a Digest of the Decisions of the Supreme Judicial Court of Massachusetts, from the year 1857 to the year 1869; or from the 9th Gray to the 102d Mass., inclusive. By EDMUND H. BENNETT and HENRY W. HOLLAND. Volume III. Boston: Little, Brown, & Company. 1872.

A digest should be made by an acute and accurate lawyer. It should be made up by an experienced book-maker skilled in all the devices of the trade. Mr. Abbott, for instance, is an excellent person to render the chaos of the United States Digest accessible by putting things where people look for them, and by a dozen convenient artifices which his experience has suggested. The very intelligent gentlemen who have done the present work shine more, as it seems to us, in the other half of the business, and manifest, perhaps, a somewhat over-scrupulous care. A state digest is not much used except by those who have access to the reports, and only want an index to them. The very fact that it is not expected to serve any other turn justifies a more general and looser form of statement than ought to be admitted in a work like the United States Digest, which many lawyers have to accept as their only report of a case. But comparisons and comments, however brief and correct, are rather out of place in a book which we only open when we want an authority, and when, as an English judge said, an ounce of precedent is worth a pound of principle. We miss the double-leading of the key-words of a sentence, which is such a convenience in Mr. Baldwin's recent Connecticut digest, and it has seemed to us that the cases do not always occur under the most obvious heads. But this latter defect is atoned for by a multitude of cross-references, a matter in which the third volume is a great improvement on the other two; and the alternative citation of the particular page and volume, thus: "See TRUSTEE PROCESS, or 10 Gray, 379," is a most excellent means of saving the reader labor. The statement of cases is not always elegant, but they have been studied with a close attention to their precise facts which is rarely shown by such works, but which is the first condition of success.

6.72

From *American Law Review* 6:737 (1872).

A Digest of the Reported Cases (from 1756 to 1870, Inclusive,) Relating to Criminal Law, Criminal Information, and Extradition, founded on "Harrison's Analytical Digest." By R. A. FISHER, Esq., of the Middle Temple, Barrister-at-Law. San Francisco: Sumner Whitney & Co. 1871.

This is a convenient and sufficiently good-looking reprint of one title of Fisher's Harrison's Digest, to which we are told in the preface the cases in the tenth and eleventh volumes of Cox's Criminal Cases have been added under their appropriate heads. It is also stated that the notes have been compared with the reports, and the citations verified.

6.73

From *American Law Review* 6:743 (1872).

Judgments delivered in the Courts of the United States for the District of Massachusetts. By JOHN LOWELL, LL.D., District Judge. Boston: Little, Brown, & Co. 1872.
This volume contains many important cases in different branches of the law. A number of them have appeared from time to time in our pages, such as *Lorway v. Lou-*

sada, p. 77 (1 Am. Law Rev. 92), asserting the jurisdiction of the district court over a suit by an alien against the consul of his nation, residing within the district, to recover fees improperly exacted; the *Becherdass Ambaidass,* p. 569 (*ante,* p. 74), in which a consul's protest against the court's taking jurisdiction of a libel for wages was respected, and several others. There are many decisions on the bankrupt law, for which we must refer to our bankruptcy digests. *Re Griffiths,* p. 431, is discussed *ante,* p. 50. The greatest dramatic interest attaches to the prize cases arising out of the late war. That time seems already so remote that we are able to see the picturesque side which is vividly brought before us by the judge's excellent statements of fact. Each is a little story. In Seventy-eight Bales of Cotton, p. 11, cotton picked up at sea by a cruiser of the North Atlantic blockading squadron under circumstances which showed that it had recently been abandoned, either by an enemy or by a neutral engaged in breaking the blockade, was held to be prize, not derelict, so far that the captors were only entitled to one half, not to the whole. The *Selma,* p. 30, arose out of the famous fight in Mobile Bay, on the question who were entitled to share in the prize. A stricter rule was applied than in the case of the ram Tennessee, which was sent to another port, and it was held that a vessel which could not have rendered any assistance in the capture was not entitled to a share merely because it was within signal distance and under the command of Admiral Farragut. The *Georgia,* p. 96, is already well known by the report in 7 Wall. 32, where this decision, that the attempted sale of the Georgia in Liverpool to a neutral, June, 1863, was invalid by the law of nations, was affirmed.

The *A. R. Dunlap,* p. 350, expresses an opinion, since sanctioned by the supreme court of the United States, that a material-man need not show that the owner had no personal credit on which the repairs could have been procured at the place where they were furnished in order to maintain his lien, notwithstanding the language of *Pratt v. Reed,* 19 How. 359.

Great Western Ins. Co. v. Thwing, p. 444, has since been reversed by the supreme court. A policy of insurance contained a covenant that the ship should not load more than her registered tonnage. The ship took on board 23 tons more than that amount, *inter alia,* 238 tons of cannel coal. The jury were instructed that if they believed from the evidence that the cannel coal was received and used as dunnage and not as cargo, it would not amount to a loading under the covenant in question. The point was ingenious, but it seems to us unsound, as the supreme court have held.

In *The Boston,* p. 464, the opinion is expressed that the owner of the whole cargo of a vessel may order her discharge at any suitable place within the port. The *Charles F. Perry,* p. 475, decides that a seaman who was shipped as cook on a foreign voyage, and who performed extra services as stevedore in a foreign port, may proceed in the admiralty for compensation for the extra services, though his wages as cook have been paid in full.

We have taken these cases at random, and must refer the reader to the book for more. The opinions, which include those delivered by Judge Lowell in the circuit court, are of course scholarly and acute. We are rather struck by an inclination to adjust the general equities between the parties in preference to a definite deduction of results from technical rules,—a tendency which a common lawyer regards with suspicion, but which the admiralty practice seems to foster.

6.74
SUMMARY OF EVENTS
UNITED STATES

From *American Law Review* 6:748 (1872).

A NEW PRACTICE ACT.—

We print in full an act[1] which will make great changes in the pleadings and practice in the United States courts.

The fifth section, adopting the practice, pleadings, &c., of the states in which the United States courts are held, seems to us a most beneficial change. It would be too much to expect the construction of a philosophic system from congress, and that of the common law has little to recommend it except its connection with substantive legal doctrines. The changes which have been made by the states are mainly in the abolition of useless technicalities, not in the substitution of new ones, which it would be a hardship to require the judges to master; and with however little judgment they may have been made, they have at least the advantage of being known to the lawyers who practise in the particular district.

The sixth section, giving similar process by attachment, &c., to that given in state courts by state laws, will probably be generally approved. Those as to the criminal law are important, and we hope especially that section eight will be liberally construed. Whatever may be the merits or demerits of our criminal law, so long as it is in force it must be supposed to have for an object that criminals should be punished. The state of things in which it was necessary to protect the accused from arbitrary power has given place to one in which the problem is to make punishment more certain, and to bring it to bear more directly on the criminal alone, as exemplified by the British Habitual Criminals Act, and the revival of whipping in certain instances. No one can think it desirable that criminals should escape through technicalities which are useless as safeguards to liberty, and only serve to make conviction more a matter of chance. It is probably true that very often punishment does more harm than good; but the way to remedy that evil is not to set up a lottery in which the party indicted may draw an escape by mere luck.

Editor's Note

1. Practice in the United States Courts, June 1, 1872, ch. 255, 17 U.S. Statutes at Large, 196. The text of the act followed this introductory note.

6.75
THE ARRANGEMENT OF THE LAW—
PRIVITY

From *American Law Review* 7:46 (1872).

In a former article* we expressed the opinion that a sound classification of the law was impossible, except on the basis of the ultimate conception *duty,* instead of the derivative notion, *rights,* which is the foundation of existing systems. In that we believed ourselves at the time to be original; for although various jurists, such as Falck and Austin, had incidentally remarked that such an arrangement was possible, none of those writers seemed at all to have considered it, or to have realized its importance, but went on to treat the law in the old way.[1] We have found, however, in a recent and able work, which is believed not to have reached this country until after the article in question was in print, and long after it was written, the following passage:—

> There is no more philosophical suggestion in Auguste Comte's writings than that in which he urges, that law should be approached and its object-matter arranged from the point of view of duties, and not from that of rights. . . . Rights, as Comte clearly saw, cannot be taken as ultimate or undecomposable phenomena in law; they require, because they admit, analysis; and this analysis is into the duties, the acts or forbearances, imposed on other persons, the claim to which constitutes the rights. In order to define any person's right, recourse must be had to the acts or forbearances imposed on other persons. Names of rights are "second intentions;" the "first intentions" of which are the duties into which they are analyzable. To take rights and not the corresponding duties as the ultimate phenomena of law, is to stop short of a complete analysis, and to make "entities of abstractions."***

The same author observes, in addition to these considerations, that "a law of 'rights' will not harmonize with ethics;"**** a subject which certainly is always approached from the side of duty, whether we agree or not with the author in denying the existence of moral rights "in the sense of claims, as rights are understood in law."

Without seeking to amplify the argument in favor of this view, or to explain it

---

*5 Am. Law Rev. 1.

**2 Hodgson's Theory of Practice(London, Longmans, 1870), pp. 169, 170 (§ 90, par. 3, 4). We have not been able to refer to the passage cited from Comte. (Cours de Phil. Pos. Leçon lvii. vol. vi. p. 454, ed. 1864.) Some of Bentham's language is also very instructive (View of a Complete Code, ch. 2, 3, 14, 19; Works, vol. iii. pp. 159, 160, 181, 195); and Kant's tables in his Doctrine du Droit, tr. Barni, pp. 60, 61, 81, are tables of *duties.* We use this word as near enough for our present purposes, but subject to an investigation, the outline of which has been sketched in our last number (pp. 724, 725), as to how far what is commonly called law imposes what are properly called duties.

It has been thought advisable to present the outline of a system without going at length into preliminary arguments in its favor, which could be expanded into a separate essay. It suffices to say in opposition to so-called practical schemes, which are sometimes formally suggested, and always implicitly by books on such subjects as telegraphs, railroads, &c., that the end of all classification should be to make the law *knowable;* and that the system best accomplishes that purpose which proceeds from the most general conception to the most specific proposition or exception in the order of logical subordination.

***Ib. p. 209, § 90, par. 53.

further at this time, we give the ground plan in the form of a table, only premising that the primary divisions have reference to the classes upon whom burdens are imposed, that is, whom the law directly addresses; and that the subdivisions have reference to those in favor of whom the burdens are imposed. The table does not profess to be complete, but only to explain the nature of the system. [See next page.]

It is obvious, however, that this scheme does not exhaust the whole body of the law. For instance, under the title, possession, we should have what is commonly made a chapter of a book on torts, and we should have no more under ownership. So under contracts, we should consider only the burdens and duties which contracts impose upon the parties to them or upon strangers. But the greater part of works on real or personal property is taken up with methods of transfer and the different estates or interests into which a valuable object may be subdivided, and of these nothing has been said. We have thus far only looked at a lateral section of the law,— at duties contemplated as existing a given instant of time;[2] it remains to make a longitudinal section, that is, to show them as continuing in time.

The mere fact that a duty is continuous, however, or more accurately, that a series of precisely similar duties is owed from a given individual to another, is not otherwise important than as making it necessary to mark the beginning and end of the series. The duty of A. not to assault B. is the same to-day as yesterday, and a description of it at any given moment is equally good at any other, and when, as in this instance, it is strictly personal, its beginning and end can be sufficiently indicated when it is described under the heads already given. We may go a step further, and say that the mere fact that there are continuous duties owed in turn to each of the series of persons who may successively fill a certain situation of fact; for instance, who may succeed each other in the possession of a thing; is not material. For, as before, a single description of the duties is sufficient, and their beginning and end, as to any particular object of them, is shown by the description of the situation to which they are incident. The duties to persons in a particular situation begin with their beginning, and end with their ceasing, to fill that situation. When you describe the situation, that is, the facts, to which the duties are incident as a legal consequence, you describe the beginning and end of the duties as to a given individual. They begin when all the facts in question concur; they end when one of those facts ceases to be true of him. Thus, if possession should be defined as the power and intention of dealing with a thing in one's own name, it follows that the duties owed to a possessor, simply as such, begin to be owed to A. or B. when he has such power and intent, and cease to be owed to him when he loses either. The modes of succession to the rights of a bare possessor create no fresh difficulty. The duties which are owed to him are incident to a continuing situation of fact, and are owed to any one who fills it, no matter how. It does not concern a stranger whether possession is rightful or wrongful. The modes of succession are, therefore, matters of fact and not of law. It is the situation of fact, and not the right of the previous possessor, which is succeeded to. There are other instances of succession, however, which require a more careful treatment, and which are harder to explain. Some continuing rights are incidents to a situation of fact, which can only be filled by the first person entitled to the rights in question. A certain individual and no other is the person

A. Duties of all the World.

1. To the sovereign
- *a.* Law of prize (applying to persons not subject as well as subjects).
- *b.* Military service—some taxes (*e.g. poll tax.*).
- *c.* Criminal law.

2. To all the World.
- *a.* Law of libel and slander (civil actions).
- *b.* Injuries to the person—false imprisonment, &c.
- *c.* Some nuisances?
- *d.* Fraud independent of contract or special relations.

3. To persons in particular situations or relations (some of this are only special aplications of the class A.2).
- *a.* Law of offices—corporations.
- *b.* Monopolies, such as patent-rights.
- *c.* Possession.
- *d.* Ownership. Easement. Rent? &c.
- *e.* Contract?
- *f.* Domestic relations.

B. Duties of Persons in Particular Situations or Relations.

1. To the Sovereign (perhaps for reasons of convenience to follow duties of all the world to the Sovereign).
- *a.* Duties of officers—impeachment, &c.
- *b.* Eminent domain.
- *c.* Taxes on property.

2. To all the World (perhaps to be put with duties of all the world to persons in the same situations. Some of these are special applications of A. 2).
- *a.* Corporations?
- *b.* Duties of land-owners not to make nuisances on their land, &c, &c.

3. To persons in particular situations or relations (including some more special applications of A. 2, and A. 3).
- *a.* Members of corporations to each other.
- *b.* Landlord and tenant, &c.
- *c.* Trustee and *cestui que trust.*
- *d.* Contractor and contractee.
- *e.* Master and servant.
- *f.* Guardian and ward. &c., &c.

with whom a certain contract was made, or to whom a certain franchise or monopoly was granted; yet the continuing rights incident to the situation of contractee or grantee may be succeeded to by another who cannot fill the situation, and the same is true of ownership as distinguished from bare possession. To explain this, it will be necessary to go into a short historical examination of the origin of *privity*.

This notion is by no means a necessary incident of every legal transfer of property. Even in modern times, the transferee may come in adversely to all the world, as is the case in some proceedings *in rem* in admiralty; and it is clear, from the symbolism employed in the infancy of law, that some of the earliest forms of transfer are based upon capture. Mr. M'Lennan, in his book on Primitive Marriage, shows this to be the case with regard to the acquisition of wives, and that the form of capture is kept up when they have become the objects of barter and sale. The spear, which was the sign of a Roman auction, seems to indicate something similar; and another illustration of the same sort will be found in the *legis actio sacramenti*, described in the fourth book of Gaius, pl. 16. The question is, how the notion arose that a transferee continued the right of the transferor, instead of acquiring a new right arising out of his own relation to the thing transferred.

The discovery that individual ownership was not the earliest form of property cannot perhaps be attributed to any single individual, but it is brought out with remarkable clearness by Mr. M'Lennan (Prim. Marr. 282). After observing that the only species of property known anywhere originally appears to have been property in common, and that the groups were at first the only owners, he says, "the history of the right of property, as we have it, is just that of the growth *inside* groups of proprietary rights distinct from the tribal. It was an advance when clan estates were recognized as distinct from the tribal; it was a farther advance when family estates were recognized as distinct from those of the clan. Barbarism was already far in the rear when individual property made its appearance."

Mr. Maine has shown clearly enough how the succession of heirs to a deceased *paterfamilias* follows from this. Inasmuch as the continuity of the family is a natural fact, no invention was needed to conceive property as remaining in the family after the temporary head had died. Heirs are called *sui heredes* in the XII. Tables; that is, heirs of themselves, or their own property, as is explained by Gaius (Inst. 2, 157), and still better by a striking passage from Paulus.* The gradual change by which the *paterfamilias* instead of manager came to be looked at as owner did not affect the devolution of the *familia* on his death. But it devolved of course in the condition in which he left it. And the heir who succeeded not to the ownership of this or that thing separately, but to the total *hereditas* or headship of the family, with certain rights of property as incident,** took this headship, or right of representing the family interests, subject to the modifications effected by the last manager.

---

*In suis heredibus evidentius apparet, continuationem dominii eo rem perducere, ut nulla videatur hereditas fuisse, quasi olim hi[[c]] domini essent qui etiam vivo patre quodammodo domini existimantur; unde etiam filius familias appellatur, sicut paterfamilias; sola nota hac adjecta, per quam distinguitur genitor ab eo, qui genitus sit; itaque post mortem patris non hereditatem percipere videntur; sed magis liberam bonorum administrationem consequuntur; hac ex causa, licet non sint heredes instituti, domini sunt: nec obstat, quod licet eos exheredare, quod et occidere licebat. D. 28, 2, 11.

**D. 50, 16, 208.

The aggregate of the ancestor's rights and duties or total *persona* sustained by him was easily separated from his natural personality, and regarded as sustained in turn by his heir, in view of the fact that it was originally his only as head of the family, and consisted of the aggregate of the family rights and duties. If we start here with succession to the entire situation of an individual in the community, on the assumption of his entire *persona*, we shall find the other and more usual examples of succession in privity easier to understand. It is very hazardous to attempt to generalize the history of legal conceptions from the example of the English law alone, because the early English law was not the spontaneous growth of the social needs, but was forced by a knowledge of the maturer system of Rome. But in England we think the course of things was this. The first succession in privity was the universal succession of the Roman law; then privity in the succession to specific things occurs when the notion of ownership was originally subordinate to a personal relation, and the succession was in the personal relation with the right over a thing as an incident, then it is extended to successions generally. Compare succession in title to land with the alienation of a chattel. The notion of privity did not at first attach to the transfer of a chattel *inter vivos*. All sales were required to be made in market overt;* and one who purchased a chattel in market overt got a good title against all the world,—he did not stand on the title of his seller.** But the case was different with regard to land. Recent investigations have shown that it was not treated as the subject of individual ownership until comparatively late times. In the beginning of the feudal period the relation between lord and man was personal, and the conception of an heir continuing the personal situation or relations of his ancestor was familiar from the universal succession which the English had received from the Roman law. Soon we see the use of a certain amount of land attached as incident but subordinate to the personal relation; an eviction did not end the duties of the vassal, but only made it obligatory on the lord to give him other land of equal value. Then a similar process took place with regard to villein services and free tenures. The only fund out of which the villein could pay his dues, or which enabled him to perform his personal services, was the land he was allowed to occupy, and in course of time the services came to be regarded as charged on the land in question. In like manner the free services were at first "all personal and uncertain as to their quantity or duration," but in course of time became definite and of a fixed value, were treated as charged upon the land just as the villein services were, and were at last commuted for money. In each case the accessory became the principal, and the principal the accessory. Instead of the land being incident to the services, the services became incident to the land.*** Bracton, who wrote while the change was going on, says, that *inter tenentem et dominum semper tenet et stat homagium quamdiu*

---

*Laws of King Edward, 1 Wilkins, p. 48; 1 Thorpe's Ancient Laws, 159; Aethelstan, 12, W. 58; Thorpe, 207; Edgar, Supp. 6, W. 80, 81; Thorpe, 275, &c., &c.; Laws of Wm. Conqueror, 2 Palgr. Comm. xcvi. § 21; cxix. n. (26); Mirror, ch. 1, § 3, p. 14, ed. 1768.

**2 Palgr. cxix. n. 26, and Leg. Cnut. § 24, Thorpe, Anc. L. vol. i. p. 391, Wilkins, p. 137, § 22, seem to show that a sale in market overt with the required form passed the title, at least after the lapse of a short time. The writers on English law generally lay down the doctrine without qualification. 2 Co. Inst. 713; 2 Bl. Comm. 449; cf. Spence's Inquiry, 475.

***See Systems of Land Tenure, Cobden Club, Morier's Essay, pp. 288, 290.

heredes ex utraque parte extiterint, et quamdiu tenens tenementum tenuerit in dominico vel servitio quod obligationem homagii inducit. (81 b.)

Of course as the services lost their personal character, it mattered comparatively little who rendered them, the superior party in the relation having the land as security. It became common therefore to give a power of substitution to the tenant by the mention of assigns in the grant. A passage from Bracton (17 b) will show the legal machinery by which this was worked out, and the origin as we suppose of privity in the English law. *Item augere potest donationem et facere alios quasi heredes, licet re vera heredes non sunt, ut si dicas in donatione habendum et tenendum tali et haeredibus suis, vel cui terram illam dare vel assignare voluerit,* &c. The rest of the passage is worth reading. The succession to a personal relation was extended to strangers by the fiction that for that limited purpose they were *quasi* heirs. In place of the universal succession to the entire *persona* of the ancestor we have a succession to a particular group of his rights and duties regarded as severable from the rest, and constituting a *persona* by themselves, as they clearly constituted a distinct personal relation. Bracton says that a freeman may hold villein land, rendering whatever services belong to it, and still remain free, since he renders them *ratione villenagii et non ratione personae suae* (Bract. f. 26, 67); that is, by reason of the special and limited relation which he has assumed, and not by reason of his general condition.

We are only attempting to explain the English law, but it would seem that an analogy may be found in the Institutes of Justinian. After stating (L. 2, t. 6, § 12) the rule that *diutina possessio* begun by the deceased is continued in favor of the heir, &c., he adds in the following section, *inter venditorem quoque et emptorem conjungi tempora divi Severus et Antoninus rescripserunt.* So that the privity between buyer and seller, which enabled the latter to avail himself of the adverse user of the former, was introduced long after the universal succession of the heir, and seems to have been suggested by it in like manner, perhaps through the medium of the testamentary sale of the *familia*. Another fact should be observed. By the law of Rome the purchaser, unlike the heir, might, if he found it to his advantage, repudiate the possession of his seller, and stand on that which he had himself obtained adversely to the other. The same thing is true of the English law.

If privity in the title to land grew out of the fact that the inferior landholders originally held their lands as incident to a personal relation with their lords, which could only be succeeded to by those who sustained their *persona* as heirs or *quasi* heirs, it is perhaps not a very violent conjecture to suppose that the application of the same doctrine to chattels bought out of market overt is a later imitation of the law of real property.

At all events, we have now said enough to make our meaning clear, when we say that the only objects of succession in privity are *personae*. Compare the ownership of a *res*—say land—with the bare possession of it. Possession, as has been explained, is the occupation of a continuing situation of fact, which may in turn be occupied by another by any means enabling him to do so, and to which certain rights are incident, however the possession was obtained. Strangers owe the same duties to the occupant for the time being, by reason of his possession, whether he is in by right or wrong. But a wrongful possessor is not an owner, because although protected against strangers, he is not protected against his disseisee. Who, then, is an owner? Reasoning from the grounds on which possession in general is protected, we say, the first of immediately successive possessors who has not wilfully abandoned possession (*e.g.*, the captor of animals *ferae naturae*), or by the doctrine of prescription, the last possessor for the period of prescription, or a claimant under a proceeding binding on all the world. Now each of these descriptions is like the cases already alluded to of a party to a certain contract, or a grantee of a particular franchise,—at any given time they do and can only apply to one individual, and no other. How, then, is a subsequent though friendly taker of the thing to avail himself of the pre-eminent advantages incident to a situation filled only by his grantor? Only by this notion of the assumption of the grantor's *persona*, the origin of which we have explained. It may not be without its significance that in the days before privity was known to the English law, the grantee found protection in a very short period of prescription,—a year and a day being mentioned in many of the early custumals as the time in which possession would ripen into title.

It is not meant that a transfer is impossible without this notion. A change of possession, with the abandonment of claim on the part of the former possessor, would suffice to give the transferee the protection which the law accords to possession in general. But without the conception of privity the title of the purchaser must have stood on the possession actually acquired by him. It is pretty clear, that even as late as Bracton's time, the rule of the Roman law obtained in England, and that the title did not pass on the sale of a chattel until delivery, as he says, *qui rem emptori nondum tradidit, adhuc ipse dominus erit* (62 a). But when the purchaser continues the legal relation of the vendor to the thing instead of assuming a new independent one; when the object of the sale is to substitute the purchaser, not to the possession merely, but to the peculiar rights of the vendor, flowing from facts peculiar to him; to separate so much of the vendor's legal *persona* from his natural personality, and allow it to be sustained by another,—a sale without delivery becomes conceivable. So do other doctrines of modern law, which stand on the identity of the buyer's and seller's legal relation to the thing, and which it is needless to go into at length. For instance, that the purchaser can add the years of adverse use by his vendor less than the period of prescription, to his own, so as to make up the necessary time, which a disseisor would not be able to do.

We proceed to illustrate the general doctrine by taking up some of the instances in which it applies and considering them a little more in detail. The successions in privity are divisible into universal and partial, or into those cases where the successor assumes the total legal personality of the predecessor, and those where he only assumes some well-defined portion of that *persona*. The best example of the former is the succession of the Roman heir, which is the more interesting, as in that case the Roman law nearly recognizes our conception that the so-called *res*, which are the objects of succession in privity, are *personae*. The *hereditas* is the first of the *res incorporales* mentioned in the Institutes,* it being there considered as an object of

---

*We cannot forbear calling attention to what seems to us a mistranslation, which we have traced back a hundred and fifty years, and which very likely could be followed much farther. The distinction between corporeal and incorporeal things is stated in Inst. 2, 2, §§ 1, 2, to be that the former are those *quae tangi possunt*, the latter *quae tangi non possunt, qualia sunt ea* quae in jure consistunt. This is constantly translated, "which consist in a right," and being so interpreted, has led to the hopeless confusion of modern

ownership. But in the Digest (41, 1, 34) we are told that it sustains the *persona* of the deceased, and that it *dominae locum obtinet* (D. 43, 24, 13, § 5), so that a succession begun by the deceased may be completed before the heir assumes the inheritance (D. 41, 3, 40), and that when the heir succeeds to it, he may have an interdict in respect of injuries to property belonging to it committed while the inheritance was lying vacant (D. 43, 24, 13, § 5). Our doctrine that letters of administration relate back to the death of the deceased seems to embody the same idea, for our executor corresponds to the Roman heir, and is another instance of universal succession.

We have said that in the beginning of the feudal times the holding of land was only an incident of a personal relation with the superior lord. When the same tenant came to hold fees of different lords, of course this was so far modified that he could not be required to perform inconsistent services; and we are told by Glanville (L. 9, c. 1, pp. 218, 220, Beames' tr.) that in that case, although he did homage for each fee, he reserved his allegiance for the lord of whom he held his chief estate; but if the different lords should make war on each other, and the chief lord should command him to accompany him in person against another of his lords, he ought to obey, saving the service due to the other lord for the fee held of him. We see, then, that the tenant had a distinct *persona* in respect of each of the fees which he held, and that a succession to one of them had no connection with the succession to another. Each succession was the assumption of a distinct personal relation, in which the successor was to be determined by the terms of the relation in question. With regard to chattels, which, Blackstone tells us (2 Comm. 386), means whatever was not a feud, the case was different. There was no distinct *persona* in respect of each of these, and we accordingly find that, from a pretty early period, the Roman law as to the devolution of all a man's property is followed by the English law as to all his property not feudal. The Roman heir, as has been said, took not as by a conveyance of so many chattels and so much land, but rather as if there had been no change of title, by a simple continuation of the legal personality by the ancestor. In like manner the executor was formerly entitled to the undistributed residue, not as legatee of those specific things, but as representing all the rights which the testator would have had after distribution, if alive. It was on the same principle, we take it, that the legatee could not assert a legal title to his legacy until the executor had assented. It may be that the modern doctrine that a residuary bequest of chattels is not specific like a residuary devise of lands is to be accounted for in the same way. The distinct *personae* sustained by the testator with reference to the several fees of which he died seised were not confused by the fact that they might all happen to be assumed by the same successor, as they had previously been by him. But the right to the residue of chattels was in its first form an incident of the assumption of the general *persona* of the testator, just as the power of the members of a corporation

---

"incorporeal hereditaments," and to Austin's attack on the division as senseless (Lect. 13). If we translate the phrase, "which exist only in contemplation of law," or "which depend on the law for existence," and notice that the first instance is the *hereditas,* which is a *universitas* distinct from its component parts (D. 50, 16, 208), and as much a fictitious thing as a corporation is a fictitious person, we shall be nearer to what the Roman lawyers had in mind, although we may not be able to justify all their examples.

over the corporate property is incident to their sustaining that *persona,* and is succeeded to, not by a conveyance of the several articles, but by the new members assuming the *persona* of the grantees of the franchise, a *persona* recognized and embodied by the law in the fiction of the corporation. When the residue came to be given away from the executor it may be conjectured that the bequest continued to be governed by the same conception.

Another instance of qualified universal succession is that of the husband to the wife on marriage. By the early Roman law she would have become his slave, and he would have taken her rights and responsibilities, if she had any, upon his shoulders. Modern times have inherited the notion, more or less modified.

Let us pass to partial successions. These include the descent of lands, and most alienations of specific things, either by act *inter vivos* or by will, where the transferee does not come in adversely to the former holder, as in the case of a proceeding *in rem* or a sale in market overt. At first sight it seems as if a corporation sole were the best illustration of partial successions. There is a continuing aggregate of rights and duties, which the law personifies, and which may be successively attributed to a series of individuals. But such corporations are rarely created except for public purposes, and the successor, although in theory of law for certain purposes sustaining the same *persona* as his predecessor, seems to come in rather by a new grant than in privity, as on account of its public character the devolution and most of the incidents of the *persona* in question are beyond the control of the present incumbent.

The true type would seem to be a corporation for private purposes, such as a modern manufacturing corporation. The continuing rights and duties, the aggregate of which constitute the *persona* in question, are incident to the grant of the franchise. Only A., B., and C. answer to the description of grantees in fact, yet their rights may be succeeded to by the assumption of their *persona,* which the law has so far recognized as severable from them as to attribute to it a distinct existence, and treat it as the owner of the rights in question, although it is very obvious that philosophically speaking the rights reside in the members.

Turning to succession in the title to land, it will be remembered that the first instance of succession in privity was derived from the Roman law, and occurred when the heirs of the first taker were named in the grant. The *persona* with which we have to deal is the fee-simple, and when assigns came to be let in they took *quasi* heirs, as has been said. But privity in this instance was not worked out to its logical result, for the estate of the assignee of the fee did not escheat upon a failure of heirs of the original feoffee, which is, perhaps, a consequence of the originally personal character of the relation of lord and man, and a reminiscence of a time when a change of tenants would have been accomplished by a surrender and reinvestiture. It is further to be noticed that the grantee comes in so far adversely to his grantor that he may acquire a new title by prescription, as has already been said.

The *persona* of an owner in fee-simple may be sustained by more than one as well as by one, just as a corporation may have more or fewer members; and it is unaffected by the death of one of the natural persons sustaining it, just as a corporation before the invention of shares was wholly sustained by the surviving members, down to the last. As Bracton says (66 b), *Heredes esse possunt plures sicut unus, et cuilibet jus descendit quasi uni heredi, propter juris unitatem,* (and 76 b) . . . *plures coheredes quasi unum corpus propter unitatem juris quod habent.* This is joint tenancy. It may be divided by dividing the land, or it may be given as if divided, with a right to partition; tenancy in commom. It may be divided laterally into a particular estate and remainders, in which case it is also divided longitudinally, thus:—

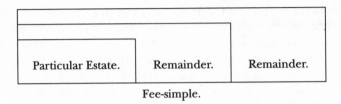

Fee-simple.

For a remainder-man has present rights as well as a probability of future enjoyment. He gets damages for an injury to the reversion, the compensation which would have gone entire to one who sustained the entire *persona* (*i.e.,* owned the fee) being now distributed between the number who collectively sustain it.

Looked at from this point of view the doctrine of corruption of blood has at least the merit of being logical. The law having put an end to the *persona* of the ancestor, those who were only entitled as supporting that *persona* could be no better off than he.

As we are not considering how one man may succeed another in the enjoyment of the same *thing,* but the same *right,* the means by which a title is extinguished and another comes in paramount to the former owner have no place in successions. In such cases the new taker sustains a new *persona* instead of the old one, as also does a grantee, when all vested and contingent claims which were outstanding at the time of conveyance have become barred by lapse of time. The successions which we are considering are successions in the support of a given *persona.* The beginning and end of the *persona* in question—*e.g., ownership*—are taken for granted as established. They would be indicated by the description of the facts to which the duties constituting it are incident. Those facts consist of being either first possessor or last possessor for the period of prescription, or a taker under a proceeding adverse to all the world. If the description ceases to be true of one and becomes true of another, the *persona* of the first is at an end, and a new one is assumed by the second. So the beginning and end of rights arising out of a contract are fixed by the terms of the contract; if an assignee of a contract surrenders his rights under that and receives a new undertaking in place of it, the *persona* which he had sustained is gone and a new one has taken its place.

When we turn to the alienation of chattels, we find the notion of privity universal in this country, and very general in England, where a sale in market overt is perhaps the exception. Still we have had reason to think that a sale in market overt was the typical sale known to the common law, and that the notion of privity had no place there. Perhaps this will explain the fact that it was impossible to limit a remainder in chattels at common law by act *inter vivos,* while in wills and testaments such limitations were permitted. A remainder could only be limited by subdividing the *persona* of the grantor. This was accomplished by testamentary dispositions, which were derived from the Roman law, as explained above. But the rights of a purchaser could not be qualified when he did not assume the seller's *persona*, but, on the contrary, came in adversely to all the world.

It has already been shown that the doctrine of privity rendered delivery no longer necessary to pass the title to a thing sold, and logically the same doctrine should have been applied to gifts, unless it was thought against public policy, inasmuch as a substitution of one individual to another under a certain *persona* does not require either delivery or consideration. The courts of common law, however, refused to go so far, on the ground that the so-called gift of a tangible thing was in substance a contract to deliver at a future time, and void for want of consideration. This reasoning is distinctively English, and the Roman law, we take it, only required delivery of a gift to pass the title, because a change of possession was necessary in all cases for that purpose. We will take up the rule of equity in a moment. Another rule of the old law was that *choses in action* were not assignable.* When the sale of a chattel interest was effected by the buyer's coming adversely into the situation of fact (possession), to which the rights were incident, it is hard to see how a contract could have been transferred. A. alone fills, and A. alone can fill the situation of person with whom, in fact, a certain contract was made. It is only by the fiction that B. sustains so much of A.'s *persona* that B. can possibly succeed to the benefit of that contract. When the notion of privity had been applied to the transfer of other chattels it was easy, even for the common-law courts, to apply it to contracts also. Those courts recognize the continuity of A.'s *persona* by compelling the suit to be brought in A.'s name just as the continuity of the *persona* under which the members of a corporation enjoy the corporate rights is recognized by the continuity of the corporate name. The same result is achieved less formally in chancery by subjecting the assignee to the equities between the original parties. Equity goes farther, and upholds a gift of a *chose in action*, logically, as we think, on the ground that it is a substitution of one to another under the *persona* of contractee,—a transaction to which, as has been said, consideration seems to be unnecessary, and with which delivery has nothing to do.

We have thus far dealt with clear cases of substitution where a successor assumes a *persona* to the exclusion of the individual who had sustained it until then. There is another class, where the new comer is introduced under a *persona* without excluding his predecessor.

We have mentioned husband and wife, and master and servant, among the par-

---

*The reason given by the English writers for not allowing the transfer of a contract, that it would encourage litigiousness, is supposed to be another perversion of the Roman law. The Institutes, after treating of those rights of property which avail against all the world, pass to *obligationes* and then to actions. *Obligationes* included contract, and also liability arising from the infraction of a legal right, which were grouped together with reference to the fact of their imposing a special burden on a certain individual, instead of an equal one on all the world. The obligation arising from having infringed a right is a mere liability to be sued, and it became a commonplace with the mediaeval civilians, when accounting for the place of the division *actions,* that actions spring from obligations as daughters from mothers. This is true of obligations of the latter sort, but is no more true of contracts than of any other right which depends on the law for protection in the last resort. The right conferred by a contract is not a right to sue any more than that given by ownership. The right to sue does not exist until the primary right has been infringed. But what was true of obligations of one sort has been applied to those of another, and

ticular relations to which duties are incident, and they are properly called "relations," because at the present day both parties to them retain to a greater or less extent their legal personality, instead of the subordinate individual being covered and extinguished by the *persona* of a *paterfamilias*. A servant can sue his master for breach of contract, as well as his master can recover from a stranger for a tort *per quod servitium amisit;* and even a wife has her separate *status*. This was not always so. Under the early Roman law the wife, children, and servants of a citizen were his slaves.* They could not be said to stand in a legal relation to him, for they had no standing before the law except as sustaining the *persona* of the family head. If they acquired property, it was he who acquired it; and he, if any one, was responsible for their torts. Without bearing this in mind, we cannot satisfactorily explain some of our modern doctrines, such as the liability of the master for the torts of his servant. If a baker sends out his man with his cart, having every reason to believe him a prudent and careful person, and the man while carrying round his master's rolls negligently runs down another in the street, it is contrary to analogy that the master should have to answer for it. Some of the writers on the Roman law, from whom Austin probably got his explanation, said that the master should have been more careful as to whom he let into his family. But he is sometimes liable when he has used the greatest care; when he has done nothing which he had not a right to, and has not been even remotely inadvertent. Such a law is easily explained, if we remember, that it originated when a servant was a slave, whom the master was obliged to keep in order as he was his cattle, and it is then manifest why it should be otherwise if he employed an independent contractor; for the latter corresponds to a free man in ancient Rome, who had a separate legal existence, and was, therefore, responsible *in propria persona*.

To the same source may be referred such notions as that marriage is not a contract, but a *status* arising out of contract; the right *in rem* of the husband to the *consortium* of his wife, and of the master to the services of his servant; and the universal succession of the husband to the rights of the wife, which has been mentioned above.

So far, however, as duties are imposed by the particular relations in question, they fall with other duties into the principal headings of the law in our first table. Our present concern is with the power of one individual to represent another, which is derived from the same source.

Where the law treats an individual as a party to a transaction in which he had no share in fact, the fiction is too bold for an effort of invention, and needs a historical explanation. There was no such doctrine in the early Roman law, which did not permit its formal stipulations and actions to be transacted by deputy. But a slave was part of the *persona* of his master; if the promise was made to him, it must bind the other party to somebody, and as the slave could acquire no rights for himself, it followed that the benefit accrued to the master. This required no fiction, but was

---

the error has been perpetuated in the name *chose in action*. Modern courts are bringing back the maxim to its true significance.

*Bynkershoek was the first to argue, in his *opusculum de jure occidendi liberos*, that the *patria potestas* was nothing else than *dominium juris Quiritium*.

the necessary result of servitude. It will be observed, moreover, that as the master's right to benefits acquired by his servants is general, and as he is liable for the latter's torts wherever a liability is imposed, the slave may be said to sustain his master's *persona* for purposes indefinite not only in number but in kind.

When the notion had become familiar that one man could acquire rights, or be subjected to obligations by another who sustained his *persona* as part of the *familia*,—the *persona* of the *paterfamilias* being the aggregate of the family rights and duties,—it did not need a great stretch to extend the power of representation to a freeman. But as the power in this case did not result from the *status* of the parties, but from agreement, instead of being general it was necessarily limited to the authority conferred, and the shadowy distinction between a servant and an agent in modern times seems to stand on this circumstance.* It is noticeable that the Roman law seems to have limited the power of a free agent to represent his principal somewhat more than we do; but when he did so he was regarded by a fiction as constituting one person with his principal, just as the slave had done in fact. In the Elzevir *Corpus* (D. 44, 2, 4, note 17) we read, Eadem est persona domini et procuratoris. Eadem, inquam, non rei veritate, sed fictione, *ideoque quod procuratori et similibus personis objici potest, objici etiam potest ipsis dominis:* nam ex quo hujusmodi personae interveniunt, censentur et ipsi domini intervenisse. But, unlike the servant, the agent retains his former legal personality for all except the purposes of his agency.

If these distinctions be remembered, and also that, in our law, even the identity of servant and master is a fiction which does not put an end to the separate personality of the servant outside the purposes of the relation, they will throw light on, as well as be illustrated by some modern doctrines. If a vendor of goods ships them on board a vessel of which the purchaser is owner *pro hac vice,* under a bill of lading making them deliverable to the buyer, the right of stoppage *in transitu* does not exist because the master of the vessel is the servant of the buyer, and his possession is the possession of the master. If, on the other hand, the goods are shipped on a vessel in the employ of third persons, the right of stoppage would remain, although the vessel was selected on behalf of the buyer. In this case the owners of the vessel would seem to be agents of the buyer; but they hold possession of the goods *qua* carriers, that is, in their capacity of independent contractors, that is, in their own name and not as supporting the *persona* of the buyer. Had he made them his agents for the purpose of taking possession, the case might be different, if the vendor would not be thereby defrauded.

Another instance may, perhaps, be found in the law of sales, where, as in England, no delivery is necessary to pass the title to goods. Suppose a written contract is made for the sale, say, of a hundred bushels of wheat, not yet ascertained, and that the seller afterwards, by the authority of the buyer, appropriates the goods to the contract. The title passes in this case at the moment of appropriation. But it is apprehended that it does so by force of the contract, which now operates as a conveyance, and that the transaction does not amount to a delivery, notwithstanding it is often called so by the judges. The seller was the buyer's agent to appropriate, but not to possess. He holds in his own name, and may still assert his lien as vendor.

*Austin, 3d ed. pp. 976, 977; table 2, note 3, C. b.

But if the agreement, instead of looking merely to the ascertainment of the goods, had expressly or by implication contemplated that the seller was to hold them in a new character, as agent of the buyer, he would thereby assume so much of the purchaser's *persona*, the possession would change without any physical transmutation, and the vendor's lien would be gone. If the sale had been made by a servant to his master, if, for instance, a coachman should sell his master a dog by oral agreement, and should continue to take care of and keep the animal in his master's stables as before, it is conjectured that it might be presumed, from the greater and more indefinite extent to which the servant supports his master's *persona*, that a change of possession had taken place.

As it is not every one who has the physical possession of a thing, who is possessor in contemplation of law, a question arises as to the test of his being so. That which is offered by the above considerations, and which is believed to be pretty nearly sustained by the English law, however it may have been with the technical system of Rome, does not depend on an intention to exclude the general owner for the time being, as has been thought by some writers, but on whether the object is held in the holder's own name or not. A servant holds his master's goods in his master's name; an agent for that purpose possesses as representing his principal; but a bailee, even a mere borrower, although he intends to yield possession as soon as demanded, holds, while he holds, on his own behalf. It seems to us that the cases of servant and borrower have been confounded from not adverting to the familiar historical facts which we have recapitulated.

We append a table, which does not profess to be exhaustive, but which will give a conspectus of the whole discussion, repeating once more the reason why these topics do not fall into the principal classification hitherto suggested. When a person becomes entitled to continuing rights formerly enjoyed by another, merely by occupying in turn the situation of fact, to which those rights are annexed as an incident,—as, to the rights of a possessor by obtaining the physical possession of a thing,—the definition of the situation in respect of which the rights are enjoyed or the duties owed, indicates the moment when any individual begins or ceases to enjoy them. But in other cases the situation is of a kind which can only be filled by the first occupant, or which, if capable of transmutation, is not in fact altered, or filled by the person who nevertheless becomes entitled to the rights or subjected to the burdens attached to it. In such cases, of course, the definition of the situation does not indicate the moment when its benefits and obligations accrue to one who does not fill it. The definition marks the beginning and end of the *persona* in question, but not the mode of determining by whom the person is supported at a given instant of time.

SUCCESSIONS.

A. UNIVERSAL, *or successions to the entire* PERSONA *of another, subject to greater or less exceptions.*

1. By will or death (executors and administrators).
2. By act inter vivos:

a. By assignments in bankruptcy (assignees)?
b. By marriage (husband to wife):

B. PARTIAL, *or successions to a special* PERSONA, *or group of rights and duties, secerable from the other rights and duties of the party first sustaining it.*

1. By descent (lands).

2. By will (lands, chattels).

3. By act *inter vivos:*

a. By voluntary change of possession (feoffment, delivery of chattles out of market overt, either with or without consideration).

b. By deed (land or chattels).

c. By other formalities, irrespective of consideration, such as transfer of shares on the books of a corporation.

d. By conveyance, either oral or in writing not under seal, for a consideration but without change of posession (chattels).

e. By simple agreement or mutual assent without consideration or change of possession (certain gifts in equity).

To which may be added SUBDIVISIONS of a *persona.*

Joint administration. Joint Tenancy, coparcenary, tenancy in common. Particular estates and remainders, &c.

REPRESENTATIONS

Or introduction of one individual under a *persona* sustained by another

1. For purposes indefinite in number and kind—slaves, servants, wives, some general agents.
2. For a definite purposes—agents.

DUTIES OF PERSONS IN PARTICULAR

Negligence *stricto sensu.*
Extreme cases, shading into
Negligence *latiori sensu*

DUTIES OF PERSONS IN PARTICULAR

Negligence *stricto sensu.*
Extreme cases, shading into
Negligence *latiori sensu*

Editor's Notes

1. Correction in Holmes's copy (OWH Papers, Paige Box 18, Item 4): . . . importance, but they all went on. . . .
2. OWH correction: . . . existing at a given instant. . . .

6.76

From *American Law Review* 7:146 (1872).

The Legal Tender Cases of 1871. Decisions of the Supreme Court of the United States, December Term, 1870, in the cases of *Knox v. Lee* and *Parker v. Davis;* with the opinions of Justices STRONG and BRADLEY, and the dissenting opinions of Justices CHASE, CLIFFORD, and FIELD. To which are added the notes of forty-four cases quoted or referred to in the several opinions above named. New York, 1872. Office of *the Bankers' Magazine and Statistical Register.* Price Two Dollars.

The case of *Hepburn v. Griswold,* 8 Wall. 603, was argued very much on the question whether the Legal Tender Act was a "necessary and proper" means of carrying out some of the powers expressly given to Congress, both by the Chief Justice giving the opinion of the majority, and by Mr. Justice Miller speaking for the dissenting judges; and the case presented the curious spectacle of the Supreme Court reversing the determination of Congress on a point of political economy.

Some arguments of a different character, which had not been adverted to in *Hepburn v. Griswold,* were presented in two communications to the *Law Review* of July, 1870, called forth by that decision, and from one of which we quote: "It is hard to understand when a power is expressly given, which does not come up to a required height, how this express power can be enlarged as an incident to some other express power. The power to coin money means, I take it, both by the true construction and as interpreted by practice: (1) to strike off metallic medals (coin); and (2) to make those medals legal tender (money). I cannot therefore see how the right to make paper legal tender can be claimed for Congress, when the constitution virtually contains the words 'Congress shall have power to make metals legal tender.' It is to be remembered, that those who deny the power have only maintained that it is not granted by implication. They are not called on to find a constitutional prohibition. It is perfectly consistent with this argument that the power to issue bills not legal tender may be claimed under the borrowing clause, and of this opinion was Mr. Madison. Mad. Pap., Aug. 16, 1787, vol. iii. p. 1346, note."

The above argument we believe to be unanswerable, and it is satisfactory to see in the later decision the majority devoting a good deal of energy to the business of overthrowing it, and Mr. Justice Field of the minority restating it in explicit language. He says: "The power to coin money is, therefore, a power to fabricate coins out of metal as money, and thus make them a legal tender for their declared values as indicated by their stamp. If this be the true import and meaning of the language used, it is difficult to see how Congress can make the paper of the government a legal tender. When the constitution says that Congress shall have the power to make metallic coins a legal tender, it declares in effect that it shall make nothing else such tender." (We should prefer to say it excludes the implication of a grant of more extensive powers.) " . . . Mr. Madison has appended a note to the debates, stating . . . that he 'became satisfied that striking out the words' (authorizing Congress to emit bills of credit) 'could not disable the government from the use of public notes, as far as they could be safe and proper; and would only cut off the pretext for a *paper currency*, and particularly from making the bills *a tender* either for public or private debts.' (Madison Papers, vol. iii. p. 1346.)" Judges Strong and Bradley are more successful to our mind in meeting the shadowy argument drawn from the spirit of the constitution,—as to impairing the obligation of contracts, &c.,—than in overthrowing this. Less attention is given than in *Hepburn v. Griswold* to the fitness of the Legal Tender Acts to accomplish their ends, which we must think a purely legislative question in the absence of an obvious fraud on the constitution.

The little book before us is convenient enough for those who do not wish to buy the twelfth of Wallace. It does not materially gain in value from the notes of the cases referred to published at the end.

6.77

From *American Law Review* 7:318 (1873).

The Code of Iowa, as reported to the General Assembly by the Commissioner for the Revision of the Statutes. Part I.

Report of Commissioners to revise the Statutes of the State of Iowa, made to the Governor of the State, in accordance with Chapter Seventy-five, Acts of 13th General Assembly. WILLIAM H. SEEVERS, of Mahaska County; WILLIAM J. KNIGHT, of Dubuque County; WILLIAM G. HAMMOND, of Johnson County; Commissioners. Desmoines: G. W. Edwards, State Printer. 1871.

Codification in India and England. A Speech by Mr. FITZJAMES STEPHEN, Q.C.

We have received some advance sheets of the draft for a Code of the Iowa Statutes, and also the report of the Commissioners appointed to make the revision in question. Without attempting to pass upon the work, which is not yet finished, we may express our satisfaction that it is in able hands. The portion of the code before us is the work of Mr. William E. Hammond, now a professor in the Iowa City Law School, and formerly editor of the *Western Jurist,* to which he contributed some criticisms of unusual excellence. If our respect for the authors of the report was less, we should less regret their avowed empiricism and distrust of philosophical methods of arrangement. In such a fragmentary work as a collection of statutes, it may be well enough to be "governed by the practical convenience of those who use the volume, rather than by any so-called scientific rules." But we regret what seems to us an ill-judged sneer at "the elaborate theories which have been devised 'out of the depths of their own consciousness,' or borrowed from foreign jurisprudence, by recent writers on classification." The most educated American lawyers are those, we believe, who would be slowest to adopt this tone. We must reiterate our profound conviction that the methods which are commonly called practical are in truth the most unpractical and destructive of sound legal thinking. A writer who takes such subjects as railroads or telegraphs, or, going a step farther, as mercantile law, or shipping, or medical jurisprudence, thinks he is doing a very practical thing. What he really does is to group his law around a fact of dramatic, instead of one of legal significance. All rules of law presuppose a certain state of facts to which they are applicable; for a rule of law is expected to be a motive of conduct, and a motive can only operate when the facts are present in which the conduct sought to be affected is possible. Rules of law, therefore, must be grouped with reference to some set of facts or other. The effort of a text-writer or codifier should be to seize those of which the presence is necessary to bring into operation a distinct rule of law. Thus, *contract* is a proper head, because the fact that a certain agreement has been made, has attached to it a series of legal consequences which would not exist without it. *Marine insurance* is a proper subdivision of contract, because the fact that the agreement was of that sort has attached to it further and more specific consequences, such as the implied warranty of seaworthiness, which cannot be reduced under any more general head. So when one, as a matter of fact, has constituted another his agent, there flows from that fact the peculiar legal consequence that the agent's actions and acquisitions in the matter in hand are attributed to the principal; and the facts under which this peculiar fiction of law, the doctrine of representation, is applied, are properly grouped together.

Telegraphs, on the other hand, is not a proper head under which to collect what is generally included there, because most of the cases stated are simply illustrations of the law of principal and agent or of contract, if the decisions are right. The circumstance that a telegraphic company was concerned is purely dramatic, and has no legal significance. The practical wisdom which seizes at the obtrusive fact in this way ends in the shears and paste of Abbott's Digests,—very good things in their way, but works which indicate to our eyes a total incapacity to deal with such problems as the codification of the United States Statutes.

Mr. Stephen's very interesting speech advocates an English code with the force and ability which characterizes all that he does. At the same time it leaves us as unconvinced as after reading Bentham and Austin.

The periodical codification of statutes is now a matter of course in the United States, but to codify the law eliminated from judicial decisions seems to us far from equally desirable. We go so far as to say that the very qualities of certainty and accuracy, which are the reputed advantages of such a code, are those in which it would prove inferior to the materials used in its construction. The best draughtsman that ever lived can feel a ground of decision more accurately than he can state it. Suppose he succeeds in stating a rule that would have sufficed for the correct decisions of all past cases, it is in the highest degree probable that some future case will require some more refined discrimination not allowed by the words of the code. Yet, if the code is law, the wrong decision must be given; for the moment the judges are allowed to look at the decisions from which the code rule was made up, and to construe it in any way consistent with them, or otherwise than according to the literal significance of the words, the code ceases to be law, whatever it may be called. Take the question of partnership as to third persons in England. The latest cases agree that most or all of the earlier ones were rightly decided; yet if the test promulgated at first, in clear words and with the utmost confidence, had passed into legislation, the last cases would have been decided wrong. The English judges at the present day are disagreed as to what the test shall be (L.R. 7 Ex. 218); yet there is probably less uncertainty than at any previous time how any given case should be decided. It is felt to fall on one side or another of a line which no hand is skilful enough to draw. The unwritten rules are stated from different points of view, in different language, by the text-writers, and their extent is shown by the cases from which they are drawn. A written rule of statute law is stated in but one form, and can only be construed from its own four corners. For, we repeat, that if more than that is allowed, the code is nothing but a text-book.

The problem with which Mr. Stephen and his predecessors had to deal in India was essentially different from the task he would like to see undertaken in England. They had to create a system, not to give an existing and well-understood system a new form. Those who wish to see a most interesting account of their monumental labors will do well to read Mr. Stephen's speech.

6.78

From *American Law Review* 7:320 (1973).

Outlines of Roman Law, consisting chiefly of an Analysis and Summary of the Institutes. For the use of Students. By T. WHITCOMBE GREENE, B.C.L., of Lincoln's Inn, Barrister at Law. New edition. London: Stevens & Sons. 1872.

This little manual is intended for the use of students who may share in the present somewhat *dilettante* interest in the Roman law. It is not so good as some German and French works of the same sort, but it has the advantage of being written in English, and of being illuminated by explanatory extracts from Maine and Austin.[1] We have several times expressed our opinion that to study the Institutes is not the easiest way to learn either law or jurisprudence, and that any one intending to be a lawyer ought to acquire a habit of thinking in terms of his own system before dallying with another.

It is not true that fundamental principles are more clearly brought out in the Roman than in the English law. On the contrary, in the former system such principles are obscured by traditions which prevented their consistent application, by historical difficulties which have to be overcome before the law can be understood, by principles of classification which have lost their significance, and by a philosophy which is no longer vital. A man should be something of a historian or of a lawyer to study the Roman law with advantage; and the learned will go to the sources. Such hand-books as this may serve to show the general topography of the country.

Editor's Note

1. In Holmes's copy (OWH Papers, Paige Box 18, Item 4), he marks "¶" here, and "no ¶" at the end of the paragraph as printed.

6.79

From *American Law Review* 7:320 (1873).

An Epitome and Analysis of Savigny's Treatise on Obligations in Roman Law. By ARCHI-
BALD BROWN, of the Middle Temple, Esq., Barrister at Law; M.A. Edin. and Oxon.;
and B.C.L. Oxon. London: Stevens & Haynes. 1872.

Many lawyers who do not skim through technical German with the same ease as the
Year-Books, or Statham's Abridgment, and yet feel an intelligent curiosity as to the
results of German learning, must be grateful for such books as this. It is a key which
opens another of Savigny's strong-boxes to many who, but for it, would never have
lifted the cover. Savigny, although pretty dull to a generation familiar with Fustel
de Coulanges and Maine, is the head of the modern historical school, and every
one who loves his profession must want to see the great man with his own eyes. We
confess, however, that we are not quite able to go along with Austin's praise of the
more famous work on Possession as "of all books upon law the most consummate
and masterly," when we read it in a bad translation. The philosophical analysis
seems to have been suggested by Kant, and the minute and constant reference to
the Roman law more or less clogs and retards the free development of principles.
Something of the same sort may be said about the work before us. Undoubtedly it
will open the reader's eyes to many details of philosophical importance which he
may have missed before, and will fortify him with many Latin texts which he is glad
to have brought up in order; but, on the whole, the chief good which we get from
it is with reference to Roman law rather than to general principles. This epitome is
too obscurely written to be read through with pleasure; but we have read in it a
good deal, with some satisfaction, and it is not without its use to a student as a book
of reference.

6.80
SUMMARY OF EVENTS

From *American Law Review* 7:578 (1873).

On January 1, 1873, was begun at New York the publication of the *American Civil
Law Journal.* Two articles in the first number concern the civil law, and another is
about Adolph Carl Von Vangerow. The prospectus, ordinarily so called, fronts us
with the more distinguished name of "Prolegomena," and is as follows:—

> The conviction that an acquaintance with the principles of the Roman law is the only
> sure basis of a legal education; the newly awakened interest therein manifested by
> students and lawyers, and a desire to facilitate the progress of those who from any
> cause are unable to attend the lectures of the great masters of the legal science at
> European universities, have induced the editors to undertake the publication of this
> journal. Its contents will mainly consist of discussions of those principles with special
> reference to the common law.
>
> The analogies and dependence of the two systems will be illustrated as far as pos-
> sible with the view of furnishing to the student and the lawyer a work of practical utility.
> The main purpose of its editors, however, is to promote in some degree the study of

the law as a science, and the consequent emancipation of our courts from their present undue adherence to precedent. The co-operation of the schools, the profession, and others interested in the advancement of learning, is respectfully solicited. As to matters respecting the editorial department, address

R. H. CHITTENDEN, 7 Dey Street, N.Y.

The journal starts with a good list of subscribers, already secured, and we wish it a success. The mere possibility of the attempt is encouraging. We have repeatedly expressed our conviction that the Roman law, as a philosophical *result*, is vastly inferior to modern law. The ambiguous, and, as the rest of the passage from Ulpian shows, perniciously false motto prefixed to this periodical illustrates the fact,—*Jurisprudentia justi atque injusti scientia*. The Roman law is a priceless mass of materials for investigations like those of the great Germans, and for the explanation of the origin and anomalies of our own system. But for the philosophy of law the "Fragment on Government" and Austin's lecture are worth the whole *Corpus*. We must add that we sincerely hope that the editors will fail in their expressed desire to diminish the weight of precedents with our courts. We believe the weight attached to them is about the best thing in our whole system of law.

6.81
SUMMARY OF EVENTS: GREAT BRITAIN

From *American Law Reivew* 7:582 (1873).[1]

THE GAS-STOKERS' STRIKE.—

The famous strike of the gas-stokers in December last, by which all London was plunged for several nights into partial darkness, at last found its way into the courts. The company prosecuted five men for conspiracy. The trial lasted only one day; the facts were simple and undisputed, substantially as follows: The stokers are hired by the company under special contracts, which require a certain notice to be given of an intention to leave work; the time of this notice varies in the contracts of different classes of workmen, ranging from one week to thirty days. Most of the stokers were combined together into a trade-union association. One of them, a member of the association, was discharged by the company, for what cause did not appear; but it was not claimed that the discharge was in violation of the contract. His fellow-members of the association demanded his reinstatement, but in vain. They thereupon, on the 2d December, refused altogether to go to work unless their demand was complied with. There was no violence towards officers of the company; but there was some violence, accompanied by a good deal of threatening, towards members of the association who had not been advised of the intention of the conspirators, and who at first hesitated to fall in with the design. The court charged the jury that the defendants had a perfect right to form a trade-union, and that the fact that their action was in restraint of trade, which would have made it an offence at common law, could not be considered in this action; but that the company alleged that the defendants "either agreed to do an unlawful act or to do a lawful act by unlawful means; and he asked the jury whether there was a combination between the defendants either to hinder or prevent the company from carrying on their business by means of the men simultaneously breaking the contract of service they had entered into with the company. This was an illegal act, and, what was more, a criminal act. If they did agree to interfere with their employers' business, by simultaneously breaking such contracts, they were then agreeing to do that which would bring them within the definition of conspiracy."

The jury were out only twenty minutes, and then brought in a verdict of guilty, but with a recommendation to mercy. This, however, the court disregarded, and sentenced the accused to imprisonment for one year. In imposing the sentence the judge said that he had told the jury that "on the question whether they were to find the defendants guilty or not, they ought not to be influenced by the suggestion that what they were attempting to do would be dangerous to the public. But it did seem to him now, when he was called on to consider what kind of conspiracy they had been guilty of, that he could not throw aside what was one of the obvious results of the conspiracy into which they entered, and what must have been in their minds; and he could not doubt that the obvious result was great danger to the public of this metropolis; that that danger was present to their minds; and it was by the acting on that knowledge and on the effect they thought it would have upon their masters' minds, and trading upon their knowledge of the danger, that they entered into this conspiracy, in order to force their masters to follow their will. . . .

"The prisoners were the principals—the chief actors; two of them were delegates chosen by the men, and therefore evidently men to whom they looked up.[2] They took a leading part in the conspiracy. Therefore, notwithstanding their good character they had unfortunately put themselves into the position of being properly convicted of a dangerous and wicked conspiracy. The time had come when a serious punishment, and not a nominal or a light one, must be inflicted,—a punishment that would teach men in their position that, although without offence they might be members of a trade-union or might agree to go into an employment, or to leave it without committing any offence, yet that they must take care when they agreed together that they must not agree to do it by illegal means. If they did that they were guilty of conspiracy, and if they misled others they were guilty of a wicked conspiracy."

Those who are interested in the immediate social aspects of this case, and who wish to hear the other side of this resort to the courts, as a move in the game between masters and men, will do well to read an able article on Class Legislation in the *Fortnightly Review* for February last, which combines much sense with some unsound notions of law. The aspect of the various instances of class legislation there collected to which we would call attention, is their relation to such essays on the theory of legislation as Mr. Herbert Spencer publishes from time to time. It has always seemed to us a singular anomaly that believers in the theory of evolution and in the natural development of institutions by successive adaptations to the environment, should be found laying down a theory of government intended to establish its limits once for all by a logical deduction from axioms. But the objection which we wish to express at the present time is, that this presupposes an identity of interest between the different parts of a community which does not exist in fact. Consistently with his views, however, Mr. Spencer is forever putting cases to show that the reaction of legislation is equal to its action. By changing the law, he argues, you do not get rid of any burden, but only change the mode of bearing it; and if the change does not make it easier to bear for society, considered as a whole, legislation is inexpedient. This tacit assumption of the solidarity of the interests of society is very common, but seems to us to be false. The struggle for life, undoubtedly, is constantly putting the interests of men at variance with those of the lower animals. And the struggle does not stop in the ascending scale with the monkeys, but is equally the law of human existence. Outside of legislation this is undeniable. It is mitigated by sympathy, prudence, and all the social and moral qualities. But in the last resort a man rightly prefers his own interest to that of his neighbors. And this is as true in legislation as in any other form of corporate action. All that can be expected from modern improvements is that legislation should easily and quickly, yet not too quickly, modify itself in accordance with the will of the *de facto* supreme power in the community, and that the spread of an educated sympathy should reduce the sacrifice of minorities to a minimum. But whatever body may possess the supreme power for the moment is certain to have interests inconsistent with others which have competed unsuccessfully. The more powerful interests must be more or less reflected in legislation; which, like every other device of man or beast, must tend in the long run to aid the survival of the fittest. The objection to class legislation is not that it favors a class, but either that it fails to benefit the legislators, or that it is dangerous to them because a competing class has gained in power, or that it transcends the limits of self-preference which are imposed by sympathy. Interference with contracts by usury laws and the like is open to the first objection, that it only makes the burden of borrowers heavier. The law brought to bear upon the gas-stokers is perhaps open to the second, that it requires to be backed by a more unquestioned power than is now possessed by the favored class; and some English statutes are also very probably open to the third. But it is no sufficient condemnation of legislation that it favors one class at the expense of another; for much or all legislation does that; and none the less when the *bonâ fide* object is the greatest good of the greatest number. Why should the greatest number be preferred? Why not the greatest good of the most intelligent and most highly developed? The greatest good of a minority of our generation may be the greatest good of the greatest number in the long run. But if the welfare of all future ages is to be considered, legislation may as well be abandoned for the present. If the welfare of the living majority is paramount, it can only be on the ground that the majority have the power in their hands. The fact is that legislation in this country, as well as elsewhere, is empirical. It is necessarily made a means by which a body, having the power, put burdens which are disagreeable to them on the shoulders of somebody else. Communism would no more get rid of the difficulty than any other system, unless it limited or put a stop to the propagation of the species. And it may be doubted whether that solution would not be as disagreeable as any other.

Editor's Notes

1. First three paragraphs by J. T. Morse, according to Holmes's copy (OWH Papers, Paige Box 18, Item 4).

2. There are no quotation marks at the beginning of this paragraph in the original.

6.82
THE THEORY OF TORTS

From *American Law Review* 7:652 (1873).

We have tried to show in an earlier number of this Review[*] that the notion of a legal duty involves something more than a tax on a certain course of conduct, although the tax may happen to be collected by means of a court of justice. Mere liability to what is called a penalty by the statute imposing it may not create a duty, it was shown, and *a fortiori* such is not the direct result of the liability to a civil action. Apart from collateral consequences, the possibility that I may have to pay the reasonable worth or market value of my neighbor's property cannot be said to amount to a penalty on conversion, much less to make it my duty not to convert it. I do not owe my butcher a duty not to buy his meat, because I must pay for it if I buy. And as liability to a civil action for the amount of the plaintiff's detriment is quite different from a punishment proportioned to the defendant's guilt, so, conversely, liability to such an action does not necessarily import culpability, as it has been thought to do by some of Bentham's followers. The liability of a master for his servant, which is one of the instances illustrative of this proposition, and which Austin tried to account for by the notion of remote inadvertence, has been explained heretofore.[**] It may safely be stated that all the more ancient examples are traceable to conceptions of a much ruder sort, and in modern times to more or less definitely thought-out views of public policy. The old writs in trespass did not allege, nor was it necessary to show, any thing savoring of culpability. It was enough that a certain event had happened, and it was not even necessary that the act should be done intentionally, though innocently. An accidental blow was as good a cause of action as an intentional one. On the other hand, when, as in *Rylands v. Fletcher*,[***] modern courts hold a man liable for the escape of water from a reservoir which he has built upon his land, or for the escape of cattle, although he is not alleged to have been negligent, they do not proceed upon the ground that there is an element of culpability in making such a reservoir, or in keeping cattle, sufficient to charge the defendant as soon as a damnum concurs, but on the principle that it is politic to make those who go into extra-hazardous employments take the risk on their own shoulders. In many of the prairie states the rule of the common law as to keeping in cattle at one's peril does not prevail. Statutes requiring railroads to fence them out are very generally in force.

---

[*] 6 Am. Law Rev. 723, 724 [see pp. 294–97 above].

[**] 7 Am. Law Rev. 61, 62 [pp. 313–14 above]. The peculiar liability for ferocious animals, which is another of those to which he alludes, is derived, we suppose, from the Roman law. In that system it seems to have been based upon the primitive notion that liability somehow attached upon the thing doing the harm. Ulpian tells us that the liability runs with the animal, and that, if it has changed hands, the action must be brought against the present owner. D. 9. 1. pr. And we read in the Institutes that a man is not liable for damage done by animals *ferae naturae*, after they have escaped, because they have ceased to belong to him. Inst. 4, 9, pr.; cf. XII. TAB. 8, 6. Yet it is obvious that the remote culpability in keeping them is as great in this case as in that of dogs or bulls. In modern times the libility would be placed upon the ground explained in the text.

[***] L.R. 3 H.L., 330, s.c. L.R. 1 Ex. 265; 3 H. & C. 774.

At one end, then, of the liabilities discussed in a treatise on torts, we should find a class of cases, some of ancient and some of modern date, in which the cause of action is determined by certain overt acts or events alone, irrespective of culpability. Such were, formerly at least, trespasses proper in general, and such are to-day those arising from some sources regarded as extra-hazardous. Again, there are other cases of acts done intentionally, but innocently, for which it is supposed indemnity might be exacted by the sufferer; as, when a man's land or easement is interfered with under an innocent mistake of boundaries.

At the other extreme from the above are found those liabilities in which culpability is in general an essential element. Such are frauds, or malicious or wilful injuries; perhaps, also, certain negligent acts *(stricto sensu)*, where the negligence referred to is the actual condition of the defendant's consciousness.

Half-way between the two groups which have been indicated lie the great mass of cases in which negligence has become an essential averment, since Bentham's ideas have got into the air, and the abolition of the old forms of action has allowed pleaders to state their case according to their own views of its essential elements. What does this modern negligence mean? Austin, following his general notion that liability imports culpability, analyzed negligence as the state of the party's mind. This seems to us unsatisfactory; and to show why, we must begin at a little distance from the subject.

The growth of law is very apt to take place in this way: Two widely different cases suggest a general distinction, which is a clear one when stated broadly. But as new cases cluster around the opposite poles, and begin to approach each other, the distinction becomes more difficult to trace; the determinations are made one way or the other on a very slight preponderance of feeling, rather than articulate reason;[1] and at last a mathematical line is arrived at by the contact of contrary decisions, which is so far arbitrary that it might equally well have been drawn a little further to the one side or to the other. The distinction between the groups, however, is philosophical, and it is better to have a line drawn somewhere in the penumbra between darkness and light, than to remain in uncertainty. For instance, a breach of warranty of quality only makes a sale voidable at most; but if the thing is different in kind from the subject-matter of the agreement, there is no sale. There is a clear general distinction; but when we come down to nice cases, where does a difference in qualities rise to a difference in kind? It is a question for Mr. Darwin to answer. In some instances a difference in name will not improbably suffice to turn the scale. Take another example nearer to our present subject. There are certain rights, an infraction of which is said not to be actionable in the absence of substantial damage. To put it more philosophically, the duty of an adjoining owner is not to refrain from abstracting a ray of light from his neighbor's ancient windows, or from digging, so that a spadeful of earth shall fall from his neighbor's land into his pit, but to refrain from substantially diminishing his light, or from digging so as to cause appreciable damage by the falling of his neighbor's soil. Fifty years ago it was left to the jury in ordinary cases to say whether the abstraction of light was substantial or not. What does this mean? If the defendant had wholly obstructed the plaintiff's windows, we presume the court would not have required the aid of a jury to hold him liable. If, on the other hand, the obstruction complained of was a foot high, and a hundred yards off, the jury would not have been allowed to find for the plaintiff. But between these clearly opposed cases there lie a great number of others which may as well be decided one way as the other, and so the exact limit of the defendant's duty is measured by the opinion of the jury. But all the elements of these cases are permanent, and there is no reason why a case should be decided one way to-day, and another way to-morrow. To leave the question to the jury for ever, is simply to leave the law uncertain. Accordingly, we read in a recent equity case* that what was left at large to the jury fifty years ago has now become a mathematical rule; that a building cannot be complained of unless its height exceeds the distance of its base from the base of the ancient windows. This instance explains the meaning of the question ordinarily left to the jury in negligence cases. They are not asked what was the condition of the defendant's consciousness. Would the fact that the defendant had taken counsel with himself, and acted as he thought prudent, exonerate him if the jury found that his conduct was not that of a prudent man? To say that he must find out at his peril is merely another way of saying that what he actually believes is immaterial. The truth is, that the cases where the character of the defendant's conduct is left to the jury lie midway between extremes which the court could determine without their aid. Suppose the whole evidence in the case was that a party, in full command of his senses and intellect, stood on the track, looking at an approaching steam-engine until it ran him down, would a judge go so far as to ask the jury if this was prudent? Supposing the whole evidence was that he attempted to cross a track which was visible for half a mile each way, and on which no engine was in sight, would the jury be allowed to find that that was negligent? The mass of cases actually tried are those which lie so near the dividing line that the standard of conduct is not clear, and is therefore referred, in the first instance, to the jury, as representing the average opinion of the community. Let us carry the analysis a little farther.

Law as law is an agent, influencing conduct by motives, and applying consequences. Before law can act, however, either upon the private citizen or the judge, when, as in civilized communities, it is not directly addressed to the individual by the sovereign, a preliminary investigation of fact has to be made. For example, the court has to satisfy itself that an ancient statute not found upon the rolls was actually enacted, before it will enforce it. It has to be convinced of the same fact as to an act of yesterday. It has to determine the meaning of the act, and the scope of precedents. A clear conviction on these points so uniformly determined judicial action, that we are apt to lose sight of the antecedent in the consequent, and to speak of the whole as a question of law;[2] although, when a precisely similar investigation is made by the same judges by the same means, by reference to statute books and reports, as to a question of foreign law, inasmuch as the consequent effect upon action is more exceptional, we find no difficulty in calling things by their right names.

This class of facts, inasmuch as their function is only to suggest a rule of law, are investigated by the court in such way as may be most convenient.[3] The fundamental fiction of the law is that all are presumed to know it, and it follows that whatever

---

* *Beadel v. Perry*, L.R. 3 Eq. 465, 467.

facts are necessary preliminaries to such knowledge may not only be judicially noticed by the courts which declare the law, but must be found out at their peril by
those who are called on to obey it. It is hard to see any distinction, whatever the
nature of the fact may be; and, although not every fact judicially noticed is a source
of law, the facts which are such are not confined to the example which has been
mentioned. They are not always to be found in any previous acts of any branch of
the sovereign body. As has been remarked heretofore,* they may not even owe their
compulsory power to their recognition by the courts, although they do not generate
rules of law in the empirical sense in which lawyers use the phrase, unless they
induce the judges to decide in the way they suggest. Lord Coke says that "a custom
cannot be alleged generally within the kingdom of England; for that is the common
law." A custom, as such, is a fact. When it is said that a general custom is law, it is
meant only that the courts will enforce a rule of conduct suggested by the custom.
This is recognized by the form of the writ in some cases reported by Lord Coke
himself, where, notwithstanding his remark, the custom of the realm is set forth at
length.** Modifications of the law are recognized much sooner in the rules of evidence than in pleading, where precedents remain of record. It ceased to be necessary to prove such customs long before it ceased to be usual to allege them. As late
as the end of the last century, Mr. Hargrave cautiously says that "it seems not only
unnecessary, but even rather improper," to recite them.*** At last Mr. Chitty is bold
enough to write "is" in place of "seems."**** Here, then, the original question of fact
has disappeared, and, in place of inquiring into the existence of a custom, the
courts simply satisfy themselves from the precedents that their predecessors have
laid down a rule of law.***** A more modern example is to be found in the rule of
the road. There, after a sufficient amount of fighting, a practice is worked out, and
a corresponding expectation generated. Then this is judicially noticed by the
courts, and it is laid down as a rule of law that men are bound to do in this instance
what by general consent they are expected to do. Take again the custom of merchants. This is a true source of law, even if its effects are confined to contracts; for
it does more than simply interpret,—it imposes consequences, irrespective of actual
intent. Moreover, the operation of such customs cannot always be justified on principles of contract, however interpreted, as is the case of an acceptor, whose liability
does not stand on any consideration moving to him from the holder.****** Indeed,
it is perhaps to be regretted that more implicit respect is not paid to such customs.
Thus, it is true, perhaps, that a contract cannot be satisfactorily made out, without
over-refining, between a bank and a stranger who has taken a check upon it from
one of its depositors. But an expectation has been generated by a well-known course

*6 Am. Law Rev. 723, 724 [see pp. 294–97 above].

** *Calye's Case*, 8 Co. Rep. 32; see also the observation of Maule, J., in *Crouch v. London & N.W.R. Co.*,
14 C.B. 255, 283.

***Co. Lit. 89*a*, note 77.

****Ch. Pl. 1st ed. 219.

*****As to special customs, see Doct. & Stud. I. ch. 10. It is immaterial whether what were called
customs of the realm were true customs. It is enough for the purposes of illustration that they were
treated as such.

******See Hardres, 485, 487, for the notion in its early form.

of dealing, and a bank which should arbitrarily disregard it would be sent to Coventry. Why should not a rule, which is more compulsory than many statutes in practice, be recognized as binding in law? However, this is not to the point of the present discussion. In some cases, as has been said, mercantile customs are a source of law, and in those the methods of ascertaining the fact have varied with the convenience of the courts. If the custom is so publicly known and understood that the conscience of the court permits it to act upon its own knowledge, it will do so.* If it can satisfy itself by an inquiry *in pais,* it is at liberty to do that, as when in *Pickering v. Barkley,* upon demurrer to a declaration on a charter-party,** the question being whether pirates were perils of the sea, "the Court desired to have Granly the Master of the Trinity House and other sufficient merchants to be brought into the Court to satisfie the Court, *viva voce,* Friday next following." Less than a hundred years ago in England it was usual to try mercantile cases before a special jury, who spoke to the custom of merchants of their own knowledge. In our day, if the court is in doubt, the fact is tried like any other, before a common jury, upon the testimony of witnesses. But however the fact is ascertained, the purpose of the evidence remains the same. The object always is to suggest a rule of law to the court, and does not differ in kind from the reading of a book of statutes. If it were possible to act up to the fiction that the court has all the law in its breast beforehand, the offer of such evidence would be as anomalous as the enactment that Messrs. Little & Brown's edition of the Statutes at Large should be competent evidence of the public acts of Congress.***

What has now been said has a direct bearing on the relations of fact and law in negligence cases. In some cases the fact, the belief of which controls the action of judges, is an act of the legislature; in others it is public policy, as understood by them; in others it is the custom or course of dealing of those classes most interested; and in others where there is no statute, no clear ground of policy, no practice of a specially interested class, it is the practice of the average member of the community,—what a prudent man would do under the circumstances,—and the judge accepts the juryman as representing the prudent man. But still the function of the juryman is only to inform the conscience of the court by suggesting a standard, just as when the finding is on a custom. To be sure the rule of law is laid down in advance, that the jury will find for the plaintiff if they find that he was using due care, and that the defendant was not. But that is a mere matter of convenience, and only amounts to adopting beforehand the standard of conduct which their opinion suggests. In a clear case, as has been said, their opinion would not be asked; but clear cases are rarely carried very far in court, and it has come to pass that negligence is regarded by many whose opinion is entitled to respect as always and in the nature of things a question for the jury. If negligence means a culpable state of mind, and it is part of the plaintiff's case to prove that, the opinion would be true; but we have tried to show that to be a misapprehension. If it means simply that in

---

*In *Gibson v. Stevens,* 8 How. 384, 398, 399, Taney, C.J., announced that the courts would judicially recognize the course of trade in the Mississippi valley, by which a transfer of warehouse receipt for grain has a similar effect to that of the transfer of a bill of lading.

**Style, 132.

***Act of Congress of Aug. 8, 1846, 9 St. at L. 75.

certain cases it is not exactly determined what overt acts will make a man liable, the function of the jury is in theory continually vanishing. For just as when a custom has been acted on it disappears and gives place to a rule of law; just as the general customs of the realm, so called, are no longer pleaded, and as the result of the findings of Lord Mansfield's special juries now appear in the pages of Kent and Story,—when the mind of the court has once been fully satisfied as to the rule of conduct in certain circumstances, it is little better than lawlessness if the same rule is not applied in similar cases thereafter. But here it is objected that no two cases of this sort ever are alike, but that each must be determined on its own shade of facts. The same idea was once prevalent as to equity, and precedent was thought to be impossible on that ground. But there are many cases which have been left to the jury in which all the facts before them could have been comprised in a short written statement. How numerous such cases may be is immaterial; for we do not propose to discuss whether it is not practically better to let many cases disappear with the fugitive tribunal which decides them, nor whether it is not desirable to abide without exact rules of conduct in some instances. All that is attempted is to point out the theory on which the jury takes any part in these decisions, and that it depends on the discretion of the court whether they shall be appealed to at all, and whether, having clearly decided to the satisfaction of the court, their vote shall still be taken if the same question is raised again.

If this analysis is correct, it will be seen that the legal liabilities defined by a book on torts are divisible into those in which culpability is an element and those in which it is not; but that the latter class may be subdivided into the cases where the facts which fix the liability are definitely ascertained, and those where the boundary line is in course of ascertainment, or from motives of policy is kept purposely indefinite.

It remains to consider the more fundamental principles of arrangement. The worst objection to the title Torts, perhaps, is that it puts the cart before the horse, that legal liabilities are arranged with reference to the forms of action allowed by the common-law for infringing them,—the substantive under the adjective law. But an enumeration of the actions which have been successful, and of those which have failed, defines the extent of the primary duties* imposed by the law, and accordingly there is no fault to be found with the contents of text-books on this subject. Torts have been thought to be infractions of rights availing against all the world. This may prove too narrow a definition, although the title includes all such rights. It contains in the first place duties of all the world to all the world; that is, duties of subjects generally to subjects generally, irrespective of any more special circumstances on either side than such as make it possible to incur a legal liability. For instance, the duty not to commit an assault and battery is imposed on all persons not excepted from ordinary rules in favor of all persons upon whom a battery is possible. The fact of possibility is merely a condition precedent, not a defined state of facts to which a peculiar rule of law attaches. A second class of duties, equally general as regards the persons on whom they are imposed, are owed, not to every

---

*The word "duties" is used to avoid a circumlocution, subject to the considerations suggested above in this article and in the earlier discussions referred to.

member of the community, but only to persons in particular situations of fact; that is, to persons distinguished from the rest of the community by certain definite marks. Such, for example, are the duties of all the world to a possessor, a patentee, or a master. The rights corresponding to both of these enumerated classes are, of course, rights availing against all the world, but there are other cases which are harder to deal with. There are some instances, undoubtedly, in which the duty seems to arise out of a special relation between the parties. Take the case of a vendor of an article known to have a secret tendency to do damage if applied to the con- templated use. It would seem, at first sight, that the duty was a consequence attached by the law to the special relation of vendor and purchaser. But the same duty would arise out of the relation of bailor and bailee, and we think reflection would show that, although the relation of the parties afforded the occasion, the duty in question was capable of being generalized into a form irrespective of the particular relation. Indeed it is believed to be one of the evils of not having a com- prehensive arrangement of the law that we lose the benefit of such generalizations as a philosophical system would naturally suggest, and cases are discussed only on the foot of the particular relation out of which they arise dramatically, but of which they are legally independent. Thus a man is employed to put up a chandelier in a public-house, and puts it up in such a way that, in the ordinary course of events, it may be expected to fall, and to do damage. The damage which might have been expected is done; but the court sees no ground for holding the defendant liable. The duty in this case arises proximately out of the relation of contractor and con- tractee, and the subject is discussed, partially, at least, in terms of contract. But the duty, if there was any, was logically antecedent to the contract,—that is, it was a duty imposed on all the world, in favor of all,—and the contract seems to have been nothing more than an opportunity for the breach.* Take again fraud in the making a contract. The breach of duty is only complete when the contract is made, but the duty not to defraud is logically anterior to the contract, and seems to be recognized as being so by the option given the defrauded party to sue in tort for the fraud. As the present object is only to illustrate the general proposition it is not considered how far the same thing is true with regard to the negligence of bailees, apart from any special duties imposed by the terms of the agreement.

There are, however, some truly special liabilities arising out of special relations of fact other than contract, which, as they are not enforced by actions *ex contractu,* are included in books on torts; for instance, the duties of a tenant for life to the remainder-man. But although such duties cannot be resolved into contracts, it is

---

* *Collis v. Seldon,* L.R. 3 C.P. 495. This case has another aspect in which it sanctions the opinions herein advanced as to negligence. The defendant was alleged to have put up the chandelier *negligently,* but Willes, J., said, "There would be no end of actions if we were to hold that a person having once done a piece of work carelessly, should, independently of honesty of purpose, be fixed with liability in this way, by reason of bad materials or insufficient fastening." That is, the court took it upon itself to say what the standard of the defendant's duty should be, without the aid of a jury, because the court had a clear opinion in this instance that it was not desirable to extend liability to the required point. Numberless other instances of the same principle might be given, but it will suffice to refer to *Ryder v. Wombwell,* L.R. 4 Ex. 32, 39; L.R. 3 Ex. 90; *Manby v. Scott,* 1 Mod. 124, 138, cited with approval by Blackburn, J., in *Bazeley v. Forder,* L.R. 3 Q.B. 559, 564; *Shipley v. Fifty Associates,* 106 Mass. 194, 199. See also *Giblin v. McMullen,* L.R. 2 P.C. 317, 336, 337; *McCully v. Clarke,* 40 Penn. St. 399.

believed that together with contracts they fall under a distinct generalization: viz., duties of persons in a particular situation of fact to persons in a particular situation of fact; or, perhaps, more concisely, duties of the parties to a particular relation of fact to each other.

It remains to be considered whether there are not liabilities analogous to the duties of all the world, admitted to properly fall within the subject under discussion, which are owed only by persons in a particular situation of fact to which the responsibilities in question are annexed as a special consequence. We think it must be admitted that there are such owed by certain limited classes to all the world. It will be observed that they shade away from duties of all the world by insensible degrees. Thus it is a duty of all not to assault with their hands,—irrespective of any more special circumstances than the condition precedent of possibility. A man with a stick is distinguished from subjects generally by facts peculiar to a narrower class. Yet it would clearly be an anomaly to describe the duty not to assault with a switch separately from the general duty not to assault. When we go a step farther to the case of assaults with deadly weapons, a distinction is taken more easily. When we get to the liability for dangerous animals it would be hard to frame a general definition irrespective of the special circumstances which would hold water. Yet this last liability is felt to be nearly connected with the preceding examples. There is an element in common between all duties which are imposed, irrespective of the special relation between the parties.[4] They cannot satisfactorily be resolved into duties of all to all, but they are discerned to tend in the same direction. It would not be instructive to generalize the duty to respect possession into a special application of the duty to keep the peace, but the two are akin to each other. The liability for ferocious animals cannot be included in a general statement that every one is liable for the consequences of extra-hazardous undertakings, because there is no certainty what will be thought extra-hazardous in a certain jurisdiction at a certain time, and the particular things which have been held so have to be considered separately; but the particular instances point to such a general principle as the tacitly assumed ground of decision.

If now the reader will refer to the table on page [[334]] of this volume, he will see that the six subdivisions of the law indicated there fall into three general groups, the members of which are philosophically connected. First, duties of all or of a special class to the sovereign; second, those which we have been discussing, duties of all to all or to a special class, and duties of a special class to all; third, duties of the parties to a special relation to each other. The analysis of the second group may be reduced to the form of a table, thus:—

	IN WHICH THE CONSCIOUSNESS OF THE PARTY LIABLE IS AN ELEMENT	DETERMINED BY ACTS OR EVENTS EXACTLY DEFINED	DETERMINED BY ACTS OR EVENTS NOT EXACTLY DEFINED
DUTIES OF ALL TO ALL.	Fraud. Willful or malicious injuries. Negligence *stricto sensu*.	Assault and battery formerly Extreme cases, shading into negligence *latiori sensu*, which are not left to the jury.	Negligence *latiori sensu*.
DUTIES OF PERSONS IN PARTICULAR SITUATIONS TO ALL.		Liability of master for servant. Ferocious animals. Cattle Other things having an active tendency to do damage; *e.g.* Reservoirs.	
DUTIES OF ALL TO PERSONS IN PARTICULAR SITUATIONS.	Maliciously causing breach of contract. Domestic relations?	Franchise or monopoly. Possession. Property. Easements exactly defined by deed, or by an arbitrary rule of law.	Prescriptive easements not exactly defined.

Editor's Notes

1. Correction, in Holmes's copy (OWH Papers, Paige Box 18, Item 4), to: . . . rather than of articulate reason. . . .

2. OWH correction to: . . . uniformly determines judicial action. . . .

3. OWH correction to: . . . suggest a course of action to the court, are investigated. . . .

4. OWH correction to: . . . irrespective of the special situation of the parties charged with them.

6.83

From *American Law Review* 7:716 (1873).

An Index of Cases Overruled, Reversed, Denied, Doubted, Limited, and Distinguished by the Courts of America, England, and Ireland, from the Earliest Period to the Present Time. By MELVILLE M. BIGELOW, author of "The Law of Estoppel," &c. Boston: Little, Brown, & Co. 1873.

This is a book for which the compiler deserves, and we hope will receive, a great deal of credit. Few people would have had the courage to attempt such a labor, fewer still the energy to carry it through with such faithful care. The method of the book leaves nothing to be suggested. It is printed in double columns on a royal octavo page. The cases criticised are in full-faced type, followed by the report and page where they are found, and the date. Then, if the same case has been reversed by a higher tribunal, the report, page, and date of the later decision follow the word *"Reversed."* If it has been overruled by a later decision in the same jurisdiction, the name of the case, in common type, and other particulars as before, follow the word *"Overruled."* If the contrary decision was in another State, *"Denied"* is put in place of *"Overruled."* If an opposite decision has been reached without discussion of the case it is indicated by the word *"Contra."* Less absolute criticism is denoted by *"Doubted,"* and cases simply proper to be considered in connection are collected under a *"See."* Every such discriminating word stands for a great additional amount of work, which the author might have declined and still have deserved praise. The dates, again, must have cost a great deal of trouble. It is, of course, impossible to speak in detail of the execution which can only be tested by long trial. Our impression, however, from random experiments, is that it will prove satisfactory. It augurs well for Mr. Bigelow's future as a legal writer that having already won high praise for more ambitious undertakings, he has not been above seeking and winning the credit of unremitting industry.

CORRECTIONS AND VARIANT TEXTS

6.4   p. 188, l. 23: Original reads "quity" for "Equity."

6.5   p. 190, l. 24: Original lacks comma after "ERLE, C.J."

6.18   p. 211, l. 25: "way-going" hyphenated at line end.

6.25   p. 230, footnote *: Original lacks period after "Md."

Index of Names

Abbott, Benjamin Vaughan, 270, 300, 320
Abinger, Lord, 288
Abrams, Jacob, 70, 92
Acton, John, 74
Adams, Brooks, 19
Adams, Henry, 19, 23, 114
Addison, C. G., 237
Allen, William, 29
Ames, Samuel, 244
Angell, Joseph K., 244
Austin, John: on arrangement of the law, 303; and the British analytical school of law, 40; on custom and law, 295; on definition of law, 215, 294–95; on distinction between *jura in rem* and *jura in personam,* 217; Holmes on narrow exclusiveness of, 266; Holmes's disagreement with on torts, 41; on incorporeal hereditaments, 219, 310n; and liability of master for his servant, 314, 326; and philosophical study of the law, 250; on rights and duties, 220

Baer, Elizabeth, 67
Baldwin, Simeon E., 245, 300
Barker, James M., 81n.146
Beaman, Charles C., 178
Bellamy, Edward, 33
Benjamin, J. P., 206
Bennett, Edmund H., 298, 299
Bentham, Jeremy, 40, 327
Bigelow, Melville M., 249, 251, 292, 298, 335
Bishop, Joel Prentiss, 222
Bispham, George Tucker, 297
Black, Hugo, 5, 98, 128n.88
Blackburn, Colin, 206–7, 228, 230
Blackstone, Sir William, 109, 277, 310
Bleckley, Logan E., 199
Bodin, Jean, 42
Bork, Robert, 126n.57, 127n.64
Bowen, Catherine Drinker, 5, 109, 110
Bracton, Henry de, 259, 260, 261, 307–8, 309, 311
Bradley, Joseph P., 318
Brandeis, Louis: and antinomies, 26; and clear and present danger doctrine, 94–96, 100, 111, 126nn. 38, 47, 57; dissent in *Baltzer v. United States,* 70; dissents in Espionage Act cases, 91;

and Holmes's bequest, 4; as source of Holmes's ideas, 111, 132n.160
Brennan, William O., 99–101, 123n.1, 130nn. 111, 114
Brewer, David, 56
Brightly, Frederick C., 242, 245
Brown, Archibald, 322
Browne, Albert G., Jr., 271, 292
Bryce, James, 250
Buckle, Henry Thomas, 74
Bump, Orlando F., 244, 267, 297
Burger, Warren E., 99
Butler, Peirce, 93
Byles, John Barnard, 190, 252

Campbell, Lord, 232
Campbell, Robert, 241
Cardozo, Benjamin, 86, 89, 110
Carlyle, Thomas, 8, 20
Castletown, Lady, 13, 33, 35, 54, 123
Chadbourn, Erika S., 6
Chafee, Zechariah, 90, 125n.29
Chase, Salmon P., 318
Chitty, 329
Choate, Joseph, 260
Clark, Charles, 225, 238, 246
Clarke, John H., 70, 90–91, 92
Clifford, Nathan, 318
Cohen, Morris R., 18, 24, 89
Coke, Lord, 260, 329
Commager, Henry Steele, 111
Comte, Auguste, 303
Conover, O. M., 201
Cooley, Thomas M., 59, 62, 268
Coppinger, Walter Arthur, 299
Corwin, Edward S., 71
Cox, Rowland, 291
Cranworth, Lord, 230
Crocker, Uriel H., 299
Currie, D., 98
Curtis, Ellen, 34, 37

Darwin, Charles, 9, 29, 327
Dehon, Arthur, 173
Dewey, John, 110, 112, 133n.169
Dicey, A. V., 240

337

Table of Cases

Colons separate case citations from page references to this volume.